ADVERTISING IN AMERICA

An Introduction to Persuasive Communication

Advertising in America

★★★★★★★★★★★ *An Introduction* ★★★★★★★★★★★

to Persuasive

Communication

STANLEY M. ULANOFF, Ph.D

Professor of Marketing (Advertising)
Baruch College of the
City University of New York

COMMUNICATION ARTS BOOKS

HASTINGS HOUSE, PUBLISHERS · New York 10016

LIBRARY OF CONGRESS CATALOGING IN PUBLICATION DATA

Ulanoff, Stanley M
    Advertising in America.

    (Communication arts books)
    Includes bibliographical references and index.
    1. Advertising—United States. 2. Advertising.
I. Title.
HF5813.U6U37   659.1'0973   76-22180
ISBN 0-8038-0369-9
ISBN 0-8038-0371-0 pbk.

Published simultaneously in Canada by
Saunders of Toronto, Ltd., Don Mills, Ontario

Printed in the United States of America

To Tooty
who has always been a source of love,
encouragement, patience and understanding.

Table of Contents

Part Five: ADVERTISING AND SOCIETY

Preface

While *Advertising in America* is a communication arts book and has a rightful place in schools and colleges of communication, it is also thoroughly grounded in the principles of marketing and is most certainly appropriate for advertising courses taught in schools and colleges of business administration.

In essence, *Advertising in America* was designed as the textbook for a first undergraduate college course in advertising entitled "Introduction to . . . ," "Principles of . . . ," or "Essentials of Advertising." It will also meet the requirements of a survey course on the subject; it will serve as well in those cases where it is the only course offered in advertising; and it will meet the needs of those who just want to know what advertising is all about.

It is a judicious mixture of the practical and the academic—the product of more than 30 years of experience in the fields of communication and education. The author has been an advertising copywriter on a number of major national advertising accounts, advertising manager of a national company, promotion writer for the *New York Times,* president of a broadcasting station in a major market, consultant to a number of advertisers and to Compton Advertising, Inc., and the author and/or editor of 18 books. In the field of education he has been on the staff and faculty of the State University of New York at Stony Brook, C. W. Post College, Hofstra University, and the New York Institute of Technology. For the past eleven years he has been a member of the faculty of Baruch College of the City University of New York, where he has served as head of the Advertising and Public Relations Division and supervisor of the Co-operative Training Program in advertising.

Advertising in America is as up-to-date as *now*. It covers such current subjects as comparative advertising, GRPs, positioning, "scratch 'n sniff," newspaper advertising preprint supplements, the "Fairness Doctrine," the resurgence of radio advertising, the new newspaper formats and the latest FTC and FCC regulations and rulings.

It tells it like it is.

Acknowledgments

I am particularly grateful to my old friend and former "boss," Dr. Walter A. Gaw who preceded me as Supervisor of the Advertising Division at Baruch College, City University of New York. It was his book, *Advertising: Methods and Media* that served as the inspiration and basis for this text.

Appreciation is due to all my present and former colleagues of the Advertising Division. For want of a better way, I shall list them alphabetically: Alfred P. Berger, Dr. Elayn Bernay, Dr. Salem K. Burnell, Robert Chamblee, Dr. Morton Jaffe, Dr. Leslie Kanuk, Thomas Killoran, James Rucquoi, and Dr. Robert Small.

I also called upon our adjunct advertising faculty who freely gave of their vast store of practical knowledge: Fred Charlton, President of Charlton Lithography, Inc.; Aaron Cohen, Vice President for Marketing of the National Broadcasting Co.; Assistant Professor David Hymes, former Sales Director of Ribolith Printing Co.; Assistant Professor Alfred Miller, Vice President for Advertising of the Omega Watch Co.; Ben Morris, Vice President Marketing Services for Merling, Marx & Seidman Inc.; and Allan G. Sacks, former Vice President and Account Manager of Hicks & Greist Advertising Agency.

I acknowledge, with due respect, the encouragement and support of my good friends, Dr. Henry Eilbirt, Dean of the School of Business and Public Administration; and Dr. I. Harold Kellar, Chairman of the Department of Marketing.

Special thanks and credit go to my benefactors at Compton Advertising, Inc. who gave me an unprecedented opportunity to observe, absorb, and keep current on the latest trends and practices in the field. I had the privilege of spending a summer at Compton as the winner of an American Association of Advertising Agencies fellowship and more recently I have served them as a Consultant. For the privilege, I am indebted to Bart Cummings, Chairman of the Executive Committee; Stu Mitchell, Chairman of the Board; and Milt Gossett, President.

I am grateful to my old "comrade in arms" Dr. Charles Winick, University Professor of Sociology at the City University of New York Graduate Center, for the chapter on "The Behavioral Sciences and Advertising"; to Myron Emery, Esq., attorney and specialist in advertising law, who wrote the chapter on that subject; and to the aforementioned Aaron Cohen, Vice President of the National Broadcasting Co., who lent his expertise to the chapter on television and my colleague David Hymes, author of *Production in Advertising and the Graphic Arts,* who gave his counsel on the chapter on print production.

I also acknowledge, with appreciation and advice of advertising and communications educators from other institutions. Professors Lee Morrison, James G. Barringer, Edw. P. Cosgrove, Felisa B. Koplon, Philip Miele, Adrienne O'Brien, Alwyn Scott, Irving Weingarten and Charles Wigutow of the New York Institute of Technology were very helpful, particularly in the broadcast media area. Too numerous to name individually but worthy of mention, indeed, are my colleagues of the American Academy of Advertising.

Invaluable background material was furnished by the American Association of Advertising Agencies, Association of National Advertisers, Association of Industrial Advertisers, American Advertising Federation, Advertising Council, Audit Bureau of Circulation, Business Publications Audit of Circulation, American Newspaper Publishers Association, Magazine Publishers Association, American Business Press, National Association of Broadcasters, Radio Bureau of Advertising, Television Bureau of Advertising, Traffic Audit Bureau, Transit Advertising Association, Direct Mail/Marketing Association, Outdoor Advertising Institute of America, Point-of-Purchase Advertising Institute, Specialty Advertising Association International, and others.

In closing, I cannot overlook the help and contribution of two of my children—my son, Roger, a graduate of the Temple University School of Communications, and now an advertising professional and an adjunct instructor in Communication Arts at N.Y. Institute of Technology; and my oldest daughter, Amy, who is a professional in public relations.

Part One

ADVERTISING

Where It All Began— Some Background

While advertising, as we know it, has had its greatest growth and development in the relatively modern times since World War I, its basic origins are long lost. Probably the first advertising took place in the dawn of history before men had a written language, even before their spoken language was well advanced. Perhaps some caveman shouted to his neighbors extolling the virtues of the stone knife, or other primitive tool created by one of their fellows. This could have been the first example of word-of-mouth advertising—the most effective form. Furthermore, it might well have accompanied the beginning of specialized labor—a skilled hunter offering to trade some of his excess meat and furs for the stone weapon made by an expert toolmaker. Later, cavemen developed artistic ability and painted scenes of daily life on cave walls and ceilings which may even have been a form of advertising.

Later still, in the more civilized society of Babylon, artisans pressed cuneiform inscriptions into wet clay for baking into bricks or tablets. Thirty centuries before the Christian era began, these were used in construction much as cornerstones are used in buildings today. They gave the name of the reigning monarch, the builder, or some other dignitary. This practice continues today in another fashion—outdoor billboards or signs, adjacent to public buildings or roads under construction, that announce the name of the governor, mayor, or other public official under whose tenure the work is proceeding.

In a parallel contemporary civilization, the Egyptians developed a picture-symbol form of writing known as hieroglyphics. The key to this ancient language, the Rosetta stone, was uncovered on the banks of the Nile by one of Napoleon's engineers. The stone, dating from 136 B.C., was an advertisement

3

for the Egyptian ruler Ptolemy as "the true Son of the Sun, the Father of the Moon, and the Keeper of the Happiness of Men." [1] *

Town criers and barkers were used for advertising purposes in Babylon, in Egypt, and later in Greece and Rome. With the invention of *papyrus,* a form of paper made from reeds growing along the shores of the Nile, written advertisements became more common. Among the first of these were notices for the return of escaped slaves.

While the powerful broadcast media of today may be said to have had their beginnings with the shouting cave man and the criers of Babylon and Egypt, outdoor advertising began in ancient Greece and flourished in Rome. Principally this took the form of signs hung in front of business establishments announcing the profession or trade of the occupant. Signs on walls also were used to announce gladiatorial combats, shows, and sports events. And in Pompeii, enterprising advertisers had signs painted along the wall of the public baths that would be seen by patrons waiting to enter. [2]

A STEP BACKWARD

Following the fall of Rome, civilization advanced very little for the next thousand years and advertising sank to its lowest ebb. During these Dark Ages, from 500 A.D. to 1450 A.D., knowledge and learning stagnated. Reading and writing were considered unmanly by the knights and noblemen, while the monks in their cloistered monasteries kept the skills alive, reading and painstakingly lettering the Bible by hand, letter after letter, word after word, page after page. The only bright spots for them in this laborious task were the initial letters of chapters or paragraphs, which they illuminated magnificently. The introduction ** of movable type and the invention of a new metal alloy by Johann Gutenberg, in 1448, was to simplify their tasks considerably and have a momentous effect on the development of advertising.

As commerce and trade began to return, the most logical way to reach the illiterate public was by means of the spoken word. In France, criers advertised wine for the taverns of Paris, and criers in England announced the wares of their clients. Doorway barkers remained the predominant advertising medium of the tradesmen, as they had been in ancient Rome.

Since the people could easily relate to pictures, the outdoor signs over English taverns multiplied rapidly, a practice soon to be followed by other trades. English shopkeepers adopted signs which identified their businesses, like the earlier three-ball sign of the pawnbroker and the red-and-white-striped barber pole. A chemist might use a mortar and pestle as the symbol on his sign; a shoemaker, a golden boot. Because there were no street addresses, the signs

* Lists of Sources are at the ends of chapters.
** While Gutenberg was probably the first European to print from movable type, the Koreans had invented the system two centuries earlier. Gutenberg did, however, invent the type-metal alloy that melted at a relatively low temperature yet was hard enough to withstand the pressure of many impressions. He also adapted the coin or wine press to printing.

were also used as a means of location. But by the time of the American Revolution, the colorful signs which had cluttered English cities were no longer in evidence, having been banned a few years earlier because of the danger of falling. And an accompanying law required the numbering of houses.

Although printing from movable type had been introduced a couple of centuries earlier, the handbills or trade cards of 17th- and 18th-century England were printed from wood and copper engravings. They illustrated and generally announced the type of business and its location. Hogarth, the famous English painter and engraver who had painted outdoor signs, designed and printed business announcements as well.

These trade cards had been preceded by handwritten announcements which were pasted up on any available wall. The practice became so widespread and space so short that new announcements were being pasted directly over others that had been slapped up only minutes before. Obviously something had to be done if a message was to have any effect. Finally a loose-knit agreement, a precurser of today's advertising code of ethics, was reached: no ad would be posted over another if the paste of the first was still damp. Since the paste of that period dried very slowly, the messages probably had a few days' exposure.

THE PRINTED WORD

The printing press reached London about 30 years after Gutenberg's first efforts and was first used to print religious books in quantity. However, William Caxton, owner of England's first press, had difficulty marketing his books. Using paper left over from one of his publishing efforts, he printed announcements explaining their availability, posting these on church doors. Caxton's effort is thought to be the first example of print advertising in Europe. It was, in fact, a more advanced version of the handwritten or engraved *siquis* or pin-up posters that had appeared earlier in England. The name *siquis* was derived from the public notices in ancient Rome which began with the words "if anybody . . . ," which in Latin was *"si quis."*

These printed announcements were followed by public registers of wants, the first of which was the *Journal Général d'Affiches* (Journal of Public Notices), published in Paris in 1612 and credited with being the first periodical. These journals, together with the English "advices," an early term for advertising, were largely want-ad media.

By this time there were printing presses in all of the principal cities of Europe. A new merchant class was coming to the fore. The age of discovery had begun and trade was opening up with the Orient and with the New World. The idea of advertising in print began to take hold.

At about the same time, newsbooks began to appear in England. First of these was the *Weekly Newes* published in 1622 by Nicholas Bourne and Thomas Archer. It measured 5 × 7 inches and consisted of 20 pages. When Bourne in 1625 merged with a rival newsbook publisher, Nathaniel Butter, Archer broke away to publish *Mercurius Britannicus.* That year Archer printed "the first newspaper advertisement published in the English language, and one of the first in any language." [3]

The second newsbook ad appeared in 1647 in Henry Walker's *Perfect Occurrences;* it promoted a book. While 22 years intervened between the first and second newsbook "advices," the success of Walker's ad encouraged a gradual increase in the number of other such publications. By 1652 the growing number of advertisements and their content appeared to antagonize some readers, a situation vaguely anticipatory of criticisms of television today.

BIRTH OF THE NEWSPAPER

Early in the 17th century the printers found a new way to occupy their presses. They published, sporadically, news or gossip sheets called "newsletters." Then in 1665 appeared the first recognized newspaper, the London *Gazette.** Surprisingly, neither the newsletters nor the newspaper sold advertising space. In fact, the *Gazette* specifically stated, in its issue No. 62 published in June 1666, that the advertising of books, medicine, and other such things were "not properly the business of a Paper of Intelligence. This is to notify once for all that we will not charge the *Gazette* with Advertisements . . ." [4]

Others, however, were eager to accept advertising. John Houghton, called "the father of publication advertising" by advertising historian Frank Presbrey, actively sought business. His *A Collection for the Improvement of Husbandry and Trade,* founded in 1682, was in a way similar to the present-day New York *Journal of Commerce.* His efforts helped to train his contemporaries.

Some of England's greatest literary talents of the early 18th century published periodicals that accepted advertising. Principal among these was Richard Steele, who published *The Tatler* from 1709 to 1711. A frequent contributor was Joseph Addison, who often wrote about advertising. In *The Tatler* of September 14, 1710, he discussed the subject at great length:

> It is my Custom in a Dearth of News to entertain my self with those Collections of Advertisements that appear at the End of all our publick Prints. These I consider as Accounts of News from the little World, in the same Manner that the foregoing Parts of the Paper are from the great. If in one we hear that a Soverign Prince is fled from his Capital City, in the other we hear of a Tradesman who hath shut up his Shop and run away. If in one we find the Victory of a General, in the other we see the Desertion of a private Soldier. I must confess, I have a certain Weakness in my Temper, that is often very much affected by these little Domestick Occurrences, and have frequently been caught with Tears in my Eyes over a melancholy Advertisement . . .
>
> But to consider this Subject in its most ridiculous Lights, Advertisements are of great Use to the Vulgar: First of all, as they are Instruments of Ambition. A Man that is by no Means big enough for the Gazette, may easily creep into the Advertisements, by which Means we often see an Apothecary in the same Paper of News

* The London *Gazette* actually began as the Oxford *Gazette* in 1665. It was published there while the court was in residence in Oxford to escape the Great Plague. It became the biweekly London *Gazette,* the following year.

with a Plenipotentiary, or a Running-Footman with an Ambassador. An Advertisement from Piccadilly goes down to Posterity with an article from Madrid; and John Bartlett of Goodman's-Fields is celebrated in the same Paper with the Emperor of Germany. Thus the Fable tells us, That the Wren mounted as high as the Eagle, by getting upon his Back. . . .

A Second Use which the Sort of Writings have been turned to of late Years, has been the Management of Controversy, insomuch that above half the Advertisements one meets with now-a-Days are purely Polemical. The Inventors of Strops for Razors have written against one another this Way for Several Years, and that with great Bitterness; as the whole Argument pro and con in the Case of the Morning-Gowns is still carried on after the same Manner, I need not mention the several Proprietors of Dr. Anderson's Pills; nor take Notice of the many Satyrical Works of this Nature so frequently published by Dr. Clark, who has had the Confidence to advertize upon that learned Knight, my very worthy Friend, Sr. William Read: But I shall not interpose in their Quarrel; Sir William can give him his own in Advertisements, that, in the Judgment of the Impartial, are as well penned as the Doctor's.

The third and last use of these writing . . . is to inform the world, where they may be furnished with almost everything that is necessary for life. If a Man has pains in his head, cholic in his bowels, or spots in his clothes, he may here meet with proper cures and remedies. If a man would recover a wife or a horse that is stolen or strayed; if he wants new sermons, electuaries, asses milk, or anything else either for his body or his mind, this is the place to look for them in.

On the dissolution of *The Tatler,* Addison joined Steele in the publication of the *Spectator.* Another literary giant and periodical publisher of the time was Daniel Defoe, author of *Robinson Crusoe.* Defoe published the *Review* from 1706 to 1712 and was called a ''hustler'' and ''one of the cleverest and most persistent advertisers of his day.'' [5]

THE PRESS COMES TO AMERICA

Though the first printing press in the New World was set up in Mexico City in 1535, it was more than a hundred years later before a press came to British North America, from England. It arrived at Harvard University, Cambridge, Mass., in 1638 accompanied by Stephen Daye. The following year the *Freeman's Oath* became the first material published in this country. More than 20 years passed before the next press arrived here, and 55 years before New York received its first printing press. But as it had been in England, the first examples of advertising were the painted signs outside taverns and inns.

The first attempt at a newspaper in British America was the *Publick Occurrences,* published in Boston in 1690 by Benjamin Harris and supressed by the colonial government after a single edition. Credit for the country's first newspaper is usually accorded to John Campbell, publisher of the *Boston News-Letter,* which first appeared in 1704. The initial issue carried Campbell's own solicitation for advertising from his readers. The third edition, dated May 1–8, 1704, carried the first paid advertising in the Colonies, under the column

STollen the 4 inftant in the Morning out of the houfe of James Cooper, near Charleftown Ferry in Bofton, feveral forts of mens Apparel, both Woollen & Linnen, by an Irifh man, fpeaks bad Englifh ; he is a young man about 22 years of Age, low Stature, dark coloured hair, round vifage, frefh coloured: he ript a fmall ftript Ticking-bolfter, and put fome of the Goods in that he carryed away. Whoever difcovers faid Perfon, or Goods Stollen, fo as both be fecured, fhall have fufficient reward at the place aforefaid.

AT Oyfterbay on *Long-Ifland* in the Province of *N. York*, There is a very good Fulling-Mill, to be Let or Sold, as alfo a Plantation, having on it a large new Brick houfe, and another good houfe by it for a Kitchin, & work houfe, with a Barn, Stable, &c. a young Orchard, and 20 Acres clear Land. The Mill is to be Let with or without the Plantation: Enquire of Mr. *William Bradford* Printer in *N. York*, and know further.

LOft on the 10 *of April* laft, off of Mr. *Shipen's* Wharff in *Bofton*, Two Iron Anvils, weighing between 120 & 140 pound each : Whoever has taken them up, & will bring or give true Intelligence of them to John Campbel Poft-mafter, fhall have a fufficient reward.

THis News-Letter is to be continued Weekly ; & all Perfons who have any Houfes, Lands, Tenements, Farms, Ships, Veffels, Goods, Wares or Merchandizes, &c. to be Sold, or Let; or Servants Run-away, or Goods Stole or Loft; may have the fame inferted at a Reafonable Rate, from Twelve-pence to Five Shillings, & not to exceed: Who may agree with John Campbel Poft-mafter of Bofton for the fame: And if in the Country, with the Poftmafter of the refpective Towns, to be tranfmitted to the Poft mafter of Bofton : & all fuch Advertifements are to be brought in Writing to faid Poft-Mafters.

All Perfons in Town & Country may have faid News-Letter every Week by the Year, upon reafonable terms, agreeing with John Campbel, Poft-mafter for the fame

These are advertisements which appeared in the *Boston News-Letter* in 1704. The one concerning the Oyster Bay real estate is thought to be the first newspaper advertisement in the United States which offered something for sale.

heading "Advertisements." Two of the three ads offered rewards for the return of stolen merchandise and the third was for real estate:

> AT Oysterbay, on *Long Island* in the Province of *N. York,* There is a very good Fulling-Mill, to be Let or Sold, as also a Plantation, having on it a large new Brick house, and another good house by it for a Kitchin & workhouse, with a Barn, Stable &c. a young Orchard and 20 acres clear Land. The Mill is to be Let with or without the Plantation; Enquire of Mr. *William Bradford* Printer in *N. York,* and know further.

It is interesting to note that the advertiser, Bradford, had been a pioneer printer; later, in 1725, he published New York's first newspaper. He was preceded as a newspaper publisher, however, by his son Andrew, who first published the *American Weekly Mercury* in Philadelphia on December 22, 1719. The *Mercury* and William Brooker's *Massachusetts Gazette*, published one day earlier, were the next two newspapers to be published in the colonies, following Campbell's *Boston News Letter.*

Probably the best-known early American publisher is Benjamin Franklin, who began as a 12-year-old apprentice in the shop of his half-brother James. James began to publish the *New England Courant* in 1721. The following year James, as Benjamin Harris had done earlier, ran afoul of the authorities by criticizing the government in print; he was imprisoned. Ben continued as editor of the *Courant* until he ran away to Philadelphia to break the bond of his apprenticeship to his brother. Here he established the *Pennsylvania Gazette* in 1728. His first issue actively sought advertising, his masthead emphasizing it rather than editorial content. He successfully competed with Andrew Bradford's *Mercury* and before long had acquired the largest advertising volume as well as the greatest circulation in British America. Franklin was a master at publicity and promoted his own causes to a great degree. By 1737 he had replaced Andrew Bradford as postmaster in Philadelphia and as public printer for Pennsylvania.

In 1741, Franklin again became a competitor with Bradford when both men began, within a span of three days, to publish monthly magazines. It was in his *General Magazine, and Historical Chronicle of the British Plantations in America,* the forerunner of the *Saturday Evening Post,* that Franklin showed his skill as a copywriter. He ran an ad for a stove he had invented called the Pennsylvania Fireplace, which is still sold today as the Franklin Stove:

> Fireplaces with small openings cause draughts of cold air to rush in at every crevice, and 'tis very uncomfortable as well as dangerous to sit against any such crevice. . . . Women, particularly from this cause (as they sit so much in the house) get cold in the head, rheums and defluxions which fall into their jaws and gums, and have destroyed early, many a fine set of teeth in these northern colonies. Great and bright fires do also very much contribute to damaging the eyes, dry and shrivel the skin, and bring on early the appearance of old age.

It can be readily seen that Franklin stressed the benefits offered by the product rather than simply describing its physical features. His publishing and advertising efforts were so profitable that he was able to establish the first newspaper chain in a number of cities throughout the colonies.[6]

While the Revolutionary War was in progress very little happened in American publishing and advertising. Before the war England had prevented the colonists from manufacturing anything that would compete with British products, hence there was little paper, printer's ink, or type. And it was not until 1796 that the United States was able to produce its first printing press.

Between the end of the Revolution and the War of 1812, newspaper circulation expanded tremendously. The Hartford *Courant,* for example, achieved a weekly circulation rate of 8,000, this despite the fact that papers were passed from neighbor to neighbor. During this period, in 1784, the *Pennsylvania Packet & General Advertiser,* the country's first "daily," appeared. Advertising in many newspapers was now illustrated with woodcuts although news stories and editorial matters were not. While wood was certainly plentiful the production of paper from wood pulp had not been developed here yet and paper was manufactured entirely from rags.

The year 1825 marked a milestone in advertising mass publication. At that time the New York *Gazette* installed a German-manufactured steam press capable of turning out 2,000 papers an hour. This innovation created a chain of events. In order to make the new press profitable it had to run at or near capacity. If it was to run at that rate, circulation would have to be increased tremendously. An important factor in raising circulation would be a reduction in price per copy, making it necessary to sell more advertising to "subsidize" the reduced subscription rate. And while the cost of the advertising might be higher, the advertiser could benefit from the greater number of readers exposed to his ad.

The application of the steam engine as a source of power became more widespread in America. Five years after the introduction of the steam-powered printing press here, Peter Cooper proved the superiority of his steam driven *Tom Thumb* locomotive over the conventional horse drawn cars. The Industrial Revolution had begun as steam went on to power textile mills and other manufactures.

The Industrial Revolution presented a problem to manufacturers similar to that which had faced the publishers of the New York *Gazette*. They now had the capacity to produce in ever increasing quantity, at a lower price. But in order to mass produce they needed mass consumption, vast numbers of people to purchase their wares. No longer could they be content to sell exclusively in their own towns or nearby communities. They needed a larger market of potential buyers.

The Civil War and the victory of the industrial North over the agricultural South continued the Industrial Revolution in earnest. The first transcontinental telegraph line had been completed in 1861; the last spike in the transcontinental railroad was driven four years after the end of the war, in 1869. And the country began to grow at a fantastic rate. Print media, which had been predominatly local, blossomed forth in the form of national magazines. These became the major vehicle utilized by mass manufacturers to reach the mass market and stimulate mass consumption.

At about this same time, the Golden Age of Journalism began to flourish in the United States and gave rise to the "Giants of the Press." It started with James Gordon Bennett and his New York *Herald* in 1835 and with Horace Greeley, who founded the New York *Tribune* six year later. The giants of the newspaper industry were not restricted to New York, however. Joseph Medill held sway over the Chicago *Tribune* from 1874 to 1899 and William Allen White became a national figure in Emporia, Kansas with his *Gazette*. But the lure of the "big city" was there. It drew Joseph Pulitzer, fresh from his success with the St. Louis *Post Dispatch,* to buy the New York *World* in 1883, and Adolph S. Ochs, who had become publisher of the Chattanooga *Times* in 1878, to purchase the faltering *New York Times* in 1896. New York also attracted

William Randolph Hearst, who in 1895 gave up the management of his father's San Francisco *Examiner* to buy the *Morning Journal.*

Shortly after Pulitzer acquired the *World,* Ottmar Mergenthaler, in 1886, introduced his astounding invention, the Linotype machine, which was to revolutionize the printing industry and make hand-set type largely obsolete. During this era too, the first illustrated daily, the New York *Daily Graphic* was published, in 1873. Not until 1919, however, did the greatest illustrated daily of them all appear, *The Illustrated Daily News.* Now New York's *The Daily News,* it too marked a milestone as the first tabloid * picture newspaper.

Competition was exceedingly intense during this period as each newspaper sought to "scoop" the other, increase circulation, and reap the rewards of greater advertising revenue.

AMPLIFYING THE SPOKEN WORD

Until 1922 the print media **—newspapers and magazines—reigned supreme as the conveyors of mass communications. That year the printed word was joined by the spoken word, but a spoken word so powerful that it could reach into thousands, even millions, of homes simultaneously. Radio, as it was called, was a direct lineal descendant of the town criers and barkers of ancient times but its message was electronically transmitted through space. It is interesting to note that the first radio commercial, like the first newspaper advertisement in this country, was for the sale of real estate.

Radio soon became a dominant means of mass communication. It brought news instantly and often directly from the scene at the time an event was happening. Moreover, it provided for the first time a means by which the President and other national leaders could speak directly to the people. It also opened up an entirely new world of family entertainment.

Following closely on the success of radio and adding new dimensions to it was television, "TV," which combines sight and action with sound. This medium represents perhaps the greatest contribution to mass communication ever developed. It was first demonstrated publicly at the New York World's Fair in 1939 but did not come into widespread commercial use until after World War II. An additional dimension—color—came into use in 1955.

An insight into its vast capabilities may be gathered from the fact that more people would see a production of *Hello Dolly* or any other Broadway hit in one showing on television than could see it in a lifetime on Broadway.***

---

* A *tabloid* newspaper has pages about 11½ × 15 inches, about half the dimensions of the standard newspaper. Traditionally, tabloids cover the news more concisely and are well illustrated.

** *Media* (singular, *medium*) are the communications vehicles such as newspapers, magazines, radio, and television.

*** The average seating capacity of a Broadway theater is 1,000. Based on nine performances a week, about 469,000 people could see the show in a year. In a lifetime of 75 years the show would have an audience of fewer than 40,000,000. The one-time showing of *The Godfather* on NBC had an estimated 90,000,000 viewers.

It is interesting to note that the broadcast media differ from the print media in that advertising bears the entire burden of supporting the broadcasts, programming, station operation, and other expenses. In short, advertising revenue pays for everything and supplies the profit.* While newspapers and magazines earn the great share of their income from the sale of advertising space, this is supplemented by paid subscriptions and newsstand sales.**

SUMMARY

Advertising as we know it today had its basic beginning in ancient times. Even then there were counterparts for the broadcast and print media as well as for outdoor advertising.

Significant milestones in the evolution of the print media were the inventions of movable type, the rotary press, and the linotype machine. The electronic (or broadcast) media are of more recent origin, the first radio commercial having been broadcast in 1922, followed a quarter century later by television. Color television, following on its heels, was introduced in 1955.

The foregoing pages are intended to serve as an introduction to the subject we know today as advertising. This review highlights the past inventive development and advancement of the means of communication and clearly demonstrates that advertising is the handmaiden of communications—as the one progresses, so too does the other. And the greater the distance the communication media can project the human voice and spread the written word, the greater the number of people effective advertising will reach and influence. Just as the mass communications media are tools of advertising, so too is advertising a tool of marketing.

Subsequent developments in the means of communicating via the mass media, and the impact of their development on advertising, will be covered in greater detail in the first few pages of each of the appropriate following chapters.

QUESTIONS AND DISCUSSION SUBJECTS

1. What is the relationship between the mass communications media and advertising? What is the relationship between advertising and marketing?

* Exceptions would be CATV (community antenna television or cable assisted television), where the viewer pays a monthly subscription; and subscription or pay television. In the latter the viewer pays for watching certain sports events or special shows that would not be available to the regular viewer. Other exceptions are member-supported television such as that of KQED in San Francisco and other public broadcasting stations.

** Certain business publications have controlled circulations, which means that they are sent free of charge to a special list of subscribers. Advertising in these publications must pay all costs.

2. When did advertising experience its greatest period of growth? When did it advance the least?
3. Who invented movable type? What was Gutenberg's contribution?
4. Why were town criers and doorway barkers used instead of signs and posters as the primary means of advertising following the Dark Ages?
5. Why did the London *Gazette* refuse to take advertising in its early editions?
6. What was the subject of the first paid ad in British Colonial America? In what newspaper did it appear? In what year?
7. What was Ottmar Mergenthaler's contribution to the mass communication media?
8. What is the greatest contribution to mass communication media developed to date? Why?

SOURCES

1. Frank Presbrey, *The History and Development of Advertising* (Garden City, N.Y.: Doubleday, 1929), 3.
2. *Ibid.*, 7.
3. *Ibid.*, 40.
4. James P. Wood, *The Story of Advertising* (New York: Ronald Press, 1958), 31.
5. Presbrey, *op. cit.*, 63.
6. G. Allen Foster, *Advertising: Ancient Market Place to Television* (New York: Criterion, 1967), 37.

FOR FURTHER READING

Foster, G. Allen. *Advertising: Ancient Market Place to Television.* New York: Criterion Books, 1967.

Presbrey, Frank. *The History and Development of Advertising.* Garden City, N.Y.: Doubleday, 1929.

Turner, E. S. *The Shocking History of Advertising!* New York: Dutton, 1953.

Wood, James P. *The Story of Advertising.* New York: Ronald Press, 1958.

What Advertising Is

Never before has the American public been exposed to so much advertising as during the past 10 to 20 years. At home and on trains, in barber shops and beauty parlors, in dental offices and in libraries, magazines and newspapers deluge us with sales messages. On subways and commuting trains, on buses and streetcars and in taxicabs, advertising rides with us. On highways, on streets and avenues of busy cities, and at the crossroads of country towns, posters catch the eye of flowing traffic. In our living rooms, kitchens, bedrooms, playrooms, and automobiles, the voice of radio bids us buy. Television with its entertainment, well studded with commercials, commands 6¼ hours per day of the average family's time.[1] Even the postman brings to our homes and offices appeals from the vendors of goods and services. Yet, surrounded and all but submerged as we are by advertising, there may be many who are at a loss to define the term correctly. As broad in scope as advertising is, many people tend to make their definitions of it too broad, too inclusive. Publicity is not advertising. Not all forms of selling are advertising. Advertising and sales promotion are not synonymous.

ADVERTISING AND PUBLICITY

Someone once said that "publicity is sent to a medium and prayed for, while advertising is sent to a medium and paid for." This distinction is, in fact, a major and a very fundamental difference between these two effective promotional tools. However, to say that publicity is free may be quite misleading to anyone unfamiliar with how it is created and placed in the several media that carry it to the public. The person or firm that plans, writes, and places publicity is paid a salary or a fee. The "free" concept arises from the fact that no money is given to the medium. The space that it occupies in a newspaper or a magazine, or the time that it commands on the air if it is broadcast or telecast, is free. Therefore, the medium may treat publicity as it pleases. It may delete portions of the publicity, rewrite it in whole or in part, or fail to use it altogether. Facing this hazard, quite naturally "publicity . . . is prayed for."

Advertising space and time, on the other hand, are purchased by the advertiser. For this reason, an advertisement, although it may be rejected by a medium for reasons of policy,* once accepted cannot be changed without the consent of the advertiser. Though a production error or a misprint may occur, an advertiser is reasonably assured that his advertisement will appear *as he prepared it, when* he wants it to appear and, within certain limitations that will be considered later in this book, *where* he wants it to appear.

Publicity, inasmuch as it is presented as a news story or feature article and not as an indentifiable attempt to sell goods, services or ideas, is more readily believed than advertising. Furthermore, studies have shown that publicity often attracts more reader attention than advertising, even when both appear on the same page and the advertising occupies larger space. However, despite these apparent advantages it is doubtful whether a consistently successful sales campaign could be carried on by publicity alone. Publicity neither could be obtained with sufficient regularity nor made sufficiently promotional to do the whole selling job. A medium will refuse publicity that is obviously promotional or commercial in character, or it may delete the promotional portions before publishing it.

Advertising, unlike publicity, can do a successful selling job alone because repeated impressions can be made for as long as is necessary and because there is no restriction on the extent of the commercialism that can be put into the sales message of the advertisement. But, even though advertising can work alone successfully, its success is likely to be greater when it is supported by publicity especially designed to supplement it.

In any attempt to distinguish between advertising and publicity it must be recognized that there are some forms of advertising that do not appear in paid space or on paid time. For example, direct-mail and specialty advertising ** do not appear in paid space or time in a medium owned and operated by interests other than the advertiser. Yet, this fact does not make them publicity. The distinguishing characteristic in these cases is the fact that the sales effort is obvious and readily identified with the party in whose interest it is created.

ADVERTISING AND PERSONAL SELLING

The salesman deals with one prospect at a time. The writer of advertising sales messages, the copywriter, appeals to many prospects simutaneously. The

---

* *The Saturday Evening Post* at one time refused to accept hard-liquor advertising as a matter of policy.

** Specialty advertising is any advertising placed upon calendars, blotters, pencils, or other items which may be given to prospects and which will serve as reminders of the advertiser and/or his product.

salesman is face to face with the prospect when he delivers his sales talk; the copywriter addresses an unseen audience. The salesman can alter his presentation to fit the special needs or even momentary moods of individual prospects. The copywriter, because he is dealing with a group unseen and unheard—except through the secondary and indirect eyes and ears of research—must be more general and all-encompassing in his approach.

Personal salesmanship always has the advantage of the spoken word—combined, when desirable, with support from the written word and aided by personal, dramatic demonstration. Advertising, except when employing the medium of television, lacks the advantage of this threefold selling impact.

While many people think of advertising as the most important selling or promotional tool, in terms of total dollar expenditure more money by far is spent on *personal selling*. This becomes more readily understandable when we consider that all of the salaries and commissions of manufacturers', wholesalers', and retailers' sales personnel throughout the country, together with their travel and other expenses, constitute a good part of the cost of personal selling. For example, in a 1967 survey of 560 industrial firms, marketing costs were found to be 14.28% of sales. The cost of advertising amounted to 1.90% of the total as compared to 7.14% for direct selling. Warehousing and distribution accounted for 2.06% and miscellaneous marketing costs made up the balance.[2] During 1973 the average cost of a single industrial sales call was $68.66.[3] It is true, however, that the cost of advertising can run as high as 50% of the retail price or more on toothpaste and other such consumer packaged good.

Only approximately 2% or $26 billion of our gross national product (GNP) is spent on advertising. But advertising enjoys some of its reputation from the glamor attached to the profession. As indicated, however, its place in the economy is a vital one. Its impact is exceedingly greater than the expenditure of funds might lead one to believe.

ADVERTISING AND SALES PROMOTION

Sales promotion is often confused with the overall term *promotion,* which encompasses all sales effort. Promotion is the combined and coordinated efforts of a business to sell its goods or services and includes all or any combinations of the several tools of selling. On the other hand, sales-promotion activity could include displays at trade shows and fairs, counter and window displays, premium plans, and contests. Advertising and sales promotion, together with personal selling, are all part of promotion.

ADVERTISING AND MARKETING

As can readily be seen, advertising has something to do with *marketing*. In fact, it has a great deal to do with it. Advertising is a component of marketing and is one of its principal selling or promotional arms. Marketing is also related to mass communications, whose media are the vehicles for advertising messages.

Professor E. Jerome McCarthy [4] has simplified the "marketing mix" by showing it to consist of "four P's"; Product, Place, Promotion and Price. *Product* consists of the planning and development of the product; *place* stands for distribution; *promotion* for selling; and *price* is concerned with the determination of the proper price for the product. Advertising falls under the third "P" and is part of the promotional mix or blend.

As has been stated earlier, promotion, or the promotion mix, is made up of personal selling, mass selling or advertising, and sales promotion. In addition to the above, publicity should be considered a part of promotion. In the past it had been deemed exclusively a tool of management, as a component of public relations, but in practice it has become an effective marketing promotional instrument as well.

ADVERTISING DEFINED

The foregoing sections of this chapter have shown that:

1. Advertising is a selling tool that usually employs *paid* space and *paid* time in the media that carry it to the market. The payment, in part, distinguishes it from publicity—which may also be used as a selling tool in print media or broadcast media. Payment also gives rise to fundamental differences that are apparent in both the use and in the effectiveness of publicity and advertising.

2. Advertising, in most cases, makes known the advertiser; publicity often hides the identity of its creator.

3. Advertising is less intimate in its approach to prospects than is personal selling. It addresses groups rather than individuals. This distinction between advertising and personal selling gives rise to additional differences in techniques and goals.

4. Advertising is but a part of the broader sales effort which is called promotion.If all of these points are put together, the following definition of advertising can be developed:

> *Advertising is a tool of marketing for communicating ideas and information about goods or services to a group; it employs paid space or time in the media or uses another communication vehicle to carry its message; and it openly identifies the advertiser and his relationship to the sales effort.*

KINDS OF ADVERTISING

What has been said above describes the major and distinguishing characteristics of advertising. But there are many kinds of advertising. Sometimes the difference is based on who does the advertising or to *whom* it is directed, and sometimes on the *ultimate aim or purpose* of the advertising.

An individual may place a notice in a newspaper stating that some article of personal property has been lost or found, that he has a used automobile for sale, or that he is seeking a job. In like manner, business firms may advertise employment opportunities that are available in their offices or factories. Such advertising is called *classified* and appears in special sections of newspapers and, to a lesser extent, in some magazines. All advertisements of a given kind are grouped together under an appropriate designating head or classification. The individual advertisements are relatively small and lack illustrations. Some similar advertisements, placed under classifying heads, carry illustrations and use display type; * they are called *classified-display advertising.*

Advertising which is not placed within classified sections of media, which usually but not necessarily is illustrated, and which is placed by business firms, is called *display* advertising. Display advertising, along with the television commercial, is what most people think of when they hear the word "advertising." Such display advertising may be *national* advertising, or it may be *retail* or *local* advertising. The former is usually done by or for a manufacturer, while the latter is placed by a retail merchant. However, the term *national advertising* is used in more than one sense. It may be employed to distinguish advertising appearing in nationally distributed media—like the big national magazines—from advertising placed in media having more restricted circulations—like metropolitan newspapers. Or still again, it may be used in connection with the advertising of a brand-name product capable of national distribution.

A manufacturer may advertise *both* to ultimate consumers and to other manufacturers, to producers of raw materials, to wholesalers and retailers, to professional people like physicians, dentists, and teachers, or to schools and colleges. Or he may advertise to such firms or people *rather than* to ultimate consumers. In either case his advertising activity outside of the ultimate-consumer market gives rise to still further classification of advertising. If his advertising is directed to other manufacturers it is called *industrial advertising.* If it is directed to wholesalers or retailers it is *trade advertising,* and if it is directed to professional people or to professional institutions like schools or hospitals, it is *professional advertising.*

Whereas *consumer advertising* attempts to sell goods or services to the ultimate user, industrial, trade, and professional advertising aim to sell goods and services to organizations or people that will employ them in the running of a business. Sometimes, in the case of professional advertising, the aim may be to induce the professional man to recommend the advertised goods or services to others. For example, a rest home may advertise in a nurses' journal, not with the thought that the nurses will be the users but with the hope that they will suggest the desirable features of the home to people who are in their care—insofar as it is within the province of nurses to do so.

In these forms of advertising, the goods may or may not be different from

* Type larger than 14 points ($^{14}/_{72}$ inch) is called display type. Script, italic, and boldface types are also display types.

Customers won't pay for lint or static streaks...you don't have to either.

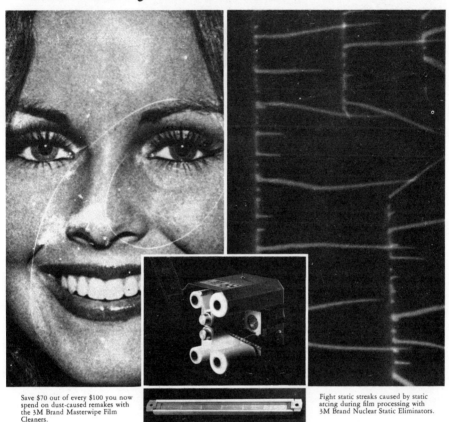

Save $70 out of every $100 you now spend on dust-caused remakes with the 3M Brand Masterwipe Film Cleaners.

Fight static streaks caused by static arcing during film processing with 3M Brand Nuclear Static Eliminators.

You get one chance in processing film and prints; lint or static streaks can ruin the results. This costs you money . . . and costs you customers. 3M Brand Static Eliminators keep static streaks from ruining film before processing. 3M Brand MASTERWIPE Film Cleaners remove lint and static from negatives for quality prints. In addition to creating satisfied customers, MASTERWIPE Film Cleaners can save you big dollars by cutting dust-caused remakes 60%-70%.

For clean negatives and quality prints, mail this coupon today.

Get more info. Circle Reader Card No. 149

Most of the advertising we see is consumer advertising, directed at us as the ultimate consumers of a product or service. This is a trade ad and it is directed at the wholesaler or retailer.

19

The flagging headline in this advertisement calls out to Doctors. It appeared in two professional magazines, *Dental Economics* and *Dental Management*, and is a professional ad. *Courtesy of Compton Advertising, Inc. and New York Life.*

consumer goods. A drill press, obviously, is an industrial commodity with a very specific and limited market. Gasoline, on the other hand, may be advertised and sold to the ultimate consumer to operate his pleasure automobile, or to an industrial user to run a bulldozer, or to the operator of a filling station to be resold by him. A diesel locomotive can be offered only in a relatively limited market; so, too, may the product of a wholesale bakery.

The buyers of goods and services that will be used in the operation of businesses or in the professions are skilled buyers to a greater degree than are ultimate consumers. They are less motivated by emotional appeals, and they have a better knowledge of comparative values and competitive prices. Therefore, the copy theme or approach made in industrial, trade and professional advertising is usually different from that found in consumer-goods advertising.

On the whole, industrial advertising and, to a lesser extent, trade and professional advertising are more long-range in the attainment of their goals than is consumer advertising, whether local or national. That is, whereas most retail advertising looks for almost immediate results and much national advertising of consumer goods expects results to follow reasonably close upon the advertising effort, industrial advertising often achieves its ends only after a considerable lapse of time. This difference is not the result of anything inherent in the advertising but rather of differences in the needs, and hence in the buying habits, of ultimate consumers and business buyers. The industrial advertiser can hardly ask a manufacturer of steel to buy a new Bessemer furnace tomorrow, but an advertiser of a candy bar or even of an automobile can request the ultimate consumer to buy immediately. A slogan common in automotive advertising during a slump in automobile sales at one time was ''You auto buy now.'' One cannot hope to move industrial goods immediately on the strength of catchy slogans or emotional appeals. Of course, some industrial-goods advertising, like some consumer-goods advertising, can expect quicker results than other industrial-goods advertising-goods advertising. But on the whole it is less productive of quick results than are appeals made to ultimate consumers.

Even advertising to the ultimate consumer may not have as its goal the immediate sale of goods or services. Rather, it may be designed to increase the prestige of the firm, to build customer goodwill, or keep a trademark or brand name before the public. Such advertising is called *institutional* or *public-relations advertising*. Sometimes the purpose of such advertising is not to sell goods at all, but to win public support for some cause—as in the case of a labor-management dispute or a government antitrust action. Sometimes institutional advertising is used to change an incorrect impression that the public has of a business firm or of its products. At other times it may be employed to build a favorable corporate image that will help the advertiser in any or all of his relationships with the public or with some segment of the public in which he may have a special interest.

Some advertising is created and is placed in media in the interest of *public service*. Examples are found in the many campaigns run through the non-profit Advertising Council. *Smokey,* the bear who works so hard to save our forests from the hazards of fire, is a familiar character across the nation. So well-known was the Advertising Council's safety slogan, "The life you save may be your own," that it appeared in such varied paraphrasings as "Drive carefully, the life you save may vote Republican," and in the army, "Drive carefully, the life you save may be your replacement." Public-welfare advertising has worked for the benefit of the general public in peacetime and in war, and undoubtedly has saved the nation many lives and much money.

Current health, safety, sociological, and other national or community problems are the general subject matter of public-relations and public-service advertising. The recent campaign against cigarette smoking is one such example. Today, a great deal of effort is expended against the disruption of our ecological balance and the pollution of our lakes and streams and the air we breathe. And major campaigns have been launched against drug abuse.

SUMMARY

To sum up, advertising is an integral part of business. Its primary function is to sell products, services, and ideas by informing the public of their good points and of their availability. Contrary to the old adage, *nobody* will "beat a path to your door" for that "better mousetrap" if they don't know who you are where you are, and what you have to offer. Advertising provides that means of communication.

QUESTIONS AND DISCUSSION SUBJECTS

1. Describe the relationship between: (a) advertising and marketing; (b) advertising and sales promotion; (c) advertising and personal selling.
2. What is the difference between advertising and publicity?
3. Name and describe the different kinds of advertising.
4. How much truth is there in the old adage, "Build a better mouse trap and the world will beat a path to your door"? What could make it agree with reality?

SOURCES

1. *Nielsen Television '75* (Chicago: A. C. Nielsen, 1975), 8.
2. "Industrial Marketing Costs—1967," McGraw-Hill Research Laboratory of Advertising Performance, June 1968, 1.

3. "Cost of an Industrial Salesman's Call in 1973," McGraw-Hill Research Laboratory of Advertising Performance, June 4, 1974, 1.

4. E. Jerome McCarthy, *Basic Marketing* (Homewood, Ill.: Irwin, 1975), 75–80.

FOR FURTHER READING

Luick, John F., and William Lee Ziegler. *Sales Promotion and Modern Merchandising.* New York, McGraw-Hill, 1968.

MacCarthy, E. Jerome. *Basic Marketing.* Homewood, Ill.: Irwin, 1975.

Mauser, Ferdinand F. *Salesmanship: A Contemporary Approach.* New York: Harcourt, 1973.

Rachman, David J. *Marketing Strategy and Structure.* Englewood Cliffs, N.J.: Prentice-Hall, 1974.

Stanton, William J., and Richard H. Buskirk. *Management of the Sales Force.* Homewood, Ill.: Irwin, 1973.

Tillman, Rollie, and C. A. Kirkpatrick. *Promotion: Persuasive Communication in Marketing.* Homewood, Ill.: Irwin, 1972.

Advertising and the American Economy

AN ECONOMY WITHOUT ADVERTISING?

In 1938, Orson Welles, a great dramatic actor and producer of the time, presented a radio broadcast based on H. G. Wells's science-fiction novel, *War of the Worlds*. It vividly described the landing of invading Martians on the New Jersey plains. Portions of the dramatic presentation followed the format of news broadcasts of the period and listeners who had tuned in late or didn't hear the beginning of the program ran screaming into the streets. Panic!

As frightening as that realistic radio broadcast of 1938 and the actual energy crisis of 1973–1974 is the fictional account, *Advertising Stopped at 10 O'clock,* presented by the National Association of Broadcasters:

ALL advertising in the United States was stopped at 10 o'clock this morning.

The nation's more than 6,600 commercial radio stations, stunned by the loss of their only revenue, announced plans immediately to suspend operations indefinitely.

All of the nearly 700 commercial television stations, also financed solely by advertising, are expected to go dark in a matter of days.

The major radio-TV networks have announced an imminent halt in all services.

The nation's newspapers and magazines, primarily dependent on advertising revenue, are trying desperately to adjust.

Many newspapers hope they can hang on—by trimming the size of editions and doubling or tripling prices to subscribers. Most magazines were pinned to the wall and ceased publication, but a few talked of joining the cost-cutting, price-boosting move.

Hundreds of thousands of people in advertising, broadcasting and the print media are looking for jobs—or soon will be. They will be joined shortly by thousands more employed in program production, equipment manufacturing and similar allied industries.

Economists predict that thousands of retail clerks in stores across the nation will be out of work within a week. They figure that, without advertising, stores won't have enough buying traffic to justify big payrolls.

Store owners and managers already are cancelling orders placed in anticipation of normal business. Manufacturers and wholesalers are slashing production and inventories and some are shutting down their plants.

Freight carriers recognize that there soon will be nothing to carry for profit and are cutting back on operations and laying off employees.

Prices are plummeting on the stock exchanges and grain and cattle markets. Many investors seem convinced that the nation is heading into a general business bankruptcy. Trading is at a standstill. There are plenty of sellers, but no one is buying.

Breadlines already are forming in areas hit hardest by widespread unemployment and demands are being heard for large doses of government aid.

To forestall panic and to deal with the fast-developing crisis, emergency meetings of the Cabinet and the Congress are underway in Washington and Governors have called special sessions of their state legislatures.

On orders of the President, all government departments and agencies are reviewing their programs and policies in a belt-tightening move designed to divert for emergency use as many spare dollars as possible.

But experts at the Internal Revenue Service are gloomy over prospects of collecting even a fraction of the taxes needed to meet even the normal requirements of government.

A leading constitutional authority warns that the nation is well down the road to dictatorship, with little chance of turning back.

Prof. I. M. Doingood of Snodgrass University, a leading critic of advertising who led citizen groups in a nationwide assault on advertising in all its forms, commented: "This is awful!"

(The professor had just been told by the university that his faculty post is being abolished because so few students have the necessary funds to return to campus next term.)

Officeholders, including those who gave the anti-advertisers lip service in their own protests on news coverage, are beginning to wonder how they'll campaign now that radio and television are blinking out and so many newspapers are folding.

A man in the Kremlin greeted the news with an enigmatic smile. What happened in America today reduced a great world power to shambles as quickly and completely as if it had been hit by a rain of nuclear bombs.[1]

THE NEED FOR ADVERTISING

Mark Twain, so the story goes, was once an editor of a small newspaper. One day he received a letter from a subscriber complaining that he had found a spider in his paper and demanding an explanation. Mark Twain is credited with replying that the spider was examining the paper to discover which merchant in town did not advertise so that he (the spider) could spin a web over the merchant's door and live a life of undisturbed peace forever after. This reply suggests the function of advertising in the American economy—it keeps the spider webs off merchants' doors and manufacturers' machines. When machines are running and doors are swinging to serve customer demand, all society benefits.

The advertising that serves this function is much advanced over its forerunners in the Old World and the early United States—the illustrative signs outside the taverns and the shops of local merchants. Such advertisements were mere pictorial notices of the availability of goods or services, though well suited to a society in which illiteracy was commonplace and needs were few and simple. Much of the early printed advertising in the United States was little more than an extension of these sign-notices to a greater number of observers through the medium of a newspaper or a magazine. Adequate for the time, such advertising was lacking in the persuasive power necessary to spark a rapidly expanding industrial society. How has this persuasive quality come to be necessary?

As was indicated earlier, the Industrial Revolution which introduced the means of mass production created the need for mass consumption. One cannot exist successfully without the other, and since manufacturers already had the facilities to produce in great quantities, they needed a larger market or pool of potential consumers. They had to broaden their horizons considerably, and exclusive ties with local merchants, developed through the years, gradually began to disappear. Marketing practices reversed themselves as the manufacturer or his representatives made sales calls on competing retail merchants and competing manufacturers placed their merchandise with the same retailer.

The greatest change of all, however, was the need to communicate with the consumer on a large scale, nationally. Although it was important to a manufacturer that the retailer *sell* his product, this merchant now carried the same or similar merchandise manufactured by a number of competing producers. It was up to the manufacturer to *pre-sell* his goods so that the consumer would demand them.

While the manufacturer was able to use salesmen to call upon the wholesale or retail merchant, he could not practically reach all of the potential consumers of his product through salesmen. The only way to get a sales message to a great number of people in a short time was through advertising by means of the mass media. And new techniques in advertising were being developed constantly until it became the great builder of mass markets that it is today.

One of the best examples of the success of the concept of pre-selling is the modern supermarket, which employs no sales clerks and merely stocks well-advertised merchandise on its shelves, the buying choice being left to the customer. This practice leads to lower-priced consumer products and services while affording a higher profit return to the seller.

Belated recognition of this principle came from the Hershey Foods Corporation. Hershey, a paradox of American marketing, had done no advertising

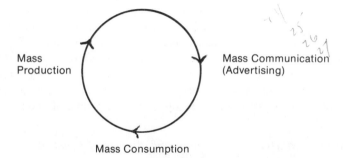

Mass Production

Mass Communication (Advertising)

Mass Consumption

The Production-Advertising-Consumption Cycle. It is possible to see any of the three elements as the initiator, but mass consumption as a result of mass communication is generally necessary to sustain successful mass production.

since its founding in 1900. It began to advertise in 1970, for the first time, after feeling the pinch of competition.

"We just want to sell more chocolate at a better profit and that's why we are going to advertise," said Hershey president Harold S. Mohler. Elaborating on this statement, he further declared, "More people are eating chocolate, but there is much more competition among the manufacturers. The need for communication with the consumer is more evident than ever to us. Supermarkets and vending machines are darn cold ways to sell a product." [2]

Of course, advertising alone is not responsible for our present industrial development or high level of living any more than are railroads, banks, or the machinery of manufacturers. Advertising is but a part of the whole economic structure—a structure created by the efficiency and effectiveness of its several parts. What, then, is advertising's special place in the economy? What function or functions does it perform?

WHAT ADVERTISING DOES

Advertising as a Tool for Selling

Advertising lowers prices and encourages competition. It is, above all, a tool for selling—its primary function is to communicate sales messages. But in performing that function fully, advertising is also an instrument of education, a molder of public opinion, and a builder of public relations.

Advertising as an Instrument of Education

Advertising, as an educator, speeds the adoption of the new and untried and, in so doing, accelerates technological advances in industry and hastens the realization of a fuller life for all. It helps reduce accidents and waste of natural resources, and contributes to building a better understanding and appreciation of American ideologies.

But advertising must be more than education. If it were no more, then one of the most powerful forces in the development and maintenance of our economic system would be greatly impaired. Advertising must be persuasive if it is to move people to action, whether that action be the purchase of a different brand of breakfast cereal or regular attendance at church on Sundays. Often advertising must be persuasive to an extent that has little in common with the impartiality of education. It is this very persuasiveness that makes advertising a great selling tool, a molder of public opinion and a builder of good public relations.

Advertising as a Molder of Opinion and Builder of Goodwill

Advertising as a molder of opinion helps to win elections, builds faith in a democratic way of life, becomes the keystone of a free competitive economy, and encourages interest in our environment and the ecology.

As an instrument of public relations, advertising helps to sell goods and ideas, but it also assists in maintaining goodwill among the various group interests that must function in harmony in a democracy.

Goodwill has been recognized as a very valuable asset and a tremendous aid to sales. A good product at a fair price is important, but so too are the many human relationships that combine to make the corner store or the billion-dollar corporation well-thought-of or disliked. Customer relation, labor relations, community relations, stockholder relations, and trade relations are important in many different phases of the operation of a business, but every one of them helps or hinders in the making of sales.

Thus advertising, in addition to its direct job of selling (pointing out the desirable features of a commodity or service and showing the potential buyers how they can derive satisfaction from a purchase), it can also do an indirect job of selling by persuading the public to view with special favor not only a particular brand but the maker of the brand as well. Furthermore, institutional advertising (or public-relations advertising) may be employed to sell more than products and services. It may be employed to sell ideas. In selling goods and services, advertising is used in the competitive battle to win men's dollars; in selling ideas, it is used to win men's minds. The moral obligations of the advertiser are greater with respect to the latter. Public opinion is powerful; and in molding it, advertising can be and is a potent force. But advertising is not a concealed effort to influence and mold opinion. Remember that the space an advertisement occupies—in a newspaper, magazine, street car, or on a poster panel—as well as the time it consumes on radio or television, is paid for by the advertiser and is readily identified with him. In this respect, advertising is more candid in its endeavor to influence thought and action than is publicity, which may appear as a newspaper story, a magazine article, or a radio commentator's opinion—showing no obvious connection with the party who inspired or created it. Publicity, in large part, is designed to *appear* as impartially written news. Because of the inability of the general public to distinguish between what is impartially gathered and presented news and what has been prepared by private interests in an effort to advance their own cause—commercial, political or otherwise—publicity is a more subtle molder of opinion than advertising.

Adolph Katz can sing today because you gave your wife a pretty négligée for her birthday.

A négligée made of Du Pont nylon looks and feels soft and luxurious. So people buy a lot of them. And Du Pont makes a profit on its nylon.

Part of that profit goes to people who have invested money in Du Pont, part goes for taxes and part goes to help support Du Pont research. From such research come new products, sometimes whole new businesses (which mean more jobs) and bold new uses of older products. One such use: surgically inject a tiny amount of specially treated Du Pont plastic into a paralyzed vocal chord. And so, hundreds of people who once could hardly speak can now speak clearly. And Cantor Adolph Katz, silenced for nine years, can once more "sing unto the Lord."

Last year, Du Pont spent $336 million in research. All of it was available because Du Pont could and did make money on nylon and other products.

That's the way our American economic system works. Profits aren't an end in themselves. They're a beginning. They make good things happen.

This message has been brought to you by the Hammermill Paper Company, of Erie, Pennsylvania, makers of fine papers. We're proud of our economic system. We want you to be proud, too.

HAMMERMILL PAPERS®

Profits make good things happen.
Just ask Adolph Katz.

This is a public relations or institutional advertisement. Note that while the Hammermill Paper Company paid for the ad, it describes an achievement of The DuPont Company, and is a tribute to the American economic system.

29

Advertising in the United States operates in a competitive arena. Claims are met with counterclaims, charges with countercharges. It is virtually impossible in some areas of operation for an advertiser to place his message before the public without challenge from opposing interests. This is especially true when advertising is employed to win public support in political or labor-management controversies. Public-opinion-molding advertising dramatically demonstrates the opposing forces in a free economy. Here the advertiser and the advertised-to are seen side-by-side at the raucous but nonetheless free round table of public-opinion formation. Excellent examples of how opposing opinions are expressed in American advertising are the National Association of Manufacturers and the American Federation of Labor advertisements that were placed in newspapers on consecutive days during the time when a labor bill was being considered in Congress.

Newspapers often become the forum for an "advertising debate." During a telephone strike some years ago, the New York Telephone Company and the National Federation of Telephone Workers, in the struggle to win public support or understanding, turned to newspaper advertising. Their advertisements appeared on facing pages of a leading New York City newspaper—a striking example of the fairness of an advertising medium in its handling of controversial issues as they are presented in paid advertising space.

Another use of institutional advertising may be found in a full-page ad run by Hunt-Wesson Foods. Hunt-Wesson was trying to show that there was no relationship between their company and another food manufacturing company with a similar name, owned by the Texas oil millionaire H. R. Hunt. The latter Hunt was politically active, while Hunt-Wesson claimed their "only business is trying to make the best food products we know how."

Not all public-relations or institutional advertising is associated with controversy. Many of the Metropolitan Life Insurance Company's advertisements undertake to contribute to the community at large. One, for example, warned the public about the need for immunization.

The Mobil Oil Corporation began its driver-safety "we want you to live" campaign in 1966. During the first five-year period, through January 1971, it ran some 50 different public-relations ads in newspapers and magazines and four television commercials, at a combined cost of about $8.5 million. These dramatic advertisements featured a large photo which took up two-thirds of the space; the copy, or text, occupied the balance.

Some of these advertisements were scheduled to run just before long holiday weekends. One that appeared before Labor Day showed a line of cars driving up a hill on a curve. The second car was about to pass. The headline asked "How is the driver of the first car going to kill the driver of the second car?" The answer that began the body copy was, "By driving too slowly." Perhaps the most dramatic of the series showed a tombstone in a cemetery for a man "who didn't want to spoil his mother's Thanksgiving dinner by being late." The stone bore the date, November 26, 1970—Thanksgiving Day.

Socony, Mobil's predecessor company, ran a similar safe-driving cam-

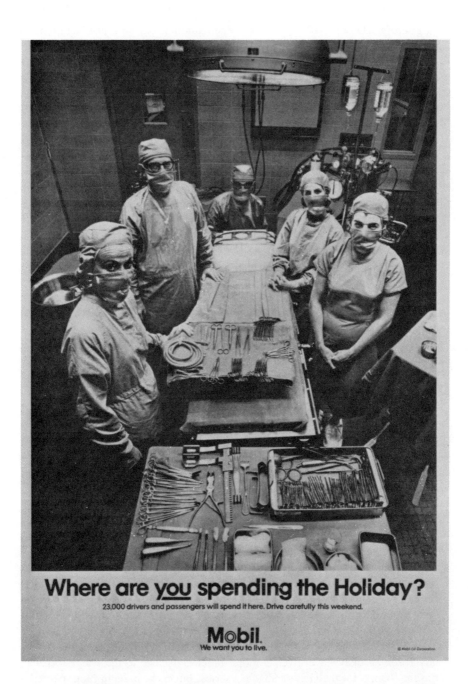

Where are you spending the Holiday?

23,000 drivers and passengers will spend it here. Drive carefully this weekend.

Mobil.
We want you to live.

© Mobil Oil Corporation

One of a series of public service ads published by Mobil in their "We want you to live" campaign. This one ran before a Fourth of July or Memorial Day Holiday that was extended by a weekend. *Prepared for Mobil by Doyle Dane Bernbach.*

paign from 1923 to 1927, in the days when automobiles were just beginning to multiply.

Public-Service Advertising—the Advertising Council

In the forefront of public-service advertising is the privately operated nonprofit Advertising Council, founded in 1942 to support the United States effort in World War II. By 1970 the nation's communications media had contributed through the Council more than $5 billion worth of advertising time and space toward "persuading individual citizens to take actions which would improve their own lot, or their community's, or the welfare of their fellow citizens."[3] And during 1973 alone the value of media contributions amounted to $570,756,834.[4]

The Advertising Council is a uniquely American institution supported by the efforts of the advertising agencies, business and industry, and the media, all of whom contribute, free of charge, their creative talents, work, time, and money. It has been estimated that they have helped:

- save more than 750,000 lives through traffic safety advertising;
- save more than $17 billion in timber resources;
- triple voluntary contributions to colleges and universities;
- alleviate the growing shortage of trained technicians for industry and government;
- find jobs for more than 1,405,000 youth, veterans, and hard-core unemployed;
- speed up mail by use of Zip Codes;
- raise U.S. Savings Bond holdings up to a record $5.9 billion a year.[5]

In addition the Advertising Council has raised money for the United Fund, helped "Keep America Beautiful," recruited volunteers for the Peace Corps and for Vista, and much more.

Institutional Company Advertising

Representative of the institutional or public relations advertising done during World War II was a series run by the Hecht Company, a department store in Washington, D.C. Hecht published a number of advertisements picturing outstanding personalities of the Axis nations (Germany, Italy, and Japan) as candidates for the "Hall of Shame." Another type or retail institutional advertisement was placed by some New York City merchants. It pictured in cartoon style an American man and woman being decorated by Adolph Hitler for services to Nazi Germany. That this couple had hoarded rationed goods was made apparent by the overstuffed closet forming the background of the cartoon. This advertisement may have given a more direct assistance to the war effort than did the "Busts for the Hall of Shame" series, but each, in its fashion, carried a wartime message to the public and at the same time reminded people of the sponsoring stores.

Shortages of consumer goods and services during the war years made

How much change does our American Economic System need: A lot? A little? None?

The more we all know about our system and how it works, the better we can decide what to preserve, what to change in the years ahead. That's why this special booklet has been prepared. Every American ought to know what it says. For a free copy, write: "Economics", Pueblo, Colorado 81009.

The American Economic System.

A public service of The Advertising Council & U.S. Department of Commerce presented by this Magazine.

One of a series of public service ads on the American Economic System prepared gratis by Compton Advertising, Inc. for the Advertising Council.

This is what little girls are made of.

Every minute, three billion cells in a little girls' body are being replaced by new ones.

The material for each new cell comes from the nutrients in the food she eats. What these nutrients do once they reach her body, and what they do with each other will make her different from every other little girl.

Her life depends on nutrition. She'll grow to live life well or ill because of it. We study nutrition. And we've learned that although poverty is the chief cause of malnutrition, it isn't the only cause.

Almost half of us are undernourished. And through nothing more than a lack of knowledge about the food we eat.

Every day we're learning more. You should learn more too.

To give you some basic information and valuable guides to preparing meals and diets, we've put together a book entitled "Food Is More Than Just Something to Eat."

Write for it. Nutrition, Pueblo, Colorado 81009. And we'll send it to you. Free.

A Public Service of This Magazine & The Advertising Council

A public service ad prepared by Compton Advertising, Inc. on a voluntary basis, without charge for the Advertising Council.

sales-promotion advertising relatively unnecessary or even undesirable. But these very shortages, plus ill will that was building up because of curt treatment by some retail sales people, made public-relations advertising highly desirable. Personal contacts with the buying public offered manufacturers few if any problems, but dealer relationships and shortages or absolute lack of civilian goods made public-relations advertising necessary to keep alive brand and company names and to maintain goodwill.

War is not the only cause of shortages. For a number of years, because capacity has not kept up with demand, an electric-power shortage has bothered the northeastern part of the country. It is particularly noticeable in the summer when air conditioners draw extra power. This shortage came to a crisis on November 9, 1965, when a total power blackout stretched along the East Coast from Pennsylvania through eight states and two Canadian provinces. For 13 hours there were no electric lights, no electric refrigeration, no radio or television reception except through battery-operated sets; neither subways, elevators, or major airports operated—in sum, nothing worked among the many electricity-powered things that we take for granted. One of the steps taken to prevent a recurrence was an interesting advertising campaign that urged people to *buy less* of the product. Under the overall theme of "Save a Watt," New York City's Consolidated Edison Company advised its customers, through the print and electronic media, on a number of ways to save electricity.

Toward the end of 1973 the nation was hit with an oil shortage. The large oil companies began to ration heating oil and gasoline to their dealers who, in turn, rationed the product to their retail customers. And their advertising, too, encouraged us to use less, and provided tips on how to save gasoline: "If you drive at 50 miles per hour instead of 60, you can save about one gallon in ten."[6]

SUMMARY

Advertising, then, may sell goods, may sell services, may educate in the process of selling, may mold public opinion, may build goodwill. In the performance of these functions it becomes a powerful force in mass communication and in persuasive selling, both necessary to a great industrial economy.

Yet it must be recognized that advertising has definite limitations. It cannot make people continue to buy a product from which they derive no satisfactions. Neither can it create new wants. How, then, can it create an increasing volume of sales?

Because of environment or other factors, some desires may be latent or unrecognized. Advertising can and does awaken them. Advertising can and does make them apparent. Sometimes personal desires may be recognized, but the urge to fulfill them may not be sufficiently strong to motivate action. Advertising can and does strengthen these desires to the point where action is taken. Thus, advertising sets in motion the human reactions that lead to the purchase of advertised products and services.

QUESTIONS AND DISCUSSION SUBJECTS

1. Describe the place of advertising in the United States economy.
2. What could happen if advertising were banned in this country?
3. Name and describe the functions of advertising, what advertising does.
4. To what uses can public-relations or institutional advertising be put?
5. What is the Advertising Council? What does it do?
6. Why would a company that has no merchandise to sell, at the time, continue to advertise?

SOURCES

1. *Advertising Stopped at 10 O'clock* (Washington, D.C.: National Association of Broadcasters, 1975), 1–3.
2. Prudence Brown, "Chocolate Town's Toothache," *Newsday,* August 19, 1969, 68.
3. *The Advertising Council Annual Report,* 1970.
4. *Advertising Council Report to the American People 1973–1974* (New York: The Advertising Council).
5. *Free Enterprise's Effective Communication Machine* (New York: The Advertising Council).
6. Amoco Oil Company, print and electronic advertising in 1973.

FOR FURTHER READING

"A Two-Way View of . . . The Advertising Story." Cincinnati: Procter & Gamble, 1974.

Backman, Jules. *Advertising and Competition.* New York: New York University Press, 1967.

Groner, Alex. *Advertising: The Case for Competition.* New York: Association of National Advertisers, 1967.

McCarthy, E. Jerome. *Basic Marketing.* Homewood, Ill.: Irwin, 1975.

★
★
★ Part Two
★
★

THE WORK OF ADVERTISING

4

Advertising Research

THE NECESSITY FOR RESEARCH

A salesman not knowing who his prospects are or where they are would waste much time wandering about making calls on people who cannot under any circumstances be induced to buy his product. Even if aware of the identity of his prospects and where they live, but knowing no more about them, he could lose many sales by making the wrong approach, emphasizing the wrong sales points. Having all of the necessary information about his prospects but lacking knowledge of his product, he would work under a great disadvantage and unnecessarily lose sales. For complete effectiveness, a salesman must know both his prospects and his product. Sales achieved without such knowledge result either from plain good luck or are made because the prospect was pre-sold the product by someone or something other than the salesman. In these situations, the salesman is either a fortunate gambler or an order-taker. A vending machine might do as good a selling job.

If knowledge of a product and of its prospective buyers is necessary for success in personal salesmanship, it is even more necessary for success in advertising, where the sales message is directed to a large and unseen audience, frequently widely scattered, of potential buyers. If the success of advertising is not to rest upon chance, marketing research and an analysis of the product must be a first step in the development of any advertising activity. Before we can talk about what form an advertising campaign or even a single advertisement should take, we must have information about the product and about the people to whom we hope to sell it. This requirement does not mean that imagination and intuition play no part in advertising. Creative intuition is the basis for much action in advertising, today as always, but it grows from known facts rather than from imagination nurtured by nothing firmer than a guess and a fond hope. Advertising more and more is getting away from unaided creative intuition.

39

And although it might appear that businessmen could solve most of the marketing and advertising problems that confront them by relying upon their own knowledge and experience without the aid of special research, such is not the case. The A. C. Nielsen Company stated that "executives are right or substantially right in only 58% of their decisions on important marketing questions" when such decisions are made without benefit of research.[1] Nielsen reports that this statistic was derived from surveys made for many important corporations.

Fresh research does not precede the creation of every advertisement. If the necessary information is at hand from previous studies and if the findings of these earlier studies are still valid, no more is needed. But if all or any part of the necessary information is lacking, then new research is required. Sometimes the desired information, or at least a part of it, can be obtained from libraries, from studies made by newspapers or magazines or other media, or from trade associations or government agencies. When this is possible, costs are less, and much time can be saved. Often, however, the needed information is not so readily available and must be obtained through field investigations conducted by the advertiser's own research staff, the research department of his advertising agency, or a firm which specializes in conducting market research.

For the advertiser, research falls into four major areas:

1. Research concerned with information about the product.
2. Research concerned with information about the market.
3. Research concerned with information about advertisements.
4. Research concerned with information about advertising media.

PRODUCT INFORMATION

Before an advertisement is visualized, before a single word of copy is written, before a model is posed or a line drawn for an illustration, there should be available answers to a number of questions about the product and about its relationship to the market in which it is to be distributed. What are the product's strong selling points and what, if any, are its weak ones? If there are any weak points, can they be eliminated or must they be met and handled by the advertising? Has the product one use or has it more than one use? If it has more than a single use, how many uses has it, and which is the most promising in terms of building sales volume? Is the product adequately and attractively packaged?

Answers to such questions give the advertiser the raw materials out of which effective advertisements and effective sales promotion can be built.

Product and Package Testing

In some respects, product testing relates more closely to the problems of production than to the problems of advertising. That is, the results of such testing are more likely to suggest changes in the ingredients, design, or manufacture of the product than they are to suggest changes in the advertising approach.

However, consumer preferences that may be discovered by such research may suggest points to emphasize in the advertising sales message.

Before placing a new product on the market, the market-wise manufacturer will run tests to determine its acceptability. Some change in design, color, flavor, or odor may spell the difference between great or small success, even between success and failure. General Motors for many years has conducted product research pertaining to automobile-design preferences among consumers and has made few mistakes in its designing. Some other automobile manufacturers would like very much to be able to make a similar claim.

The need for such testing is not limited to any particular class of products. Almost all manufacturers do extensive product research in test markets before introducing nationally. Some tests concern color preferences. Others concern design, shape, unit size, or other variables. Hard goods and soft goods, goods with a dominant style factor and goods with little or no style factor—all are subject to product tests.

When a new package is to be put on the market, whether it is a container for a new product or for an old, established one, questions must arise concerning its effectiveness as a sales tool. Is it the best design that could have been developed with regard to the marketing problems at hand? Is it superior to the old package? How will it compare with competitors' packages? Are the colors right? Is the lettering too large?—too small?—too thick?—too thin? These and other questions must be answered. Sometimes the answers are obtained from an expert in the field of packaging, sometimes from conferences of client and advertising-agency executives, and sometimes by taking the problem directly to the public with consumer-market tests.

In one case of developing a new package, the commercial artist commissioned to do the job submitted more than 60 separate designs over a period of three months before one finally was selcted as the "right" package for the product. Often, drawings of the proposed package are not enough—models must be made of each proposed design. These models are then shown to a group of consumers selected on some predetermined sampling basis, or they are shown to a consumer panel * or to executives of the client's firm. When the consumers are involved, we have true package testing. Where the firm's officers make the decision, guessing—maybe extremely good guessing, but still guessing—has been substituted for testing.

MARKET INFORMATION

Information about the product and its package is not all the raw material that is needed to do a successful marketing job. In addition to such information, the sales and advertising staffs must have facts about the market, about the people who are the buyers and the potential buyers of the product, where they are to be found, and a variety of other data concerning them and their activities.

---

* A *consumer panel* is a comparatively permanent group of people maintained by an advertising agency or research organization for purposes of research and testing.

The Domestic Market

Stretching East and West between the two great oceans of the world and extending from the Rio Grande on the south to the border of Canada on the north lie 3,628,130 square miles of land, lakes, and rivers. To these, Alaska adds 586,400 square miles and Hawaii 6,423 square miles to form the 50 states of the United States of America. Other territory includes Puerto Rico, the Virgin Islands, Samoa, and Guam. Within the reaches of this great land, one city stands 4,950 feet above sea level and another all but dips its streets in the tidewaters of the ocean, standing but four feet above the sea. More than 67 inches of rain fall annually upon one community; another rarely sees the sun darkened by a cloud. Residents of one locality watch the mercury in their thermometers climb to a normal maximum summer high of 104° while in another locality people live comfortably under a normal maximum high of only 75°. Normal winter temperatures vary as much as 68° from one place to another even with Alaska excluded from consideration.

Upon this land of marked topographical and climatic differences live more than 210 million people,[2] of whom a little more than half are women. More than 20 million range from 15 to 19 years of age, another 18 million are between the ages of 20 and 24, and more than 50 million are between 25 and 44 years old.[3] These people are not scattered evenly over the land, nor are their numbers divided evenly among the residents of big cities, farms, and small towns. Alaska has an average of but 1 person per square mile; New Jersey has 979.[4] Neither do these people remain in one place. Over the years there have been sizable migrations from rural areas to urban areas and from cities to suburbs. The forefathers of some of these people fired on the British at Concord; 400,000 arrived in the United States for the first time in 1973;[5] others came today. It is estimated that 45 million held high-school diplomas in 1975 and that 15 million had college degrees.

This is market information, in a very general sense. But an advertiser has need for much more specific kinds of market information. Most of it must be found by hard digging in answer to sharp questions about what people need, what they will buy, what they can buy, how they buy, and about all the other W and H words and ideas that are used to ask questions in the English language.

Location and People

A market is usually associated with a geographic location and may be identified in terms of a particular location or place. But a market also must consist of people willing and able to buy the product or potentially willing and able to buy it. A business-finance executive effectively dramatized the importance of the concept of the market as comprised of people when he said:

> I can recall when the New York Curb Exchange was located on the sidewalk and when an order was consummated by a clerk snapping his fingers under the belly of a horse drawing a wagon loaded with beer barrels down the street. There was activity there—people buying and people selling. There was a market. On the other

hand, I visited an exchange in Europe during the depths of the Great Depression of the 1930's. This exchange was housed in a beautiful building with all of the then most modern equipment and trappings. But there were no people—no buyers, no sellers. There was no market.

A location becomes important or loses its importance depending upon what people are doing and thinking. In turn, what people are doing or thinking with respect to the purchase of products may be somewhat conditioned by physical location. Where rainfall is unusually heavy and the drying of laundry consequently difficult, people may be more receptive to a drying-machine advertisement than are people in sections of the country that have only occasional showers. The rugged winters of the North are more conducive to a favorable attitude toward heating units, insulation materials, and storm windows than are the milder climates of more southerly areas. Even movements of population may result in part from a quest for more attractive climate or greater economic opportunity, which in turn may depend on the physical characteristics of location. Therefore, it is both difficult and impractical to divorce the concept of the market *as a place* and the market *as people*. It must be both; each has its impact upon the other.

For the advertiser, the information needed about the market divides into two broad areas:

1. Information related to the economic and sociological factors that are having or will have impact upon the marketing situation in general.
2. Information more directly related to the sale of the particular product as distinct from other products on the market. This information would relate to the buyers or potential buyers of the product as a class and to buyers and potential buyers of the particular brand. It would be concerned with the competitive situation, motivation of consumers, and so on.

Information concerning the first area is usually obtainable from government agencies and from secondary sources. Information concerning the second area more often must be obtained firsthand. In this second area, the advertiser must obtain both quantitative and qualitative data. He must know how many people are buyers of the product as a class and how many are buyers of his particular brand; he must know if these buyers are men, women, or children. If they are women, it might be desirable to know whether they are housewives or working women. More than 30 million women are employed in the major occupation groups as listed by the Bureau of Labor Statistics. These women have less time to buy than the housewives, frequently need different kinds of products, and may well be interested in different kinds of advertising appeals. The advertiser will want to know the age and income of his buyers and where they live, what they read, and what kind of entertainment they enjoy. In what quantities they purchase the product, how often they buy it, and from what type of retail outlets they obtain it are all of concern if the advertiser is to plan the most effective advertising possible. Whether there is a difference between the *buyers* and the *users* of the product is of great importance. If such a difference does exist, he must determine whether the buyer or the user is the more influential party in the choice-making and buying.

Only when the advertiser has this kind of information is he prepared to solve the problems associated with writing the most effective copy, designing the best layouts, and buying the best media to carry his message to the most productive markets.

Research studies reveal many things of interest to advertising and marketing people. A considerable number of them can be found in the pages of the *Journal of Marketing,* published by the American Marketing Association; the *Journal of Marketing Research;* in the *Journal of Advertising,* published by the American Academy of Advertising; and in the *Journal of Advertising Research* of the American Research Foundation.

One such study of four American social classes made by Kim Rotzoll [6] indicated that consumption standards focused on two levels. The social classes studied were the Lower-Lower, the Upper-Lower, the Lower-Middle and the Upper-Middle class. The findings demonstrated that the "American standard" or "level for the Common Man," already attained by the Lower-Middle class was the consumption goal sought by the two lower classes. On the other hand, the consumption aims and aspirations of the Upper-Middle class centered on the achievements of the Upper class. People in the Upper-Middle group are highly ambitious and education played a part in their spending. It manifested itself in the purchase of experience types of intangibles that leave "only a memory." These included such things as travel, education, hobbies, and recreation.

Another study, on the personality traits and temperament of automobile owners,[7] was made by Professor Ralph Westfall at the University of California, Los Angeles. His findings indicated that there did not seem to be any marked personality differences between the owners of compact and standard cars but that there appeared to be differences between the owners of those two types and the owners of convertibles. Car owners scoring high in one or more of the characteristics *active, vigorous, impulsive, dominant,* or *sociable,* particularly those with high scores in *active,* were more likely to buy a convertible than the average car owner. On the other hand, less likely purchasers of a convertible were those who ran low in the aforementioned characteristics, not including *dominant.* Professor Westfall's findings also corroborated those of an earlier study by Franklin B. Evans, who found no significant personality differences between the owners of Chevrolets and Fords.

Age and Sex of Prospects

The importance of making an appeal to the more influential party in consumer buying activities is recognized in the historic advice of the *Ladies' Home Journal:* "Never underestimate the power of a woman." A comparable piece of sage advice was carried in a West Coast newspaper advertisement: "It doesn't matter who wears the pants, it's who picks them out that counts." A few years ago, a company manufacturing and selling a product used almost exclusively by men had assumed that it was also bought by men. However, research showed that women were the largest buyers and that they bought the product as a gift for men. This discovery led to a restyling of the product and a resulting sizable increase in sales. All this might lead one to assume that women are always the dominant influence in making buying decisions as well as the chief purchasing agents for American homes, but that is not always so.

Consider children. Mothers are the buyers of ready-prepared packaged cereals, but the processors of these cereals have found it profitable to aim much of their broadcast advertising, premium offers, and package designs toward children. Toys, and probably much clothing for children, are bought in accordance with the wishes of Junior and Sissie.

And consider husbands. One manufacturer of high-priced appliances even suggested in an advertisement that "Behind every purchase there is the shadow of a man." A study made a number of years ago for *True—The Man's Magazine* revealed that in the homes studied the husband was the dominant influence in making brand choices in 12 product and service classes studied. These 12 classes were beer, liquor, automobiles, tires, work shirts, life insurance, air conditioners, television sets, electric shavers, shaving cream, outboard motors, and air travel.

However, in most buying situations, others of the family may make their impact felt. The *True* study revealed that in a sample of 107 urban homes the original suggestion to purchase a new automobile was made by the husband and that in most cases he decided on the make which would be bought. Choice of model, however, was a mutual decision of husband and wife, and the wife selected the color and upholstery. The major influence in 103 households in the selection of a brand of work shirt, although resting with the husband in most cases, varied with the income status of the family. The wives in lower-income families exerted more influence over the purchase of work shirts than did the wives in higher-income groups. In 101 households studied, husbands exerted the major influence on the brand selection of portable television sets, but the original decision to buy arose most often from a conflict of family interests concerning program preferences. In more than half of the households studied, the man's preference determined the brand of the most recently purchased electric shaver. Even in some cases where the shavers were gifts, the husband was able to influence brand selection. In shaving cream, husbands almost exclusively were responsible for selection of brand, with long-standing brand loyalties playing an important role in the purchases.

A more recent syndicated study on male influence was concluded by the Simmons Organization in 1972. The report, "The Male Expression of His Brand Influence," indicated that the man of the house also exerted influence on many grocery, food, beverage, and toiletry products that had always been considered to be entirely within the purview of women. In a listing of 64 of these products—including such items as shampoo, bacon, tea, yogurt, canned tuna, and pretzels—it was shown that 58.4% of male users had "High Influence" as far as the choice of brand of regular ground coffee was concerned. (The report defined the "High Influence" category as those males who either "influence it completely" or exercise "quite a bit of influence.") The lowest-ranking categories or the list over which men exerted a "high" degree of influence were packaged instant potatoes and rice mixes, each of which claimed 30%.[8]

In a further effort to document the influence of strength of men in the marketplace, Charles D. Hepler, publisher of *Reader's Digest,* pointed out that "in any given two-week period, 4 out of 10 shoppers in supermarkets are men. And in a typical two-week period, 70% of *all* men visit the supermarket." He concluded that they weren't "there just to squeeze the Charmin." [9]

In the past, men usually went to the supermarket with a list made out by their wives. This is not the case today, according to *Chain Store Age:* "The power of the male supermarket shopper is *real.* Over half of male customers are the *primary* shoppers for their households." [10]

Income and Social Class

Where the advertiser discovers that the dominant buying influence with respect to his product rests with women, his problems may still be complicated by the fact that all women may not think or act alike when selecting and buying products and services. Macfadden-Bartell publishes a number of periodicals. Among these is a Women's Group consisting of eight magazines led by *True Story* and *Photoplay.* In the early 1940s the publisher became aware of the unique appeal these magazines held for the blue-collar working-class woman. They have been studying her since that time.

An early study made for the then Macfadden Publications by Social Research, Inc., indicated that there were marked social and psychological differences between the wives of white-collar workers and the wives of skilled and "service" workmen,* and that these differences were reflected by different behavior in the market place. In many cases there was little or no difference in income received by the white-collar worker and the skilled laborer; the differences observed did not therefore stem from differences in "spending levels" but rather from a more basic and inherent characteristic bred of social background. The two groups of women might, and to a large extent did, buy the same products, but they bought them for different reasons.

That study stated that the wife of the blue-collar worker needed "reassurance that the world will treat her well" to a far greater extent than did the wife of the white-collar worker. "She wants reassurance," says Macfadden, "that the products she buys for her family, and particularly for her children, are safe, and that she, herself, is on secure ground in having faith and confidence in these products. Advertising should give her that assurance." In enlarging on the contrast between the white-collar worker's wife and the wife Macfadden had chosen to call the "Familiar Stranger," the statement was made that "Since the social horizons of the Familiar Stranger are more limited than those of [the white-collar worker's wife], she feels a great need for the personal satisfaction of prettying-up her home, and, in fact, her children. . . . Advertising,

* *Service workmen* include policemen, bus drivers, firemen, postmen, and the like—producers of services rather than of tangible products.

then, probably is better received when it conveys some of this prettied-up atmosphere, when it is not purely factual in its presentation. A product which fits in
with the Familiar Stranger's more serious striving for average-woman status
and, at the same time, proves emotionally gratifying has, according to Social
Research, the strongest appeal.''

As late as 1965, a more current Social Research study ''found the workingman's wife to be as housebound and family centered as her grandmother
before her.'' [11] However, shortly thereafter signs of ''interesting shifts in values'' [12] began to take place. These indications gave rise to the latest study,
''Working Class Women in a Changing World,'' concluded in mid-1973 by
Social Research.

The new study covers a relatively short span of years; however, it bridges
a period of great social change, resulting from the Vietnam War and other factors. It includes the effects of such major movements as Consumerism and
Women's Liberation.

The study shows the workingman's wife to be less homebound than she
had been and more active in community affairs. Her social contacts and friend-
ships, previously centered on relatives, are now widening and she has become
more like the conventional Middle-Class woman of an earlier period. While the
gap between the two has narrowed considerably, it still remains because the
Middle-Class woman has changed, too.

It is interesting to note that the Working-Class woman is dropping her adherence to the old Protestant ethic and is seeking more immediate and self-cen-
tered gratification. As for Women's Liberation, it is meeting its greatest resistance among workingmen's wives who cling ''to their traditional role of being
dependent on their men'' although they are less reluctant to complain about the
drudgery of housekeeping and child-rearing.

Consumerism, as well, has made few gains among the wives of workingmen.

> Since the mid 60's, the workingman's wife has gone a long way in acquiring
> the complement of appliances and equipment Middle-Class people have long held
> essential if they are to be served, entertained, and otherwise catered to in the style
> they crave. Thus, Working-Class ownership of such items is up appreciably and,
> more important, basic attitudes toward many goods and services have shifted.
> Fewer things are rated now as ''luxuries'' and more are seen as becoming in the na-
> ture of ''necessities.'' Also, the kinds of things which are especially prized and
> sought after have changed in a way that points to a markedly new set of values.
> Thus, products and services which save the woman work, make her comfortable,
> entertain her, enable her to go away from home—such things as dishwashers, air
> conditioners, stereos, personal cars, baby sitters, etc.—are things which are find-
> ing appreciably greater favor in her eyes. Things which are more closely geared to
> work—such as kitchen stoves and sewing machines—have lost part of their appeal.
>
> All in all, the Working-Class woman is the most enthusiastic and pleased of
> consumers (dissatisfied only in the sense that she cannot consume as much as she
> would like). Thus, she tends to believe the quality of goods and services has been
> improving over recent years (higher-status women are more inclined to question

this). Likewise, she is more receptive and positive in her orientation toward advertising than is the Middle-Class woman, particularly in acknowledging her use of it
as a source of ideas. As a relatively fresh and recent participant in many consumer
areas, she quite likely uses this source to guide as well as motivate her consumer
behavior.[13]

The Teen-Age Market

Another area with which many advertisers must concern themselves is the
teen-age market, estimated at $9½ billion and steadily growing. Studies made
by Eugene Gilbert and Company, a leading research firm in this field, have
shown that the teen-age population either buys or exercises a dominant influence upon the purchase of a large number and wide variety of consumer goods
and services.

Studies made of the readers of *Seventeen* magazine show that 58% of girls
aged 13 to 19 do the weekly family food shopping. In 23% of the cases the
girls made the shopping list themselves; another 18% made out the list together
with their mothers; and 3.3% did not use a list.[14] Close to eight million girls
between 14 and 17 years of age spent $3,143,540,000 for fashion and non-
fashion merchandise in 1973 in preparation for high school [15] and in the same
year 1,149,000 women entering colleges spent a total of $398,026,000, at the
start of the term, for wearing apparel, things for fun and work, and things for
their rooms.[16] *Seventeen* points out that not only do teen-age girls have all this
money of their own to spend, but they also influence family spending amount-
ing to billions of dollars more for major purchases, and they have impact upon
the market as receivers of gifts on all manner of special occasions such as birth-
days, graduations, back-to-school, off-to-college, and so on. This age group
also has a great market impact as new homemakers. Studies made for *Seventeen* shows that "more than one million (8.9%) teen girls are already engaged.
The median age of engagements is 17.3 with wedding bells only 6.8 months
away." [17]

According to studies of the spending habits of teen-age males, the influence which they exert, like that of their sisters, is felt across a wide range of
products and services and manifests itself both in terms of purchases made by
the teen-agers themselves and by their influence upon family spending.

Motivation Research

The questions concerning what makes people buy or fail to buy, or buy
one brand rather than another fall within the broad area of market research that
relates to the selling of particular products or brands. Although these are questions that probably always have been of some interest to advertisers, increased
interest has been generated in recent years by motivation research.

Motivation research, or MR, differs from earlier efforts to find answers to
the question of what makes people buy. It is based upon a belief that the
reasons why a consumer accepts or rejects a product are frequently not known

to him and often are not the ones that appear most obvious. To discover the real reasons for buying, the research worker must conduct depth interviews * and then engage in psychoanalytical interpretations of the findings.

The actual techniques employed in sampling and in obtaining information, as well as the relative importance given to Freudian psychology, group-behavior patterns, and cultural and environmental factors in interpreting data, vary among motivation-research workers and are beyond the scope of this text.

Motivation research has a number of critics, some of whom question its value as a marketing research tool and some of whom express doubts about whether its procedures are scientific. Others criticize it on ethical grounds, suggesting that it is wrong to probe into man's subconscious to discover ways of motivating his actions in the market place. But, regardless of all the criticism, motivation research has been widely used by advertisers, and many an advertising appeal has been changed as a result of its findings. For example, a campaign for a food product that had placed emphasis on the attractiveness of a fine and fit figure changed to an "hors d'oeuvres or snacks" appeal when motivation research indicated that many people were associating the product with dieting. Another advertiser removed a design element from his package when MR showed that customers viewing the package blinked their eyes more than customarily. A shoe manufacturer changed the illustrations in his advertisements from pictures showing shoes alone to pictures of men wearing shoes when motivation research indicated that this might lessen a dislike among men for buying new shoes.

So, whether one accepts the position of the critics or of the advocates of motivation research, the fact remains that it has molded advertising of several important companies and probably will continue to exert an influence for some time to come.

Gathering Information

The advertiser may obtain the information he needs in any one way or in a combination of ways. Among the methods available to him are the following:

1. The placing of observers in strategic locations or in places predetermined by the nature of the research with the purpose of making a physical count of the occurrence to be measured.
2. The obtaining of answers to specific questions by use of: (a) personal interviews; (b) written questionnaires; (c) telephone interviews.
3. The use of an experimental program to test the product, the package, the advertising approach, or the marketing practices of the advertiser.
4. The employment of a consumer panel or dealer panel, depending upon the nature of the information sought.

* *Depth interviewing* is a method of personal interviewing that employs a comparatively small sample and no formal set of questions. The interviewer in conversation with the respondent attempts to gain an insight into his reactions. Completeness of detail is a major aim of the interview and an important characteristic of the technique.

Neither time in an elementary course in advertising nor space in an elementary advertising textbook permits a detailed study of these and other research methods that the advertiser may use. But, in general, it may be said that if the problem at hand can be solved by an answer to the question "How much?" or "How many?" the use of observers and a physical count may prove quite satisfactory. Examples of the use of this method are found in traffic counts for evaluation of poster or store locations and in style counts to determine style or color popularity trends in shoes, ready-to-wear, and the like. However, the questionnaire method is recommended if the solution to the problem demands an answer to the question "Why?"

In employing the questionnaire method, the advertiser will not question the entire group (or *universe*) in which he is interested unless it happens to be comparatively small, as in the case of people employed in certain kinds of businesses. Instead, he will send interviewers or questionnaires to what he regards as a *reliable* and *representative sample*.* Sometimes the interviewers are given the freedom to question whom they please. However, this system has the decided disadvantage of readily creating a bias in the sample should the interviewers happen to question people predominantly of one sex or of approximately the same age or income level or other characteristic. To guard against this shortcoming, the sampling procedure is often predetermined and carefully regulated by the research office to give the interviewers no discretion whatsoever. Sampling may be done on a *random* basis (similar to drawing names from a hat), on an *area* basis (in which an area—presumably representative of a considerably larger area of which it is a part—is established as the location for a prearranged schedule or interviewing), or on a *stratification* or *quota* basis (where for the purpose of interviewing a percentage is selected among the particular type of the entire group of people, occupations, locations, and so on, with which the advertiser is concerned).

If the questionnaire is a written one, considerable care must be taken that questions are not so phrased as to precondition responses, that questions may not be interpreted in more than one way, and that they are adequate to supply the advertiser with all of the information he needs or which he can reasonably hope to obtain.

The telephone type of interview has been used with good results in radio and television audience research, as we shall see in a later chapter.

The experimental method is effective in the testing of a new product, a new package, or any promotional element such as a book jacket, display stand, or self-merchandiser. A publisher wishing to know which of two jackets placed on a novel would sell the more books selected two groups of retail book stores that were as nearly alike as possible. In one of these groups of stores, he placed his novel with jacket A, and in the other group he offered the same book in jacket B. Sales of the books in jacket B were sufficiently greater than sales of

---

* A sample is *reliable* if it is sufficiently large to give accurate results; it is *representative* if it contains an accurate presentation of the characteristics of all of the several component parts that comprise the total of which it is a part.

PLEASE TELL US ABOUT YOUR NEW
1976 CAR

By completing this questionnaire you will be telling car manufacturers your opinion of your new 1976 car, and helping them design future models to fit the wishes of buyers like yourself. To keep your answers confidential, you may detach the label below with your name and address on it. Please do not remove the lower portion of the label as it identifies the model type and the assembly plant where your car was built. We need this information to analyze your answers. Please return this questionnaire in the enclosed postage paid envelope. The pen enclosed is to express our thanks for your help.

Please Remove Name and Address

PLEASE DO NOT REMOVE

PLANT CODE

WRITE IN YOUR NEW CAR'S —

MAKE _____   SERIES NAME OR NUMBER _____
(see example)

		EXAMPLE	
		MAKE	**SERIES**
		Nova	Concours
		Coronet	Brougham
		Montego	MX
		Gremlin	Custom

BODY STYLE:
- ☐ 2-dr. Sedan/Hard Top
- ☐ 3-dr. Hatchback
- ☐ 4-dr. Sedan/Hard Top
- ☐ Convertible
- ☐ 2 Seat Station Wagon
- ☐ 3 Seat Station Wagon
- ☐ Van

Type of Engine? ☐ Gas   ☐ Rotary   ☐ Diesel

Which engine do you have? ☐ Standard   ☐ Optional

Number of cylinders? ☐ 4-cyl.   ☐ 6-cyl.   ☐ 8-cyl.

Did you buy this car ☐ New   or   ☐ Used

What month did you take delivery of this 1976 car?_____ How many miles has it been driven to date? _____

BELOW IS A LIST OF ITEMS THAT ARE AVAILABLE ON MOST CARS

PLEASE CHECK THOSE ITEMS YOU HAVE ON YOUR CAR

- ☐ . . Power Brakes
- ☐ . . Power Steering
- ☐ . . Automatic Transmission
- ☐ . . Automatic Transmission w/Overdrive
- ☐ __ Manual Transmission
- ☐ . . Power Windows
- ☐ . . Power Seats
- ☐ . . Air Conditioning
- ☐ . . Adjustable Steering Wheel
- ☐ __ Cruise Control

- ☐ . . AM Radio
- ☐ . . AM/FM Radio
- ☐ . . AM/FM Stereo Radio
- ☐ . . Cassette Tape Deck
- ☐ __ 8-Track Tape Deck
- ☐ . . Citizens Band Radio
- ☐ . . Power Trunk Lock
- ☐ . . Bucket Seats
- ☐ . . Sun Roof
- ☐ __ Vinyl Roof

CHECK ONE ONLY

- ☐ . . Power Door Locks
- ☐ . . Remote Side View Mirror
- ☐ . . Rear Window Defogger
- ☐ . . Anti-Spin Rear Axle
- ☐ __ White Wall Tires
- ☐ . . Convenience Group (extra lights, mirror, etc.)
- ☐ . . Fuel Injection
- ☐ . . Miles Per Gallon Gauge
- ☐ . . Steel Belted Radial Tires
- ☐ . . Regular Bias Tires

WHEN YOU PURCHASED YOUR 1976 CAR DID YOU . . .

☐ Dispose of a car (owned or leased)   ☐ Keep your previous car   or   ☐ Didn't own a car

PLEASE TELL US ABOUT YOUR PREVIOUS CAR . . .

Make _____ Series Name or Number _____ Year Model, 19 _____

Body Style:
- ☐ 2-dr. Sedan/HT
- ☐ 3-dr. Hatchback
- ☐ 4-dr. Sedan/HT
- ☐ Convertible
- ☐ 2 Seat Station Wagon
- ☐ 3 Seat Station Wagon
- ☐ Van
- ☐ Other _____

Was it bought ☐ New or   ☐ Used ⟶ (if used) **Year Bought?** 19 _____

Important

Everything considered and on the basis of your overall experience, how would you rate this previous car?

☐ Good   ☐ Fair   ☐ Poor

A questionnaire sent to new car buyers by General Motors. *Courtesy of General Motors Corp.*

those in jacket A to warrant the conclusion that jacket B would do the better selling job and that the novel should be marketed in all retail outlets in that jacket.

Consumer panels and dealer panels are often maintained by magazines or other media, by advertising agencies, and by research organizations for the purpose of providing answers to a variety of marketing and advertising questions. For example, a panel may be used to provide information about any one or a combination of such things as the number and brands of products purchased, about radio and television programs tuned-in, about consumer or dealer reactions to new products or new packages or to advertising appeals, and about current opinions in the marketplace.

Panels, like samples, vary in size as they do in purpose. One organization may have a panel consisting of five or six thousand families selected to represent the population of the United States, whereas another organization may have a panel of a few hundred people representing a restricted area or a specific trade.

ADVERTISEMENT INFORMATION

A significant part of advertising research relates directly to the advertisement itself. As it becomes more expensive to reach prospective customers through the media, it becomes increasingly more important to have the strongest, most effective advertising message possible. Consequently, in recent years the field of creative research has mushroomed into an important phase of advertising research.

Creative research, a good part of which is related to copy testing, has three principal components or stages:

A. *Research which helps to create the strategy.* What should the advertisement tell the consumer about the product?
B. *Research which helps in the choice of the creative executive.* What is the best combination of art and words to interpret and communicate the strategy to consumers?
C. *Post-evaluation of the advertising.* How well did people respond to what was said or offered?

Generally speaking, in the first two stages, creative research seeks to explore the elements of message comprehension. Such subjects as word or phrase connotations, picture associations and their meaning, are examined in terms of what they really mean to the consumer. Do consumers understand the story line or, if a demonstration is being utilized, how well is it being perceived?

Advertising impact is also looked for in the first two stages of creative research. Major package-goods advertisers like Procter & Gamble and General Foods consider the impact measurement to be very helpful in evaluating their advertising messages. Impact is deemed important because if consumers cannot recall the message, the message content becomes relatively meaningless.

Advertising impact is usually measured through "playback" type research. Consumers are asked to relate the content of the advertising message some time after the advertisement has run.

Stage three, post-advertising testing, usually measures consumer attitudes. Did my advertising message change the consumer attitude towards the product? If so, what precisely did occur?

Key elements in any copy-research activity include the following:

1. *The means of evaluating.* The system to elicit and record the response.
2. *Size, makeup, and location of audience.* The number of people being interviewed or exposed to the ad or commercial, who they are, and where it is taking place—home? street? theatre?
3. *Point in time.* When the advertisement is being measured—now, or a day after it appeared.
4. *Experimental design.* How many responses or attitudes are being measured? Is the strategy a new or an old one?
5. *Stage of development.* Is the commercial or ad finished and worthy of presenting on the air or publishing, or is it in a very rough stage?

Pre-Testing Print Advertisements

While a number of methods are employed for the testing of print ads, a few of the systems are in more common usage.

Essentially, copy testing consists either of having the respondents rank alternate versions of ads and answer questions about them at the time of the viewing, or asking them to recall information about the ads immediately following the viewing or at a later date. The former method is known as a *consumer jury test.* Examples of the letter are the *dummy magazine test* and the *portfolio test.* In each of these recall methods the viewer is exposed to noncompeting ads, as well as editorial matter, along with the ads to be tested. Gallup and Robinson use *Impact—The World Today,* a dummy magazine they created, for their tests. Another qualitative copy research service is the Starch *Impression Studies. Impression Studies* reports on how many readers showed personal involvement and on how many expressed positive, mixed, indifferent, or negative attitudes toward the entire ad and toward the copy and illustration separately. For the purposes of comparison, Starch provides average comparisons.

Pre-Testing Television Commercials

As with print ads, television commercials are tested prior to "airing" before the general public. Because of the great expense involved in television production and the great expense of air time, there is often a question as to the degree of completion before testing. Obviously, for the sake of realism, the commercial that most resembles the finished thing is best.

In this area, test methods generally fall into two broad categories—contrived and natural. Under the first system, respondents are drawn to a theatre by means of an invitation through the mail or are invited to see a "TV preview" by a representative of the research firm who gives them a "free" pass. This method was pioneered by Dr. Horace Schwerin and is being used today by a number of research firms including McCollum-Spielman, an organization headed by former Schwerin associates. In essence, the audience is exposed to a television program with commercials properly interspersed throughout. Prior to the viewing the audience members complete a questionnaire and at the conclusion of the program they answer additional questions. The degree to which opinions about the product or service have changed is the measure of the effectiveness of the test commercial.

In the second category, respondents view the television programs and commercials under more normal viewing circumstances or conditions. They see them in their own homes, and in some of the methods they are not even aware that they are being tested. Test markets are selected and test commercials are aired along with the regular programming. Random telephone calls are then made to a sample of the population. Alternate versions can be tested in matched markets. The Milwaukee Advertising Laboratory has divided four counties of Greater Milwaukee into two matched markets of 750 families each. The television sets of each panel member have an electronic meter installed that can be controlled for split runs. Simultaneous testing of alternate versions is also accomplished by means of cable television. Half the population of the sample sees version A and the other half sees version B.

Post-Evaluation of Print Advertisements

A number of syndicated research services conduct post-evaluation studies and reports of print ads and their effectiveness.

Daniel Starch & Staff, Inc. publishes syndicated studies generally based on its *Advertisement Readership Service*. Each year Starch conducts studies on over 900 issues of more than 100 magazines (consumer, business, trade and farm), daily newspapers, and Sunday supplements. Readers' observations of ads are measured as "Read Most," "Associated," and "Noted" in declining order. These ratings are also assigned to the components of each ad, including headline, subheads, illustration, copy blocks, logo, and other details. *Adnorms Reports* is a summary of ads studied in the *Advertisement Readership Service;* it provides norms for 36 different size and color units and 109 different product categories. The reports furnish a means for comparison of current ads. *Ad-Track—Relating Marketing Objectives to Advertising Performance* can serve as a marketing/advertising data bank. It provides additional data on product and/or brand usage, purchase, and identification, on the demographic characteristics of readers of a client's advertising, and on which sex influences the purchase of products or brands. Another Starch report is *Impression Studies*. This report and the Gallup and Robinson magazine *Impact* are also employed in pre-testing, as was mentioned earlier in this chapter.

Readex, Inc. provides three studies: *Reader Interest Reports, Ad Component Rating,* and *Red Sticker Reports.* All are readership studies, conducted through the mail, of ads in consumer and farm magazines.

Other studies of advertising effectiveness are conducted by the Opinion

Research Corporation, Audience Studies, Inc., the Harvey Communication Measurement Service, Chilton Ad-Chart Services, and the Magazine Publishers Association.

Post-Evaluation of Television Commercials

In addition to Schwerin and the other services mentioned under the pre-testing of commercials are the Starch *Viewer Impression Studies* and Gallup and Robinson's *Total Prime Time (TPT) Studies* and their *TV Impact* report.

Like the *Reader Impression Studies,* the Starch *Viewer Impression Studies* provide a qualitative report based on random interviews conducted over the telephone with approximately 200 viewers in one or more local areas (depending on the geographic distribution of the commercial).

The *TPT Studies* are conducted in Philadelphia, employing a modified probability sample of 1,400 adults (over 18 years of age). Interviews are conducted in person the day following the broadcast and cover the previous night's prime time period. By referring to a roster, respondents are asked if they recall seeing the commercials, which the interviewer identifies by brand name. They are then asked to answer a series of questions, on those that they recall, related to specific sales points, and to rate the commercial's persuasiveness.

MEDIA INFORMATION

The fourth area of advertising research with which we are concerned is that dealing with the media.

A great number of research studies, similar to those already discussed, are produced by the media themselves. These are designed to show advertisers and advertising agencies the medium's readers' (or listeners' or viewers') affinity for certain products and services, including automobiles,[18] liquor,[19] tools and construction equipment,[20] sports and hobbies,[21] and others. Often these media studies are demographic and psychographic and set forth their subscribers', listeners' and/or viewers' spending powers, levels of education, income, sex, personality traits, and so forth. In addition to the research that is done by advertising agencies and by the media themselves, there is a sizable area of media research that is done by associations in the field, by private research companies, and by members of the academic community.

In an effort to maintain standards for the preparation and evaluation of media research studies, both the American Association of Advertising Agencies and the Association of National Advertisers have published guides. *Recommended Breakdowns for Consumer Media Data* is the result of work begun in 1963 by the American Association of Advertising Agencies (AAAA). It was revised, for the second time, in 1970. The Association of National Advertisers (ANA) published *Evaluating Marketing and Media Research Studies*.

THE ADVERTISING RESEARCH FOUNDATION

The Advertising Research Foundation, or ARF, was organized in 1936 under the joint sponsorship of the American Association of Advertising Agencies and the Association of National Advertisers. It is a nonprofit enterprise supported by its more than 400 members comprising advertisers, advertising agencies, and advertising media. The membership also includes associate members from foreign countries, related associations, other research organizations, and universities. The ARF operates in all areas of research important to advertising. Several of its publications are widely regarded as standard references on both the print and broadcast media, and for motivation research.[22]

Important contributions of the Advertising Research Foundation include the *Journal of Advertising Research,* published every other month, and the Open Audit Plan proposed at ARF's 16th Annual Conference in 1970.[23] The plan offers registration to all advertising research services" and provides ARF-sponsored spot auditing of operations at no cost to the research companies." Another important contribution is the preparation of a publication titled *Criteria for Marketing and Advertising Research.*

SUMMARY

Research is vitally important to all phases of advertising. It furnishes needed information concerning the product, the market, the ad itself, and the media. While this chapter has covered the subject in some detail, additional information on research will be found in a number of the other chapters, particularly Chapter 28, "The Behavioral Sciences and Advertising," written by Dr. Charles Winick, and Chapter 26, "Broadcast Ratings and Services."

QUESTIONS AND DISCUSSION SUBJECTS

1. Why is research necessary in advertising?
2. Into what four areas is advertising research divided?
3. How do product and package research relate to advertising?
4. Define a market.
5. What two broad areas of information about the market are needed by advertising people?
6. Discuss motivational research.
7. How can an advertiser get the information he needs? Explain.
8. Name and describe the key elements in copy research.
9. What methods are used for researching advertising copy? Describe them.
10. What types of information can be learned about media through research?

SOURCES

1. *A Brief Description of Nielsen Food Index and Nielsen Drug Index* (Chicago: A. C. Nielsen Co.).
2. U.S. Department of Commerce, *Statistical Abstract of the United States 1974* (Washington, D.C.: Government Printing Office, 1974), xiii.
3. *Ibid.,* 6.
4. *Ibid.,* 12.
5. *Ibid.,* 97.
6. Kim Rotzoll, "The Effect of Social Stratification on Market Behavior," *Journal of Advertising Research,* VII, No. 1 (March 1967), 22–27.
7. Ralph Westfall, "Psychological Factors in Predicting Product Choice," *Journal of Marketing,* XXVI, No. 2 (April 1962), 34–40.
8. Jane Personeni, "Male Influence," a Memorandum from *Readers' Digest,* October 9, 1972.
9. Charles D. Hepler, "Meet the Men in Your Market," *Advertising Age,* May 28, 1973.
10. *Loc. cit.*
11. *Working-Class Women in a Changing World,* New York: Social Research, Inc., 1973.
12. *Loc. cit.*
13. *Loc. cit.,* 13, 14.
14. *Teen Age Girls Today.* (New York: *Seventeen,* 1968), 78.
15. *The High School Study.* Report No. 16 (New York: *Seventeen,* 1974), 3, 5.
16. *The College Freshman Report.* Report No. 22 (New York: *Seventeen,* 1974), 2–3.
17. *Teen Age Girls Today, op. cit.,* iv.
18. *The 1970 Mechanix Illustrated Automotive Survey* (New York: Fawcett Publications, 1970).
19. *Thirty-sixth Liquor Report,* January–June 1969 (New York: *True,* 1969).
20. *The 1969 Mechanix Illustrated Home Improvement Study* (New York: Fawcett Publications, 1969).
21. *True Leisure Time Survey 1967* (New York: Fawcett, 1967).
22. *Handbook of ARF Technical Services* (New York: Advertising Research Foundation, 1965), i.
23. Paul E. J. Gerhold, *The Open Audit Plan* (New York: Advertising Research Foundation, 1970), 6.

FOR FURTHER READING

Bartos, Rena. *The Future of the Advertising Agency Research Function.* New York: American Association of Advertising Agencies, 1974.

Boyd, Harper W., Jr., and Ralph Wesfall. *Marketing Research: Text and Cases.* Homewood, Ill.: Irwin, 1972.

Campbell, Roy H. *Measuring the Sales and Profit Results of Advertising.* New York: Association of National Advertisers, 1969.

Journal of Advertising.

Journal of Advertising Research.

Journal of Marketing.

Journal of Marketing Research.

Lucas, D. B., and S. H. Britt. *Measuring Advertising Effectiveness.* New York: Mc-Graw-Hill, 1963.

Schoner, Bertram, and Kenneth P. Uhl. *Marketing Research: Information Systems and Decision Making.* New York: Wiley, 1975.

5

Identification
in Advertising

Trademark
Counterfeiting
Brought
Death Penalty

PARIS, FRANCE—A team of student geologists surveying ancient building foundations in a small hamlet outside of Paris yesterday unearthed 16th Century court records which established a dramatic precedent of penalty for unfair trade practices.

The Court records reported a case brought before the French judiciary in 1592 that resulted in the death of a trademark counterfeiter.

According to the translation of the manuscript penned in old French, Monsieur Pierre Blanque produced low quality gold and silver cloth on which he impressed the words "La Gilt Lamé" and the symbol of the famous quality house of Le Premier Francais, manufacturers of expensive fabric used by the Lords and Ladies of the Royal Court.

When apprehended, the records relate, Blanque denied the charges but evidence was uncovered in the back room of his Left Bank atelier that proved to the Court he was the culprit.

He was sentenced to be hanged and the sentence was executed within three days of the final judgment.[1]

This stylized news item is a fictional version of an actual historic event that took place in 16th-century France. It shows the importance and value of a "good name" and the extreme to which the authorities went in protecting a trademark. While today the sentences meted out by the courts for the infringement of trademark rights are far less severe, the intent to protect the property of the owner of the identification device remains the same.

WHY IDENTIFY?

A retail store may advertise raincoats and derive full benefit from the advertisement. The advertisement identifies the store but not the maker of the raincoats. The reputation of the store is known to its clientele and others in the area from which it draws business. On the basis of this reputation and the description and price of the coats given in the advertisement, people go to the store, inspect the merchandise, and accept or reject the offer. But whether they buy or not, the advertisement has called their attention to a particular stock of raincoats available at a particular store.

A manufacturer, however, when he advertises, must identify his merchandise if he is to derive full benefit from the advertising. He cannot advertise raincoats as such without also promoting the coats made by his competitors. He must advertise and sell his coats under his company name, under a brand name, or if he distributes through an exclusive agency, under the name of the store or group of stores that handle his line. To do otherwise would be to advertise the product generically, or as a class, rather than to promote his own brand. This kind of product-class advertising is done at times by trade associations or groups acting cooperatively or by a company that controls the entire output of the product. The Tea Council, for example, tells us to "Take tea and see"; De Beers Consolidated Mines, Ltd., informs us that "A diamond is forever." This is good advertising for an association, and most members of a trade or industry would contribute to its support. It is also good advertising for an organization that is the exclusive manufacturer or distributor of a product. But few manufacturers are so philanthropically inclined that they will advertise an unidentified product for the benefit of their competitors.

The need to identify arises not only when an entirely new product is introduced to the market, but also whenever a variation of an established product is offered. The first automobile to bump over the cobblestone-paved streets of a city or to mire on a mud-rutted country road bore a distinguishing name as has every motorcar that has followed it right up to the streamlined, chrome trimmed, multicolored versions of today. The problems involved in identifying a newly invented product may be somewhat different from those associated with identifying subsequent variations put on the market by competing manufacturers, but the basic need to identify is the same.

IDENTIFICATION DEVICES

In practice, several devices may be used to identify a product. They are the *trademark, trade name, brand name, trade character, slogan,* and *package*. At times some of these are combined and used as a single device—the brand name may be used as the trademark or as part of the trademark; or when the same picture may be used as a trademark and as a trade character. At other times they may be employed as separate and distinct devices.

Trademark and Brand Name

A *trademark* is a pictorial device, number, letter, symbol, or word that identifies the origin of a product and under law may perform no other function than that of identification. The *trademark* and *brand name* may be the same.

But, when so used, the brand name must do no more than identify. It may not be descriptive of the product. When a brand name is also the trademark, it is usually a word used by a multiproduct manufacturer to identify one particular product or line of products. The brand name frequently is used in association with an overall trade name (sometimes called a *house mark*) that a manufacturer applies to his entire product line. For example, *Ritz* crackers, *Uneeda* biscuits, and *Lorna Doone* cookies are all a part of the *Nabisco* line produced by the National Biscuit Company. A brand name as such has no separate legal status. In marketing terminology, however, the term *trademark* is sometimes used in a restricted sense to mean a pictorial device or symbol as distinguished from a word; then the expression *brand name* is applied to the "word" marks. In service organizations the *service mark* is the equivalent of the *trademark*. An example of a service mark is the greyhound dog of the Greyhound Bus Company.

Trade Name

A *trade name* or "commercial name" identifies the business; a *trademark* identifies the product. The same word or name may be used as the principal component in the corporate title of a business and also on the products of that business. A pair of examples is Quaker Oats and the Quaker Oats Company. When this occurs, however, technically the trade name is not being used on the product. What happens at times is that the identical word used as the trade name is often also the trademark. In some cases the trade name is emphasized on the packages to establish more strongly a family identity among many products marketed by the same firm. The drug trade offers good examples of this practice.

Trade Character

A *trade character* is a picture of a person or of an animal. Some trade characters readily brought to mind are the *Jolly Green Giant,* the *Frito Bandito,* and *Mr. Peanut.* They are often, but not necessarily, caricatures. They may or may not be the same picture as the trademark. Trade characters identify products or businesses, but are also employed to obtain attention and sustain interest in advertising. A number of years ago Piel's Beer introduced two animated comic characters. Enough interest was generated by "Bert and Harry Piel" so that the time of their appearance on television could be announced with the expectation that people would tune in to catch their latest antics, as an audience might tune in on any regular entertainment feature. Yet Bert and Harry surely could not be seen without calling to mind Piel's Beer. They were attention-getters and interest-holders, but they were also identification devices.

Packages

While the package serves a number of other important purposes, it can be a strong factor in product recognition and identification. One such distinctive package was the Log Cabin syrup container, a can in the shape of a log cabin.

What a way to

You're looking at some of the brands and names of companies that sell gasoline. Some people say oil companies are a monopoly. If so, it's the world's most inept "monopoly."

This "monopoly" is so inept that it offers the world's richest country some of the world's most inexpensive gasoline.

This "monopoly" is so inept that it lets everybody and his brother horn in on the action. Did you know that of the thousands of American oil companies, none has larger than an 8.5% share of the national gasoline market?

In fact, this "monopoly" is so inept that you probably wouldn't recognize that it is a monopoly

run a "monopoly!"

because it looks so much like a competitive marketing system.

People who call us a monopoly obviously don't know what they're talking about.

Union Oil Company of California
: os Angeles. California 90017

Although designed for another purpose, this ad illustrates the trademarks of the gasoline companies.

63

The function of the package as a product identifier has greatly increased in importance in recent years owing to the tremendous growth of self-service merchandising in this country. So important is the package in modern marketing and advertising that it will be treated in greater detail in the next chapter.

Slogans

Although *slogans* are primarily a part of the advertising copy, it should be recognized that they may also possess value as identifiers of the product. This is especially true of those slogans that have been used by companies for many years and have had a considerable weight of advertising placed behind them. Although studies have shown that some people are not able to associate a slogan with the correct product, enough people do make the association correctly to justify recognition of the value of the advertising slogan.

EFFECTIVENESS OF IDENTIFICATION

The question of the relative strength of the several identification devices is difficult if not impossible to answer, because the strength of any given identification device will depend upon the skill with which it has been conceived and the manner in which it has been presented. However, there are some generalizations that probably can be made.

It has already been seen that the trademark may be a picture, a symbol, a word or words, or any combination of these. The pictorial or design type of trademark enables the consumer to recognize a product visually; so do the trade character and the package. But a customer rarely, if ever, will ask for a product by describing any of these devices. "I want some of that cleanser used by Josephine the lady plumber" would be an unusual way of asking for *Comet*. "Where do I find that toilet tissue Mr. Whipple is always squeezing?" undoubtedly would get the customer *Charmin,* but this request is not likely to be heard in the local supermarket. More common, perhaps, would be the statement, "I don't recall the name, but it comes in a blue and red package." Even this is not the common expression of consumer demand. Nevertheless, these visual aids to recall are very effective and valuable identification devices. They have always been important and, in this day of self-service supermarkets and other types of self-service merchandising, they are increasingly so. The more aids that the consumer's memory can be given and the greater the number of product associations that can be established, the better. Therefore, it is perhaps not a question of which kind of identification device is the strongest but rather a problem of developing several or all of them.

The "word" trademark is the identification device by which the product is asked for in the market place. It therefore assumes special significance and is subject to greater dangers in the competitive struggle for markets than are the other identification devices.

Identification devices have a long history of use to connect products with their makers. The ruins of a prehistoric city on the island of Crete revealed to exploring archaeologists broken bits of lamps with trademarks impressed in the clay. The bricks made in ancient Egypt carried not only the identification mark of the owner of the brick works but a mark to identify the slave laborer who made each brick. Later, in the Middle Ages, guilds required their members to identify their wares with distinguishing marks. In those early times the trademark appears to have been employed as a means of tracing inferior workmanship to its source. If the buyer of merchandise in medieval England found that his purchase was not up to standard, the blame could be placed on the specific artisan who made the faulty wares. In like manner, the knights of France of the same period could trace, if they lived, a defective piece of armor to its maker.

As time passed, it became apparent that good workmanship as well as poor could be traced through the trademark, and these identification devices began to assume a new significance in trade. In fact, some of the trademarks had become such valuable commercial assets by the early 17th century that counterfeiting of marks was a problem.

Today, the trademark, trade name, and brand name are the manufacturer's assurance that his product will be recognized in the marketplace and that any goodwill built up by him through his advertising and business practices will be reflected in consumer demand for his particular products. Yet, it should be recognized that there is no intrinsic value in a trademark. It is but a word or a symbol, and its value depends upon what it stands for in the minds of consumers. This, in turn, depends upon the reputation of the manufacturer and upon the product. When both are good and the trademark has come to signify this fact, then and only then does it assume real value. Once established, this

---

E:T•N   **Eaton Corporation**

The Board of Directors is pleased to announce that the Company's shareholders at a meeting on Wednesday, April 21, 1971 approved a change in the corporate name to:

It is effective immediately. Significantly shorter than the previous name Eaton Yale & Towne Inc., we believe the new name will project a clear and memorable identity, endorsing all of the Company's products and divisions efficiently. The distinctive mark from this day on will stand for Eaton Corporation.

A formal announcement of a corporate change of name.

value can be enhanced by the weight of advertising that is placed behind the trademark. That is, a trademark symbolizing the virtues of the manufacturer and the product may be weak or strong as an identifying device, depending upon how effectively and how extensively it has been promoted, primarily through advertising.

Within a short time after the Chrysler Corporation had introduced its new "pentastar" trademark, it is estimated to have spent $65 million publicizing it, and the Cities Service Company reportedly paid $20 million or more to promote the new image envisaged in its *Citgo* logo.[2]

More impressive, however, in terms of the cost of promotion of an identifying device, is the estimated $125 million spent by the Standard Oil Company of New Jersey, over a period of one year, to change its name. In 1972, the Company replaced the three names it had used—Humble, Esso, and Enco, each in different parts of the country—and adopted the coined word *Exxon* for universal use. The advertising campaign announcing it in the broadcast and print media cost an estimated total of $25 million; physically changing the names on gasoline pumps and other equipment, at their gas stations thoughout the country, cost approximately another $100 million.[3]

While the company retired some of its old trademarks—including *Jersey Standard, Humble,* and *Enjay*—it will continue to protect *Esso* and *Enco.* However, *Exxon* will serve as both the corporate and the brand name.

In selecting the new name the company had decided that it shouldn't be longer than four or five letters. A computer search turned up 10,000 words which were finally whittled down to six. These six were checked out in more than 100 languages to make certain that they didn't mean anything offensive or ridiculous to anyone. In the course of this research, which took more than three years, some 7,000 people were interviewed throughout the world. *Exxon* was finally selected because it was easy to pronounce in most languages and satisfied the requirement of not being vulgar or objectionable in any language.[4]

An interesting sidelight that developed from the research was that *Enco* means "stalled car" in Japanese—certainly no name for a gas station.[5]

REGISTRATION AND THE LANHAM ACT

Although an advertiser is not necessarily required by law to register his trademark * and although an unregistered trademark has protection under common law,** there are definite advantages associated with registration. Therefore, in the creation of a trademark, care should be taken to assure that the new trademark is registerable.

Advantages to be gained by registration include:

* Manufacturers of products from precious metals are required to register their trademarks.
** Under common law, priority of use is an important consideration. If an advertiser can prove that his trademark was in use before another, even a registered mark, his rights to use it will be protected.

1. Evidence of validity and ownership.
2. Incontestability of the trademark under specified circumstances after the first five years of registration. This means that after five years of unprotested, or unsuccessfully protested, registration the registrant acquires permanent right to use the mark for his class of goods, with certain exceptions enumerated in the trademark law.
3. The right to prevent the importation of foreign-made goods bearing an infringing trademark.

The most recent Federal legislation pertaining to the registration of trademarks is the Lanham Act, which became effective in 1947. Under the provisions of this law a trademark, provided it complies with the provisions of the law, may be registered for a period of 20 years. Thereafter, registration may be renewed. However, during the sixth year after the date of registration, the registrant must file an affidavit showing that the trademark is still in use. If such action is not taken by the registrant, the Commissioner of Patents will cancel the registration. Affidavits showing use also must be filed when registration is renewed at the end of each 20-year registration period.

The Lanham Act provides for registration under either the principal register or the supplemental register. If a trademark does not fall under the specific prohibitions for registration given in Section 2 of the Act, and if it distinguishes the goods to which it is to be applied, it may be registered under the principal register and secure all of the benefits previously described as associated with registration. Requirements for registration under the supplemental register are less strict; many trademarks not registerable under the principal register would be registerable under it. However, many of the advantages of registration would be lost by so doing. For example, registration under the supplemental register is not *prima facie* evidence of ownership; neither does such registration give the registrant the right to have the importation of goods into the United States stopped when such goods bear an infringing trademark. Supplemental registration may be upgraded to the principal register if the trademark has been used exclusively for the preceding five years.

Registration in the supplemental register is of particular importance to American exporters. Trademark registration is necessary in many foreign countries for full protection of legal rights, but a number of countries will not permit American firms to register their trademarks unless they are first registered in the United States. Under such circumstances, if the American company were required to have a registration on the principal register, it might be unable to comply with legal requirements.

The duration of the registration is the same under both the principal and supplemental registers. Under the supplemental register, the trademark must have been used for one year prior to application for registration. However, if the applicant requires a domestic registration as a basis for protection in one or more foreign countries, registration may be granted immediately.

The Lanham Act also provides for the registration of *service marks,** *certification marks,*** and *collective marks.**** Slogans may also be registered if they distinguish the applicant's goods. Packages and configurations of goods may be registered in the supplemental register if they are capable of distinguishing the goods of the applicant. This kind of registration may be especially helpful as the basis for corresponding registration in foreign countries, and here again the supplemental register is a device for assisting the American exporter.

Certain things are not registerable, and these the creator of a new trademark should avoid. An advertiser may not register anything in the public domain. In other words, he may not register anything that belongs to the public as a whole. For example, he may not register a color, as such, or a geometric form, as such. These are things to which he has no personal claim, things that anyone has a right to use. However, he may create an original design comprised of geometric forms, and this will be registerable. In like manner, he may color his trademark, but this act is quite different from registering the color as a trademark. He may not register geographic names or family names unless they have acquired a secondary meaning. This means that if such names are merely geographical designations or surnames they may not be registered. But if, through use, they have acquired a meaning that associates them with a specific product, in the mind of the public, they are registerable. Obviously, the trademark of a new product has acquired no secondary meaning. Therefore, the creator of a trademark for such products should avoid surnames and geographical names. The same holds true for any name that might be judged to be descriptive of the product. A name like "puregold" might be said to be descriptive of jewelry. The fact that the two words are written as one would make no difference. Furthermore, unless the jewelry in question was made of pure gold, such a name would be regarded as fraudulent. "Puregold" as a name for a cake mix, although perhaps suggesting a golden color for the cake, conceivably could obtain registration. It could be argued that the name is not really descriptive of the flour and certainly the public would not be led to believe that it contained gold. Such names as *Tastee* Bread and *Pittsburgh Plate Glass* existed before the trademark law.

Also not registerable are coats of arms of the United States or any foreign country, any state or national flag, or any mark that is fraudulent or misleading.

PROTECTION OTHER THAN REGISTRATION

The protection of a trademark starts with its creation and lasts throughout its life. We have noted that descriptive names, as a rule, cannot be registered.

---

* *Service marks* are identification marks or symbols for businesses such as banks, laundries, insurance companies, and the like, that render *services*. They are distinguished from *trademarks,* which identify *products*.

** *Certification marks* are marks or symbols that identify a company that certifies, approves, or otherwise gives testimonial to the products or services of others.

*** *Collective marks* are trademarks or service marks used to identify members of a collective group, such as an association or a union.

Registration can come only after such names have acquired a secondary meaning or have come to mean one particular product to the public. An advertiser would be unwise to adopt such a name with the intent of using it until after it has acquired a secondary meaning. In the first place, if the name is original and distinctive (which a descriptive name is not) the trademark is in a far stronger legal position. In the second place, there is nothing to stop a competitor from using a descriptive word in its purely generic or descriptive sense, and by so doing he may destroy any claim to exclusiveness that the original users might have hoped to establish. Therefore, the advertiser who uses an original and distinctive name as his trademark has a mark of greater legal strength and greater market potential.

The creator of a trademark, whether it be a name, a design, or a picture, should take care that it does not resemble another existing trademark in meaning, appearance, or sound. If the meaning of words is the same, even though they are spelled differently, or if the two pictures or designs are the same or very similar in appearance, registration will not be granted. In such cases, confusion is said to exist, and the new trademark is regarded as infringing on the existing one. Identical trademarks have been acceptable though, when used on totally unrelated products. Probably no one would associate the General Motors *Cadillac* with *Cadillac* dog food despite the fact that the latter also used the auto company's $\vee$ symbol (although in an era of conglomerates and business diversification such a relationship is not beyond the realm of possibility).

Even when the trademarks are not associated with competing products, however, the new mark will be denied registration if there is danger that the public will think the new product comes from the company that owns the original trademark or think it is endorsed or otherwise approved by the owner of the original mark. Such was the case with *Look* magazine and a cosmetic bearing the name *Look*. Although it is doubtful that the public would have believed that the publisher was making cosmetics, it might have been thought that the magazine had endorsed the new cosmetic. Inasmuch as magazines sometimes do endorse products or give new products editorial support, the chance of confusion in such a case was very real.[6]

If the trademark is to be a design, it should not be a feature of the product that is or might become common to other products. For example, Sylvania used, as a distinguishing mark for its flash bulbs, a blue dot that resulted from a manufacturing process. This dot was a functional part of the product and at one time was protected by patent rights. However, once the patent rights expired, others could use the process that resulted in the blue dot. The Federal District Court of New Jersey held that the dot was not a valid trademark. A useful feature of a product cannot become the exclusive property of a manufacturer through its use as a trademark.[7] This case was affirmed on appeal, by the United States Court of Appeals, November 22, 1957.

Finally, the newly created trademark should be checked for possible infringements. A lawyer should make this check and register the mark. (After application has been made to the U.S. Patent Office but before the patent has been granted, the advertiser may use the words "Patent Pending" on his product and in his advertising.)

Once registered, the trademark should not be used without some indication that it is a registered mark. This is usually made by printing under it, often in small type,

Registered U.S. Patent Office

or the abbreviation

Reg. U.S. Pat. Off.

Frequently the symbol ® is used to indicate registration. When the trademark name appears in the advertising for the first time in each piece of copy, it should be followed by an asterisk with an accompanying footnote explaining that it is a registered trademark. Whenever the trademark name appears in the advertising copy, it should be set in capitals. The trademark should be affixed to the product or, if this is not possible, as in the case of packaged flour, to its container.

Registration in foreign countries as well as in the United States is necessary if the product is going into the export trade.

It may be wise for an advertiser whose business is entirely within a single state to consider the advisability of state registration. Most states have some form of trademark registration. Again, advice of a lawyer is recommended.

It should be emphasized that registration is no guarantee against infringement or loss of property rights in a trademark. If the trademark is a name or includes a name, there is danger that the name may become generic—that is, instead of designating only the product of one particular manufacturer, the name may come to designate the product as a class. *Aspirin* was once a trademark, and its owner enjoyed full property rights to it. But the public began to think and speak of the acetylsalicylic acid tablet as "aspirin" regardless of what company sold it. Eventually, the trademark *Aspirin* became the generic noun "aspirin," and property rights were lost. A similar fate was shared by *nylon, cellophane, linoleum, milk of magnesia, shredded wheat, escalator,* and many, many more. *Thermos* is one of the most recent well-advertised and seemingly well-protected trademarks to lose its exclusivity.

Companies must be on constant guard to protect their trademarks from this danger. Any use of the trademark name by a writer or publisher in a generic sense or in a manner that might lead one to believe it to be other than a trademark, should be protested immediately. The Coca-Cola Company, owner of the registered trademarks *Coca-Cola* and *Coke,* has used the following letter effectively for this purpose:

> The attached clip from your fine paper mentions our product, Coke, but in "down style."
>
> I hate to bother you again about this, but the Lanham Trademark Act makes it necessary for us to notify editors of such use of our trademarks or stand the risk of losing them.

We greatly appreciate the publicity. But, unfortunately, lower casing or other usage which can be construed as generic is actually damaging to us.

For that reason we will be very grateful if you will remind the members of your staff (or possibly the proofreaders) that both "Coke" and "Coca-Cola" are registered trademarks and therefore are entitled to the same typographical treatment as a proper name.

Records of such letters as this indicate a company's policing activities of its trademark and serve in court to help prove that every reasonable means has been employed to preserve the "identifying distinctiveness" of its trademarks.

EDITORS: Our legal name since 1969 has been RCA Corporation and not Radio Corporation of America. There are no periods between the letters RCA.

RCA News

RCA Corporation
30 Rockefeller Plaza
New York, N.Y. 10020
Telephone (212) 598-5900

Release Immediately   June 11, 1975

Some companies have undertaken extensive educational campaigns to protect their trademarks. A number of them have published booklets and manuals, among which are *The GAF Trademark Manual,* the Pittsburgh Plate Glass *How and Where to Use Trademarks, The Case for the Upper Case* of the Coca-Cola Company, *The Goodyear Trade Mark Manual, Remington Rand Trademarks,* and 3M's *The Bug Book.* Du Pont, too, has published booklets and has made motion pictures that tell those who sell the Du Pont products how to use its trademarks so as not to jeopardize property rights in them. Other companies make it a point to provide the public with a class name for their products as well as a trade name or brand name. For example, Johnson & Johnson not only places the brand name *Band-Aid* on the package but also an additional statement like "cloth strips" or "plastic strips" and "adhesive bandages." *Anacin* is identified on the package as "analgesic tablets." The statement "Q-tips— cotton swabs" gives additional information that is both helpful to the customer and protective to the company. This practice serves a double purpose in the market. The consumer is given additional information that tells him what the product is, if he is unfamiliar with the grand name, and the general public is provided with a generic "handle" by which it can identify the product as a class in each case. By supplying such "generic handles" the companies are helping to make their trademarks or brand names distinctively identifying, thereby protecting their property rights.

Property rights in a trademark also can be lost by abandonment. That is, if the registrant stops using the trademark with no intent to again employ it, another company may pick it up and use it. Failure to take action to stop another company from using your trademark is still another way in which property rights may be lost. It is important to note in this connection that registration, in itself, is not enough to protect a company's rights to trademark. The registrant must be constantly vigilant to see that there are no infringements and must immediately initiate a protest if and when they occur. If the protest is not honored by the infringer, court action is necessary. The government takes no action to guard registered trademarks against infringement. The policing action is the responsibility of the registrant. That this policing may be far from a simple task is seen in the estimate that about 55,000 editorial mentions of a single well-known trademark name are made every year.

OTHER IDENTIFICATION CONSIDERATIONS

The creator of a trademark has considerations other than those related to registration with which he must concern himself. The new trademark should be as easy to remember as possible. In this aspect of the creative work, a knowledge of psychology and some field research are most helpful. However, pure weight of advertising may offset some weaknesses in the trademark design.

The new trademark may be a *picture;* examples are *Aunt Jemima,* extolling the merits of her pancake mix, or RCA Victor's fox terrier who had listened through the years to *his master's voice.* It may be a *coined* or *created word* like *Kodak* or *Yuban,* a *dictionary word* like *All* or *Tide,* a *personal name* such as *John Hancock* or *Betty Crocker,* or a *place name* as in *Waltham,* or *Elgin* watch. It may be a *design* or *symbol* composed of geometric forms like Ballantine's three-ring sign. It may be a combination of letters or numbers like the *IBM* or *7-Up* trademarks, or it may be combinations of pictures, letters, words, numbers, designs, and/or symbols. Which form it should take cannot be stated as a generalization. It is the task of the individual advertiser to decide which will do the best job of identifying his product under the circumstances peculiar to his business, product, and market.

If the trademark is a picture of a person or even, under some circumstances, a picture of an animal rather than a word or a design, it carries the risk of going out of style or otherwise becoming outdated as time passes. This is especially likely to happen if the trademark is a picture of a woman. The style of women's clothing changes rapidly. Women's hair styles also change. Even what is considered fashionable in the feminine form is subject to change. What starts out as a very modern-appearing trademark may become quite outmoded in a few years. In time, such a trademark, if unchanged, may suggest a long-established company. However, there is sure to be a long interval when it appears amusingly out-of-style. Of course, the trademark can always be changed and brought up to date. Although this entails extra cost and effort that might have been avoided by the selection of a trademark less subject to outdating, valuable publicity may be derived from the change. A few years ago the changes in a company's trademark over a period of years were made a feature presentation in a national magazine. A change in a trademark can also be made of value in stimulating public interest in a company's advertising. It has been made the subject of a contest on at least one occasion.

Several trademarks and trade characters have passed through a series of interesting evolutionary developments. Quaker Oats' old gentleman in quaint attire who became, in 1877, "America's first registered trademark for a breakfast cereal" [8] was changed a number of times until, in 1946, he was reduced to a smiling head-and-shoulders symbol. In 1970 his head was further modernized to a semisilhouette that could easily be reproduced in one color. The image of Betty Crocker has been changed four times since its first use in 1936. RCA modified in the circle with lightning trailing from the leg of the "A" to modern, bold, distinctively designed block letters. Heinz dropped its perennial "57," and the John Hancock Mutual Life Insurance Company replaced the historic signature with block letters. "Ma Bell," in her fifth change since 1889, simplified AT&T's familiar blue bell in the circle by removing the inscription. Psyche, the White Rock trademark, changed her hairdo, altered her position on the rock, lost weight, and finally "talked." The Fisk Tire boy finally changed his pajamas. But changes, in these cases and others, were made gradually and none was drastic. The change should never be so extensive as to destroy a continuity of identity in the trademark or trade character, unless the company is prepared to back it with a massive promotion campaign.

If the trademark is a name, some special considerations are involved. It has been said that a brand name should have good oral qualities or that it should sound pleasing when spoken. This reasoning is developed further by the observation that the vowels have a more pleasant sound than the consonants in the English language. Although this may be true and possibly could be applied in a number of cases, the creation of a brand name or trademark is a specific problem related to a particular product and cannot be approached in terms of generalizations. It is far more important that the name fit the product than that it have good oral qualities. *Schlitz,* replete with consonants, is an excellent name for beer. Among other things, it suggests a Germanic origin, and Germans generally are regarded as brewers of fine beers. But *Schlitz* as a brand name for perfume fills one with misgivings, however. A name rich in vowels fits a French perfume; one with the so-called harsh-sounding consonants—the *f*'s, the *s*'s, and the *z*'s—may be fine for a beer.

It also has been said that a brand name should be easy to pronounce. Again, in general, this is probably true. But in this day of the spoken advertising word of radio and television, such advice is of less significance than it once might have been.

Of major concern in creating a trademark that is in whole or in part a brand name is the selection (or coining) of a name that can be protected.

ORGANIZATIONS AND ASSOCIATIONS IN THE FIELD

The United States Trademark Association was founded in 1878. It is a nonprofit organization supported by the annual dues of its members. The USTA has three types of members; *regular, supplementary,* and *associate.* The former two are owners of trademarks, the latter are all others who have an interest in trademarks and trade names. At present, the Association has close to 1,000 members in all classifications. These members include companies owning trademarks, lawyers specializing in trademark work, advertising agencies, business associations, package designers, public-relations counselors, and others.

The purpose of the United States Trademark Association, according to its by-law, is:

> . . . to protect the interest of the public in the use of trademarks and trade names and to promote the interest of the members of the Association and trademark owners in general in the use of their trademarks and trade names, and to obtain, collect, and disseminate information concerning the use, registration, and protection of trademarks and trade names in the United States and its territories and in foreign countries.

The Trademark Reporter, the official journal of the United States Trademark Association, is issued bimonthly to all members. Among other valuable services performed by USTA was the publication of a book, *Trademark Management—A Guide for Businessmen,* which has become a recognized authoritative source in the field.

Also engaged in work to educate the general public and the retail trade to the value of brands is the Brand Names Foundation, Inc., founded in 1943 as a nonprofit organization. Currently, the Foundation has more than 500 members comprising manufacturers, advertising agencies, leading advertising media, and retailers (associate members).

Advertising space and time are contributed by such media as newspapers, magazines, transit advertising, radio, and television to carry the messages of Brand Names Foundation to the public and to the retailers of the nation. The value of the time and space thus contributed in a single year, estimated at $15 million, gives an idea of the extent of the program.

Brand Names Foundation says that the story it has to tell is essentially the story of American free enterprise:

> The manufacturer of the branded product stakes his life-long reputation on each unit of goods he offers to the public. The consumer makes his choice each time he makes a purchase. It is a continual town hall forum of public airing and election. Product identification makes this possible.

A year-round program of retailer education, including the Retailer-of-the-Year Competition, is also a part of Brand Names Foundation work. Here, the emphasis is on the fact that "the preselling of brand names achieved by advertising results in lower sales costs, faster turnover and more satisfied customers."

SUMMARY

While trademarks have their origin in ancient times, it was not until relatively recently, along with the advent of mass communications and advertising, that expendable household and similar products were identified by their manufacturers. At that time, it became clear that if the manufacturer wanted repeat business, he would have to identify or put his name on his product and advertise it.

Identification by means of a trademark, service mark, brand name or trade name is of value to the consumer as well as to the manufacturer or distributor. The consumer benefits because he or she is reasonably assured of a product or service that meets a certain standard established by the manufacturer or service company. The consumer also has a place to turn to if there is a query or a complaint. The manufacturer or service company, on the other hand, has a name or a symbol that will grow in value as he promotes it and strives to improve his product or service.

QUESTIONS AND DISCUSSION SUBJECTS

1. What differences are there, relative to the identity or brand name of merchandise, between the advertising done by a retailer and that done by a manufacturer? Why?
2. Name six identification devices. Describe them.
3. What current marketing trend has made the package an important identification device?
4. Name as many distinctive packages as you can think of. Describe them.
5. How many product or service advertising slogans can you remember? Name them.
6. Which trade characters readily come to mind?
7. Discuss the merits of the packages, slogans, and trade characters you have named, together with the trademarks of those companies. Do any have negative aspects?
8. Must a trademark be registered in order to have protection under the law?
9. Name three advantages of registering a trademark under the Lanham Act.

SOURCES

1. The United States Trademark Association (New York).
2. Gordon Weil, "Uprating Images: Many Firms Adopt New Corporate Symbols in Bid to Improve Recognition, Lift Sales," *The Wall Street Journal* August 1, 1968, 22.
3. *Time,* May 22, 1972.
4. Exxon Corporation, data, 1975.
5. Exxon Corporation, date, 1975.

6. S. A. Diamond, "Brand Name Choice Must Avoid Confusion, Patent Office Rules in Cowles-Jergens Case," *Advertising Agency Magazine,* January 3, 1958.

7. S. A. Diamond, "Useful Feature of Product Can't Become Trademark," *Advertising Agency Magazine,* December 21, 1956.

8. Clarence Newman, "At 93, the Quaker Man Goes Mod," *Newsday,* September 24, 1970, 96.

FOR FURTHER READING

"A Guide to the Care of Trademarks." U.S. Trademark Association, 1974.

Borchard, William M. "When ® Should and Should Not be Used." *Executive Bulletin,* U.S. Trademark Association, No. 18 (1975).

Campbell, Hannah. *Why Did They Name It . . . ?* New York: Ace Books, 1964.

Diamond, Sidney A. "How to Use a Trademark Properly." *Executive Bulletin,* U.S. Trademark Association, No. 9 (April 1971).

Fey, Dorothy. "The Name of the Game: Trademarks," *The Practical Lawyer,* Vol. 14, No. 6 (October, 1968), 81–90.

Holcomb, Charles A. *Trademarks . . . An Orientation for Advertising People.* New York: American Association of Advertising Agencies, 1971.

Perine, H. Ford. "Brand Names = Famous Products = Freedom of Choice," *Boot & Shoe Recorder,* July 1969.

"Private Brands: The Inside Story," *Changing Times,* November 1965.

"Renewed Vitality for Very Large Corporations," *Design Sense 58, A Marketing publication of Lippincott & Margulies,* 1968.

Sarnoff, Robert W. "Anatomy of a New Trademark," *Saturday Review,* April 13, 1968.

"Trademark Stylesheet." U.S. Trademark Association, July, 1969.

U.S. Department of Commerce. *Q & A About Trademarks.* Washington, D.C.: U.S. Patent Office.

$$\begin{matrix} \star \\ \star \\ \star \\ \star \\ \star \\ \star \end{matrix}$$ 6

Packaging

Within the memory of some of our senior citizens, butter was cut and sold from a tub; flour and sugar were scooped from barrels and sold by weight; coffee was sold loose in bean form or ground for the customer by the grocer; crackers were sold from barrels, and milk from large tin containers. And as it was in the grocery stores, so was it in other kinds of retailing establishments, for these were the days of little or no packaging. Manufacturers' packages, for the most part, consisted of bulk containers designed for shipping the product and possibly for temporary storage in the retail store until the product could be sold. Retail packaging, in large measure, was done in plain wrapping paper, in plain paper bags, or in boxes bearing no identification.

In sharp contrast are the stores of today. Packages of varied shapes and sizes, formed from a wide variety of materials and replete with colors and identifying symbols and brand names, are arrayed on the shelves, counters, floor display racks, and stands. In present-day supermarkets, 10,000 items compete for the customers' attention and dollars. Not infrequently, the package is a major factor in this competition, especially in self-service stores. In these, the package has assumed a role of self-merchandiser of the product; it must identify favorite brands to old users and induce non-users to try its contents for the first time.

When one realizes that 77%, better than three out of four, of all of the grocery sales in this country today are made by supermarkets, and that a parallel trend toward self-service is taking place in drug and variety stores, the importance of the package in modern merchandising need not be argued.

But it is not only in supermarkets and other self-service stores that the package has come to play a dominant role in advertising and selling. Cosmetics and perfumes, regardless of where they are sold, depend heavily upon their containers for customer appeal. In fact, packaging plays a large part in the

At the end of the last century and the beginning of this one, most foods were not packaged as we know them today. Milk was taken out of a large can by the grocer and ladled into the container the customer brought with him or her; butter was cut from a large tub, etc. *Courtesy of the National Cash Register Co.*

selling of products as diversified as watches and beer, sterling-silver flatware and onions, office supplies and toys.

The kinds of packages used to carry this great variety of goods differ both with the product and with the purpose or goal of the seller.

Variation in package style with respect to package contents is obviously expected: one would not package a fine watch in the same manner as onions, nor eggs in the same sort of container as bolts and nuts. With respect to the goal or purpose of the seller, variation in package design may be wide indeed. Always, the package must serve as a *container* of the product and should help to sell the product. But in performing this selling function, the package may become any one or a combination of things in addition to being a container. It must also be a *dispenser* of the product. It may help *build a product image* of fine quality, durability, femininity, or whatever else the advertiser wants associated with his product. It may have a secondary use and so serve as a *premium*—an extra value—obtained at the time of purchase. In many cases it may be an *attention-getter*—a stopper of a store's flow of traffic at the place where a particular packaged brand is displayed.

It may seem that packages and packaging encompass so broad an area of merchandising that any consideration of the subject more appropriately belongs in a general text on marketing than in an advertising book. But it belongs to advertising because the package is advertised, because it performs advertising functions, and because there is a strong and close relationship between package advertising and other advertising. One packaging expert points out that if a paperboard package or a can label is opened at the seams and spread out it offers a larger advertising area than is available in almost any advertisement short of a billboard. The package is one means of carrying the advertiser's sales message in both words and pictures to the very point where purchases are made—the retail store. In addition, it often furnishes copy for the advertiser's messages carried in other media, as when a new package is developed or a new feature is added to an old one. For example, entire advertising campaigns were built around the first use of the pull-off beverage-can top, and the wide mouth *Chug-A-Mug* beer bottle. Also, when R. J. Reynolds changed the camel on its cigarette package "consumers felt the product was somehow different without the familiar symbol." The company quickly reinstated the "traditional package and apologized in full-page ads." [1]

Above all, the present trend in advertising agencies to provide wider marketing services to their clients naturally leads them more and more into the area of packaging. In a survey made as long ago as 1957, of 100 advertising agencies, 90 said that they considered packaging a logical agency function. Writing for *Printers' Ink,* Gustav L. Nordstrom, Executive Director of the Folding Paper Box Association, said, "Packaging today is advertising. More and more it is being recognized by inclusion in the advertising and sales budgets of manufacturers who once considered packaging costs exclusively a part of production." [2]

FUNCTIONS OF PACKAGES

As Containers

The package is, and must be, first and always, a container for the product. In this capacity its chief function is that of holding and protecting the product. But, in serving this function, it also can be an aid in selling. If it is so designed that it protects the product from damage in shipment, from becoming stale, or otherwise deteriorating on the dealers' shelves or while in possession of the ultimate consumer, it is at once a saving to the manufacturer and an added selling feature of interest to the consumer.

Many of the new packaging materials used today have made it possible to do an excellent job both in protecting the product and in adding to the effectiveness of the package as a selling device. For example, some of the transparent film wraps adequately hold and protect the product while displaying it to advantage. Metal foils not only protect the contents of the container but also lend beauty or attention-getting qualities to the package. Plastics serve admira-

Illustrated here are packages made of a number of materials—glass, metal, paper, plastic and aluminum foil. *Courtesy of Lippincott & Margulies, Inc.*

bly as containers for many products and add a safety factor by providing an unbreakable container. Even the more traditional packaging materials have been improved to make modern packages more effective in holding, protecting, and selling their contents. For example, the "crushproof" cigarette package, the amber-green glass wine bottle that protects its contents from damage by "flavor-stealing light rays," and various wax wraps that keep cereals and crackers "oven fresh" are all made from improved versions of packaging materials long in use. A revolutionary development that may eliminate the need for refrigeration is presently in use in Europe and Japan; the food is heat-processed in its package—a flexible plastic film pouch. The process had been awaiting approval by the Department of Agriculture for use by housewives in this country, although it had been tested successfully by the United States Army. In July 1975 the Army advertised for suppliers of food in this new packaging to replace the traditional field rations (remembered by millions of veterans as K rations and C rations). Since the new packages are smaller, more flexible, lighter, and more compact than the former cans and cartons, they will simplify logistics both for the individual soldier and for the Army as a whole.

Whether or not a package is a good container depends in large part on the materials from which it is made and on the manner in which it is constructed.

What constitutes the best material and the proper construction depends upon the characteristics of the product. Some products are hydroscopic and must be protected from moisture in the atmosphere; others are fragile and must be protected from breakage; still others may deteriorate in strong light and so must be packed in opaque materials or materials that will reduce or filter out damaging light rays; and foods that are to be frozen must be freezer-packed. In short, the materials used in the package should be dictated by a consideration of what will best hold and best protect the product. The same consideration also holds true for the manner in which the package is constructed.

As Dispensers

Every package must be a dispenser of its contents at least once, and many packages dispense their products over a more or less extended period of use. For example, the entire contents of a cake-mix package may be used at one time, hence this package is a one-time dispenser. On the other hand, an aerosol can of shaving cream may dispense its contents repeatedly over a period of several weeks. But a package, whether used once, a few times, or many times, if it is to perform at maximum effectiveness as a selling device, must make it easy for the user to obtain its contents. If it can assist him in obtaining them, so much the better.

The olive bottle tht permits easy removal of the olives, the catsup bottle that does not present its user with an "all or nothing" alternative, and the shoe-polish can that does not require a set of burglar tools to open it are indeed a boon to the consumer. More seriously, the package that is a satisfactory dispenser of its product can be a factor in obtaining new sales and in building brand loyalty. This feature is a merchandising assist that is especially helpful to manufacturers who produce a product in which there is but slight difference among brands.

Considerable emphasis has been placed on the advertising of packages with respect to their special product-dispensing qualities. Aerosol cans * offer a notable example. Others include metal cans with tops that pull completely off to serve individual dessert snacks, and coffee cans that can be reclosed with accompanying plastic covers.

Whether or not a package is a good dispenser may depend upon one feature or a combination of features and will vary with the type of product to be dispensed. It may depend upon so simple a feature as an easily removed cover or any device that will facilitate opening the package—for instance, a screw cap rather than a cork. It may depend upon the construction of the package so as to permit easy removal of the contents—for example, the wide-mouth jar as compared with the narrow-necked bottle. It may depend upon a feature that will assist the user to apply the product without removing it from the package ex-

---

* Aerosol cans were developed during World War II for use by our armed forces. They were first employed to spray insect repellants and paints, and were great labor-saving devices. Today, however, gaseous propellants such as Freon are believed to reduce the earth's ozone layer, allowing penetration to the surface of more ultraviolet rays, which can cause skin cancer.

Can-opening is quick, easy and safe even for youngsters, with the help of ScotchTab, a pressure sensitive closure used to seal cans of Libby, McNeill & Libby nectar. The closure, a 3M Company product, now provides "peel and pour" convenience on three nectar flavors, apricot, peach and pear. Twelve-ounce cans of the nectar are now in national distribution, and Libby's plans to use ScotchTab on 5½-ounce cans of the nectars as well as on tomato juice.

cept as it is used—for example, the pressurized metal paint container that sprays the paint or the squeeze bottle that sprays the deodorant. It may depend upon some feature that will overcome an undesirable condition associated with the removal of the product from its container—for example, the no-drip spout that eliminates stickiness on the syrup bottle.

As Premiums

The secondary-use package is one especially designed for some use in addition to that of containing and dispensing the product. Once emptied of its original contents, such a package can be used for another purpose. The cheese glass that subsequently may be used for fruit juice and the liquor bottle that serves as a decanter or can be converted into a table lamp are examples. In a real sense such packages are premiums that offer the buyer of the product an extra value. However, the secondary-use package is not be confused with a

A magazine ad featuring the easy open can. *Used by permission of Hunt-Wesson Foods, Inc. All Rights Reserved.*

package that contains a premium as part of the enclosure or that bears a coupon or other redeemable element exchangeable for a premium. Such practices involve premium promotions and will be discussed in Chapter 24.

The secondary-use package may be employed in a number of ways to promote sales. A few of the possibilities are mentioned:

Seasonal Promotions. A number of years ago, a brand of tea was packaged in a novelty ceramic tea pot, which in turn was enclosed in a box with traditional Christmas holly design. Although tea normally would not be sold as a Christmas remembrance, the novelty of this package accomplished the sale of a satisfactory amount of the product for this purpose. In addition to selling a product for a purpose for which it would normally not be bought, this promotion also effected a sampling of the product at no cost to its distributor. Some people who received the tea as a gift may not have previously used it. Some of these people may have liked it enough to become regular users of the brand once having sampled it.

Another well-known example of seasonal promotions through secondary-use packages is the featuring of decanters and other types of secondary-use bottles by the liquor industry every Christmas season. This has been a traditional holiday promotion, often with the decanter or gift bottle selling at the same price as the regular bottle.

Long-Term Promotions. In some cases a promotion through the use of secondary-use packages may extend over a long period, several months or even years—for example, cereal packages with cutouts for children printed on their panels or candy especially gift-packed in a box that can be used afterward to hold jewelry or sewing equipment.

Secondary-Use Package-Sets Promotions. An effective promotional plan is the employment of packages that suggests their collection and use as sets. A dairy company ran a summer promotion of cottage cheese by packaging it in plastic mugs of different colors. After a few weeks, the containers were changed to plastic bowls in colors matching the mugs. This packaging technique induced customers to collect a set of matching mugs and bowls with a resulting increase in the sale of cottage cheese. In honor of the Nation's Bicentennial, Log Cabin packaged their syrup in a set of historical collectors bottles.

Use of Shipping Cartons in Promotions. Even in the case of large household appliances where the only package involved is a shipping carton, the secondary-use promotional idea can be employed. One company selling such a product constructed its shipping cartons so that they might be reassembled as play log cabins. The outside of the carton was lithographed to resemble logs, and provision was made for cutout windows and a door.

As Identifiers and Attention-Getters

The package, by its configuration, color, design, and copy, identifies the product and brand. This has been an important function of the package for many years, but with the increase in self-service retail selling, quick and easy identification of brands has become absolutely essential to effective selling.

The same features—configuration, color, pictorial design, and copy—that make the package an identification device also make it an attention-getter. This function has increased in importance since the rapid growth of self-service merchandising. The customer may be stopped by an attractive package and induced to buy a product that he otherwise would not have bought. In a later chapter it will be seen that large quantities of goods are bought on impulse, and the package often may play a large part in stimulating the impulse to buy.

If the package is to identify a brand, it must possess a degree of distinctiveness. This can be attained by means of its shape, its color or combination of colors, its pictorial design, the picturing of the trademark or trade character, and obviously by the prominent display of the brand name. Caution must be employed, however, in the use of some of these devices. An odd shape may detract so much from other desirable qualities of a package as to offset any advantage of identification. While the peculiar shape might add to the ability of the package to identify a particular brand, it might make the package difficult to

The most beautiful bottle of Bourbon in American history.

The Old Grand-Dad Bicentennial Decanter. About $22.

*Prices may vary according to state and locality. Kentucky Straight Bourbon Whiskey, 86 Proof, Old Grand-Dad Distillery Co., Frankfort, Ky 40601

A handsome secondary use package is this Bicentennial decanter advertised in national magazines during 1976. *Courtesy of National Distillers.*

stack for storage or display purposes, increase the cost of manufacturing the package, increase shipping charges, complicate the filling operation, and make it difficult to empty the package of its contents. On the other hand, there are product areas where such adverse results would not occur or would not be of serious consequences if they did. Stacking of packages might be of importance in the grocery field, for example, but would be of little concern to the jeweler. Increase in cost due to manufacturing and shipping of odd-shaped packages might present an insurmountable obstacle in staple goods but in the case of many luxury goods be readily offset by high profit margins on the sale of even a few more units.

The features in package design that are used as attention-getters are the same as those employed to make the package an identifier—shape, color, pictorial design, and copy (including brand name). But, the manner in which they are used differs considerably among different classes of products. Although the same elements—the printed word, pictures, and color—might be employed to direct the public's attention to a circus and to the opening of the grand opera, the manner in which they would be used would be quite different. The same is true in packaging. The attention-attracting package that contains cigarettes, a breakfast cereal, or a detergent will use color, the printed word, pictures, and package configuration quite differently from the package containing perfume or cosmetics. Either package will employ these attention-getting features in a manner guite different from the patent medicine package. Therefore, generalizations concerning what colors to use, what kind and size of print to employ, what shape the package should be, where on the package the various elements should be placed, are misleading and dangerous. Information and advice of this kind must be related to the packaging of a specific product under known marketing conditions.

There are principles which if applied in the design of a package will give predictable results. Whether or not we wish such results must depend on the individual situation. A light-colored package will appear larger than one of the same size in dark colors. The use of a pictorial design featuring a sunburst, a series of dilating circles, or any other element that will direct the eyes of the observer to the edges of the package will tend to expand it and create the optical illusion of greater size, whereas a dark-colored border will have the opposite effect. If the circus-broadside approach in display is in order, then large, easily read lettering to spell out the brand name is better than a lighter type or script. Also, under such circumstances, color combinations should be sought that make brand names and pictorial elements stand out sharply. (Highly readable color combinations characterize automobile license plates.) Color used in this kind of packaging should make the package stand out on the dealer's shelf as well as make the brand name easily distinguishable and readable. A hardware product at one time was packaged in a dull green package with black lettering. Under these conditions neither the brand name nor the package was readily noticeable. When the company changed the color combination to blue on metallic silver, the package was a standout among its competition, the brand name was easy to read, and the package as a whole literally "flashed" a call to customers from the shelves or counters where it was displayed.

Most packages in the food field, as well as packages containing soaps and detergents, dentifrices, and cigarettes, are of the flashy-display kind. Usually these packages contain some copy in addition to the brand name—for the most part, recipes or directions for use. Often such recipes or directions suggest new or different uses that, if accepted by the consumer, will result in increased consumption of the product. For example, the copy on a ready-to-eat cereal package may state that, in addition to being a breakfast food, the contents may be used to make cake or candy, and provide recipes for doing so. A detergent package may have copy informing the reader that the contents may be used to clean paint brushes as well as to do the normal household cleaning jobs. This copy usually is placed on the side panels of the package, leaving the larger front and rear panels for the brand name, picture or design element, and any special promotional announcements like premium offers or contests.

Packages designed for esthetic effect rather than for mass-display impact, or those created to give the impression of luxury or "conservative elegance," will not use loud colors and heavy type. They usually will contain a minimum of copy.

SPECIAL FEATURES OF PACKAGES

Package Size and Multiple Packaging

Obviously the size of the package is dictated by the product that it is designed to hold. Almost any quantity of aspirin tablets will require a smaller package than three tennis balls. But, should the aspirin package hold 6 or 300 tablets, the tennis-ball package one or a dozen balls? In other words, what size should a package be for the product class or for the kind of product? The answer to this question requires considering such things as (1) the buying habits of consumers with respect to quantity of the product; (2) the sizes offered by manufacturers of competing brands; and (3) the average speed of product consumption as related to the rapidity of product deterioration.

Quantities purchased by customers at any one time may or may not be firmly fixed as a buying habit. That is, by promotional effort on the part of the manufacturer, customers may be induced to buy in larger quantities, either in single-unit or multiple-unit packages. Soft drinks and beer were long offered almost universally in single 12-ounce bottles or cans; many brewers and manufacturers have found customers attracted both to 16-ounce and even larger containers and to smaller ones—8 ounces or 6 ounces. "Odd" sizes like 7 ounces and 11 ounces have been offered with some success. The once traditional case of 12 or 24 bottles has almost given way to the 6-pack, but some markets have accepted 8-packs. Milk, long sold in quart cans or cartons, is increasingly well accepted in half-gallons and larger sizes, while pints, half pints, and various single-serving sizes are also used to reach buyers in special sales outlets— delicatessens, snack bars, school lunchrooms, and the like.

The cigar industry found that it could increase sales by offering a package of two or more cigars to smokers accustomed to buying a single cigar at a time. The "large economy size" package is traditional for many products. On the other hand, it might be difficult to educate the public to buy chewing gum by the pound. In other words, the strength of the buying habit as related to size of purchase varies among different kinds of products.

Sales volume may be increased not only by increasing the size of the package but also by combining packages and selling two or more as a unit. Examples of this kind of packaging are numerous: in beverages, in soaps, and in dry or ready-to-eat cereals. The number of areas is increasing: motor oil, flashlight batteries, glassware, detergents, and many other products are offered in multipacks. But, just as care must be taken before increasing the size of a package so, too, some study of the situation should be made before deciding to multipack a commodity. In case of nonfood products, would a multipack or a single large package offer the consumer the greater advantages? If there is danger of fast deterioration after the package has been opened, there may be decided advantages in a pack composed of two or more relatively small packages within one big package. If the product is used in more than one place in the home, the multipack offers some advantages. A pack containing two, three, or more cakes of soap that can be placed in the bathroom and kitchen may be more desirable to many customers than one large cake of soap. A pack holding two packages of toothpaste may be better suited to a two-bathroom home than a large package containing a single tube.

If the product is a food, different questions must be answered before deciding on a multipack. There might be little point in offering a multipack of the same kind or same flavor unless the opening of a single large package might result in rapid deterioration. If the producer is planning to offer a number of different flavors or several different varieties, as in the case of a pudding dessert or ready-to-eat cereals, the question of consumer preferences becomes important. What are the most popular flavors or the most desired varieties? Are preferences so strong for one or two flavors or varieties as to make customers hesitate to buy a multipack that contains lesser favorites as a part of the selection? Or, are the majority of buyers sufficiently interested in change to make the choices offered in the multipack a real attraction?

In product areas of keen competition the size of the package must be the same as competitors' packages or very closely approximate it. Any appreciable difference in size of package must be offset by a price difference or by superior quality of product.

The question of speed of deterioration as related to speed of use in determining package size is not as important today as formerly because of improvements in home refrigeration and storage facilities on the one hand and superior packaging techniques and materials on the other. Outer and inner wraps of waxed paper, plastic, and foil, tight-fitting lids, pressurized push-button dispensers, aseptic canning which obviates the necessity of freezing, and a variety of other devices help keep products fresh, crisp, and otherwise unspoiled over longer periods of time than was once possible.

Inserts, Outserts, and Premiums

Packages can serve as advertising and promotional tools in a way quite apart from anything considered thus far. Through the use of an *insert* (a leaflet or circular) or an *outsert* (a paper band or leaflet fastened to the outside of the package), the package can be used to carry information concerning its own contents, advertising about other products made by the same manufacturer, recipes, coupons, announcements of contests or premium offers, and statements of special offers or sales. The package can also be made to carry the premium so that the customer receives it immediately upon purchase of the goods. In past promotions of this sort, toothpaste manufacturers have packed tooth brushes with their products, toilet-soap manufacturers have included soap dishes with theirs, and detergent manufacturers have packed towels or dinnerware in their packages. These premium promotions have generally been supported by point-of-purchase and other advertising.

Gift Wraps

Another promotional idea associated with packaging that has proved successful in some areas of merchandising is prepurchase gift wrapping. That is, packages already gift wrapped are delivered by the manufacturer to his retail outlets. Such packaging saves time at the retail level and makes attractive displays at Christmas and other holiday seasons. This practice has long been prevalent in the liquor industry during Christmas, often in combination with secondary-use containers.

CHANGES AND IDENTIFICATION PROBLEMS

Many manufacturers and distibutors have chosen to carry one or more elements of design through all of the packages in their lines. These elements may be the trade name, a color, a pictorial design, or any combination of all of them. Such practice serves to establish a readily recognizable "family relationship" among products of different kinds made by the same manufacturer or sold by the same retailer. Such packaging is common in the drug field where a single firm may market a large number of different kinds of products and where the corporate image of the firm may mean much in establishing public confidence in the product.

Even where this practice is not followed, a manufacturer will want to establish through his package a means of quick and easy brand recognition. This, as has been seen, is accomplished by distinctiveness of package design and by advertising or otherwise promoting the package. The longer the distinctive package is on the market, the stronger is its brand-identifying ability likely to become. This raises the question as to whether it is wise to change package design frequently or drastically. It is probably true that frequent change in any given package should be avoided, but once it has been decided to make a change, there is no reason, why it cannot be as great as the advertiser wishes.

Change in package can be made without danger of loss of customer recognition of the product and brand in one of three ways:

1. The change can be so slight as not to destroy the customer's association between package and brand. This presents the problem of whether so small a change is worth making.
2. A two-stage change can be made in which a transitionary package carries identity over from the old to the new package. The cost associated with this practice may make it impractical.
3. A radically new package can be introduced with sufficient weight of advertising so that a new association between package and brand is quickly built in the minds of buyers. This approach probably has most to recommend it.

Any plan to change a package must also be weighed against costs. Such considerations go beyond initial costs of creating the design and subsequent manufacturing costs; they include any complicating factors in use of filling machinery or in labor costs associated with filling the new package, any resultant shipping and storage costs, and so on. The planning and adoption of a new package entails far more than the creation and acceptance of a "pretty" design.

A problem of different nature confronts the manufacturer who produces two or more competing brands. S. C. Johnson & Son, for example, which manufactures a number of competing floor waxes, embraces them all under its corporate trade name. On the other hand it is rather difficult to identify a family relationship among Procter & Gamble's many competing brands of detergents.[3]

TRUTH IN PACKAGING

Until about 1966, with relatively minor exceptions, most manufacturers had complete freedom as far as their packaging was concerned. A few, mainly the drug and textile manufacturers, were bound by stringent regulations. But now these problems face all manufacturers since the Fair Packaging and Labeling Act of 1966 has come into force. It is a "truth in packaging" law administered by the Federal Trade Commission and the Food and Drug Administration. While the title of this law mentions "packaging," it is concerned principally with the "label," and there principally with the text or copy. The FDA sets the standards for the labeling of foods, nonprescription drugs, and cosmetics, the FTC those for such items as furniture polish, light bulbs, soap, and similar products. The Department of Commerce is also directed by the Act to reduce the proliferation in packaging sizes through voluntary agreements with industry.

There has been an urgent need for such a law for quite some time; unfortunately, the regulation that finally passed was weak and practically ineffectual. In fact, the FTC's list of items to be regulated was whittled down by more than half as a result of court challenges. Typical of the goods removed from the FTC's packaging jurisdiction were toys, jewelry, and paint. In addition there were numerous delays in getting the labeling regulations into force. Confusing terminology continued to perplex the consumer. The same 3¼-ounce tube of toothpaste was called "giant" by Pepsodent, "large" by Crest, and "medium" by Colgate. Equal confusion existed in detergent and other product package sizes.

THE RETAILER'S PACKAGE

In any discussion of packaging, one is inclined to think only in terms of packages used by the manufacturer. However, many products are not packaged for retail distribution by their manufacturers but are placed in bags or boxes by the retailer at the time he sells them. Such bags and boxes can be mere containers or, like the manufacturers' packages, they can do a selling job for the retailer.

There can be little doubt that the average customer would prefer to carry purchases away from a store in an attractive box or bag rather than in a wrap that looks like an oversized lunchsack or a bundle of laundry. Furthermore, the name of the store on its wrapping paper, tape, ribbon, bags, and boxes advertises the store to all who see them as they are carried by customers through the streets and on buses or trains.

Gift wrapping or packaging can be as much of a promotional aid to the retailer as it is to the manufacturer, and there is no store too small to employ it. Shopping bags are a convenience to the customer and a goodwill builder and advertising medium for the store. They also are incentives to more purchases and to impulse buying. Make it easier for the customer to carry more and he may buy more; refuse him this aid and he may forgo a purchase that otherwise would have been made.

Smart packaging also can help such businesses as laundries and dry-cleaning establishments to merchandise their services.

So, the package as a sales promoter and as an advertising device is, or can be, important to manufacturer and to retailer, to big business and to small, to sellers of tangibles, even to some sellers of services, providing serious thought is given to its development and use.

SUMMARY

In the not so distant past, grocery and dairy products, among others, were sold to the consumer, loose. They were dipped out by means of a ladle into a jar brought by the customer, as in the case of milk. Solid objects like butter, cheese and crackers were wrapped in paper by the grocer.

Similar to trademarks, as the means of mass communications developed and advertising became recognized as a principal means of promotion, manufacturers began to package their wares and put their names on them.

Packages are made of many substances, principally paper board, steel ("tin" cans), aluminum, plastic, glass, wood, burlap and other fibers.

While the package provides the last opportunity to advertise and sell the product on the shelf of the supermarket—a very important function—its most important job is to properly contain and protect the product. Next in importance is the ability of the package to dispense its contents.

QUESTIONS AND DISCUSSION SUBJECTS

1. What is a secondary-use package?
2. Name three ways in which a secondary-use package can be used to promote sales.
3. What is the primary purpose of the package?
4. What other functions may a package perform?
5. Define or explain the following: (a) insert; (b) outsert; (c) retail package; (d) multi-use package.
6. Explain the relationship between packaging and advertising.
7. Name several packaging materials and give examples of products packaged in each.
8. What is the purpose of a multipack?
9. Discuss the Fair Packaging and Labeling Act.
10. Describe recent innovations in packaging.

SOURCES

1. Walter P. Margulies, *Packaging Power* (New York: World, 1970), 20, 21.
2. Gustav L. Nordstrom, "Packaging Today Is Advertising," *Printers' Ink,* April 26, 1957, 116.
3. Margulies, *op. cit.,* 5.

FOR FURTHER READING

AIGA Packaging. New York: American Institute of Graphic Arts, 1972.
Favre, Jean-Paul. *Color Sells Your Package*. New York: Hastings House, Publishers, 1970.
Herdeg, Walter, ed. *Graphis/Packaging 3*. New York: Hastings House, Publishers, 1977.
Margulies, Walter P. *Packaging Power*. New York: World, 1970.

Visualization and Layout

When advertising people say "visualization" they often bewilder beginners or outsiders, for they use the word in many related meanings, sometimes with more than one meaning in the same utterance.

So what is visualization? It has to do with seeing ideas, with making ideas and the abstract seeable, with "seeing" an advertisement before any part of it is printed on paper or flashed on a screen. It is a process. It is also the tangible result of that process—a sheet of paper with a sketch that will ultimately be seen by readers or viewers. And the visualization, either process or result, may apply to an entire ad or only to the pictorial element of the ad. As this chapter discusses it, visualization refers chiefly to the process of creating the entire ad. After visualization comes *layout,* usually (but not always—in advertising, "always" is rarely applicable).

When visualization refers to the overall print advertisement, it encompasses all of the components—headline, body copy, illustration, logotype, whatever. In the process, discussions or "brainstorming sessions" are held and decisions are made as to which of the elements are to be included, what weight each should have, and how they should be collectively treated and presented. The same kind of visualization is also done for television commercials.

In a narrower sense, visualization refers only to the conceptualization of the illustration—what it should contain and how it should be presented. In this chapter we are concerned chiefly with the broader interpretation, the advertisement as a whole.

To illustrate: A family about to build a new home needs to decide what architectural style it wants, how large the house is to be, how many rooms it is to have, what kind of finishes will be used, and many more details. This planning is comparable to the visualization process in the creating of an advertisement and results in a decision as to what, for this particular family, seems the ideal house. But to pass this idea over to a builder by merely giving him an oral description of the proposed building could hardly be expected to result in a structure resembling the "dream home." To be sure that the finished building duplicates the idea or visualization, an architect must prepare detailed working drawings to instruct each of the many technicians involved on how to proceed with his particular phase of the work. From these same drawings the family for which the house is to be built can see its ideas presented in a more concrete form than in the "word picture" of the discussion phases of the planning. Such working drawings are somewhat comparable to the *layout* in print advertising and to the *storyboard* in television commercials.

In advertising, the process of visualizing gives form to an idea. The layout converts this idea into a concrete presentation that (1) enables the advertiser to better appreciate what his finished advertisement will look like and (2) gives the creative people and technicians the information they need to create an advertisement that makes the visualization come to life.

VISUALIZATION

The visualization of an advertisement, its conception, may take place in a plans-board meeting, a brainstorming session, or in the same activity called by almost any name. It generates the ad in the course of thinking, planning, and discussion of the various ways in which a sales idea can be developed. Few advertisements spring fully shaped from the head of an advertising man, as legend holds that Athena sprang from the head of Zeus. Most advertisements are planned, worked over, and reworked. Often dozens of rough drawings are made of different possible presentations before the final form the advertisement is to take is decided upon. Probably the most effective evolution of an advertisement—from the time of the initial idea until the final layout is approved by the agency staff and client—is accomplished by a free exchange of ideas between the copywriter and art director. It is for this reason that such planning sessions have become so popular among modern advertising agencies.

Any advertising goal can be attained in more than one way. Any sales message is capable of more than one means of expression. It is the task of the visualizers to create the most dramatic, the most efficient, the most effective way of presenting the sales story under the circumstances related to the particular problem at hand.

Consider the problem posed in selling the idea of smallness to an automobile-buying public that has long been conditioned to think in terms of "bigger = better" is no easy task for the visualizer. It was tackled boldly and effectively in a Volkswagen advertisement—the photograph of the car, the headline, and the VW logo put the point across with succinctness and great dramatic punch. The concept of smallness was emphasized in the photograph by showing the Volkswagen at a distance, small and isolated against a large and severely plain background. The contrast was pointed up by the brief, positive statement of the headline, centered just under the photograph, and even by the logo—large enough to be readily identifiable and standing out plainly from the surrounding copy area. This copy tells enough to leave the observer of the advertisement with a knowledge of what is being advertised and with the essential of the sales message. The visualization that can do this is a difficult one to improve upon.

Another, and in many respects less effective type of visualization, employs an indirect approach. The headline in one such advertisement read, "Like an open book." Its illustration pictured a book open on a table, a pair of eyeglasses beside it, a lamp in the right background, and a bouquet of flowers in the left background. Such a headline and illustration tell the observer nothing of the selling message contained in the copy; they refuse even to let him know what is being advertised. The advertisement might be selling anything. In fact, an identical headline and illustration were used by two different companies to sell things as widely different as a *service* and a *day bed!*

The hope of the visualizer who uses the indirect approach may be that the observer's curiosity will compel him to read the copy to find out what the advertisement is all about. This is taking a long and unnecessary chance. An appeal to curiosity is an appeal to prospects and to nonprospects alike. To arouse curiosity among those who are not logical prospects for the product or service being advertised can do the advertiser little good. It is reasonable to expect that prospects will make up a larger percentage of those drawn by an advertisement that makes clear what is being advertised and what it will do for its buyers than of those drawn by an advertisement that makes an approach dependent upon reader curiosity. Consider, for example, an advertisement very similar in visualization to the one just described. The illustration is again an open book with a lamp and flowers. The headline reads, "Let there be light." The product advertised is a set of books. How many readers of the magazines containing this advertisement will skip over it because they think of it as selling light bulbs, for which they have no immediate need? Of those who do not read the advertisement for this reason, how many might be prospects for the set of books and desirous of more information about them? This is, of course, a question that cannot be answered. But if the visualizer thinks his problem through, no such question need arise.

All this does not mean that the indirect approach is never good. In a magazine directed to those interested in horses, a motor oil advertisement picturing a horse and colt with the headline reading, "His character is written in the stud books," might be reasonably effective; but it would be poor in a general magazine. If the indirect appoach ties in closely with reader interest, it is far more likely to be effective than if it is only a curiosity-stimulator in a mass-circulation publication. But, even as a mere curiosity-stimulator, it can be effective if it is repeatedly used so that an association is established between a unique visualization and the product. In other words, if an advertiser consistently uses an indirect approach in order to inject an element of interest into his copy that otherwise might not be obtainable, and if this technique becomes characteristic of his advertising, the danger of losing prospects because of their inability to recognize what is being advertised has been removed or substantially lessened.

The indirect approach can be effective when employed in a tickler campaign or in a series of advertisements designed to snowball curiosity until the climaxing advertisement breaks the suspense by satisfying that curiosity. In such cases, the approach is indirect only to a point—the point when the suspense is broken by a very direct tie-up of the campaign with the product or service being advertised.

The indirect approach can be varied by the use of symbolism to visualize the sales message. However, the symbols employed should be readily understandable to the audience addressed, if they are to result in an impressive and effective advertisement. Symbolism is achieved through the choice of unusual setting, model poses, and lighting. An understanding of it is not dependent upon specific knowledge but upon the ability of the observer to see and relate to the artistic mood that has been created.

Often advertising ideas are visualized by a pictorial dramatization of the headline. In such visualizations the approach may be either direct or indirect, depending upon the character of the headline. The product picture retains its strength as a story-teller or an attention-stopper. In fact, it can be stronger in both of these areas than many an indirect visualization.

A pictorial presentation of the results of a test provides still another visualization possibility. This kind of visualization has the strength of the direct approach and forcefully calls attention of the observer to a selling point of the product.

Interesting visualizations are accomplished by a contrast of ideas. Such a visualization might show a "before and after" situation or show the "old" contrasted with the "new."

A selling point also can be visualized dramatically by showing a detail of the product. The detail can be pictured very much enlarged, as if seen under a magnifying glass, or it can be shown by picturing the product in cross section or by showing only that part which it is wished to emphasize.

Other visualization possibilities include showing the product alone, showing the product in a setting, and showing the product in use. Sometimes a unique manner of reproduction is employed in combination with other visualizing techniques to give a different and effective approach to the sales story. One advertiser, in an effort to find a different illustrative and copy approach, explored unusual art techniques and finally chose the age-old technique of wood engraving. The extra time and expense required for the many step process of making wood engravings were, in the opinion of the agency, well justified. The result was novel, attention-getting, and a wide departure from the frequently used type of illustration. Furthermore, the wood-engraved illustration provided a printing plate which is virtually foolproof on paper stocks ranging from those in newspapers to those in glossy magazines, and provided an effect impossible to duplicate even by scratchboard * and photoengraving.

After the visualizer has decided what his sales story is to be, he must

* A method in which artwork is created by scratching an India-ink-coated drawing surface so that the white paper strikes through, thus producing the picture in white lines against a dark background.

decide upon the manner of telling it. If it has been decided that showing the product in use is the best visualization, there are still several ways to tell the story. An illustration—possibly a reproduction of a photograph or painting—may be employed with accompanying copy written in a serious vein. Possibly it will be thought that humor would make the best appeal, and the visualization of the product in use may be presented in cartoon style. Or, an all-copy advertisement with no illustrations may be regarded as the most effective presentation. In short, visualization goes beyond the problem of deciding *what* should be in the sales story and includes the decision as to *how* the story may best be told.

Color vs. Black-and-White

Whether the advertisement should be in color is a question that may arise somewhere during the visualization process. Color costs money—considerably more than black and white—both to prepare the ad and to run it in the magazine or newspaper. The difference can be expected to come to about 37% for black plus one color (usually referred to as two-color), to about 70% for "full color" (black plus three colors). If the ad fills a page, the difference may be less than it is for a part page. These percentages can easily work out to $10,000 or $20,000 per insertion—figures that aren't petty cash in any budget. Clearly, careful consideration should be given to this matter of additional cost during the process of visualization.

The costs for television production in color are also considerably higher than those for black and white. Today, however, virtually all television production is in color.

Color may be used for any one or a combination of the following reasons:

1. To attract attention to the advertisement.
2. To attract attention to a special feature in the advertisement.
3. To present the product in a more realistic or lifelike manner.
4. To create an atmosphere or mood.

The first use of color, as an attention-getter that performs no other function for the advertisement as a whole, has least to be said in its favor. Certainly, an advertisement must be seen to do its job. But ways other than the the use of color can be employed to attract attention; most of these ways add nothing to the space cost. An unusually attractive or unique layout, a forceful copy appeal, a compelling headline or a striking illustration may do a far better job of getting attention than a splash of color—and at the same time perform additional functions. The color might get its attention as a pushcart peddler of fruits and vegetables would by standing on his head and singing "Home, Sweet Home"—but would it add to or detract from his sales? Surely, he could devise other methods of attracting attention that would tie in with his products and be more likely to help him sell his goods. The same is true of color. It will attract attention to a greater or lesser degree, depending upon the conditions under which it is used. In a medium that is entirely or predominantly black-and-white, color will stand out as an attention-getter. In a medium that is entirely or predominantly in color, additional color will be far less effective as an attention-getter. But effective or not, color adds to the cost of the advertisement. The advertiser must determine whether another device would be just as effective, and whether the color is helping to sell the goods as well as attract attention. It may do no more toward boosting sales than the song and acrobatics of our peddler.

The use of color to attract attention to a specific feature of the product or a special selling point in the copy is more justifiable than the use of color as an overall attention-getter. To conclude our analogy with the fruit peddler, he would change his tune from "Home, Sweet Home" to "Life Is Just a Bowl of Cherries."

The use of color to present the product in a more realistic or lifelike manner has much to be said in its favor. A national magazine emphasized this point some years ago when it ran a full-page newspaper advertisement picturing a table on which were displayed food and wine. The advertisement was in black-and-white. The headline read, "What This Ad Needs Is Color." It surely did! The psychological impact of color, especially when associated with food, is undeniable.

Ready-to-wear clothing, rugs, home furnishings, and many other products can be made much more appealing to prospective customers when pictured in color The increasing use of color in the catalogs of big mail order houses is in itself a strong indication of its value as a sales-boosting device. These organizations are not spending money simply to make their catalogs look prettier; for them, color sells goods or it isn't used. Seed catalogs in particular demonstrate an effective, sales-producing use of color.

Closely associated with use of color to present the product in a more life-like manner is its use to create an atmosphere or feeling tone. Goodyear ran two truck-tire advertisements that demonstrated this use of color very dramatically. One pictured a truck and trailer being driven over barren and rocky land with red, orange, and yellow as the predominating colors. The effect was to create a feeling of intense heat. The other advertisement showed a tanker truck; in the landscape the dominant colors were green, white, and blue. Here the feeling was one of cold.

Such temperature suggestion is not the only effect conveyed by color. Blue may suggest sadness or depression; a pink or rose tone, happiness or gaiety. Subtle colors and shading may suggest quality or exclusiveness. Harder, sharper colors, on the other hand, may create an impression of ruggedness or coarseness. And the suggestive powers of color can work toward the negative in selling as well as the positive. One well-known designer believes that light blue should not be used on milk cartons or in the advertising of milk and that green is to be avoided in the packaging and advertising of bakery goods. Light blue, it is felt, suggests "thin" milk, and green suggests mold.

The theme of an advertising campaign may be such that none of the reasons just considered for employing or rejecting color will decide whether or not it should be used. Assume that the advertiser is engaged in a campaign designed to emphasize the long and impressive record of public service his firm enjoys. Suppose, further, that it has been decided to visualize this by use of old-fashioned-appearing advertisements in which the illustrations will resemble woodcuts. The use of color in such advertisements would be quite out of character.

The choice of medium in which the advertisements are to be run may dictate the advisability of using color, irrespective of other considerations. If the medium is printed on a poor-grade paper stock, a black-and-white advertisement would probably be far more attractive than one in color. If an excellent color reproduction can be obtained, but the majority of competing advertisements are in color, black-and-white might stand out better. If color has been used consistently by a particular advertiser over a long period of time, a change to black-and-white may result in some "surprise-attention" value and some word-of-mouth publicity.

LAYOUT

Roughs, Finished Layouts, and Comprehensives

Depending upon the use to which they are put, layouts may be very rough presentations, crudely drawn, giving only the minimum of detail necessary to convey an idea, or they may be carefully developed pieces of art, almost as detailed as the finished advertisement. If the purpose of the layout is to give agency personnel a more concrete presentation of a visualization or to serve as a guide for the copy and production staffs, a rough drawing may be all that is needed. A *rough layout* may start out as a small drawing designed merely to help its creator convey to another member of the agency staff what he has in mind. Several of these small layouts or *thumbnail sketches* may be made to obtain a better idea of the various ways in which the advertisement might be presented. When one is finally selected, a "rough" or rough layout is made in the size that the final advertisement will assume. Proportions of the various elements—copy blocks, illustrations, logo, and so on—will be accurate. But the copy may be indicated by horizontal lines, the headlines may be very roughly lettered, and the illustrations may be represented by the crudest of sketches. A rough layout is often all that is needed by a professional advertising staff.

If the layout is to be submitted to the client, a more detailed work-up is desirable and sometimes necessary. These *finished layouts* have carefully drawn illustrations. Headlines are lettered so that they will resemble closely the typeset headlines of the finished advertisements; and other elements—logo, trademark, coupons, and so on—are indicated in a manner that makes them recognizable even to the untrained observer. These layouts enable the client to see what his advertisement will look like when completed and make it easier for him to suggest changes to his agency at a time when they can be made with minimum difficulty and expense.

At times, the layouts that are submitted to clients are made to look as

Two steps in the creation of an advertisement—a rough layout with a very sketchy indication of copy and art, and a comprehensive layout which closely approximates the appearance of the final printed advertisement. *Courtesy of Castle & Cooke, Inc.*

The finished advertisement as it appeared in several leading magazines. The advertisement appeared in full color. *Courtesy of Castle & Cooke, Inc.*

100

much like the finished advertisement as possible. These very carefully developed, detailed layouts, or *comprehensives,* may even have copy set in type and pasted into position in place of the horizontal lines generally used to indicate copy. If the final advertisement is to have color, the finished layout is also colored. Subheadlines as well as headlines are lettered and so are the logo and slogan. Little or nothing is left to the imagination of the client in a comprehensive.

One of the jobs of the visualizers and layout artists is to decide upon the arrangement of the several component parts of the advertisement. If it consists merely of a headline, an illustration, copy, and a signature, as many advertisements do, the problem is comparatively simple. But as more elements are added, the problem becomes increasingly difficult. If the advertisement consists of a headline, a subheadline, two or more illustrations, two or more copy blocks, a trademark, a slogan, a coupon, and a signature, then it offers a variety of possible arrangements from which to choose. The arrangement of these several elements not only must result in an overall pleasing appearance of the advertisement but must also place emphasis on the most important parts. Therefore, a first step is the evaluation of the component parts of the advertisement to determine their relative importance in the sales message that the advertiser wants to convey to the market. Once this decision is made, the task becomes one of determining what manner of emphasizing the more important elements will be used.

Emphasis

Emphasis may be obtained by location of the page on which the advertisement appears, by size, by the use of color, by the use of white space, or by the action in the advertisement directing the reader's eyes to the important element. In a Champion International advertisement, an important feature, hence the one to be emphasized, was the picture of a room after it was remodeled. However, the visualization called for three illustrations—the original room, the remodeled room, and a picture of the six kinds of Weldwood from which the buyer could make a choice. Emphasis on the remodeled room was achieved in three ways: (1) by placing the illustration at the very top of the page, even above the headline, (2) by making the picture of the remodeled room larger than that of the original room, and (3) by the use of color in the illustration of the remodeled room and black-and-white in the picture of the original room. The picture of the six kinds of Weldwood had to be colored to give the woods a natural appearance and make the illustration more meaningful to the reader. Color at this point also helped tie in the black-and-white illustration with the colored one appearing above it and thus made for greater unity among the three illustrations.

Heavy black type and light script alike can emphasize a point. Emphasis often can be obtained as effectively by restraint as by spectacular display. Generous use of white space can be more compelling in its emphasis than all the type and all the exlamation marks in the printer's font. The device employed to obtain emphasis in any given advertisement will depend upon several considerations. It will depend upon the medium in which the advertisement is to appear. It will depend upon the product or service being advertised. It will depend upon the theme stressed in the copy. It will depend upon the type of audience sought. It will depend upon what the competition is doing. And finally, it will depend upon the judgment, experience, and good tast of the advertiser.

Gaze Motion

Partly as a matter of emphasis, but also as a matter of giving the advertisement greater coherence and unity and of preventing the loss of the reader's attention to competing advertisements, the layout artist attempts to incorporate gaze motion into the ad. Gaze motion is the direction that the advertiser would like the reader's eyes to take in looking at an advertisement—the order in which his attention moves from one element in the advertisement to another. One way it is guided in the layout is by the actual or implied action shown in the illustration. That is, the advertisement may picture a person walking or running in a particular direction or an automobile being driven in a particular direction. The reader's eyes tend to move in this direction. Or the action may be implied, as when an inanimate object is so placed in an illustration as to point in a particular direction, or when a model may look or point in a given direction. The reader's eyes tend to move in the direction of the implied action. Gaze motion may also be achieved by the more obvious devices of an arrow, or a dotted line.

If the principles of gaze motion are incorporated into a layout, action or implied action never will lead the reader's eyes off the page or toward competing advertising. If an automobile is pictured pointing off the page or in the direction of another advertisement on the same page, one or more people will be pictured standing in front of the car looking back at it. These figures act as a baffle to the gaze motion of the reader, catching his eyes as they move in the direction the automobile is facing and turning them back toward the car.

Coherence and Balance

The art director must be concerned with tying together the several parts of the advertisement so that it will possess coherence and so that the reader's eyes will be directed through it in a predetermined manner, but he must also balance the several elements. Without balance an advertisement will have an unpleasant appearance. It will look wrong, appear to be falling off the page, leaning or toppling over. Balance may be *formal* or *informal*. Formal balance is attained by placing objects of equal value on either side of the optical center of the advertisement and equal distance from it. The optical center is a point located about five-eighths of the distance up from the bottom of the advertisement and at an equal distance from each side. It is the point that the reader would name as the center of the page if asked to do so without the aid of a ruler or other measuring device. Formal balance, although pleasing in appearance, lacks the life and dramatic possibilities that may be obtained by informal or occult balance. However, it may give classic simplicity that would prove effective for some forms of advertising.

An example of formal balance.

An example of informal balance.

In informal balance the several elements are arranged on either side of the optical center and above or below it in such fashion as to achieve balance without symmetry. As in a see-saw, balance is obtained by moving the object of greatest weight nearer the fulcrum. The weight of the elements in an advertisement may be a matter of size, degree of blackness, color, or shape.

Layout and the Small Advertiser

Good layout perhaps is more important to the advertiser who uses small space than it is to the one who can afford full-page and double-page spreads. The small advertiser cannot depend upon the impact of big space to attract attention. Neither can he depend upon it to hold competing advertisements at a safe distance. Faced with comparatively small space in which to arrange the component parts of his advertisement, and knowing that his advertisement will be surrounded by competition, his layout problems become harder to solve and also more compelling in their demand for satisfactory solution than those of the big advertiser. But with some experimentation and much imagination, surprising layout effects can be obtained in considerably less than full-page space units. One advertiser, for example, bought two one-third pages on facing pages of a magazine. These spaces were located on the outer-sides of the right-hand and left-hand pages; editorial matter lay between them, on the inner portions of each page. The two advertisements were tied together by their background treatment. A *benday* (shading) in the form of a crescent was applied to each advertisement so that the open sections of the two crescents faced each other. The overall appearance became a shaded circle broken by the editorial matter of the magazine that separated the two advertisements. This circle pulled the two one-third page advertisements together and gave much the same reader impact that might have been obtained from a double-page spread. Thus, by a simple layout device, the two one-third-page spaces were made to approximate a two-page space in effectiveness.

Advertisements of considerably smaller size than one-third page can be made distinctive through well-planned layout. A check of the classified and classified-display sections of any newspaper usually will give examples of advertisements that, by virtue of their layouts, stand out amid surrounding competition.

PITFALLS FOR THE BEGINNER

Perhaps one of the most common mistakes of the beginner in advertising is to make his visualizations too complicated. He wants too many things in the illustration, too many words in the copy. In general, as a visualization grows in complexity it loses in strength. The complicated visualization is likely to lead to a cluttered layout. The art director is faced with the problem of getting so much into the layout that strength of simplicity is lost to the confusion of minor detail. In most cases, the simpler and more direct the visualization, the simpler will be the layout and the better will be the resulting advertisement. It is far better to have one important selling point understood and remembered than to have a dozen selling points missed completely or soon forgotten.

THE TELEVISION STORYBOARD

While visualization for television production may take the same discussion and planning as for print ads, the layout for a television commercial consists of a series of drawings, each representing a scene that will run for several seconds on the TV screen. Each drawing consists of one frame of a sequence that will include motion. This drawing "freezes" the representative frame of a particular scene. Below each drawing appears the script for that scene, including the directions for the director, cameraman, and talent. This combination of the copy and art, called a *storyboard,* serves as a guide in the casting or selecting of performing talent, and in set design; it also provides the producer, director, and cameraman with a script and a planned layout of what is to be put on film or video tape.

Also, in the early stages of the television production, before anything has been put on film or tape, the storyboard helps the agency's management people, the client, and others to visualize what the finished commercial is going to be like.

SUMMARY

Visualization is a mental process that enables one to see or picture "images" in his or her mind, without the benefit of a printed or projected

JANITOR IN A DRUM

texize

First industrial-strength cleaner for home use

"CLEVELAND" :30 Seconds

OPEN WITH HEAD-ON BOW SHOT OF SS PRESIDENT CLEVELAND STEAMING TOWARDS CAMERA.

ANNCR (VO): The President Cleveland

...home for a cleanup...

these men can't waste time

with stubborn dirt,

that's why they use,

industrial-strength Janitor-in-a-Drum! (SOUND: BOOM OF DRUM)

(DRUM BECOMES PRODUCT PACKAGE IN HOME.) The same industrial-strength cleaner

you can use at home to cut cleaning down to size.

Tough enough for a playroom floor...

tame enough for a baby's highchair.

(SOUND: BOOM OF DRUM) Janitor-in-a-Drum from Texize... it does the work — not you.

A *photoboard*—the same as a storyboard except that it is produced after the completion of the commercial and uses actual photographs from the release print or video tape.

image. It can be likened to the "picture" one conjures up when listening to a descriptive radio commercial. The tangible result of that mental process is a sketch put down on paper. In its broader sense visualization refers to the conceptionalization of the entire ad rather than of the illustration alone. It is in the former meaning that it has been considered here.

Visualizations often evolve into layouts, which are like blueprints or representations of the ad. Layouts range in completeness from rough and thumbnail sketches to finished layouts and comprehensives. The comprehensive is complete and leaves nothing to the imagination—it resembles the printed ad most closely.

QUESTIONS AND DISCUSSION SUBJECTS

1. What are some meanings of *visualization?*
2. How would you differentiate between layout and visualization?
3. Give an example of the indirect approach.
4. Knowing the many advantages of color, when might it be a good idea to use black and white?
5. Define "rough," "thumbnail sketch," and "comprehensive."
6. Bring to class an advertisement that employs gaze motion.

FOR FURTHER READING

Art Direction Magazine, ed. *Creativity.* New York: Hastings House, Publishers, annually.

Berrien, Edith Heal. *Visual Thinking in Advertising.* New York, Holt, 1963.

Bockus, H. William, Jr. *Advertising Graphics.* New York: Macmillan, 1974.

Dair, Carl. *The Organization of Space.* New York: Westvaco Corporation, 1966.

Herdeg, Walter, ed. *Graphis Annual:* International Advertising and Editorial Graphics. New York: Hastings House, Publishers, annually.

Herdeg, Walter, ed. *Graphis/Diagrams:* The Graphic Visualization of Abstract Data. New York: Hastings House, Publishers, 1974.

Herdeg, Walter, ed. *Photographis:* International Advertising, Editorial and Television Photography. New York: Hastings House, Publishers, annually.

Longyear, William. *Advertising Layout.* New York: Ronald Press, 1954.

Stankowski, Anton. *The Visual Presentation of Invisible Processes.* New York: Hastings House, Publishers, 1967.

★
★
★ **8**
★
★
★

Copy and Communication

Advertising copy is the advertiser's sales message. The term *copy* usually refers to the sales messages that appear in print, the written portion of the message, exclusive of the illustration. However, the term is sometimes used in a broader sense to include everything in the advertisement—headline, subheadline, logotype (the advertiser's signature and address), slogan, and picture. But more common usage restricts the term to the headline, the subheadline, and the main body of the sales message. The term *copy* also includes the spoken sales message, as broadcast over radio or television, which must be written before it is delivered. Therefore, the copywriting job must be done whether the advertising is written for publication in a print medium or written for oral delivery.

Advertising copy is first and last a means of *communication*. The advertiser has a product or a service that he wishes to sell. He wants to tell potential buyers about it. In this capacity he is the *sender* of the message, the *communicator*. On the other end of this communication channel is the *receiver,* the one to whom the communication is addressed. He is the prospect, the potential buyer. This potential buyer may or may not be aware of any need or desire for the advertiser's product or service. Lacking awareness, he must be made aware. Having awareness, he must be stimulated to action manifesting itself in the purchase of the product or service or in some other behavior that the advertiser might wish—for example, clipping and returning a coupon.

So, on one end of the advertising channel we have the

SENDER

and on the other end we have the

RECEIVER.

The job of the copywriter and of the media man, who places the copy in a vehicle that will carry it to the market, is to establish intelligible communication between sender and receiver. To accomplish this, the copywriter works with symbols, the media man with vehicles to carry these symbols from sender to receiver. If the wrong symbols are used, they will either not be understood or will be misinterpreted by the receiver, and communication will break down.

The ideal communication occurs when the receiver understands the message exactly as it was intended by the sender, and reacts accordingly. If, however, the wrong media are used, the symbols, no matter how intelligible they may be, will not reach enough receivers and the communication will be ineffective. Let us leave the problems of the media man until a later chapter and concentrate here upon the copy job.

THE SYMBOLS OF COMMUNICATION

The three kinds of symbols most commonly used to communicate written ideas from person to person are:

1. Pictures
2. Words
3. Numbers

The copywriter is concerned with all three, but works for the most part with words. Unfortunately, the word-symbol is most likely of the three, to be misinterpreted or misunderstood. There is little chance that the receiver will fail to comprehend the meaning of the sender when the symbol is "2," "60," or "89." A picture also usually interprets the sender's idea to the receiver with little or no confusion in meaning. Words, however, often present both sender and receiver with problems. Do they mean the same thing to both parties? How well are they understood by the receiver? Will the choice of words stimulate the desired action, or would other words of similar meaning but different connotation be better? These illustrate the kinds of questions to which the advertising copywriter must address himself. He must realize that if there is ambiguity in a piece of advertising copy the receiver will rarely take the time and trouble to clarify a meaning that is obscure to him. Either the meaning is clear or the message is lost.

Let us examine the word-symbol more closely and determine, if possible, wherein the breakdowns in communication most frequently occur. The symbol "dog" will convey to the receiver the general thought of the sender. There may be a difference in the image this symbol creates in the minds of the sender and and the receiver with respect to breed. But the general concept of "a member of the canine species" is conveyed. If the sender wishes to transmit a more specific picture, he may use a word-symbol designating a particular breed such as "collie" or "cocker spaniel." Depending upon the receiver's knowledge of dogs, this more precise symbol results either in a mental image closer to that of the sender or in a mental image no more explicit than that conveyed by the symbol "dog." However, "collie" and "cocker spaniel" are symbols capable of exact definition through readily available reference books, and such definitions are often assisted by picture-symbols.

Now let us suppose that the symbol used is the word "good." Here, the mental image of the sender and that of the receiver may be very different. Even the sources for definition and interpretation may be of little help. Under such circumstances, there is a chance of partial or even complete breakdown of communication. Word-symbols that describe subjective evaluations or abstract ideas are likely to give the communicator the most trouble, especially if the audience addressed is a large and heterogeneous group. Also word-symbols that large segments of the population, may seldom use fail partly or completely to communicate the idea of the sender to the receiver. For example, the word "aroma" was used in a test to determine word comprehension in a coffee advertisement. A sizable percentage of the people questioned said that they did not know what the word meant but thought that it had something to do with *love (amour)*. Another coffee advertisement of a few years ago asked the reader if he had had his "bouquet" for breakfast that morning, and further complicated the symbolism by picturing a bunch of flowers in the advertisement. One cannot help wondering how the word "bouquet" was interpreted by many readers of the advertisement.

If communication is to be effective, symbols should be readily intelligible and should mean the same things to both sender and receiver. If there is a suspicion of weakness in either respect, a different symbol or set of symbols should be used, or else an adequate interpretation of the questionable symbolism should be made. This might be done by an additional word explanation, by a picture, or by both.

The precise statement is more desirable than the generalization as a conveyor of ideas. To say that an automobile is economical to operate may mean different things to different people, depending upon the size of their incomes and their past experiences with automobiles. To say that the car can be operated on x dollars a month or can run y miles on a gallon of gasoline under stated conditions is far more meaningful to every reader. The reader receives and is able to interpret the communication in the same terms that the sender had in mind.

The word-symbol that evokes no mental picture communicates nothing. But, to evoke a mental picture may not be enough. Some words are far more effective in this respect than others, although the basic meaning may be the same, and these are words the copywriter should use. Mark Twain once said that the difference between the right word and *almost* the right word is the difference between the lightning and the lightning bug. Winston Churchill's reference to "blood, sweat, and tears" would have been somewhat less effective had he said, "danger to life and limb, hard work, and unhappy times." Patrick Henry might have been less impressive had he said, "Should we evaluate life and peace more highly than freedom—Heaven forbid," instead of "Is life so dear, or peace so sweet, as to be purchased at the price of chains and slavery? Forbid it Almighty God!"

Not only do individual words create mental pictures of varying vividness and impact, but the manner in which words are put together in clauses and sentences has much to do with the image that is registered in the reader's or listener's mind. John Randolph, a political enemy of Henry Clay, might have said, "Clay is brilliant but corrupt." Instead, he said, "Henry Clay, so brilliant yet so corrupt, like a mackerel cast on a rock in the moonlight he shines and stinks." The meaning of both statements is the same The imagery is far different. One is a harsh statement; the other is perhaps one of the most caustic sentences ever uttered in a political speech.

The dramatic impact of words is probably more apparent in political utterances than in commercial writings, but as word-symbols move men in areas of political activity, so can they also move them in areas of marketing activity. Yet the copywriter must not strive merely for effect or startling dramatic impact upon his audience. What was said in the chapter on visualization about gaining attention applies equally to copywriting: the getting of attention merely for attention's sake is poor advertising strategy. If the copy is to do an effective selling job, the mental image created by the word-symbol must relate to the product, idea, or service being advertised. A piece of copy that gains attention and is remembered *as a piece of copy* is of questionable value to the advertiser. A piece of copy that gains attention and causes the reader to remember the product has done its job well.

THE AIMS OF COPY

Good copy is not an end in itself. An ad that wins prizes for its artistic excellence or entertainment value is not necessarily one that does its job. In most cases that job is to sell a product, a service, or an idea, by means of informing, educating and persuading the public. The good copywriter never loses sight of that goal.

The sale may be expected to follow closely upon the appearance of the copy in an advertising medium, as in mail-order selling and in much retail advertising. On the other hand, the sale may not necessarily be expected to follow immediately the appearance of any given piece of advertising copy. In manufacturers' or national advertising, the cumulative effect of several advertisements may educate buyers to a brand preference and eventual purchase of the advertised goods. Still again, the goal of copy may be to stimulate interest in a product and possibly provoke inquiry from prospects but not actually to close the sale; the closing is left to personal salesmanship. Such copy aims are frequently found in industrial advertising and in the advertising for large consumer household appliances and automobiles.

Even within any one of the broad classifications of retail, national, or industrial advertising, the relationship between the copy and its expected effect may be of short or long duration, depending upon whether the copy is promotional or institutional in character. If the copy is promotional—whether it is retail, national, or industrial—returns from it are expected to be realized over a shorter period of time than if it is institutional. Much institutional copy is of a public-relations character and, therefore, comparatively long range with respect to anticipated results. It endeavors to "sell" the company, for if the company is accepted by the public, its products will be more in demand.

SELLING FEATURES

Irrespective of *when* the copy is expected to do the selling job, the *how* of accomplishing the task is about the same. First, the *attention* of prospects must be gained. Immediately thereafter, or even better—simultaneously, their *interest* must be aroused, *not* in the copy as such but in the offer being made. This should be followed or accompanied by the prospect's *acceptance* of the sales story as factual. Next, the prospect's *preference* for the advertised brand must be established. Finally, the prospect must be stimulated to take the *action* the advertiser wishes him to take, whether it be to buy, to inquire further about the offer, or to act in some other manner in accordance with the requests or suggestions made in the copy.

Attention

Attention must be obtained, or the copy will be passed over and never read. We have seen that a reader's attention may be attracted to an advertisement in a number of ways. The illustration, a unique layout, the use or non-use of color, and the headline may individually or in combination be employed as attention-getters. If only the copy element in the advertisement is considered, then, obviously, the headline becomes the major attention-getting device because it normally would be seen and read before the body of the copy. A leading copywriter states that "on the average, five times as many people read the headline as read the body copy." [1] Therefore, whether the rest of the copy is read would depend to a considerable extent upon the ability of the headline to attract attention and arouse sufficient interest to induce the reader to continue further into the reading matter of the advertisement.

In writing headlines, as in writing the main portion of the sales message, it should be remembered that copy sells because it convinces the reader or listener, convinces him that he needs or would like to have the product or service offered. Both the body of the copy and the headline must be addressed to the specific needs and desires of a specific audience.

The headline can be a statement of fact providing *news,* possibly a scientific discovery, or it may promise a *benefit.* It may be in the form of a question, a plea or a command, or a statement; but with few exceptions it should let the reader know what the advertisement is selling. What was said concerning the direct and indirect appaorch in visualization applies equally to the headline; it is, of course, a part of any visualization.

No matter how much of an attention-getter a headline may be or how believable its accompanying text may prove, the advertisement will not sell power lawn mowers to apartment dwellers who have no lawns and never expect to have them. These nonprospects might be induced to read a part of the copy by a curiosity-arousing headline, but it should be recalled that in gaining reader-ship of some nonbuyers this technique may lose the attention and readership of some real prospects who fail to recognize the relationship of the advertisement to their needs. If the copywriter is selling lawn mowers, he should direct both the headline and the accompanying copy to people who do have lawns. This is known as *flagging*. It flags or calls the attention of a particular type of person or a specific segment of the population. This selective method singles out those who have an interest and excludes all others. Maybe some writers, as well as some salesmen, might sell the proverbial refrigerator to the proverbial Eskimo, but the same advertising dollars or sales effort spent in somewhat warmer regions would build far better sales volume.

Not only should the copywriter address the appropriate audience for the product or service that he is attempting to sell but in addition *he should be sure that he knows what he is selling!* People rarely buy mere physical *products;* they buy *benefits* or *satisfaction.* Few buyers, if any, purchase just an au-tomobile. They buy transportation, social prestige, recreation, convenience, or some combination of these, even all. The advertiser who discovers the domi-nant motivating appeal among any group of prospects and sells them this satis-faction has an effective piece of copy and a decided competitive edge on the advertiser who has not made this discovery. One advertiser found that his ad pulled better when a *curiosity* headline reading, "How to be Up and About with a Backache," was changed to a *promise* or offer of *satisfaction:* "She Suffered from a Backache, Then Got Relief." In the first headline the adver-tiser was selling the ability to still function although troubled with a backache. In the second headline he was selling relief from a backache. Which would you rather buy? The answer is obvious and the premise is borne out by David Ogilvy who says that, "headlines that promise a benefit sell more than those that don't." [2]

A third advertisement in this series carried another *curiosity* headline, "Johnnie 3-Way to the Rescue." This also failed to do as well as the *promise* headline selling "relief." Here, the observer was not told in the headline what was being sold. Curiosity, perhaps, was supposed to lead him into the body copy. But maybe a person's curiosity is somewhat dampened by a backache. Many people with backaches, excellent prospects for the remedy, may have been too much annoyed by their ailment to care about reading the rest of the copy—never mind who Johnnie 3-Way was or whom he was rescuing.

News and *command* headlines have already been mentioned. An example of the former is, "New Diet Chocolate! No Calories and tastes Like the Real Thing!" A command headline might read, "Put a Gizmo Battery in Your Car! It Will Start in Arctic Cold!" This is a command coupled with a promise.

Interest

Once the reader's or listener's attention is obtained, the body copy must catch and hold his interest. If it fails to do this, the initial gaining of attention will have accomplished little.

Nothing is more interesting to a prospect than himself and his own problems. Therefore, copy addressed to him in terms of himself, his interests, and his problems will hold his interest—or nothing will. The refrain of some verses on copy written by Victor Schwab of Schwab, Beatty & Porter, Inc., is a course in good copywriting in its own right. It reads:

> So tell me quick and tell me true
> (Or else, my love, to hell with you):
> Less—how this product came to be;
> More—what the damn thing does for me! [3]

These lines proclaim again the old advice, too frequently ignored, to take the "you and your" approach in copy and forget the "me and mine." If this is done, the copy will gain and hold reader interest—not the interest of all readers of a publication, but the interest of those who count, the prospects for the product or service being advertised.

The people at Comptom Advertising agency follow a simple creative philosophy: Find the most meaningful benefit the product has to offer; present it in the most interesting and persuasive way possible.

Acceptance

Attention and interest are of little value unless the sales message is believed—accepted by the prospect. Acceptance may be, in many cases, the result of a reputation built by the advertiser over a period of years. The corporate image of many firms may be one of fair dealing, quality product, and truthful advertising so that their copy claims are accepted without question merely because of the logos or signatures over which they appear. But such a reputation and the accompanying acceptance of advertising claims are earned over a period of time. There are more immediate ways in which the copywriter may gain acceptance or belief in his writings.

Proof of the copy's claim may be offered:

1. In an indorsement by an independent testing laboratory or accrediting institution.
2. In a testimonial of a satisfied user of the product, provided that the testimonial comes from a person whose word is meaningful to the audience addressed by the copy.
3. In descriptions and results of tests conducted by the advertiser to substantiate his claims.
4. In tests that it is suggested the consumer himself may try.
5. In cases cited where the product has performed as claimed.
6. In a statement concerning materials and construction associated with the manufacture of the product.
7. In a statement of guarantee.

Acceptance of copy claims is also increased by:

1. Elimination from the copy of such incomplete comparisons as "The A-1 Washer washes faster and does a better job."

2. Avoidance in the copy of omissions of information pertinent to an understanding of a statement or claim made. For example, "10,000 questionnaires were sent out and 90 percent of the replies received were favorable." (How many were received?)
3. Avoidance of weasel words in the copy or of exaggerations in text or illustrations.
4. Avoidance of overly emotional appeals in the copy.

Of course, the manner in which the copy is presented may be such that none of these means of gaining acceptance is used. In fact, they may be directly contradicted. For example, exaggeration may be employed and with good effect. The "white tornado" employed in the television commercials for Ajax liquid cleanser illustrate this point. The commercials are humorous and no one actually believes that a tornado is unleashed from a bottle to clean up a home. Yet the viewer gets the message from the tone of the copy that this is a strong cleaner.

Preference

Assume that the reader's attention has been attracted to a particular advertisement, that he has found it interesting, and that he has read the complete sales message. Assume also that he has believed the claims set forth in the copy. There still is a next objective that has not yet been accomplished. Other advertisements in the same medium and other advertisements elsewhere trying to sell similar products may have achieved among readers the same degree of attention, interest, and believability. Therefore, the claims made in any given piece of copy must not only be accepted by the reader as true, but they must also be of such character as to establish in his mind a definite brand preference for the advertised product. Only trade or association advertising can afford to sell a product as a class. The hat industry may try to sell the idea that men should wear hats, but Stetson would prefer men to wear Stetson hats, and Knox would rather they buy Knox hats.

The task of creating brand preference presents the copywriter with comparatively few problems when competing brands present recognizable differences. But the job becomes increasingly difficult as product differentiation becomes less apparent. Unfortunately for the copywriter, in many cases the differences among brands are small. It is in such situations that the danger of slipping into generalizations and unsupported claims becomes greatest and that the copy is least likely to be believed. It is under such circumstances that the copywriter is tempted to write such statements as

"Relieves pain faster"

and the reader is likely to ask,

"Faster than what? Faster than any other product or faster than when nothing is used?"

It is also in these situations of minute product differentiation that one is most likely to find advertisers A, B, and C each claiming to use only the most costly ingredients or only the best raw materials in the manufacture of their respective products. These claims may be quite true; they may all indeed buy the most expensive and best raw materials available, but when all three advance the claim it has little in it to build brand preference; the same-claim ads may even create doubt in the minds of readers.

When writing about products too similar to their competition to set them apart, the copywriter must exercise special care that in attempting to gain brand preference he does not lose audience acceptance of his claims.

The slogan, if properly conceived, can assist in building a desire to try a specific brand or in serving as a reminder that a specific brand has a quality that should make it attractive to consumers. The slogan "When it rains it pours" associates Morton Salt with the desirable feature of not clogging the salt shaker in damp weather. The Coca Cola slogan, "The Pause that Refreshes," associated that brand with a very desirable characteristic for a soft drink. These and other good slogans are abbreviated sales messages that summarize more lengthy sales arguments in a dramatic or in an easy-to-remember manner. These longer arguments may or may not appear in the body of specific pieces of copy, but they are major selling points for the brands in question.

Slogans are employed in two principal ways. A slogan may be created early in a firm's history and be used for many years, sometimes for the lifetime of the business. Alternatively, a slogan may be created to emphasize the major sales message of a specific campaign and discontinued at the termination of the campaign. Pan American Airlines, which for years had used the slogan "The world's most experienced airline," added to their repertory the catchy singing commercial "Pan Am makes the going great." TWA added "Up, up, and away." And "Coke" created a new slogan that told us, "It's the real thing." General Electric's old standby, "Progress is our most important product," was joined by the admonition, "Don't be a bulbsnatcher" for a special campaign. And the A & P gave us "W-E-E-E-O-O-O *w*here *e*conomy *o*riginates," which they dropped in 1975.

In practice, slogans may be used as headlines, as an integral part of the copy message, or as an appendage to the copy—a sort of postscript to the main sales message. Slogans are also used on packages and may, at times, be the subjects of product-promotion contests. Not infrequently the slogan is a repeated portion of a radio or television commercial.

Action

As has been seen, the goal of most advertising is to evoke action from the audience to whom the copy is addressed. It may be expected to take place immediately upon the reading of the advertisement, or it may not be expected until considerable time has elapsed, but action of some type and at some time is usually the goal and is certainly hoped for, if not expected.

If the readers were logical prospects, and if the copy has succeeded in each of the areas just considered—if it has obtained attention, has aroused interest, has been believed, and has created the desired brand preference—then action could and often would follow as a natural sequence of events. However, inasmuch as action is wanted, action should be asked for. One authority in copy evaluation contends that the advertisement must contain a request for action and, when appropriate, a *command* to act.

It would be a mistake to think that the needs for attracting attention, stimulating interest, securing acceptance, establishing brand preference, and motivating action have the same relative importance in every advertisement. The importance of each varies with the copy task at hand, the kind of advertisement for which the copy is being written, and the medium in which it is to appear—all related considerations.

Not many readers of a magazine or newspaper can be expected to seek out manufacturers' advertising. Readers are looking for information or entertainment from the editorial content of the publication and usually have no concern at the moment with chewing gum, soft drinks, automobiles, or soap. Their interest must, then, be diverted to an advertiser's product message in which they may have little or no immediate interest. For this reason, the job of attracting attention and of arousing interest is more important in the case of national or manufacturers' advertising copy in newspapers and magazines than it is in some other forms of advertising.

However, readers of classified advertisements, catalogs, retail advertising, and some advertising for theatres and other kinds of entertainment do have an interest in the advertised products or services that cause them to seek and read the advertisements. An unemployed man may read carefully the help-wanted advertisements in the daily newspaper. A man inspired by the first signs of spring may seek and read a seed catalog. A woman in her role of household buyer may search the newspaper page by page to find the retail store offerings of the day. A couple in search of an evening's entertainment may hunt out and read the motion picture and theatre advertising. In each of these cases, the attention and interest of the readers already exists, and the copy may be less concerned with attracting attention and building interest. However, the tasks of gaining acceptance, creating preference, and stimulating action remain important.

These three copy objectives lose some of their importance only when the copy task is to sell a necessity that enjoys virtual monopoly of the market. Here, there would be little need for creating brand preference; but the copy must still win acceptance and the stimulation to action may still be desirable, as in public-utility advertising. Even though the utility may enjoy a quasi monopoly, there are substitutes in certain areas of use. For example, at the present time one has small choice but to use electricity for lighting one's home, but it can be heated by electricity, oil, coal, or gas. One can use as few or as many electrical appliances as one chooses. The utility, whether privately owned or government operated, needs customer acceptance and may be very much interested in proving to the community that it is doing a conscientious and efficient job. Thus, even in the case of a monopoly, the copywriter must concern himself with preferences, with getting his claims believed, and with obtaining action.

MEDIUM AND AUDIENCE

Advertising copy should be written to fit both the medium in which it is to be placed and the audience to whom it is directed. Even when a specific medium is selected because its audience is the one the advertiser is seeking, the copy should be written to fit both; the more so, if the medium appeals to a general audience. A medium may have characteristics that place definite limitations on copy, irrespective of the audience addressed. Billboards and other forms of outdoor advertising are seen chiefly as their "readers" walk or drive past. No one stops to examine them; they are seen briefly in passing. Therefore, copy in the outdoor medium is limited to a few words. Advertisements in trains and buses are before their audiences for a longer period of time, and their copy can be somewhat longer than that found in the outdoor advertising medium. Such advertising is removed some distance from the reader, so lettering must be large enough to be readily legible. This consideration, as well as others that will be discussed in a later chapter, limits the length of copy in transit advertising.

Newspapers and magazines, because they and these other media are read under quite different conditions, can successfully present advertisements with lengthy copy. Some people do contend that even in newspapers and magazines the copy should be kept short. However, there is evidence that length of copy does not materially reduce readership. Indeed, David Ogilvy contended that "if you are advertising a product which has a great many different qualities to recommend it, write long copy; the more you tell, the more you sell." [4] This position was further supported by Daniel Starch, who said that "whether anybody reads it or not depends on the advertisement, what it says, and how it says it." [5]

The restriction on length of copy imposed by the character of some media automatically excludes the possibility of writing educational or even promotional copy when these media convey the message. The few words of copy that characterize most outdoor advertising are adequate for reminder or reinforcing advertising and for some forms of institutional advertising, but they would hardly accommodate either the development of a sales story necessary to the introduction of a new product or to the sort of detail about product differences that might be required in highly competitive advertising.

Restrictions on length are not the only limitations placed on copy by the media in which it appears. Certain kinds of educational and institutional copy are better suited to magazine than to newspaper presentation. Magazines are likely to be read in leisure time rather than when a person is hurrying to or from work. In contrast, newspapers are frequently read during spare moments, on buses or trains, or when the reader has only limited time. Even when a newspaper is read at home and at leisure, it is usually read for different reasons than magazines. It may be read for the advertising it contains, whereas magazines seldom are. It may be read for spot news, but not often for entertainment. The opposite is true of most magazines. Magazines are read for entertainment or for information of a kind not found in newspapers. These differences in reading habits and the difference in editorial content of the two types of publications make the one more suitable than the other for certain kinds of copy. The Metropolitan Life Insurance Company places its health-care advertisements in magazines. This choice is wise, for it is less likely that persons looking at a newspaper would take time to read a lengthy advertisement concerned with prevention of pneumonia than would persons reading magazines, who probably have more time to spare and are in a different reading frame of mind. In such cases, it is not a matter of length of the copy or the kind of readers that suggests one or another of these media, but rather the content of the copy.

Copy should be written with some regard to the editorial content of the medium in which it will be placed and the conditions under which it will be read, but it should also be written in terms of the kinds of readers the advertiser wishes to influence. It makes considerable difference whether the copywriter is addressing women or men, adults or children, fishermen or golfers, farmers or bankers. Consider the following copy examples:

WE'RE RIGHT AROUND THE CORNER!
"Hi! Bob and I have been bike-riding and we thought it would be rather fun to drop in and visit. But I called so we wouldn't catch you with cream on your face or something. . . . Wonderful! We'll dash right over."

Isn't Jennie considerate? She knows how she'd feel if someone popped in on her without giving her a chance to look her best. She calls friends before she drops in, calls home when she's delayed. No wonder she's popular with her friends—and her family too.[6]

—Bell Telephone System

Can you guess to whom this copy was addressed? It appeared in *Seventeen*. Compare it with the following:

"Now I feel as if I'm still next door instead of in another town!
"They just finished installing the phone and I couldn't wait to call! I love the house and the town looks nice but, gosh, it feels strange to be so far away.
"Promise me one thing: let's keep in touch by telephone. That way we'll still feel like neighbors."[7]

This Bell Telephone copy appeared in the *Saturday Evening Post,* a long-time general-purpose cosumer magazine. In the same month the following appeared in *Holiday:*

TELEPHONE AHEAD FOR RESERVATIONS
Vacation hours are precious, and accommodations are often scarce. A telephone call does your looking for you and lines things up in advance. And if you plan to visit friends along the way, be sure to telephone ahead and let them know when you will arrive. Welcomes are always warmer when travelers are thoughtful.[8]

The first piece of copy is addressed to teen-age girls, the second to some-what older women, and the third to the travel-minded, vacation-minded reader. Note the difference in approach and language in each. The audiences in these cases had differences either in age or in interests. Audiences, of course, have many other differences that would require the copywriter to change the copy approach and the language. Among such differences might be the prospects' degree of familiarity with the advertised product and their recognition of a need for it. The Kohler Company placed the following ad in a general weekly:

YOUR OWN ELECTRICITY WHEN REGULAR SERVICE IS CUT OFF

Safeguard health, property, against failure of electricity for lights, automatic heat, refrigerator, freezer, appliances. Used in homes, hospitals, public and indus-trial building everywhere.

WHERE REGULAR SERVICE DOESN'T REACH

For camps, trailers, trucks, drilling rigs, excavators, boats. . . .

On-the-job electricity for lights, power tools wherever needed. Sizes to 100 KW, gasoline and diesel. Write for Folder D-45.[9]

Compare this with the copy, placed in *Yachting* by the Albina Engine & Machine Works, that reads:

Featuring two independent cone clutches, the Albina Utility Power Take-off can be operated by direct or remote control, utilizes chain or lever operation. Avail-able in single or double pulley models, has sealed bearings that require no lubrica-tion. Adaptable to any marine engine. Weight approximately 25 lbs.

Operates . . .
- Bilge Pump
- Anchor Windlass
- Generator
- Hydraulic Equipment

[Illustration]

Direct from Engine
No Maintenance
Long Service

Write Factory for Full Details.[10]

Emphasis in the Kohler copy is on uses, with a minimum amount of space given to construction detail. This copy is addressed to a general audience who may or may not be aware of the uses or need for electric generating plants. The Albina copy is addressed to a more selective audience, being placed in a publication designed to serve yachtsmen. Although there is a listing of uses to which the product may be put, emphasis throughout the copy is on construc-tion.

THE BROADCAST MEDIA

While the basic principles for writing copy remain the same for both the print and broadcast media, copy for radio and television must conform to a dif-ferent dimension. Time is the governing factor in broadcast advertising, in contrast to space in newspapers and magazines. Everything that has to be said in a radio or television commercial generally has to be said within 8 to 60 seconds. This means approximately 120 words for a one-minute commercial based on the rule-of-thumb of two words per second.

Like the print ad, the broadcast commercial has a job to do—sell a product, a service, or an idea. Radio does it entirely with sound—the human voice, music, and a wide variety of special sound effects. Television does it with sound plus a sequence of pictures in motion, and usually in full color. Unlike the print media, radio and television accomplish their tasks with the spoken word. Television is able to support its sound or audio effort with the video picture. Radio must rely on more descriptive words and sound effects to create a similar image in the human mind. For example, the radio scriptwriter might have an actor say, "See that green-eyed monster breathing fire!" In another situation he might have the narrator set the stage by saying "A policeman bursts into the room." In television, the action would be obvious to the viewer and therefore not require verbal description.

Guide to Effective Radio Copy

The Radio Advertising Bureau, Inc. (RAB) prepared the following *Guide to Effective Radio Copy* consisting of "8 do's" and "4 don't's."

The 8 Do's

1. *Know what you're writing about.* Use fact sheets, telephone interviews, look into RAB files, keep up to date on business trends. All station staff members—but especially copywriters—should visit accounts to get the feel of the retailer's problems and copy possibilities.
2. *Talk about customer benefits.* Remember what the listener asks herself: "What's in it for me?" Talk directly to your listener and tell her what it'll do for her beauty, her convenience, her happiness, her family.
3. *Use action words.* "Get to the big RETAILER sale today," is better than "There's a big sale at RETAILER today." Words should get listener actively thinking about going into the store and buying the merchandise— soon.
4. *Omit unnecessary words.* You don't have that many. Instead of "Whatever you choose, be sure it's from RETAILER, you can be sure it's bound to please," "Try RETAILER, they're bound to please." Even better, "Shop RETAILER for bargains."
5. *Mention the account's name as often as you can.*
6. *Keep it simple.* Short sentences outpull long ones every time.
7. *Write copy for the item's customer.* Decide who's most likely to buy the merchandise and talk directly to him or her.
8. *Read the script out loud to yourself.* Lots of things look good on paper, but don't read well. Does copy flow? Any tongue twisters? Radio writing is for the ear alone.

And a Few Don't's

1. *Don't write poetry.* See No. 8 above. Copy that sells merchandise beats deathless prose on the air.
2. *Watch the superlatives.* They often weaken your story when they're hard to believe. Stick to the story and the customer benefits instead of superlatives.
3. *Don't die at the end.* Some commercials start out enthusiastically with a big production effort, then run down at the end. Build and hold because it's the close that lingers on.
4. *Don't use dialog unless you're sure.* You need a real ear for language, otherwise dialog sounds phoney.[11]

Since radio is primarily a local medium, some of the guidelines listed above are directed toward retail advertising.

The Television Storyboard

Radio and television commercials are written in the form of scripts that clearly indicate the dialog, the announcer's part, the accompanying music, the sound effects (SFX), and in television, directions for the camera. (See the following glossary of terminology for storyboards and scripts.) The television copywriter must always keep in mind the strength of his medium. Because television is principally visual, the copywriter should rely on the picture and use it to the greatest advantage.

Once it has been approved, the television script is translated into a *storyboard* that contains all of the elements of the script plus illustrations. Each scene—that is, each particular action or sequence of actions—is represented on the storyboard by a single picture. Directly below each illustration is the dialog for that particular scene, together with the audio and video directions for producing it. In preparing the storyboard, the artist works closely with the copywriter to make certain that he depicts on paper precisely what the copywriter had visualized (they often work as a team on visualization).

Format or Structure

While Book and Cary list and describe 13 structures for television commercials,[12] approximately four or five are in general use. There are, of course, variations, and often two or more of these formats are combined in one 30- or 60-second commercial.

The principal formats are the *problem-solution* and the similar *slice of life* and *story line* structures. In essence each tells a story of an everyday problem and offers a solution. *Chronology* follows basically the same pattern but uses a documentary-film approach, while the *suspense* format builds up curiosity. The *spokesman* structure, also known as the *presenter* and *stand-up pitch,* is essentially just that—an announcer describing and selling a product or service. A *testimonial* is a form of "word-of-mouth" advertising. It could be an interview

VIDEO

OPEN OF ECU OF FRIENDSHIP CONTAINER
DESIGN ON BACK OF FRIENDSHIP T-SHIRT.
CAMERA STARTS PULLBACK IMMEDIATELY.

AUDIO

MUSIC: (STEVE ALLEN PLAYING PIANO AS
HE SINGS JINGLE)
STEVE ALLEN (V.O.) (SINGS): Put a
little Friendship ...

VIDEO

PULLBACK REVEALS THAT T-SHIRT IS
WORN BY MAN PLAYING PIANO AND
SINGING.

AUDIO

... in your life!

VIDEO

ZOOM IN ON CONTAINER AS HE DIPS IN
SPOON, TAKES OUT SPOONFUL.

AUDIO

Light. Smooth. Delicious. Because
Friendship Cottage Cheese is made
the old-fashioned way -- (EATS)

VIDEO

CUT TO CLOSEUP OF ALLEN AGAIN AS
HE PUTS SPOON IN CONTAINER JUST
AFTER TAKING A BITE.

AUDIO

-- with all natural ingredients.

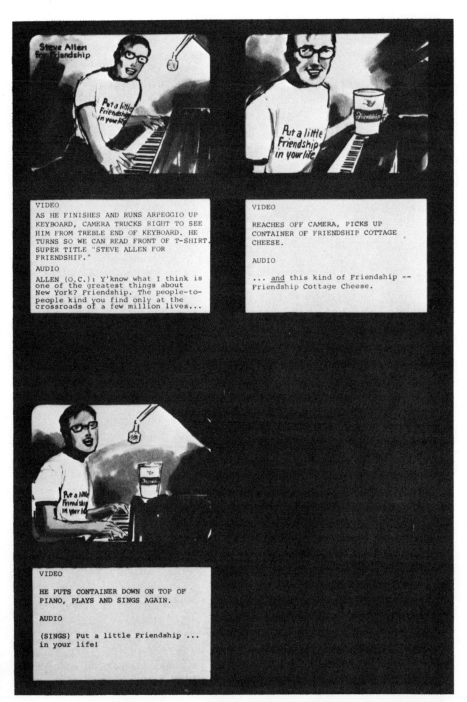

A storyboard for a TV commercial selling Friendship Cottage Cheese and featuring Steve Allen as the spokesman.

with a "real life" Mrs. Jones at the supermarket, or a statement from a celebrity who has some logical association with the product or service.

All of the above can be, and often are, combined with a *demonstration* that shows the product in use. Sometimes the result is compared, side by side, to a competing one, as in the Comet "Lady Plumber" commercials.

Length of Television Commercials

For years the one-minute production was the standard television commerical. It was found, however, that the 30-second commercial can deliver 75% to 92% of the effectiveness of the 60-second commercial[13] and the trend among major advertisers has swung in favor of the shorter commercials. While station and network time costs for the 30-second commercial are more than half those for the one-minute commercial, in light of its greater proportional impact it would appear to be an economically sound choice. Indeed, many multi-product manufacturers utilize the 60-second spot time for two different products back-to-back, or "piggyback," to take advantage of the one-minute price rate. Many advertisers created the 30-second and shorter spots from the one-minute commercial, cutting down the longer version through judicious copy-writing and editing. The other alternative was to "shoot" both at the same time. In the latter case, only the scenes that differed required additional filming or taping; scenes that were alike could be lifted from the 60-second commercial. In 1974, 76% of television commercials were 30 seconds in length and another 17% were 60s piggybacked.

More Effective Communication

Experience has demonstrated that the television commercials which communicate most effectively are basically imaginative, direct, simple, and interesting. Many film techniques that are exciting and different often tend to distract the viewer. *Direct voice,* where the performer is seen while he is talking, is more effective than *voice over,* where a speaker is heard but is not seen in the video picture. By the same token, sparing use of *supers,* printed titles or messages superimposed over the picture, is recommended. In short, a simple construction is usually better than a complex one.

SOME TERMINOLOGY FOR STORYBOARDS AND SCRIPTS.

Beauty Shot.   Close-up of the product.

Boom.   A movable or telescoping support for a microphone, lighting fixture, or camera. Hence, also, a movement of the camera from a low position to a high position or from a high position to a low position: e.g. "boom up."

Cut.   To jump directly from one scene to another.

Direct Voice (DV).   *See* Sound on Film.

Dissolve.   To fade one scene into a superimposition of another scene until the second scene finally takes over.

Close-Up (CU).   The head of a person, a package, or a product fills the entire screen.

Dolly. A movable-carriage platform for a camera. Hence, also, a movement of the entire camera in and toward the subject or out and way from the subject.

Extreme Close-Up (ECU). A shot which isolates one feature or detail.

Long Shot (LS). A shot which shows a person full length, or any subject at a comparable distance from thecamera.

Matte. The joinging of two different pictures so that they appear as one. With a matte, there is no ghost image where one element blends into the other. *Compare* Split Screen.

Medium Close-Up (MCU). A shot of a person from the chest up, or of any subject at a comparable distance from the camera.

Pan. A movement of the camera head pivoting from side to side.

Sound on Film (SOF). Live sound, where the performer is actually talking on camera. Also called *Direct Voice (DV)*.

Split Screen. Two scenes on the screen at the same time, each having a different portion of the screen. They are not superimposed over each other. *Compare* Matte.

Super. Titles that are superimposed over a scene on the screen.

Sync. Synchronization between picture and sound.

Truck. A movement of the camera laterally—usually used to follow people from one action to another.

Voice Over (VO). The voice of an announcer or actor who is not on camera and does not appear physically in the scene.

Wide Angle (WA). A shot which includes a relatively wide rea.

Wipe. One scene appears to push the other off the screen.

Zoom Back. A camera-lens operation that makes the viewer seem to move rapidly away from a subject first seen from a relatively close viewpoint, while remaining in constant focus.

Zoom In. A camera-lens operation that makes the viewer seem to move rapidly toward a subject first seen at a greater distance, while remaining in constant focus.[14]

OVERVIEW: KEEPING COPY CONTEMPORARY

While certain basic principles may be established for copywriting, in view of successful precedent, it must be recognized that copy, like communications, is a dynamic rather than a static matter. Mores change constantly; what might be considered extreme or shocking at one time or in one year might be quite natural and acceptable in another; witness the increasing permissiveness in our society during the 1970s. Although it is not recommended that the copywriter make a habit of far-out extremes or shock tactics for their own sakes, it is essential to keep abreast of current tastes and trends, avoiding such total reliance upon the good old tried-and-true that the message seems stale, stodgy, or old-hat. Many of the most successful and memorable campaigns have dared to defy the "sacred cows" and to set new trends and standards. While eccentricity and iconoclasm are not ends in themselves, and are seldom to be condoned, sound basic judgment must be dovetailed with a real awareness of the current scene to achieve the freshest, most dynamic, and soundest copy and communication.

SUMMARY

Written communication is accomplished by means of three symbols—pictures, words and numbers. Of these, words are the most likely to be misunderstood or misinterpreted. Words should be used that have the same meaning to the communicator (the sender) as they do to the receiver.

Advertising copy to be effective, must gain attention, arouse interest, be accepted by the prospect and above all, it must evoke action.

Copy should be written for the audience at which it is aimed and for the medium in which it is to be placed. Obviously, a drug manufacturer would not use the same technical terms to the consumer that he would to a doctor and to a pharmacist, nor would he try to reach them through the same media. By the same token but for other considerations, because of the nature of the medium, copy used in outdoor advertising should be considerably shorter than that used in a magazine or newspaper ad.

QUESTIONS AND DISCUSSION SUBJECTS

1. How would you define "copy?" What may it include?
2. Describe effective communication.
3. What are the symbols employed in communication?
4. What is the principal aim of copy?
5. Name the five steps copy employs in accomplishing the selling job.
6. Give examples of headlines that *flag, promise, command,* and give *news.*
7. What is the relationship between copy and the medium?
8. In what way would your copy differ if you were writing for an outdoor advertising billboard as opposed to a newspaper ad; a newspaper ad as opposed to a radio commercial; a radio commercial as opposed to a television commercial?
9. Name and describe the principal formats used in television commercials.
10. Is it a good idea for a copywriter to defy convention in his copy? Explain.

SOURCES

1. David Ogilvy, *How to Create Advertising that Sells* (New York: Ogilvy & Mather, 1975), 3.

n of Victor Schwab of Schwab, Beatty & Porter, Inc.
of an Advertising Man (New York: Atheneum, 1963),

Advertising Readership and Results (New York: Mc-

on of the Bell Telephone System.
on of the Bell Telephone System.
on of the Bell Telephone System.
on of Kohler Co., Kohler, Wisconsin.
sion of Albina Engine & Machine Works, Portland,

Copy (New York: Radio Advertising Bureau, Inc.).
Cary, *The Television Commercial: Creativity and Crafts-*
ker Communications, 1970), 9–28.

: Television Bureau of Advertising, 1975).

FOR FURTHER READING

Bedell, Clyde. *How to Write Advertising that Sells.* New York, Toronto, London: McGraw-Hill, 1952.

Book, A. C., and N. D. Cary. *The Television Commercial: Creativity and Craftsmanship.* New York: Decker Communications, 1970.

Burton, Philip W., B. Kreer, and J. B. Gray, Jr. *Advertising Copywriting.* Englewood Cliffs, N.J.: Prentice-Hall, 1962.

Clarke, George T. *Copywriting: Theory and Technique.* New York: Harper, 1959.

Diamant, Lincoln. *The Broadcast Communications Dictionary.* New York: Hastings House, Publishers, 1974.

——. *Television's Classic Commercials: The Golden Years 1948–1958.* New York: Hastings House, Publishers, 1971.

Fehlman, Frank E. *How to Write Advertising Copy that Sells.* New York: *Printers' Ink* and Funk and Wagnalls Company, 1950.

Glim, Aesop. *Copy: The Core of Advertising.* New York, Toronto, London: McGraw-Hill, 1949.

Ogilvy, David. *Confessions of an Advertising Man.* New York: Atheneum, 1963.

——. *How to Create Advertising that Sells.* New York: Ogilvy & Mather, 1975.

Reeves, Rosser. *Reality in Advertising.* New York: Knopf, 1961.

Steinberg, Charles S. *The Communicative Arts.* New York: Hastings House, Publishers, 1970.

Terrell, Neil. *The Power Technique of Radio and TV Copywriting.* Blue Ridge Summit, Pa.: Tab Books, 1971.

Wainwright, Charles A. *Television Commercials: How to Create Successful TV Advertising.* Revised Edition: New York: Hastings House, Publishers, 1970.

Winick, Charles, and others. *Children's Television Commercials.* New York: Praeger, 1973.

Print - Media Production

In preceding chapters we have seen the steps necessary to the creation of an advertisement—visualization, layout, and writing the copy. However, once the artist or photographer has delivered the artwork and the copywriter has completed the copy, the advertisement is still a considerable distance, measured in time and work, from its appearance in a medium. At this point in its development, the advertisement consists of original artwork and typewritten copy that must be reproduced in some manner in the various media that have been selected to carry it to the buying public. The job of converting this artwork and copy into a form that will make possible multiple reproduction of the original layout falls upon the production staff of the advertising agency or advertising department of the advertiser's firm, working in conjunction with printers and specialists in the graphic arts.

METHODS OF PRODUCTION

The three major methods by which advertisements are reproduced in the print media are: (1) *letterpress,* (2) *gravure* or *intaglio,* and (3) *offset lithography.* Each has certain advantages, depending upon the production problems of the advertiser; the final choice must be based on such considerations as the size of the run or number of copies to be reproduced, the effects to be achieved in the art, the limitations imposed by the medium to be used, and cost.

Letterpress

Letterpress prints from a raised surface, a surface that rises in *relief* from a surrounding cutaway area. The familiar office rubber stamp is an example of a letterpress printing device. Its printing surface shows a mirror image of what it will print; thus .M.A on the stamp becomes A.M. on the paper when the stamp is inked and pressed against it. The image on the letterpress printing plate can be either letters or pictures; the plate can be as small as the rubber stamp or as big as a two-page newspaper spread; the material of the plate can be rubber but is usually metal or plastic.

Letterpress printing is used extensively in advertising. Many magazines and large metropolitan newspapers are printed by letterpress so that the advertiser who uses them has no choice of process, unless the use of inserts is permitted.* Some direct-mail pieces and many catalogs also are printed by letterpress. And though letterpress printing is being supplanted in many media by other printing processes, advertising people will need to work with letterpress as long as the big media use it—newspapers in particular.

The reading matter in letterpress is usually set in metal type, letter by letter. Artwork—pictures, designs, photographs—goes through a more complex process before the reader sees it on paper.

Artwork falls into two broad classes: (1) line art and (2) halftone art. Newspaper cartoons and comic strips are examples of line art; newspaper "photos" are halftone art, as are printed reproductions of oil paintings, watercolors, and the like. Printed halftones render the finely varied shading that one sees in such originals; in line-art pictures, such shading cannot be rendered so accurately, but it can be approximated. Either line or halftone art can be printed by any of the three major methods; however, each method produces its best results if the art is prepared to fit that method.

Line art is executed by drawing sharp lines with pen, crayon, or brush. Shading effects are produced by the varying thickness of the lines and by their spacing, but there is no true gradation of tone. Such art may be reproduced in color as well as in black-and-white, but regardless of the color or colors used, each line has the same tonal quality. For example, in a black-and-white line drawing there are no true grays. Halftone art, on the other hand, shows the gradations of tone or shading seen in photographs, oil paintings, water colors, or pastels.

The reproduction of either line art or halftone art by letterpress involves a process called *photoengraving*. In reproducing line art the original art is photographed and the image is transferred to a light-sensitive plate. Then all nonprinting surfaces are etched and routed away, leaving only the raised lines that duplicate the original art. The ink rollers of the press can put ink only on these raised surfaces, and they, in turn, transfer the ink to the paper, thus reproducing the original art.

Although line art cannot be made to look like a photograph or a painting, it is possible to obtain a shading effect by the use of *benday* screens or any one of several patented devices. These devices utilize, variously, a decal principle, a transparent overlay with various designs imprinted upon it, or an especially treated paper. They superimpose or bring out patterns (parallel lines, dots, cross hatch, herringbone, or other) on the surface of the photographic film, the

* An insert is an advertisement printed by the advertiser, often on special paper stock, and subsequently bound into a publication.

plate, or the artwork. The pattern is thus combined with the original art—giving the effect desired by the artist but never quite achieving halftone qualities.

Sometimes an advertiser, in order to obtain an effect that will attract reader attention, will use a *reverse line plate*. Such a plate produces a solid black background with white illustration and lettering. The white is not ink but merely the white of the paper which shows in contrast against the black in those areas where the plate has deposited ink. Artwork for a reverse plate is done in heavy lines, and lettering is set in heavy or bold type. This is necessary because fine lines tend to fill with ink and do not show up as clear, sharp, and white when printed.

The photoengraving of halftone art involves the use of a *halftone screen*. The basic halftone screen is made by mechanically cutting fine parallel lines into the surfaces of glass plates, then putting two of these plates together so that the lines cross each other at right angles much as do the wires in a window screen. Such a halftone screen is designated by the number of lines per inch—thus, an 85-line screen, a 120-line screen, and so on upward; the printed halftone may be described as an 85-screen halftone, or the like. The higher the number, the finer the screen and the more faithful the shading in the resulting halftone illustration. Smooth printing paper will accept 200-line or even finer screens, whereas newsprint paper may demand an 85-line or even coarser screen.

Photographing the art through the halftone screen divides the image into a pattern of equidistant dots much as the window-screen wires make a pattern of equidistant holes. The halftone dots, however, are of different sizes; where the art has light tones or white areas the dots are small or may even disappear; where it has dark areas, the dots are large and may even blend together. The combination of big and little dots with little or much white space between them produces the shading in the image of the art. This image is transferred to the printing surface in much the same way as the line-art image, and the nonprinting areas are similarly etched below the surface. The raised areas can then take ink from printing-press rollers and transfer it to paper, thus producing a printed picture.

In a coarse-screen halftone the dots are readily discernible to the unaided eye, but in fine screen halftones a magnifying glass is needed for seeing the dot structure. This is why the finer-screen halftones look more like photographs and original paintings than do those made by coarser screens. The finer the screeen the better the reproduction.

Live models or actual objects are not photographed through a halftone screen; only the pictures of these objects are photographed.

When a picture is taken through a halftone screen, the resulting dots will cover the entire negative, foreground and background alike. The manner in which the background is treated produces several kinds of halftone printing plates. For example, if the background is left untouched so that the graying effect of the screen extends to the edges of the illustration, is it called a *square halftone*. If the background effect of the screen is entirely routed away or re-

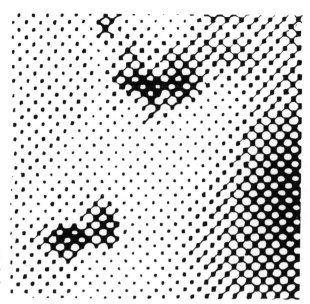

This greatly enlarged section of a halftone reproduction shows the dot structure.

moved so that the foreground objects stand out against the background color of the paper, it is a *silhouette halftone*. When the background is treated so that it is darkest in areas nearest the foreground object and fades off in a soft cloud effect, it is a *vignette halftone*.

A *highlight* or *dropout halftone* is achieved by the removal of the halftone dots in certain areas so that the white of the paper upon which the picture is printed is completely free of the halftone screen. This results in a bright or highlighted area.

It is also possible to combine halftone and line art in a *combination plate*. The production of such a plate is accomplished by stripping together halftone and line art negatives and reproducing them on a single plate. Type can be combined with a halftone and be free of the shading effects of the screen by use of either a *mortise* or a *surprint*. In a mortise a section of the halftone plate is cut out so that copy set in type can be inserted. In a surprint the negative of the line art copy is superimposed on the halftone negative, and combined on a single plate. In the halftone with mortise the copy can be changed merely by inserting new material in the cut-out section, but in a surprint no change is possible once the plate has been made.

It is possible to make what is called a *line Velox plate*. This is usually done when cost is a major consideration and when quality of reproduction need not be the best. In producing such a plate, a screened Velox photograph of the artwork is made. This is a photograph on paper where the emulsion has been broken into a dot structure by the use of a coarse halftone screen. A line photoengraving is made directly from this print, and each dot reproduces as line art. The resulting picture has the characteristics of both line art and coarse halftone art. The Velox print should be made the same size as the plate, because any reduction would tend to have the same effect as the use of a finer screen and would result in a blurring of the illustration.

Duplicate Plates

An advertiser very often places the same advertisement in several different publications and, although some of them may make plates for him from his original art, in many cases he must provide the plates himself. Then one original plate is not enough to meet newspapers needs. To make additional originals would be far too costly and entirely unnecessary. Furthermore, any plates he furnishes for rotary presses must be curved, but the original plate is flat. There are several methods by which duplicate plates may be made from the original. These methods result in duplicates called *stereotypes, electrotypes, plastic plates,* and *rubber plates*.

An impression of the original plate can be made in plastic or in a *papier-maché*-like substance. Such an impression or mold is called a *matrix* or *mat*. The mat is light in weight and is easily and inexpensively shipped. It can be used either flat or curved and can be reused. Most often, mats are used in reproducing advertisements that are scheduled for newspapers. When a newspaper receives a mat it is placed in a special device into which molten type metal is poured. This metal flows about the contours of the mat and produces a metal printing plate called a *stereotype* or *stereo,* which is a duplicate of the original plate. It should be appreciated that the mat itself is not the printing plate. It is merely a mold and has neither the strength to withstand the pressures of a printing press nor the correct formation of printing surfaces. The letters and illustrations on a mat are depressed or sunken surfaces. These, when filled with metal, produce the raised letters and illustrations that will print by the letterpress process.

An *electrotype* or *electro* is made by making a wax impression of the original plate. Silver, which is a conductor of electricity, is dusted over this mold, and the mold is placed in an electrolytic bath that coats it with copper. The resulting copper shell is then backed with a heavier metal to enable it to withstand the pressure of the printing press. An electro, although more costly to produce than a stereo, gives a sharper reproduction of the artwork and copy. If long press runs are to be made, the duplicate plate is coated with nickel instead of or in addition to copper. A *nickeltype* is good for about 300,000 to 400,000 impressions, whereas a copper-faced electro is good for a run of approximately 250,000.

In an improvement in the process, molds of Tenaplate or plastic are substituted for the wax mold. Other materials used in making molds for electros are Vinylite, which will produce 7 to 10 electrotypes, and lead, considered by many printers to be the best for four-color engraving.

When plates are to be used on a flat-bed press, they are mounted on bases so that the printing surfaces are of the correct height when the plates are placed on the press. This standard height, .918 of an inch, is called *type high*. If all

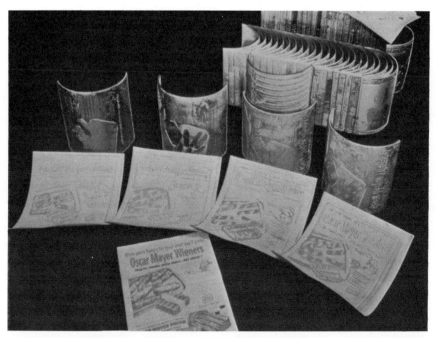

Newspaper cast stereotypes of a four-color advertisement, together with the mats and a color proof, ready for the press room.

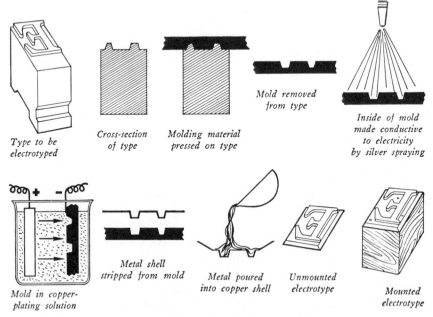

Type to be
electrotyped

Cross-section
of type

Molding material
pressed on type

Mold removed
from type

Inside of mold
made conductive
to electricity
by silver spraying

Mold in copper-
plating solution

Metal shell
stripped from mold

Metal poured
into copper shell

Unmounted
electrotype

Mounted
electrotype

Steps in the process of creating an electrotype. *Courtesy of the International Association of Electrotypers & Stereotypers, Inc.*

plates and type were not this exact height it would be impossible to obtain satisfactory printing results.

Most magazine publishers will accept *duplicate originals* (a conflicting title!) in lieu of original engravings for process color work. They are used when an ad which requires original plates is running simultaneously in more than one publication. In effect they are high-quality electros which duplicate the fineness of the original plate at a lower cost.

Plastic plates, which cost less to produce than electros, offer further economy. Since they weigh about one-sixth as much as electros, shipping costs are reduced considerably, and though they are very light they are strong, stable, and "wear like iron." The platemaking process is a relatively simple one. A sheet of plastic is used to make a matrix from an electro or from the original plate under heat and pressure. After about 20 minutes the cured or hardened matrix is dusted with thermoplastic vinyl powder which in turn is placed under heat and pressure to produce the plastic printing plate. A limitless number of plates can be made from the matrix.

A similar process is followed in the production of rubber plates. In this case the printing plate is made from a sheet of unvulcanized rubber. Flexible rubber plates are used in *Flexography,* a rotary web-fed letterpress process ideal for printing on packaging film, foils, and gift wrap.

Gravure

Gravure, or intaglio, prints from ink-carrying cells recessed into a surface. In this respect it is the opposite of letterpress. The surface of the plate is the nonprinting area in gravure. The picture and copy to be reproduced are cut or etched into the plate. When the plate comes in contact with the ink rollers of the press, ink is forced into the incised or etched areas and the surface of the plate is thereafter wiped clean. When plate and paper make contact, the ink is drawn from the recesses and produces printed copies on the paper. A transparent ink is used so that the thickness of the ink deposited on the paper determines the intensity of color reproduction. The amount of ink deposited on the paper depends upon the depth of the etching in different areas of the plate. This, in turn, is determined by the amount of light passing from the positives of the original art work to sheets of carbon tissue used in transferring the picture to the metal plate or cylinder.

In making gravure plates, positives of the original artwork on transparent film are used. The image is transferred by photography to the copper rollers or cylinders used in gravure printing by the use of a gravure screen and carbon tissue. The gravure screen is the opposite of the letterpress screen in that it makes dots that are etched *into* the printing surface rather than left standing to form the surface. The image is laid on the metal in the form of a gelatin coating through which the metal of the cylinder is etched—shallow or deep according to the solubility of the gelatin, and deepest where the ink is to be strongest. This process, as already explained, produces the different shadings—ink intensities—in the finished gravure reproduction.

The cost of platemaking is comparatively high in gravure, and only certain paper stocks can be used for printing. However, the process lends itself well to long runs, and very soft gradations of tone are obtainable. It is used in advertising in some magazines and catalogs. It is also used in producing some direct-mail pieces and in the printing of our paper money and postage stamps.

Offset Lithography

Lithography prints from what to the naked eye appears as a flat surface, and works on the principle that oil and water will not mix. Artists many years ago discovered that if they drew a design with an oily crayon on a polished but porous stone and then dampened the stone with water, the water would not adhere to the crayon image but would wet the stone. Then they could apply a greasy or oily ink; this was repelled by the water-wet stone but clung to the crayon design. The inked design could then be repeatedly transferred to paper to make as many copies as the artist desired. This process was called *lithography,* a word derived from the Greek word *lithos,* meaning "stone," and *graphos,* meaning "writing"—literally, "writing from stone."

Modern offset lithography, although considerably more complex, works on the same basic principle that grease and water will not mix. Today, instead of the stone, a thin metal (sometimes plastic) plate is used. This plate, so thin that it will wrap around the press cylinder, is grained or roughened by rolling steel, or glass balls back and forth across its surface, which during the operation is dusted with a fine abrasive. The purpose of the graining is to give the metal some of the moisture-retaining qualities of the old lithographic stone. After the graining the plate is coated with a water-soluble substance that is sensitive to light, so that a photographic image of the original art or type may be transferred to the surface of the plate. The dark areas of the original become ink-accepting areas and the white areas become water-accepting areas. When the plate is fastened to the press cylinder, moistened, and inked, it can produce a copy of the art or type at every turn of the cylinder.

In offset lithography, unlike letterpress and gravure, the printing is not done directly from the inked plate to the paper. Rather, the plate first prints on a rubber-blanketed cylinder; this blanket, in turn, reprints or *offsets* the image on the paper. For this reason, the lettering on an offset plate is not reversed as it is in letterpress or gravure. On the letterpress plate or rubber stamp we see the letters A.M. in the mirror form .M.A but on the offset plate they appear as A.M. because they will go onto the blanket as .M.A and then onto the paper as A.M. for normal reading.

Printing from the rubber roller instead of from the unyielding surface of a metal plate permits the use of a wider variety of papers. Offset lithography also makes possible economies in platemaking, because halftone negatives can be stripped into line art negatives and both halftone and line art can be reproduced on a single lithographic plate.

Offset lithography is widely used in advertising in the printing of packages, direct-mail pieces, catalogs, outdoor posters, labels, and tags. Newspapers and magazines are also printed by this process.

Xerography

Xerographic printing employs static electricity to transfer an image from the original (hand-drawn, typewritten, or printed) to the printed copy. Static electricity has been experienced by everyone who has walked across a wool rug and touched a metal doorknob; it is static electricity that makes a comb attract hair. In *xerography*, this attraction is produced and controlled to deposit black powder onto paper. The major and original commercial system utilizing this principle is Xerox. IBM, Saxon, and 3M have also introduced electrostatic copiers.

In operation, the original work to be copied is inserted into the machine. The machine is then activated, causing a bright light to reflect the original image onto a mirror. The mirror, in turn, projects the image onto a highly polished cylinder as a pattern of static electric charges which in turn attract a small amount of black powder (the Xerox "ink"). This black powder is thereafter attracted to and deposited on a sheet of paper, in the same pattern. This sheet is passed through a heating unit to fuse and "fix" the powder and then emerges from the machine an exact duplicate of the original. While earlier Xerox machines took a little longer to produce the printed copy, Xerox machines in use today can mass produce 7,200 copies per hour. Some models are designed to copy photographs and halftones, and others will proportionately reduce the size of copies from the original.

The Xerox will also make master offset plates for the Multigraph office litho machine, substituting the master plate for the blank paper and following the same process described above. Xerox and 3M also offer full color reproduction by means of the electrostatic process.

Conversion Systems

Serving a purpose similar to duplicate plates, conversion systems make it possible to utilize letterpress plates and type in offset lithography. While it is impossible to use the letterpress type directly, a *reproduction proof*, or *repro*, pulled from the inked surface, can be photographed and the resulting negative used to make an offset plate.

There are a number of such conversion systems. Among them are Brightype, where the letterpress plate itself is photographed after polishing. Similar to it is Verticon. Another process is 3M's Scotchprint, which utilizes a sheet of plastic with high ink receptivity and follows the same procedure for making a reproduction proof. It produces a negative directly without camera or darkroom, as does Converkal. This latter system is activated by the type, which is heated prior to contact. Cronapress is a DuPont process, a little more complicated than the others, utilizing a vacuum and a "bouncing ball" that also produces a negative.

Silk Screen

Another method used for reproducing some forms of advertising is the silk screen process. This is a stenciling process in principle and is most commonly used in poster reproduction when runs are comparatively short. It is most economical in runs up to 5,000 copies. It presents two major advantages, aside from cost: (1) It imposes less limitation on the size of the advertisement that can be produced on a single sheet of paper. (2) Printing can be done on paper, cardboard, cloth, glass, and many other surfaces. (It is used for printing on T-shirts.)

Color Reproduction

When the advertisement has a colored illustration, a separate plate must be made for each color. A full-color advertisement can be reproduced by using the three primary colors (red, yellow, and blue) plus black. Let us assume that a full-color advertisement is to be reproduced by letterpress. The original art work is photographed four times, each time through a different color filter. The resulting negatives are called *color-separation negatives*. These are not colored pictures like Kodachromes but are "black-and-white" translucent and transparent screened negatives. Each of the three color filters has removed all but one of the primary color values as they appear in the original art. That is, one filter has removed all but the red values, another all but the yellow, and so on.

A separate plate is made from each of the four negatives. These plates, each inked with the corresponding primary color or with black, and printed one upon the other, result in a full-color reproduction. Progressive proofs are made from each color plate and show how these plates are combined in printing to give the desired result. The progressive proofs are used to indicate to the printer the color intensity and the plate register. In other words, colors are matched against the original art, and inasmuch as four plates are printing successively one upon the other, a check is necessary to determine if the elements on each plate are falling into proper *register* with each other.

We know that a halftone reproduction is produced by means of a series of dots. In making a color halftone it is necessary to re-angle the halftone screen each of the four times a photograph is taken of the original art. This must be done so that the dots created by the screens will not fall in the same identical place on two or more negatives or plates. If this were to happen, dots would be superimposed on dots in the printing, and the desired effect would not be obtained. In printing colored pictures, as opposed to painting, colors are not directly and physically mixed. Instead, the large number of fine dots of different colors are interspersed on the paper and create an optical illusion. The viewer does not see a large number of blue dots interspersed among a large number of yellow dots; he sees green. The eye does the mixing, and the viewer sees the color that would be achieved in painting by the physical mixing of the same primary colors.

In reproducing color work by gravure or lithography it is necessary, just as in letterpress, to make separate cylinders or plates for each color.

Artwork

The advertiser may find that he wishes to use only a part of the picture portrayed in his original artwork. For example, his original art may show the full figure of a man, and it may be decided that the illustration in the advertisement should show only the head and shoulders. In such a case the advertiser may indicate on the back of the photograph of the original art or on a tissue overlay those portions which he wishes to include in the engraving. This process is called *cropping,* and the marks used to indicate deletions are called *crop marks*. The photoengraver, guided by these crop marks, will then exclude the unwanted portions of the art when the plate is made.

In general, the safest practice is to place directions or crop marks on the tissue overlay. Whether they are put on the back of the art or on the overlay, two cautions are to be observed: (1) not to write with ink that may strike through the writing surface and show on the picture; (2) not to make a pressure imprint that will show on the face of the art or photo. If writing or marks must go on the back of a photo, a soft china-marking pencil or crayon should be used. Paper clips should not be used with art or photos; they are very likely to make scratches and almost certain to make pressure imprints.

When artwork or photographs of the original art are sent to a client for approval, or to the photoengraver, they should never be folded. A fold is difficult to remove and it may crack the surface of the paper. Such a crack or even a fold, if not completely removed, will show up in the engraving.

Very often original art is created in a larger size than that planned for the finished advertisement; this practice has two advantages. First, it is often easier for the artist to draw or paint in the larger size; second, the imperfections that are difficult to avoid in hand-created art will tend to disappear when the picture is reduced in size by photography. However, it should be recognized that some detail also will be lost in reduction; the greater the reduction the more the loss. Therefore, the original art should not be made more than two or three times the size for printing.

If the original art is smaller than the space to be filled in the advertisement, it can be enlarged or "blown up"; the *blow-up* should not be more than twice or three times the size of the original.

When a piece of art is blown up or reduced the proportions do not change. If the art is square, so is the blow-up or the reduction; if the art is half as tall as it is wide, so is the blow-up or the reduction. Suppose, for example, a photo is 3½ inches high and 4½ inches wide; then it can be blown up to 7 by 9 inches but not to 7 by 10 inches, or can be reduced to 1¾ inches by 2¼ inches but not to 1¾ inches by 2½ inches. Advertisers often need to change the width or height of a piece of art to make it fit an ad space; then they need to know what the other dimension will become. This can be found in several ways; those who dislike arithmetic often use what is called the *diagonal method*. Consider, for example, that 3½-by-4½-inch photo, and suppose its width must be reduced to 2½ inches—how high will the reduction be? To find out, first draw a rectangle the size of the photo—4½ inches wide and 3½ inches high (*the original should not be marked*). Then draw a diagonal from the lower corner to the opposite upper corner. On the lower edge of the rectangle mark a point 2½ inches from the side where the diagonal meets it. From this point draw a line perpendicularly upward to the diagonal. Measure this line; it is the height of the reduction (just over $1^{15}/_{16}$ inches).

If you must enlarge the art to (say) 5¼ inches wide, you can use the diagonal method also. Again, draw the rectangle 4½ inches wide and 3½ inches high, but run the lower edge out beyond 5¼ inches on the right; draw the diagonal from the lower left to the upper right and run it about 1½ inches beyond

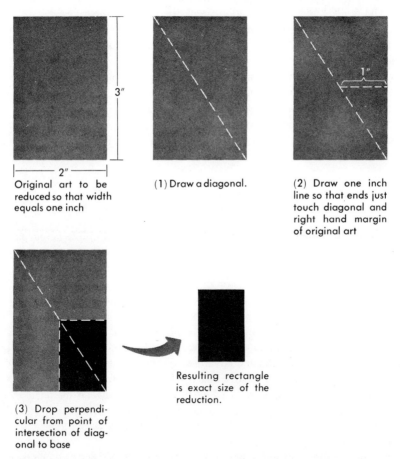

3″

|——— 2″ ———|
Original art to be reduced so that width equals one inch

(1) Draw a diagonal.

1″

(2) Draw one inch line so that ends just touch diagonal and right hand margin of original art

(3) Drop perpendicular from point of intersection of diagonal to base

Resulting rectangle is exact size of the reduction.

The Diagonal Method. When art must be reduced or enlarged, one dimension is usually known or established. The diagonal method does not require arithmetic computations. It gives an exact and accurate result regardless of the measurement units.

the upper corner. Then draw a perpendicular line from the 5¼-inch point on the lower edge upward to meet the diagonal. Measure this line and you have the height of the blow-up (it should be just over $4^1/_{16}$ inches).

As was said, there are several ways to find the dimensions of blow-ups and reductions. Some people perfer the diagonal method; some like to use arithmetic or algebra; others prefer slide rules and similar devices; some even have the art photographed in the new size and measure it. It is wise to use two methods to make sure of a correct result.

It was said that proportions do not change in blow-ups and reductions. This is usually true but not always strictly so, for there are processes that can make a distorted blow-up or reduction, one proportionately longer or wider than the original. But the results of this kind of distortion may not be good if the distortion is more than slight. In any case, if distortion is to be used, someone who really knows the operation should be in on the figuring.

If the artwork is hand-created, rather than a photograph, it may be produced by any one of several art methods including pencil, crayon, charcoal, water color, oil, scratch board, and wood engraving. Choice of art method (also called art medium) depends, in large measure, upon the effect that the advertiser wishes to create and upon the advertising medium in which the advertisement will be reproduced. Choice of art method often determines choice of artist because many artists are specialists with respect to the art medium in which they work. Even when an artist works in several art media, he usually excels in only one.

TYPOGRAPHY

During the three centuries they have been in the English language, the words *typography* and *typographer* have taken on numerous meanings, chiefly bearing on the arts and crafts of using and arranging type. Around 1916, *typography* began to mean the profession or business of setting display type for advertisers, and *typographer* to mean a person in this business. Now, the typesetters are sometimes called compositors, typographers being specialists in the choice and arrangement of type for appearance or effect. In this latter sense, typography has great importance in advertising, since the chosen type face creates a "feeling tone" for the advertisement as a whole. Some years ago, a trade journal in the printing field set each story in a different type face to demonstrate how type could be selected to fit and emphasize an intended mood. Black boldface type would look ridiculous in an advertisement for a Parisian perfume, just as an advertisement for diesel locomotives would look wrong set in a fine script.

Although there are more than 6,000 different type faces, they can be classified in six recognized type families. These are (1) Gothic, (2) Old Style Roman, (3) Modern Roman, (4) Text, (5) Decorative, and (6) Transitional. The

6,000-odd kinds are variations and combinations of the characteristics of these six families, or they are artistic creations.

Although a beginner in advertising need not be able to recognize on sight any large number of type faces, an understanding of a few of the outstanding characteristics of the six type families is helpful. The paragraphs of the illustration will give a few basic points about each family.

This paragraph is set in Gothic, sans serif bold. It will be noted that this is a sans serif type which means that the bars and feet of the letters have no flourishes but begin and end as straight lines. (The accompanying diagram of a piece of type will give the student an understanding of the various terms used in reference to parts of letters and type.) It also should be ncted that the letters of the Gothic family of type are made up of circles and straight lines. The "O" is a perfect circle, the "C" is a circle with a piece cut out, the "D" is a half circle with a straight line. The "T," the "H," the "I" and so on, are combinations of straight lines only. Furthermore, the· letters are of the same weight and thickness throughout.

This paragraph is set in Caslon Old Style, which is of the Old Style Roman family of type.

This paragraph is set in Bodoni Modern and is an example of Modern Roman. The vertical strokes in Modern Roman have greater variation of thickness than do the corresponding parts of Old Style Roman. Note, for example, the first down stroke of the capital "M." It is very thin, but the next stroke of the same letter is thick, the third is thin and the fourth thick. This variation of stroke provides considerably more contrast than is found in Old Style. Another difference between Old Style and Modern is that the serifs in the latter are almost flat, whereas the serifs in the former tend to round into the letters.

𝔗his paragraph is set in 𝔠loister 𝔗ext, sometimes called 𝔒ld 𝔈nglish. 𝔍t is an example of the fourth family or text and is not extensibely used in advertising, primarily because it is difficult to read. 𝔍ts major use is to create atmosphere or effect, and it is most frequently used around the 𝔠hristmas season.

This paragraph is set in script because Decorative includes the scripts. It is a family widely used in display advertising.

Transitional is composed of type faces that have some of the characteristics of Old Style Roman and some of Modern Roman. Baskerville, in which this paragraph is set, is one example. Another is Scotch Roman, in which this sentence is set.

Most type families have five different sets of alphabets. These are:

1. Lowercase letters—not capitals.
2. Uppercase letters—capitals.
3. Small capitals.
4. Italic lowercase.
5. Italic uppercase.

A single type family may contain many shades and weights as well as condensed forms, boldfaces, and bold italics—and, of course, several sizes. A condensed type is one in which the letters are narrow so that more of them can be accommodated in a line of type.

Measurement of Type

Type sizes are measured in units called *points;* a point is faintly less than $1/72$ of an inch, an inch faintly more than 72 points. However, a letter in 72-point type may not measure 72 points from top to bottom; to see the 72 points it is necessary to visualize some such sequence of letters as "Ip" or "Hq." If the type size is 72-point, then the distance from the top level of the I or H to the bottom level of the p or q will be 72 points. (Some novelty letter designs don't fit this statement, but the principle holds generally.)

In most type families, the tops of the capital letters are the highest points in a line, the bottoms of the letters g, j, p, q, and y the lowest points; the downstrokes are called *descenders.* Letters like a, c, e, and so on do not reach the highest or lowest points. The letters b, d, f, h, i, j, k, and l rise as high as the capitals; the upstrokes are called *ascenders.* The capital Q may have a short or a long descender; the capital J in some forms descends to the extreme lowest level. The letters g and t usually do not ascend as high as the capitals and the tall lowercase letters.

The type sizes that advertisers use range from 5-point (a little smaller than $1/14$ of an inch) to 144-point (2 inches). Even larger letter sizes may be needed; when they are, it may be necessary to set type in an available size, pull a proof, and enlarge or blow up the proof by photographic methods. Large "type," indeed "type" of any size, can be hand-lettered by an artist. Type larger than 14-point is regarded as *display* type; type smaller than 6-point generally is considered too small for practical use in advertising except, possibly on coupons. Not all type faces come in all sizes, and not all typographers have all the sizes of every type face.

In some old books, type sizes are called by such names as *agate, nonpareil, pica,* or *primer;* this name system is obsolete and survives only in the dimension terms *agate, pica,* and less commonly *nonpareil* (5½-point, 12-point, and 6-point).

The space beneath some letters (which the descenders occupy in other letters) is called the *shoulder* (the word makes sense in referring to metal types, as is shown in the illustration). When this space is the only space between lines of type, the type is said to be set *solid.* More space can be put between lines; the

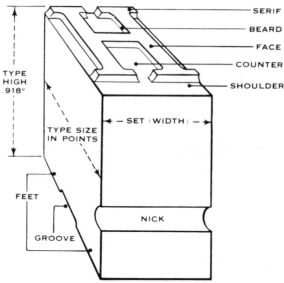

A Single Metal Type—a Capital H. This illustrates the meaning of many terms that occur in typography; some of the terms are used in connection with "cold type."

additional space is called *leading* and the type is said to be *leaded* (pronounce these words *ledding* and *ledded,* not *leeding* or *leeded*). When type is set in metal, this space is achieved by inserting thin strips of lead between the lines to space them apart. If the lead strips are 1, 2, 3, 4, or 5 points thick, they are called leads; if 6 points or more, *slugs.* Leads and slugs are lower than *type high* (see the illustration). The space between lines may be called leading even when the type is "cold," that is, set without metal. The leading is used to improve appearance and perhaps readability. Here is a table [1] for such leading:

Type Size	Minimum Leading	Maximum Leading
6-point	solid	1 point
8-point	solid	2 points
10-point	solid to 2 points	4 points
12-point	2 points	6 points
14-point	3 points	8 points

Spacing between words and letters seldom needs to be measured; when necessary, it is usually measured in points.

Line length and column width are measured in *picas;* 1 pica equals 12 points, almost exactly $\frac{1}{6}$ of an inch. Many newspaper news columns are 10 picas wide (1⅔ inches; but the inch measurement is rarely used), plus varying between-column space. Newspaper classified-ad lines are 9 picas long (1½ inches).

This line i

This line is set in 36-

This line is set in 18-point type.

This line is set in 12-point type.

This line is set in 10-point type.

This line is set in 8-point type.

This line is set in 6-point type.

This paragraph is set in 8-point type set solid. That is, no leads have been used between the lines. If a long piece of copy is set solid it is not as easy to read as it would be if more space were allowed between the lines.

This paragraph is set with 2-point leading. That is, leads measuring 2 points have been inserted between the lines. Compare this spacing with the paragraph above where no leads were used. Leading makes for easier reading and a cleaner appearing page.

This paragraph is set with 5-point leading. In other words, leads measuring 5 points have been inserted between the lines. Too much white space between lines of printed matter can make reading more difficult and may make the page less attractive in appearance than if more conventional spacing were used.

Type Size and Leading. The three paragraphs at the bottom, all demonstrating leading, are set in the same type. The leaded paragraphs give a strong illusion of larger type size.

The height or depth of an advertisement, from top to bottom, is measured in inches or picas for many purposes; it is also measured in *agate lines* or *lines*. *There are 14 agate lines in an inch; 1 agate line equal* $1/14$ *of an inch.* *

* Publications charge for advertising space by the agate line, 1 column wide. This practice refers back to the time when classified advertising was set in agate type (about 5½-point). Though not entirely rational, agate-line measurement is the custom of the business. Agate lines will be considered in more detail in Chapter 18.

Type Design

As already indicated, choice of a type face should be made in terms of the product advertised and the particular qualities of the product that the advertiser wishes to emphasize. Stuart and Gardner say: "Black type should be used for advertising concrete mixers, stone walls or Barnum and Bailey's circus that's coming to town. . . . Misguided advertisers believed that if twenty-four point black type would sell four hundred cans of soup, then forty-eight point black type would sell eight hundred cans. In other words, they reasoned that heavy type meant heavy sales. Such reasoning is utterly ridiculous." [2] A copy chief of a well-known advertising agency some time ago lamented a similar use of heavy black type to sell a cleaning compound. It appears that the rule of fitting the type to the product and to the product-story is too often violated.

Even more important to good advertising than appropriateness of type face is legibility of type face. Ease of reading depends upon a number of things. First, a simple, clean-cut face like Caslon is easier to read than are the more decorative letters of Old English. Legibility should not be sacrificed for effect or atmosphere. Ease of reading also depends upon the proper use of capitals and lowercase. Copy set in all capitals is harder to read than copy set in the more customary combination of capitals and lowercase. Occasionally, words or headlines may be set in capitals if neither the words nor the headlines are very long. It has been demonstrated by tests that when long, polysyllabic words are set in capitals, the eye has from 20% to 50% more difficulty in separating the syllables than when the words are set in either lowercase or a combination of capitals and lowercase. There is also a direct relationship between legibility and the size of type in relation to the length of line. In other words, there is an optimum line length for each point size of type. One authority recommends that the maximum line length for 6-point type be 10 picas, for 8-point type 13 picas, for 10-point type 15 picas and for 12-point type 21 picas.

Other factors that enter into the legibility of type are orderly arrangement of all component parts of the advertisement, use of strong contrasting colors, adequate spacing between lines and paragraphs, and proper margins.

HAND LETTERING

Hand lettering is done by an artist working with a pen or brush. After he has completed the job, the lettering is then reproduced, like any other hand-created art, by any of the processes described earlier. That is, it is photographed and subsequently reproduced on the printing plate.

Hand lettering is more flexible than type. It can be created in any size. Its lines can be curved. Its letters can be partially superimposed one upon another. It can be stretched or condensed to fit a given space. Its most common use in advertising is in headlines and subheads.

TYPE MARKING (PROOFREADERS' MARKS)

Capitals are indicated in the typewritten copy by underlining three times any material that is to be set in this manner. For example, the typewritten copy reading:

These are the best widgets on the

market regardless of price.

would appear in print as follows:

These are the BEST widgets on the
market REGARDLESS OF PRICE.

If small capitals are desired, the material is underlined twice. A single underline indicates that italics are wanted. The typesetter understands these symbols, and their use reduces any chance of misunderstanding and resulting error.

Typeset copy should be checked carefully for typographical and other errors before it is sent to the printer or lithographer. An error in the original material is very likely to be carried over to the typeset page or photoengraving. If an error appears in the plate, it cannot be corrected; a new plate must be made. If an error occurs in material set in type, corrections can be made, but making many corrections can be costly. Corrections of errors for which the advertiser is responsible or any changes he makes after type has been set are billed to him as *author's alterations*. If the errors are the fault of the printer, corrections are made at no expense to the advertiser.

An advertiser normally will want to see proofs of his advertisement before the final printing. Such proofs should be carefully read for errors. When correcting proofs it is wiser to use proofreaders' marks rather than detailed corrections in the margins of the proofs. Proofreader's marks are standard symbols universally understood by printers, and their use will avoid misunderstandings and resulting errors.

A branch office of a business firm, in checking proofs on a direct-mail piece for the home office, had occasion to question a price. The following notation was made on the margin of the proof opposite the questionable price listing: "J.P., is this OK?" The proof was returned to J.P. at the home office. He sent it back to the printer without rereading. A few days later 5,000 copies of the mailing piece were delivered with "J.P., is this OK?" printed after the price listing. Moral: Never write personal notes on proofs. If you must write a note to the advertising manager, to a client, or even to the printer, write it on a separate sheet of paper and address it as you would a letter. Reserve margins of proof for corrections only, and indicate these by using the proofreader's marks.

Proofreaders' Marks

X Change letter	**⏞** Paragraph	**v** Apostrophe
X Broken or bad letter	**No⏞** No paragraph	**v** Quotation
⊥ Push down space	**wf** Wrong font	**=/** Hyphen
⊙ Turn over	**stet** Let it stand	**=** Straighten lines
𝓳 Take out; delete	**⊓** Raise	**tr.** Transpose
∧ Left out; insert	**⊔** Lower	**Caps** Capital letters
# Insert space	**⋃** Less space	**s.c.** Small capitals
V Even spacing	**C** Close up	**l.c.** Lower case
⊏ Move left	**⊙** Period	**ital.** Italics
⊐ Move right	**/** Comma	**[/]** Insert brackets
□ Em quad space	**⊙** Colon	**≡** Capitalize
¦M One-em dash	**;/** Semicolon	**//** Align
¦¦M Two-em dash		

Example of Use of Proofreader's Marks

Proofreader's mark should be used when making correc- ⌢ **S**

X tions in copy⊙Their use will reduce the [chance fo error **r**

through mis understanding. This so is because all printers **tr**

Caps. in america as well as in other parts of the world understand **⊓**

l.c. ———— their meaning. Students of advertising should be familiar

with these marks and their proper use.

Proofreader's Marks, with Examples of Use.

TYPESETTING

At one time all type was set by hand, but as time passed, mechanical methods were developed for doing the job. However, even today some type is still hand-set, particularly for headlines. This method, although slower and more costly than machine setting, offers the advertiser greater flexibility and an opportunity to employ some unusual type faces that are not available in machine set type. Good type composition is easy to obtain in hand-set type, because the typesetter or compositor can maintain uniform and balanced space areas between words and letters by employing optical rather than mechanical spacing. A "composing stick" is used in setting type by hand. This is a tray that is held in the hand and into which are placed the type characters as they are taken from the type case. As the compositor places the type in the tray, he spells out the words and sets the lines to read from left to right, but upside-down, so that when they are reversed in printing they will read correctly from left to right.

Hot Type

Mechanically set type for letterpress printing is cast from molten metal as it is set—hence the name *"hot type"* or "hot-metal type." Linotypes and Inter-types (which are much alike) are widely used typesetting machines. They have keyboards somewhat like typewriters. When depressed, a key releases a brass mold or *matrix* corresponding to the letter on the key. These matrices are as-sembled in proper order to form words; other keys release varible-thickness spacebands to go between words; when the words and spaces fill a line, the molten type metal is forced into the matrices to cast the line in one solid piece. The matrices are returned to a magazine or storage compartment for repeated use. The lines of type (also called slugs) are used in the printing operation.

Linotypes and Intertypes set type rapidly and provide a wide choice of type faces in sizes ranging from 5 points to 48 points (sometimes even larger). As compared with hand-set type, however, they have a few disadvantages. Their spacing is mechanical; the compositor is not as intimately in control of the type as he is in hand setting. And since the type is cast in lines, the correc-tion of any error requires resetting the entire line. Suppose the word "advertis-ing" were incorrectly set "advretising." In hand-set type the "r" and the "e" could simply be transposed; in Linotype or Intertype, the entire line must be reset and recast. All the lines to the end of the paragraph may have to be thus reset if the correction changes the length of the line. (The same is necessary in any kind of typesetting.)

Monotype, another method of mechanical typesetting, accommodates type faces ranging from 5 to 18 points and display type as large as 60 points. It dif-fers from Linotype and Intertype in that it casts one type character at a time. The Monotype system comprises two units, one of which perforates a ribbon that causes the second unit to cast the desired characters. The keyboard mecha-nism of the first unit can be changed to meet the requirements of special com-position. This method adapts itself well to tabular and chart work, as well as to the setting of type for books, catalogs, and magazines.

When large display type is needed, as in headlines or when especially clear or sharp reproductions are desired, the Ludlow method of typesetting may be used. This method offers display type ranging in size from 12 to 72 points and in a variety of assortments. The method itself consists of a combination of hand-set matrices and machine-cast type. The line of matrices is set by hand, then placed in a casting machine that produces the line of type.

Photocomposition–Cold Type

The type produced by the Linotype, Intertype, Monotype, and Ludlow is all hot type, cast in hot metal from metal matrices. So-called *cold type,* on the

Linotype machine. *Mergenthaler Linotype Company.*

other hand, is produced by a phototypesetting machine from photographic matrices. Cold type is employed principally in offset lithography, though it may be photoengraved for use in letterpress.

Three of the leading photocomposing machines are manufactured by the same companies that produce the hot typesetting machines. In fact, there is a physical family resemblance between the respective cold and hot mechanical typesetting systems. Most phototypesetting machines operate in basically the same fashion. Each has a typewriter-like keyboard and a photounit, and as an end result produces a photographic image on film or paper. With the exception of the Intertype Fotosetter, the keyboards of all the machines produce a punched or perforated tape which is fed into the photographic unit for the automatic production of type. The Fotosetter, Fotomatic, and Fototronic, developed by Intertype, are tape operated. Other important phototypesetting systems are the Mergenthaler Linofilm, Monotype's Monofilm, Photon, the ATF Photo Typesetter, the Friden Justotext, Alphatype, and the Mergenthaler Linocomp and Addressograph Multigraph Comp/Set 500 direct entry phototypesetters. As this is written, numerous innovations, improvements, and new systems are in prospect.

Typewriter Composition

In effect, typewriter composition is also cold type and can be readily used in offset lithography. These composing machines are generally automatic electric typewriters which can adjust spacing and change type faces and which will do line justification so that all type ends evenly at the right-hand margin.

Among the machines which can meet these requirements in varying degrees are the IBM Electromatic and Executive, the Remington Rand Statesman, the Varityper, the Fairchild Lithotype, and the Friden Justowriter.

The standard office machines, manually operated and electric, which do not have these capabilities, also serve a purpose in composing type for direct mail advertising letters where close similarity to an original letter is generally desired. To produce the personal effect of an original typed letter there are a number of machines that operate from punched paper tape, automatically typing as many originals as required. The body of the letter is punched on the paper tape by a special machine. Other machines use magnetic tape. The typist inserts it into the automatic electric typewriter, rolls in a letterhead, and types the name, address, and salutation. The machine then automatically types the balance of the letter. This process can be repeated for as many letters as are desired. The tape can even be set up to stop at certain points in the body of the letter so that the typist can manually insert variations or *"variables."* These may repeat the person's name, address, or other message. The machine will then complete the body of the letter. Automatic typewriters that operate in this manner include the Auto-Typist, Robotyper, Hooven, and Flexowriter.

The Computer

Today's computers can perform a number of functions in the printing process ranging from the composition or setting of type to actual direct high-speed printing. More than 400 daily newspapers, presently, are using computers to set type. Coming generations of computers, some presently on the drawing boards, will do even more—faster, better, and more efficiently. Some are even being used to improve color reproduction.

All of us who have suffered through the pangs of learning spelling and grammar are well aware of the complexities of the English language. In addition to knowing when to end a page, where to end a line and how to justify it so that it ends flush at the right-hand margin, the computer, with proper programming has mastered the essentials of the rules of hyphenation—where to split or break a word at the end of a line. Along with the rules, it has also memorized the great list of exceptions. With this capability, the computer is able to convert "idiot tape"—punched paper tape that had no provision for proper spacing, line justification, and hyphenation—into a tape that will properly operate a typesetting machine. The advantages are at least twofold. The output of the human operator is greatly increased since he or she is relieved of a number of time-consuming functions, and the typesetting machine operates far more efficiently with computer-processed tape.

Computerized typesetting is ideal for newspapers, directories, catalogs, and price lists, and has also been used in book publication. A similar experimental system for automatic phototypesetting utilizes a Flexowriter for the input via IBM punched cards; a computer addition to the Photon 560 has also been developed. Improvements of this system are applicable to other photocomposition machines.

As has already been stated, computers can not only do the typesetting but can also do the printing. The use of computer-printers in the direct-mail advertising field seems to be a widening trend. Here, the printing is done directly by the computer (rather than through a tape produced by it for use in a typesetting machine, whose issue is then used for printing). Obviously such direct computer printing saves a number of steps. It also offers a great deal of flexibility. It can hyphenate words at the ends of lines and will accept preprogrammed computer-inserted variables, including names and addresses, to personalize each individual letter. The variable is printed in the same type face at the same time so that it is indistinguishable from the rest of the letter. The computer-printer also offers another attention-getting feature that can be used effectively in an advertising letter—it will print the words of the letter in a shaped format such as a star, a circle, or an arrowhead.

The Xerox 9200 Duplicating System, which can deliver two impressions per second, has a computerized programmer that controls the entire system.

PAPER

Paper is always a factor that must be considered in planning and producing print advertising. When an advertisement is scheduled for newspapers or magazines, the advertiser must work within the limits imposed by the paper employed by these media unless, as is sometimes the case, they will permit him to use inserts. If an insert is permitted, the advertiser can produce his own advertisement on a paper stock of his choice, and the newspaper or magazine will insert it as a part of the publication. Probably many readers have seen an occasional sheet of foil or other unusual material inserted in their daily newspapers, and it is not at all uncommon to find inserts in trade and industrial magazines.

In direct mail advertising, dealer displays, catalogs, and posters, the advertiser has a wide choice of paper which can often make the difference between an excellent or a poor reproduction of artwork. Also, paper, like type faces, illustrations, choice of words, and use of color, can create a feeling tone or atmosphere. For example, poor paper can make an otherwise attractive direct mail advertising piece look cheap, whereas good paper can help it to appear rich and distinctive.

SUMMARY

Print production in advertising encompasses all of the steps that are taken after the approval of the comprehensive layout until the ad appears in newspapers and magazines.

The three principal methods of printing are letterpress, gravure, and offset lithography. Letterpress prints from a raised surface, gravure from a surface with etched or incised areas, and lithography from what appears to be a planar or flat surface. Other methods of reproduction include xerography and silk screen.

Full-color ads are reproduced by means of the color separation process. In letterpress, four photos are taken of the original artwork. Three are taken through different color filters which filter out all but one primary color. The resultant black and white negatives, represent consecutively red, yellow, blue, and black. Plates made from these negatives, when used with the corresponding ink color and superimposed over each other, will give full-color reproduction.

Type comes in many sizes and designs. It is up to the art director and production people to select the face and size that best represent the ad.

While type was originally set by hand, and still is, there are two principal categories of mechanical typesetting. One is called hot type because the type is cast from molten metal in the machine. In most common use are the Linotype and Intertype, each of which has a keyboard resembling a typewriter. The other category of typesetting is called cold type, because it produces type by means of a photographic process. Both the Linotype and Intertype companies, along with others, have photocomposition machines on the market. All have typewriter-like keyboards.

The computer also functions as a typesetter and can do direct high-speed printing, as well.

QUESTIONS AND DISCUSSION SUBJECTS

1. Tell how an advertisement is reproduced by offset lithography.
2. Explain how a four-color advertisement is reproduced.
3. What are the advantages of using proofreader's marks when correcting copy?
4. Describe at least two processes by which line art may be given a shading effect.
5. What are the major considerations that should be given to a choice of type face for an advertisement?
6. Each term in the right-hand column defines or is related to a term in the left-hand column. Indicate which terms match by placing in the blanks of the left-hand column the correct numbers from the right-hand column.

_____ Stereotype   1. A stenciling technique
_____ Silk screen process   2. Matrix
_____ Pica   3. $^1/_6$ of an inch
_____ Line art   4. Indicates a deletion in artwork
_____ Mortise   5. Capital letters
_____ Crop mark   6. ⊓
_____ Diagonal method   7. ⊏
_____ Uppercase   8. No gradation in tone
_____ Raise   9. Reduction in art work
_____ Move left   10. Section of halftone plate is cut out

SOURCES

1. David Hymes, *Production in Advertising and the Graphic Arts* (New York: Holt, 1966).
2. Edwin H. Stuart and Grace Stuart Gardner, *Typography, Layout and Advertising Production* (Pittsburgh: Edwin H. Stuart, Inc., 1947).

FOR FURTHER READING

ATA Advertising Production Handbook. New York: Advertising Typographers Association of America, Inc., 1963.

Bahr, Leonard F., *Advertising Production Handbook*. New York: Advertising Typographers Association of America, 1969.

Bockus, H. William, Jr. *Advertising Graphics*. New York: Macmillan, 1974.

Dalgin, Ben. *Advertising Production*. New York: McGraw-Hill, 1946.

Hymes, David. *Production in Advertising and the Graphic Arts*. New York: Holt, 1966.

Latimer, H. C. *Advertising Production Planning and Copy Preparation for Offset Printing*, 3rd edition. New York: Art Direction Book Co., 1974.

McNaughton, Harry H. *Proofreading and Copyediting: A Practical Guide to Style for the 1970's*. New York: Hastings House, Publishers, 1973.

Pocket Pal. New York: International Paper Co., 1975.

Schlemmer, Richard M. *Handbook of Advertising Art Production*. Englewood Cliffs, N.J.: Prentice-Hall, 1966.

Stuart, Edwin H., and Grace Stuart Gardner. *Typography, Layout and Advertising Production*. Pittsburgh: Edwin H. Stuart, Inc., 1947.

The Electrotype and Stereotype Handbook. Cleveland: International Association of Electrotypers & Stereotypers, Inc.

Wales, H. G., D. L. Gentry, and M. Wales. *Advertising Copy, Layout and Typography*. New York: Ronald Press, 1958.

Wright, John S., Daniel S. Warner and Willis L. Winters, Jr. *Advertising*. New York: McGraw-Hill, 1971.

$$\begin{matrix} \star \\ \star \\ \star \\ \star \\ \star \\ \star \end{matrix} \quad 10$$

Broadcast-Media Production

WHAT THE AGENCY PRODUCER DOES

Within the advertising agency, the agency producer is responsible for the production of television commercials. He works closely with the account executive, the copywriter, and the art director, advising them on the production capabilities of the medium and on what can or cannot be done. And if it can be done, he lets them know what it will cost. Being a creative individual himself, he contributes ideas and may come up with an economical alternative solution that is feasible for accomplishing the same purpose. He makes cost estimates and times the script (storyboard).

At this point it is interesting to note that the title *agency producer* is, in a way, a misnomer. Actually, he does not produce the commercial. "He organizes and plans the production job, hires suppliers, is in charge during shooting and is responsible for the end result." [1] In smaller agencies the task is often performed by an art director or copywriter.

Once the script and storyboard have been approved by the agency creative team (copywriter, art director, and producer), by the copy supervisor or creative director, and by the agency account group, client approval must be obtained. This is usually accomplished by the account executive in a meeting at the client's office. Although they aren't always required, it is a good idea to have the copywriter and art director and even the agency producer accompany the account executive; they can often better explain the storyboard and production schedules, and are on tap if a technical question arises that the account man can't handle.

Competitive Bidding

Following the client's approval, the agency producer invites competitive bidding for the actual production of the commercial from several outside pro-

154

TV tells the world,
"MISTER SALTY Pretzels are crisplier"

(Silence)

(Music)
"MISTER SALTY is a pretzel . . .

crunchy to eat.

He's got fresh, light taste you just can't beat.

Gonna tell you why he's so special

MISTER SALTY is a crisplier pretzel.

Eat 'em anytime pretzels are fun

get MISTER SALTY a crisplier one.

Pretzels that are crisplier are best to munch

MISTER SALTY as a snack goes . . .

crunch, crunch, crunch.

ANNCR: MISTER SALTY the crisplier pretzel by NABISCO.

A photoboard of an animated cartoon commercial.

155

duction companies or studios. The bidding is done on the basis of the story-board submitted by the agency producer. The choice of the contract production company, however, is not necessarily made on the low bid but rather on fair cost from the best qualified producer. Under some circumstances, competitive bids might not even be sought, as where a production company offers special or unusual qualifications that are needed for a particular commercial. For example, a production company might have a director who is particularly good at working with children, and the *talent* in the commercial might be a 5½-year-old girl.

Most advertising agencies follow the competitive bidding system, even the small number that have their own in-house production facilities. But practice varies. For instance, one of the biggest advertisers, employing a number of advertising agencies, had an arrangement with a large production company. While this production company did not get preferential treatment, the client required that its agencies include that production house as one of the bidders.

Once the bids are in and a selection has been made, the agency seeks client approval on the production-cost estimate. With that in hand the next step is *casting,* or hiring talent.

Casting

The agency producer must furnish the casting director a copy of the story-board and information about the number and types of talent that the commercial requires. The casting director, often a woman, has files of actor's photos and résumés, including their film and stage credits. The casting director will select a few for each role and arrange an audition or casting session. The candidates appear before the agency's creative team involved in the commercial to read their lines. If there are two or more roles with dialogue, the candidates are usually auditioned together and read their parts opposite each other. Those selected are then presented to the account group and to the commercial production company's director for approval. This latter's concurrence in the approval is important to the agency, to avoid a claim of "poor talent" in the event that the production company has to reshoot some scenes or the entire commercial.

Once the final selections have been made, the casting department notifies the actors when and where to appear. It also arranges with the agency's business department to prepare talent contracts. On the day of the shooting, the agency producer has the additional chore of getting the contracts signed by the actors. Particular care must be taken in the preparation of contracts so as to avoid paying to *extras,* who appear on camera but do not have speaking parts, the rate and *residuals* * paid to players. While an extra who actually plays a full player's speaking part can be properly compensated, an extra does not receive residuals unless he has a speaking part on camera. A contract which calls for "a player or an extra" carries the higher pay scale and residuals regardless of the part played.

---

* *Residuals* are paid to an actor each time the commercial is broadcast.

Actors' pay scales are governed by the union to which they belong, either the Screen Actors Guild (SAG) or the American Federation of Television and Radio Artists (AFTRA). However, well-known or "name" actors and those with a reputation usually are paid "over scale." The scales include varying grades of pay for each task an actor is required to perform, including wearing of special costumes or using technical things such as scuba equipment.

PreProduction Meetings

The last step, before the actual shooting and the bulk of the production money is spent, is the *preproduction meeting*. At this point, the commercial has been approved, the production house selected, the talent recruited, and the location, if any, chosen. Called by the agency producer, the meeting is usually held at the agency. It is usually attended by a representative of the client, by the agency's creative team and account executive, and by the production company's producer, director, cameraman, and set designer. Others who may be present for specific purposes include the stylist, propman, musician, production manager, animator, makeup man, and hairdresser. For example, the hairdresser might not ordinarily attend the meeting but she (or he) would be needed if the product under consideration was a shampoo or a hair spray, or if the commercial required a special hairdo.

The importance of this meeting cannot be overemphasized. It is a complete and thorough review of all details and procedures. It is the final opportunity for the copywriter, the art director, and the agency producer—the agency's creative team—to make changes or otherwise resolve differences and improve the commercial before the cost of such changes becomes excessive. Such things as special effects, unusual props or properties, and production and casting problems are covered in the meeting. Most important of all is the visualization of the commercial, as they would have it filmed, presented by the agency producer and art director.

SHOOTING THE COMMERCIAL

Following the weeks of preliminary creative work, meetings, preparation, making arrangements, coordinating, and so forth, the day of the shooting finally arrives.

At the production company's studio or on location, work begins early, as last-minute preparations and adjustments are made on the set. On hand from the agency are the producer, art director, and copywriter. The latter two may be needed to assist the agency producer in the rewriting of the script or in experimental shooting. To avoid overcrowding, other agency people, with the exception of the account executive, generally do not come to the studio. The client may have a representative present to observe. And, of course, the talent is there.

At the filming, the biggest contingent is the people from the production company and the freelance specialists they have hired (hairdresser, makeup, and the like). The studio producer does overall supervision. The director is in charge of the set or location, guides the cameraman, orders lighting effects, directs the talent, and coordinates with the producer. The sound engineers, off to the rear, stand by their recording equipment as the sound is brought to them via the microphone extended over the set by means of a boom. The assistant camerman loads the film, makes the proper lens adjustments, and focuses the camera. The cameraman, looking through the camera viewer, frames the scene and calls the director and/or the producer to approve it. Then the agency producer and possibly the art director take a turn at seeing what the camera sees.

Once all-around approval is obtained, the scene is ready for filming. A buzzer sounds the warning; the door is locked and ''Silence'' signs are lit. The actors are in position, the camera and the sound tape are rolling, the clap-sticks attached to the slate are slammed together in front of the camera lens to synchronize the separate sound track and picture, and the scene and *take* are identified both by voice and in writing (on the slate). Then the actors say their lines and play their parts. A script girl times the take and makes note of the director's comments or decision. If the director is satisfied he will say ''Print that''; if not, it will be taken over and over again until he is satisfied. In any event, a number of takes are made to allow for subtleties and possibilities not observed during filming. It is far less expensive to do them at this time than it would be to recall the talent, crew, and others at some later date.

Each scene in the storyboard is shot in the same manner but not necessarily in sequence. Filming out of storyboard sequence may save a great deal of time and money if, for example, the first and last scenes call for the same set and intervening scenes take place on other sets. In this case, the first and last scenes are shot one after the other, followed by the remaining scenes. They are put into proper sequence later by the editor.

In changing scenes, the *grips* and the *props* or handymen may have to move the properties,* the sets, and/or the camera; and the *gaffer,* as chief electrician, may have to readjust the lights.

Barring unusual circumstances or an extremely complicated script, a 30-second or a 1-minute commercial can be filmed in one or two days at the most. (Often 30-second and shorter variants are filmed at the same time as the 60-second commercial, utilizing the same talent, sets, and other resources).

On Location

While most scenes can be duplicated on a studio set, it makes sense to use the real thing whenever possible. A storyboard may call for a beach scene, or for skiing. In such cases the filming is done *on location*. If the season is right and there is an appropriate beach nearby, operations and participants are moved to the beach. Prior to the move the assistant director (AD) scouts the location and arranges for a dressing van or trailer, sanitary facilities, and meals. However, if it is winter in New York or wherever the advertising agency is located,

* Both properties and the men who move them are called ''props.''

it will be necessary to shoot the commercial on location in Florida, Puerto Rico, or some other warm climate. Under these circumstances it might be advisable to take along only key personnel. The production company's producer may also elect to rent camera equipment at the site rather than carry it with him and pay the additional air fare for extra baggage.

Today, with air transportation so readily available, air fares relatively inexpensive, and flying time so short, it is fairly common to shoot on location in Paris, Rome, London, Hawaii, or any other place specified in the storyboard. In these cases the same procedure for hiring certain personnel at the site is followed. In fact, for many American commercials shot in Europe, a foreign production company is given the contract. Europe does not lack for superior producers, creative directors, and professional cameramen and their efforts certainly can add to the realism of the commercial. Even the talent can be hired overseas.

Realism in Commercials

"In the past, the heat of old-fashioned studio lights, the lack of studios with proper equipment (refrigerators, freezers, and stoves), inferior color film, and less sophisticated cameras meant that a variety of techniques and ingredients were used to ensure that food products looked realistic in finished print ads and commercials." [2]

While it is possible to enhance the attributes or appearance of a product by means of mock-ups or dummies, color correction, photographic techniques, and special lenses (closeup, zoom, telephoto, wide angle, "fish eye," etc.), these practices are not followed, today, by reputable advertisers or advertising agencies. In fact, most of the larger agencies and manufacturers have explicit guidelines on this subject, prepared by their legal staffs. They also get, prior to shooting, legal-staff clearance on television product demonstrations. This new awareness sometimes rules out the filming of a food product, for example, that might not be particularly photogenic. However, advertisers would rather err in this direction than use a technique that might incur the wrath of the FTC and self-regulatory agencies or the enmity of the consumerists. It is interesting to note that the consumers' best interests may not always be served, in such cases, and that they can be denied a new and worthwhile product or recipe. If an enhancing technique were used to show a particular food product honestly, as it actually is in life rather than as it appears without enhancement on the television tube, the advertiser would probably run afoul of current regulations. Yet there might actually be no deception or misrepresentation.

Film vs. Tape

While *video tape,* * generally referred to simply as "tape," is used predominantly in regular daytime television programs and in substantially better than

---

* Video tape is plastic film, two inches wide, coated with magnetic iron oxide. It can record both sound and image and play them back instantly. It closely resembles the narrower home audio recording tape.

half of nighttime television, many commercials are still produced on motion-picture film with an audio track.[3] Film is easier to handle on location and is used for spot news apparently for the same reason. Even when television commercials are taped they are often duplicated on 16mm film for spot broadcasting. On the other hand, sports events are often produced on tape, as is evidenced by the instant replay. In this case, however, the camera and tape equipment can be based in the press box, which offers some of the facilities of the studio. New innovations about which we will be hearing more are the video cassette and video disc.

At this juncture it should be pointed out that tape has the decided advantage of instant replay, an immediate rebroadcast of the take that has just been made, while it may be hours or days before film can be processed for viewing. The editing of video tape formerly presented a problem. However, that disadvantage has been reduced. The principal drawback to tape, other than the difficulty of portability, is that duplicate tapes cost more than film copies.

Most commercials were produced on color film even during the period when there were more black-and-white television sets than there were color receivers, and despite the greater cost of color production.[4] Since color transmission is compatible, it could and can be received also on such black-and-white sets. As color sets became more numerous, it made sense to produce commercials with that extra dimension.

As for film size, 35mm provides a much larger frame and greater definition than 16mm. While, for the most part, the more expensive 35mm film and equipment are used for television commercials, the smaller 16mm camera is sometimes used to achieve particular results. It is more portable, it can be hand-held, and it is the equipment used by television stations and networks for spot news coverage. It is used on occasion when commercials require a similar live, spontaneous effect. In addition, 16mm film and equipment are very welcome for low-budget films and commercials, and are being used with greater frequency.

Although the subject of this section is Film vs. Tape, there is a third option—to broadcast live. In the early days of the medium, live programs and live commercials were the general order of business. Today, these are the exception rather than the rule, and for good reason. With live action there is no opportunity to correct mistakes or improve performance, whereas both tape and film can be edited to broadcast a combination of the best takes. Both can also be shot in any sequence and edited later. The rare use of live commercials today would be on local television. Even when a personality like Johnny Carson or Ed McMahon introduces a commercial ''off the cuff'' on the *Tonight* show, the entire program is taped earlier in the evening for broadcasting later that night. Advance transcribing on film or tape also makes possible network programs that can be broadcast nationally at different times to accommodate the four time zones in the United States.

Sound

Background music and voices called for by the storyboard, other than those that appear directly on camera (DV, direct voice), are usually recorded at a sound studio. This may be a private commercial studio or the agency's recording studio if it has its own. An announcer who does not appear visually in the commercial but whose voice is heard (VO, voice over) records his part on audio tape. He repeats his lines until the agency producer is satisfied as to time, expression, sound, and other qualities. The copywriter is on hand at this recording session in case it becomes necessary to rewrite awkward passages or otherwise edit the script. In the same fashion, the musicians or singers go through their parts and the sound effects (SFX) are recorded, as well.

Announcers, musicians, and singers are hired through the agency's casting director, the same as other talent. The pay scale for musicians is set forth in the Television and Radio Announcements Agreement of the American Federation of Musicians (AFM).

Original lyrics and music are generally contracted for on a speculative basis, with the agency reimbursing the composer and lyricist for out-of-pocket expenses pending acceptance or rejection of the work. Such costs are usually high, ranging from $2,000 to $5,000. Stock music, considerably less costly and readily available in great variety, is often used instead. Music is generally "developed with a particular target audience in mind." [5] It serves as an attention-getter and "can also be used to create a mood, to highlight action, or to emphasize a product benefit or selling phrase." [6]

When the recording session is completed, the individual audio tapes of voice, music, and sound effects are again recorded on separate 35mm magnetic film. The sound engineer then "mixes" the three. Each is placed on its own reel, timed, adjusted for sound and quality levels, and synchronized. A single track combining all of the sound finally emerges from the mix.

Essentially the sound process described above is the one followed for radio commercials and programs other than live broadcasts of news, disc-jockey, and talk programs. "Dialogue" talk shows, where the listener can telephone the station and be heard on the air, are taped and broadcast with a seven-second delay so that they can be monitored or censored and profanity—if any—edited out.

Screening

Following the shooting sessions, the agency's producer and art director, together with the production company's director and editor, as a group, view all *rushes* or *dailies*. These rush prints, provided by the photo processing laboratory from the negatives shot the preceding day, form the basis of the *work print* or *rough cut*. This first edited copy of the commercial consists of the preferred take, selected by the group, of each scene in proper sequence and length. The work print is not yet adjusted for pacing or mood. Scenes start and end abruptly since the film does not yet have fades, wipes, and dissolves to ease the transition from scene to scene. This first agency screening of the work print is limited to the small creative group. It gives them an opportunity to criticize their own work and to make recommendations. The agency producer serves as the chairman of this group and is responsible for the execution of all recommendation agreed upon.

Like the first screening, the presentation to the account group is an *interlock* session where the film and sound track, still separate, are run simultaneously in synchronization, giving the effect of a composite print. The agency producer, together with the art director and copy supervisor, presents the recommendations. He then reports back to the creative group on the decisions.

The next interlock session is with the client. The agency producer, accompanied by those who attended the previous screening, presents the film along with combined agency recommendations. The account people record the client's approval as well as all decisions. They then follow through in their normal procedure as liaison between the client and the creative group.

Editing

Perhaps the most important step in the production of a television commercial (or of any film, for that matter) is the editing. There is no question that the skill of the editor can make or break a film.

The editor mounts the film on a Moviola, the trade name for a viewing machine that he can speed, slow, stop, and reverse. The Moviola can also run the separate sound track "in sync" with the film. The editor selects the best takes and splices them in chronological sequence. With the agency producer's approval, the editor then runs the film through and marks it with a grease pencil or felt marker for cuts, wipes, fades, dissolves, other optical effects, titles, and the like. These are added at an optical laboratory. A new negative is then made with all of the necessary additions and deletions. The film is accurately timed and the sound-track negative is finally recorded directly on to it to produce what is called the *printing negative*.[7] The first film made from it is called the *answer print*.

Client approval is obtained at a meeting attended by the agency producer, account group, art director, and copy supervisor. Hopefully no corrections will be required since at this stage of the game they would be extremely costly. Once the client has approved the answer print the agency producer's and art director's responsibility for it is over, and they are ready to produce the next commercial.

To the Television Screen

The answer print, however, does not go directly to your television screen, although, in effect, it becomes the first *release print*. Sufficient numbers of release prints or *air prints,* which are the finished commercial, are reproduced from the printing negative to satisfy the schedule made by the media department. These are then sent out for broadcasting by the traffic department to the television stations with which the media department has made contracts.

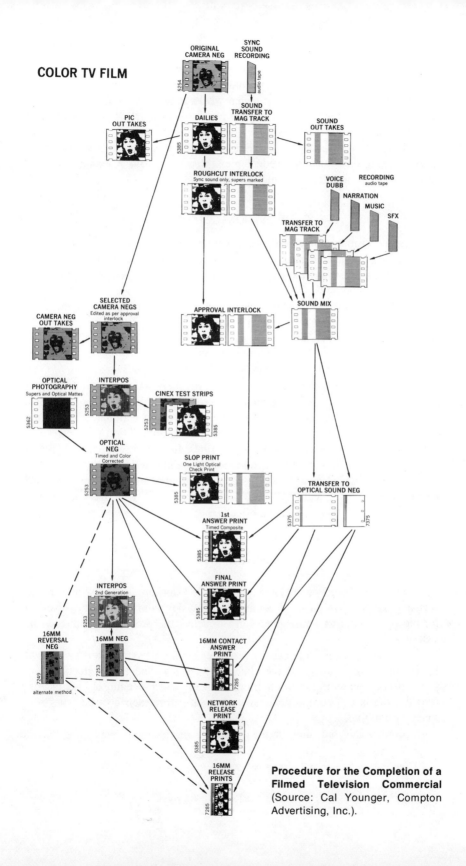

COLOR TV FILM

Procedure for the Completion of a Filmed Television Commercial (Source: Cal Younger, Compton Advertising, Inc.).

The entire production from the time the client approves the storyboard to the final approval of the answer print normally takes from four to six weeks for live action on film. This goes up to ten weeks if animation is involved, since filming the cartoon action is a lengthy process—each frame or picture of an animated-cartoon film requires an individual drawing (and sound-picture film runs 24 frames per second).* For live action on tape, in contrast, as few as seven working days may be needed, plus three more days if existing or stock film clips are to be integrated into the tape.

THE TELEVISION COMMERCIAL

The television commercial is less than 30 years old, yet it has played and continues to play an important part in our lives. This would be the case even if its only contribution were to pay the way for the rest of our entertainment and news on television.

But the commercial has also become an art form in its own right. Commercials are recognized internationally as film art; no wonder, in light of the fact that a tiny commercial requires nearly all of the care, preparation, and attention that goes into a full-length feature film. And the commercial must tell its story in 60, 30, or even 8 seconds.

Each year awards are made to writers, producers, talent, and other participants in the production of prize-winning commercials. Presentations are made at a gala annual function recognizing "the outstanding national, regional and local broadcast advertising of the past year." The competition for these CLIO awards in the United States was begun in 1960. In 1966 it was expanded to an international competition and the following year radio was added.

While the CLIO awards are based on creativity, artistic effects, and production techniques, the EFFIE awards, initiated in 1971, judge commercials (and print ads) on their marketing effectiveness.[8]

SUMMARY

The agency producer is the expert on television production within the advertising agency. He puts the completed television commercial storyboard up for bid by production houses and helps to select the production company that will do the job.

Following casting, the agency producer calls a preproduction meeting attended by representatives of the client, the agency, and the production company. It is a complete run-through of all details and procedures. This meeting provides the last opportunity to make changes before their cost becomes relatively prohibitive.

Commercials are shot in the studio or on location, depending on the

* Tape runs at the rate of 30 frames per second.

budget and extent of realism to be achieved. Extreme care is exercised not to exaggerate the benefits of the product and to remain within FTC regulations and the advertising industry self-regulatory guidelines.

Although video tape offers many advantages and is used for most television programs, film is still used for many television commercials.

After the commercial has been shot, the voice over and the background music are recorded. The film is then edited for chronological sequence, content, and timing. Effects such as dissolves, fades, and wipes are added, and the sound track is joined to it. The television commercial is now complete as a printing negative; the first print from it is called the answer print. Subsequent release or air prints are made from the printing negative for distribution to the televison stations that are under contract to broadcast the commercial.

QUESTIONS AND DISCUSSION SUBJECTS

1. Describe the procedure for turning a storyboard into a commercial.
2. On what basis does the agency producer select a company to produce a commercial?
3. Name the people who select and approve the talent that appears or is heard in a commercial.
4. What is the significance of the preproduction meeting?
5. Are the scenes in a commercial filmed in the same sequence as seen in the actual broadcast?
6. What are the two principal means of recording commercials? Which is most often used for regular television programs?
7. Describe the advantages and disadvantages of each.
8. What is the editor's contribution to the commercial?

SOURCES

1. John D. Burke, "Writing and Producing Television Commercials for National Advertisers," *Encyclopedia of Advertisng & Marketing* (Blue Ridge Summit, Pa.: Tab Books, 1974).
2. John A. Howard and James Hulbert, *Advertising and the Public Interest* (Washington: Federal Trade Commission, 1973), V12.
3. A. C. Book and N. D. Cary, *The Television Commercial: Creativity and Craftsmanship* (New York: Decker Communications, 1970), 49.
4. *Ibid.*, 48.
5. Howard and Hulbert, *op. cit.*, V7.

6. *Ibid.,* V6.
7. G. F. Seehafer and J. W. Laemmar, *Successful Television and Radio Advertising* (New York: McGraw-Hill, 1959), 233.
8. *Clio Awards Teacher's Guide* (New York: CLIO Enterprises, Inc., 1972), 48.

FOR FURTHER READING

Book, A. C., and N. D. Cary. *The Television Commercial: Creativity and Craftsmanship.* New York: Decker Communications, 1970.

Diamant, Lincoln. *The Broadcast Communications Dictionary.* New York: Hastings House, Publishers, 1974.

———, ed. *The Anatomy of a Television Commercial.* New York: Hastings House, 1970.

McGuinn, D., and R. M. Mumma. *Some Important Things I Believe a Young Account Representative Should Know About Broadcast Affairs.* New York: American Association of Advertising Agencies, 1969.

Madsen, Roy. *The Impact of Film: How Ideas Are Communicated through Cinema and Television.* New York: Macmillan, 1973.

Margulies, R., W. B. Moseley, and D. H. Wallace. *Some Important Things I Believe a Young Account Representative Should Know About Television Commercial Production.* New York: American Association of Advertising Agencies, 1967.

Millerson, Gerald. *The Technique of Television Production.* Ninth Revised Edition. New York: Hastings House, Publishers, 1972.

Ogilvy, David. "How to Make Successful Television Commercials," in his *How to Create Advertising that Sells.* New York: Ogilvy & Mather, 1975.

Seehafer, G. F., and J. W. Laemmar. *Successful Television and Radio Advertising.* New York: McGraw-Hill, 1959.

Wainwright, Charles Anthony. *Televison Commercials: How to Create Successful TV Advertising.* Revised Edition. New York: Hastings House, Publishers, 1970.

★
★
★
★
★
★
★

11

The Campaign

THE IMPORTANCE OF THE CAMPAIGN

The campaign is the sum total of a company's advertising effort toward a particular objective during a specific period of time.

The placement of a single classified advertisement may accomplish an advertiser's purpose. However, except for this and other such isolated uses of advertising, it is difficult to conceive of one advertisement being very effective. It may appear at times that a single advertisement has done a completely satisfactory job, but in the great majority of cases this seemingly single advertisement actually is one marcher in a long line of advertisements or other marketing promotional efforts. What degree of its success is attributable to it as an individual advertisement and what degree to its predecessors? The answer is difficult, if not impossible, to determine. But one may be reasonably sure that earlier promotional efforts contributed in some measure to its success. For example, it may appear that some one advertisement, placed simultaneously in two or more daily newspapers, has accomplished all that a retail store might desire in the way of attracting customers to a sale. However, it is very likely that many past advertisements placed by the store over a period of months and years have built a reputation or a "store personality" that helped the single sale-announcement advertisement do the successful job that it seemingly accomplished alone. The same is true of the occasional public-relations advertisement that may appear as a one-time insertion to meet an emergency and nonrecurring situation. Its success, beyond doubt, depends upon its merits as an individual advertisement. But perhaps, to an even greater extent, its success depends also upon the seemingly unrelated advertising that has gone before. The "corporate image" that the sum total of the firm's advertising has built in people's minds makes it possible or impossible for this one public-relations advertisement to do the job expected of it.

Today, General Electric sailed a ship across the Atlantic, rolled steel in Mexico and turned on the lights in Spain.

More examples of how GE technology serves people worldwide.

Aboard the Japanese supertanker, S. T. Energy Transport,
a General Electric automatic control system makes possible remote
operation of the ship from a single console.
In Mexico, GE drives, instrumentation and process control systems
help the nation's steel industry keep up with the impressive
growth in demand for industrial and consumer products.
At Alcantara, Spain, equipment built by General Electrica Española
powers and controls western Europe's largest hydroelectric plant.
Technological advances in industrial automation from
General Electric are serving the needs and wants
of customers everywhere.
In marine, industrial and utility applications,
General Electric people are making progress around the world.

Corporate ads generally cover the broad picture rather than a particular product or service. They are called institutional ads and emphasize the "corporate image." *Courtesy of GE.*

In sum, the advertiser needs to think not in terms of single advertisements only but rather in terms of overall campaigns. One or two advertisements normally are not enough to do a selling job. Even a larger number of successful but uncoordinated advertisements can lose much of the force that such weight of advertising should carry. Single victories are not sufficient. The military man must plan each battle so that it may be won, but at the same time he must see the individual battle as but a part of a complete campaign. A series of uncoordinated battles fought with no overall strategy in mind is not likely to win a war against an enemy who fights a well-coordinated campaign, planned in advance. So, too, with the advertising man in his competitive struggle for markets—an occasional advertisement or even a number of uncoordinated advertisements are apt to be disappointing in their results.

To stay with the military analogy a little longer, we see that a campaign is made up of several individual but nonetheless related battles and that the war often is made up of several campaigns. These campaigns in turn are related and aimed toward the accomplishment of the final goal of victory. In like manner, in advertising we have campaigns made up of individual advertisements, and we have a competitive "war" made up of several campaigns. At this point the analogy begins to break down, for in advertising there is no final victory—no end to the "war." It is fortunate that there is none. In a competitive economy, the continuing struggle of competitor against competitor supports progress, an up-spiraling standard of living, the very life of the nation.

THEME

Both in advertising and in military terms, the campaign is a planned, organized, coordinated, continuing effort to gain a specific objective. Usually it is conducted under a theme or slogan. Military slogans, with which we are all familiar, include; "Remember the Alamo," "Remember the *Maine,*" "Make the world safe for Democracy," and "Remember Pearl Harbor." Advertising themes, with which we are perhaps a little more familiar, include: 7-Up's "The Un-cola," Alka-Seltzer's "Try it. You'll like it," "Schaeffer is the one beer to have when you're having more than one," Hallmark's "When you care enough to send the very best," "Milk is a natural," "As long as you're up get me a Grant's," Morton Salt's "When it rains it pours," and others.

GOAL AND OBJECTIVE

If final victory cannot be the goal of an advertising campaign or, for that matter, of a series of campaigns, then what is the goal? In attempting to answer this question, a distinction should be drawn between immediate objective and ultimate goal. The *ultimate goal* is always *to sell* a product, a service, or an idea. The immediate objective may vary from campaign to campaign within a company or among campaigns of competing companies. For example, when a new product has been developed, the obvious objective of the initial campaign is to get the product accepted by those people who are thought to be its potential buyers and users; there may be little or no direct competition. But as the market for this new product is developed, competition enters, and a new campaign is created. The immediate objective shifts; now it is not to gain acceptance for a new product but to gain preference for a particular brand. The immediate objectives of the two campaigns are quite different and the means of attaining them of necessity must be different, but the ultimate goal of each is the sale of the product. Under other circumstances the immediate campaign objective may be to better the public relations of a company. If the public relations effort is directed toward consumers, there is an evident tie-in with sales, and the ultimate goal of selling the company's product may be clearly seen. However, if the campaign's public relations effort is directed toward the labor public or the government public with the objective of preventing a strike or avoiding restrictive legislation, its relationship to sales of the product may be less direct. Nonetheless, the ultimate goal of the campaign still remains that of selling—this time, selling an idea rather than the product: the idea that the company is a good place to work, that hours are right, that pay is adequate, that there should be no strike; or the idea that the restrictive bill should not become law.

From the advertiser's point of view, the value of this concept of the ultimate goal of any and all advertising campaigns lies in the emphasis it places on sales. Although immediate objectives may differ, the advertiser should never lose sight of the fact that his advertising, regardless of what form it assumes, is created to sell something. If the ultimate goal is other than this, then there may be a question as to whether advertising is the proper tool for its accomplishment.

The advertiser must further keep in mind the fact that the selling which is the ultimate goal is *continued* selling, the creation of *brand loyalty,* which impels the customer to return time and time again to repurchase the brand. This is particularly the goal in advertising grocery products and other such items that are expendable and replenished frequently, but it is also the goal in advertising products as large as automobiles, which might be purchased only once every two to six years. Continued selling is also the goal in advertising every kind of service, whether it be rendered in a barber's chair or offered by an airline that carries a vacationer to the Orient.

The significance from the viewpoint of the advertiser of the concept of the immediate objective of an advertising campaign lies in the recognition that advertising problems differ and that the ultimate goal, a sale, is not always obtained in the same way. There are, indeed, many ways to accomplish the sales goal. These ways establish the immediate objectives. Consider, for a *few* examples, several ways of increasing sales, any one of which might set the immediate objective of an advertising campaign as a step toward the ultimate goal of selling more product.

1. Stimulate buying by people in new places or more places.
2. Stimulate buying by more people in places where the product is already bought—reach a new segment of the market.
3. Stimulate buying more of the product by people who already buy it.

A campaign of the first type is in order whenever the marketing programs enter a new geographic market area.

A campaign of the second type might include advertisements directed to an age group, ethnic group, or social-status group whose members had not been buyers of the product. It might also include placing advertisements in previously unused media. An excellent example is the promotion of Johnson & Johnson's Baby Shampoo. First it was advertised for babies; then mother was told that if it is good enough for baby then it's good for herself too. The next stage in the campaign promoted the ''baby'' product to men.

The third type of campaign, in particular, offers innumerable opportunities for advertising ingenuity and strategy. Following are a few examples:

Stretch the selling season. Soft drinks were once almost exclusively hot-weather items; Coca-Cola's advertising has built it up as an all-year and all-climate beverage. Automobile antifreeze was once solely a winter item; advertisers have programmed their campaigns to fit the longer cold-climate winters and have also pointed out the value of antifreeze as an all-weather radiator protector.

Discover and promote new uses. The 3M Company, especially when Scotch tape was relatively new on the market, demonstrated many different ways of using it; advertisements invited suggestions from users, who were rewarded in cash if their ideas were deemed worth advertising. Food manufacturers promote cooking contests that use their products, and they publicize the new recipes that win the prizes. The Arm & Hammer Company has advertised numerous uses for ''baking soda'' other than for baking. These range from deodorizing kitty litter and refrigerators to extending the power of laundry bleach and neutralizing chlorine in swimming pools.

Promote multiple-unit sales. When soft drinks and beer are sold in six-packs, buyers consume more cans or bottles. If ball-point pens are sold by the dozen, a user need not buy a new pen (perhaps a competitor's) so soon.

Promote convenience-unit sales. The single candy bar is a classic example of this kind of unit; advertisements for the innumerable kinds of candy bars sold them to millions who did not buy boxed candy. Alka-Seltzer's two-tablet packets, which come in boxes of 18 packets, can be easily sold because it is convenient to carry in pockets or purses.

Reward quantity consumers. Advertising of quantity discounts or ''large economy sizes'' is common. Giving premiums for proofs of purchase can also be advertised.

Let it be emphasized that these are only a few examples. The immediate objectives of advertising campaigns are as varied and numerous as are the

One way to increase sales of a product is to find additional uses for it, and then advertise it.

Packaging in multiple units makes for greater unit sales for Coke. The Cluster Case® made of a single ply kraft paper holds 24 cans. A simple perforation break splits it into two 12-packs and a paper zipper divides each into two 6-packs. *Courtesy Mead Packaging.*

problems of advertisers. To cite them all probably would be impossible. A few of the more common objectives are: to obtain leads for later personal solicitation, to keep a brand name before the public, to sell goods by mail, to correct mistaken notions about a firm or a product, and to introduce a new product, a new package for an established product, or a new style or model. An interesting objective is that of creating a *product image* or *corporate image*. An advertiser may feel that he can best sell his product if he can get the consumer public to think of it in a particular way. For example, he may decide sales can be increased if the product is given an aura of prestige, is associated with "fine living," and is made synonymous with top quality. A campaign may be developed to create such a product image in people's minds by always presenting the product in association with objects or symbols that represent the desired characteristics. A corporate image is created in much the same way, except that the associations are made to relate to the company rather than the product. One of our large corporations has done a good job of associating itself with *progress,* another with *integrity of product.* Some retail stores have built themselves reputations as bargain shops, others as exclusive establishments.

Still other immediate objectives might include meeting competition, answering a charge of competitive claim, encouraging the buying of more of the product along with a related item through cooperative advertising. A campaign might aim to meet the challenge of a substitute—a new, entirely different product which can perform the same or a similar function, such as plastic film as opposed to aluminum foil.

COMPARATIVE ADVERTISING

A strategy which began a long time ago, but has come into more popular use in the last few years, is comparative advertising. Essentially it is the practice of making specific comparisons by naming or showing the competitor's product or name in advertising. It is a strategy that is generally employed by manufacturers or service companies that have not attained the top position in their fields. While comparisons can show that the advertiser offers features superior to those of his competitor, they can also demonstrate that a much lower-priced product has the same features the more expensive competitor has.[1]

POSITIONING

Another means of achieving a goal or objective is a strategy called *positioning*—putting the advertiser's product or service into a place or position in the buyer's scheme of how the product is to be used. An example of positioning might be the decision to market baking powder as a refrigerator deodorant, as was done by Arm & Hammer.

According to Al Ries, president of Ries, Cappielo, Colwell and a champion of positioning, "It is not what you do to the product, it's what you do to the mind. It is how you position your product in the mind of the prospect or potential customer—the special niche that you give to it."

Which is the $1.85 Pen?
COMPARE & SAVE

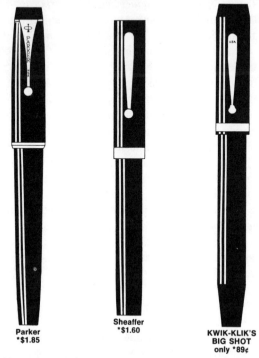

Parker	Sheaffer	KWIK-KLIK'S
*$1.85	*$1.60	BIG SHOT only *89¢

*All prices are based on minimum orders, however, the comparison and saving remain the same as the size of the order increases.

WHAT THE BIG SHOT HAS THAT ITS COMPETITORS DON'T

BIG SHOT is Flexible.
It accepts the standard size ink cartridge readily available at stationary stores _as well as_ the Jumbo refill.

Parker's and Sheaffer's DO NOT!

BIG SHOT has a specially designed square hole (patent pending) that lets more air into the barrel and allows the cartridge to breathe properly. The square hole has greater structural strength than the round one and will prevent wiggling of the writing tip.

Parker's and Sheaffer's DO NOT!

BIG SHOT has a slip fit "push-on, pull-off" cap instead of a threaded one for greater ease and convenience.

Parker's and Sheaffer's DO NOT!

BIG SHOT offers a _FREE_ Trademark Reproduction Service. It will turn your **BIG SHOT** "portable billboard" into a "Broadway Spectacular.

Parker's and Sheaffer's DO NOT!

See other side for complete details.

June, 1976 KWIK-KLIK WRITING INSTRUMENTS 6291

LITHO U.S.A.   SEE OTHER SIDE

Comparative advertising. Note the use of competitor's names and products. *Courtesy of Stacie-Island Pen Co.*

174

Examples already mentioned illustrate positioning. When Coca-Cola broke out of the summer-drink category it repositioned itself as a beverage for all seasons. In like manner the orange growers of Florida began a campaign, in 1973, to reposition orange juice as a drink for all times of the day, rather than one merely for breakfast. Other examples are Lava soap, which had been a product used by mechanics and laborers, but was repositioned as a soap for mothers to use on kids; Lipton's dried soups (particularly the onion soup) were repositioned as principal ingredients for dips; and Slender, Carnation's diet drink, was repositioned as a meal substitute or a snack for non-dieters and re-named Instant Breakfast. It was followed up by Special Breakfast—a bigger instant breakfast.

MARKETING STAGES

In planning the campaign, an important factor to consider is the marketing stage of the product. A completely new product, a new invention, for which no counterpart exists, obviously must be treated differently from one that has competitors. (In effect, however, practically every product has competitors, even a new product that obsolesces old ones and even if the old ones don't accomplish exactly the same thing as well or as efficiently.) The first airline didn't have to compete against other airlines. It was in the *innovative* or *introductory market development stage*. The company name was of only minor importance because no one else offered the same kind of service. The primary job of advertising was to introduce, establish, educate, inform, and sell air travel in general. It would tell about the excitement of flying and describe the scenic beauty of flying among the clouds. And it would compete against surface travel, emphasizing the time-saving advantages, much as the Air Transport Association, the industry spokesman, might do today. On the other hand, once a second airline appeared on the scene, the competition was between airlines. Each airline tried to sell itself by showing its advantages over the other. Now, among others, TWA, Pan Am, Eastern, American, and United compete against each other as well as against foreign air carriers who fly the same routes.

While the example offered here is simplified to illustrate a point, it is important to indicate that despite the fierce competition and the highly developed state of the industry, airlines continue to promote the primary demand. Up until a few years ago statistics showed that a large percentage of Americans had never travelled more than 200 miles from their homes. Reduced fares for members of the armed forces and for young people, special "take me along" rates for wives, and lower-cost family travel plans were efforts to induce added selective demand and to enhance the primary demand. Airline advertising continues seeking to stimulate *both* primary and selective demand.

Many advertisers are long past that first innovative stage. And if the product or service offered is any good, the innovator is going to have plenty of company in the second, or *competitive stage*. Success breeds competition, and the lead time for the innovator to retain his exclusivity and reap his unchallenged reward is extremely short if he is not protected by a patent. Often the product or service does not lend itself to patent or copyright protection, and the imitators swarm in. The "Johnny-come-latelies" enter full-blown upon the competitive stage, sometimes with added features forcing the innovator to meet their challenge. Successful products and services, whether or not they were once innovations, spend most or all of their lives in the competitive stage.

While a successful product or service rarely, if ever, leaves the competitive stage by achieving complete market dominance, some have been advertised for many years and have achieved a certain measure of recognition by the public. Some have become common household terms. By virtue of this status and the weight of the promotion that has gone before, these advertisers feel that they can be effective with a simple reminder, like Coca-Cola's "It's the real thing." However, this *reminder stage* can be effective only with that segment of the population that has been exposed to the past advertising and the product's reputation. Since a new generation is always entering upon the scene, the advertiser must simultaneously continue his campaign in the competitive stage.

It should be noted that while the overall product, such as an automobile, might be in the competitive stage, a particular feature of the car might be in the innovative stage. Such a feature, might be a new type of bumper which would withstand an impact of 25 miles an hour and protect the car and its occupants. Of course, such an innovative feature, if exclusive to a single make of car, would greatly enhance its overall competitive position.

LENGTH OF THE CAMPAIGN

The duration of the campaign is often determined by the length of customary media contracts and the periods covered by the syndicated media research organizations. Campaigns rarely extend beyond a year. On occasion, however, successful campaigns, characterized by appealing slogans and the accomplishment of objectives and goals, do run longer.

Some experts claim that media schedules are arbitrary and bear no relationship whatsoever to people's buying habits. Nevertheless, a valid argument could be made for the 13-week segments in which most broadcasting contracts are offered. These roughly follow the four natural seasons, running a few weeks ahead. The broadcast year generally begins in the middle of September, following the summer hiatus. This date coincides with the opening of schools and colleges, and covers most of the fall season. It ends a few weeks short of Christmas, which is in the next 13-week segment, and so on through spring and summer in subsequent 13-week cycles. And an advertiser can sign for 13, 26, 39, or 52 weeks.

The other major factor determining the length of campaigns is the four-week period used by the media research organizations as the basis for their reports. These four-week segments are a carryover from old radio network programming. Arbitrary or not, they are short and are very popular among users of spot television. Since the research organizations cover the print media in the same four-week cycles, they influence campaign length likewise.

The customary magazine contract periods vary according to frequency of publication. Weekly magazines offer a discount for 13 insertions, while monthly periodicals base their rate structure on the number of their issues for the year.[2]

OTHER TYPES OF ADVERTISING AND PROMOTION

The advertising activity of a complete campaign may be extended well beyond that which appears in the major publication and broadcast media. Outdoor advertising, transit advertising, and direct mail advertising may play important roles. Sales promotion in the form of specialty advertising, premiums, trade shows, contests, catalogs, ads in the Yellow Pages,[3] and various types of dealer aids or point-of-purchase advertising also may become important elements in the advertising plan. In addition, promotional activities other than advertising and sales promotion, but coordinated with them, may be made vital parts of the campaign strategy. These might include publicity and public relations (especially in its consumer relations aspects). All of these activities that are a part of the complete campaign must be related to the distribution pattern of the company and the activities of its sales force. Finally, the campaign directed to the ultimate consumer will be supplemented by a campaign directed to the dealers, properly timed so that its impact will result in adequately

DISPLAY AD

Types of advertisements found in the Yellow Pages. *Courtesy of AT&T and the Yellow Pages.*

stocked retail shelves to serve consumer demand stimulated by the consumer campaign.

The interdependence of the advertising function with other promotional and marketing activities of a business is demonstrated in present-day advertising agency services, which, as has been indicated in an earlier chapter, extend well beyond advertising as such to include almost all promotional and merchandising activities.

Publicity

We have already seen that publicity is more thoroughly read and more readily believed than advertising, but that it is not as consistently obtainable and that it cannot be as commercially promotional. Because of its advantages it can do a selling job. Because of its limitations, it cannot be depended upon to do that job alone. Therefore, publicity becomes an excellent supplement to any advertising effort if properly coordinated with it. That is, the publicity program should not be developed as something separate and apart from the advertising, but should be closely tied in with it with respect to both content and timing.

There is a distinction between company or *institutional publicity* and *product publicity*. It is the latter that must be coordinated with the advertising campaign. Some newsworthy events will occur that should be publicized but that will have little or nothing to do with the advertising campaign currently running. A promotion, a retirement, the hiring of a new executive, the settlement of a threatened labor dispute are all news and may serve the company well as publicity releases, but they contribute little directly to the advertising effort.

Marketing activities are often newsworthy enough to obtain considerable publicity. Introduction of new models, development of new products or significant improvements in old ones, new package designs, opening of new retailing establishments or branches, and the running of contests are all news and might be expected to get publicity in consumer and dealer publications or on the air. Staged or "created" news is also important as a means of obtaining publicity. Such events as the Macy's Thanksgiving Day Parade and the Tournament of Roses Parade get nationwide publicity and have unquestionable commercial value to their sponsors.

So the advertiser has at hand numerous events occurring in the normal operation of his business that can be converted into business-news publicity. He has in addition the opportunity of legitimately creating as many other newsworthy events as his imagination, time, and budget will permit.

Although the daily newspaper probably forms the backbone of most publicity programs, the consumer magazines, trade publications, radio, and television offer excellent opportunities and frequently decided advantages as publicity media.

In addition to the press release covering spot news stories, the advertiser may obtain publicity by inviting a paper to cover a newsworthy event directly. In this case, the reporter rather than a publicist will write the story. In general, such coverage is more likely to result in a published story than is the news release written by the company's publicity department and sent to the newspaper—partly because a member of the newspaper's staff wrote the story but more because of the character of the news event, which would have to be of some importance to warrant direct coverage in the first place. Much of the news sent out as publicity releases would not justify a paper's sending out a staff member to cover it.

Publicity may also be obtained through the use of feature stories, photographs, remarks passed by radio and television commentators, interviews of company representatives on radio or television programs, comments made by columnists, and speeches made by company officials. It should be kept in mind that every event has more than one publicity possibility. For example, the introduction of a new-model automobile probably is good for a spot news story and some pictures of the car. It is possible also that a feature story concerning some of the problems and human-interest aspects of designing and creating the new model may be developed for a Sunday supplement or a magazine. In like manner, a talk given by a company executive has a three-way publicity possibility: (1) an announcement that the talk is to be given, including such detail as when, where, and why; (2) a broadcast of the talk at the time of its delivery; and (3) a follow-up story about the talk that was given and of any on-the-scene happenings of interest or reactions to the speech.

Once publicity has appeared, its value to the overall campaign can be kept alive and considerably enlarged by a number of advertising devices. Reprints of the publicity story can be made and used as direct mail pieces. The story with the publication's logo can be reproduced as a poster display for store windows and counters. It can be republished in the company's magazine and distributed to dealers or customers. Reproductions can be inserted in salesmen's portfolios as an assist in making a sales presentation to customers. And the list of possibilities for getting secondary impact and value from publicity does not end here. An alert advertiser, awake to the opportunities presented by each publicity-advertising situation as it arises, can find other ways of extracting the last drop of usefulness from his publicity breaks.

Public Relations

Public relations is the broader category that encompasses publicity. Although primarily employed to cover a much wider range of operation than product promotion, it can be related to the advertising campaign strategy. In its broadest application, public relations has at least an indirect effect upon the sales-promotion activities of a business because, in general, the better a company is thought of, the more readily will its advertising claims be believed and the more readily will people be willing to try its products. Furthermore, there is a very definite interrelationship among the several publics of a business so that an improvement in relations in any one area is likely to be reflected in one or several other areas. Improvements in labor relations, in community relations, or in some other area may, therefore, have beneficial results in customer relations as well. However, it is in the more narrowly defined field of customer relations that the public-relations program most directly relates to the advertising activities.

A good customer-relations program should recognize that consumers are interested in product information, and this, in turn, should be reflected in the advertising copy. Further, since a satisfactory sales volume built up by excellent advertising may be ruined by unsatisfactory servicing of the product, the customer-relations program should anticipate this danger and provide means through the proper channels for an adequate and effective product-service system. Proper handling of complaints can turn potential ill-will to goodwill. This involves not only a satisfactory settlement of each complaint but a study of the complaints so that unsatisfactory aspects of the product or service can be corrected. All inquiries from consumers and potential consumers should be promptly answered.

In short, a public-relations program that recognizes areas of possible customer dissatisfaction and resentment and removes them, one that recognizes what customers want and, insofar as possible, gives it to them, will materially strengthen the company's advertising efforts, increase their effectiveness, and contribute to the overall campaign.

SOME CAUTIONARY THOUGHTS

Today many large advertisers rely, in the main, on television. Procter & Gamble alone puts more than 90% of its advertising budget into television. In most of the larger agencies, 70% to 90% or more of the media dollar is spent on TV. However, even those advertisers that are completely sold on television usually supplement their television selling effort through the use of other media and sales promotion.

While many advertising people agree that the effects of advertising are cumulative and that the benefits are residual, Leo Bogart, in his book *Strategy in Advertising,* finds this extremely difficult to measure:

> Advertising planners find the concept of accumulation too convenient a crutch to discard it merely on the grounds that it has no basis in valid communications theory. Under "laboratory" conditions it may be possible to measure the communications effects of an individual message in a series, in isolation from the effect of all the preceding messages. In real life it cannot be done. Campaigns in advertising exist only in the dreams and schemes of advertising generals.[4]

SUMMARY

All advertising is done to achieve a particular objective. The sum total of that advertising effort, in a specific time frame, is called the campaign.

In most cases no single ad accomplishes the objectives set forth by an advertiser. The successful campaign is usually the cumulative effort of a number of ads together with publicity, public relations, and other sales promotional efforts.

While the ultimate goal of most business is sales, objectives are steps in that direction. Objectives might include expanding the geographic market for a product or service, stimulating more people in the present geographic area to buy, and encouraging those who presently buy to buy more. Other objectives might be to introduce a new product, meet the challenge of a competitor, promote a new package or a new use. Objectives are as numerous and varied as are the advertiser's challenges and problems.

Comparative advertising is a strategy of making specific comparisons with a named product or service offered by a competitor.

Positioning is a strategy aimed at achieving a goal and an objective. Essentially positioning is finding a new use or a different segment of the market for a product and "selling" the area to prospects or potential customers.

QUESTIONS AND DISCUSSION SUBJECTS

1. What is the basis for the concept of "immediate objectives" and the "ultimate goal" in advertising campaigns, and of what significance is this concept to advertisers?
2. By what means may the value of publicity be kept alive and extended beyond the publication and distribution of the publicity as such?
3. What are the several means by which an advertiser may obtain company and product publicity?
4. Show how public-relations activity can be made to support effectively a company's advertising program.
5. Why is it difficult to measure the effect of a single advertisement?
6. List some objectives of campaigns.
7. Explain and give an example of positioning.
8. What effect does the marketing stage of the product have on the advertising?
9. Explain the relationship between publicity, public relations, and advertising.

SOURCES

1. Stanley M. Ulanoff, *Comparison Advertising: An Historical Perspective* (Cambridge, Mass.: Marketing Science Institute, 1975).
2. Leo Bogart, *Strategy in Advertising* (New York: Harcourt, 1967), 153–155.
3. *The Yellow Pages in Marketing and Advertising* (American Telephone & Telegraph Company, 1937).
4. Bogart, *op. cit.,* 157.

FOR FURTHER READING

Dudley, Homer M., Irwin Gross, and Yorom Wind. *Advertising Measurement and Decision Making*. Boston: Allyn & Bacon, 1968.

Gerlach, John T., and C. Anthony Wainwright. *Successful Management of New Products*. New York: Hastings House, Publishers, 1968.

Glatzer, Robert. *The New Advertising: Great Campaigns from Avis to Volkswagen*. New York: Citadel, 1970.

Steinberg, Charles S. *The Creation of Consent: Public Relations in Practice*. New York: Hastings House, Publishers, 1975.

Ulanoff, Stanley M. *Comparison Advertising: An Historical Perspective*. Cambridge, Mass.: Marketing Science Institute, 1975.

★
★
★
★
★
Part Three

MANAGEMENT

The Advertising Agency and the Advertising Department

THE ADVERTISING AGENCY

In 1842 Volney Palmer started a business in which he hoped to operate as an exclusive sales agent for a group of newspapers. His plan was to sell space in these papers to advertisers and in return for his services to obtain 25% commission from their publishers. This "newspaper advertising and subscription agency" was the forerunner of the advertising agency of the present, although it planned or created no advertising. (Palmer is, however, reputed to have written advertising copy, at times.)

Palmer's hope for an exclusive agency operation was short-lived, if indeed it ever materialized at all; he soon had competition from other agents as well as from the selling activities of the newspaper publishers themselves. He did, however, sell space, and by 1848 had offices in Philadelphia, New York, Boston, and Baltimore.

All agencies in this period operated solely as space brokers. That is, they sold space for a commission paid by the publisher but they performed little or no other service for either publishers or advertisers. Virgil D. Reed, speaking before the Forty-third Annual Conference of the Association of Canadian Advertisers, Inc., said of these early agencies, "Up to the emergence of the service agency, only poetic license and convenience could justify the use of the term *advertising* agency."

In 1865 an advertising agent, George P. Rowell, began operations as a "space merchant" rather than a "space broker." Rowell bought space in about one hundred newspapers and resold it in small units to advertisers. He advertised "an inch of space a month in one hundred newspapers for one hundred dollars.'' In 1870 Rowell also published a newspaper directory, the first in the United States, which came as something of a shock to his competitors. They felt that he was placing between two covers and making available to all advertisers the knowledge upon which their agencies were based.

In 1887 another agency man, J. Walter Thompson, offered to advertisers his exclusive ''List of Thirty'' magazines. Thus, between 1865 and 1880 the space-broker agency was largely replaced by the space-merchant agency. But there was still no widespread or significant attempt on the part of the agencies to render any creative advertising services or to place the advertising in the space they sold.

Between 1870 and 1880, however, forces were in operation that were destined to cause the space-merchant agency to evolve into the service agency. The publishing of the Rowell directory perhaps was a first step in this direction, even if a feeble one. Then, about 1875, some agents began to solicit advertising for one or a few newspapers instead of for a large number of smaller and widely scattered papers. These agents eventually became known as *newspaper representatives,* but in those early times they were serious competitors of the space-selling advertising agencies. By 1880, service agencies began to develop, and by the turn of the century they were very much in evidence.

In 1918, a Report on Agency Services made by a national committee of the American Association of Advertising Agencies contained a statement of agency service standards. This statement remains today, with minor changes, the *Agency Service Standards of the American Association of Advertising Agencies.* It states:

> Agency Service consists of interpreting to the public, or to that part of it which it is desired to reach, the advantages of a product or service.
>
> Interpreting to the public the advantages of a product or service is based upon:

1. A study of the product or service to determine the advantages and disadvantages inherent in the product itself, and its relation to competition.
2. An analysis of the present and potential market for which the product or service is adapted:
   As to location
   As to extent of possible sale
   As to season
   As to trade and economic conditions
   As to nature and amount of competition
3. A knowledge of the factors of distribution and sales and their methods of operation.
4. A knowledge of all the available media and means which can profitably be used to carry the interpretation of the product or service to consumer, wholesaler, dealer, contractor, or other factor. This knowledge covers:
   Character
   Influence
   Circulation: Quantity, Quality, Location
   Physical Requirements
   Costs

Acting on the study, analysis and knowledge as explained in the preceding paragraphs, recommendations are made and the following procedure ensues:

5. Formulation of a definite plan.
6. Execution of this plan:
   a. Writing, designing, illustrating of advertisements, or other appropriate forms of message.
   b. Ordering the space, or other means of advertising.
   c. The proper incorporation of the message in mechanical form and forwarding it with proper instructions for the fulfillment of the contract.
   d. Checking and verifying of insertions, displays or other means used.
   e. The auditing and billing for the service, space and preparation.
7. Co-operation with the sales work, to insure the greatest effect from advertising.

   The above outline of agency service has been made by the Association more clearly to define what it is, so that advertisers and media may know what to demand and agencies may know what may be expected of them in dealing with the problem of advertising.

An individual agency is, of course, free to determine with its clients what services it will perform.[1]

Agency Services

The major goal of advertising agency service, after agencies first became truly service organizations, was to increase the effectiveness of the client's advertising. Although the major goal of present-day advertising agencies has not changed, the number of variety of services rendered by the modern agency have increased considerably.

The advertising agency of today is more of a *marketing* agency. In addition to performing the strictly advertising services of copywriting, procurement or creation of artwork, production, purchasing of time and space, and placement of advertisements, the modern agency engages in many related functions. In performing these additional services an agency may create trademarks and trade characters, design or redesign packages, handle publicity and public relations for clients, conduct sales research, conduct sales training, produce internal and external house organs, prepare for clients such special literature as training manuals or even books pertaining to the clients' products or services, conduct or supervise market research, design merchandising displays, and—sometimes—create new products.

Some of the new and broader role of the modern advertising agency is seen in a definition given by Marion Harper, Jr., a former president of McCann-Erickson, Inc., in a speech before an annual meeting of the Association of National Advertisers:

> The modern advertising agency is an independent, professional, business service organization, planning and performing mass communication and sales development services that are integrated into the marketing and public relations programs of business and other private and public institutions.[2]

In developing the concept of an advertising agency as "an independent, professional, business service organization," Mr. Harper said:

> The independent organization offers many advantages for product quality and enterprise incentive. In its independent capacity, the advertising agency is enabled to be, and is obliged to be, objective in its counsel and free from captive opinion. It can develop marketing knowledge and skills in any and all areas of American business and apply them, as appropriate, to develop an advertiser's opportunities.
>
> . . . The agency maintains a creative and professional idea-creating and problem-solving team of a hundred or more specialized communications and sales development skills. This team can go to work almost instantly. . . .[3]

Thus, the value of a modern agency to its clients depends on expanded service, made more effective by the objective view the agency takes of its clients' advertising problems. This service is backed by skilled and highly specialized professional staffs, which many individual advertisers would find it financially impossible or highly uneconomical to maintain.

Agency-Media Relations

The various advertising media, were it not for advertising agencies, would have to maintain much larger and more costly sales departments. Quite obviously, instead of selling their space or time through relatively few advertising agencies, the media would have to sell to a very large number of widely scattered advertisers.

It was apparent at an early day in advertising that advertisers would be more interested in buying space in media if their advertisements were productive. This meant that the media became interested in having the best possible use made of the space they sold. Publishers felt that it would be necessary for them to help advertisers (some newspapers still do help small advertisers), but they realized that embarrassment might result from the need for handling competing accounts. The advertising agencies relieved them of this embarrassment in most cases.

In general, media feel that advertising agencies are of service to them in the following ways:

1. The advertising agency develops new business.
2. The agency reduces the hazards of advertising and thereby the mortality rate in the medium's business.
3. The agency advocates the idea of advertising in competition with other means of sales promotion.
4. The agency creates the advertising messages, which are an essential element in the sale of space or time that media have to sell.
5. The agency develops and improves advertising techniques and thereby increases the productivity of advertising.
6. The agency simplifies the medium's credit operations and reduces the cost of these operations.
7. The agency carries the cost of credit losses.

8. The agency simplifies the mechanical preparation of advertising and reduces the medium's cost.
9. The agency reduces the medium's cost in following up advertising schedules to meet publication or broadcasting deadlines.

Note points 6 and 7—the agency is solely liable for payments to media. The agency contracts with the medium for time or space in its own name—not the typical agency relationship practiced in business law.

It is important to recognize that the advertising agency looks with an impartial eye upon all media available for use by its clients and is neutral among media. It seeks to develop advertisers—not newspaper advertisers or television advertisers or magazine advertisers or radio advertisers or any other sort of advertisers differentiated by media. The agency seeks to use advertising and to develop the client's business. The agency can be expected to have only one prejudice—a prejudice in favor of advertising as a way to promote the sale of the client's goods or services.

The medium reserves the right to reject an advertisement or to ask for a change in any part of it. However, the medium may not make any change in an advertisement without the consent of the agency.

Agency Organization

An advertising agency may be a one-man-and-a-secretary operation, or it may be an organization employing hundreds of people and having branch offices in every important country in the world. Its annual billings may be as little as a few thousand dollars or may approach a billion.

Although agencies may be organized in any number of ways, they usually follow either a departmental or a group format. In departmentalized operations such functions as copywriting, print production, television production, art, media, and research are set up as separate departments. Larger agencies may have, in addition, departments for market development, information services, direct marketing, publicity, public relations, accounting, new business, and law. Each department is supervised by an executive, often a vice president, who is responsible for its operation; each department is responsible for serving all of the agency's clients.

In contrast to this departmental type of organization is the group type, wherein a group of specialists is assigned to one or more accounts. Such a group cuts across departmental lines and includes copywriters, television producers, artists, media specialists, research workers, and so on. The group is responsible to a creative-group head, who is often also a vice president, and to the account executive who represents the accounts assigned to it. The account executive is an employee of the agency who serves as the liaison officer between the agency and one or more clients. He may or may not be expected to serve also as a new-business man. Sometimes research, media, or some other area of the agency operation may not be represented in the group. In such cases the service or services not represented are obtained by each group from the departments involved.

A TYPICAL ADVERTISING AGENCY ORGANIZATION CHART

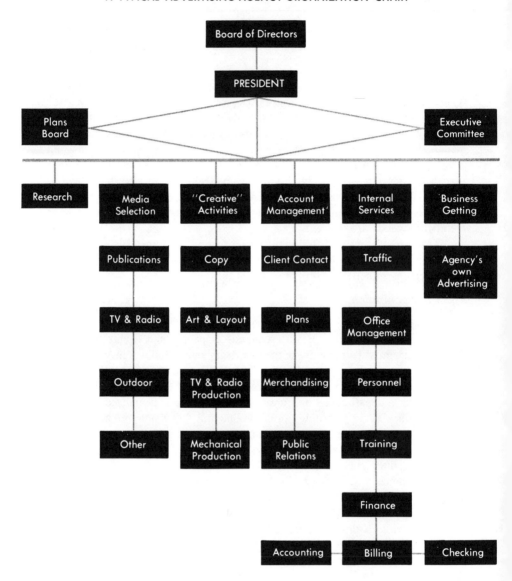

Most agencies also divide their functions on the basis of creative and management responsibilities.

There is often considerable variation from agency to agency in the extent to which various departments are developed. Some agencies may have large art departments while others may maintain a skeleton staff of artists, depending to an appreciable extent on freelance art to serve their needs. Public relations may be a well-defined department in some cases; in others, it may be a function

190

handled through a subsidiary organization. Research may be handled by a single department, or it may be subdivided as media research, marketing research, and so on.

Size and Scope

It is estimated that "some 6,000 firms design, create and produce the messages which stimulate people to buy." [4] As has been stated, these range in size from the one-man agency to such giants as J. Walter Thompson with annual billings of well over $867 million,* and the Interpublic Group which has billed more than $1 billion. *Advertising Age,* in its annual agency compilations, showed that 698 U.S. agencies billed out a record $13.6 billion during 1974! Of that amount, more than one-third, close to $5.6 billion, was billed by the top ten American advertising agencies, with the least of them producing more than $335 million in business.[5]

While these figures may seem impressive, and they most certainly are, the total expenditure for advertising is a mere 2% of our nation's gross national product. The bulk of the business is in the hands of a relatively small number of advertising agencies. Twenty-five of them had billings of more than $100 million each, and together with the remaining 47 agencies that made up the over-$25-million category they accounted for more than 75% of the $13.6 billion recorded in *Advertising Age.* [6]

A further indication of the relatively small size of the agency business is the number of people employed in it—approximately 65,000. Of these, only a fifth are in the creative end of the industry. They total 13,000—5,400 copywriters, 5,300 artists, and 2,300 involved in broadcast production.

Other Types of Agencies

The organizations described above are the traditional advertising agencies, sometimes called *full-service* houses. In contrast to them are a number of variants that have arisen relatively recently. Principal among these are *house agencies* organized by advertisers to handle their own advertising. Some provide all the services offered by full-service agencies while others utilize the services of specialty firms that furnish elements of advertising on a piecemeal or *à la carte* basis. These include independent media buying services and what are popularly known as *boutiques,* which offer creative services, ideas, and copy.[7] Andrew Kershaw, president of Ogilvy & Mather, in an address to the American Marketing Association on the future of advertising, described boutiques as "one-man advertising firms" which "sell good merchandise, in beautiful surroundings, at a high price, but do not offer satisfaction or your money back." [8] He pointed out that although they are doing very well the total billing of all boutiques was less than the annual increase alone of the J. Walter Thompson business. Kershaw did not see them as a threat to the great established full-service houses, for which he foresaw continued growth. On the other hand he

---

* These and the following figures include billing by the agencies' foreign divisions or affiliates.

said, "the good boutique, if it is successful, will become a large, full-service agency. The bad boutique will sink without a trace." [9] This contention has been supported by John Crichton,[10] president of the American Association of Advertising Agencies; by Bart Cummings,[11] chairman of the Executive Committee of Compton Advertising and past president of the American Advertising Federation, and by others.

Media buying services, the other challenge to full-service agencies, are seen by Kershaw as an example to follow and emulate in improving agency media departments. In addition he stated that the buying services "have opened our eyes to new profit possibilities." [12] Crichton's opinion is that "if the client were to take over media services, the total dollars he is likely to save are small by comparison with the share of market gains or losses." [13]

While the future of the traditional advertising agency certainly appears secure, the American Association of Advertising Agencies, in 1971, nevertheless saw fit to publish a position paper on the subject. *The Case for the Full-Service Agency* enumerates its advantages over the house shop, the advertiser's in-house agency that utilizes a boutique, and a media buying service on a fragmented "do it yourself" basis. These advantages are:

1. Centralization of responsibility and accountability.
2. Simplified coordination and administration.
3. Greater objectivity.
4. Sales-oriented creative work.
5. Synergistic experience.
6. Stronger pool of talent.
7. Promoting professional and financial strength in the marketing area.
8. May be even less costly.
9. Simplifies corrective change.
10. Better working climate and esprit de corps.[14]

In an attitude of "beat 'em at their own game," Ogilvy & Mather in New York is willing to offer the service of its individual specialized departments piecemeal to clients on a negotiated-fee basis.[15] They reason, logically, that they already have the departments and that they are functioning.

THE ADVERTISING DEPARTMENT

If one were to stop a description of the organization of the advertising business with a discussion of the advertising agency and the various regional and national associations, the story would be left less than half told. Practically all large advertisers, and many smaller ones as well, have their own advertising departments. This is true regardless of the kind of business operation in which they are engaged. Manufacturers, wholesalers and retailers, makers and sellers of consumer goods and industrial goods, advertising media, and all manner of service organizations may, and often, do have their own advertising departments. Depending upon the size of the business firm of which they are a part, these departments may range in size from one man working at advertising on a part-time basis to more than 100 employees. The head of the advertising department is commonly called an advertising manager, although he may be known as an advertising director, a vice president in charge of advertising or marketing, or by some other title. Regardless of title, his function is to manage his department and to assume responsibility for the firm's advertising.

It is common practice for manufacturing firms and service organizations, especially the medium-sized and larger ones, to use an advertising agency as well as maintain their own advertising departments. Division of work between the agency and the advertising department varies considerably. Factors and problems of internal organization and external marketing operations of individual advertisers will determine this relationship. However, in general, the advertising department will tend to handle some or all of the noncommissionable work, whereas the agency performs those tasks that are commissionable and also any others, on a fee basis, that the advertiser elects to have it handle. In other words, the advertising department (retailers excepted) usually will not be concerned with creating advertisements, purchasing advertising time and space, or placing advertisements in media. The department may or may not handle direct mail, the company's house organ, point-of-purchase advertising, the preparation of sales-training or other literature, trade shows, contests, dealer aids, and the like. It will be primarily concerned with the initial choice of an advertising agency and any subsequent change in agency affiliations. It also will be very much involved with the aproval of agency-submitted ideas, plans, and advertisements. In this connection, the advertising manager and the account executive work closely together. The advertising department usually informs company salesmen about forthcoming advertising campaigns and individual advertisements so they will be fully aware of the company's promotion efforts. Matters of advertising budget and advertising expenditures, of course, are also of vital concern to the department.

The organization of large advertising departments may be along product lines or functional lines. If a company produces a large number of different products, the advertising department may have specific subdepartments or divisions that are each responsible for a class or group of products. Often the responsibility for a product rests with a product manager whose position is analogous to that of an agency's account manager. On the other hand, if the company produces but one or a few products, the organization of the advertising department may be similar to that of a departmentalized advertising agency—one division being concerned with copy, another with production, and so on. In such cases the copy division may be concerned with direct mail, preparation of company literature, and similar jobs, whereas the production division would purchase company printing and take care of graphic-arts needs of the advertising department as a whole.

In Retail Stores

The advertising department in a retailing establishment differs from the typical manufacturer's advertising department chiefly in that it performs most or all of the advertising job. Usually, retailers do not use advertising agencies.

Hence, the whole burden of the company's advertising falls on the advertising department, which writes copy, prepares artwork, handles production detail, purchases space and/or time, places advertisements, and checks results. In addition, it may assume many of the functions performed by nonretailing advertising departments—producing catalogs, handling direct mail, and so on.

Three major reasons contribute to a retailer's not using an advertising agency, (1) The nature of his business is such that a company-operated advertising department is better adapted to the tempo of operation than an outside organization. (2) Much retail advertising is not commissionable. (3) Local advertising rates are usually lower than national rates.

The retailer requires more day-to-day change in his advertising than does the manufacturer. Sales and special events, one-time or short-term offers, leader merchandise offers to meet a sudden competitive situation, changes in offers or cancellations of advertisements because of sell-outs or inability to replenish stocks, tie-ins with local events, even changes dictated by the weather—all are a regular part of the retailer's advertising calendar. The retail advertising department is geared to such change and speed; many agencies are not. Also, operations are made easier by the proximity of the retail advertising department's staff to the merchandise to be advertised and to the store's buyers, who must approve copy and illustrations.

Much retail advertising appears in newspapers and at local rates which, as has been stated, usually are lower and carry no agency commission. Therefore, if an advertising agency handled this advertising, it would have to be on a basis other than that of media commission.

In large retail stores, advertising is often set up as a subdivision of a sales-promotion department. Other divisions of such a department might be publicity, public relations, store and window display, comparison shopping, and research. An advertising manager is generally the head of the advertising division and under his supervision are art, copy, production, and other areas directly pertaining to the advertising function.

In operation, the buyers for each of the merchandise departments of the store submit their requests for advertising to the advertising department or division. Such requests are based on the individual buyer's advertising budget and his estimated sales for the period to be covered by the advertising requested, usually one month. The advertising department then prepares a store schedule of advertising based on these requests. This often necessitates some adjustments in the original requests. Thereafter, detailed requests for specific advertisements are submitted by the buyers as advertising is need. These requests are checked by the advertising manager against the basic plan and budget. Advertisements are then created by the advertising department; these, when approved by the buyer whose merchandise they cover, are ready for publication. Normally, before the advertisements are run, sales clerks are shown proofs so that they will be aware of what the store is featuring in its advertising from day to day. Where this practice is neglected, the store is missing an opportunity to increase the effectiveness of its selling effort.

After the advertisements have been run, checks are made to determine their effectiveness. Although such checks usually are impossible to make on most manufacturers' advertising (mail order excluded), they are possible in retail advertising because of the more direct relationship between store advertising and sales.

As in most areas of human activity, there are exceptions to the general practice. Occasionally a retailer will be found who does most or all of his advertising through an advertising agency.

SUMMARY

The advertising agency as we know it today evolved from an agency, established in 1842, that more closely resembled a space broker. Thirteen years later the space brokers began to be replaced by the space merchant. The latter actually bought space in publications which he resold in small units to advertisers.

The real forerunner of today's full-service advertising agency, however, appeared by 1880. A report of the 4As, in 1918, listed services provided by advertising agencies that are, for the most part, the bill of fare offered by the modern agency.

In addition to the normal functions of copywriting, art layout, production, and placement, today's agency may provide some marketing services. These include public relations and publicity, package design, creation of trademarks, sales and market research, sales training, and more.

The media prefer to work with the advertising agency rather than directly with the advertiser. The agencies are professionals and relieve the media of a large number of tasks, for which the media allow a customary commission of 15%.

There is no set pattern of agency organization. Most, however, follow the departmental or group formats. In departmental organization each specialty, such as copy or art, is an entity unto itself. In the group set-up, copywriters, artists, researchers, and others work as a team.

Advertising expenditures amount to approximately 2% of the U.S. gross national product. The industry is relatively small, with some 6,000 agencies ranging in size from one-man firm to those employing many hundreds. In addition to the traditional full-service agency, there are specialty firms offering expertise in one particular area—copy, media buying, etc. Practitioners predict that the successful specialty house will evolve into a full-service agency and that the unsuccessful one will fall by the wayside.

Parallel to the advertising agency is the advertising department of the advertiser or client. Like the agencies, these departments range in size from one person to more than 100. Generally, the department will perform only those advertising functions that are not commissionable, leaving the commissionable tasks to the agency. However, the advertising departments of retail firms do everything that the agency does, as well, because retailers generally do not employ advertising agencies.

QUESTIONS AND DISCUSSION SUBJECTS

1. To what present-day advertising function can the first advertising "agencies" be compared?
2. Explain the difference between "space broker" and "space merchant."
3. How did the agencies which began to develop in the 1880s differ from their predecessors?
4. List as many as you can of the services performed by a present-day advertising agency. Can you think of others they could offer?
5. Why do the media prefer to do business with agencies rather than advertisers? Give seven (of the nine) reasons why.
6. Describe the two principal organizational arrangements employed by agencies.
7. What choices are available to the advertiser other than the traditional or full-service agency? Do you recommend them?
8. What do you see as the future of the advertising agency? Discuss it.
9. What is a *boutique?*
10. Give three reasons why a retailer would not ordinarily use an advertising agency.
11. What are the functions of the advertising department in a retail enterprise?

SOURCES

1. Reproduced with permission of the American Association of Advertising Agencies.
2. Marion Harper, Jr., "The Evolving Functions of the Modern Advertising Agency," a viewpoint presented at the 1956 Annual meeting of the Association of National Advertisers.
3. *Loc. cit.*
4. James V. O'Gara, "Billings of U.S. Agencies Top $11.3 Billion in 1972," *Advertising Age* February 26, 1973, 1.
5. James V. O'Gara, "U.S. Agency Billings Hit Record $13.6 Billion," *Advertising Age,* February 24, 1975, 1, 16, 53.
6. *Loc. cit.*
7. Andrew Kershaw, "The Changing Face of Agency Services," an address before the American Academy of Advertising, March 12, 1973.
8. Andrew Kershaw, "1980: Alive and Well and Living on Madison Avenue," an address before the American Marketing Association, September 8, 1970.

9. *Loc. Cit.*

10. John Crichton, *Do We Have to Repeat History?* (New York: American Association of Advertising Agencies, 1970).

11. Barton A. Cummings, "Full Service Agencies vs. à la Carte," *Journal of Advertising,* 2 (May 1973), 12–15.

12. Kershaw, "1980," *op. cit.*

13. Crichton, *op. cit.,* 5.

14. John Monsarrat, *The Case for the Full Service Agency* (New York: American Association of Advertising Agencies, 1971), pp. 7–17.

15. Kershaw, "1980," *op. cit.*

FOR FURTHER READING

Advertising—A Guide to Careers in Advertising. New York: American Association of Advertising Agencies, 1975.

"The Centennial of the J. Walter Thompson Company." *Advertising Age,* December 7, 1964.

Gerson, Irving B. *Tomorrow's Advertising Agency.* Chicago: Geron Howe and Johnson, 1970.

Miracle, Gordon E., and Bernard M. Bullard. "Evolution of Advertising Agencies," a paper presented at the American Academy of Advertising National Conference, April 20, 1975.

Weinberg, Charles. *Advertising Management.* New York: Harper & Row, 1974.

What Advertising Agencies Are What They Do and How They Do It. New York: American Association of Advertising Agencies, 1976.

13

Management and Organization in the Advertising Business

While creativity is generally acknowledged to be the most important function of the advertising agency, the people who manage the agency obviously play an important part, as well. They hire the creative people, pay their salaries, obtain new business, work with the client, and generally supervise day-to-day operation.

ACCOUNT MANAGEMENT

The management person with whom the client comes into contact most is the account executive. He is the liaison between the client and the agency. He is one among three degrees of account managers. In order of increasing importance they are the account executive, the account supervisor, and the management supervisor.

According to a brochure prepared by Compton Advertising for its clients and prospective clients, an advertiser should expect from his agency's account manager these services:

> You should expect your account manager to be an intelligent businessman with a thorough understanding of *your* business. He should be able to see things through your eyes, and at the same time bring a fresh, objective viewpoint to your problems, needs and opportunities.
>
> He should represent your interests at the agency, and take responsibility for coordinating the activities of all the various specialists in the agency departments. He should plan and manage the total agency effort on your account, arrange the workload in proper priorities, and put the empahsis where the results will be most

productive in relation to your objectives. He should be able to motivate other people to do their best work on your behalf, and to get it done on time.

You should expect him, in addition, to be frank and open with you . . . a constant source of new ideas . . . a good presenter and an even better listener.[1]

In a similar "new business" pamphlet, Kenyon and Eckhardt described its account people's responsibility for clients' corporate profits as opposed to corporate sales:

One of the great fallacies of much of yesterday's marketing thinking was the undue emphasis it placed on sales and the small emphasis it placed on profits. A lot of people have mistakenly used the so-called "marketing concept" to build themselves a sales-oriented bureaucracy, rather than a profit-oriented business.

We believe that all of this has got to be changed—and that, in any healthy future advertiser-agency relationship, it will be changed.

At K&E our account people—that is to say our account executives, account supervisors, and management supervisors—approach our clients' advertising problems first on a profit basis, on the basis of the advertiser's own profit objectives, not on some vague thing called a marketing basis, or a research basis, or even a creativity basis. They're instructed to build their plans and recommendations, to the greatest extent possible, and to the degree that a particular advertiser will allow it, on an intimate knowledge of a client's profit goals—the cold-turkey, dollars-and-cents returns he seeks on investments.

Obviously, to do this requires a kind of business maturity and savvy, undreamed of in an old-fashioned agency. It involves working with clients in a different, much more intimate, highly confidential way. It requires the use of business tools, figures and compilations which never used to be looked at by most agency men.

Among these, for instance, is a whole series of what we at K&E call "critical numbers"—the relationships in a client's operation and those of his competitors, of profits to sales, advertising to sales, sales to sales goals, profit to profit goals for different product and product lines, over a period of years, and in the face of new and varied types of competition.

Sure, it requires a lot of hard work, skillful work, hard-headed business work, to understand and use such tools, but we find that this is where sound advertising planning should start, and we expect to do more and more of such work in the years ahead.

We also believe that concentration on profit objectives helps to clarify the role of advertising in a corporation's over-all activities.

Advertising, viewed in the light of profits, is not just an attempt to build an "image" or win a high broadcast or readership rating or achieve a so-called "communication goal." It is one of several powerful forces which, together with a corporation's research, production, distribution, pricing, and other factors, are directed along dollars-and-cents lines. And when you recognize this, it is much easier to assess the contribution which advertising should be called upon to make.

Finally, we believe that, in the long run, the concentration by an agency on a client's profit objectives will help to clear up the confusion and duplication of activities and responsibilities between advertiser and agency which now hamper many of these relations.

Not only the role of advertising itself, but the highly specialized role and important contribution of the advertising agency are then seen in a new light.[2]

David Ogilvy, in an institutional newspaper ad run in 1972, sees his Management Supervisors stimulating the agency "service departments to do great work for clients": [3]

Our Management Supervisors are equivalent to the partners in great law firms. They must be stable, courageous, professional and imaginative.

They must work in partnership with our creative people—neither bullying them nor knuckling under to them.

This is not a job for lazy, frightened mediocrities, nor for superficial "contact" men.[4]

OVERALL AGENCY MANAGEMENT

In advertising agencies as in any other industry, there are people responsible for the running and operation of the business. Ogilvy offers advice here, too:

The key to success in management lies in this concept of PARTNERSHIP. Partnership between the Heads of our offices and their colleagues at the Round Table.* Partnership between our 57 offices around the world.

Happy partnerships are as difficult to sustain as happy marriages. The challenge can be met if those concerned have clear-cut divisions of responsibility and don't poach on the other fellow's preserves.

"Why beholdest thou the mote that is in thy brother's eye, but considerest not the beam that is in thine own eye?"
Superior service to our clients depends on making the most of the men and women on your staff.

Give them challenging opportunities, recognition for achievement, job enrichment, and *responsibility*.

Treat them as grown-ups—and they will grow up.

Help them when they are in difficulty. Be affectionate and human, not cold and impersonal.

Give outstanding performers spectacular rewards. Nothing is too good for our make-or-break individuals.

Encourage free communication *upward*. Senior men have no monopoly on great ideas.

Nor do art directors and copywriters. Some of the best ideas come from clients, account executives, researchers and others.

Don't be a hermit

Do not summon people to your office—it frightens them. Instead, go to see them in *their* offices.

A Chairman who never wanders about his agency becomes a hermit, out of touch with his staff.

Never hire relatives or friends.

* The Round Table refers to top management at Ogilvy & Mather.

Sack incurable politicians.

Crusade against paper warfare. Encourage your people to air their disagreements face-to-face.

Discourage secrecy.

Discourage poaching.

Compose sibling rivalries.

Avoid duplication of function—two people doing a job which one could do.

Disciplines

In all our departments, our top people must instill a healthy discipline. Due dates must be met. The staff must arrive on time. Telephones must be answered politely. Security must be policed.

It is also the duty of our top people to sustain unremitting pressure on the *professional standards* of their staffs. They must never tolerate mediocre creative work or sloppy plans.

In our competitive business, it is suicide to settle for second-rate performance.[5]

Perhaps the best summary of what an advertiser can expect from his agency management people is presented by Compton Advertising:

The ability to build a strong and effective staff—to select strong people and to provide for them organizational structures and procedures and an environment which will achieve meaningful interrelationships, strong incentives and involvement, and performance at peak levels.

The ability to keep that staff ever in the vanguard of new thinking, new ideas, new processes—to keep their thinking stirred and flexible.

The desire and know-how and courage to run a profitable agency operation—for without profits no agency can offer the type of meaningful current and long-term incentives which make possible the accomplishment of the above goals.

As deep an involvement in the output of the agency—its advertising product—as in administrative matters. Internally this means an open-door policy to those key employees trained to keep their management well informed, or gentle but firm intrusion into those operations run by traditional loners. Externally, it means sufficient continuing contact with client management so that agency management involvement can lend meaningful and broad perspective to agency recommendations.

A climate of moral leadership and pride-in-organization aimed at achieving maximum output with greatest efficiency, at putting forth one's best possible effort, at producing advertising which is effective and compelling while equally being honest, in good taste, and a credit to the client and the advertising profession. In the fiscal area, such leadership entails achieving accurate cost accounting, prompt billing, prompt paying, strict accountability, and a willingness to open the books whenever requested to client audit and review.

An involvement in the world in which we all live and a willingness to contribute time and effort not only to worthwhile social, religious and humanitarian causes—but perhaps even more importantly a willingness to commit to and fight for the competitive free enterprise system which has made this country great.[6]

BRANCH MANAGEMENT

Very few, if any, of the large advertising agencies do not have branch offices in their own country and throughout the world. As early as 1848, Volney Palmer in his pioneer "agency" had three branch offices in the principal cities of the Northeast.

Not only do the agencies have offices in the largest metropolitan areas, but some also maintain branches near the home offices of their principal clients. For example, an agency with an automobile account might have a branch office in Detroit and an agency representing Procter & Gamble might have an office in Cincinnati.

The selection and retention of branch managers then becomes another important function of agency management. While there is no great wealth of literature on this particular subject, David Ogilvy provided some information relative to the way it is handled at his agency:

> Our offices must be headed by the kind of men who command respect. Not phonies or zeros.
>
> *Qualifications for the Heads of Our Offices:*
>
> 1. High standards of personal ethics.
> 2. A *big* man, without pettiness—a formidable individual.
> 3. Stable, guts under pressure, resilence in adversity, a keep keel.
> 4. Brilliant brain—not a safe plodder.
> 5. Commitment—dedicated, a hard worker.
> 6. A streak of unorthodoxy—the urge to innovate.
> 7. The courage to face tough decisions, including firing non-performers.
> 8. Inspiring enthusiasm—with infectious gusto.
> 9. Decisive—speed in grasping nettles.
> 10. Ability to hire and promote good people.
>
> If you treat your lieutenants as subordinates, they will be less effective in their jobs; they will come to resent their subordination.
>
> Our Top Management in each country should function like a Round Table, with none of the overt discipline of a military hierarchy and its demeaning pecking order.
>
> An egalitarian structure encourages independence, responsibility and loyalty. It reduces dependence on ONE MAN, who is sometimes absent, often fallible and always mortal.[7]

AGENCY OWNERSHIP

Advertising agencies in the beginning were regarded as a personal type of business. They were owned entirely by their principals, as individuals or partnerships. Later, even when many assumed the corporate structure which offered limited liability, management still owned all of the stock. It was not until 1962, in a period when it was very fashionable to "go public," that Papert, Koenig, Lois became a public corporation. During the 1960s, more advertising agencies sold their stock to the public. Principal among these were Foote, Cone & Belding and Wells, Rich, Green. By 1973, the agencies that had become publicly owned corporations included J. Walter Thompson, Grey Advertising, Interpublic, Ogilvy & Mather, Doyle Dane Bernbach, and Needham, Harper & Steers. Hesitantly on the brink were Batten, Barton, Durstine & Osborn and Carl Ally.[8] Finally BBD&O went public but Carl Ally had not, as late as 1976.

Where agencies have become public corporations, some shares of stock are kept in the hands of management. And the value of the stock, being established by the market, helps in the recruiting of personnel and makes it easy to handle retirements, employee stock options, and profit sharing.

The public corporate structure has also enabled some agencies to diversify. J. Walter Thompson, for example, is in the casualty insurance business in Puerto Rico. It also leases vehicles and industrial equipment, and is a partner in a travel agency. Wells, Rich, Green produced a full-length feature motion picture, and Doyle Dane Bernbach is the successful manufacturer of plastic-hull sailboats.

On the negative side of the public corporate situation was Clinton E. Frank, a Chicago-based agency that had sold its stock to the public. The management became disenchanted with the results. In a falling market the value of their stock had depreciated considerably and by the end of 1973 the firm had begun to buy back its outstanding shares. A year later, Wells, Rich, Green took advantage of a deeply depressed stock market to buy back their stock.[9]

HIRING AND RECRUITING

In Chapter 11 it was stated that advertising agencies employ approximately 65,000 people. (This total does not include those employed in manufacturers', wholesalers', and retailers' advertising departments, in the media, and in other phases of advertising.) Of the relatively small number at the agencies, many possess highly specialized skills, particularly the 13,000 creative people. "The creative function," according to Ogilvy, "is the most important." It is therefore incumbent on management to seek out and hire the best people it can find. Here is his recipe for accomplishing the task.

> Your paramount *hiring* problem is this: Advertising is one of the most difficult functions in industry, and too few brilliant people want careers in it.
>
> 1. Make a conscious effort to avoid recruiting pedestrian hacks.
> 2. Create an atmosphere of ferment, innovation and freedom. This will attract brilliant recruits.
> 3. If you ever find a man who is better than you are—hire him. If necessary, pay him more than you pay yourself.
>
> In recruitment and promotion we are fanatical in our hatred for all forms of prejudice. We have no prejudice for or against Roman Catholics, Protestants, Negroes, aristocracy, women, Jews, agnostics or foreigners.[10]

Before World War II a young college graduate usually began his advertising career in the mail room or traffic department of an agency. If he had the ability he worked his way up. Depending on his own particular skills, he climbed the ladder leading to a top position in management or in the creative side of the business. Many who followed this path rose to the presidency or chairmanship of some of the world's largest agencies.

Shortly after World War II and up until a few years ago, BBD&O and some of the other larger agencies conducted training programs for beginning account managers. For the most part, however, these programs no longer exist. Today, the agencies seek their beginning junior account people from among recent Master of Business Administration (M.B.A.) graduates with a Marketing and/or Advertising specialization. Some also advance able young people from Media and other departments.

One unique arrangement is the cooperative training program of Baruch College, the senior School of Business of the City University of New York and the largest School of Business in the United States. Approximately 15 seniors majoring in advertising are selected each semester for this practical course. They attend a one-hour seminar at the college, along with their other courses, and work 15 to 20 hours each week at a participating advertising agency, advertiser, or medium. In addition to receiving three semester hours of credit and getting paid for their work, they get practical experience which often leads to full-time employment at the cooperating firm. Long-time participants in the program are Ted Bates, Carl Ally, and Leber Katz Partners, among others.

Baruch College's advertising cooperative program provides benefits to all concerned. The students get on-the-job training and an opportunity for full-time jobs on graduation; the company gets the skilled young people it needs; and the course instructor maintains his contacts with working practitioners.

AGENCY COMPENSATION

Advertising agencies customarily receive a 15% commission * from media for the space and time they purchase for client use. For example, if a medium's published rate is $1,000 for a given amount of space, the agency's commission of 15% amounts to $150. Therefore the total amount due the medium from the agency is $850, or $1,000 less $150. The medium usually allows 2% cash discount, but this discount is a percent of the amount billed to the agency, not of the list price of the space—in other words, 2% on $850, or $17. This cash discount is normally passed on to the client by the agency. Therefore, the client pays the agency $1,000 (the list price of the space) less $17 (the cash discount received by the agency), or a total of $983. The agency, it will be recalled, paid the medium $833 for this space, so the difference ($983 less $833) represents the agency commission of $150 or 15% on the list price of the space. The following figures may make this somewhat clearer:

* The commission for outdoor advertising is usually 16⅔%.

1. List price of space or time $1,000
2. Agency commission (15%)   150
3. Cost of space or time to agency (line 1 less line 2)   850
4. Cash discount (2% of line 3)   17
5. Agency pays medium (line 3 less line 4)   833
6. Client pays agency (line 1 less line 4)   983
7. Agency retains   150

The income from commissions allowed by media accounts for about three-quarters of the total income of the larger agency. About 20% of the income comes from the agency's own *percentage charges* on materials and services purchased for clients. These percentage charges are added to the cost of materials or services purchased by the agency for a client. Such materials and services might include finished artwork, photography, plates and mats, typesetting, research incidental to the creation of the advertisements, and so on. The remaining 5% of the income represents fees for special services performed by the agency that are not incidental to the creation of the client's advertising. Examples of such services would include, among other things, handling a client's publicity and public relations, preparing a client's house organ, or conducting a major market-research job. In general, the performance of any such work that is not commissionable would command a *service fee*.

Fees and percentage charges, unlike commissions, are not uniform from agency to agency, and there are some services that are billed to the client at cost by some agencies. Most agencies apply a charge of 17.65%, which is equivalent to the 15% commission.

Smaller agencies earn a lesser amount of their total income from media commission and a higher percentage from fees than their larger counterparts.

The profit incentive for the advertising agency is to earn the commissions allowed by media, together with its own percentage charges and the fees paid for its creative work. If the results are successful for the advertiser, they are also successful for the agency. If they are not, the advertising stops and the agency loses the account in question. For this reason, the agency business has attracted the aggressively independent businessman—one who is willing to take the risk that his agency won't be paid at all if its creative work is not used. The agency is paid by the advertiser only after the advertising has appeared. Also, because the agency is rewarded in proportion to the use made of its creative work, the agency owner is encouraged to hire the best creative people he can find. This means that the best possible creative organization is put behind the service and development of advertising.

In recent years, the commission method as a means of compensating advertising agencies has been questioned by some advertisers, and in 1954 the Department of Justice started an investigation of the advertising business for possible antitrust violations. One practice under question at the time was that of setting uniform agency commissions. Complaints were issued by the Justice Department against the American Association of Advertising Agencies and five leading media associations. All six denied the charges but agreed to stop any practices that were questioned by the government. This *consent decree* affected practices related to the granting of advertising-agency recognition by media associations, restrictions on rebating of commissions by agencies, and restrictions on the use of speculative presentations by agencies—more than it affected, in any direct manner, the commission method of agency compensation.

In 1956 the Association of National Advertisers sponsored a study of the advertising business by Professors Albert Frey and Donald Davis of Dartmouth College. Considerable emphasis in the final report on this study was placed on the question of agency compensation, 150 pages out of a total of 275 being devoted to this subject. The report indicated that there was some dissatisfaction among advertisers, and to a lesser extent among media, with the commission method of agency compensation. However, in the opinion of many in the advertising business, the Frey Report gives an overall endorsement to the commission method. It is pointed out in the report that if the views of those who consider the media commission method of compensation satisfactory are combined with those who consider it not satisfactory but practical, one obtains in every category—advertisers, agencies and media—an overwhelming endorsement of the commission method. On this basis, advertising managers, agencies, and media record between 80% and 90% acceptance of the commission basis of compensation. Therefore, it is unlikely that any major change in the means of compensating advertising agencies will occur in the near future. There has been, however, a trend over the past several years for a larger percentage of total income to be derived from fees and other charges. With the expanding services rendered by agencies, this trend is likely to continue.

An advertising agency must be "recognized" by a medium before it can receive a commission. Recognition, in most cases, was recommended or granted by the media associations prior to the consent decree of 1956. At present, individual media rather than their associations decide whether they will give an agency commissions. The rate of agency commission is determined by each medium and is allowed on whatever conditions the medium may choose to establish.

Variations of the commission basis of compensation are employed by almost all advertising agencies. Such variations include: (1) media commission plus percentage charges added to cost of materials and services purchased for the client; (2) media commission plus percentage charges added to cost of materials and services purchased for the client plus charges for services performed inside the agency or by the agency's employees; (3) a fee agreed upon with the client, crediting media commissions; (4) a percentage of the client's expenditure, crediting media commissions; (5) the agency's cost of handling the account (or cost plus), crediting media commissions; (6) a minimum fee; or (7) a fee plus a percentage of the client's profits.

Although there are any number of combinations of compensation systems, the principal alternative to the straight commission is the 100% fee basis. In 1964 Bernard Gallagher in his report on *The Standard Procedure for Advertising Agency Selection and Compensation* [11] recommended the 100% fee compensation. In support of this position the report states that the writer had discussed the situation with the chief executives of over 25 leading advertisers, all of whom favored the 100% fee. The report also indicated that General Foods operated on a fee basis with two agencies—Young & Rubicam and Ogilvy & Mather. The latter also had 100% fee agreements with a number of national advertisers that included Sears Roebuck, KLM, Shell Oil, American Express, and Nationwide Insurance.

Like all compensation arrangements, the 100% fee basis would be negotiated and agreed to by both client and agency. According to Gallagher it should include guaranteed compensation for all direct and indirect costs plus a 15% profit.

David Ogilvy is a particularly outspoken advocate of the fee system. He summed up the case for fees vs. commissions, thus:

Fee or Commission?

We offer our clients a choice of fee or commission. Fees offer four advantages:

1. The advertiser pays for what he gets—no more, no less.
2. Every fee account pays its own way. Unprofitable accounts do not ride on the coat-tails of profitable accounts.
3. The agency has an incentive to provide noncommissionable services.
4. Unforeseen cuts in advertising expenditure do not result in temporary personnel layoffs.

   Then there is the commission system, and some clients prefer it. Both systems will continue for years to come. We should be open-minded about them.[12]

Nevertheless, the commission basis seems to remain the predominant compensation system. The American Association of Advertising Agencies in the 1976 edition of *What Advertising Agencies Are—What They Do and How They Do It* [13] show commissions as the principal form of agency compensation. In an address before the 59th annual meeting of the Association of National Advertisers Edward L. Bond, Jr., chairman of Young & Rubicam and at the time chairman of the 4As, thought "that the basic commission system will continue to be the nucleus of agency compensation. But much greater use will be made of special fee arrangements to supplement it." [14] Ogilvy & Mather, which had pioneered the fee system in 1960 and predicted that it would replace commissions by 1970, acknowledged that commissions still accounted for more than three-quarters of the income for all agencies in 1973. And at that time only half of Ogilvy & Mather's income came from fees.[15]

AGENCY-CLIENT RELATIONS

Although the relationship between an agency and any given client may vary as the needs and problems of the clients differ, some basic patterns of relationship have developed. For example, it is usual for an agency not to handle competing accounts. That is, at any one time an agency will not handle the advertising for two different advertisers who market the same or very similar products. In turn, the client usually agrees not to hire the services of a second advertising agency without the knowledge and consent of the first agency. It is also customary for an agency to obtain approval from the client for all expenditures made by the agency in connection with the client's advertising. It is customary for the agency to pass on to its clients any cash discounts allowed by media, providing that the client pays the agency's bill in time to permit the agency to obtain the discount. If a client fails to pay the agency for time or space in which its advertising appeared, the agency is liable to the media. However, the agency usually is not responsible if media or suppliers of materials fail to meet their obligations. In a more recent development, advertising agencies have become liable for the promotional claims they make on behalf of their clients, even if the client warrants that they are true.

New Business

The secret to growth in the advertising agency business is to help present clients increase their profits so that they, in turn, will increase their advertising budgets, and continue the upward cycle. In addition, management has another important growth resource—new business, the acquisition of new accounts or clients.

In the early days of the industry it was the usual practice for the account manager to seek out his own clients and bring them to the agency. This practice persists today among the smaller agencies. In the larger agencies, however, account managers are assigned to clients. They have very little to do with the acquisition of new business, with the possible exception of having participated in initial presentations.

Most of the leading agencies have new-business departments staffed with top-level executives whose prime job is to seek out, solicit, and acquire new accounts.

There are many different ways in which a new account can come to an agency. As has been stated, it can be solicited by the agency, but very often the initiative comes from the client. The client may simply call in the agency and offer the account to it, or may ask a number of agencies to present bids. Bids can result in elaborate and costly presentations by the competing agencies. These bids can include complete campaigns with examples of print ads and television commercials. Sometimes, but not often, the prospective client offers to pay for or share the cost of the presentation.

New clients are not always welcomed by agencies. They may be competitors of existing accounts, they may be expensive or troublesome to handle, or the cost of making the bid may be too high. David Ogilvy had this to say about new business:

> The most difficult decisions are which new accounts to take and which to reject. The primary considerations should be:
>
> 1. Does anyone in our Top Management really want the account? We should never take a new account unless at least one of our key men can approach it with tremendous enthusiasm.

2. Are we convinced that good advertising can sell the product?
3. Would the marriage be a happy one? Unhappy marriages do not fructify—and they do not last.
4. Has the account potential for growth?

The prime responsibility for new business must lie with the Head of the office. Our Heads should not allow Management Supervisors to spend too much of their time in this area; their prime responsibility must always be to our present clients.[16]

International and Multinational Agencies

While it is recorded that an American advertising agency had a foreign office as far back as 1899,[17] multinational agencies are a relatively recent innovation. United States agencies have either established their own branches or bought into existing foreign agencies in countries around the world. Each multinational agency, with its principal headquarters in the United States, owns varying shares of its individual foreign affiliates. However, it appears to be the general rule that foreign nationals—natives—are placed in the principal management and creative spots in their own countries. The logic is self-evident—nationals of the country can certainly relate better to their compatriots.

As we stated above, the big international move by American agencies is relatively recent. Members of the American Association of Advertising Agencies had only 44 offices outside North America in 1952. Twenty years later these had grown tenfold to well over 400. And the international billings of these agencies, during 1972, comfortably exceeded $2 billion.[18]

Each of the 20 leading American advertising agencies owns all or a part of at least one foreign agency. While in most cases the highest percentage of billing is from the United States, top-ranking J. Walter Thompson bills $466 million outside the country and $401.5 million here. Five of the other top agencies are in a similar position with a greater share of their billings coming from foreign markets.[19]

Up to this point we have discussed only American advertising agencies. While it is true that the agency is an American creation, in recent years there has been a great deal of advancement in this field in other parts of the world. The greatest areas of growth have been in Japan, Western Europe, Canada, and Great Britain. Of the world's top 55 advertising agencies, 17 are *not* American-owned or affiliated. Eleven of these are Japanese, including the world's first-ranking agency, Dentsu Advertising Ltd., with $907.7 million in billing. With this exception, the next top 12 biggest world advertising agencies are American.[20,21]

ADVERTISING ASSOCIATIONS

The advertising business, like most other areas of commercial and professional activity, has its trade associations and other organizations designed to support and better the position of the industry.

American Association of Advertising Agencies

Of the several associations and groups of agencies in the advertising field, perhaps one of the most influential and best-known is the American Association of Advertising Agencies, the "4As," which was established in 1917. This association is national in scope and comprises 392 advertising-agency members, who place approximately 75% of the advertising handled by all United States agencies and who employ more than half of the people working in agencies in this country. Its members agencies are organized into three regions and 20 councils. These handle local problems. Twenty national committees and the executive office of the Association in New York City are concerned with the broader problems of the industry. The stated purposes of the 4As are:

1. To protect, strengthen, and improve the advertising-agency business.
2. To advance the cause of advertising as a whole.
3. To give service to its members.

The 4As has worked with other associations in the advertising field to bring to advertising broad benefits that could not have been achieved without cooperative effort. For example, in 1936 the 4As and the Association of National Advertisers (ANA) established the Advertising Research Foundation. In like manner, the Traffic Audit Bureau had a three-way sponsorship from the 4As, and ANA, and the Outdoor Advertising Association of America. As we shall see in a later chapter, the major functions of the Traffic Audit Bureau are to certify traffic counts, evaluate poster locations, and conduct research in the outdoor medium. The 4As also helped found the Advertising Council; it obtains the volunteer agencies for the Council's campaigns, underwrites the agencies' share of Council financing, names agency representatives on the Council Board, and distributes campaign material to the advertising agencies throughout the country. It also seeks out blacks and other minorities for employment in the industry.

These and other projects with which the 4As is associated all work toward the advancement of advertising by providing the advertiser and the advertising agency with the basic factual material necessary to do a scientific and economical job.

Association of National Advertisers

The Association of National Advertisers, organized in 1910, is an association of more than 400 business firms engaged in national advertising. Hence its membership, which includes 90 of the 100 largest users of advertising, comprises advertisers rather than advertising agencies. The ANA has a staff of full-time workers, a Board of Directors, five Policy Committees, and many task groups to do the work of the association. Like the 4As, ANA has worked in the broader areas related to the advertising business and advertising interests. It has been actively associated with the work of the Advertising Council, assisting in the distribution of campaign materials. The ANA states that its major purposes are:

1. To provide a clearing house for members where advertisers can pool their mutual interests.
2. To provide the means for advertisers' collective dealings with advertising media.
3. To provide the means for advertisers' collective dealings with government.
4. To provide the means for advertisers' collective dealings with advertising agencies.
5. To provide the means for building sound public, community, and employee relations in order to maintain a healthy climate for business and for advertising.

American Advertising Federation

The organization that was to become the American Advertising Federation came into being in 1905 when a number of advertising clubs, notably those in Chicago, Cincinnati, Detroit, St. Louis, Cleveland, and Indianapolis, associated themselves in an effort to improve advertising procedures and to eliminate abuses which were all too common at that time.

The first truth-in-advertising campaign was organized and promoted by this group in 1912. Further, the recommendations by President Woodrow Wilson in 1914 that a Federal Trade Commission be formed and the subsequent activation of the Commission in 1915 were the results of the efforts of this group of clubs. Clubs in various cities also formed vigilance committees to publicize and upgrade the standards of advertising. Out of this particular activity the Better Business Bureaus developed.

The movement for better advertising spread rapidly not only across the United States but into foreign countries as well, and the clubs involved became known for a time as the Associated Advertising Clubs of the World. However, the depression of the 1930s caused this group to shrink to national proportions, and it became the Advertising Federation of America. More recently, it moved its headquarters from New York to Washington, D.C., and again modified its name to the American Advertising Federation, or AAF.

In its effort to create a better understanding of advertising, the AAF works with colleges and secondary schools as well as with the general public. It sponsors an annual high-school essay contest, serves as a clearing house for information related to the advertising business, and through its Educational Committee plans to work with educators to improve advertising education.

The Federation takes active leadership to combat unfair and discriminatory taxation of advertising. There have been efforts by several states in recent years to enact gross sales taxes or special taxes on advertising. It should not be inferred that the AAF opposes all legislation designed to regulate or control advertising. In fact, the Federation has supported constructive legislation.

The American Advertising Federation is a nonprofit horizontal organization representing all advertising interests—agencies, advertisers, service organizations in the advertising field, and media. Its membership consists of these several different types of advertising business plus the advertising clubs and associations.

American Academy of Advertising

The American Academy of Advertising was established in 1953 as a national organization with a major objective of elevating and maintaining standards of advertising education and business practice. Its membership comprises college and university professors of advertising, and advertising practitioners (associate members) who wish to contribute to the teaching of advertising at the college level. The Academy is affiliated with the American Advertising Federation. Its purposes are:

1. To coordinate the effort to advance advertising education.
2. To assume leadership to appraise advertising.
3. To emphasize the value of professional education for advertising.
4. To study, evaluate, and improve advertising education.
5. To stimulate research concerning advertising education.
6. To develop closer liaison between academic disciplines.
7. To encourage closer cooperation among teachers of advertising.

Association of Industrial Advertisers

The idea for a national organization of industrial advertisers was conceived in 1921 at the Atlanta Convention of the Associated Advertising Clubs of the World (AACW). In 1922, the forerunner of the Association of Industrial Advertisers (AIA) began as a department of the AACW. It became a separate group several years later and was known until 1959 as the National Industrial Advertisers Association. That year it assumed the name it now bears. The following year it spun off the predecessor organization of the Marketing Communication Research Center. However, relations between the two groups continue to be close.

AIA has a membership of more than 3,000 professionals from companies engaged in business-to-business selling, advertising agencies serving such firms, business magazines, and companies providing consulting and other supporting services. AIA represents its entire industry—advertisers, advertising agencies, and media. Members belong to 35 chapters throughout the United States and Canada, with new chapters being formed in other parts of the world.

The association is very education-conscious. It offers four student scholarships annually and places ads in 58 undergraduate college newspapers "explaining how advertising contributes socially and economically." Its principal objective, as stated in its constitution, is to develop the art and science of advertising and marketing to business and industry."

International Advertising Association

While all of the advertising associations covered in this chapter are essentially American, the International Advertising Association, or IAA, has a worldwide membership of more than 2,600 employed in advertising, marketing, and related fields. Both the individual members and a number of corporate sustaining members represent advertisers, agencies, and media.

IAA members are located in more than 75 countries and have 40 Chapters in the principal advertising centers of the world. (Since some countries do not have a Chapter, all members do not necessarily belong to one.) Association World Congresses, which boast attendances of greater than 1,000, had been held annually, until 1974, after which they were scheduled on a biennial basis. The 25th World Congress was held in Buenos Aires in May, 1976. In addition to the Congresses are special conferences, symposia and seminars conducted in the advertising metropolises of the world.

IAA governing bodies are a 160-member World Council representing all countries in which there are members, and a 47-member Board of Directors. The World Secretariat is located at IAA headquarters in New York City. It is headed by an Executive Director, who serves as Managing Director of the Association. A European Secretariat is based in London.

IAA Standards and Objectives are expressed best in their own words:

1. The primary goal of IAA is to advance the level of advertising and marketing proficiency throughout the world for the benefit of the consuming public. IAA encourages strict adherence to codes of ethics, such as the International Code of Advertising Practice of the International Chamber of Commerce, and seeks to enhance the prestige of advertising. IAA is dedicated to improvement in every facet of communications among business, government and the public.

2. IAA informs its members around the world of trends and developments affecting their interests, and stimulates among its members the interchange of ideas, experiences and skills. The Association has been doing this since its founding in 1938 through a series of World Advertising Congresses, Chapter and Regional meetings, special reports, educational projects, answering of inquiries and periodic publications.

3. Above all, IAA is constantly aware of its full responsibility to recognize the interests and safeguard the well-being of consumers everywhere.

ADS

Formerly known as Alpha Delta Sigma, ADS changed to its present name in 1971. As the "national professional advertising society" it has 32 active undergraduate chapters on 32 campuses throughout the country. The primary purpose of the society is to give advertising students an opportunity to meet important people in the field and to gain practical experience. It also provides the opportunity to develop employment contacts prior to graduation.

In addition to the college chapters, there are ADS professional chapters in 10 principal cities in all parts of the nation. Many of the professional members are former members of undergraduate chapters.

ADS is affiliated with the American Advertising Federation.

Public Utilities Advertising Association

The Public Utilities Advertising Association represents public utilities advertisers. It has no paid officers, and no headquarters as such. The PUAA is affiliated with the American Advertising Federation. Its "Standards of Practice,'' which were adopted by the founders in 1922 and are still maintained intact by the Association, are:

1. To consider the interests of the public foremost.
2. To claim no more, but if anything a little less, in our advertising than we can deliver.
3. To refrain from statements in our advertising which, through ambiguity or through incompleteness, are likely to be misleading to the public, or unjust to competitors.
4. To use every possible means, not only in our own individual advertising but by association and cooperation, to increase the public's confidence in advertised statements.

Advertising Association of the West

The Pacific Advertising Clubs Association was organized on the Pacific Coast in 1903. This regional association later became the Advertising Association of the West, or the AAW. Like the 4As and the AAF, it works to advance the interests of the advertising business and has a strong educational interest and program. The several advertising clubs of the West run educational projects of various kinds, and the permanent educational committee of AAW coordinates these operations. It is affiliated with the AAF.

League of Advertising Agencies

The League of Advertising Agencies, established in 1951, also serves advertising agencies but is more local in character than the 4As. Among its functions is the gathering and disseminating of information of value to its agency members and to advertisers.

Other Associations

Among related associations is the Business/Professional Advertising Association (B/PAA), which has been in existence for more than 50 years and has a membership exceeding 3,000 professional marketing communicators. It is based in New York City.

Another such association is the Marketing Communications Executives International.

Of paramount importance is the Council of Better Business Bureaus which sponsors the National Advertising Division (NAD) and the National Advertising Review Board (NARB).

Advertising Agency Networks

A number of advertising agencies in different parts of the country have formed what are known as agency networks. Each network is composed of independently owned and noncompeting agencies. The member agencies of each network interchange information, ideas, and services that enable individual agencies to better serve their clients. The first of these was the First Advertising Agency Network, established in 1928.[22]

With 49 member agencies, the Affiliated Advertising Agencies Network, organized in 1938, is one of the largest of these groups. It has offices in more than 40 major cities in the United States as well as offices in Japan, Canada, Colombia, the Philippine Islands, and Australia.

The Continental Advertising Agency Network, functioning in the United States and Canada, was formed in 1932. The Midwestern Advertising Agency Network operates in the area within a day's train ride from Chicago and was started in 1948. Other networks are the National Advertising Agency Network organized in 1932, the National Federation of Advertising Agencies established in 1951, and the Transamerican Advertising Agency Network started in 1938. Another is the Mutual Advertising Agency Network.

Today, there are 10 networks with a total of 327 member agencies and combined billings of $1,005.5 million.[23]

SUMMARY

In addition to those people who perform the creative functions of the advertising agency, management plays an important and necessary part. Management, among other things, runs the agency, hires the creative staff, pays salaries, seeks new business, and serves as the liaison with the client. The latter function is performed by account management.

Many agencies also maintain branch offices in principal cities in this country and throughout the world.

Advertising agencies began as individual proprietorships and partnerships. Although some later became corporations, to take advantage of the limited liability offered by that form of business structure, stock ownership remained with management. During the 1960s, it became fashionable to become a public corporation and sell stock to the general public. A number of agencies followed this trend. However, a severely depressed stock market encouraged some of those that had gone public to buy back their stock.

The commission allowed by the media is the principal method of agency compensation. Another method is the fee, a sum of money agreed upon jointly by the agency and the client. Other systems of compensation are generally combinations of the aforementioned two.

A relatively recent trend is the multinational agency. American agencies have either established their own branches in foreign countries or have bought into existing foreign establishments.

As do most businesses and professions, advertising has its trade associations. Principal among these are the American Association of Advertising Agencies, which represents advertising agencies; the Association of National

Advertisers, which represents advertisers; and the American Advertising Federation, which represents all advertising interests.

QUESTIONS AND DISCUSSION SUBJECTS

1. By what three titles are account managers known? Describe their job.
2. What are some of the responsibilities of the overall agency management?
3. What have been the traditional patterns of agency ownership?
4. Name the advantages to the agency offered by public ownership of its stock.
5. Who is responsible for claims made in advertising—the advertiser or the agency?
6. Which is the predominant method of agency compensation? Explain it.
7. Who pays the agency under the system you described in answer to question 6?
8. Name and describe alternate systems of agency compensation.
9. What are multinational advertising agencies? How do they operate?
10. Name the principal advertising associations. Which segments of the population are represented by each?

SOURCES

1. *What Should You Expect from Your Advertising Agency?* (New York: Compton Advertising, 1973).
2. David C. Stuart, *The K&E Viewpoint* (New York: Kenyon & Eckhardt, 1966).
3. David Ogilvy, "How to Run an Advertising Agency," in his *How to Create Advertising that Sells* (New York: Ogilvy & Mather, 1975), 23.
4. *Ibid.*
5. *Ibid.,* 22, 23.
6. *What Should You Expect from Your Advertising Agency? op. cit.*
7. Ogilvy, *op. cit.,* 22.
8. Margaret D. Pacey, "Up the Flagpole," *Barron's,* April 22, 1973, 3+.
9. *Loc. cit.*
10. Ogilvy, *op. cit.,* 23.
11. *The Standard Procedure for Advertising Agency Selection and Compensation* (New York: The Gallagher President's Report, 1964).
12. Ogilvy, *op. cit.,* 23.
13. *What Advertising Agencies Are—What They Do and How They Do It* (New York: American Association of Advertising Agencies, 1976).

14. Edward C. Bond, Jr., in an address before the 59th Annual Meeting of the Association of National Advertisers.
15. Andrew Kershaw, "The Changing Face of Agency Services," an address before the American Academy of Advertising, March 12, 1973.
16. Ogilvy, *op. cit.,* 23.
17. Pacey, *op. cit.,* 3.
18. *Report to Stockholders—1973 Annual Meeting* (New York: Ogilvy & Mather, 1973), 4.
19. "72 Agencies Billing Over $25,000,000," *Advertising Age,* February 24, 1975, 30.
20. "World's Biggest Agencies," *Advertising Age,* March 31, 1975, 1.
21. "Billings of 740 International Agencies," *Advertising Age,* March 31, 1975, 34–43.
22. Benjamin J. Katz, "Growth Effects in Agency Network Functions," a paper presented at the American Academy of Advertising National Conference, April 14–22, 1975.
23. *Ibid.*

FOR FURTHER READING

Aaker, D. A. and J. G. Myers. *Advertising Management.* Englewood Cliffs, N.J.: Prentice-Hall, 1975.
Advertising—A Guide to Careers in Advertising. New York: American Association of Advertising Agencies, 1975.
American Association of Advertising Agencies. *A Handbook for the Advertising Agency Account Executive.* Reading, Mass.: Addison-Wesley, 1969.
Barton, Roger, ed. *Handbook of Advertising Management.* New York: McGraw-Hill, 1970.
Borden, Neil H. and Martin V. Marshall. *Advertising Management, Text and Cases.* Homewood, Ill.: Irwin, 1959.
King, William R. "A Conceptual Framework for Ad Agency Compensation," *Journal of Marketing Research,* May 1968, 177–180.
1974/1975 Roster and Organization of the American Association of Advertising Agencies. New York: American Association of Advertising Agencies, 1974.
Weinberg, Charles. *Advertising Management.* New York: Harper and Row, 1974.
What Advertising Agencies Are—What They Do and How They Do It. New York: American Association of Advertising Agencies, 1976.

14

Computers and Advertising

Just as the steam engine was the driving force behind the Industrial Revolution, the computer has served as the spark, or brain, for a second revolution, not in industry alone but in every phase of modern life.

The computer, with its great capacity for electronic data processing, is a major phenomenon of our times. It has been characterized as an extension of the human brain and can perform an astronomical number of mathematical calculations within a single second.

THE "SUPER BRAIN"

It is difficult for one not familiar with computers to comprehend their amazing speed and capabilities. In effect, they have successfully made time stand still, reducing the work of hours to *nanoseconds,* making it possible to perform in a single second the computations that could take a man a lifetime. A nanosecond is a billionth of a second, or more dramatically—one thousandth of a millionth of a second. In more descriptive terms, there are as many nanoseconds in one second as there are seconds in 30 years.

Just imagine how many computations could be made in the blink of an eye, or the time it takes to read this sentence! And the economy-minded will be glad to know that these millions of calculations per second cost only a few pennies per million calculations.

If these figures seem startling, then consider the fact that there are computers presently on the drawing boards that will make calculations at hundreds of times the current rate, at a considerably lower cost.

Analog and Digital Computers

Much time could be spent explaining the differences between analog and digital computers, but it need not be spent here. It is enough to say a few things about analog computers and proceed thereafter to look into the uses and capacities of digital computers, the ones that are at least for the present of most use to advertising people.

One kind of analog computer was explained in Chapter 9—the diagonal method for computing the size of a blown-up or reduced piece of art. One needs no digits or counting or arithmetic to use this kind of computer, although its results can be measured and expressed in numbers. A slide rule also is an analog computer—an operator gets a result from the positions of the two moving parts of the rule (it is an incidental and additional fact that the moving parts are scaled in a system of numbers and digits). The works of a clock are an analog computer, although we can translate the positions of the clock's hands into digits or can show digits on a screen without hands. Some mathematicians have remarked that truly digital calculators cannot exist in principle—that all calculators are analog calculators though some can be *thought of as if* they were digital.[1] In this chapter, we deal with digital computers and need not worry about the exact subtleties or the subtle exactitudes; we put digits into the machines and we get digits out of them.

The digits go into the digital computers as events that can be counted. These may be keystrokes, air puffs, openings or closings of electric circuits, electronic pulses, magnetic pulses, light pulses—or still other events, some of which have yet to be invented. The computer counts these events, adds the counts or subtracts them; if necessary, it repeatedly adds or subtracts to achieve multiplication or division. The computer does this work, but must be told what to do. It reports the results of its operations in digital signals (on dials, screens, scoreboards, printouts, or other); it may translate the digits into words or even into pictures.

From Fingers to Abacus to Computer

Numbers, which are the basis of digital computers, may well have been invented before writing. What we call Arabic numerals were invented by the Hindus shortly before the beginning of the Christian era and had become fully accepted in Europe about the 15th century. From that date, modern skills in mathematics began to improve rapidly.

The early use of the human hand as a calculator is suggested by the very word *digit;* it meant *finger* before it came to mean *numeral.* Not too long after the human hand came into use as a calculator the *abacus* was invented. It is still in use in the form of several kinds of wire-and-bead devices in the Orient and in the Soviet Union; other kinds of abaci were grooves cut into the top of a counter; into these grooves a user could place pebbles (a pebble is a *calculus!*). We may think of the abacus as a device for computing in units, 10s, 100s, 1,000s, and so on; but it need not be so in principle and indeed many abaci used in Europe had grooves for computing in I's, V's, X's, L's, C's, and so on, of Roman numerals.

In the 17th century, Europeans needed more effective calculating machines. In 1614 the Scottish mathematician John Napier developed a system for

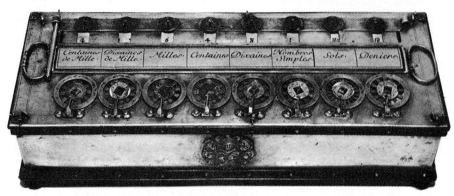

The abacus was man's most common calculator for over 3,000 years, until Blaise Pascal invented the first mechanical adding machine in 1642. Toothed wheel counters carried numbers to the next column. *Courtesy American Federation of Information Processing Societies.*

multiplication which employed number-marked sticks that came to be called "Napier's bones." The Frenchman Blaise Pascal's adding machine arrived on the scene about 28 years later. It employed six geared wheels, each divided into parts marked 0 through 9, which worked much like today's electric or gas meter or like an automobile's odometer. In 1672, the German mathematician Baron von Leibnitz invented a forerunner of the desk calculator; it could add, subtract, multiply, and divide. In 1885, William Burroughs presented his adding machine, the descendants of which are still being produced by the company that bears his name.

Meantime, about the beginning of the 19th century, the French inventor Joseph-Marie Jacquard had devised a system of punched cards to control the operation of a loom in weaving intricate patterns. About 1823, Charles Babbage in England planned and began construction of his computer, an "analytical engine," applying punched-card controls to mathematical operations. The analytical engine was never completed but Babbage's ideas (including memory and decision functions) were available to later workers in the computer field. One dramatically successful punched-card system, developed by Dr. Herman Hollerith, was used for the tabulations and computations of data from the United States Census of 1890; improved systems have been used since.

The modern digital computer dates back to shortly before the start of World War II. Appropriately named the Mark I, it was begun by Howard Aiken in 1937 and began operations at Harvard University seven years later. Because it was electromechanically operated, credit for being "the first" is often accorded the all-electronic ENIAC. Developed between 1939 and 1945 at the University of Pennsylvania under the sponsorship of the United States Army, it had 18,000 vacuum tubes. It could perform 5,000 additions in one second. While a number of other computers were developed, each more advanced than its predecessor, the UNIVAC, introduced in 1951, was the first produced by a commercial company for business rather than military data processing and scientific computation. Since that time, IBM and other manufacturers have been producing generations of revolutionary new computers. As of the end of 1974 it was estimated that there were 40,000 computer installations in the United States with an estimated 175,000 operating computers, and it was predicted that there would be 200,000 by 1980.[2]

COMPUTER LANGUAGE

While computer programmers and operators have to know the computer language, account executives and others who merely utilize the output of computers do not. Knowledge of the rudiments of programming, however, would seem an advantage to the latter group. The language "spoken" by the computer is a mathematical one and is based on the binary system rather than the decimal. The latter system, with which all of us are familiar, consists of 10 digits ranging from 0 to 9. The binary system (a very ancient one, now being taught as part of the "new math") uses only the two digits 0 and 1. In the computer the 0 and 1 can be translated in a number of ways. The 0 can represent "Off" and the 1 can mean "On"; or they can mean simply "No" and "Yes." Indeed, 0 and 1 can be used to differentiate between low and high voltage, closed or open circuit, or the values in any other two-value system. The computer computes in the binary system. Data on punched cards or paper tape are converted from decimal to binary notation in the computer, and the results from binary to decimal in the printouts. Data on punched paper tape may be in either binary or decimal notation. Data on magnetic tape are usually in binary notation although they may be fed to the tape via decimal notation.

The state of the art has advanced to the point where the programmer can write instructions for the computer in a form of stylized English. One such computer language is COBOL or Common Business Oriented Language. Another computer language is FORTRAN (Formula Translation), which relies on mathematical and algebraic terms.[3] Both COBOL and FORTRAN are problem-oriented languages (as opposed to machine-oriented) and must be translated into machine language. Other problem-oriented languages are ALGOL (Algorithmic Language), PL/I, RPG (Report Program Generator), and BASIC.

Future computers may accept directions in everyday English—typed, printed, even spoken (these capacities are claimed for some of them even as this is written). However, it is more likely that high-school and even grade-school students will learn FORTRAN and other computer languages almost as routinely as they now learn arithmetic.

Memory Banks (Storage Devices)

Although all computers operate in similar fashion and perform essentially the same functions, there are a few varieties of memory banks. In one type, a computer's "knowledge" is stored on doughnut-shaped, pinhead-size ferromagnetic ceramic cores, strung on crisscrossed wires within a frame. In appearance they resemble square tennis rackets. These wire frames are stacked in units. A basic unit, only 5 inches by 3 inches, would contain over 150,000 magnetic cores each capable of retaining one bit of information, the binary digits 0 or 1.[4] A typical computer might have a number of these core-storage units, each containing 2.5 million or more of the ferromagnetic "doughnuts" packed with electronically coded data.

The great speed of the computer can be readily appreciated when we realize that this giant memory bank can be tapped within a millionth of a second. The retrieved data then can be fed directly to the user, or the computer can be programmed to utilize it to solve problems or make calculations.

Other storage systems employ drums, disk packs, data-cell devices, and tape units. Basically, however, all operate in the same way—information is converted into a series of magnetic impulses and stored. Storage devices have been compared to mail boxes in a post office in that each box has an assigned number. In like manner, each storage location, which holds a specific unit of data, has an "address." When properly programmed, the computer is able to locate and extract the data required. Unlike the mail box, however, the unit of data still remains in the storage location (unless it is intentionally removed), regardless of the number of times it furnishes the information. In this respect it closely resembles the human brain.

Storage devices are also called *internal memories* as compared to *external memories,* the term used for the various input systems.

How It Works

The usefulness of the computer lies in its fantastic speed, permanent memory, extreme accuracy, and automatic operation. It works in nanoseconds and remembers millions of facts. In addition to remembering facts, it accepts and recalls instructions as well; and while the human brain sometimes forgets, the computer can be relied upon to cull out the needed information in a fraction of a second. Its accuracy is unparalleled and it can make calculations of 10 decimal places or more at lightning speed. However, its performance is dependent both upon the skill of the programmer and on the data that have or have not been fed to it. The computer's supreme capability, automatic operation, is a result of its ability to remember instructions and to perform them in proper sequence.

Input/Output

Like an extension of the brain, the computer pursues much the same operational sequence that would be followed by a human being in solving problems. The first step involves the feeding in of the known facts or data and of the program or instructions, using a computer language. This is known as *input* and can be accomplished in any of several ways, depending upon the compatibility of the computer. There are numerous input systems. Data stored on cards, tapes, or disks outside of the computer can serve it as an external memory and can be compared to the reference books, telephone directories, calendars, maps, and the like which people consult to supplement the data stored in their internal memories or brains. *Output* is the product of the computer—the transcribing of data from the internal storage bank of external memory, or the solution to a problem accomplished by utilizing the data from the memories together with the input instructions.

The input/output system familiar to most laymen is the *punched card*. It is the system most frequently used and predates the computer, having been perfected by Dr. Herman Hollerith to facilitate and speed up the 1890 Census. Dr. Hollerith was chief of the tabulating section of the United States Bureau of the Census. Whereas it had taken seven years to tabulate the 1880 Census, that of 1890, with a greater population, was completed in less than three years with Hollerith's punched cards.[5] Later Dr. Hollerith left government service to offer his system to industry. The company he founded later merged with others to become the International Business Machines Corporations, and Hollerith's cards are commonly known as IBM cards. Punched cards are usually used for furnishing additional information and programming or giving instructions to the computer. Similar to the punched cards is *punched paper tape*, which is about ¾ of an inch wide. Adding machines, cash registers, typewriters and other similar equipment can be fitted with a device that will automatically punch the tape as a second record of whatever is typed, tabulated, or transacted on the machine.

Magnetic tape is one of the principal computer input and output media. Like the tape used in home audio recorders, it is a thin ribbon of plastic film coated with iron oxide, which can be magnetized. It offers a major advantage in that one ten-inch reel holds the data equivalent of 250,000 punched cards and can be read much faster. While punched cards and punched tape might be used for programming instructions and supplemental data, magnetic tape generally holds the principal external data and, like the others, can be inserted into the computer whenever that information is required. It is stored outside the computer for repeated use and when its data is no longer needed, new information put on it will erase the previous input or output.

Similar to magnetic tape are magnetic disks. Resembling phonograph records, but larger, they are capable of furnishing or receiving data at an even faster rate than tape.

A more recent innovation in input devices is *magnetic ink* which enables the computer to read numbers and other symbols, printed in the special ink. The most common use of magnetic ink is on checks and deposit slips, where codes representing the individual's account and one representing the bank are printed, starting in the lower left hand corner. A computer can read this code, properly identify the bank and the account, prepare bank statements, and so forth. Another advanced input system is capable of reading printed paper documents.

Once the computer has been fed the necessary external data and has been programmed or given the appropriate instructions, it can be activated. And then the computer, working at lightning speed, utilizes the input data and instructions, calls upon its internal memory bank, performs the necessary calculations, and furnishes data for the solution of problems.

The solution or output can be delivered by any of a number of means,

Input-output devices make it possible to "type" business or scientific data directly into a computer which displays the results of its calculations on a television-like screen. *Courtesy American Federation of Information Processing Societies.*

including the aforementioned *punched card, magnetic tape,* and *magnetic disk.* A very common one is the *electric typewriter,* which can also receive input as well as deliver data. One of the most dramatic output methods is the *high-speed printer,* which disgorges printed data at the rate of better than 1,200 lines a minute—the equivalent of a full 8-hour day's work for a typist typing at the rate of 60 words a minute. Other delivery devices include *display lights,* which give the answer in a binary code; and *graphic display units,* which resemble a television screen and transmit images such as distribution curves and lines on graphs or charts; and a sound device that transmits audible messages.

ADVERTISING AGENCY COMPUTERS

Advertising agencies put computers to work as soon as efficient computers became available within the cost tolerance of the business. As early as 1967, approximately 15 agencies owned computers or leased them for full-time use; in 1969 the number was 31, according to a 4As' survey. To serve their customers, Batten, Barton, Durstine & Osborn developed Mediametrics, the first agency media-planning computer model of consequence. BBD&O also produced the mathematical model SIMAD (System for Integration of Marketing and Advertising Data). Young & Rubicam offered HAMM (High Assay Media

Model). Interpublic devised Midas (Marketing Communications Decision Analysis Systems).

Electronic data processing and other computer service are available to advertising agencies (as to other businesses) in a number of ways. Direct ownership or full-time lease of a computer offers complete control and economy (if the agency can use enough of the machine's time). But unused computers waste money rapidly; the owning agency may have to lease or rent time to other users in order to cover expenses.

Other plans and patterns include cooperative arrangements, time sharing, remote batch processing, and the use of independent data-processing services. Computers are also available through the syndicated research services, custom information companies, and the leading broadcast station representatives (which check television time availabilities and do billing and ordering).

A number of agencies have shared computers on a cooperative basis for media planning purposes. One such arrangement, organized under the leadership of Compton Advertising, was COMPASS. Members of this group included Compton; D'Arcy; Doyle Dane Bernbach; Ted Bates; Cunningham & Walsh; Ogilvy and Mather; Grey; Foote, Cone & Belding; Tatham-Laird & Kudner; and Leo Burnett. These worked with the Diebold Group, a consulting firm.[6] Following the first years of operation the COMPASS cooperative lost Ted Bates as a participant and reorganized under the name COUSIN (Compass Users Inc.) to develop better ways to apply the basic COMPASS system.[7] Other scaled-down models of COMPASS have continued with seven or eight agencies participating.[8]

Similar to the voluntary arrangements for cooperative agency computer use are the client-initiated interagency operations. Some advertisers who manufacture or produce a number of products use different advertising agencies for each or several of their wares. This diversification of accounts is very common among large advertisers in the automotive, food, and drug industries. In the latter two categories, General Foods, Proter & Gamble, Colgate, and Bristol-Myers, as multi-agency advertisers, have found it necessary to coordinate the efforts of their agencies by means of common computer use.[9] In other words, all of the advertising agencies that handle a particular manufacturer's products would share a computer or would be linked, in a computer net, together with the client.

Another type of computer service available to advertising agencies is the data-processing service bureau. These bureaus are independent firms which will perform specific computer operations for advertising agencies, or for any other customer.

COMPUTER APPLICATIONS IN ADVERTISING

An indication of the types of computer applications available to advertising agencies can be readily seen in a perusal of a directory of data-processing service bureaus. This list, published by the American Association of Advertising Agencies clearly shows that the greatest availability is in the management and accounting areas. In 1976, 63 of the firms provided client profit and loss analysis, 64 offered to prepare the agency payroll, and 43 would do agency billing and/or income analysis.[10]

While 21 of the data-processing service companies would tabulate and list consumer research questionnaires, and 30 would do statistical analysis of marketing data, only 17 would prepare media estimates. As to other media application, 9 firms would do redistribution of media circulation/coverage analysis with client selling areas, 20 would do media selection, and 12 of the data services would do analysis of competitive media usage.

The computer is a remarkable management and marketing tool. In advertising, its superbrain and microsecond reaction have use in a wide number of applications. A list prepared by the 4As shows the following:

Preparation of Media Estimates
Preparation of Clients' Media and Production Billing
Preparation of Payments to Media and to Production Suppliers
Preparation of Insertion Orders and Contracts to Media
Agency Billing and/or Income Analysis
Agency Payroll
Client Profit and Loss Analysis—Including Analysis of Agency Time Records
Talent Payments
Tabulating and Listing Consumer Research Questionnaires
Redistribution of Media Circulation/Coverage Analysis with Client Selling Areas
Determining the Relationship of Client Sales Dollars or Units to Advertising Dollars
Media Selection Using Mathematical Techniques Such as Linear Programming, Simulation, etc.
Decision-Making Model Building for Specialized Agency Use
Direct-Mail Addressing and Mailing Services
Yellow Pages Advertising Market Selections and Program Costs
Statistical Analysis of Marketing Data
Analysis of Competitive Media Usage
Spot TV Control System Network and Spot TV Audience Analysis
Key Punching and Verifying Analysis of Client Sales Data
Personnel Administration General Ledger and Related Accounting Data
Post Buy Analysis Tie Into Business and Technical Abstracts
Budget Control
Radio Efficiency Analysis
Aging Accounts Receivable [11]

Additional related computer uses include: market forecasting, a number of other media analyses, typesetting, printing, creating or coining trademarks and brand names, and other diverse uses such as operating the electric-light spectaculars on the sides of the Goodyear blimps and outdoor advertising spectaculars.

Attesting to the importance of information management in advertising, the 4As conducted a seminar on "The Impact of the Computer on Advertising Agency Management and Operations" during the spring of 1972. One bid for the future use of electronic data processing that emerged from this meeting was a plea for "the communality of computer systems." The common system was likened to the standard railroad track guage used throughout the United States and most of Europe.[12]

Hunt-Wesson Foods made a novel use of the computer when in August 1970 it offered computer planned and balanced menus to consumers through advertising in 155 newspapers and 5 magazines. The ad included a coupon which asked for certain pertinent data relative to the size of the family and the food budget. At Hunt-Wesson's Computer Meal Planning Center in Dayton, Ohio, the data in the coupon were processed through a computer. The computer was programmed to plan a month's menus specifically for the requesting family. It was geared to process up to 30,000 plans a day, and produced a 10-page printout for each applicant, consisting of nutritionally balanced meals for each of 30 days. The printout also included recipes for the major dishes, and tips for shopping, health, and homemaking.

An example of computer application by an individual ad agency is provided by Ogilvy & Mather. O&M, which leases equipment for electronic data processing, divides its computer use into three major categories: Media, Accounting, and Administrative.

Under the *Media* heading, it lists the following applications:

Reach and Frequency (TV, Magazine, TV and Magazine)
Network Program Evaluation

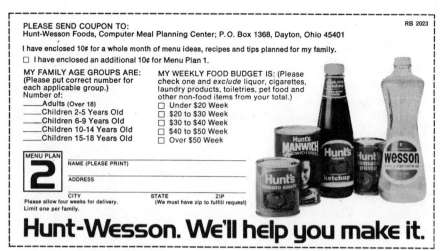

```
1st DAY OF YOUR COMPUTERIZED MENU PLAN

BREAKFAST                    LUNCH

MIXED FRUIT CUP              BEAN WITH BACON SOUP
FRENCH TOAST, SYRUP          GRILLED CHEESE, BACON
BACON                          SANDWICHES, RELISHES
MILK, COFFEE                 PEARS, CREAM
                             MILK, TEA


DINNER                       TIP:

SPAGHETTI WITH MEATBALLS     WHEN PLANNING YOUR OWN
GARLIC BREAD                 MENUS, INCLUDE AT LEAST
ANTIPASTO SALAD              ONE VITAMIN C RICH FOOD
ICE CREAM CAKE               PER DAY, SUCH AS CITRUS
MILK, TEA, COFFEE            FRUITS, TOMATOES AND RAW
                             CABBAGE.
```

Computer Application to Consumer Service. A menu plan designed for a family of four on a weekly food budget of $30 to $40 (in 1970).

Media Delivery
Piggyback Schedules
Market Target Evaluator
Geographic Media/Sales Planner
Spot TV System
Documentation

In the *Accounting* area, O&M employs computers for:

Cost Accounting
General Ledger
Media Payments
Travel and Entertainment Expenses
Production Billing
Media Billing Analysis

The *Administrative* uses of electronic data processing are in:

Profit Sharing
Employee Benefits Statements
Mailing Lists
Personnel

In order to tie in with its branch office in Los Angeles, Ogilvy & Mather use a time-sharing network where data from its principal office in New York are exchanged, via local telephones, through a computer in Cleveland.

It can be readily seen that the computer serves the agency predominantly as an aid in management, marketing, research, and media. Little application has as yet been found in the creative areas of copywriting or art. However, one computer-research-company official contends that the machine does enhance creativity, and while it cannot create advertising copy, it can point the copywriter in the right direction.[13]

The computer is an excellent example of man's technology which produces machinery more advanced than his ability to employ it. Current-generation computers are still performing functions that could be handled by first-generation models.[14] While studies indicate that the computer is not being used nearly as much as it could be, it is certainly conceivable, in light of present trends, that applications in the above mentioned areas will increase considerably and new uses will be found.[15]

SUMMARY

The computer, a product of modern technology based on principles and discoveries made hundreds of years ago, is capable of making mathematical calculations and retrieving stored information at lightning speed. It is used widely in education, business, industry, government, and elsewhere.

Electronic data processing is put to a number of uses in advertising. It is a remarkable management and marketing tool, performing many accounting and research functions. In addition, it is used for such diverse tasks as printing direct mail letters, addressing envelopes, typesetting, creating trademarks and brand names, and operating the electric lights on outdoor advertising spectaculars.

QUESTIONS AND DISCUSSION SUBJECTS

1. In what way has the computer been compared to the steam engine?
2. What is the difference between the analog and the digital computer?
3. Which type is currently being used in advertising?
4. Who was Dr. Herman Hollerith? What were his contributions to computer technology?
5. When was the first modern digital computer put into operation?
6. Explain how the binary system is used in computers.
7. What are COBOL and FORTRAN?

8. How does the computer storage system operate?
9. Name some data input/output systems.
10. What uses do advertising agencies make of computers?
11. What was COMPASS?

SOURCES

1. *Digital Computers* (Washington, D.C.: Department of the Army, 1970), pp. 3–7 in particular. John von Neumann, "The General and Logical Theory of Automata," in James R. Newman, ed., *The World of Mathematics* (New York: Simon and Schuster, 1956), vol. 4, especially pp. 2074–2076. A. M. Turing, "Can a Machine Think?" in Newman, *op. cit.,* especially pp. 2102–2105.
2. "Computer Abuse to Become Billion Dollar Threat," *The Gallagher President's Report,* August 20, 1974.
3. M. Keshin, R. F. Lyman, K. Ross, and J. St. Georges, *Some Important Things I Believe a Young Account Representative Should Know About Electronic Data Processing* (New York: American Association of Advertising Agencies, 1969), 8.
4. *You and the Computer* (Schenectady, N.Y.: General Electric, 1965), 13.
5. *Ibid.,* 17.
6. Thayer C. Taylor, *The Computer in Marketing* (New York: Bill Publications, 1970), 73.
7. Keshin *et al., op. cit.,* p. 20.
8. *Loc. cit.*
9. *Ibid.,* p. 21.
10. *Data Processing Service Bureaus Serving 4A Agencies* (New York: American Association of Advertising Agencies, 1976), pp. 37–58.
11. *Loc. cit.*
12. John Boyd, "Communality of Systems Among Agencies," in *The Impact of the Computer on Advertising Agency Management and Operations* (New York: American Association of Advertising Agencies, 1972), pp. 15–22.
13. Taylor, *op. cit.,* p. 72.
14. *Ibid.,* p. 2.
15. E. L. Bailey, *Computer Support for Marketing* (New York: National Industrial Conference Board, 1969), pp. 3, 6, 7.

FOR FURTHER READING

Bailey, Earl L. *Computer Support for Marketing.* New York: National Industrial Conference Board, 1969.

Barnett, Michael P. *Computer Typesetting.* Cambridge, Mass.: MIT Press, 1965.

Cooper, M. J. *What Computers Can Do: A Guide for the Plain Man.* Princeton, N.J.: Brandon/Systems Press, 1970.

Digital Computers. Department of the Army Technical Manual (TM 44–210). Washington, D.C.: Department of the Army, 1970.

Halacy, D. S., Jr. *Computers: The Machines We Think With.* New York: Harper & Row, 1962.

The Impact of the Computer on Advertising Agency Management and Operations. New York: American Association of Advertising Agencies, 1972.

Introduction to IBM Data Processing Systems. White Plains, N.Y.: IBM, 1967.

Keshin, M., R. F. Lyman, K. Ross, and J. St. Georges. *Some Important Things I Believe a Young Account Executive Should Know About Electronic Data Processing.* New York: American Association of Advertising Agencies, 1969.

Martin, E. W., Jr., and William C. Perkins. *Computers and Information Systems.* Homewood, Ill.: Irwin/Dorsey Press, 1973.

Rushforth, J. M., and J. L. Morris. *Computers and Computing.* London: John Wiley & Sons, 1973.

Taylor, Thayer C. *The Computer in Marketing.* New York: Bill Publications, 1970.

You and the Computer. Schenectady, N.Y.: General Electric, 1965.

15

Auditing Groups and Standard Rate & Data Service

There was a time when media people, if indeed not all advertising people, were forced to rely upon intuition as almost their sole guide in the selection and use of advertising media. Guesswork plus experience were the ingredients of the mix that, hopefully, would result in an advertisement being properly placed in a medium that would carry it to the desired market. There was little assurance that this hope would actually be realized, for these were the days of no standards in media evaluation, and little or no scientific media research.

Over the years, various associations, auditing groups, and research organizations have been created so that the media people of the present have at their disposal a rather formidable and certainly a most useful array of tools and services to help them in their work. To treat each of these tools and services in detail would require a book in itself. Therefore, this chapter undertakes merely to introduce those unfamiliar with the field to some of the many areas from which the advertiser can draw information and assistance that will help in solving media problems.

AUDITING GROUPS

One of the handicaps of advertising in earlier days was the total lack of definitions and standards concerning circulation. An advertiser could never be sure of what he was buying with his media dollars. This situation, unfortunately, still exists in some parts of the world. But in the United States and Canada, organizations have been developed that have as their function the measuring, checking, and verifying of circulations of various media and media groups.

AUDIT BUREAU OF CIRCULATIONS

The Audit Bureau of Circulations (ABC) is a nonprofit association founded in 1914 to establish and maintain standards for circulation fact-finding and fact-reporting. It currently verifies and reports on approximately three-quarters of all published print media circulation available to advertising buyers in the United States and Canada. Thus circulation information, which prior to 1914 begged for dependable description and reporting, is today accurately defined and reported to advertising buyers in accordance with terms and standards mutually approved by the tripartite industry interests of ABC members. And in addition to the raw verified-circulation data ABC can provide related information, and it can provide these jointly in combinations and formats to answer an almost endless variety of marketing needs.

ABC membership includes approximately 1,200 advertisers and advertising agencies, more than 1,800 daily and weekly newspapers, and 625 business publications, magazines, and farm publications.

While publisher members pay in about 91% of the Audit Bureau's annual $2.5 million budget, the majority of those on ABC's 33-man elected Board of Directors are advertiser and advertising-agency representatives. To further insure buyer control of ABC, its Board Chairman must be chosen from among the advertiser or agency members. Directors are elcted at ABC annual meetings, and each serves, without compensation, for 200 to 250 hours a year on ABC matters.

Carrying out the directives of the Board, a staff of about 170 does the day-to-day work of the Audit Bureau at headquarters in Chicago and in offices in Toronto and New York; 70 specially trained field circulation auditors visit the offices of publisher members.

A basic standard for membership eligibility for most publishers is that the publication have at least 70% of its total distribution qualify as paid circulation under the ABC rules. Two exceptions to this standard exist: A publication may be elected to provisional membership with less than 70% but more than 50% paid, provided its publisher agrees to attain the regular membership standard within three years. Special standards, for business publications only, provide membership eligibility on the basis of at least 70% paid or 70% nonpaid-direct-request, or a combination of paid and nonpaid-direct-request equal to at least 70% of total distribution.

The services supplied by the Audit Bureau have greatly expanded in recent years to meet the growing needs of media buyers and of marketing people generally.

ABC provides two basic reporting services. The semiannual *Publisher's Statements* contains the circulation claims of each publisher member. The annual *Audit Report* is based on the actual findings of the field auditor's examination of a publisher's records. The *Audit Report* verifies or corrects claims made to ABC in preceding *Publisher's Statements*.

The Audit Bureau's computer-generated Data Bank Services provide spe-

TV GUIDE

RADNOR, PENNSYLVANIA 19088

Magazine Publisher's Statement

Average Paid Circulation
For Six Months Ending December 31, 1975
19,168,096

Publisher's Compilation - Subject to Audit

Audit Bureau of Circulations
123 North Wacker Drive - Chicago, Illinois 60606

ABC Audit Report-Magazine

PENTHOUSE

New York, New York

CLASS, INDUSTRY OR FIELD SERVED: The full range of sophisticated male entertainment, from outspoken contemporary comment to photographic essays of the world s most beautiful women.

1. AVERAGE PAID CIRCULATION FOR 12 MONTHS ENDING JUNE 30, 1974:

Subscriptions:	166,592	
Single Copy Sales:	3,660,952	
AVERAGE TOTAL PAID CIRCULATION		3,827,544
Advertising Rate Base and/or Circulation Guarantee during Audit Period.to 9/1/73	2,000,000	
since 9/1/73	3,500,000	
Average Total Non-Paid Distribution	6,459	

2. PAID CIRCULATION BY ISSUES: (Total of subscriptions and single copy sales)

1973		1973		1974		1974	
July	3,360,215	Oct.	4,018,797	Jan.	3,684,975	Apr.	3,944,991
Aug.	3,646,795	Nov.	3,659,487	Feb.	3,820,456	May	3,892,523
Sept.	3,918,356	Dec.	3,987,827	Mar.	3,897,193	June	4,098,915

AVERAGE PAID CIRCULATION BY QUARTERS for the previous audit and period covered by this report:

Calendar Qtr. End.	1971	1972	1973	1974
March 31	569,674	1,319,800	2,991,478	3,800,875
June 30	643,591	1,605,164	3,280,801	3,978,810
September 30	753,125	1,943,070	3,641,789	
December 31	1,064,032	2,482,817	3,888,704	

AUDIT STATEMENT

A comparison of the average total paid circulation shown in this report with Publisher's Statements for the period audited, shows an addition to verified circulation in excess of that claimed in Publisher's Statements of an average of 29,954 copies per issue, which addition is accounted for by additional single copy sales, publisher having overestimated returns in compiling statements to the Bureau.

The records maintained by this publication pertaining to circulation data and other data as reported for the period covered have been examined in accordance with the Bureau's bylaws, rules and auditing standards. Test of the accounting records and other auditing procedures considered necessary were included. Based on ABC's examination, the data shown in this report present fairly the circulation data and other data as verified by Bureau auditors.

February, 1975.
(04-0843-0 - #114939 - EKH - DB)

M-2—1-74—200

AUDIT BUREAU OF CIRCULATIONS
123 North Wacker Drive, Chicago, Illinois 60606

cialized studies on individual- or multipublication analyses. These studies, made to the specifications of the media buyer or researcher, relate circulation, households, demographics, cost, product marketing information, reach, frequency, and other data.

ABC *FAS/FAX* reports on member publications are published semiannually. They deal with basic circulation, population, and household coverage. Separate volumes report information on: United States daily newspapers, Canadian daily newspapers, and weekly newspapers for both countries. A fourth volume providing data on all periodical members is distributed on August 15 and February 15.

While the Audit Bureau's basic *Publisher's Statements* and *Audit Reports* for publications within media divisions are standardized and directly comparable, the kinds of data reported differ among these divisions, recognizing that each type of medium has its own appeal to the advertiser. For example, daily newspapers must relate circulation sales to ABC-defined market areas (city and retail trading zones or primary market areas); magazines and farm publications provide total circulation figures; business publications relate circulation to breakdowns of uniform vocational analyses.

In addition to quantitive information, circulation quality is reflected through report data on subscription prices, arrears, subscription-producing efforts (use of premiums, contests, special offers, etc.) and other incentives.

ABC newspaper reports break down an actual day's total distribution by market area, and by towns and counties receiving 25 or more copies. Comparative housing-unit figures are given for each listing, and a supplementary county "adjusted figure" relates the one-day gross distribution in the breakdown to average paid circulation for the period covered by the report.

Special for its newspaper-member reports, too, are local market-area maps. Like those for the 950 ABC-defined market-areas, the individual maps visualize the geography of local market conditions, not circulation penetration. If not specifically shown elsewhere in the report on an optional basis, circulation-to-household coverage can be quickly computed from data included in each report for either market areas or counties. In 1974, ABC added a Newspaper Audience Research Data Bank providing standardized basic readership and audience characteristics.

Magazine and farm-publication reports show a state (and/or provincial) breakdown of circulation, with special breakdowns on an optional basis for regional or special demographic editions.

Magazines with over 500,000 circulation are required to provide a further breakdown of circulation by county population size. A similar type of breakdown is optional for farm publications.

On business-publication members, ABC reports a business or occupational breakdown of subscribers or recipients. Since 1926, it has been mandatory that these breakdowns be uniform for publications serving the same field or profession and, therefore, be directly comparable, publication to publication, line for line. ABC business publications are also required to report on the percentage of subscriptions renewed in each report period.

Recognizing the concern of media buyers over problems in maintaining data files, ABC has initiated summary *Audit Reports*. These are two- and four-page digests of the full *Audit Reports* that may run as many as 180 pages. Full reports are made available to media buyers as an optional service.

One of the most important features of the *Audit Report* is the auditor's statement that appears on the cover sheet or first page. This statement either verifies the publisher's claims or calls attention to differences between the auditor's examination and the claims of the publisher. Through a procedure of double-checking the field auditor's work, by experienced house auditors, the advertiser is assured accurate facts and figures as a basis for his advertising research and expenditures.

ABC report services are purchased mainly by advertising agencies but are available at cost to any member. Reports can be purchased on a complete-member basis or on selected individual member-publications to match the marketing needs of users. Besides the *Audit Report* and *Publisher's Statements, FAS/FAX* reports, Data Bank Services, and special report services, ABC makes available complete sets of semiannual *Publisher's Statements* for each publication division in bound volumes known as *Blue Books*.

Besides the wealth of circulation data compiled over its history of more than 115,000 field audits, the Audit Bureau maintains a complete library of the latest United States and Canadian census information. Through "ABC Estimates" it has established procedures for updating census-produced population and housing figures.

Through cooperation with the Bureau of Advertising, American Newspaper Publishers Association, ABC is incorporating local market-research information into its computer data bank, thus providing an extension of the Audit Bureau's own market area analyses.

To the Audit Bureau of Circulations, serving the needs of its members has been an ever changing challenge. Each ABC report contains facts and figures bearing on quantity, quality, and distribution of circulation, and on circulation methods. In no instance does ABC attempt to evaluate any of the data that it reports—interpretation is left to those who use these reports.

In a unique industry cooperative venture ABC has joined with the Business Publications Audit of Circulation (BPA) in a market comparability program. The Joint ABC/BPA Banking Market is studying two ABC-audited and four BPA-audited banking publications. By January 1979 they will provide an analysis of 10 categories in banking by occupational and title classification.

Business Publications Audit of Circulation

Business Publications Audit of Circulation, Inc., formerly Controlled Circulation Audit, was founded in 1931. Like ABC, it is a national, independent, nonprofit corporation of advertisers, advertising agencies, and business and special-market publications.

BPA's function is to issue standardized statements of the circulation of its publication members; to verify the accuracy of the figures shown in those statements by means of an auditor's examination of any and all necessary publisher records; to issue, at least once a year, a report made by the corporation on each publication member; and to disseminate pertinent circulation data concerning its publication members for the benefit of advertisers, advertising agencies, and publishers.

In fulfilling these objectives of organization, BPA audits business and special-market publications with paid circulation, with nonpaid circulation, or with any combination of the two. It audits circulation only—not readership, purchasing power, or buying influence. It audits only qualified or controlled circulation: that for which the mailing address, publisher's restriction of circulation to his field, and a business/occupational breakdown of recipient qualifications may be verified according to one or more standard sources of circulation qualification.

BPA's field auditors visit each publication member once each year to examine circulation records. During this audit, the publisher must prove that his publication's circulation conforms to the definitions he has set for it. The audit must also verify the publisher's claim that the publication's recipients are qualified—that all recipient names, titles, and addresses meet BPA standards.

BPA believes these requirements are essential to the establishment of precise, reliable, and nonpromotional circulation information which may serve as a sound basis for media evaluation and selection.

To disseminate these data, BPA annually issues regular circulation reports for each publication member; semiannual *Publisher's Statements,* printed on green stock, which are checked and released subject to audit; and the annual BPA *Audit Report,* which is printed on buff stock. Its contents are "examined and verified" by a field auditor prior to release. BPA also publishes a series of special Marketing Services audits which report circulation and marketing data beyond that contained in the basic circulation audit reports.

As of mid-1975 BPA had 644 publication members, 116 advertiser members, and 98 advertising-agency members.

Traffic Audit Bureau

The Traffic Audit Bureau was formed under the joint sponsorship of the American Association of Advertising Agencies, the Association of National Advertisers, and the Outdoor Advertising Association of America. It is a nonprofit organization and performs two main functions: (1) the auditing of the circulation values of outdoor advertising and (2) the conducting of special research on traffic as related to outdoor advertising.

The Traffic Audit Bureau states that in making an audit of a poster plant it determines how many people can see each poster panel and how readily it can be seen. This determination necessitates making a traffic count and rating a poster panel in terms of what TAB calls its "space-position value" or relative visibility (SPV).

In making its traffic counts, TAB does not include all persons moving in the area of the panel. TAB states that only one-half of all pedestrian and automobile traffic and one-quarter of all mass-transportation traffic are included.

Not counted are people who walk or ride in a direction away from that in which the panel faces, or people in buses or streetcars whose seats face them away from the poster. The figures thus adjusted represent what TAB calls "effective circulation."

The space-position value is determined by (1) the number of panels in a location, (2) the angle of the panel to the flow of traffic, (3) the unobstructed distance over which the panel may be seen, and (4) the speed of the passing traffic. Each panel is rated on these four factors according to a scale in which 10 is the maximum.

Having determined the effective circulation of each panel, TAB then computes the total effective circulation of the average showing of a given size (number of panels). *Circulation,* as the term is used in outdoor advertising, means the number of people who have a reasonable opportunity to see any one or more of the panels in a showing. All circulation figures are expressed on a daily basis.

Having rated the space-position value of each panel, TAB then adds the ratings of all panels and divides the sum by the number of panels to determine the average SPV of all panels in the plant.

The Traffic Audit Bureau also makes studies of outdoor circulation and traffic patterns in specific markets. These studies cover such topics as the difference in strength between different-intensity showings, the number of people

Form D														TAB
			SPACE POSITION VALUATION TABLE											
			Code and Scale of Values for Poster Panels											
						TYPES OF PANELS								
	APPROACH			Angled Single (AS) Angled nearest the Line of Travel (AE)		All Other Angled (A)				Parallel Single (PS) Parallel End of a Group (PE)		All Other Parallel (P)		
							In a Two Panel Facing		In a Facing With More Than Two Panels					
PEDESTRIAN	VEHICULAR													
	Fast Travel	Slow Travel	CODE	VALUE	CODE	VALUE		CODE	VALUE	CODE	VALUE	CODE	VALUE	
LONG APPROACH			1AS	10	1A	10		1A	9	1PS	8	1P	7	
Over 125 ft.	Over 350 ft.	Over 250 ft.	1AE	or (100%)		or (100%)			or (90%)	1PE	or (80%)		or (70%)	
MEDIUM APPROACH			2AS	8	2A	7		2A	7	2PS	6	2P	5	
75 to 125 ft.	200 to 350 ft.	150 to 250 ft.	2AE	or (80%)		or (70%)			or (70%)	2PE	or (60%)		or (50%)	
SHORT APPROACH			3AS	6	3A	5		3A	5	3PS	4	3P	3	
40 to 75 ft.	100 to 200 ft.	75 to 150 ft.	3AE	or (60%)		or (50%)			or (50%)	3PE	or (40%)		or (30%)	
FLASH APPROACH			AF	4 or (40%) 3 or (30%) 2 or (20%) 1 or (10%) 0 or (0%)	AF	3 or (30%) 2 or (20%) 1 or (10%) 0 or (0%)		AF	3 or (30%) 2 or (20%) 1 or (10%) 0 or (0%)	PF	2 or (20%) 1 or (10%) 0 or (0%)	PF	1 or (10%) 0 or (0%)	
Under 40 ft.	Under 100 ft.	Under 75 ft.												

The Basis for Space-Position-Value. An evaluation table used by the Traffic Audit Bureau. *Source:* Traffic Audit Bureau, Inc.

WABC-TV
NEW YORK CITY
(Airdate August 10, 1948)

ABC TELEVISION SPOT SALES, INC

TvB

An ABC Owned Station
Subscriber to the NAB Television Code
Media Code 6 233 0500 0.00
American Broadcasting Co., Inc., 1330 Avenue of Americas, New York, N. Y. 10019. Phone 212-581-7777.

1. PERSONNEL
Vice-Pres. & Gen'l Mgr.—Kenneth H. MacQueen.
General Sales Manager—John Bonanni.
Local Sales Manager—Lee Gannon.
National Sales Manager—Burke Liburt.

2. REPRESENTATIVES
ABC Television Spot Sales, Inc.

3. FACILITIES
Video 116,000 w., audio 11,000 w. (FCC equivalent 316 kw at 1,000 ft.); ch 7.
Antenna ht.: 1,378 ft. above average terrain.
Operating schedule: 6:20 am-sign-off Mon thru Fri; 7:25 am-sign-off Sat and Sun. EST.

4. AGENCY COMMISSION
15% to recognized agencies; no cash discount.

5. GENERAL ADVERTISING See coded regulations
General: 1a, 2a, 2b, 3a, 3b, 3c, 3d, 4a, 5, 6b, 7b, 8.
Rate Protection: 10m, 12m, 13m, 14m.
Contracts: 20b, 24a, 24b, 25, 26, 29, 31a, 31b.
Basic Rates: 40b, 41b, 41c, 42, 44a, 45a, 47.
Comb.: Cont. Discounts: 60b, 60d, 60e, 61b, 62b.
*Cancellation: 70a, 73a, 73b.
Prod. Services: 80, 82, 83, 84, 86, 87b.
(*) Advertiser or station may terminate contract by giving the other party 4 telecasts prior written notice on all announcements. No such notice shall be effective until 28 days after the start of each schedule.
Affiliated with ABC Television Network.
10-second station breaks must share visual station ID except as otherwise provided.
Station reserves the right to reschedule announcements or station breaks to accommodate any revision of program schedules or to avoid conflicting products.
Product Protection
While no guarantees are made, the station will make every effort to secure a 10 minute spread between competitive products. In no case will credit be given for a product conflict.

6. TIME RATES
Rates temporarily have been withdrawn by station.

11. SPECIAL FEATURES
COLOR
Schedules network color, film, slides, live and tape. Equipped with high band VTR.

12. SERVICE FACILITIES
Address all commercials & commercial instructions to:
Director of Operations & Continuity
77 West 66th Street
New York, N. Y. 10023

13. CLOSING TIME
72 hours prior film, slides, artwork.
Submitted by Jerry Russell.

WCBS-TV
NEW YORK CITY
(Airdate July 1, 1941)

TvB

CBS Owned
Subscriber to the NAB Television Code
Media Code 6 233 0550 5.00
CBS, Inc.; operated by CBS Television Stations, 51 W. 52nd St., New York, N. Y. 10019. Phone 212-765-4321.

WNBC-TV
NEW YORK CITY
(Airdate July 1, 1941)

NBC Television Network

NBC Spot Sales

TvB

An NBC Station
Subscriber to the NAB Television Code
Media Code 6 233 0600 8.00
National Broadcasting Co., Inc., RCA Bldg., 30 Rockefeller Plaza, New York, N. Y. 10020. Phone 212-247-8300. TWX 212-640-5788.

1. PERSONNEL
Exec. Vice-Pres. & Gen'l Mgr.—Arthur A. Watson
Station Manager—Monte G. Newman.
Sales Manager—Diran R. Demirjian.

2. REPRESENTATIVES
NBC Spot Sales.
Atlanta, Dallas & St. Louis—Bomar Lowrance & Associates.
Eastern Canada—NBC Spot Television Sales. (N. Y. office)
Pacific Northwest & Western Canada—Simpson/ Reilly & Associates Co.

3. FACILITIES
Video 30,000 0w., audio 5,130 w.; ch 4.
Operating schedule: 5:55-1:45 am. EST.
Antenna ht.: 1,440 ft. above average terrain.

4. AGENCY COMMISSION
15% to recognized agencies on net charges, studio charges production services and station-built programs.

---

5. GENERAL ADVERTISING See coded regulations
General: 2a, 3a, 7b.
Rate Protection: *10f, 14f.
Contracts: 25, 26, 29.
Basic Rates: 40a, 43a, 47a.
Comb.; Cont. Discounts: 62a.
Cancellation: 70a.
Prod. Services: 87b
(*) Unit & Prime time classifications, 28 days from date of announcement.
(†) Either agency or station may terminate contract by written notice to the other at least 28 days, or 4 telecasts prior to the effective date of such termination. No such notice shall be effective until the expiration of at least 28 days after the first broadcast.
Affiliated with NBC Television Network.
Verbal Commercial Changes: When a client or an advertising agency requests that station run a different film, tape or commercial copy from that already or originally scheduled, the station is only responsible for such change when it is in writing and received within 72 hours (not including Saturdays and Sundays). Verbal requests are at client-agency risk and there can be no credit or makegood if such instruction delivered verbally, results in a different film, tape or commercial copy being televised from the one that was requested as a verbal change. Announcements ordered every other week are subject to preemption by announcements running on consecutive weeks.
Advertiser Accommodation Plan. Announcements are sold at reduced rates in return for the station's right to adjust schedules and furnish suitable replacements (or credit) for any announcements preempted, with prior advertiser approval.
Payment date: All charges are payable on the 15th of month following month of telecast unless earlier date of payment has been specified by agreement. Challenge of specific items of billing will not justify delay in payment of undisputed charges.
Product Protection
While we strive to maintain ten (10) minutes separation between competitive announcements, make-goods will only be offered to competitive advertisers running within the same commercial break.
Station retains right to make final determination as to whether products or services are competitive.
Retail Accounts—Protection is limited only to competitive products or in the case of department stores only to competitive departments. In no case will credit be given for a product conflict, suitable make-goods will be offered.

POLITICAL
Time and facilities are sold for political broadcasting on basis of conformity with company policies the Federal Communications Act, and rules and regulations of Federal and State governments

6. TIME RATES
No. 41 Eff 9/8/75—Rec'd 9/17/75.
Rate Designation: Preceding station break spots are considered part of the commercial content of programs beginning at :29 or :59. Such spots are no so considered with programs beginning on the hour or :01, :30 or :31.
All times are approximate.

7. SPOT ANNOUNCEMENTS
PRIME TIME CLASSIFICATIONS
7:29-11 pm Mon thru Fri; 6:59-11 pm Sat & Sun.

	30 sec	30 sec
1	10000 *7	5000
2	9000 *8	4500
3	8000 *9	4000
*4	7000 *10	3500
*5	6000 *11	3000
*6	5500 *12	2000

(*) Preemptible on no notice by higher rate advertiser.
Prime 20 sec: 75% of 30 sec.
Prime 10 sec: 50% of 30 sec.
OTO adjacencies to network specials, when available, take current classifications unless notified 7 days in advance. Rates quoted subject to reclassification on 7 days' advance notification.

8. PARTICIPATING ANNOUNCEMENT PROGRAMS
Rec'd 11/21/75.

	30/20 sec
MON THRU FRI:	
Today—6:59-9 am	400
Not For Women Only—9-9:28 am. R.	400
Day Rotation—9:28 am-3:59 pm. R.	600
PM:	
Robert Young Family Doctor—3:59-4:59. R	1000
News Center 4—4:59-5:58. R.	1200
News Center 4—5:58-7. R.	1500
The Eleventh Hour—11-11:30 Mon thru Sun. R	4500
Tonight Show—11:30 pm-1:01 am. R.	1600
Tomorrow Show—1:01-2:01 am Mon thru Thurs. R	400
Midnight Special—1:01-2:31 am Fri.	700
Great Great Show—2:01 am-concl Mon thru Thurs. R; 2:31 am-concl Fri; 1:01 am-concl Sat	125
SAT:	
Children's Adjacencies—6:59 am-1:30 pm.	500
PM:	
Various—1:30-5:58	300
Kukla Fran & Ollie—5:59-6:30	500
Weekend Varieties/Sammy—11:30 pm-1 am Sat/Sun	125
SUN:	
Various—sign-on-6:29 pm	300
Meet The Press—various	500
6:29 pm	900
Sunday Film Festival—1:01 am-concl.	250
R—Rotates	

60 sec: 200% of the 30 sec.
10 sec: 50% of the 30 sec.

10. PROGRAM RATES
Daily 7 pm-midnight, 1 hr. | 10,700

11. SPECIAL FEATURES
NEWS SPONSORSHIPS

	60 sec	30 sec
News at 7:25/8:25 am Mon thru Fri	800	400
News Center 4—4:59-7 pm Mon thru Fri	3000	1500
The Eleventh Hour—11-11:30 pm Mon thru Sun, approx 5 min	9000	4500

Rates include time & talent.

COLOR
Schedules network color, film, slides, tape and live. Equipped with high band VTR.

---

12. SERVICE FACILITIES
Send film to Room 929; Videotap to Room 572; and commercial instruction send to Traffic Department Room 317-H.

13. CLOSING TIME
2 weeks prior initial program; program material 1 week; 72 hours film, slide and artwork
Submitted by Jim Zafiros.

WNEW-TV
NEW YORK CITY
(Airdate April, 1940.)

Metromedia Television

METRO TV SALES

TvB

Subscriber to the NAB Television Code
Media Code 6 233 0650 3.00
Metromedia Television, Division of Metromedia, Inc., 205 E. 67th St., New York, N. Y. 10021. Phone 212-535-1000. TWX 212-867-6978.

2. REPRESENTATIVES
Metro TV Sales.

WNJU-TV
LINDEN-NEWARK
(Airdate May 16, 1965)

Spanish

Media Code 6 233 0675 0.00
WNJU-TV Broadcasting Corp., 1020 Broad St., Newark, N. J. 07102. Phone 201-643-9100.
New York Sales Office: 711 5th Ave. Phone 212-233-6240.

1. PERSONNEL
Vice-Pres. & Gen'l Mgr.—Carlos Barba.
Director of Sales—Jerry O. MacFarland.
Business Manager—Dominick Cascio.

3. FACILITIES
Video 234,000 w., audio 46,800 w.; ch 47.
Antenna ht.: 1,182 ft. above average terrain.
Operating schedule: 4:30 pm-midnight Mon thru Sat; 4 pm-midnight Sun. EST.

4. AGENCY COMMISSION
15% to recognized agencies on net time charges; no cash discount.

5. GENERAL ADVERTISING See coded regulations
General: 1a, 2a, 2b, 3a, 3b, 3c, 3d, 4a, 5, 6a, 7a.
Rate Protection: 10i, 11i, 12i, 13i, 14i, 15, 17.
Contracts: 20a, 21, 22a, 22b, 22c, 24b, 25, 27a, 28, 29, 31a, 31b, 32b, 32d, 34.
Basic Rates: 40b, 41a, 43a, 44a, 45c, 47, 49, 50.
Comb.; Cont. Discounts: 60f, 61c, 62a.
Cancellation: 70j; 71, 72, 73b.
Prod. Services: 80, 83, 84, 86.
Product Protection: 10 minutes.

6. TIME RATES
No. 11 Eff 8/1/74—Rec'd 11/11/74.
A—Mon thru Sun 6-10:30 pm.
B—Mon thru Sun sign-on-6 pm & 10:30 pm-sign-off.

7. SPOT ANNOUNCEMENTS

CLASS A					
	1 ti	3 ti	5 ti	10 ti	15 ti
60 sec.	235	205	175	145	115
30 sec.	135	115	95	80	65
20 sec.	115	100	85	70	55
10 sec.	90	80	70	55	40

CLASS B					
60 sec.	110	95	85	70	55
30 sec.	65	55	50	40	25
20 sec.	50	45	40	30	25
10 sec.	40	35	30	25	20

8. PARTICIPATING ANNOUNCEMENT PROGRAMS
Rec'd 11/11/74.

CLASS A					
	1 ti	3 ti	5 ti	10 ti	15 ti
60 sec.	250	230	210	190	160
30 sec.	145	135	120	110	90
20 sec.	125	115	100	90	75

CLASS B					
60 sec.	125	110	95	80	65
30 sec.	75	60	55	45	40
20 sec.	60	50	45	35	30
10 sec.	50	40	35	30	25

9. PACKAGE ANNOUNCEMENT RATES
ROS
75% of the applicable time classification fixed-position rates.
ROS rates apply only to schedules with a weekly minimum of 7 spots. ROS spots will be shown at station's discretion.

10. PROGRAM RATES
Mon thru Sun 6-10:30 pm, 1 hr. | 1300

11. SPECIAL FEATURES
COLOR
Schedules network color, film, slides, tape and live. Equipped with high band VTR.

WOR-TV
NEW YORK CITY
(Airdate October 5, 1949)

TvB

Subscriber to the NAB Television Code
Media Code 6 233 0750 1.00
RKO General, Inc., 1440 Broadway, New York, N. Y. 10018. Phone 212-764-7000.

(This listing continued on next page)

Part of a page reproduced from the SRDS Spot Television edition. *Courtesy of SRDS.*

Some of the titles in the SRDS series.

going outdoors during specific periods of time, and how many of these people have an opportunity to see posters, as well as other factors important to the outdoor advertiser. Studies of this kind were made in Cedar Rapids, Iowa, and Fort Wayne, Indiana.

STANDARD RATE & DATA SERVICE

An advertiser must concern himself with rates as well as with circulations. Information on both may be obtained from rate cards published by the individual periodicals and broadcast stations. These cards usually show rates and breakdowns of circulation, indicating something of the quality as well as the quantity of circulation. They also provide specifications on the mechanical requirements for the medium, thus supplying the advertiser with information that he must have for the preparation of plates, films, and other technical details. Most publishers and broadcast station operators have adopted similar formats for their rate cards in keeping with recommendations of the Association of American Advertising Agencies.

An advertiser engaged in placing national advertising in many different media would need to obtain, file, and keep up-to-date a large number of such individual rate cards—a burdensome and costly process. Because of the volume of information required, the need for having current material in usable form, and the low cost of the services, large advertisers and advertising agencies generally subscribe to *Standard Rate & Data Services* (SRDS). Standard Rate & Data Service, Inc., publishes a set of paper-bound reference books for each major medium, such as *Newspaper Rates and Data*. These books give information on personnel, addresses, rates, closing dates, mechanical requirements, circulations, and other facts of importance to advertisers for each of the several different classes of media. The SRDS books are published at regular stated intervals and cover the types of media under the following headings: Newspaper, Consumer Magazines and Farm Publications, Weekly Newspaper, Business Publication, Transit Advertising, Spot Radio, Network, Spot Television, Print Media Production, Medical/Paramedical Edition of Business Publications, and Canadian Advertising. The most recent of the SRDS publications is *Direct-Mail List Rates and Data*.

It should also be noted that each SRDS periodic reference is itself an advertising medium. Each one solicits and accepts ads pertaining to the medium for which the reference book furnishes data. For instance, *Newspaper Rates and Data* carries advertising from newspapers pointing out why advertisers and advertising agencies should use their publications.

SUMMARY

In the early days of advertising, advertisers and agency media buyers had no reliable method of judging the circulation of media. The first step in this direction was the creation of the Audit Bureau of Circulations (ABC) in 1914. The Business Publications Audit (BPA), established in 1931, filled a gap by auditing controlled circulations of certain business publications. Both the ABC and BPA do an excellent job of covering the principal print media. The Traffic Audit Bureau (TAB) performs the same function for the outdoor advertising industry.

Standard Rate & Data Service, or SRDS as it is more commonly known, is one of the greatest services ever furnished to advertisers and media buyers. In addition to the information customarily found on media rate cards, SRDS provides specifications on the media mechanical requirements, deadlines for submission of copy, and other pertinent and useful data. This information is provided in separate volumes for each of the major types of media. The data are brought up to date periodically.

QUESTIONS AND DISCUSSION SUBJECTS

1. What gave rise to the need for the auditing groups?
2. Do auditing groups exist in all countries today?
3. What are the major differences between ABC and BPA?
4. What services are offered by SRDS that are of value to advertisers?

5. How does TAB determine the space-position-value of an outdoor advertising location?

FOR FURTHER READING

Barton, Roger. *Media in Advertising*. New York: McGraw-Hill, 1964.

Bennett, Charles O. *Facts without Opinion*. Chicago: Audit Bureau of Circulations, 1965.

Brown, Lyndon O., Richard S. Lessler, and William W. Weilbacher. *Advertising Media*. New York: Ronald Press, 1957.

McClure, Leslie W., and Paul C. Fulton. *Advertising in the Printed Media*. New York: Macmillan, 1964.

Myers, Kenneth H., Jr. *SRDS*. Evanston, Ill.: Northwestern University Press, 1968.

Broadcast Ratings and Services

The extent to which an advertiser is able to convert a station's potential audience into an actual audience depends, in large measure, upon: (1) the kind and quality of the program that he puts on the air, (2) the time of day or night of the telecast or broadcast, and (3) the kind and quality of programs being telecast or broadcast at the same time over other stations. The degree of success that he achieves in building an actual audience is, of course, of vital concern to him. For this reason, program ratings are crucially important.

A *rating* is a measure of the audience size obtained by a given program. However, the different ratings measure audiences in different terms. The reason for variations in approach is that advertisers and agencies need different kinds of information in making evaluations of programs.

Ratings may be stated in terms of *homes/households* or in terms of *people*. If stated in terms of homes, they may be expressed as (1) a percent of all United States homes or (2) a percent of homes in a specific area. The time involved in computing ratings also varies. The rating may be based on the average minute, on 15 minutes, or on the total period of the broadcast. Still another difference exists in that the rating may be in terms of a single broadcast, or it may be a measure of the cumulative audience obtained over one week or four weeks.

There are also *local ratings* and *network ratings*. The network ratings are based on network programs only and cover all listening or viewing in a group of cities. Local ratings, as the term implies, show the audiences of specific programs irrespective of whether the programs are of local or network origin. Generally, in the major markets, local ratings are made available once a month.

Rating, both local and network, has as a major purpose the informing of advertisers and agencies about how many homes and people listen to or view programs and about when these people do their listening or viewing. Both broadcast stations and advertisers use these reports. The stations subscribe to them because they use ratings both as a sales tool and for programming purposes. For example, a station can tell by looking at ratings whether its 8 o'clock program is doing as well as a competitor's 8 o'clock program; and if it is not, steps can be taken to remedy the situation.

The advertising agencies use ratings because they need something to keep them informed about the listening and viewing habits of people. A time buyer living in New York City cannot have an accurate knowledge of what program preferences are in some distant city without the aid of the ratings or some similar service.

Broadcast ratings generally fall into the following principal categories:

1. Sets in use.
2. Share of audience.
3. Total audience.
4. Program rating.
5. Average audience.

The most basic concept in the rating system for television network program evaluation is the *average audience** measure—the size of the audience during the average minute of the program. This is an A. C. Nielsen Company figure and is reported as a rating index or percentage based on the number of homes reached.

The rating furnished by different services are not always comparable. Popularity of programs differs in urban, small-town, and rural communities. One program may have more urban audience than small-town or rural audience, whereas another may rate just the opposite. There also are differences in living and viewing habits in diferent sections of the country that may affect audience size irrespective of the quality of the program. Such differences may be revealed by the ratings. For example, 10:30 p.m. is regarded as an excellent time in New York City but as a poor time in a city where the habitual time of retiring is earlier. Therefore, it is not possible to tell what a *national rating* will be from a *metropolitan-area report*.

A single report should not be regarded as a typical rating for a program. One large advertising agency feels that there should be an average of at least four reports to determine a rating level. This same agency warns against comparing summer and winter ratings. Inasmuch as there is a high seasonal factor in television, if winter and summer programs are being analyzed, share of audience rather than ratings should be the basis of comparison.

---

* The *Nielsen average audience* is defined as the number of television homes that were tuned to the program during the average minute as a percent of all television homes able to receive the program. This figure is obtainable only through the use of a meter recording of audience listening habits.

RATING METHODS

Diary

This method is employed by Nielsen, American Research Bureau, and Videodex for their television ratings, and by Media Stat for radio.

Essentially, randomly preselected homes are furnished with diaries that are kept close to the televeision set or radio. Each member of the household is supposed to make entries about what he or she has seen and/or heard. Diaries provide basic viewing information along with data on audience characteristics. The system is relatively inexpensive and makes available a great deal of information. Its principal drawback is in the human element—getting people to make the entries and getting them to return the diaries at the close of the test period.

Mail

Like the diary method, mail surveys furnish a great deal of data at low cost. Questionnaires can be mailed anywhere in the United States (and in Canada and Mexico, for that matter) for the same relatively low postal rate.

The method is used principally by Home Testing Institute, which offers what it calls a TVQ score based on a questionnaire mailed to approximately 2,000 children (over age 6) and adults. This sample provides opinion data on network television programs, as well as demographic data on the respondents.

Mechanical Recorder (*Meter*)

The best-known of the electronic metering devices is the Audimeter, more recently called the Storage Instantaneous Audimeter. This is a registered trade name owned by its user, the A. C. Nielsen Company. Nielsen places the SIA in 1,150 homes preselected in accordance with an area probability design. This population sample, representing a cross section of the United States, differs from the samples employed in other rating services in that it does not change except for a normal turnover each year of about 15% to 20%. The fixed sample permits finer delineation of audience trends, according to Nielsen, and allows the tracing of program audience cumulation and duplication over several weeks.

Nielsen Television Index initiated a new Storage Instantaneous Audimeter beginning with the 1973–1974 television season. This device makes possible the daily production of national program rating data on all network sponsored programs between 6 and 11 p.m., New York time. Networks subscribing to the service receive daily ratings on either the first or second working day following the telecast. Each meter is connected electronically to a central-office computer that automatically retrieves the stored data at least twice a day. The new system virtually eliminates nonresponse and delays in collecting tuning information, because no action whatsoever is required on the part of the sample household.

All television sets in a household are measured, including battery-operated portables, and the stored data shows whether a set is on or off, what channel is selected (including CATV and UHF), and for how long. Another feature of the system is that subscribers can receive daily reports (via dial telephone access to a time-sharing facility) as printout in their offices.

Another such mechanical recorder is Arbitron.

Personal Interview (Roster Recall)

Interviewers may go from door to door querying people about the programs they saw and/or heard the previous day. In this personal-interview method, the respondent is aided by a roster of programs handed to him by the interviewer. The list helps him to recall what he has seen. In addition to program information and preferences, the interviewer also collects detailed demographic data. While some might consider this method costly, in fact it is not because reports generally cover a period of four to eight weeks.

The roster-recall method is currently being employed by The Pulse Inc., which publishes reports on radio audience measurements.

One weakness in the personal-interview method is the possibility that the respondent might want to improve his image in the eyes of the interviewer and therefore select programs that he didn't watch but that are culturally more acceptable than the ones he actually did see. This drawback could also distort results in the diary, mail questionnaire, and telephone coincidental methods, but to a lesser extent. Another distortion might occur from those who refuse to answer questions in personal interviews and in the telephone coincidental method.

Telephone Coincidental

This method consists of a personal interview conducted over the telephone—at precisely the time the respondent is watching television. The obvious advantage of this system is the spontaneity and accuracy of responses given while the information is fresh in the mind of the viewer. The number of questions that can be asked are necessarily few; however, the system does make possible the speedy reporting of ratings, often the very next day.

The telephone coincidental method saw considerable application when radio was the principal broadcast medium. C. E. Hooper, Inc. currently provides rating on radio use based on this method, as does Trendex, which furnishes ratings for television network specials.

THE RATING SERVICES

The broadcast media created a need for kinds of media research differing from those that had been employed for measurements in print media. To serve this need, many types of rating services have been developed. Some furnish their reports periodically on a syndicated basis, that is, to any firm or individual who subscribes to the service. Others work only on a custom basis for individual clients. A few of the important services are considered in the following pages.

The American Research Bureau(Arbitron)

The American Research Bureau, known as Arbitron, has employed both the diary and instantaneous meter outlet methods. Up until May 1972, the American Research Bureau placed diaries and meters—also called Arbitron—in television homes in the New York area: diaries alone were furnished to television homes in other markets throughout the country. The metering was then suspended, but the use of diaries continued. Starting in the fall of 1974, meters were again placed in 500 New York homes with television, as well as in 500 Los Angeles television homes. In addition, Arbitron measures 207 other markets or Areas of Dominant Influence (ADIs). (These, according to the rating service, are "now the most widely accepted market definitions.")

Arbitron issues from three to eight reports a year, depending on the size of the market, for the 209 ADIs. These reports provide audience composition and household response for all qualifying television stations in the market. They are based on data furnished by some 400,000 diaries (a 55% return on those sent out), and on the Arbitron meter readings.

American Research Bureau ratings are shown as a percent of the market population—that is, of all television homes within the signal strength of a program's lineup. The ADI reports rate all stations by quarter-hours for every hour of the day. If the station has adequate rating levels, a set of figures for audience composition is included in the report. Samples for the ADI reports range from about 400 to 1,600 television homes per month.

C. E. Hooper, Inc.

Hooper, a wholly owned subsidiary of Daniel Starch and Staff, employs the telephone coincidental interviewing technique. It provides a rating service for approximately 100 markets. Reports are issued from one to twelve times a year in these markets. Information includes Radio Sets in Use and Share of Radio Audience Demographics. Most reports measure quarter-hour periods on a Monday-through-Friday basis although many also contain weekend listening information on client request. Reports cover the hours of 7 a.m. to 10 p.m.

"Hooper" formerly was the important "buy and sell" tool used by advertising agencies, but it is now used principally by radio-station management as a preliminary report, or intelligence, to prevent the stations from becoming locked into a particular position by other rating services before they have a chance to change it.

Hooper also publishes reports on out-of-home radio audiences as follows:

Business Establishment Surveys. These reports are telephone coincidental surveys of retail business establishments listed in the "Yellow Pages" of the telephone directory—beauty shops, barber shops, dental offices, and so on. These are usually done for the "beautiful" music stations and the reports contain information on business establishment radio sets-in-use and the share of audience for all such stations.

College Audience Studies. These studies, employing the telephone coincidental method, assess the 18–24-year-old radio-listening audience to a degree that is not available elsewhere.

A. C. Nielsen Company

The Nielsen Company is the most famous of the rating services. As was stated earlier, it uses an electronic recorder called the Storage Instantaneous Audimeter as the basis for its sampling procedure. Tuning, as Nielsen's basic measure, is regarded as a very workable and readily definable criterion for audience measurement. The national reports issued by Nielsen measure all sponsored television network programs. The reports are issued twice a month, each report covering two weeks of viewing or listening.

In addition to the national reports, Nielsen also produces individual city reports for television. Nielson's Designated Market Areas (DMAs) are comparable to Arbitron's ADIs. Nielsen's local reports include an average of four weeks to assure average conditions. The *Nielsen Station Index,* as the Nielsen local reports are called, also includes cumulative audience data, frequency of viewing, and audience composition. The Nielsen local reports are derived from meters and diaries. If the two kinds of records do not agree for any given home, that home is omitted from the rating report for that particular day.

Additional features of the Nielsen services include information on the audience composition and viewers-per-set, cost efficiencies for all sponsored network programs, the duration of viewing or how long the average home views a program, and minute-by-minute audience profiles. Audience statistics by market and home characteristics (such as county size, territory, age of housewife, and family size) can be had. Special reports can be purchased on program duplication and audience for a spot schedule.

Nielsen reports measure both the average-minute audience and the total audience of a program. They can measure the audience of a particular commercial and can trace television habits. The national reports measure 52 weeks in a year and provide a continuous trend of ratings.

The Pulse, Inc.

Pulse employs the roster-recall method for rating radio programs. Personal interviewers are used exclusively. In order to find more people at home, they begin interviewing late in the afternoon. When a visit is made, all members of a household who are available are interviewed. The interviewing employs an aided-recall technique, using printed rosters that contain, simply, station identification information—call letters, dial position, and slogans. Pulse believes that simply showing this roster would be misleading and would result in unreliable data. Therefore, the interviewers first determine family activity before using the printed roster. When an interviewer finds that there has been no listening, the roster is not shown. Only when a family is found to have devoted time to radio is the roster employed, and then it is accompanied by intensive probing.

NATIONAL *Nielsen* TV RANKING

(Estimates supplementing National Nielsen TV Ratings Report)

EVENING

Rank NAA	Program Name	Prog. Type · Dur. · Ntwk. Freq.	Nielsen Avg. Audience % — This	Last	Share of Audience % — This	Last	Program Coverage
	AVERAGE FOR ALL 113 PROGRAMS		11.9				
1	ALL IN THE FAMILY	CS 30 C1	21.2	20.6	40	34	99
2	*STARSKY AND HUTCH	OP 60 A1	20.7	25.5	42	46	99
3	M*A*S*H	CS 30 C1	20.0	24.2	38	39	99
4	*BARETTA	OP 60 A1	19.4	22.7	38	39	98
5	NBC SUNDAY MYSTERY MOVIE	SM VAR N1	18.7	17.0	36	32	99
6	JIGSAW JOHN	OP 60 N1	18.6	16.6	34	30	97
7	LAVERNE AND SHIRLEY	CS 30 A1	18.2	21.5	37	36	99
8	HAPPY DAYS	CS 30 A1	18.1	22.5	40	41	98
9	MAUDE	CS 30 C1	17.9	18.7	32	30	97
10	MARY TYLER MOORE SHOW	CS 30 C1	17.6	16.9	39	35	99
11	ONE DAY AT A TIME	CS 30 C1	17.4	21.5	32	34	94
12	*ABC MOVIE SPECIAL(S)	FF 115 A1	17.3		33	33	94
12	BOB NEWHART SHOW	CS 30 C1	17.3	17.1	37	34	98
14	KOJAK	OP 60 C1	17.2	15.8	33	30	99
15	SWITCH	PD 60 C1	16.9	17.2	32	31	96
16	MEDICAL CENTER	GD 60 C1	16.6	15.4	30	26	98
16	PHYLLIS	CS 30 C1	16.6	16.6	35	30	98
18	SIX MILLION DOLLAR MAN	A 60 A1	16.3	17.1	33	36	99
19	BARNABY JONES	PD 60 C1	15.8	12.1	31	22	94
19	JOE FORRESTER	OP 60 N1	15.8	16.6	29	29	97
21	BIONIC WOMAN	A 60 A1	15.6	19.0	34	36	99
22	*ABC MOVIE SPECIAL(S)	FF 115 A1	15.2		29		95
23	*LAST DETAIL,THE(S)	CS 30 A1	15.1		29		98
23	WELCOME BACK,KOTTER	CS 30 A1	15.1	16.4	35	34	96
25	POLICE STORY	OP 60 N1	14.9	20.3	31	39	97
26	WONDERFUL WORLD OF DISNEY	FV 60 N1	14.8	11.7	34	28	99
27	*ABC THEATRE(S)	GD 115 A1	14.7		29		98
27	CANNON	PD 60 C1	14.7	14.9	28	25	98
29	DINAH AND FRIENDS	CV 60 C1	14.5	14.8	31	30	97
29	DONNY AND MARIE	GV 60 A1	14.5	15.1	34	32	98
31	BARNEY MILLER	CS 30 A1	14.4	16.2	32	31	96
31	BRONK	OP 60 C1	14.4	13.8	28	26	95
31	NBC THURSDAY NIGHT MOVIES	FF 120 N1	14.4	15.5	29	28	98
34	ROCKFORD FILES	PD 60 N1	14.3	17.3	31	33	96
35	*ROOKIES, THE	OP 60 A1	14.2	15.6	27	28	97
36	HAWAII FIVE-O	OP 60 C1	14.1	15.5	28	28	97
36	*KELLY MONTEITH SHOW	CV 30 C1	14.1		29		97
38	*McCORMACK FOR PRESIDENT(S)	P 5 C1	13.9		30		99
39	SONNY AND CHER SHOW	GV 60 C1	13.8	13.6	28	29	99
40	ELLERY QUEEN	SM 60 N1	13.7	11.8	28	25	99
40	JEFFERSONS, THE	CS 30 C1	13.7	15.7	35	35	99
40	SANFORD AND SON	CS 30 N1	13.7	14.1	33	31	98
40	60 MINUTES	DN 60 C1	13.7	15.0	31	36	99
44	GOOD TIMES	CS 30 C1	13.6	16.6	28	28	97
44	*HARRY O	PD 60 A1	13.6	15.7	27	29	97
46	DOC	CS 30 C1	13.5	15.2	32	33	97
47	JOHN DAVIDSON SHOW	GV 60 N1	13.5	15.9	29	30	94
47	*McCORMACK FOR PRESIDENT(S)	P 5 A1	13.4		27		98
47	POLICE WOMAN	CS 30 N1	13.4	14.9	25	24	94
47	RHODA	CS 30 C1	13.4	15.0	30	29	98
47	STREETS OF SAN FRANCISCO	OP 60 A1	13.4	17.6	27	31	96
52	FRIDAY NIGHT CBS MOVIES	FF VAR C1	13.3	12.9	28	26	95
53	*S.W.A.T.	OP 60 A1	13.2	14.6	24	23	96
54	*JACKSONS, THE	CS 30 C1	13.1		29		97
54	NBC SATURDAY NIGHT MOVIES	FF 120 N1	13.1	14.1	29	29	98
56	ABC MONDAY NIGHT BASEBALL	SE VAR A1	13.0	13.0	24	24	98
57	*BLUE KNIGHT	OP 60 C1	12.7	14.4	26	26	95
57	BEST OF SANFORD AND SON	CS 30 N1	12.5	14.4	25	25	94
59	*EMERGENCY	GD 60 N1	12.0	13.0	29	29	99
60	PRACTICE, THE	CS 30 N1	11.9	12.5	27	26	96
61	*LITTLE HOUSE-PRAIRIE	GD 60 N1	11.8	12.6	26	24	96
61	WALTONS, THE	GD 60 C1	11.8	13.0	27	26	99
63	*BERT D'ANGELO/SUPERSTAR	OP 60 A1	11.7	10.1	25	21	85
63	[illegible]	SE 90 A1	11.7	9.5	23	17	92
65	*U.S. OLYMPIC SWIM. TRIALS(S)	SE 90 A1	11.6		22		98
66	*AMERICAN PARADE(S)		11.6		22		99
67	CBS EVENING NEWS-CRONKITE	N 30 C5	11.4	11.9	28	28	95
67	CITY OF ANGELS	OP 60 N1	11.4	11.2	22	21	99
67	*RETURN-GREATEST DETECTIVE(S)	FF 90 N1	11.4		23		98
67	*TONY ORLANDO AND DAWN	GV 60 C1	11.4	9.4	26	18	98

EVENING (Contd)

Rank NAA	Program Name	Prog. Type · Dur. · Ntwk. Freq.	Nielsen Avg. Audience % — This	Last	Share of Audience % — This	Last	Program Coverage
71	ABC FRIDAY NIGHT MOVIE	FF VAR A1	11.2	14.1	24	27	97
72	*ABC SATURDAY NIGHT MOVIES	FF 90 A1	10.8	12.6	24	26	91
73	*ENTERTAINMENT-FAME AWARDS(S)	AC 120 N1	10.7		26		98
74	CHICO AND THE MAN	CS 30 N1	10.3		19		93
75	MAC DAVIS SHOW	GV 60 N1	10.1	10.0	23	20	93
76	NBC NIGHTLY NEWS	N 30 N5	10.0	10.6	25	24	99
77	*FREEMAN(S)	CS 30 A1	9.9		24		93
78	VIVA VALDEZ	CS 30 A1	9.8	11.7	22	24	89
79	GOOD HEAVENS	CS 30 A1	9.7	10.4	24	23	92
80	*REALLY ROSIE(S)	EA 30 C1	9.5		21		98
81	CBS SUNDAY NEWS-DEAN	N 15 C1	9.4	7.8	22	18	83
81	*NBC NEWS SPECIAL REPORT(S)	N 30 N1	9.4		27		97
83	*I'VE GOT A SECRET	QP 30 N1	9.3		20		89
84	MOVIN' ON	GD VAR N1	9.2	9.2	20	16	86
85	CBS SATURDAY NEWS-RATHER	N 30 C1	9.1	9.7	27	28	92
86	TONIGHT SHOW	GV VAR N5	8.3	8.0	31	30	99
87	*COACHES ALL AMERICAN FTBL(S)	SE 190 A1	8.0		19		98
88	SARA	GD 60 C1	7.7	8.4	18	19	92
89	ROOKIES-11:30 P.M.	OP 60 A1	7.5	7.2	23	21	95
90	*UNDERSEA WORLD-J.COUSTEAU(S)	DO 60 A1	7.4		17		90
91	ABC NEWS-REASONER	N 30 A5	7.2	7.3	18	17	99
92	NBC SUNDAY NIGHT NEWS	N 30 N1	6.8	6.7	18	19	84
92	WED. MOVIE OF THE WEEK	FF 60 A1	6.8	7.7	24	27	95
94	*CBS NEWS SPECIAL REPORT(S)	N 60 C1	6.7		25		97
94	*GOODALL-ANIMAL BEHAVIOR(S)	DO 15 A1	6.7		15		82
94	MANNIX	PD 70 A1	6.7	6.9	24	26	96
97	*CBS EVENING NEWS	N 30 C1	6.5	9.6	17	26	89
97	LATE NIGHT CBS MOVIES	FF 105 C5	6.5	5.4	27	24	88
99	*POL. SPIRIT OF '76(S)	N 30 A1	6.2		21		94
99	*U.S.OPEN GOLF-FRI(S)	SE 30 A1	6.2		13		98
101	*FRIENDS(S)	GV 80 N1	5.9		20		94
101	NBC SATURDAY NIGHT NEWS	N 30 N1	5.9	4.9	18	14	86
103	*ABC NEWS CLOSEUP(S)	DN 60 A1	5.2		10		98
104	ABC WEEKEND NEWS-SUN.	N 15 A1	5.2	5.9	12	14	97
105	MAGICIAN, THE	PD 50 A1	5.0	4.8	30	29	96
106	*SATURDAY NIGHT	GV 85 N1	4.9	6.6	26	25	91
107	ABC WEEKEND NEWS-SAT.	N 15 A1	4.5	5.9	13	13	95
108	MONDAY NIGHT SPECIAL	FV 60 A1	4.4	4.5	16	18	94
108	ABC NEWS-KOPPEL	N 30 A1	4.3	4.9	13	14	74
109	TUES. MYSTERY OF THE WEEK	SM 60 A1	4.3	4.5	17	19	98
111	MIDNIGHT SPECIAL	PC 90 N1	4.1	4.0	26	26	98
112	TOMORROW SHOW	CC 45 N4	3.1	2.8	21	22	95
113	*NBC NEWS SPECIAL REPORT(S)	N 30 N1	2.1		17		90

WEEKDAY DAYTIME

Rank NAA	Program Name	Prog. Type · Dur. · Ntwk. Freq.	Nielsen Avg. Audience % — This	Last	Share of Audience % — This	Last	Program Coverage
	AVERAGE FOR ALL 42 PROGRAMS		5.9				
1	ALL IN THE FAMILY M-F	CS 30 C5	9.7	9.1	35	33	99
2	AS THE WORLD TURNS	DD 60 C5	9.7	9.4	36	37	99
3	MATCH GAME '76	QP 30 C5	9.6	9.1	32	30	98
4	HAPPY DAYS M-F	CS 30 A5	9.5	7.6	41	35	96
5	ANOTHER WORLD	DD 60 N5	9.1	8.9	31	31	99
6	YOUNG AND THE RESTLESS	DD 30 C5	9.0	8.5	37	37	96
7	GUIDING LIGHT	DD 30 C5	8.6	8.0	33	33	99
8	SEARCH FOR TOMORROW	DD 30 C5	8.4	8.2	34	35	99
9	DAYS OF OUR LIVES	DD 60 N5	7.6	7.0	28	27	99
10	ALL MY CHILDREN	DD 30 A5	7.5	6.9	29	28	99
11	DOCTORS, THE	DD 30 N5	6.8	6.3	26	26	99
12	PRICE IS RIGHT	AP 60 C5	6.8	6.5	38	37	97
13	BREAK THE BANK	QP 30 A5	6.5	6.2	25	26	97
13	LOVE OF LIFE	DD 25 C5	6.5	6.4	28	30	98
15	CBS MID-DAY NEWS-EDWARDS	N 5 C5	6.4	6.3	27	28	92
15	$20,000 PYRAMID	QG 30 A5	6.4	6.1	23	24	98
17	EDGE OF NIGHT	DD 30 A5	6.2	6.0	22	21	95
17	TATTLETALES	GD 30 C5	6.2	5.7	21	19	90
19	RHYME AND REASON	QP 30 A5	6.1	5.5	23	22	98
20	ONE LIFE TO LIVE	DD 30 A5	6.0	6.0	20	20	95

* Telecast one week only in this report interval.
= For definitions of Program Type abbreviations see pocketpiece.
(S) Special or Pre-empting Program

These data are confidential and subject to same permissible uses as NTI Ratings Reports.
Telecasts with curtailed station facilities are excluded.
Programs are rated in terms of total duration.

1

The new Nielsen Audimeter.

Pulse interviews over 500,000 families a year. The data it furnishes can be applied directly for programming, for buying or selling time, or for other activities associated with radio advertising.

Pulse also makes available much qualitative data for network programs including product usage information and family characteristics.

Daniel Starch and Staff

Starch, which in the past produced TV Commerical Impression Studies and other television reports on a syndicated basis, now does them on rare occasions, and only on order.

Interviews were conducted by telephone one hour immediately following the program. Respondents were selected at random in test cities chosen from among 30 cities on the basis of a geographical spread and the ratings of the programs being studied.

Starch still retains the capability, however, to do the studies when required, and they continue to prepare their reports on print media advertising.

Trendex

Trendex maintains the largest continually active staff in the world. Its operations are located in more than 600 cities throughout the United States and are available for rating both radio and television programs. The telephone coincidental method is employed to this end. Random telephone calls are made during the presentation of the program that is to be rated, and questions are asked concerning the program—the channel over which it is being received, the composition of the audience, and other matters.

Surveys can be done locally, regionally, or nationwide, depending upon the needs of the clients—and results can be obtained overnight, for delivery next day.

Qualitative studies of television program audiences involving program reaction, intention to view next week, and awareness of program promotion are conducted periodically—usually in the fall and midwinter when new schedules are established.

Like Starch, Trendex no longer does broadcast-oriented research to the same extent as in the past; all audience studies are done on a custom basis. In fact, these studies are only a small part of Trendex operations; consumer, market, and opinion surveys now account for more than 90% of its total gross business.

Leading National Advertisers (LNA)

The LNA Multi-Media Reports summarize brand expenditures in six media—including network television, spot television, and network radio—showing top-line brand totals. LNA is a successor to the N. C. Rorabaugh Co., which formerly published a quarterly report on spot television advertising based on the detailed activity reports supplied by more than 300 television stations located in over 200 television markets throughout the United States.

Other Broadcast Rating Services

While some of the broadcast rating services which had been important in the past are now active in other areas, a few new firms have entered the field. These include Market Trends in Radio, of Chicago; and The Source, based in Los Angeles. Others, mentioned in this chapter, include Videodex, Media Stat, and Home Testing Institute.

THE BROADCAST RATING COUNCIL AND CONTAM

As a result of Congressional hearings early in 1963, the National Association of Broadcasters established the Broadcast Rating Council to create a new minimum standards for rating services, to accredit them, and to audit them. At the same time, the Committee on Nationwide Television Audience Measurements (CONTAM) was created to investigate the aspects of national television ratings questioned by Congress. CONTAM is a joint research group consisting of representatives from the three national television networks and the National Association of Broadcasters.[1]

CONTAM's first report, published in February 1966, showed three noteworthy facts: (1) The results of small random samples used in measuring the television-viewing behavior of large numbers of television houses are statistically accurate. (2) There was a small amount of bias introduced into the diary- or meter-based sample by the refusal of some member of the sample to cooperate; however it is far less significant than in the past. (3) The ratings obtained by the American Research Bureau (Arbitron) and Nielsen in measuring the same programs on the same days, despite great differences in procedure, were remarkably similar.[2]

The fourth study sponsored by CONTAM was presented at the Advertising Research Foundation Annual Conference in October 1969. It concluded that the difference between telephone coincidental audience-size estimates, and those obtained from meters were apparently caused by placing too much weight on sample units giving less than full information (no answer, busy signal, language difficulty, etc.). In other words, if disconnected phones are misidentified as nonanswering phones, and are assumed to be nontuning households, a sizeable underestimate of audience results.[3] These findings were borne out by two later studies, one completed at the end of 1969 and the other in the spring of 1970.[4]

SUMMARY

In the same way that advertisers in the print media want to know the circulations of newspapers and magazines, so too do they want information relative to the audiences of television and radio programs. These data are provided by a number of rating services which determine the size and make-up of the audiences.

The techniques or methods employed to measure audiences include diaries, mail surveys, mechanical recorders or meters, personal interviews, and telephone coincidental. The principal rating services are Arbitron, Hooper, Nielsen, The Pulse, Daniel Starch and Staff, and Trendex.

Rating services are accredited by the Broadcasting Rating Council, which was established by the National Association of Broadcasters. The Council also sets minimum standards. A further control is provided by the Committee on Nationwide Television Audience Measurements (CONTAM).

QUESTIONS AND DISCUSSION SUBJECTS

1. In what respects do the rating services of the following differ: (a) American Research Bureau; (b) C. E. Hooper, Inc.; (c) A. C. Nielsen Company; (d) The Pulse, Inc.; (e) Trendex; (f) Daniel Starch and Staff.
2. Why do advertising agencies employ the rating services, and what uses do they make of the ratings?
3. Why do radio and television stations subscribe to the rating services?
4. On what grounds have the ratings sometimes been criticized?
5. Why do advertisers and agencies frequently subscribe to more than one rating service?

6. Why are the ratings furnished by different services not always comparable?
7. What is CONTAM?

SOURCES

1. Martin Mayer, *How Good are Television Ratings?* (1966), 4, 5.
2. *Ibid.*
3. *How Good Are Television Ratings? (continued . . .)* (New York: Television Information Office, 1969), 1, 26, 27.
4. *Television Ratings Revisited . . .* (New York: Television Information Office, 1971), 7, 8.

FOR FURTHER READING

Bellaire, Arthur. *TV Advertising: A Handbook of Modern Practice.* New York: Harper, 1959.
Head, Sydney W. *Broadcasting in America: A Survey of Televison and Radio.* Third Edition,. Boston: Houghton Mifflin, 1976.
Steiner, Gary. *The People Look at Television: A Study of Audience Attitudes.* New York: Knopf, 1963.

Part Four

MEDIA

★
★
★ 17
★
★

Media Evaluation and Use

AN INTRODUCTION TO MEDIA

After an advertisement has been created it must be brought to the attention of prospective customers in some manner. The vehicles through which this is accomplished are called *advertising media,* or, if spoken of in the singular, *advertising medium.* Frequently, in everyday use, the term *advertising* is dropped and reference is made to *media* or to a *medium.*

The leading advertising media are newspapers, magazines, radio, television, direct mail, outdoor advertising, and transit advertising. Outdoor advertising includes poster panels, painted signs, and electrical advertising displays—all erected on structures out-of-doors. Transit advertising includes the advertising carried on both the inside and outside of such mass-transportation vehicles as buses, suburban railroad cars, street cars, and subways. The transit medium also includes the posters placed on station platforms or within stations or airport terminals, as well as any advertising that might appear on timetables and schedules.

There are also several other media such as specialty items, match books, motion pictures, and even various forms of sky advertising that make use of airplanes and lighter-than-air craft. Reference is sometimes made to major and minor media. But almost obviously, what is a minor medium to one advertiser may be major to another. Therefore, any such references must refer to the degree or extent of overall use and not to the importance any medium has for individual advertisers.

The principal media are generally grouped into two broad categories: (1) the electronic or broadcast media—television and radio; (2) the print media—newspapers and magazines chiefly, plus direct mail, some outdoor advertising, point-of-purchase advertising, specialty advertising, and transit advertising.

The men and women who create advertisements—the copywriters, the art-

257

ists, and the production people—must know in what medium each advertisement is scheduled to appear. Therefore the media or medium must be chosen even before the first step of visualization can be made. Selection of the best medium to do a specific job in terms of market coverage is a problem that every advertiser, large or small, must solve. It is by no means an easy problem. First, there is the task of choosing among different types of media. Once this choice has been made, the advertiser must decide which medium or media within the type or types chosen best suit his needs. For example, if magazines have been selected as the best media for the job at hand, there still remains the problem of determining which specific magazine or magazines to use out of the many that are available. If television or radio is the chosen medium, the advertiser must decide whether to use a network or individual stations. If he decides on a network, there is still a question of which network to use; if individual stations are his choice, he must decide which stations. Slide rules, computers, and reference books will help but they alone will not solve the problem—they will not give all the answers. Behind the mechanical aids, behind the current statistics, behind the rate cards and the Standard Rate & Data Service (SRDS) publications, there must be a solid body of knowledge and good judgment to do the thoroughly constructive media job that present-day competitive markets demand—judgment built of experience and occasionally supported by what one agency calls "flashes of creative imagination."

PROBLEMS IN EVALUATION

Big advertising budgets do not eliminate media problems. Rarely, if ever, does the media man have all the dollars that he would like to have in order to accomplish all the things he would like to do. The media problem is still further complicated by the increasing number of carriers from which selection must be made. Information published in 1975 mentioned approximately 695 commercial TV stations,[1] 4,422 AM radio stations,[2] 2,468 FM radio stations,[3] 1,768 daily newspapers,[4] 641 Sunday newspapers,[5] 9,379 country (or weekly) newspapers,[6] 4 national newspapers,[7] 4 newspaper supplements,[8] more than 1,200 consumer and farm magazines, and some 800 outdoor advertising plants,[9] all of which can be used effectively to sell a client's products or services. In addition there are car cards and station posters, specialty advertising of various kinds, direct mail, motion-picture advertising, and a number of other means of reaching potential markets.

Interdependent Elements in the Media Plan

Because of this wide choice in media and because of changing marketing situations, the advertising agency of today has to be better informed in more areas than it used to be. It has to be staffed with well-rounded people who are closely related to the client's special marketing problems and who have the ability to determine which forms of available media are best able to give the most complete and convincing expression to a special selling idea.

COMPARISON OF ADVERTISING OF MAJOR MEDIA IN 1973 AND 1974

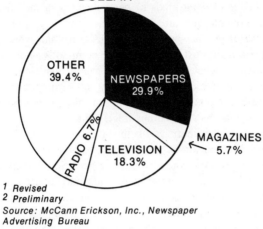

SHARE OF ADVERTISING DOLLAR

OTHER 39.4%

NEWSPAPERS 29.9%

RADIO 6.7%

TELEVISION 18.3%

MAGAZINES 5.7%

1 Revised
2 Preliminary
Source: McCann Erickson, Inc., Newspaper Advertising Bureau

		1973[1]		1974[2]		Per cent
		Millions	% of Total	Millions	% of Total	Change
Newspapers	Total	$ 7,595	30.3%	$ 8,000	29.9%	+ 5.3
	National	1,111	4.4	1,193	4.4	+ 7.5
	Local	6,484	25.9	6,807	25.5	+ 5.0
Magazines	Total	1,448	5.8	1,525	5.7	+ 5.0
Television	Total	4,460	17.8	4,850	18.3	+ 9.0
	Network	1,968	7.8	2,165	8.2	+10.0
	Spot	1,377	5.5	1,460	5.5	+ 6.0
	Local	1,115	4.5	1,225	4.6	+10.0
Radio	Total	1,690	6.7	1,790	6.7	+ 6.0
	Network	70	0.3	70	0.3	0.0
	Spot	380	1.5	380	1.4	0.0
	Local	1,240	4.9	1,340	5.0	+ 8.0
Farm Pubs		65	0.3	65	0.2	0.0
Direct Mail		3,698	14.7	3,920	14.8	+ 6.0
Business Papers		865	3.4	915	3.4	+ 6.0
Outdoor	Total	308	1.2	335	1.3	+ 9.0
	National	200	0.8	220	0.8	+10.0
	Local	108	0.4	115	0.5	+ 6.0
Miscellaneous	Total	4,951	19.8	5,240	19.7	+ 6.0
	National	2,573	10.3	2,735	10.3	+ 6.0
	Local	2,378	9.5	2,505	9.4	+ 5.0
Total	National	13,755	54.8	14,648	55.0	+ 6.0
	Local	11,325	45.2	11,992	45.0	+ 5.0
GRAND TOTAL		$25,080	100.0%	$26,640	100.0%	+ 5.9

An advertising agency executive dramatically illustrated the problem that faces the modern media man by citing a hypothetical situation in which an agency, faced with creating a media plan for a client, asks a media man to go into his office and work out the plan behind closed and locked doors. Faced with such a situation, what does the media man need for the job?

First of all, he requires a complete picture of the client's marketing position—knowledge of what kinds of people represent the client's prospects, where they live, how old they are, whether they are women or men, how often they buy the type of product produced by the client and what they use it for. Further, the media man must know what the competitive position of his client is—more specifically, what his share of the overall market is, how this varies by market size and by regions of the country, how competitive his prices are, whether he is selling a quality brand for more than his competitors or a more popular brand for less than his competitors. This media man must also know his client's pattern of distribution, whether the product can be bought from a large number of different kinds of retail outlets or whether it is sold through exclusive agencies. He must know whether distribution is national, regional or local—whether it is primarily urban or extends into suburban and rural areas. Knowledge must be obtained concerning how much purchasers can spend per case or per box, how much volume it will take to "pay out" successfully, how important are special promotions, and whether there are peaks in demand that suggest special promotions at certain times of the year.

No start can be made in considering what media plan should be employed for taking the client's product story to the consumer until the media man obtains this background information. Therefore, the media man becomes dependent upon the research and marketing departments of the advertising agency and upon the client to help him determine the product's present marketing position as well as its future marketing objectives.

But, even after all this information has been obtained, the media man is not able to proceed with the media plan without further aid from beyond his closed and locked doors. He may know that the product's distribution is concentrated primarily in metropolitan areas, that the best prospects are found among larger and younger families, that the product is priced lower than competitors' brands, that it responds well to advertising and promotions, that it is bought primarily by women in grocery stores, that it sells best in the fall and winter months, and that, on the average, a family uses three packages a year. He may know all this and more, and still he is not yet able to start on media evaluation and selection.

What additional information must he have before he can prepare a media plan that will generate the proper weight toward the people that are the best prospects and still match the advertising weight to any seasonal peaks? The answer is that he cannot possibly proceed intelligently until he knows what kind of story is to be told about the product.

The media man has learned what kinds of people have to be reached to sell his client's product, but he must also know what kind of sales story is going to be told to these people and in what manner it is to be delivered—written, spoken, or both. Therefore, he once more becomes dependent upon other members of the advertising agency team. He must learn what the copy, art, television, and radio groups have planned. He must know whether the copy platform will contain a theme that depends upon the use of demonstrations to make a sale, or whether it is a matter of creating an atmosphere of quality and prestige to build an impression of brand leadership. He must know whether the copy story needs illustration to support it, whether color is vital to an effective demonstration. He must know whether the copy story is highly competitive, whether it contains a long list of reasons why the product should be bought or is a short appeal based on a key slogan that requires frequent repetition.

This mass of information is vital to the media man before he can start to consider media plans. One theme may depend upon daytime television for its most effective presentation. Another may best fit into the pages of a high-quality prestige magazine. Still another may call for the use of spot radio and outdoor posters, or possibly a news announcement story that fits naturally into the columns of a daily newspaper.

Even when the media man is informed of the copy strategy that will be used, he still needs one more piece of information. He must know as completely as possible the kind and amount of advertising weight that is being applied by his client's competitors. He needs complete information about this competitive advertising in terms of dollars spent and consumer advertising impressions made, by market sizes and regions, as well as by seasons. He must know where advertising pressure is being directed in terms of age and income groups. The media man knows that if his plan is to be thoroughly competitive, one of his objectives must be to make his client's advertising dollars more efficient than those of his competitors.

The purpose of the advertising agency executive in describing the problems of this hypothetical media man was to illustrate the fact that agency functions cannot be regarded as separate, unrelated activities, that media evaluation and use are far from simple problems, and that like all other functions they are completely dependent upon close teamwork among several agency departments.

Media plans, if they are to be sound, practical, and creative, must stem from marketing considerations, copy strategy, and a complete awareness of the activities of competitors.

Considerations in the Choice of Media

Media evaluation, selection, and use are more important than they used to be. The reason for this can be traced to two basic developments. The first is the growing importance of all forms of communication. The second is the increased competition in many areas of present-day business. The growth in the means of communication has made the advertising business considerably more complex than it once was.

Today, media recommendations, like all marketing proposals, are more difficult to make and require far more study than they did in the past. In the second decade of the present century, the advertising man still chose among national magazines, newspapers, and perhaps outdoor and transit advertising as carriers of his sales messages. Then along came radio, and new advertising techniques had to be developed. Dollars that once had flowed largely into newspaper and magazine advertising now had another powerful medium into which they could be diverted. Next came television, which soon became a major contender for media-budget dollars.

An advertising budget of a million dollars in 1939 would have bought a pretentious advertising program composed of magazines, newspapers, and probably network radio, with adequate frequency in each. Today, with three or four times that sum, a company is far less important as an advertiser than it would have been with less than a million in the 1940s.

Not only does the advertiser of today have more places where he can spend his media dollars, but moreover in many areas there is more competition to fight. Under these conditions, the present-day advertiser cannot afford many mistakes in his product, his selling strategy, his copy theme, or his media plan.

Today's advertiser has a choice among media of big circulations. A single issue of one national monthly magazine, *Reader's Digest,* is read by more than 44 million people. And an average issue of one national weekly magazine, *TV Guide,* has more than 42 million adult readers. A telecast of one of the children's classics, according to a newspaper estimate, was seen by more people during the course of a single show than could have witnessed it had it played to a full house on Broadway, two performances a day, seven days a week for a century. A showing of *The Godfather* over the NBC network had an estimated audience of 90 million.

The major audience studies that are being conducted for leading publications and by broadcast measurement services, although subject to certain margins of error, represent important contributions to the overall attempt to bring more science into the business. They are the major bases for information on coverage and penetration of programs and publications, and they are invaluable sources in telling the advertiser what kinds of people, with respect to income, age, and other important considerations, are being reached through their properties. These characteristics are important and deserve the full attention of the advertiser, but if and when emphasis is placed on total audience, the advertiser should be aware of the limitations involved in this concept. For example, let us say that 13 issues of a particular magazine *reach* a total of 73 million people. When these figures are reviewed in terms of the *frequency* with which these people are reached it is found that of the total number, 36 million read one to three issues, about 21 million are reached four to seven times, and 16 million eight to thirteen times.

If an advertiser is going to be completely realistic in his appraisal of media values, he should be interested primarily in the "hard core" of regular readers who see eight to thirteen issues, and next most interested in those who are reached four to seven times, and perhaps relatively little interested in the mass of 36 million people who see three or fewer issues. The same thinking applies to any mass-media audience, not to magazines alone.

Repetition is the key aspect of advertising. This is a basic principle, one that has been drummed into the thinking of advertising people for years. And although it cannot be determined by slide rule or computer exactly how many times a prospect must be reached to convince him that he should buy a particular product, the goal of every advertiser is to gain the greatest possible frequency with the largest groups of potential customers that his advertising dollars will buy.

There is, however, another school of thought about frequency and repetition. Agreeing that they are important, this school holds that the same results can be attained with less frequent pitches to a large audience than with 13 pitches to a smaller one, that a short and intensive campaign is more effective in gaining maximum audience recall than 13 ads or commercials spread over a full year.[10]

People's interests in products differ not only from product to product but according to the particular circumstances of any individual at the time his attention is directed toward a given product. A new-model automobile may have great intrinsic interest for most people at certain times, but, on the other hand, there are also times when it may not be so easy to arouse interest in a 15-cent bar of candy. However, there are surely times when many individuals may be more interested in candy than in automobiles. To make sure of creating interest in such areas of product selling requires reaching and selling the prospects over and over again; an appraisal of a medium's audience must be related to its hard core of frequently reached people. The advertiser must be concerned with how many people and how many families a medium delivers with sufficient frequency to enable him to make a sale. Thus he must concentrate weight in the media in the geographical areas where he can reach his market most efficiently, striving for the utmost in continuity.

Some studies have provided ample documentation for this proposition. For instance, take the case of an advertiser who must decide between two ways of reaching a consumer audience through national magazines. One way involves the use of thirteen pages in one magazine; the other way calls for the use of six pages in one magazine and seven pages in another of equal size. The first plan, that of concentrating the thirteen pages in one publication, will get him a hard-core audience of frequently reached people two to three times as large as he can get by going into the two magazines. Or again, suppose that the advertiser is choosing between every-week use of a nighttime half-hour television program and an alternate-week use of two programs. The programs are similar in content and size of audience. By concentrating his advertising on one program he ends up with a hard-core audience of frequently reached viewers that may be eight to ten times as large as he could get by splitting his efforts between the two programs, according to the statement of a leading advertising agency.

With the tremendous increase in advertising competition facing any national advertiser today, considerations of this kind are very important. With all the sales messages that surround the consumer in all forms of media it is difficult enough to make an impression in depth. If the client's advertising dollars are going to be spent with maximum efficiency, more information about the hard core of media audiences must be had so that more ingenious ways of reaching the best prospects and selling them with the greatest possible frequency can be devised.

Another vital step in refining and improving the values of media research is that of completing the circuit that relates media penetration to product use. It is important to measure the total size of the audiences reached by any medium. But, what the advertiser really wants to know if, say, he is selling first-aid kits, is which medium delivers the most *families that use or could be convinced to buy first-aid kits*—and delivers them most efficiently. If the advertiser is selling cosmetics, he is interested in the total number of women reached by the service magazines; but he is much more interested, or should be, in learning which of these publications will deliver most efficiently the *women who are the greatest users of cosmetics*. It is through this kind of media analysis that much of the risk involved in spending the client's advertising money can be reduced.

The advertiser is not really spending his money to reach just *people,* but to reach *people who buy specific products or who use specific services*. It is the advertising agency's responsibility to show him where such people can be reached in the greatest number for the least money and in the right kind of environment that will permit his sales message to work most effectively. This reference to the "right kind of environment" means that the quality of the prospects must be regarded in direct relation to their confidence and belief in the integrity of the publication or the television or radio program under consideration. It is in this area that the media man, once all the figures are available, may decide to override the statistical conclusions and base his appraisal on judgment. This is the difference between a media recommendation that stems solely from figures and one that combines scientific research with inspiration and imagination.

Direction

When Alice inquired of the Cheshire Cat in Wonderland which direction she should take, the cat replied that it depended largely upon where she wished to arrive. So, too, in media selection, before a path can be chosen, the goal must be determined. There are no sure paths to success, no foolproof formulas in the media side of the advertising business any more than there are in any other business where "art" plays at least as important a role as "science."

Some companies place a major portion of their advertising budgets in television, others are heaviest in newspapers, still others place the weight of their advertising money in consumer magazines, and each may be selling a satisfactory volume of goods. So, in the final analysis, *which* medium is used and *how* it is used are of equal importance. A medium must be used so as to give the simplest, most believable, and most dramatic expression to the product story. If one advertiser makes such use of a medium and another does not, the latter disappointing results may appear to be springing from an unhappy choice of medium but may be, in reality, the result of a less dynamic employment of the medium.

But even when the goal or final destination is known, the choice of medium may not always be readily apparent. There may appear to be several paths, any one of which seemingly leads to the same place. However, when such a situation is reduced to its bare essentials, there is no such thing as identical paths in media plans. The roads may look alike, but they will end up in different places. Different media serve different purposes. Different copy themes call for different media selection. Finally, after all the facts are weighed, no two plans are exactly alike.

MEDIA STRATEGY

A factor beyond selection of media is involved in obtaining the best possible results. The advertiser whose *strategy* in the use of media is to relate his advertising message directly to the audience served by the medium is thereby compounding the value he gets from his advertising dollars.

Usually a marketing plan consists of four parts:
1. A selling plan.
2. A copy plan.
3. A media plan.
4. A promotional plan.

But the strategy dimension often can be added. It may involve the ingenious timing of an advertising message, the selection of an unusual or conspicuous position, the harnessing of the flexibility of certain forms of media, or the selection of a medium with particular strengths that will permit the product story to work with maximum effectiveness. Sometimes it involves the degree of weight, the number of pages or the number of commercials that are applied at a particular time. There are no set rules, standards, or sources that can be used to arrive at this kind of media thinking. It is at this point that the judgment, the experience, and the creative skills of the media man come into full play. It is at this point that the media man becomes a truly important member of the agency team.

Probably a review of the past century of advertising would reveal that more progress has been made in media research since the 1960s than in all the years that went before. Media research is the kind of research that tells how many people were reached with this magazine or that television show, what proportion of the audience is in the younger or the older age groups, how the audience is divided by various sizes of markets or by income groups, and so on. But possibly a little too much time is being spent in the quantitative measurements of media and too little in the more creative area of the *dynamics of media strategy*.

The dynamics of media strategy is concerned with the more resourceful and imaginative uses by which the medium itself almost becomes a part of the product story. Three examples will show more clearly what is meant and why advertisers will need much more of this kind of thinking if they are to do the job required of them.

Some years ago, someone put forth the idea that the station break was a natural, a perfect time for an advertising claim about the value and dependability of a particular brand of watch.

During the competitive struggle for market leadership, a food company used a seven-page section of four-color bleeds in a national magazine that dramatically presented all of its ready-mixes to the consumer and to the trade. Later, these sections were also mailed in large, colorful envelopes to every important grocery man in America. At the time this was done, the use of multipage advertisements was in its infancy, and the impact was great.

Another instance of the dynamic use of media lies in the copy format that was employed by some advertisers when the *Reader's Digest* first started to accept advertising. This copy technique, still used today, consists of adapting the copy to the *Digest's* editorial style and layout. The result is informative editorial-type advertising that presents a logical story about the product in the same documentary style that is used by the magazine's editors. However, overuse of this technique has reduced its effectiveness.

The people responsible for the development of these dynamic approaches to the selection and use of media may or may not have been deeply involved in the statistical appraisal of media values. But whether they were or not, it is apparent that they were making serious efforts to break away from the commonplace in media use and to approach the job with imagination and resourcefulness. By so doing they went far toward increasing the value received for the advertising dollars that they spent.

All advertisers and all advertising agencies have the same opportunity to buy media to advertise products or services. They can buy space in newspaper X at 55 cents per line, a spot on television station Y for $160, a 100-showing of outdoor posters in city Z for $1,460, or a black-and-white page in monthly magazine Q for $15,500. Incidentally, the lowest price is not necessarily the best choice. In advertising, cost is computed by a simple formula: the rate charged by the medium is divided by the circulation or readership count or the audience count or the traffic count; then the result of this operation is multiplied by 1,000; the resulting figure is the *cost per thousand* or *CPM*. The CPM concept makes it possible to compare media rates on the same basis.

However, being sure that their advertising dollars are being spent in the places that will give a maximum impact and exposure for the money should not be regarded by an advertiser or his agency as the whole job. The skill and imagination that an advertiser or an agency employs in the use of media make the difference between an ordinary campaign and an inspired one. Consider some historic examples.

When Astronaut Neil Armstrong made that historic "one small step for a man, one giant leap for mankind," a number of the products of the inventive genius of American industry went with him and his crew mates aboard Apollo

XI. Most of their manufacturers tied promotions to the occasion, which was the greatest newsmaking event of the decade if not of the century. Tang, an orange-colored citrus fruit drink, advertised itself as the drink that accompanied the astronauts into space.

In like fashion, other companies gear their advertising to coming events and holidays. Western Union, for example, ran its ads for its Candy-Gram in newspapers the day before Christmas. The headline said, "This is the only gift you can send *today* across the country in time for Christmas!" How can better timing be achieved for making a sale than when the prospects are at a psychological buying peak?

An advertisement for Pan American Airways suggested that the readers might like to "fly like Peter Pan" and told why Mary Martin took Pan American to Paris. On the very evening of the day that this advertisement appeared in the newspapers, some 65 million people, after weeks of advance publicity, were waiting to see Mary Martin fly like Peter Pan in her television performance of the Barrie story.

Timing was the key to dynamic strategy in these advertisements. But there can be more than timing.

When the state of the nation's ecology became "important" many advertisers climbed aboard the bandwagon to show what they or their products were doing to preserve or improve the environment. Petroleum refiners took lead out of their gasolines and let us know about it in their advertising. The Humble Oil Company (now Exxon) did an entire series of radio and television commercials showing that their drilling operations, onshore and offshore, do not disturb the ecology.

A number of years ago, Marlboro cigarettes entered the filtertip free-for-all. Here was a quality product that over the years had come to be known as a woman's cigarette. The advertising campaign was designed with one basic objective—in the words of the advertising agency, "to take Marlboros out of the boudoir and endow them with masculinity." Rugged characters—sailors, fighters, and cowboys—were shown in Marlboro ads with tattoos on their hands and wrists. But the choice of media also played an important part in attaining the goal of the campaign. What could be more masculine than big, black newspaper pages with king-size subjects, or than full-color magazine ads and television commercials showing these men in action?

Similarly, Johnson & Johnson developed a hair shampoo which they advertised exclusively for babies. By no strange coincidence it was called a "baby shampoo." As soon as they had achieved success in that segment of the market they began to advertise that, in effect, what was good for Baby was good for Mom, and finally it was demonstrated to be good for Dad too. Johnson & Johnson follow the same marketing policy with their baby powder and other similar products.

Some time ago, a 24-sheet poster (billboard) showing a baby stretched across its length, completely unclothed and with no accompanying copy, appeared in virtually every city, town, and community throughout the nation. The suspense was great. People called, wrote, and wired the outdoor advertising plants to find out what the poster was all about. Ten days later, timed to within a day of the introduction of the new model, the copy "Smooth as a New Ford!" was stripped in. Here, surely, was a dynamic use of the outdoor medium.

The dynamic approach can be applied to television as successfully and in some respects more easily than to print media. Television can deliver more in terms of product demonstration than can possibly be achieved in any other way. The Heinz Ketchup humorous Western style "shootout" is a good example of this. Here a Heinz catsup bottle and a competing brand advanced toward each other in gunfighter style. They then turned over and the "thin watery" contents of the competitor poured right out while Heinz thick ketchup, pouring slowly, only partly emptied its bottle—"the slowest ketchup in the west, east, north and south." Here the medium of television, with sight and sound, permitted a clear demonstration of a selling point in a unique and simple manner, yet more dramatically than could have been accomplished in any other medium.

Sometimes the dynamic strategy in media use results from the fact that the medium itself is an unusual one, or is ideally located, or both. Such is the case with Kodak's Colorama. When the advertiser is in the business of selling film and cameras, it is logical that an effective advertising approach might be to show the end result of using these products as colorfully and as dramatically as possible. It is difficult to think of a better application of this logic than showing beautiful color photographs, far larger than life-size, to the legions of people who walk through Grand Central Station in New York City. This is one of the most heavy-traffic areas in the world—a place that many people pass through on vacations carrying cameras they will use. And here the Kodak Colorama displays spectacular color photographs created with the Eastman Kodak Company's products.

There are many examples of media dynamics for magazine advertising. Two will serve our purpose. French's Mustard and other food products gained importance by association with highly appetizing and colorful food illustrations. By using facing half-pages in major women's magazines, the French's products dominated the entire two-page spread at the cost of only two half-pages. Color and wise use of magazines space helped to increase the stature of the products, as well as the readership of the advertisements.

For years *Better Homes and Gardens* ran a monthly perforated gate-page of recipes that could be detached and inserted into the *Better Homes and Gardens Loose-Leaf Cookbook*. What more dramatic use of magazine space could Kraft have made than to buy this gatefold pull-out page and present a variety of cheese recipes for the readers of this magazine to clip out and add to their permanent recipe files!

Knowing *which* medium to use in any given case is of utmost importance, but, once having made the choice, knowing *how* to use the selected medium most effectively is equally vital to success in today's highly competitive markets.

SUMMARY

The advertiser today has a vast array of media from which to choose for delivering his message. Principal among these are the broadcast or electronic media, consisting of television and radio; and the print media, namely newspapers and magazines. There are many more from which to choose in each category as well.

The choice of media must be made before the creative team begins its work. First, the broad class of media must be selected—magazines, for example. Then, the specific magazine or magazines must be chosen—those whose readerships match the demographic profile of the users, or sought-after users, of the product or service, and whose circulations coincide with the advertiser's geographic area of distribution or market. The budget and many other considerations must also be taken into account by the agency media buyer.

Media dynamics and strategy recommend that the copy be related to the editorial content of the medium and the audience served by it. Timing is another important factor, particularly when an ad or commercial can be tied into a current newsworthy event.

QUESTIONS AND DISCUSSION SUBJECTS

1. Differentiate between *media* and *medium*.
2. Name the various kinds of media available to advertisers.
3. What information must the agency media man have about the client and his product or service in order to do an effective job?
4. What must the media man know about the advertising campaign?
5. Why is the media job more complicated today than it was 25 years ago? 30 years ago? 50 years ago?
6. For what reasons might a media director choose a particular medium?
7. Why would an advertiser choose to buy time every week on a half-hour program as opposed to alternating every week or two different programs? Why might he choose the two different programs?
8. What people does an advertiser want to reach?
9. Name the elements of an advertising plan.
10. Define the dynamics of strategy. Give examples of its use.

SOURCES

1. *Nielsen Television '75* (Chicago: A. C. Nielsen Co., 1975), 4.
2. *Dimensions of Radio* (Washington, D.C.: National Association of Broadcasters, 1975), 1.
3. *Ibid.*
4. *Facts About Newspapers 1975* (Washington, D.C.: American Newspaper Publishers Association, 1975).
5. *Ibid.*
6. American Newspaper Representatives, 1975.
7. *Ayer Media Facts 1972–73* (Philadelphia: N. W. Ayer, 1973), 11.
8. *Ibid.*
9. Outdoor Advertising Association of America, Inc., 1975.
10. Eugene Pomerance and Hubert Zielske, "How Frequently Should You Advertise?" *Media/Scope,* September 1958, 25–27.

FOR FURTHER READING

Barton, Roger. *Media in Advertising.* New York: McGraw-Hill, 1964.
Blum, Eleanor. *Basic Books in the Mass Media.* Urbana: University of Illinois Press, 1972.
Bogart, Leo. *Strategy in Advertising.* New York: Harcourt, 1967.
Cook, Harvey R. *Selecting Advertising Media: A Guide for Small Business.* Washington, D.C.: U.S. Government Printing Office, 1969.
The Roper Organization. *Trends in Public Attitudes Toward Television and Other Mass Media 1959–1974.* New York: Television Information Office, 1975.
Roth, Paul M. *How to Plan Media.* New York: Media Decisions, 1974.
Schiller, Robert D., ed. *Market and Media Evaluation.* Toronto: Collier-Macmillan Canada, 1969.

Newspapers and
Sunday Supplements

NEWSPAPER ADVERTISING BACKGROUND

Newspapers and industry in the United States grew together, each contributing to the development of the other. The newspapers depended upon the revenue from advertising for their support and growth; industry benefited from the markets that newspaper advertising helped to build.

The first regularly issued newspaper in the United States was the *Boston News-Letter,* started in 1704. The first advertisements that it carried, probably the first published in any American newspaper, were concerned with the sale of a piece of real estate on Long Island, in Oyster Bay, New York, and with the offering of rewards for the return of some stolen property and the capture of a thief. As far as is known these advertisements were the first paid newspaper ads. The advertisement for the Long Island real estate is credited with being the first American newspaper advertisement to offer something for sale.

The first newspaper to use illustrations in advertisements was the *Pennsylvania Gazette,* which Benjamin Franklin published in Philadelphia in 1728. These first illustrations were woodcuts. At that time American newspapers were published weekly or at even less frequent intervals. More than half a century elapsed between the birth of Franklin's *Pennsylvania Gazette* and the first publication of a daily newspaper, the *Pennsylvania Packet & Daily Advertiser.* This daily also was published in Philadelphia, the first copy being issued in 1784. It is perhaps significant that the word *advertiser* appeared in its title. Since that time many other newspapers have used that word in their names— and probably with good reason, because even today newspapers, as a group, account for more advertising linage than any other medium.

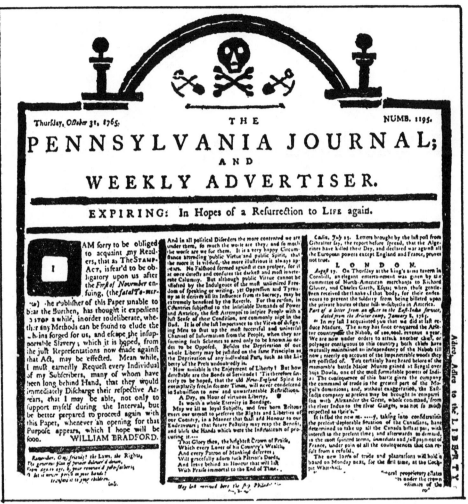

This special "tombstone" edition of William Bradford's *Pennsylvania Journal and Weekly Advertiser* was a protest against the Stamp Act.

The publication of this daily newspaper did not, however, launch a new and great force on the American scene. Newspapers still had a long way to go. The daily newspaper in this country in those days possessed few enduring qualities.

However, in the early 1820s, improvements in papermaking machinery and the introduction of power-operated newspaper presses appreciably reduced the cost of publishing. These developments, combined with the expanding business opportunities of the time, helped to build the importance of newspapers as an advertising medium and to make possible the "penny press." The first newspaper to sell for as little as one cent appeared in 1833.

Also, there was considerable growth in the number of newspapers. It is estimated that by 1847 there were 2,000 in the United States, and by 1854 this number had doubled.

During the first half of the 19th century, advertisements in newspapers were still primarily concerned with the sale of real estate, rewards for the return of runaway slaves, notices of the arrival of ships, and notices of slave auctions. There were only occasional announcements of goods offered for sale by retailers.

In 1835 the *New York Herald* was established. This newspaper, instead of publishing merely legal notices and political news, carried human-interest stories. This practice appreciably widened its audience, and was an important step toward making newspapers a mass-circulation advertising medium. Civil War news also was a circulation builder, crowding advertising off the front pages of American newspapers, a position which it was never to regain in this country—except in a very limited number of publications.

Between the end of the Civil War and the early 1890s, the rotary press, typesetting machines, and the use of halftones made it possible to print more attractive-looking newspapers and to print them more quickly.

In 1869 George P. Rowell published the first directory itemizing all newspapers published in the United States. This directory not only listed the names and locations of newspapers, as had been done for English newspapers in an earlier directory published in London, but also gave circulation figures whenever they were obtainable. The reliability of these figures was frequently uncertain, for the audited circulation was still many years in the future.

Rowell, who was an "advertising agent" as well as a publisher, made advertising contracts with newspapers in several sections of the nation so that he was able to "sublet" advertising space in a list of papers covering specified areas.

The first advertisers to employ what might be called a national campaign in newspapers were the vendors of patent medicines. However, through the closing decades of the 19th century and the early part of the 20th, many new national and regional advertisers turned to the pages of newspapers to carry their sales messages to the new and rapidly expanding markets of a fast-growing nation.

Manufacturers—ranging all the way from those making such pennies-priced items as soaps, polishes, and cigarettes to those making automobiles selling for many hundreds of dollars—used the pages of newspapers to carry their advertising to the American public.

AUDITING AND TRADE GROUPS

In 1914 the Audit Bureau of Circulations (ABC) was organized as a nonprofit corporation designed to establish standardization of definitions with respect to circulation claims and to conduct careful audits of circulations of publisher members. Prior to the founding of ABC there had been two short-lived attempts to measure and audit circulations scientifically. But, for the most part, in pre-ABC days, circulation figures came from a variety of sources. Some were sworn statements of publishers, some were just claims, and some were even gathered by actually counting papers as they came off the presses.

As industry became more concerned with the need for reliable market data, many privately operated research organizations came into being. Several of these worked, at least in part, in the field of newspaper and magazine advertising. Daniel Starch and Staff was a pioneer in readership studies of newspaper and magazine advertising.

American Newspaper Publishers Association

The American Newspaper Publishers Association (ANPA) is the only trade association exclusively for daily newspapers in the United States, Canada, and the offshore islands. It has served the daily newspaper business since 1887. Its 1,075 members represent more than 90% of total daily and Sunday circulation in the United States and 82% of daily circulation in Canada.

In 1971, ANPA moved its headquarters offices from New York City to Reston, Virginia, a suburb of Washington, D.C. The ANPA staff of professional and technical newspaper specialists, with supporting secretarial and clerical personnel, numbers more than 100 persons.

The principal objectives of the ANPA are to help solve problems of individual newspaper members and to advance the daily-newspaper publishing business. The ANPA's staff of specialists provides a wide variety of services to members and to the general public.

The ANPA represents its members in legislative and legal activities and advises them on labor relations. It furnishes economic data and information on newsprint supply and demand, and it fosters news research. The association provides credit information on more than 1,200 advertising agencies to its member newspapers and advises them on tariff and traffic regulations. In addition, the ANPA serves in a public relations capacity, issues publications, and engages in educational activities.

Newspaper Advertising Bureau

Formerly part of ANPA, where it was known as the Bureau of Advertising, the Newspaper Advertising Bureau (NAB), assumed its new title in 1973. It supports newspapers by conducting "how to" seminars for their sales personnel, on local and national advertising and on cooperative programs. The NAB also compiles and furnishes data on newspaper audiences and advertising, and generally promotes advertising in newspapers. New York City serves as NAB headquarters.

National Newspaper Association

Another newspaper organization is the National Newspaper Association (NNA). This group, which has been in existence for close to 90 years, represents community newspapers—weeklies and dailies. Its membership consists of state newspaper publishers' associations as well as individual country newspapers.

The NNA's primary function is a lobbying one and it is therefore based at the national seat of government, in Washington, D.C. It has active committees on Federal Legislation, Better Newspaper Content, Newspaper Cost Study, Government Workshop, Public Notice, Printing and Production, Freedom of Information, Schools of Journalism, Promotion, Public Relations and Community Service, and Suburban Newspapers and Daily Newspapers.

The association supports the Freedom of Information Center at the University of Missouri, is one of the founding members of the American Council for Education in Journalism, is a contributor to the Junior College Journalism Association, and provides career material for high-school students. It also conducts annual international Study Missions.

The NNA produces three publications: *Publishers Auxiliary,* which comes out every two weeks; a newsletter called *Trends,* and the monthly *Byliner.*

In the area of advertising-space sales the NNA supports the wholly owned American Newspaper Representatives, Inc., which sells and services national advertising for members. This is done on a convenient "one-order-one-bill-one-check" basis.

NEWSPAPERS TODAY

In 1974, 1,768 daily newspapers, 641 Sunday newspapers,[1] and 9,379 country weeklies were printed in the English language in the United States—a big jump from the six weekly newspapers published in Benjamin Franklin's day. There had been a five-year period, from 1954 through 1958, during which the number of dailies declined markedly; even some leading and well-known ones closed down. The declining trend seems to have been stemmed, although during the next decade New York City lost the *Herald Tribune* (1966) and the *World Journal Tribune* (1967). The decline resulted in part from the competition of other advertising media and in greater part from the increased cost of newspaper production. In recent years, both Sunday and daily editions have rather steadily increased in number.

In 1920 there were 2,042 daily newspapers. From that year, with relatively minor exceptions, dailies steadily declined in numbers until 1945, when there were 1,749. During the years through 1974 there was some fluctuation, up and down. In all there was a net gain of 19 daily newspapers for a total of 1,768. During that same period the total circulation of all newspapers showed a general upward trend through 1973, with a slight drop in 1974. Although the circulation kept pace with the increase in adult population until 1965, the gap began to widen from that point on.[2]

Since the end of World War II the increase in the amount of money spent on newspaper advertising rather consistently exceeded the growth rate of the nation's GNP for the same period. Whereas the expenditure on newspaper advertising has increased during recent years, the newspapers' portion of the total amount spent on advertising has remained at around 30% since 1945 [3]—the result, in large part, of the growth of television. While newspapers still command the largest share of the advertising dollar, their strength is in local and retail advertising, not in national.

Types of Newspapers

Newspapers are classified on the basis of publication frequency as *dailies* or *weeklies,* and in accordance with the areas in which they are primarily distributed as *urban* or *rural*. In a broad sense the first classification is interrelated with the second. Most daily newspapers are published in cities and are circulated among urban populations, whereas most weeklies are published in suburbs, small towns, and villages and find their readers among rural and suburban populations. However, this relationship does not hold among foreign-language newspapers and other newspapers appealing to minority segments of the population, such as the Negro or black-oriented press and the "neighborhood" newspapers. These papers are published, whether daily or weekly, irrespective of the size of the community in which they originate.

Another category is the *national* newspaper. These are published daily in newspaper format and are distributed on a national basis. Among them are *The Christian Science Monitor, Wall Street Journal, The National Observer,* and the *Army Times*.

Under most circumstances an advertiser will be less concerned with the frequency of issue of a newspaper than with the kind of market it reaches. The decision to use large metropolitan dailies, country weeklies, foreign-language papers, the black press, neighborhood papers, or some combination or all of these must depend upon the marketing and advertising goals of individual advertisers.

The Metropolitan Daily Press

News of local, regional, national, and foreign events, business and financial reports, comics, items of special interest to women, special features, comments on sports—all are to be found in the metropolitan daily newspaper. This breadth of appeal to a wide variety of interests makes the big city newspaper a mass-circulation medium. But, unlike mass-circulation magazines, newspapers are distinctly local in character. Newspapers, with few exceptions, are seldom bought and read by many people outside of the cities and surrounding trading areas in which they are published.

This mass circulation within limited or local areas makes the newspaper an excellent medium not only for local advertisers but also for national advertisers who wish to spot their sales messages according to needs dictated by local marketing conditions. Furthermore, the metropolitan dailies have deadlines for accepting advertising that are close to the time of publication. For this reason, newspaper advertisements can be made to tie in with current events, announce special sales, quote prices subject to frequent change, and, in general, be very timely.

The metropolitan dailies may be published as morning or evening papers, or may be issued in several editions throughout the day. The relative importance of morning and evening newspapers is a subject that has been discussed many times in advertising texts and in training groups in advertising agencies. However, it is a subject in which generalizations are of little or no value. On the whole, there is greater relative strength in morning papers in the East and in evening papers in the South. This difference occurs because in the South there are a large number of small-town dailies that are published in the evening, while in the East there are several outstanding morning papers such as the *New York Times* and the *New York Daily News*. But in the final analysis, the choice between a morning and an evening newspaper will depend not only upon location of market but also upon the aims and problems of the individual advertiser.

The Country Press

The country press consists of 9,379 all-paid-circulation newspapers, most of which are published in small towns and villages throughout the United States. The rest are published in suburban areas and, for this reason, are more directly in competition with the large city newspapers. However, suburban and small-town weeklies alike are unable to compete with daily newspapers, radio, and television in the coverage of spot news events. They must seek other means of building and maintaining circulations. Their chief attraction to readers is that they carry detailed home-town news that is not available in the metropolitan dailies or through broadcasts received from neighboring metropolitan areas. This local news attracts readers, and it is further claimed that it results in the country newspaper often being read more thoroughly and kept about the home longer than the big-city daily.

Although these newspapers are supported in large part by the advertising of local merchants and by the publication of legal notices, they do contain national advertising and can be of considerable value to the advertiser who seeks coverage of rural or suburban markets.

Individually, the average weekly with a circulation of little better than 2,000 plays a relatively small role in any national advertiser's sales program. Collectively, weekly newspapers deliver a total circulation of somewhat less than half that of the dailies. Recognizing that the national advertiser must be interested in many weekly papers, a large proportion of weekly newspaper publishers are represented by one or more of the sales organizations that specialize in selling this medium to national advertisers. These organizations not only sell space in their member newspapers but also take care of handling insertion orders, checking copies, billing, and most of the other detail work that would otherwise make the handling of thousands of widely scattered small-town weeklies a slow and tedious task. Two organizations representing country newspapers on a national basis are American Newspaper Representatives, Inc., which represents more than 7,000 hometown papers, and U.S. Suburban Press, Inc. which acts as advertising sales agent for some 100 weeklies and small-circulation dailies in big city suburbs.

The Foreign-Language Press

Some sections of the United States, chiefly large cities, have concentrations of foreign-born. Where such concentrations are sufficiently large, it has become profitable to publish foreign-language newspapers. These papers have little in common with each other, each being edited to build a circulation among members of a particular language group. *El Diario-La Prensa,* which serves the Spanish-speaking population of the metropolitan New York area and has a circulation of close to 67,000, is an example of one of the successful foreign-language papers.

The advertiser who is marketing a product that has a special appeal to a foreign-born or ethnic group and who believes that his product can best be brought to the attention of such a group through sales messages written in its own tongue is the user of advertising space in these newspapers. However, it should be recognized that in the homes of foreign-born parents with American-born children, the English-language newspaper is likely to be found as well as the foreign-language paper.

It is common practice when placing advertising in foreign-language newspapers to submit copy in English and to leave the translation and proofreading to the paper, which usually assumes these responsibilities. Large advertising agencies, however, have their own translators and so create their own advertisements for these publications.

Other Types of Newspapers

There are approximately 225 black-oriented or Negro newspapers in the United States, consisting in the main of weeklies but including semiweeklies, biweeklies, and one daily. The latter is *The Chicago Defender,* which has a reported circulation greater than 35,000. The biggest of the black-oriented newspapers are New York's *Amsterdam News,* with a circulation of 70,359, and Detroit's *Michigan Chronicle* with 41,686. Both are weeklies.[4,5]

Whereas the foreign-language papers are often read to the exclusion of other newspapers in the community, this generally is not true of the black-oriented newspapers. These build their circulation by giving consideration to news of particular interest to the black population, but on the whole the interests of the black population extend to the metropolitan dailies or home-town weeklies as well.

Until 1941, much advertising in the black newspapers consisted of mail-order offers, some of questionable character. But censorship by the publishers has eliminated the objectionable advertisements in large measure, and today several large national advertisers use the pages of the black press, often employing specially prepared advertisements.[6]

Advertising space may be purchased directly from the individual newspapers or through representatives that handle several papers. For example: Amalgamated Publishers, Inc., which represents 81 papers in major cities, is one of the principal sales representatives of black-oriented newspapers.

There are also college, labor, shopping, military, financial, and religious newspapers. The names of these groups are self-explanatory with the possible exception of the city or suburban shopping newspaper, sometimes called the pennysaver, which is usually a weekly and contains little if any editorial material. It is customarily filled with retail advertising and is distributed free.

NEWSPAPERS AS AN ADVERTISING MEDIUM

Every advertising medium has certain characteristics that make its use especially advantageous to some advertisers. Many of these characteristics are common to several media, whereas some are peculiar to a single medium. Whether a particular characteristic with its attending advantages is significant to any given advertiser will depend upon his advertising problems and goals. Obviously, what might be regarded as an advantage by one advertiser might not be so regarded by another, nor even by the same advertiser under different circumstances.

Newspapers possess certain characteristics that give them special value as an advertising medium. Among them are the following:

1. *Newspapers serve a special local market and usually saturate it with coverage.* Regular newspaper readership is 88% among families with annual incomes of $15,000 or more, dropping to 64% among families with incomes of $5,000 or less. The same correlation holds true for level of education—only 64% of those without a high-school education read a daily newspaper regularly, as compared to 83% of high-school graduates and 87% of those who completed college.

2. *Daily newspapers cover a very wide range of subjects and contain something of interest to everyone.* News about current events at home and abroad, the world of sports, the financial and business pages, the comics, the women's and social columns, the editorials, and the various special features—all combine to make the newspaper a medium that is read by the whole family.

3. *To many local advertisers the use of the daily newspaper is almost a necessity.* Department stores and supermarkets, in particular, rely heavily upon newspaper advertising to attract customers. The national advertiser is supplied with an authoritative medium for carrying his sales messages to most of the families of the community. That is, behind the advertising that appears in the daily newspaper lies a background of reliable reporting of current news that makes the paper an accepted authority of communications. This authority tends to carry over to the advertising.

4. *Newspapers provide the national advertiser with a high degree of specificity in terms of geographical areas covered.* The advertiser can place his sales messages in the markets where he believes they will do the most good and avoid those in which he thinks there would be considerable waste. He can open new markets, one by one or several at a time, as con-

ditions dictate. He can use newspapers to bolster a declining market or to meet increased competition in specific local areas.

5. *Newspaper deadlines are so close to time of publication that it is possible to tie in advertising with current events.* An urgent or topical message can be delivered upon as little as 24 hours' notice. For example, when New York city newspapers were carrying stories and pictures of the arrival of the ocean liner *United States* in New York harbor on her maiden voyage, a petroleum company's advertising, announcing that the ship had used its products, appeared in the same newspapers and on the same pages as the news stories and pictures. The same type of advertising, for cameras, beverages, and other items, accompanied the news of United States accomplishments in space.

6. *Newspapers are local media.* Because of the local character of newspapers it is possible to make an easy tie-in between national and retail advertising. Many manufacturers have special supplements whereby the manufacturer pays part of the cost of retail advertising that features his products.

7. *Newspapers are published daily.* This fact, together with the fact that they have very little audience turnover, makes it possible for the advertiser to reach his audience with almost any desired frequency. From the information that is available it appears that newspapers are being read as much today as ever. Furthermore, there is no evidence that newspapers suffer any marked seasonal fall-off of readers. Therefore, a continuous year-round series of repeated contacts with nearly every consumer in any given market is possible through this medium.

Services to Advertisers

Most newspapers will assist local advertisers with layout and copy for their advertisements. They will also set type. Often space salesmen prepare complete advertising campaigns for buyers and potential buyers of advertising space in their papers. It will be recalled that foreign-language newspapers will also assist advertisers with translations and proofreading of their copy. These several services are most frequently used by smaller advertisers who do not have their own advertising departments or advertising agencies.

Some papers will help advertisers lay out routes for salesmen within the city and trading area served by the paper. Most papers have available general marketing information for the area within which they are distributed, and more or less detailed information on their own circulations. Such information is of special interest to out-of-town advertisers who use the newspaper; it serves as a supplement to information that they may already possess on local conditions or on the character of the readership of the different papers in the community.

Several newspapers make continuing studies that are of interest to advertisers. For example, about 30 papers make studies annually or oftener within their trading areas of the number of families using particular brands of products; about 10 papers make annual studies of brand availability in their cities; and 10 make monthly studies of grocery inventories.

Many newspapers publish special sections, from time to time, that are of value to some advertisers. The year-end-review sections of the *New York Times* are examples. Special sections in other papers deal with such events as the Pasadena Tournament of Roses, the Indianapolis Memorial Day 500 Race, and with special product lines or services such as automobiles, apparel, and travel. In addition to these are the advertising supplements that appear in many Sunday newspapers. They are generally purchased by an independent organization, company or association which sells space to its members or to related organizations and industries. It is also responsible for obtaining the editorial matter for the supplement and for giving complete copy to the newspaper ready for type-setting and reproduction. If the supplement is to appear in a number of different newspapers it is usually printed in advance by the advertiser and furnished in bulk to the several newspaper publishers as a complete entity to be inserted into the paper and distributed.

Color

During the past few years more and more newspapers have made run-of-paper (ROP) color* available to advertisers. An advertiser currently can obtain full-page units-in-black-and-three-colors in 1,156 newspapers, full-page units in black-and-one-color in 1,499 papers. The newspapers that accept ROP full-color advertisements account for 82% of total circulation of all daily newspapers; those that accept black-and-one-color account for 91%.[7] Studies have indicated that both male and female readership is increased by better than 50% through the use of color. Under such circumstances it is not surprising that ROP color is becoming increasingly popular with advertisers.

Newspapers can also offer two other types of full-color printing to their advertisers. Since 1958 a method known as *Hi-Fi* had been in use. *SpectaColor,* a competing full-color system, was introduced four years later. Both are delivered to the newspapers on preprinted rolls and are processed along with the newspaper's other pages. Hi-Fi repeats the advertisement so that regardless of where it is cut the reader will have at least one full copy of the ad. SpectaColor is an improvement over this, designed to present ads that are in-register; it requires special electronic controls. The newspapers that offer Hi-Fi number 1,550 and account for 94% of the total daily circulation; 432 newspapers, representing close to 50% of the entire circulation, offer SpectaColor.[8]

A number of newspapers offer *split runs*. That is, alternate papers of any given edition carry alternate pieces of advertising copy. This circulation split is obviously of value to the advertiser who wishes to test his copy. In general, there are restrictions as to the size of copy, and there is usually a special charge for the service.

* Color not restricted to special sections of the paper but available to the advertiser without the need of buying preferred positions or special sections.

SELLING ADVERTISING SPACE

In most newspapers, advertising space is sold by the *agate line*. It is common practice to drop the word *agate* and to refer to newspaper advertising space as consisting of so-and-so many *lines* or as being composed of a specified amount of *linage*. An agate line is a measurement of space $^1/_{14}$ of an inch from top to bottom and one column wide, irrespective of the width of the column. It should be clearly understood that the agate line is a measurement of space and has nothing to do with the lines of type or printed matter except as such material must be related in size and volume to the quantity of space purchased. In other words, 14 agate lines or 1 column inch would accommodate one line of 72-point type or two lines of 36-point type set solid, and so on.

The average newspaper column is about 1½ inches wide and in standard-size newspapers like the *New York Times* it is 300 (agate) lines deep. In the tabloid-size paper the average column is about 200 lines deep. The standard-size paper normally has eight columns to the page,* hence a page is equivalent to 2,400 lines ($300 = 8$). The tabloid usually is a five-column paper with a depth of 200 lines, making the page equivalent to 1,000 agate lines (200×5). The ANPA reports that in 1974 there were 976 papers with eight-column formats, 150 with six columns, and 80 more with nine columns, each format having varying page and column widths. It should be appreciated that these figures are general and that an advertiser must check each newspaper individually or use one of the reference sources.

Most newspapers will not sell less than an established minimum amount of advertising space to an advertiser. For example, the majority of papers will not sell less than 14 agate lines on one column, 28 lines on two columns (total 56), 56 lines on three columns (total 168), and so on. Also, they customarily charge for an entire column when an advertisement approaches full column depth even though the entire column is not bought.

Newspaper Rates and Contracts

Newspapers quote their advertising rates as either *flat* or *open*. A *flat rate* is one that is not subject to either quantity or frequency discounts. That is, no matter how much linage an advertiser uses or how frequently he places advertising in the paper, the rate remains the same. An *open rate* is one that is subject to quantity and frequency discounts. Under such an arrangement the paper has a sliding scale of rates that decrease as the amount of space used or the frequency of insertion of advertisements increases.

Newspaper advertising space may be purchased on a *run-of-paper* (ROP) basis that permits the publisher to place the advertisement anywhere he pleases within the paper, or on a *preferred-position* basis that allows the advertiser to

---

* Because of rises in postal rates and in the cost of newsprint, the *Los Angeles Times* in January 1975 reduced its page width by ¾ of an inch and introduced six 2-inch columns. Many newspapers have followed suit including the *New York Times* which joined them in September 1976.

state where he wants the advertisement to appear. Such positions are usually those next to reading matter, those at the top of a column, those on a special page, or those in a special section such as the sports or women's pages. If an advertiser specifically orders a preferred position, he is charged a premium over the ROP rate. If, however, such a position is merely requested, the newspaper may elect to honor the request and make no extra charge.

Besides the ROP and position considerations, there are four broad divisions upon which rates are based. They are (1) classified, (2) classified display, (3) retail, and (4) national. There are some important rate differences between retail and national advertising that deserve attention. Retail advertising, according to the view of most newspapers, is any advertising that is placed by a merchant who sells to consumers through one or more retail outlets that he owns or controls, usually located in the community where the newspaper granting the local or retail rates is published. Retail advertising space is noncommissionable* and is subject to quantity and frequency discounts.

National advertising, as defined by most newspapers, is advertising placed by others than those classed as local or retail advertisers. With certain exceptions, newspapers use a flat rate for the national advertisers. Not only are local advertisers given rates that are lower than those charged national advertisers, but many newspapers give local advertisers an opportunity to earn substantial discounts by increasing their frequency or volume or both, while denying national advertisers this privilege. This situation obtains in all but 25 out of a total of 1,768 daily newspapers. The fact that the Sunday supplement group (for both magazine sections and comics) has given the national advertiser a similar incentive to use more space or to make more insertions apparently has not influenced those who direct the sale of advertising space in daily editions.

The newspaper advertising contract, if one is involved, may specify that the advertiser will use a certain amount of linage or that he will make a given number of insertions during the contract period. In the former case, the contract is known as a *space contract;* in the latter case, it is called a *time contract*. In neither case is the advertiser obliged to fulfill the terms of the contract with regard to the amount of linage used or the number of insertions made. The contract serves as a basis for monthly billings of the advertiser, with subsequent adjustments being made to fit the actual use made of advertising space. For example, if an advertiser has a space contract in which he has agreed to purchase 10,000 lines at $1.00 per line and the paper's rate card indicates that amounts of space below this figure sell at $1.10 per line, the advertiser is billed monthly for the space he uses at the rate of $1.00 per line. However, if at the end of the contract period he has failed to use at least 10,000 lines, he is billed an additional 10 cents for every line that he did use during the contract period. This is called the *short rate* and represents the difference between the contract rate and the actual earned rate. On the other hand, if the paper's rate card indicates that

---

* No commission is given to advertising agencies by the great majority of newspapers for selling retail advertising space, whereas commission is given for selling space to national advertisers.

the use of 15,000 lines or more entitles the advertiser to a 90-cent rate and the advertiser actually uses this amount instead of the contracted 10,000 lines, the paper will rebate at the rate of 10 cents a line. Thus the contract does not bind the advertiser to use any specific amount of space or to make any specific number of insertions, but serves to establish the rate per line he will be billed as that which exists at the time of the signing of the contract.

If the advertiser is working under a time contract and there is no specification concerning the size of the advertisements which must be placed, he may maintain his contract rate by using minimum-space advertisements in off-seasons and large-space advertisements during the better selling seasons. These minimum-space advertisements are called *rate holders* because they hold the rate at the contract price by maintaining the agreed frequency of insertion.

Most newspapers, if they offer an open rate, will grant retail or local advertisers a quantity or frequency discount whether they have a contract or not. But, inasmuch as rates are subject to change and tend to vary with the circulation of the paper, it is often to the interest of the advertiser to have a contract. Furthermore, newspaper advertising contracts usually are subject to cancellation should the advertiser wish to terminate the agreement.

As was noted earlier in this chapter, there has been a great increase in the availability and use of ROP color in daily newspapers. The additional cost for color varies according to the amount of space purchased, with the average premium for a full page in one color being about 19% over the black-and-white space cost and the average premium for full color about 34%.

The Milline Rate

One of the indices used in space buying is the milline rate. This is the rate per line per million circulation and is determined by multiplying the line rate by 1,000,000 and dividing by the circulation. That is,

$$\frac{\text{line rate} \times 1,000,000}{\text{circulation}} = \text{milline rate.}$$

The milline rate is obviously not an actual rate charged by the newspaper. Rather, it is a device that provides a common denominator for comparing papers with different rates and different circulations. For example, newspaper A with a flat rate of $1.70 and a circulation of 891,995 has a milline of $1.91, while newspaper B with an open rate of $2.05 and a circulation of 557,244 has a milline of $3.68.* The milline rate of paper B is 92% higher than that of paper A, but care is necessary in dealing with the milline, as it is necessary in dealing with any quantitative index that does not reflect audience characteristics. It is quite possible that qualitative characteristics of a medium's audience

* The arithmetic is:

$$\frac{1.70 \times 1,000,000}{891,995} = 1.91 \qquad \frac{2.05 \times 1,000,000}{557,244} = 3.68$$

might offset the difference in cost reflected by a purely quantitative consideration.

Combinations

Many newspapers are individually owned and advertising space in them is sold on an individual-paper basis. There also are situations where two or more papers are controlled by a common interest. In these latter cases the advertising in the papers is sometimes sold on a combination basis. These newspapers offer *combinations*—a publisher who owns two newspapers in a city quotes a separate rate for each of his papers and a third rate when both are used; use of the combination is optional. In actual practice there are several types of combinations. The most common is the morning and evening papers in combination; a second is the daily paper combined with the Sunday paper; and a third is the combination editions in an all-day paper of which several editions are put out each day. There are also the dual-city and tri-city combinations where the publisher controls the papers of two or three cities and sells their advertising space in combination.

One possible disadvantage of a combination is that there is likely to be considerable duplication of circulation. An extreme example of this is found in the case of a publisher that does not offer a subcription to its morning paper without the evening edition. On the other hand, there are some papers that have a relatively small circulation in the city but big circulation in the suburbs for their morning editions with the reverse situation existing for the evening papers.

SUNDAY SUPPLEMENTS AND COMICS

Sunday Newspapers

Sunday newspapers have larger circulations in general than their daily counterparts. They also reach beyond the metropolitan areas in which they are published to a greater extent than do the dailies. Some evidence of the larger circulation of the Sunday papers is seen in the fact that the total circulation for 1,768 daily newspapers is 61,877,197 whereas the total circulation of only 641 Sunday newspapers is 51,678,726.

The make-up of the Sunday paper is usually different from that of the daily. Because more complete coverage is given to many topics, what appears in the dailies as departments is often presented as whole sections in the Sunday papers. This is often the case with such topics as sports, society, business, travel, and classified. In addition, many Sunday papers carry such special sections as magazine supplements and comics. Although not all Sunday papers carry either or both of these two types of special sections, those that do account for a high percentage of total Sunday-newspaper circulation.

Magazine Supplements

Sunday supplement magazines have made a notable recovery since their decline that began in 1958. At that time advertising revenue stood at a peak of $117.4 million; it had dropped to 66.6 million by 1965. During that period one of the "big four," Hearst's *American Weekly,* fell by the wayside, and in 1969 it was followed by *This Week.* Four reasons accounted for the demise of these two giants and for the overall decline in Sunday-supplement magazine advertising.

First, major advertisers, principally Procter & Gamble, Lever Bros., General Foods, Colgate, and others shifted their mass marketing efforts to television. Second, national magazines showed, by including the "pass along" reader in their studies, that they offered more readers per advertising dollar than the supplements. Third, when market segmentation became important the supplements did not offer regional editions. Fourth, many newspapers carried more than one supplement, which resulted in wasteful duplication.

By 1969, the annual advertising revenue for the 176 Sunday magazines had exceeded $200 million, with a substantial share of it going to the two remaining national "giants"—*Parade,* published by Whitney Communications, and Downe Communications' *Family Weekly. Parade* is king of the supplements with a 1975 circulation of well over 19 million through 109 newspapers.[9] Advertising revenue came close to $39 million in 1970 and in the first quarter of 1971 exceeded the previous year by 42%. Well over half of the new revenue was from tobacco advertising which had been banned from television.[10]

Family Weekly, which appears in small newspapers with an average circulation of 31,000 in contrast to the large newspapers which carry *Parade,* boosted its 1970 advertising income to $19.2 million in 253 newspapers. It too showed an increase of better than one-third at the beginning of the following year, largely from cigarette advertising.[11] In 1975 *Family Weekly* appeared in 307 papers.[12]

The 416 newspapers which carry either *Parade* or *Family Weekly* pay for the privilege at a given rate per thousand circulation. However, they do participate in advertising profits.

Parade and *Family Weekly* are edited nationally with regional editions, and are supplied in bulk to the newspapers that carry them, the paper's name being included in the masthead. Though their editorial content and appearance are essentially the same in every paper in which they are included, they now offer the flexibility of individual markets.

It is also possible for advertisers to buy another package of large-circulation publications from Metropolitan Sunday Newspapers, Inc. This group, which goes under the name of *Sunday,* is owned by 47 independent major local supplements banded together for the purpose of better obtaining national advertising. It has a circulation of close to 22 million. *Sunday* also furnishes editorial matter. Three members of the group are the *New York Sunday News,* the

Chicago Tribune, and the *Philadelphia Inquirer.* They had formerly operated as the First Three Market Group, which arrangement expired in June 1971.

Other such supplements are *Tuesday* and *Tuesday at Home,* each of which has a circulation exceeding 2.3 million. The former is published on the second Sunday of each month and the latter on the fourth Sunday. Both are distributed by the same 23 newspapers.

In addition to these comparatively large-circulation supplement magazines, a number of Sunday magazines are published independently by individual newspapers. The largest and most important of these independents is The *New York Times Magazine,* which carries more pages of soft-goods advertising than any other magazine, including consumer magazines. It has a circulation of more than 1.5 million. Another such independent is the *Los Angeles Times Magazine,* which boasts of the greatest individual total advertising linage. Its 2,722,000 lines exceeded that of the *New York Sunday News Magazine* in 1969. The latter, however, is the circulation leader of the supplements, with a net paid circulation of 2,990,698.[13]

Sunday Comics

All of the leading Sunday newspapers except the *New York Times* carry comic sections. In fact, the Sunday newspapers that carry comics account for 97% of all Sunday-newspaper circulation.

Although advertising revenue for the remaining national magazine supplements has increased over recent years, advertising in the comics has declined. While there had been an upward swing since the mid 1960s (reaching approximately $15 million in 1969), the comics dropped about $3 million in advertising revenue the following year. This was caused in large part by a change in campaigns by Coca-Cola. Presently, however, the comics are maintaining the same $12-million level of advertising income.

There are two national groups of comics, *Metro* and *Puck.* In adition, several comic sections are published independently by individual newspapers. In the case of the two national groups, advertising space can be ordered as a package. *Metro Comics* is a combination of syndicated comics put together by individual newspapers. *Puck,* on the other hand, is supplied to subscribing newspapers in bulk. There are also a number of smaller regional groups that are not affiliated with either *Metro* or *Puck.* This lack of affiliation does not mean that they may not carry many of the same comic features as the two large groups but rather that they are not joined together in a major national sales group. The combined circulation of *Metro, Puck,* and these independents is about 48 million.

Metro accounts for 70 Sunday newspapers with a total circulation of 21,586,399. Although *Puck* has 105 subscribing newspapers, its near 17 million circulation is more than 25% less than its competitor.[14] Both groups offer plans including additional newspapers and circulation, extending to some independents as well as to some of the competition. However, as with Sunday magazine supplements, great care is taken to avoid duplication of circulation.

Audiences

The trend has been for the big-city newspapers to drop both *Parade* and *This Week* and to publish their own locally edited supplements. The two national magazine supplements, on the other hand, have become very strong in suburban markers.

The *Metro* and *Puck* comic-section coverage is primarily in metropolitan areas. Audience composition for comic and magazine supplements differs considerably. About 28% of the total audience for comics is made up of children from 7 to 17 years of age. Among the adult audience more men than woman read the comics, although the percentage difference is not great. The magazine supplements, on the other hand, have slightly more women readers than men. Children account for only 12% of their readers.

Advertising Costs

If figured on a basis of cost-per-thousand-delivered-audience, color advertisements in the most widely used space sizes are less costly in the Sunday magazines and comics than in the regular sections of the Sunday newspapers. In turn, the comics are less expensive than the magazine supplements. The quality of art reproduction in the magazines is far superior to that in the comics.

The range in cost-per-thousand-delivered-audience among the different magazine supplements is not great and would not be very significant as a consideration in selecting one magazine rather than another.

Advantages to Advertisers

An advertiser may obtain a degree of selectivity in his audience depending upon his use of the different sections or supplements in the Sunday papers. Magazines and comics, as we have seen, although appearing in the same paper, do not have identical audiences.

Sunday papers get into the home to a greater extent than daily papers. Therefore, all members of the family can and do read them. Usually, more time is spent with the Sunday paper than with the daily, and Sunday papers purvey broader coverage than their daily counterparts.

The advantages that the Sunday magazines offer the advertiser include high-quality reproduction and intensive individual market penetration. Also cost-per-thousand-delivered-audience is substantially lower than that of national magazines. Finally, magazine supplements, as distinguished from other sections of Sunday newspapers such as sports, society, financial, and the like, are written for family readership.

It should be appreciated that while Sunday magazines offer heavy coverage of almost every metropolitan market in the United States, they do not constitute a national advertising medium in the same sense as the national consumer magazines.

Estimates indicate that some 120 million Americans read comics regularly, accounting for approximately three out of four who are old enough to read.

Further advantages of the Sunday comics as an advertising medium include the fact that they reach all members of the family and have a low cost-per-thousand-delivered-audience as compared with other media. Inasmuch as approximately 80% of all Sunday newspapers carry comics, and these papers represent as much as 97% of Sunday-newspaper circulation, it is possible to obtain intense family coverage with them. Further, they offer the advertiser color at the lowest cost-per-thousand among print media.

SUMMARY

The growth of the newspaper and other industry in the United States had been interdependent. Newspapers first appeared on a regular basis in this country in 1704. These early papers were weeklies or monthlies and it was not until 80 years later that the first daily newspaper was published.

Newspaper advertising, through the first half of the 19th century, dealt mainly with real estate, mercantile announcements, and legal notices. Patent-medicine vendors were what might be called the first national advertisers. They were followed in order by a long list encompassing the range of consumer products.

The creation of the nonprofit Audit Bureau of Circulations in 1914 was a giant step toward the substantiation and verification of media circulation claims. A number of private research firms also appeared on the scene, providing marketing data.

Daily newspapers, which are published in urban areas for the most part, number under 2,000, and there are approximately 600 Sunday papers. More than 9,000 weekly newspapers represent the rural and suburban areas. In addition to these customary newspapers are those that serve special markets or segments of the population. These include the foreign-language press and the black-oriented newspapers.

While the number of newspapers published has declined, circulations are up. By the same token, although the total number of dollars spent on newspaper advertising has grown, the percentage of the advertising dollar spent in newspapers has remained stable for 30 years, in the face of competition from television.

As an advertising medium newspapers offer certain unique features. They serve a particular local market and saturate it with coverage. Dailies contain something of interest to everyone. Retailers, particularly department stores and supermarkets, rely heavily on newspaper advertising; national advertisers get a high degree of specificity in the geographical areas of the papers' circulations. These two features facilitate cooperative advertising. The fact that newspaper deadlines are close to publication time makes it possible to relate advertising to news events. And the consistency of newspaper readership enables advertisers to reach it with practically any desired frequency.

Often newspapers publish special supplement or editions which are tailor-made for certain advertisers. Many newspapers also offer ROP color and split runs. Advertising space is usually sold by the agate line and column width. Contracts call for a flat or open rate, and space may be purchased on an ROP or preferred-position basis. The four types of newspaper advertising are classified, classified display, retail, and national—each of which carries a different rate.

Sunday newspapers offer many more features than the dailies, including magazine supplements and comics.

QUESTIONS AND DISCUSSION SUBJECTS

1. What is the cost of a newspaper advertisement that is 56 lines deep on two columns when the line rate is $1.10?
2. What would be the cost of a newspaper ad that is 3 inches deep on two columns when the line rate is $1.10?
3. Using *SRDS*, determine the milline rate of the *New York Times* and the *New York Daily News*.
5. Why do national advertisers use newspapers when they can reach nationwide audiences with network televison and national magazines?
6. How does *Sunday* differ from *This Week?*
7. Define or explain *rate holder* and *short rate*.

SOURCES

1. *Facts about Newspapers 1975.* Washington, D.C.: American Newspaper Publishers Association, 1975.
2. *Loc. cit.*
3. *Loc. cit.*
4. *Newspaper Rates and Data,* April 24, 1975, 202, 763–765.
5. "The Largest Ethnic Markets, Jewish, Black, Spanish Language," *ANNY*, November 20, 1970.
6. "Black Press Does Its Own Thing, Spurs Readers' Heavy Buying," *Advertising Age,* April 20, 1970, 192.
7. *1973 Newspapers Offering ROP Color, HiFi and SpectaColor* (New York: Newspaper Advertising Bureau, May 1973).
8. *Loc. cit.*
9. *Newspaper Rates and Data,* April 24, 1975, 716.
10. Philip H. Dougherty, "Special Sunday Sections Making Good Gains," *New York Times,* February 28, 1971, 15.
11. *Loc. cit.*
12. *Newspaper Rates and Data,* April 24, 1975, 715.

13. "Sunday Supplements in Big Comeback After Sag," *Advertising Age,* April 20, 1970, 146.

14. *Newspaper Rates and Data,* April 24, 1975, 678–679.

FOR FURTHER READING

Arnold, Edmund C. *Profitable Newspaper Advertising.* New York, Harper & Row, 1960.

Barton, Roger. *Media in Advertising.* New York: McGraw-Hill, 1964.

Brown, Lyndon, Richard S. Lessler, and William W. Weilbacher. *Advertising Media.* New York: Crowell Collier & Macmillan, 1964.

Hynds, Ernest C. *American Newspapers in the 1970s.* New York: Hastings House, Publishers, 1975.

Kauffman, Jack, and Stanford Smith. "The Outlook for Newspapers." Remarks to a group of security analysts in New York City, December 11, 1974.

McClure, Leslie W., and Paul C. Fulton. *Advertising in the Printed Media.* New York: Macmillan, 1964.

"Recommended Interim Sizing Charts for Preparing National Newspaper Advertising Materials." Bulletin No. 3272, American Association of Advertising Agencies, July 9, 1975.

Shover, William R., ed. *Promoting the Total Newspaper.* Washington, D.C.: International Newspaper Promotion Association, 1973.

Udell, Jon G. *The Growth of American Daily Newspapers.* Madison: University of Wisconsin, 1965.

Consumer Magazines

MAGAZINE HISTORY

Magazines were not always the great advertising medium that they are today. Many early publishers of magazines in the United States were not interested in accepting advertising for their publications and their magazines were not especially attractive to advertisers as conveyors of their sales messages.

Several magazines started as external house organs of book publishers. Although some used these magazines to advertise their own books, many thought that advertising of other products would lower the quality of their publications. However, this was not the attitude of all publishers. Some would accept advertising if requested to do so; some even actively sought it. But such publishers sometimes found it hard to sell advertising space because of their small circulations. Unlike magazines of the present, when 89% of United States adults read an average of eight different magazine issues each month,[1] none of the 18th-century magazines is thought to have had an annual circulation over 1,500; today, in contrast, *Reader's Digest's* monthly paid circulation exceeds 18 million and *TV Guide* claims 18,382,000 average paid circulation each week.[2]

These small circulations were the result of a combination of factors that for many years were not entirely eliminated or corrected. For one thing, editorial content of the early magazines lacked originality. Stories were copied from English or other foreign publications or, if of domestic origin, were often poorly written. Added to this general unattractiveness of editorial content was the fact that 18th-century American life left little leisure time for magazine reading for the majority of the population. Also, subscription prices were high for those times.

There weren't many advertisements in the 18th-century magazines and those that did appear were most often printed notices without illustrations. When illustrations were used, they were woodcut reproductions that usually

THE

𝕎𝖔𝖗𝖈𝖊𝖘𝖙𝖊𝖗 𝕸𝖆𝖌𝖆𝖟𝖎𝖓𝖊.

NUMBER VIII.   VOLUME III.

For the *Fourth* Week in MAY, 1787.

WORCESTER, *(Maſſachuſetts)* Printed by I. THOMAS, by whom Subſcrip-
tions, Eſſays, &c. &c. for this Work are taken in.

[Price SIX PENCE Single.]

DAVID HAMMOND,

HEREBY acquaints all thoſe Gentlemen whom he ſup-
plies with the WORCESTER MAGAZINE, that the preſent quarter of
a year, which he propoſed to ride, will expire the laſt week of this month, at which
time he hopes and expects prompt payment from ALL his Cuſtomers, and that
none will requeſt he ſhould be put to the trouble of calling another time for payment of ſervices he will then have performed, eſpecially as he now acquaints them,
that he ſhall then quit the buſineſs, for the preſent, and the trouble and expence of
his making journies, after that time, to collect the ſmall ſums which will be due to
him, will be more than his circumſtances (and he hopes the generoſity of his cuſtomers) will permit.   He returns thanks for all favours, and is the
Publick's humble Servant,   DAVID HAMMOND.
Wincheſter, May 9th, 1787.

Now for Mule Colts !

WILL Cover this Seaſon, at
the Stable of the Subſcriber, in
WOODSTOCK, four miles and an half ſouth
of DUDLEY Meeting-houſe,

A Famous JACK.

The terms are, that the ſubſcriber engages all
the Mule Colts that are propagated from ſaid
Jack, unleſs a particular agreement, and will
pay the owner from 12 to 15 dollars, as they
may be for goodneſs ; they will be worth four pounds, upon an average, at four
months old, free from any expence of ſaid Jack.   Or otherwiſe for the ſingle Leap,
One Dollar ; Two Dollars for the Seaſon ; or Four Dollars if inſured.   Good
Paſturing for Mares, by their humble ſervant,
Woodſtock, April 24, 1787.   STEPHEN TUCKER, 2d.
☞ N. B.   Said Tucker hath two covering JACKS, one of which is for ſale.

To Cover for the Seaſon,

THE noted HORSE, formerly owned by
SAMUEL MOWER, of WORCESTER, has been
owned for this year paſt by Capt. NEWELL, of CONWAY,
and is now re-purchaſed by ſaid SAMUEL MOWER, who
will keep him for the purpoſe of Covering, at his Stable, one
mile and an half ſouth of the Meeting-houſe in Worceſter, where conſtant attendance will be given.   Said Horſe is now ſeven years old, and ſtill maintains the character which he eaſily eſtabliſhed.

A page of advertising
from the *Worcester Maga-
zine* of May, 1787, illustrated
with woodcuts.

were symbolic of the advertised product rather than a picture of the merchandise itself. That is, a woodcut of a house indicated that the accompanying copy
was concerned with selling or renting a home, but the illustration was not a picture of the actual house with which the advertisement dealt.

In 1870, Roswell Smith published the first issue of *Scribner's Magazine*
and set a turning point in the history of magazine advertising. Smith made
serious and effective efforts to obtain advertising for *Scribner's,* which in 1881
was renamed the *Century.* The success of Roswell Smith's efforts is evident in
the fact that by 1890 the *Century* was carrying the advertising of 910 business
enterprises. Other publishers followed Smith's example, and during the closing

decades of the 19th century sought advertisers and built circulations that would attract and hold them.

Advertising agents also contributed to the development of magazines as an advertising medium. In the 1890s, J. Walter Thompson, founder of the advertising agency that bears his name, published his list of 30 magazines, known as the *Thompson List of Thirty*. It included practically all of the magazines then available in the United States. Mr. Thompson had persuaded the publishers to sell him the space on their back covers. He then proceeded to divide these covers into ¼-page spaces and sell them to advertisers. He thus became the exclusive contractor of magazine advertising space for an extended period. Later, Stanley Resor and Helen Lansdowne, of the J. Walter Thompson Agency, introduced the first vegetable cooking fat, Crisco, in magazine advertising that was modeled after the editorial pages of the publications in which it appeared. The Resor and Lansdowne team is also credited with persuading another client to use the first every-issue color-page magazine campaign in the United States. Another advertising agency man, James Webb Young, induced *Redbook* magazine to run what is believed to be the first split-run insertion in history.

The changing attitude of magazine publishers toward the acceptance of advertising, increasing magazine circulations, and the efforts of creative and progressive advertising agents were not the only factors that helped build magazines as a major advertising medium. Improvements in the graphic arts, new inventions, changes in the postal laws, increasing literacy among the American people, release from long hours of burdensome work as mechanization of industry and agriculture progressed, a rapidly expanding economy, and changes in the formats of magazines—all were contributing factors.

Patent-medicine advertisers played an important role in the development of magazines as an advertising medium from the 1860s until after the turn of the century. Those were the days when medicines were offered as sure cures for ailments which even today pose formidable problems to medical science. Although this kind of advertising helped early magazines to survive, some of the more far-sighted publishers realized that legitimate advertisers and magazines alike would be harmed by it and in the 1890s started to eliminate it from their publications. Despite this action, patent-medicine advertising of questionable character persisted well into the 20th century. However, the crusading spirit of some magazines publishers and the development of new industries that were destined to become heavy users of magazine advertising space finally drove patent medicines from the pages of all but inferior magazines.

The Rise and Development of Associations

Although magazines had started to become an advertising medium of growing importance as early as the 1870s, most of the trade associations and other organizations worthy of note in the field were not developed until the 20th century.

The Quoin Club was organized by magazine interests in 1903, with its chief function being the handling of advertising-agency relations. In 1921 this organization became the *Periodical Publishers Association of America* (PPA). Its present function is as a credit-rating bureau for magazine publishers.

The *Magazine Publishers Association* (MPA) was formed in 1919 as the National Association of Periodical Publishers. The MPA is a nonprofit membership corporation. It gathers and disseminates information of interest and value to its members, conducts a long-term program to attract new manpower to the industry, maintains a complaint department to protect both the public and publishers from the operations of fraudulent or unauthorized solicitors of magazine subscriptions, holds conferences at the operating level of the business, and performs many other valuable services for its publisher members.

The *Magazine Advertising Bureau* (MAB) was formed in 1943 to promote magazines as an advertising medium and to serve as a center of information about magazine advertising for advertisers, advertising agencies, and publishers. On January 1, 1959, it merged with the Magazine Publishers Association and now operates as the marketing department of the MPA.

The *Central Registry of Magazine Subscription Solicitors* was founded by the MPA to protect publishers' door-to-door subscription sales as well as to protect the public against abuses in this area. The Central Registry establishes and is responsible for the maintenance of acceptable standards for the personal solicitation of magazine subscription sales.

The *Publishers Information Bureau, Inc.* (PIB) was started in 1919. Its membership includes the major magazine publishing companies and its purpose was to provide statistical information about general magazine advertising. It issues monthly cumulative reports, on an annual basis, on the volume and cost of display advertising carried by more than 85 general magazines and three newspaper supplements. These reports consist of data on approximately 150,000 ads each year, showing space size and characteristics and the one-time rate for each ad. Data are grouped by industry—Automotive, Food, and the like. A further breakdown is provided by monthly summary reports for more than 300 product categories. In these, for example, Food is categorized as Cooking Products and Seasoning, Dairy Products, Prepared Foods, Meats, and so on, and each of these has subclassifications.

Both the PIB and the Periodical Publishers Association are related to the MPA and serve MPA members exclusively. The PPA obtains financial reports from advertising agencies doing business with its members and makes credit ratings available to the publishers.

Another MPA-related group is the *American Society of Magazine Editors,* founded in 1963. Its membership consists of the chief editors of close to 100 magazines published in the United States. The Society is concerned with the editorial content of the medium and its contribution to adult education and the nation's growth and progress. It meets quarterly, and sponsors an annual Editorial Conference in Washington, D.C., attended by editors and publishers and in addition by leading government officials, educators, and scientists.

Membership in the *Magazine Advertising Sales Club* includes approxi-

mately 200 executives and representatives concerned with advertising space
sales. The club, which was founded in 1963, provides a forum for members to
hear talks by prominent advertising and agency executives. It also sponsors
workshops and seminars on magazine advertising space sales.

MAGAZINES TODAY

The magazines of today offer the advertiser a large and varied group from
which to make his selections; *Standard Rate & Data Service* lists over 1,200
consumer or general-readership magazines and farm publications. In addition to
these there are other magazines not listed in SRDS as well as a very large
number of business, trade, and professional magazines. These periodicals differ
greatly in editorial content, reader characteristics, space costs, and other ways
that are significant to advertisers. Because advertising budgets are limited and
because individual advertisers have different problems and goals, there is
always the need for making evaluations and selections among the many magazines from which the advertiser may choose.

Types of Magazines

Magazines are classified according to frequency of issue as weeklies,
monthlies, and so on, or according to their editorial content as general magazines or class magazines. The classification of *general* or *mass-circulation*
magazines includes publications like the *Reader's Digest* that have editorial
content of a broad, general interest. The *class* publications, in contrast, have
editorial content aimed at specific interests or hobbies; Examples are *Sports Illustrated, Field & Stream,* and *Holiday.* In fact, it would not be easy to name
an area of human interest or activity that does not have at least one magazine
devoted to it.

In addition to these broad kinds of classification, subdivisions or more narrowly defined classifications exist. For example, there are magazines that appeal predominantly to women. Among these are the three major *women's service magazines—McCall's,* the *Ladies' Home Journal,* and *Good
Housekeeping. Home service magazines* have a more specialized content than
the women's service group; among these are *American Home, House & Garden,* and *Better Homes and Gardens.* There are also magazines that appeal to
younger women and girls, such as *Seventeen* and *Ingenue.* Still another specific
classification is the *news magazine* group that includes *Time, Newsweek,* and
U.S. News and World Report.

Problems of Selection

In space buying, the advertiser must first choose among one or more of
these various fields of specialization. Then, having made this choice, he may
be faced with the need of selecting one or a few magazines from the group that
represents the class he elected to use. For example, assume that the advertising
problem is such as to suggest the women's service group. As already noted,

there are three major magazines in this area. Each has a multimillion circulation. If the advertising budget or policy consideration does not permit the use of all three, a choice must be made. Therefore, it becomes necessary to evaluate each with respect to editorial excellence, circulation strength, audience characteristics, cost per thousand readers, and other qualitative and quantitative factors. It is necessary to be aware of any difference among the magazines as to emphasis in editorial content. That is, does one of the "books" devote more space to home furnishings, to the preparation of meals, to babies, or to any other specific subject or subjects than do the others? The answer to this question is important insofar as any such editorial emphasis might be related to the product or service to be advertised.

If the advertising problem at hand suggests the need for reaching the teen-age female market rather than the older women, the advertiser must turn to and analyze an entirely different group of publications. Here, he will know or discover that *American Girl* is read by younger teen-age girls, whereas *Compact* and *Seventeen* appeal to an older teen-age group. If the advertiser is seeking as wide a market as possible he may think it desirable also to consider *Scholastic Magazine,* which is distributed in junior and senior high schools. Of course, such a magazine probably would have as many boy as girl readers, but it would give the advertiser an opportunity to broaden and strengthen his program, if that is his aim. In short, if a particular field of publications offers the type of audience that represents the best market for a particular product or service, it becomes necessary to evaluate each magazine in that field and to rate each in terms of its importance to the advertiser in question.

Circulation Trends

Unlike newspapers, magazines have experienced an increase in circulation at a rate that matches the increase in United States households. Since 1950 the number of households has grown approximately 63% and magazine circulations as a whole have increased a like amount. The number of magazines entering homes annually increased from an average of 79.5 copies in 1950 to 87.9 copies in 1970.[3] Circulation per 100 adults was 26.5 in 1914, 132.8 in 1950, and 168.9 in 1970, but dropped to 154.8 in 1972, according to MPA figures.[4]

Although the total number of magazines sold annually has shown a substantial increase, the student should recognize that the total circulation available to advertisers increased markedly when the *Reader's Digest* began to run ads in April 1955. The demise of the *Saturday Evening Post,* in contrast, had a negative effect on circulation in 1969 and the following year, as did the passing of *Look* and *Life,* the latter at the end of December 1972. For a two-year period, 1944–1945, newsstand sales of magazines accounted for the predominant part of their circulation; since then an increasingly higher proportion of circulation has come from subscriptions. From the viewpoint of the advertiser, this subscription basis has both advantages and disadvantages. The more circulation that a magazine sells on subscription basis, the greater will be its hard-core audience, or those people who receive 50% or more of all issues of a magazine in a year. Recently, however, because of rising postal rates, publishers are taking a more kindly look at newsstand sales. They and their advertisers recognize that these are the most voluntary type of circulation and provide a good measure of the editorial strength of the magazine.

Increases in circulation through subscription have reduced newsstand sales despite the fact that both kinds of sales have been promoted by publishers. One publisher has stated that for every 100 new subscribers gained, 30 have been converted from newsstand buyers, whereas another publisher stated that as many as 50% of his subscribers were formerly newsstand buyers. On the other hand, such publications as *TV Guide, Playboy,* and *Penthouse* are distributed mainly through newsstands, while *Family Circle* and *Woman's Day* can be purchased only at supermarkets.

Circulation and Distribution

The circulation of consumer magazines as a whole does not vary much from month to month. In 1969, for example, October circulation was 8.6% of the year total, June 8.1%.[5] However, circulations of individual magazines may vary sharply. For example, one magazine with an average circulation of 4,702,000 had a difference of nearly a million copies between its high and low points. This fluctuation was not due entirely to seasonal factors but, as with most magazines, occurred primarily because of heavily promoted special editorial features.

Except for the farm and small-town magazines, the circulation distribution of magazine groups generally tends to match the population by market size for the United States as a whole. This is especially true of large-circulation magazines like the general weeklies, the women's service group, and the digest magazines.

Magazine circulation tends to be lowest in the South and Southwest, to be higher in the Northeast and Midwest, and to peak in the West. Farm magazines, however, are very strong in the South and Central regions, weak in the East.

Recent Trends

Beginning in 1969 a number of magazines changed size. Most of these changes can be attributed to the rise in postal rates that was announced earlier and took effect in May 1971, and to other economic reasons. With two exceptions all of the modifications were reductions from what had been known as *"Life* size" (680 lines) to *Time's* 429. These included *American Home, Holiday, Esquire, Vogue,* and *McCalls.*[6] *Boy's Life* went from *"Life* size" to *Fortune's* 632 lines; and *Popular Science* reversed the trend going from 224 lines to *Time* size. Later, *Fortune* too, reduced its dimensions, as did *Ladies' Home Journal.* More recent postal rate increases have also had their affect on publishing economy.

Probably the greatest blow to magazine publishing came with the passing from the scene of four stalwarts of the industry. The first of the giants to fall in recent times was *Colliers*. It was followed into oblivion by the *Saturday Evening Post,* which like *Colliers* was a weekly general mass-circulation magazine that featured fiction and nonfiction articles and stories. The *Post* traced its descent back to the magazine Benjamin Franklin published in colonial times. Poor management, the competition of television, obsolete equipment, and the economy finally overwhelmed it. It had changed publishers a number of times and in January 1969 published its "last" edition. But relatively soon the *Saturday Evening Post* announced that it was going to publish again in its former size (680 lines) and format, as a quarterly. The first reborn issue of 500,000 copies was dated June 1, 1971, and appeared on the stands on May 25. The issue ran 168 pages, of which 58 were advertising. While it had come to publish nine issues a year in 1975, this *Post* was not the erstwhile giant.

More recently *Life,* a leader and mainstay of American magazine publishing for many years, was also forced to give up. It had been a mass-circulation pioneer of photojournalism but couldn't compete with the immediacy and the variety that televison offered. Rising costs for labor, materials, and postage proved insupportable. Near the end, in an attempt to make its advertising rates more palatable to advertisers, *Life's* management held down its weekly circulation; this, however, only delayed the inevitable, and *Life's* issue of December 29, 1972, was its "last" (talk of reviving it persists, perhaps as a monthly for newsstand sale only). The passing of *Life* was preceded by the demise of *Look,* a bimonthly magazine that had been its principal competitor in the field of photojournalism. It is interesting to note that the publishers of *Life* subsequently published another magazine—*People*—which is sold principally at newsstands and stores, with few subscriptions delivered by mail.

The departure of these leaders in the field was not offset by the 86 new magazines that were introduced in 1970 and the 76 the following year (as opposed to 24 magazines that sold, merged, or discontinued service in 1970 and 20 in 1971).[7]

Competition

Although more money has gone into advertising in magazines in recent years, they have received a lower proportionate share of total advertising dollars spent annually. This decrease, in very large part, has been the result of competition from television.

Before the advent of television, radio was the main rival of consumer magazines for the advertising dollar.* Expenditures for radio advertising rose steadily and overtook the magazines in 1939. Television barely began to make itself felt as an advertising medium in 1949. By 1953 magazines had reversed radio's trend and passed it. The following year television took its toll on magazines and radio, surpassing both in advertising revenue. Through the succeeding years television has increased its lead over the other two media and magazines have maintained their superiority over radio.

---

* Newspapers have earned the largest share of the advertising dollar since before 1935.

In a number of self-serving promotional publications, MPA has stated the case for magazine advertising as opposed to advertising on television. "Prime Prospects Read More, View Less . . . And Pay Less Attention When They Are Viewing" states its argument in its title: that prime prospects read more magazines and watch less television. It is based on a special computer analysis of Simmons's 1968 *Selective Markets and the Media Reaching Them.* A like claim is made in *Weight of Evidence on Changing Levels of Communication Effectiveness,* based on 21 major studies that include Simmons, Starch, Hooper, and others. A similar publication, *The 1970's: New Demographics . . . New Patterns of Media Consumption,* contends that white-collar workers and households with incomes of $15,000 and more favor magazines over television. And the booklet *Trends in Magazine and Television Advertising Costs* indicates that magazines delivered more readers per dollar in 1970 as compared to 1965. In addition, it reiterates the point that magazines reach the people who are likely to buy, at a lower cost per thousand than television.

The Magazine Publishers Association discusses what audiences believe in the booklet *Credibility: The Medium and the Message,* based on a 1969 Gilbert Youth Research Study. This booklet holds that young people believe magazine editorial matter twice as much as they believe television and radio programs and that advertising in magazines is nearly two times as appealing as television advertising, three times as compared to radio. On the other hand, television advertising is found to be more deceptive, silly, annoying, and unbelievable than magazine advertising; radio advertising was found to be slightly less unbelievable and deceptive than magazine advertising.

Quite to the contrary is the report, *An Extended View of Public Attitudes Toward Television and other Mass Media, 1959–1971.* This study, conducted by the Roper Organization, was published in 1971 by the Television Information Office, a division of the National Association of Broadcasters. It states that 49% of the people believe television as opposed to 9% for magazines, 10% for radio, and 20% for newspapers. When asked which of the media they would "most like to keep" if they were limited to just one, 58% chose television and 5% magazines; newspapers were favored by 19% and radio by 17%. The same question asked of college-educated and upper-income groups produced like results, slightly more favorable to each of the other media as opposed to television but still overwhelmingly in favor of the latter.

This situation points up some of the problems facing the advertiser and the media buyer.

Television has developed primarily as a medium of entertainment. It has presented the kinds of programs that deliver the largest audiences for a given time period. This vast audience has made television an increasingly desirable medium for advertisers and is probably the reason that many look to it as a means of obtaining millions of delivered advertising impressions with a high degree of frequency.

The fact that television is predominantly a medium of entertainment has opened an opportunity for magazines to become increasingly important as a medium for dependable information. This very fact may mean that the authority with which magazines address their readers, always a strong point with them, will increase in the future. Actually, there has been a trend in recent years for magazines to reduce the amount of fiction offered and to step up the number of service and informative articles. It is very possible that in this area magazines will find their greatest competitive strength against television.

Value as an Advertising Medium

As is the case with all advertising media, magazines have certain advantages to offer the advertiser—some of which are peculiar to the magazine medium and some of which are found to a greater or lesser degree in other media as well. Among the more outstanding of the advantages of magazines as an advertising medium are the following:

1. *Quality.* Magazines offer the advertiser high-quality reproduction of his advertisements both in black-and-white and in full color.
2. *Audience selectivity.* It is possible by the proper selection of magazines to obtain an audience that is especially receptive to a particular product or service. Certain magazines by virtue of their editorial content appeal to people particularly interested in certain hobbies or occupations. If the advertiser's product or service is associated with this special hobby or occupation, he obviously reaches a select market and eliminates some waste circulation that might sell nothing for him in a less selective medium. Such selectivity need not be in terms of hobbies or occupations but can be in terms of age, sex, and in some cases even of geographical location.
3. *Message life.* Magazines are kept around the home for relatively long periods of time, giving the advertiser's message a longer life than it might enjoy in some other types of media. For example, a study of one magazine showed that of all the people in the United States ten years of age and older, 12.6% live in households that either save back issues of the publication or clippings from it, or both. Furthermore, these back issues are read even after having been in the home for a considerable time.
4. *Secondary readership.* Magazines tend to be passed along from the original purchaser to others who, although they do not buy the publication, are nevertheless good prospects for the advertised products that appear on its pages. Because this secondary circulation is not reflected in the advertising rate, it represents a bonus to the advertiser. Another type of secondary readership occurs when magazines are read in reception rooms of professional and business offices, in barber shops and beauty parlors, in doctors' and dentists' offices, and in public libraries. Magazines, to a greater extent than other print media, enjoy this kind of secondary circulation.
5. *Prestige and authority.* Most magazines have considerable prestige and are accepted as authoritative sources of information in their fields of editorial specialization. Much of this prestige and authority is carried over to the advertising in such magazines. That is, people are willing to accept as au-

thoritative not only the information contained in the editorial matter but also much of the advertising. Evidence of this acceptance is seen in the practice of some retail merchants who display signs in their windows stating that such-and-such merchandise is as advertised in *Harper's Bazaar,* or *Vogue,* or the *Reader's Digest,* or some other well-known magazine. These merchants recognize and are employing the prestige of the magazines to help sell the merchandise.

6. *Editorial reinforcement.* The editorial content of the class magazines and the women's and home service publications helps the advertiser by indirect suggestion and by putting the readers in a buying frame of mind. For example, when a story about the latest boating equipment appears in *Yachting* or *Motor Boating* it may stimulate the reader's interest and receptiveness to advertising for such equipment. A story in a home service magazine on how to make a cellar into a playroom may place a reader in a frame of mind that will cause him to seek out advertisements for wallboard, paint, floor tiles, and other materials mentioned in the article as necessary to do the job.

7. *Consumer selectivity.* The distribution pattern of magazine circulation enables the advertiser to obtain national coverage among those people who presumably are best able to make purchases of specific products by reason of income, age, or other characteristics.

8. *Variety of format.* Magazines make a variety of layout possibilities available to advertisers—bleeds, spreads, multipage units, gatefolds and others that will enable them to make dramatic and dominant displays.

9. *Market selectivity.* Magazines are becoming more flexible as an advertising medium. At present more than over 230 consumer and farm magazines offer some form of regional edition or split run. In some cases publishers offer geographical splits, in other cases they put out regional editions, and in still other cases they give numerical splits. Publishers have divided their regional editions according to markets, to Postal Service ZIP code zones, and to county. *Newsweek* and other mass-circulation magazines provide the advertiser with an amazing selectivity in market coverage hitherto impossible to obtain. All this adds up to the fact the major national magazines are becoming attractive as advertising media, for the first time, to a group of advertisers who do not enjoy national distribution of their products. This flexibility is also a help to the national advertiser who wishes to introduce a product on a limited basis before going into national distribution or one who wishes to meet regional competition without carrying additional advertising weight into national markets.

SELLING AND BUYING MAGAZINE ADVERTISING SPACE

Magazines, like newspapers, quote an agate-line rate, but by far most advertising in magazines is sold in terms of multiple-page units, double pages, pages, and fractions of a page. Many publications have a flat rate per page for each insertion, with fractional parts of a page either selling for a proportionate price or for slightly more. For example, in some cases a page might cost $20,000 per insertion, ½ page $10,000, and ¼ page $5,000. In other cases a publisher who charges $20,000 for one page might ask $11,000 for ½ page and $6,000 for ¼ page. This latter practice amounts to giving a quantity discount, inasmuch as the cost per line goes down as the amount of space bought for any single insertion is increased. Many publishers also offer a frequency discount, which reduces the cost of any given amount of space per insertion as an advertiser increases the number of his insertions over a contract period. For example, a magazine may offer a page of space on a one-time insertion basis at $23,475, on a 13-time insertion basis at $22,301, on a 26-time basis at $21,597, on a 39-time basis at $20,839, and on a 52-time basis at $20,190, if the insertions are made within a specified contract period. The contract period is usually one year and starts with the first insertion. In the case of a monthly magazine, the number of insertions usually required to obtain a frequency discount is 3, 6, 9, and 12.

The fractional part of a page that can be purchased depends upon two things: (1) the minimum amount of space that any particular magazine will sell and (2) the format of the magazine. If the magazine has a four-column page, the fractions are ½ pages, ¼ pages, ⅛ pages, and so on. However, if the magazine has a three-column page, the divisions are in terms of ⅓ pages, ⅙ pages, and the like, plus perhaps horizontal ½ pages.

The size of the page, as far as the advertiser is concerned, is the portion set in type rather than the overall size that includes the margins. This is called the *plate size* as distinct from the *trim size,* which is the size of the entire page—type and margins—as seen by the reader of the publication. The term *trim size* is derived from the cutting or trimming of magazines on the top, bottom, and outer edge after binding and before they are delivered to the subscriber or newsstand.

If the advertiser wishes, he may purchase a *bleed* page. In this case, a larger plate is provided by the advertiser so that when the magazine is trimmed the illustration or background color of the advertisement runs to the edges of the page leaving no white margins. Bleeds usually cost approximately 15% to 20% more than comparable nonbleed pages.

Magazine publishers charge more for space when colored advertisements are run than for the same space when black-and-white advertisements are used. For an example, one magazine quoted a black-and-white page at $5,820, a two-color page at $7,215, and a four-color page at $8,630. The MPA shows a cost per page per thousand circulation of $4.32 for black and white as compared to $5.98 for four-color in 1970. It should be recognized that these are space costs only. All additional costs associated with purchasing the art work and the necessary color plates are also borne by the advertiser.

If an advertiser wants an advertisement reproduced in a manner other than that employed by the magazine he wishes to use, or if he wants his advertisement printed on a special paper stock, some magazines will permit him to print his own advertisements. The publisher then binds these advertisements into the magazine as inserts. When they are used, the advertiser is concerned with a minimum of two pages of space, the front and back of each insert sheet. The magazine section of *Standard Rate & Data Service* and the business-publication section of the same service give the advertiser information concerning which magazines provide this service, and the rates.

In magazines, as in newspapers, it is possible for the advertiser to buy preferred positions if he is willing to pay the premium that such space commands. The preferred positions in magazines are the covers and the two facing pages in the middle of the book, the *center spread* as it is called. The covers are referred to as the *first, second, third,* and *fourth* covers. The first cover is the front cover, the second cover is the back or inside of the front cover, the third cover is the inside of the back cover, and the fourth cover is the outside or back of the back cover. Consumer magazines usually do not sell the first cover for advertising purposes, but trade and industrial publications sometimes do.

Other positions, such as the pages facing the second and third covers, the page immediately before the editorial pages in the magazine, and the pages facing any regular special feature of the magazine, are regarded as *secondary positions*. These are not so highly regarded as the preferred positions but are thought to be superior to locations elsewhere in the book. In some cases, an advertiser is required to pay a premium for these locations although not so much as for preferred positions. In other cases, these secondary positions are given without additional cost to advertisers who use large quantities of space or hold longterm contracts with the magazine.

Space-Buying Tools and Information

The advertiser who is considering buying advertising space in a magazine or in magazines has at his disposal several tools and sources of information that will assist him in the task of selecting a publication and purchasing the necessary space.

Every magazine has a rate card on which are given the rates, the units of space that are available, the mechanical requirements, the dates of issue of the publication, the closing dates for advertising copy, and a statement of guaranteed circulation or the rate base of circulation. The mechanical requirements do not apply to the problems of space buying but are of interest to the production departments of an agency or advertiser's department. Closing dates for four-color advertisements may run as much as eight to ten weeks in advance of issue dates. Usually the closing-date advance for black-and-white space is less than that for color—in most cases, five to six weeks.

With respect to guaranteed circulation, the inference is that during a specified period, usually the calendar year, the magazine will average out the guaranteed circulation or give a rebate to its advertisers.

Since most advertising agencies deal with many magazines, it is more convenient for them to use *Standard Rate & Data Service* (SRDS) than individual rate cards. If a magazine is not listed in SRDS other sources may be used.

Ayer's Directory, the *Standard Periodical Directory* and *Ulrich's Periodical Directory* would be such references. Additional sources would include publications in fields allied to the editorial coverage of the magazine being sought. The Association of National Advertisers and the Magazine Publishers Association are still other possibilities.

As it does for the newspaper advertiser, the Audit Bureau of Circulations provides the magazine advertiser with facts upon which his evaluation of space may be made.

Research and evaluation data on magazines, which are available to advertisers and advertising agencies alike, may be divided into five broad categories: magazine audience (size, characteristics, and behavior); market information; advertising effectiveness; advertising volume; and editorial content. Such studies appear on a continuing basis. In addition, magazine publishers may commission custom reports by such firms as Simmons, BRI, Starch, Sindlinger, and Hall.

A list of research studies offered by consumer magazines may be found in the current edition of *Bibliography of Consumer Research.* Sources of *Consumer Magazine Information* is also excellent. Both are published by the Magazine Advertising Bureau.

Innovations

In the past three decades a number of new ideas were introduced into magazine advertising. Some were expansions of older concepts, such as gatefolds, which now appear as double and triple covers and verticals. Some were radically new, like ads that can be seen as three-dimensional and others that exude the distinctive fragrance of the product being advertised.

Multipage Units. While two-page units had been fairly common in *center spreads* and the other parts of the magazine, a trend to three or more pages began in the early 1950s. A 12-page ad for the Chrysler Corporation appeared toward the end of 1954 in *Life, Look,* and the *Saturday Evening Post.* Probably the biggest multipage unit was the 100 pages run by Celanese Corporation in *Harper's Bazaar* in 1967. The following year Uniroyal placed 40 full-color pages in the May *Reader's Digest.*

Inserts. The insert trend began in 1957 with a detachable General Mills cookbook that was included in *Coronet.* This was followed in other magazines by Ford's *Car Buyers' Guide,* DuPont's *Garden Clinic Guide,* 3M's *Gift Wrapping Guide,* the Institute of Life Insurance booklet *The Facts of Life,* and others, not to mention redeemable coupons and card inserts with unduplicated numbers to be brought to dealers for prizes.

Samples. Although some products do not lend themselves to this application, a number do qualify in size, dimension, and lack of bulk. Some of these which have been used are Johnson & Johnson Band-Aids, Scott towels, Curtiss candy, Miracle Air grape-flavored powder, Glidden's Spred Satin latex paint, and Vanity Fair lanolin facial tissues. Kotex supplied a sample of a new product in a 1975 issue of *Seventeen.*

Fragrant Ads. Distinctive aromas have been incorporated into products by three methods—perfumed ink, cotton pads sealed in aluminum packets, and microencapsulated 3M "scratch and sniff" strips and their more recent "Microfragrance." The first of these was an ad for Baker's coconut that appeared in a 1957 issue of *Better Homes and Gardens.* In 1960 Vicks featured the scent of its Sinex nasal spray in *TV Guide,* and during 1964 the readers of *Harper's Bazaar* were treated to the fragrance of Ondine perfume. The appearance of "scratch and sniff" strips increased the use of aromatic ads in 1967 and the years following. Passport 360, a men's cologne, was advertised in *Playboy* in this manner, as was Imprévu perfume in *McCall's* and Lifebuoy soap in *Redbook* and *Reader's Digest.* A liquor company also lauded the bouquet of its bourbon using this method. "Microfragrance" ads for Softique appeared in *McCall's, Ladies' Home Journal,* and *Woman's Day* at the close of 1974.

Recordings. Audio messages have been employed as another form of magazine insert. Music and/or sales messages are impressed into thin sheets of vinyl in a process similar to the making of traditional phonograph disks. They can be detached and played on a home record player. In 1959 Remington promoted its electric razor on such a platter—"Music to Shave By," which ran in *Look.* Regional editions of the November 1964 *Ladies' Home Journal* carried audio messages for the Lutheran Laymen's League. Recordings have also been used quite frequently in business publications. (The *Advertising Age* issue of February 24, 1975 carried a 33⅓ r.p.m. sound sheet.)

Pop-Ups. Although pop-ups have been used principally for children's magazines, they have been employed for adult attention in business periodicals. *Jack & Jill* ran a series of six 4-page color pop-up ads on behalf of Wm. Wrigley, Jr., Co. These ads, which appeared during 1964, complemented Wrigley's television advertising, which featured zoo animals.

Invisible Ink. To pull prospects into its dealers' stores, Ebonite ran a four-color spread in *Look* promoting its bowling balls. All the ads carried coupons; 5,000 of these were randomly overprinted with a special ink which showed up only under the proper light at the dealer's store, entitling the bearer to a free bowling ball.

3-D. Shortly after World War II, three-dimensional photography caught the public fancy as a hobby and was used in motion pictures and in magazines. The drawback was the need for special glasses for viewing and the inconvenience these entailed. This contributed to loss of popularity and early abandonment. However, a number of years later *Look* magazine developed a 3-D photo process, Xograph, which did not require viewing glasses. At first it was used for editorial purposes, later for advertising. Advertisers who have used Xograph include Pfizer, International Harvester, Eastman Chemical Products, Rust-Oleum, BOAC, American Express, and Wallace Silversmiths.

Cooperative Advertising of Related Products by Different Companies. Companies producing related products have taken facing pages and used the same theme and format to promote their respective wares. An example might be a brewer and a baker running ads promoting beer and pretzels. Advertisers have similarly shared a page, a spread, or a gatefold. Cooperative advertising has also resulted in multiple-page inserts tied by a basic theme. The Edison Electric Institute, together with a number of electrical-appliance manufacturers, sponsored the "Live Better Electrically Medallion Home" promotion in magazines. A 1968 issue of *Fortune* had a 60-page insert promoting industry in Illinois, sponsored by 39 advertisers.

Some Other Innovations. Others among numerous new departures include the use of such print production materials as metallic ink and sheets of aluminum foil or plastic instead of conventional paper stock. Other developments are checkerboard layouts and rotogravure and offset sections.

SERVICES TO ADVERTISERS

Magazines, like newspapers, provide a number of services for those who use their advertising space. While the majority of advertisers who use magazine space have their own plates made, magazines—like newspapers—will, if requested, set type for the advertiser.

Some magazines make their advertising pages attractive to local as well as national advertisers by publishing an edition or several editions that have limited distribution as compared with the regular edition that circulates nationally. The advertisers who use this limited edition do not pay the same rate as those who use the nationally distributed edition. Furthermore, they escape paying for the waste circulation outside of the markets in which their products are available.

Many magazines offer the advertiser a *split run,* or opportunity to place alternate advertisements in alternate copies of the same edition. Inasmuch as these advertisements can occupy identical space and can be related to identical editorial matter and competitive advertisements, the split run provides an excellent device for research and for testing copy or layout.

Most magazines will furnish the advertiser with reprints of his advertisement at a regular scheduled rate. A reprint, as the name implies, is a printed duplicate of the advertisement as it was run in the magazine except that it is printed on a separate sheet of paper and without any editorial material. There is usually a printed line that states the advertisement is a reprint from such-and-such magazine as of the specific date. Reprints are used by the advertiser for promotional purposes.

SUMMARY

Although there were a number of greats during the "Golden Age of magazines" in the 18th century, no magazine approached the circulation of today's periodicals. Magazines of that era had circulations that did not exceed 1,500 as compared to more than 17 million for today's *Reader's Digest* and *TV Guide*.

Most advertising of the time did not have illustrations and those that did have them used woodcuts.

A milestone in magazine publishing was established in 1870 by Roswell Smith. His *Scribner's Magazine* actively sought advertising and made a positive attempt to interest business and industry in placing advertising in the publication. It was eminently successful and other magazines followed suit. Other contributions to magazine advertising were the *Thompson List of Thirty*, color, and split-run insertions along with new developments and inventions, more favorable postal laws, growing literacy, more free time, a booming economy, and new magazine formats.

A substantial share of advertising, in the early days, was done by the self proclaimed "cure-all" medicines. Although a small amount of dubious patent medicine advertising continued into the 20th century, reputable publishers began to eliminate it in the 1890s.

Like most of the other media, magazines are represented by an association—the Magazine Publishers Association (MPA). Founded in 1919, it provides marketing data and other information to its members and others.

Magazines are divided into a number of categories—frequency of issue, whether they are general (mass-circulation) or class publications, and again whether they are women's service magazines or home service magazines. Another category is the news magazine group.

Magazine circulation has been increasing at a rate that matches the increase in United States households. The average number of magazines entering homes increased from approximately 80 copies in 1950 to 88 in 1970.

Rising postal rates and higher labor and production costs forced a number of magazines to reduce their physical dimensions. Similar conditions also forced four of the leading magazines to cease publication.

While more money is going into magazine advertising, competition from television has reduced the magazines' overall share of the advertising dollar. The MPA has published a number of pamphlets giving reasons why magazines are better buys for advertisers than television.

As an advertising medium, magazines offer a number of advantages—high-quality reproduction, audience selectivity, message life, secondary readership, prestige and authority, editorial reinforcement, consumer selectivity, and variety of format.

Advertising space rates differ from magazine to magazine. Many offer a frequency discount. Depending upon their capabilities, they may offer color and/or bleed pages. Most magazines offer preferred positions, at a premium. Information on rates and other specifications may be found in the magazine's rate card, SRDS, and other directories.

Magazines are innovators. Over the past twenty years they have introduced a number of exciting advertising concepts that include ads with the fragrance of the product, pop-ups, 3-D, sound recordings, and more.

QUESTIONS AND DISCUSSION SUBJECTS

1. Why were some early magazine publishers reluctant to accept outside advertising?
2. What were some reasons for low magazine circulations in the 18th century?
3. Describe an 18th-century advertisement.
4. Name some of the services performed by MPA for its members.
5. Classify magazines into categories and subcategories, giving an example of a current magazine for each.
6. What have been the recent trends in the magazine-publishing field?
7. How can you explain the demise of the mass-circulation magazines *Colliers, Life,* and *Look?*
8. Does your explanation signify that magazines are declining as a medium and that fewer magazines are entering the field? Explain.
9. Which month is the greatest for magazine circulation? Which is the lowest? What is the difference between the highest and lowest months?
10. List some advantages of magazines as an advertising medium. List some disadvantages. Compare with other media.
11. Name and describe some innovations in magazine publishing.

SOURCES

1. *Rediscovering* (New York: Magazine Publishers Association), 7.
2. *Ayer Media Facts 1975* (New York: N. W. Ayer, 1975), 14.
3. *Rediscovering, op. cit.,* 4.
4. Circulation of All A.B.C. Magazines (New York: Magazine Publishers Association), 1.
5. *Magazine Circulation by Months, 1969* (New York: Magazine Publishers Association), 1.
6. Thomas Collins, "Ailing Magazines Turning a New Leaf," *Newsday* (January 28, 1971, 13A.
7. *Rediscovering, op. cit.,* 5.

FOR FURTHER READING

Ford, James L. C. *Magazines for Millions: The Story of Specialized Publications.* Carbondale, Ill.: Southern Illinois University Press, 1969.

Mott, Frank Luther. *A History of American Magazines*. Cambridge, Mass.: Harvard University Press, 1930–1968.

Peterson, Theodore. *Magazines in the Twentieth Century*. Urbana, Ill.: University of Illinois Press, 1964.

Wolseley, Roland E. *The Changing Magazine: Trends in Readership and Management*. New York: Hastings House, Publishers, 1973.

Wood, James Playstead. *Magazines in the United States*. New York: Ronald Press, 1971.

Business and
Farm Publications

The first known businesspaper appeared sometime during the 15th century: *News Tidings of the House of Fugger.* This publication was created and operated largely in the interest of Jacob Fugger of Augsburg, an extremely wealthy German businessman of that time, to whom it brought business news from markets of the then known world. *News Tidings* continued publication during the 16th and into the 17th century, during which time the House of Fugger occupied a position of great wealth and power. Also during the 16th century, an Englishman, Thomas Graham III, started a business news service that supplied his countrymen with information and news that they needed in a world of expanding business opportunities. The *Philadelphia Price Current,* started in 1783, is considered the first independent businesspaper to be published in the United States. When the Civil War began, 78 years later, only 30 such papers were available to American businessmen. Today, *Business Publications Rates and Data* lists some 2,400 publications under 308 separate market classifications. It would be difficult to find any area of business activity that does not have one of more magazines associated with it.

BUSINESSPAPERS TODAY

The businesspapers, or trade papers, of the present have a combined distribution of close to 65 million [1] and during 1973 some 27,000 advertisers [2] spent $978.9 million to reach them.[3] Furthermore, this audience has been growing and still is. The number of managerial and professional workers in the United States has increased considerably in recent years, but businesspaper circulation has grown even more. While the count of managerial and professional workers rose from 7,200,000 in 1940 to 18,576,00 in 1969—an increase of 158%—the distribution of businesspapers rose from 13,700,000 to 63,604,000—an increase of more than 364%. This growth responds to the increasing size, complexity, and variety of business enterprises and their supporting specialties, especially those in the technologies and sciences. As business and industry have grown larger and more complex, there has been a rapid growth in many of these specialty functions. New business publications have arisen in these fields. Such publications as *Laser Focus, Oceanology International,* and *Datamation* serve fields and functions that were not even in existence at the end of World War II. Furthermore, the complexity of manufacturing and engineering operations has forced the business manager and technical man to depend more than ever on techical, professional, and business publications as sources for "postgraduate education." For example, scarcely any engineer whose degree antedates 1960 was taught in college such subjects as acoustoelasticity, bionics, biomechanics, cryostatics, electroluminescence, fuel cells, magnetohydrodynamics, thermoelectricity, fiber optics, lasers, microminiaturization. Yet these terms are in general use in industry today.

In recent years, along with consumer magazines, business publications have introduced a number of advertising innovations. The more dramatic include Xograph, or illustrations that give a three-dimensional effect, aromatic or fragrant ads, inserts of actual products, other novelty inserts, and pop-ups. In 1967, issues of *Nation's Business* and *Better Buildings* carried, as four-page inserts for Butler Manufacturing Company, a three-dimensional pop-up of a prefabricated building. And a 33⅓-r.p.m. record was on an insert in the February 24, 1975 issue of *Advertising Age.*

The American Business Press

The national trade association in the businesspaper field, the American Business Press, Inc. (ABP), was started in 1906. It was first known as the Federation of Trade Press Associations, and became the Associated Business Publications in 1916. At one point it was known as the Associated Business Papers, Inc. In 1964, it merged with National Business Publications and received its present name. As the earlier title of the national association indicates, there were several regional groups in operation at the time of its founding in 1906. Of these, the Chicago Trade Press Association continues today as the Chicago Business Publications Association. This group has the distinction of being the oldest businesspaper organization in the United States.

Among other activities of ABP has been the publication of a wide range of booklets, folders, films, and research reports dealing with marketing to business and industry and demonstrating the effectiveness of business advertising. ABP is also the primary source of statistical data on business and industrial advertising and produces annual surveys on the subject. It also grants annual awards for the best advertising in business publications.

Other publications of ABP include the *Manual of Recommended Prac-*

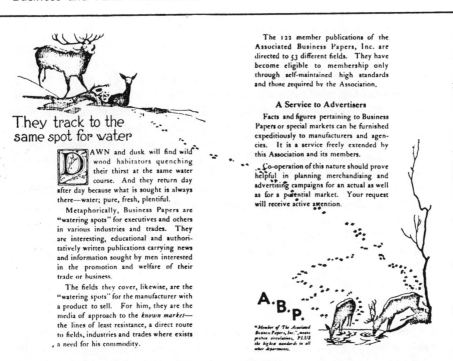

They track to the same spot for water

DAWN and dusk will find wild wood habitators quenching their thirst at the same water course. And they return day after day because what is sought is always there—water; pure, fresh, plentiful.

Metaphorically, Business Papers are "watering spots" for executives and others in various industries and trades. They are interesting, educational and authoritatively written publications carrying news and information sought by men interested in the promotion and welfare of their trade or business.

The fields they cover, likewise, are the "watering spots" for the manufacturer with a product to sell. For him, they are the media of approach to the *known market*— the lines of least resistance, a direct route to fields, industries and trades where exists a need for his commodity.

The 122 member publications of the Associated Business Papers, Inc. are directed to 53 different fields. They have become eligible to membership only through self-maintained high standards and those required by the Association.

A Service to Advertisers

Facts and figures pertaining to Business Papers or special markets can be furnished expeditiously to manufacturers and agencies. It is a service freely extended by this Association and its members.

Co-operation of this nature should prove helpful in planning merchandising and advertising campaigns for an actual as well as for a potential market. Your request will receive active attention.

A.B.P.

"Member of The Associated Business Papers, Inc.", means proven circulations, PLUS the highest standards in all other departments.

THE ASSOCIATED BUSINESS PAPERS, INC.
Reprint from Printers' Ink, issue of February 17, 1921.

Headquarters 220 West 42d Street · NEW YORK

A Historic Promotion Document. The first advertisement in ABP's continuing campaign to promote business papers as an advertising medium. It appeared as a two-page spread in *Printers' Ink,* February 17, 1921. *The American Business Press.*

tices, a number of booklets containing research data and promotional materials, the making of cost studies, and the granting of awards for the best advertising in industrial, institutional, professional, and merchandising papers.

Types of Businesspapers

The editorial content and the advertising differ markedly among the many types of business publications. However, they are all devoted to the technical, industrial, business, or professional interests of their readers and in this respect differ from the general press, which is devoted to the broader interests of larger segments of the public if not of the public as a whole.

Businesspapers can be divided into four major classes or groups:

1. Industrial businesspapers.
2. Institutional businesspapers.
3. Professional businesspapers.
4. Merchandising or trade businesspapers.

A fifth group, usually considered separately from the businesspapers, consists of farm or agricultural publications.

Under the industrial classification, the publications may be divided further into vertical, horizontal, and "umbrella" magazines or newspapers. A *vertical publication* is one that is designed to serve the needs of a specific industry and may contain material of interest to workers in different kinds of jobs within that industry. The *horizontal publication,* in contrast, has articles of interest to only one kind of worker (chemical engineers, for example), but these workers might be in several different industries. The *"umbrella" publications* are general in scope, like *Fortune, Sales Management,* or *Business Week, and serve management at all levels.*

Pipe Line Industry is an example of an industrial businesspaper. It serves the needs of men and industries concerned with the transportation of oil and gas by pipe lines.

Institutional businesspapers serve workers in such businesses as the operation of hotels, or the maintenance work of schools and hospitals. *Hospital Management* is an example.

Professional businesspapers are those directed to the interests of professional people—doctors, nurses, engineers, architects, or others. *Architectural Record* is an example.

Merchandising businesspapers are concerned with the needs and interests of the nations's wholesalers and retailers. The approach taken in both editorial content and in the advertising in these publications differs from those taken in the industrial, institutional, and professional papers. The ultimate product buyers are the users of the products purchased. On the other hand, the problems of the wholesalers and retailers are not those of the ultimate user but those of the middleman. *Progressive Grocer* is a merchandising businesspaper.

Format

Businesspapers, regardless of the classification into which they may fall, range in format from newspapers to slick magazines. Some are issued as dailies, some as semiweeklies, some as weeklies, and some at less frequent intervals. Both format and frequency of publication depend upon the needs of the industry, business, or profession that the paper is designed to serve. In areas where there is much happening and where it is important that news of these events reach the people in the business as soon as possible, the businesspaper is likely to take the form of a newspaper and to be published daily or weekly. If, on the other hand, the industry or business is one in which there are many technical problems or in which the results of scientific experiments must be reported, the needs of readers may best be served by a magazine issued at less frequent intervals—because of the greater length of the articles, the possible need for accompanying pictures, charts, and graphs, and the less frequent occurrence of vital news.

Readership and Circulation

Businesspapers are read because their readers need them. The need is a consequence of the environment in which modern men live and conduct business—an environment vastly different from that as recent as a few generations ago.

Until the 19th century, man moved across limited stretches of the earth no faster than he could be carried or drawn by elephant, camel, ox, burro, or horse, and upon the sea no faster than he could be borne by fickle winds. His light by night was furnished by burning wax or oil. His toil by day was of his own muscle, aided when he was lucky by animals pressed into his service. He lived under the shadows of pestilence and famine and died young. Then came the discoveries and inventions that triggered the Industrial Revolution, and within two centuries the stable world altered—both in appearance and in way of life—for millions of its inhabitants. The speed of discovery and invention increased as each short year sped by. Man has virtually abandoned his work animals in many parts of the earth; he has learned to light his cities with the throwing of a switch; he travels faster than the speed of sound; he hears and sees, in his own living room, distant events at the moment of their occurrence; he swallows drugs that free him from age-old killers; he casts chemicals upon the ground and the shadow of famine is removed; he pierces the vastness of space with giant telescopes and with his satellites, rockets and astronauts; his dreams of distant planets and worlds to conquer have become a reality.

So rapid and so constant has change become that the best-trained engineers, chemists, physicists, doctors, and business men must continue to read and to study or soon find themselves quite inadequate in their respective callings.

The businesspaper was an important but probably dispensable factor in the success of Jacob Fugger and his descendants over two or more centuries. But to the business and professional man of today it has become a necessity. The American Business Press points out that ''a 1960 graduate who stopped searching out knowledge from the printed page could scarcely design today's products . . . or work on today's management team . . . or run today's wholesale and retail businesses. . . . And to hold their own—not to speak of moving ahead—men must know more than the changing techniques of their callings. They must keep up, too, with changing times, fluctuating markets, economic conditions, government regulations, and the moods and desires of the public.'' The business press in very large measure helps them do this.

Business publications are peculiarly suited to serve the needs of the merchant, the industrial worker, and the professional man in these rapidly changing times. These publications are created and edited not to entertain but to inform their readers. They are read—both their editorial content and their advertising—because their readers know that they must keep up with changing conditions and new developments in their businesses and professions. They are read because their readers know that new ideas and inspiration may be drawn from their pages as well as useful current facts. The story is told that the inventor George Westinghouse, after working unsuccessfully with hand brakes and steam, finally got his idea for an air brake from a businesspaper article that described how compressed air had been used to cut through a mountain. Henry Ford states in his diary that a businesspaper story gave him the first detailed description of a new gasoline engine called the "Kane-Pennington" motor. Thus, the businesspaper not only keeps its readers informed of what has happened but gives them, many times, the inspiration for new inventions and new and better methods of conducting their businesses.

Circulation of businesspapers, as was seen in an earlier chapter, is audited either by the Audit Bureau of Circulations or by the Business Publications Audit of Circulation.

Businesspaper circulation is very selective inasmuch as the editorial content of these publications is directed at people in particular areas of employment or at people holding particular jobs. In some markets, for example, there may be several publications, each one of which is designed for a special group of workers. Furthermore, there appears to be a trend toward even greater specialization of coverage. ABP points out that business magazines are specializing more in order to pinpoint specified markets.

Not only are businesspapers read but so, too, is the advertising that they contain. Studies made by the Advertising Research Foundation show that 97% of businesspaper readers read the advertising. An ABP survey showed that 96.6% of a group of leading merchandisers read trade papers regularly.

Businesspaper Advertising

The advertiser in the industrial and business publication knows that there is a sizable turnover of important and influential personnel in key buying positions and in positions that influence the decisions to purchase industrial and business products and services. Some of the turnover is the result of promotions, some the result of retirements, and so on. Such changes make it difficult for the salesman of industrial goods and services to keep in contact with all of his prospects. However, the businesspapers follow these people and maintain, as the salesman frequently cannot, a more or less continuous contact.

Often there are hidden influences in the decision to purchase business and industrial products. A suggestion of a foreman, or of a secretary, or of a filing clerk may start the chain of events moving that results in a purchase. These people cannot normally be reached by the manufacturer's salesmen, but they can be reached by his advertising in industrial and business periodicals. The American Business Press, Inc., states:

> . . . the investor who is getting the most out of his businesspaper advertising dollar is the one who realizes that the businesspaper reader is different. That he reads not for relaxation, not to while away leisure hours, and not to be entertained. He knows that this businesspaper reader is looking, on both editorial and advertising pages, for information and ideas which will help him make extra profits, help

him get ahead at his place of business, and, if he's already the top banana, to whale the daylights out of his competitors.

So he, the sophisticated advertiser, treats his businesspaper advertising differently. He separates it in his mind and in his planning from his consumer advertising. He and his agency produce specialized ads for specialized audiences—and the sales figures are a joy to behold.

He finds out that *buying power* per thousand . . .

He researches his markets to find out what prospective buyers want to know—and need to know—about his product . . .

Having researched his markets, the successful businesspaper advertiser then tells prospective buyers why it is to their advantage to buy his brand. In short copy—or in long copy. "Tell All"—in as many words as a good copywriter needs to tell the story.

The ABP has published a check list of factors that make good businesspaper advertising. The 20 points of the check list follow:

Objectives

1. The objectives of a good businesspaper campaign are clearly defined.
2. The objectives are specific, attainable, readily understood.
3. No single advertisement tries to cover too many objectives

Coherence

4. Headline, picture, copy and typography work together to produce a unified, easily read advertisement.
5. Headlines lead naturally and logically into the copy, and work with the copy to convey the sales message quickly and concisely.

Illustrations

6. Illustrations are chosen because they contribute to the sales story, and not merely to embellish the advertisement.
7. Illustrations are honest, convincing.

Typography

8. Typography is designed for clean appearance and easy reading.

Copy

9. Desirably, the copy shows a benefit from the purchase and use of the product (such as savings in cost of labor, greater operating efficiency, higher profits).
10. Good businesspaper copy is simple and specific.
11. It emphasizes what the advertiser can do for the prospect, not what the prospect can do for the advertiser.
12. The copy tries to help the reader solve problems by giving him helpful ideas.
13. The copy does not hesitate to ask the reader to do something, such as write for literature, ask for specific proposals, or send in an order.
14. It makes it easy for the prospect to act, by giving him the essential information needed for action.
15. The copy, being sincere and straightforward, does not oversell.
16. It talks directly to the prospect in his language (not down to him or up to him).

17. The length of copy is determined by the demands of the sales argument, not by any arbitrary idea of the relative merits of short or long copy.

Color

18. Color (when used) contributes to the sales message and is not merely decorative.

Product Uses

19. If the advertisement shows the product in use, it illustrates and describes the use in a way that will appeal to a worthwhile number of prospects.

Correlation

20. The advertisement, when part of a campaign, has a family resemblance to other advertisements in the campaign by effective use of headlines, layouts, picture treatments, typography, and logotype.

FARM AND AGRICULTURAL PUBLICATIONS

Farm and agricultural publications have dual personalities. Both editorial content and advertising are aimed at the farmer as a businessman and as a producer and are also directed toward him and his family as consumers. While many statistics on consumer magazines include the farm journals, and *Standard Rate & Data Service* has a section for agricultural publications in its *Consumer Magazine* edition, it is more useful to discuss them in this book as businesspapers.

Farm publications started many years ago as media in the magazine field. Their growth was rather slow at first, but, as farmers realized the value of having publications edited for the express purpose of helping them in their farming operations, they began to show more interest until at present there are 34 farm publications that are members of the Agricultural Publishers Association.

The Agricultural Publishers Association, or APA, was organized in 1915 for the purpose, as stated in its by-laws, ". . . to develop the usefulness of farm publications, to promote a spirit of cooperation among them, to coordinate their efforts and to perform for them such common services as otherwise would be duplicated by their individual efforts, to use various means to promote a public understanding of the field they service, and to cooperate with other associations and/or individuals or firms in such research and promotional efforts as are to the common good of the membership."

In 1948 the APA established Farm Publications Reports, Inc., as a separate company. Its purpose was to measure and classify the advertising appearing in member farm journals. Statistical studies encompassing these data are made available to the members as well as to interested advertising agencies.

Farm and agricultural publications may be broad in coverage or they may have editorial content directed toward a particular kind of farming. They are divided into national, regional, state, and specialized groups. The national publications include *Farm Journal, Progressive Farmer,* and *Successful Farming,* in order of revenue and circulation. Among the regional farm journals are

Capper's Farmer and *Wallace's Farmer.* Typical of the state publications are the *Wyoming Stockman Farmer,* the *Montana Farmer-Stockman,* the *Washington Farmer,* and the *Alabama Farmer.* The specialized publications include such titles as *Hoard's Dairyman, Poultry Tribune, Shorthorn World,* and *Soybean Digest.* Magazines like the *Western Fruit Grower* have a dual regional-specialized status. At present, by providing regional editions, national and specialized publications are offering an increased degree of flexibility to the advertisers who use their pages.

Despite the fact that farming remains a way of life for only a small percentage of Americans and although this figure decreases each year, the readership of agricultural publications is truly impressive. *Farm Journal,* for example, has a circulation of just under 2,000,000. *Progressive Farmer,* the next in size, claims more than 1,100,000 readers [4]; more regional in nature, it covers about one-third of the states—from Texas to Delaware. State farm journals have considerably fewer subscribers. These circulation figures had been much higher in 1969, only a short time earlier.[5]

In light of the facts mentioned above—the nation's farm population has fallen from 18,712,000 in 1956 to 9,000,000, a drop of more than half; and in approximately the same period the number of farms diminished by 25%, or 1,000,000 farms, leaving a total of less than 3,000,000—farm magazines voluntarily cut their circulations. *Farm Journal* reduced its circulation by a full third and the others followed suit. This was accompanied by an equal drop in advertising pages. The outcome, however, is a positive one. Farm publications also raised their advertising rates and cut their operating expenses. Increased rates were justified by the fact that farming today is prosperous and highly profitable. Although there are fewer farms, they have become bigger and richer, in a short period of time. American farms have increased by one-third in size, and income has more than doubled in the past 10 years.[6]

SUMMARY

Business or trade papers had their beginnings in 15th-century Germany. The first businesspaper in the United States was published in 1783, the last year of the Revolutionary War. The growth of trade papers was slow in this country with only 30 in existence at the start of the Civil War. Today, however, there are some 2,400 of them representing 308 different market classifications, and their distribution growth rate exceeds the rise in managerial and professional employees by more than 225%. It is hard to think of a business, industry, trade, or profession that does not have at least one trade paper associated with it.

There are four categories of businesspapers—industrial, institutional, professional, and merchandising. Farm and agricultural publications can be considered a fifth category. The first, industrial, can be divided again into vertical, horizontal and umbrella publications.

Trade papers come in all recognized sizes and formats. They are newspapers and magazines and are distributed as dailies, weeklies, monthlies, and at other frequencies.

They are a prime source of the latest information in their particular fields and a means for the practitioner to keep abreast of developments in his business, trade, or profession. By the same token they provide an ideal medium for advertisers to reach these highly specialized markets.

Farm publications serve a dual market. They reach the farmer both as a businessman and as a consumer. Although there are relatively few farmers in the United States and their numbers decline each year, some farm journals claim circulations of 1 and 2 million. Farm publications have voluntarily reduced their circulations. At the same time they raised their advertising rates to match the rise in size of American farms and the greater profit they produce.

QUESTIONS AND DISCUSSION SUBJECTS

1. Why have businesspapers become increasingly important to their readers?
2. According to the ABP's check list, what factors make good businesspaper advertising?
3. Into what major classifications may businesspapers be divided?
4. (a) In what respects do farm publications differ from other types of businesspapers? (b) Of what significance are these differences to advertisers?
5. What is the importance of farm publications as an advertising medium?
6. Explain the great drop in circulation of agricultural magazines.
7. Define, identify, or explain: (a) ABP; (b) APA; (c) BPA; (d) *Business Publications Rate & Data;* (e) vertical publication; (f) horizontal publication; (g) umbrella publication; (h) institutional publication; (i) industrial publication.

SOURCES

1. "Info/File '74," *The Case for the Business Paper* (New York: American Business Press, 1974), 53.
2. "Business Press Has 27,000 Advertisers," *Advertising Age,* November 21, 1973, 104.
3. "Info/File '74," *op. cit.,* 51.
4. "Farm Magazines Look Up As Prices Soar," *Advertising Age,* November 21, 1973, 85.

5. *Loc. cit.*
6. *Loc. cit.*

FOR FURTHER READING

Editorial Department Management, vols. 1, 2, and 3. New York: American Business
    Press, 1970 and 1972.
Editorial Presentation, vols. 1 and 2. New York: American Business Press, 1970.
Editorial Research. New York: American Business Press, 1970.
Elfenbein, J. *Business Journalism.* 2nd revised edition. Westport, Conn.: Greenwood
    Press. Reprint of 1960 edition.
Elfenbein, J. *Business Paper Publishing Practice.* Wesport, Conn.: Greenwood Press.
    Reprint of 1952 edition.
Ford, James L. C. *Magazines for Millions.* Carbondale, Ill.: Southern Illinois University
    Press, 1969.
Smith, Roland B. *Advertising to Business.* Homewood, Ill.: Irwin, 1957.
Wortman, Victor. "The Farm Market: Breaking Away From Tradition," *Printer's Ink,*
    May 1, 1964.
Writing and Editing for the Business Press. New York: American Business Press, 1965.

21

Radio Advertising

EVOLUTION OF BROADCASTING [1]

One of the most dramatic developments of 20th-century technology has been the use of radio waves—electromagnetic radiations traveling at the speed of light—for communication. Radio communication designed for reception by the general public is known as *broadcasting*. Radio waves of different frequencies (number of cycles per second) can be "tuned." Hence, signals from many sources can be received on a radio set at the listener's choice.

In everyday language the term *radio* refers to aural (sound) broadcasting, which is received from amplitude-modulated (AM) or frequency-modulated (FM) stations. *Television,* another form of radio, is received from stations making simultaneous visual and aural transmissions. AM radio, sometimes called standard broadcasting, was the earliest broadcast service and operates on relatively low "medium" frequencies. FM and TV are newer and occupy considerably higher frequency bands.

Radio communication was born of many minds and developments. In the 1860s, the Scottish physicist James Clerk Maxwell predicted the existence of radio waves. The German physicist Heinrich Rudolf Hertz * later demonstrated that rapid variations of electromagnetic energy can be projected into space in the form of waves similar to those of light and heat. In 1895, the Italian engineer Guglielmo Marconi transmitted radio signals over a short distance, and at the turn of the century he conducted successful transatlantic tests.

The first practical application of radio was for ship-to-ship and ship-to-shore telegraphic communication. Marine disasters early demonstrated the speed and effectiveness of radiotelegraphy for saving life and property at sea.

---

* His contributions have been internationally honored by the adoption of *Hertz* as the basic unit of wave frequency for broadcasting. The frequency 1 kc/s (one kilocycle per second) is called a kiloHertz (abbreviated kHz) and 1,000 kHz is called 1 megaHertz (1mHz). They were formerly called kilowatts, megawatts, etc.

The new communication medium was first known as *wireless telegraphy* or *wireless*. American use of the term *radio* is traced to about 1912 when the United States Navy, feeling that "wireless" was too inclusive, adopted the word *radiotelegraphy*. Use of the word "broadcast" (originally a way of sowing seed) stems from early Navy practice, the broadcast of orders to the fleet. Now the word is used to describe radio service to the public.

The origin of the first voice broadcast is a subject for debate. Claims to that distinction are made for "Hello, Rainey," said to have been transmitted by Nathan B. Stubblefield to a neighbor, Rainey T. Well, in a demonstration near Murray, Ky., in 1892. "First" claims are also made for an impromptu program from Brant Rock, Mass., by Reginald A. Fessenden in 1906, which was picked up by nearby ships. There were other early experimental voice transmissions. Lee De Forest put singer Enrico Caruso on the air in 1910, and there were transatlantic voice tests by the Bell Telephone Company at Arlington, Va., in 1915, but it was not until after World War I that regular radio broadcasting began.

The identity of the "first" broadcasting station is also a matter of conflicting claims. This is due largely to the fact that some pioneer broadcast stations developed from experimental operations. Although KDKA, Pittsburgh, did not receive a regular broadcasting license until November 7, 1921, it furnished programs under a different authorization before that date. Records of the Department of Commerce, which then supervised radio, indicate that the first station issued a regular broadcasting license was WBZ, Springfield, Mass., on September 15, 1921. (WBZ is now assigned to Boston.)

The First Commercials

In 1919 Frank Conrad, a Westinghouse Corporation engineer, borrowed music records from a shop to make some experimental broadcasts. The owner of the shop asked that credit be given him during the broadcasts for use of the records. Thus occurred what might be regarded as the first radio "commercial," although commercial radio as such was not yet born. The Conrad experiments were sufficiently successful to warrant the construction of Station KDKA by Westinghouse in 1920. In 1922 Station WEAF (New York) offered to sell time for the purpose of advertising goods or services. Shortly after this offer was made, a real-estate firm broadcast a ten-minute program giving details of a real-estate development in Jackson Heights, New York City. This was the first sponsored program as well as the first paid commercial.

The Start of the Networks

There was experimental network operation over telephone lines as early as 1922. In that year WJZ (now WABC), New York City, and WGY, Schenectady, N.Y., broadcast the World Series. Early in 1923, WEAF (now WNBC), New York City, and WNAC, Boston, picked up a football game from Chicago. Later that same year, WEAF and WGY were connected with KDKA, Pittsburgh, and KYW, Chicago (now in Cleveland) to carry talks made at a dinner in New York. President Coolidge's 1923 message to Congress was broadcast by six stations.

In 1926, the National Broadcasting Co., a subsidiary of Radio Corporation of America, started the first regular network with 24 stations. In its first coast-to-coast hookup, in 1927, it broadcast a football game. In that same year, the Columbia Broadcasting System, first called the Columbia Phonograph Broadcasting System, was organized.

For some years NBC operated two networks, the Red and the Blue, but in the early 1940s the Federal Communications Commission adopted chain broadcasting rules. These prohibited one organization from operating two networks serving the same area at the same time. RCA sold the Blue Network to Edward J. Noble in 1943; it ultimately became the American Broadcasting Co. (In 1968 ABC itself was given a limited exception to the dual-network rule in order to operate four radio networks each providing a specific service.)

Television broadcasting and frequency-modulation (FM) radio broadcasting emerged from their experimental stage just before the United States entered World War II. Wartime restrictions retarded expansion of radio facilities, although the emergency produced new techniques and apparatus that are in use today. In the decades following the war, broadcasting expanded domestically, and the development of communication satellites has opened new possibilities for international relay.

The Rise and Development of Associations

The National Association of Broadcasters (NAB) came into being in 1922. Its original purpose was to promote the development of radio broadcasting. Following the advent of television it was known, for a while, as the National Association of Radio and Television Broadcasters. In 1933 it promulgated a code of ethics for member stations which served as a guide for all station broadcasts, including commercials. There are separate codes for radio and for television and they are revised from time to time to keep them current. Today, the NAB is the trade association of the radio and television industry. Its membership consists of close to 4,000 radio and television stations with associate memberships being granted to the seven networks.

The Radio Advertising Bureau, Inc. is an organization of over 1,600 radio stations, radio networks, and station representatives. Its function is to sell the concept of radio advertising to advertisers and agencies. It does this through personal calls, through research, and through printed promotions. In addition, the RAB provides its members with services designed to help make their own selling efforts more effective. For example, it turns out printed "presentations" that tell how to use radio, case studies, and tapes of successful commercials. The RAB is credited by some with having played a major role in revitalizing radio in the early 1950s.

The Nature of Broadcasting in the United States

Although educational and other noncommercial stations share the airwaves, the United States broadcasting system for the most part is commercial.

Being commercial, it is supported by revenues from those who advertise goods or services to the audience. Advertising messages are presented as commercial *spot announcements* before, during, and after programs, or as part of *sponsored* programs.

Broadcast stations are licensed to serve the public interest, convenience, and necessity. Because radio channels are limited in number and are part of the public domain, it is important to entrust the use of them to licensees with a sense of public responsibility. By law, each license must contain a statement that the licensee does not have any right to operate the station or use the frequency beyond the term of the license. The maximum term of license is three years, which is renewable.

The Assignment of Call Letters and Frequencies

International agreement provides for national identification of a radio station by the first letter or first two letters of its assigned call signal, and for this purpose the alphabet is apportioned among nations. Broadcast stations in the United States use call letters beginning with K or W. Generally, those beginning with K are assigned to stations west of the Mississippi River and in territories and possessions, while W is assigned east of the Mississippi. However, KDKA, Pittsburgh, and some other eastern stations authorized before this system went into effect have retained their K calls, and similarly some pioneer stations west of the Mississippi have kept their W calls. Most of the early broadcast call signs contained only three letters. These combinations were soon exhausted and stations were assigned four-letter calls. Since many AM licensees also operate FM and TV stations, a common practice is to use the AM call letters followed by "FM" or "TV."

Radio *frequencies* differ in characteristics, and each service is assigned to a frequency band to suit its needs.

The AM aural service, sometimes called standard broadcast, occupies the band from 535 kHz to 1605 kHz. Radio waves travel with the same speed as light, and are of different *frequencies* (cycles per second) and *wavelengths* (distance between comparable points in successive cycles). Frequency and wavelength vary inversely with each other. The latter term was formerly used generally to describe a radio signal, and still is in some other countries; but in the United States the term *frequency* is much more common. The medium frequencies, those of the AM band, are usually referred to by their number of *kilocycles per second,* or, for short, *kilocycles;* the prefix *kilo* means "thousand." The higher frequencies are usually referred to by the number of *megacycles* (1,000 kilocycles or 1,000,000 cycles) *per second,* or, for short, *megacycles.* The term *gigacycle* has come into use in more recent years (it means 1,000,000,000 cycles or 1,000 megacycles) to describe the much higher frequencies now being used in many services although not in broadcasting as such. The term *Hertz* as a synonym for *cycle per second* has recently been agreed upon internationally and domestically, along with its derivatives kiloHertz, megaHertz, etc. The usable frequency spectrum has constantly expanded upward with developing technology, so that what were once high frequencies are near the low end of the total spectrum used. Frequencies for AM stations are assigned at 10-kHz intervals beginning at 540 kHz, providing 107 frequencies. The center frequency consists of AM broadcast channels, from 540 to 1600 kHz.

Frequencies for FM broadcasting occupy the range from 88 to 100 megaHertz, with 100 channels of 200-kHz width each; the lowest 20 of them are reserved for educational use.

Although "AM" and "FM" are often used to refer to the standard broadcast and FM broadcast services, these terms more properly apply to the methods—*amplitude modulation* and *frequency modulation*—used to impress aural or visual intelligence on the carrier wave. The AM principle is used not only in the standard broadcast but also in the picture portion of television and in the international shortwave service. The FM principle is used both in the FM broadcast service and in the sound portion of television.

In all the broadcast services, the same aural or visual channel can be used by stations in different places if the stations are far enough apart not to interfere with one another or with stations on adjacent or technically related channels. Thus several stations can often use the same channel.

How Radio Works

Without being too technical, this is how a radio station works:

A person talks into a microphone as if it were a telephone. His voice sets up vibrations of varying intensity and frequency. The lower the pitch the slower the vibration. A cycle, or wave length, is one complete performance of a vibration.

In the microphone these vibrations are converted into electrical impulses which are then greatly amplified at the transmitter before being put on the *carrier* wave. The intensity and frequency of the carrier wave are constant. This wave, by itself, does not transmit music or speech, so it is varied to correspond with the fluctuations of the speech or music received at the microphone. This is called *modulation*.

In AM transmission, the audio waves are impressed on the carrier wave in a manner to cause its amplitude to vary with the audio waves. The frequency of

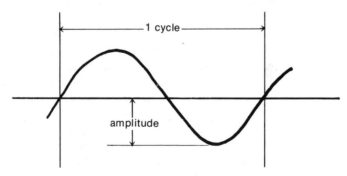

Cycle and Amplitude.

the carrier remains constant. This is known as amplitude modulation. In frequency modulation (FM), the amplitude remains unchanged but the frequency is varied in a manner corresponding to the voice or music to be transmitted.

These modulated waves radiate from the antenna tower at approximately 186,000 miles per second (the speed of light). Those portions of them that follow the contour of the ground are called groundwaves. Those that radiate upward are called *skywaves*. At night, the skywave portions of transmissions in the standard broadcast (AM) frequencies are reflected back to earth by electrical particles in the ionosphere * portion of the atmosphere. This lets the listener hear more distant AM stations at night, but also increases interference. Daytime reception is dependent on groundwaves.

Radio waves may pass through buildings and other objects but are subject to absorption or interference. As in the case of ripples on water, radio vibrations weaken with distance. Seasonal disturbances and sunspot periods can throw them off course and cause "freak" reception.

AM broadcast stations use medium-frequency waves. That is to say, they transmit 540,000 to 1,600,000 wave cycles per second, or 540 to 1,600 kilo-Hertz. At 540,000 wave cycles per second, the distance between the crests is approximately 1,800 feet.

The so-called shortwave (international long-distance) broadcast stations transmit in the frequency range 6 mHz to 25 mHz (1 mHz = 1,000,000 cycles/second). These waves are sent out, one after another, so rapidly that the distance between their crests (wavelength), is only about 150 to 37 feet. FM and TV stations, broadcasting in the very high and ultra high frequencies, send out even shorter, or *very short,* waves (The word *shortwave* came into use before there was technology to use these other parts of the spectrum.) The modulated radio wave from the radio station is "picked up" by the receiving antenna; that is to say, the wave sets up in the receiving antenna a current having the same frequency characteristics as the one transmitted. In the receiver the audio and carrier waves are separated by a device called a detector or demodulator. The carrier wave, no longer needed, is dissipated while the audio wave is relayed to the loudspeaker where it is transformed back into the sound that is heard by the listener.

Simultaneous broadcasting from two or more stations, including *networks,* depends upon wire, cable, or radio connecting facilities (common carrier or private). Most live-talent radio network programs are sent over telephone circuits, many across the continent, for rebroadcast. For local broadcasts, stations usually employ wire connections between studio and transmitter, but some use radio links.

Broadcast programs can also be picked out of the air for rebroadcast. TV, because of its characteristics, cannot be sent over ordinary wire lines but depends upon coaxial cable or micrawave relay. Both of these methods also

* Also called the Kennelly-Heaviside layer, after the two men who discovered the phenomenon in 1902.

handle AM and FM transmission as well as telephone and telegraph communication.

In the AM service, antenna height above ground is not usually a matter of much importance. The entire antenna structure acts as the antenna and usually varies in height with the frequency of the transmission. Few AM antennas exceed 1,000 feet in height and most are considerably less.

By contrast, in FM and TV, where transmission follows *line of sight,* service depends on the location of the receiver in relation to the transmitting antenna. Here, antenna height is extremely important. While FM and TV antennas themselves are short, they are often situated atop natural or manmade structures which give greater height, such as tall buildings, mountain tops, or tall antenna towers specifically built for this purpose. Television towers may extend more than 2,000 feet above ground level.

RADIO AND ADVERTISING

Despite the fact that many of the nation's major advertisers are still users of radio, there have been some rather important shifts in the way this medium is used.

Before television nearly two-thirds of all radio sets were located in the living rooms of American homes. Mass-audience programs took the advertiser's sales messages into most homes where his programs were heard by all or most of the family. Then, about 1949, television started to move in and rapidly encroached upon what was once radio's exclusive territory. Swiftly, it took over the living rooms of the nation and, with them, the mass audiences. Today, thanks to the transistor, few radio sets remain in the living rooms. The rest are scattered about the house, installed or carried in automobiles, even carried in the hand or in the pocket to beaches, playgrounds, parks, picnics, indeed almost anywhere.

But, although television took over what had once been the mass audiences of radio, a new role developed for the latter medium. Advertising leaders heavily committed to television often employ radio as a supplementary or supporting medium or, not infrequently, as a major medium for selling brands that are not leaders in their product class. For the large advertiser, radio has become a medium less dominating than television but one that has contact with an audience throughout much of the day and night. Although people do not listen to radio for as many consecutive hours as they did before television came into their homes, their listening is scattered throughout most of the waking hours of the day. They get the radio news and the radio weather in the morning and again at night, either at home or in the automobile. They listen to music as a background to other activities in which they are interested. And commuters driving from the suburbs get much-needed traffic information on their way between home and work.

The distribution of radio receiving sets is an indication of this change in listening habits. Radio Advertising Bureau surveys show that home radio sets are in only 47% of the living rooms, whereas they are located in 71% of the bedrooms, 56% of the kitchens, 40% of the studies and dens, 22% of the dining areas, and 20% of the laundry rooms.[2] This means that no matter where in the home a person happens to be the chances are good that a radio will be close at hand. Often, the location of the sets relates to the kind of activity the listeners will be engaged in and can be made to tie in with the advertising of related products. For example, a housewife at work in the kitchen may be especially receptive to a commercial dealing with foods or with cleaning compounds for pots and pans; a man driving an automobile may be more susceptible to automobile-accessory advertising. Incidentally, more than 96% of all persons 12 years of age and older listen to radio during an average week.[3] Considerable out-of-home listening is attributable to the increase in the number of portable transistor and automobile radios. The RAB indicates that 91% of new cars are sold equipped with radios. The Radio Advertising Bureau also places the number of radios in automobiles in 1975 at 100,400,000 or 95% of all cars in the United States.[4] Boats also account for an increasing amount of out-of-home listening. Listening out-of-home extends even to places of business.

Though television emerged as a medium of consequence in 1952, with approximately 40% national penetration, radio has continued to grow. In 1975 the number of radio sets in working order was close to four times the number that existed in 1952 and sales of radios were up close to five times. Money spent for radio sets had also increased more than fivefold.[5]

Radio's place as an advertising medium has changed as a result of the many changes brought about by television. Large advertisers do not depend upon it as they once did to carry the major burden of new-product announcements or promotions nor do they use it to reach mass audiences at one time. Neither is radio the prestige medium for them that it once was. Instead, the large advertiser of the present uses radio to do a supplementary but important job of frequent selling. It is a medium used to reach people wherever they happen to be. In addition to the receiving sets in homes and autobobiles, many additional sets are in such public places as restaurants, garages, barber shops, and the like. The average automobile set alone is estimated to be in use 62.4% of driving time.[6] Of the privately owned sets, a vast number are battery-powered transistor portables that can be carried from room to room within the home or taken out-of-doors and used in locations where other types of radios cannot be played.

For these reasons and because radio is a highly efficient medium (on a cost basis) for delivering the advertisers' messages, it fills an important place in the advertising programs of both large and medium-sized advertisers. In fact, the limited-budget client has become the economic foundation on which radio rests.

Another indication of the increasing importance of radio as an advertising medium is the fact that the number of commercial stations has increased during recent years. The sale of 54,200,000 radio receiving sets in 1974 alone demonstrated a strong consumer interest in the medium.[7] This sale figure is especially

significant when one realizes that the average household in the United States
had 5.5 radio sets in 1975 and that 98.6% of American homes have at least one
radio in working order.[8]

Programming

Before television took its place in the mass communication scene, programming of the typical radio station resembled that of today's television—early morning news followed by programs for the preschool generation,
then women's programs and "soap operas" (*Ma Perkins, Our Gal Sunday,
Stella Dallas,* etc.), followed by programs for the youngsters returning from
school. These included *Jack Armstrong: The All American Boy, Little Orphan
Annie, The Green Hornet,* and others. Later in the afternoon *The Lone Ranger*
was heard. News was generally broadcast at seven in the evening when the man
of the family was home. Such news reporters and commentators as Gabriel
Heatter, H. V. Kaltenborn, and Edward R. Murrow, to cite a few, were
household names. These were then followed by music, mystery, dramatic,
and/or comedy programs catering to the entire family gathered around the big
console radio in the living room. A typical music program was the *A&P Gyp-
sies;* typical programs of other categories were *The Inner Sanctum* for mystery,
the *Lux Radio Theater* for drama, and *Amos and Andy,* Eddie Cantor, and Fred
Allen for comedy.

The advent of television changed all that. Radio stations have revolu-
tionized their programming to appeal to special segments of the population. In
music alone there are at least ten varieties, ranging from "rock" to classical
and including numerous specialties. And there are any number of radio stations
that air one particular program type, "from dawn to dusk," for their clientele.
Some stations broadcast only news from sign-on to sign-off, and others offer
talk shows or "dialog radio," where the listener has the opportunity to call the
station and hear his own opinion or comment on the air.

All an advertiser has to do is match his market profile to the station audience.

Coverage and Circulation

Coverage is defined as the area or the number of homes equipped with
radio receiving sets that can pick up a clear signal from a transmitting station.
Coverage is not synonomous with circulation. *Circulation* refers to the number
of homes that actually tune in the station.

The factors that affect coverage are mostly mechanical or physical and
may be related to the transmitter, the receiver, or both. On the receiving end,
the type and power of the receiver will have an effect on coverage, as will the
location of the receiver and the kind of building in which it is located. The factors that affect coverage on the transmitter end are the power of the transmitter,
the location and height of the antenna, directional factors with respect to the antenna, antenna efficiency, transmission frequency, and topography. The more
power a station uses, the greater is the coverage; the more care taken with the

physical installation of the transmitting equipment, the less will be the loss of power.

As was explained earlier, AM stations may have two different areas of coverage, one during the day and the other at night. The daytime radio wave (ground wave) follows the curvature of the earth as far as station power permits. The nighttime radio wave (skywave) covers a larger area. Skywaves are lost in space during the day, but at night they are turned back toward the earth by the ionosphere layer. The usual effect of this layer of ionized atmosphere is a widening of the station's coverage after dark. Its advertising effect, however, is negligible except for national advertisers.

Obviously, circulation must fall within a station's coverage, and so, to this extent, it is limited by the same factors. However, circulation is rarely if ever as great as coverage. This would mean that every receiving set capable of picking up a station's signal would be tuned-in on a specific program. Although such a situation might be approximated under certain unusual conditions, commercial broadcasts can hardly count on such circulation.

The circulation that a program enjoys depends upon the time of day or night that it is broadcast, the character and quality of the program, and competing attractions on other programs—including television as well as radio—that are presented at the same time.

Reach and Frequency

In media planning and research it is necessary to have parameters, standards, and means of measuring and comparing advertising weight. Coverage and circulation, already mentioned, are two of these. Others used in the broadcast media are *reach, frequency,* and *gross rating points.*

Reach represents the percentage of different individuals exposed to a particular radio or television station in a single week or over a four-week period. Synonymous with reach is the term *cumulative audience,* more commonly known as "cume." *Frequency* * is the average number of different times that individuals are reached during the same periods.[9]

In effect, reach measures the breadth or width, the geographic range, of a particular radio or television station, program, or commercial—how many people it covers under its blanket. Frequency measures the other dimension—depth. It accounts for the impact of the coverage. Frequency is the embodiment of the repetition factor in advertising.[10]

Together, reach and frequency provide an ideal method of measuring advertising weight. They account for the extent to which a commercial or a campaign reaches the population, and the number of time that it does so.

Gross Rating Points

Gross rating points (GRP) are a relatively new method of evaluating the weight of broadcast advertising campaigns. In its simplest form, a single *rating*

---

* The term *frequency,* used in this sense, has been known to confuse some people who have in mind the *frequency* of the broadcast signal that is measured in kilocycles/second or in kiloHertz.

point represents 1% of the base used for the total audience under study, for example, all radio listeners or all television homes within specifically designated geographic boundaries. If for example, the program being rated was heard or seen by 20% of the listeners or viewers in the area it would have a weight of 20 rating points. If the program were broadcast two times a week during the rating period (usually four weeks) the commercial's GRP would be 40.

While a rating point "provides a common base for all markets and to some extent reflects the advertising weight of a radio campaign, . . . a gross rating point in itself accounts for the total advertising weight in a market but does not distinguish between how many people are reached by the advertising and how many times." [11] Using the example given above, the commercial that had 40 points also could have reached 10% of the audience base an average of four times a week, and still have the same GRP.

The Radio Advertising Bureau solved this problem by relating GRP's and reach and frequency, and came up with a new planning approach.

> This relationship is based on the allocation of a common number of announcements per station in a market. The GRP method, once a desired level has been set up as a goal, determines the number of stations to be used in each market and the number of announcements. Both these factors will vary by market for a common GRP level but the reach and frequency of the schedule will be identical in all markets. [12]

Essentially, a GRP is "the sum of the ratings of all the programs in a given plan or schedule. It can be divided by the reach to find the frequency or by the frequency to find the reach. [13]

Spot Radio

The terms *spot radio* or *spot broadcasting* are not synonymous with *spot announcement, radio spot,* or *spot commercial.* Actually, there is considerable confusion in their use outside the advertising business. Even people in phases of advertising other than radio or television are not always clear about them.

Spot radio or spot broadcasting refers not to announcements only but to entire programs ranging in length from 8 to 60 seconds to an hour. The important consideration in such broadcasts is the geographical areas involved and not the time employed. In other words, the advertiser "tailor makes" his own network if the existing networks don't suit his requirements. The advertiser selects one or more stations in terms of market locations and puts on a program or announcement of whatever length he believes suitable.

A spot announcement, radio spot, or spot commercial, on the other hand, is a short announcement (that can be used on spot radio or spot broadcasting) and is thought of more in terms of units of time than in terms of geographical location.

Both sets of terms have their counterparts in television and are employed in exactly the same way.

Spot radio may be used for a number of reasons but is especially suited to:

1. Introduction of a new product where the advertiser does not wish immediate national distribution.
2. Introduction of a new product when national distribution is not desired at any time.
3. Promotion of a new use for an established product, especially if it is desired to make the promotion on a limited test basis.
4. Support of special promotions in specific markets.
5. Enlistment of dealer support in specific markets.
6. Meeting increased competitive pressure in specific markets.
7. Taking advantage of and developing specific market opportunities.

One of the major advantages of spot radio is its flexibility. Its use permits selection of those markets offering the advertiser the greatest sales opportunities and exclusion of those offering less promise. It also makes possible the selection of a specific station within a market that might not be available through a network. Audience preferences for programs sometimes differ in different parts of the country. Spot radio permits the scheduling of programs to fit the tastes of different regions. Listening habits also vary from place to place with respect to the time of day most people turn on their sets. Spot radio permits programming in different stations to meet local time preferences more closely. Finally, programs on spot radio can be discontinued in some locations and continued in others to take advantage of seasonal variations in demand for the advertised product.

Spot radio may permit a dominance in a regional or local market or in a selected group of markets that, because of budget limitations, would be impossible to achieve on a national scale. This dominance may be important in introducing a new product. For example, assume that product A has a national potential but that limited production forces its introduction on a regional basis. The objective of the advertising campaign is to tell as many people as possible—as often as possible, and in as short a time as possible—about the product. Spot radio lends itself ideally to these objectives. By starting the campaign on a large scale, a carry-over effect is achieved. The impact of the early part of the campaign starts people thinking about the product. They seem to hear about it every time they turn on a radio. As the campaign is tapered off and subsequent reminders are broadcast, these tend to reinforce the idea of size and importance. That is, they have the cumulative effect of making the smaller expenditures of the latter part of the campaign seem greater than they really are. The same thing could not be accomplished without the use of spot radio, because the initial impact could not be made sufficiently great with the limited budget assigned to the launching of product A.

When radio was the only broadcast medium, its audiences tended to concentrate on two of the major networks. Advertisers with large radio budgets, who could make long-term commitments on stations affiliated with these networks, were able to tie up the best availabilites. As a result, the less frequent users of radio time were forced to take lower-rated availabilities. However, since the rapid growth of television, this is no longer the situation. The radio audience of the present is more evenly distributed, and it is distributed over a large number of stations. Also, the more popular local programs are sold on a participating announcement basis so that announcements are available on programs broadcast during times when the number of sets in use is greatest. This basis makes it possible for today's short-term buyer of radio time to obtain rating levels as good and at as satisfactory cost-per-thousand figures as do the heavier users of the medium.

Today, larger audiences can be accumulated through spot schedules than through network buys. The reason is that the greater flexibility in station selection makes it possible to distribute the number of spots per market according to local rating levels.

Local Advertisers

Radio always has been and continues to be a useful and valuable medium for local advertisers. It offers the local merchant a quick and relatively inexpensive means of reaching his entire urban and suburban market. Whereas an available metropolitan newspaper may not reach every family in a local advertiser's trading area, the coverage of the local radio station is probably such that, given the right program, the advertising can obtain a circulation representative of the majority of families in the area.

Networks

A network comprises a group of stations permanently joined by telephone lines. This enables the network to broadcast an advertiser's program simultaneously over all the stations in the network. The network itself is made up of a limited number of company-owned stations (usually seven) together with affiliated independently owned stations that are bound to the network by contractual agreements.

Networks may be regional or national in extent. There are four national radio networks: (1) the Columbia Broadcasting System, (2) the American Broadcasting Company, (3) the Mutual Broadcasting System, and (4) the National Broadcasting Company. These networks are competitive not only in their attempt to obtain advertisers but also in their efforts to gain as large a share of the listening audience as possible. As a result of this competition a wide variety of broadcasting opportunities is available to advertisers.

The local stations affiliated with the network get the benefit of sponsored and sustaining programs put out by the network, as well as maintenance of telephone lines. In return, the local stations give the network an option on part of their broadcasting time. This time may be purchased by the network at a lower rate than others would have to pay for it. The time thus purchased by the network is sold by it to national advertisers.

By using a national or regional network, an advertiser can arrange through a single contract for broadcast time that will carry his program over many stations in many markets. If he wishes, he can broadcast his program simultaneously over all of the stations of the network for which he has contracted. But, should he believe that the different time zones will result in a loss of his best prospects in some sections of the country if the program is carried by all stations simultaneously, he may repeat his program but use only a part of the network facilities for each broadcast.

Another advantage claimed for the networks is that their studios are located in New York, Chicago, and Hollywood—thus facilitating the obtaining of top quality dramatic and musical talent. Also, inasmuch as the network program is staged in but one station, better control is possible than in spot radio. Last-minute changes in program or commercials are more easily made.

Network radio, however, is less flexible than spot broadcasting. Therefore, the advertiser has less selectivity in markets and may obtain more waste circulation under certain circumstances. For example, if his distribution is not adequate in all areas covered by the network or if he is selling a product that has regional variations in sales because of climate or other factors, he will be less able to eliminate waste than in spot radio.

It is not possible today, as it once was, for an advertiser to obtain at any one time a large audience through the use of a single network. However, because of the change in radio-listening habits of the public, a sizable audience can be reached over a period of time. For this reason, participating-announcement programs in network radio have become increasingly popular with advertisers. By means of strategic placement of commercials over a period of time on different days and at different times of day, an advertiser can obtain a reasonably large audience. However, audience figures will vary considerably depending upon what specific plans are purchased.

The efficiency of the networks makes them especially attractive to national advertisers. Particular times can be selected to reach specific audiences; however, a lower cost-per-thousand is attainable if run-of-station schedules are used.

A network for national defense purposes was established by the FCC in cooperation with military and civil defense agencies. This Emergency Broadcast System, is based on voluntary participation by the broadcast industry. EBS facilities are for the primary purpose of giving emergency warning and advice to the public in the event of hostile attack, but they are put to peacetime use in alerting audiences to serious weather and other emergencies threatening life and property.

Frequency-Modulation Radio

Although interest of advertisers in frequency modulation radio had been relatively limited, there are indications that it may become an increasingly important medium. The number of FM commercial broadcasting stations has grown steadily so that in 1972 there were 2,468.[14] In 1974 there were 33,900,000 new AM/FM receiving sets sold as compared to fewer than 2,000,000 in 1960.[15] Studies indicate that the majority of male heads of FM households are professional people and have higher than average incomes.

These factors, together with its nonstatic reception, combine to make FM a seemingly attractive advertising medium.

FM advertising rates are lower than AM rates but, unlike AM, night rates are higher than day rates. Many FM stations are owned by the same people who own the AM station in the same town. In the past it was very easy for the owners of joint facilities to save money and use the same programming on FM that they had on AM. However, in order to encourage the growth of the newer service, the FCC now requires that in such cases of joint ownership, at least 50% of the FM station's programming must be original, in cities with populations greater than 100,000. Those stations that are exclusively FM generally accept fewer commercials per hour than AM stations and normally will not broadcast "hard sell" announcements.

SUMMARY

Radio, as a means of communication, developed from the work and inventive genius of many men in many countries. Rudimentary discoveries were made in the latter half of the 19th century. Wireless or radiotelegraphy first employed electrical impulses in the form of Morse code (dots and dashes) to communicate. The first voice broadcast was made in 1892 and the first broadcasting stations were established in the early 1920s. Shortly thereafter, in 1922, the first sponsored program as well as the first paid commercial made their debuts. The networks had their origin in the middle of the decade.

For the most part radio and television broadcasting in this country is done by commercial stations. That is, they are supported by the fees paid by those who advertise to the audience. There are also educational and other noncommercial stations but they are far fewer in number. All stations are licensed by the FCC to serve the public interest.

There are two types of radio broadcast service—AM, or the standard broadcast, and FM, which is in more limited use but provides a clear sound with less static and outside interference.

Radio was replaced by television as the medium for advertisers seeking to reach the mass audience. However, radio changed its programming to fit specific markets. A further boost came from the transistor, which placed additional radios in our homes, on our persons, and in our cars. Radio made a spectacular comeback and today is a major medium to be considered seriously by advertisers.

Media buyers and advertisers are concerned with coverage and circulation, reach and frequency, and they evaluate advertising campaign by means of gross rating points.

QUESTIONS AND DISCUSSION SUBJECTS

1. The text states that despite the fact many of the nation's major advertisers are still users of radio there have been some rather important shifts in the way the medium is used. What have these shifts been?
2. What indications exist that radio still is and probably will continue to be an important advertising medium?
3. What, if any, are the indications that FM radio may increase in importance as an advertising medium?
4. For what reasons might a large national advertiser use spot radio?
5. (a) What are the advantages associated with the use of network radio? (b) Would these advantages be equally important to all advertisers? Why or why not? (c) What, if any, are the disadvantages of network radio from the advertiser's point of view?
6. Is radio a medium that can be effectively used by small advertisers? Why or why not?
7. What does an advertiser mean when he speaks of "coverage" in radio? When he speaks of "circulation"?

SOURCES

1. The author is grateful to the Federal Communications Commission for the use of material from the pamphlet *Broadcast Services,* published in October 1970. This information will be found from the beginning of the chapter to the section, "Radio and Advertising."
2. *Radio Facts: RAB Pocket Piece 1975* (New York: Radio Advertising Bureau, 1975), 3.
3. *Ibid.,* 10.
4. *Ibid.,* 4.
5. *Ibid.,* 1.
6. *Ibid.,* 4.
7. *Ibid.,* 1.
8. *Ibid.,* 3.
9. *Major Discoveries about Radio Reach and Frequency* (New York: Radio Advertising Bureau), 2.
10. *Loc cit.*
11. *Radio Planning Approaches* (New York: Radio Advertising Bureau, 1969).
12. *Ibid.,* 16.
13. *SSC&B Media Guide Book,* second edition, 1974–1975 (New York: SSC&B Inc. Advertising, 1974, 9.

14. *Dimensions of Radio* (Washington, D.C.: National Association of Broadcasters, 1974), 1.
15. *Radio Facts, op. cit.*, 2.

FOR FURTHER READING

Allen, Lousie C., Audre B. Lipscomb, and Joan C. Prigmore. *Radio and Television Continuity Writing*. New York: Pitman, 1962.

Chester, Giraud, Garnett R. Garrison, and Edgar E. Willis. *Television and Radio*. New York: Appleton-Century-Crofts, 1963.

Hilliard, Robert L., ed. *Radio Broadcasting: An Introduction to the Sound Medium*. Second Edition. New York: Hastings House, Publishers, 1976.

Hilliard, Robert L. *Writing for Television and Radio*. Third Edition. New York: Hastings House, Publishers, 1976.

Lichty, Lawrence W., and Malachi C. Topping. *American Broadcasting: A Source Book on the History of Radio and Television*. New York: Hastings House, Publishers, 1975.

Radio Facts: RAB Pocket Piece 1975. New York: Radio Advertising Bureau, 1975.

Seehafer, G. F., and Jack W. Laemmar. *Successful Television and Radio Advertising*. New York: McGraw-Hill, 1959.

Taylor, Sherril W. *Radio Programming in Action*. New York: Hastings House, Publishers, 1967.

Wolfe, Charles H. *Modern Radio Advertising*. New York: Funk & Wagnalls, 1953.

22

Television and
Screen Advertising

EVOLUTION OF TELEVISION [1]

❘ The start of television as a medium for carrying the advertiser's messages took place only a few short years before the middle of this century. But its beginnings as a device for transmitting images or pictures date back to the 19th century. ❘

Men of many lands contributed to the development of television. Like aural radio, television was made possible by electronic discoveries in the late 19th and early 20th centuries. In 1884 Paul Nipkow, a German, patented a scanning disc for transmitting pictures by wireless. In this country Charles F. Jenkins began his study of the subject about 1890. The English physicist E. E. Fournier d'Albe conducted experiments in the early 1900s. In 1915 Marconi predicted "visible telephone."

In 1923 the physicist Vladimir Zworykin, a Russian-born American, applied for a patent on the iconoscope camera tube. In the years following there were experiments by E. F. W. Alexanderson and Philo T. Farnsworth in the United States and John L. Baird in England. In 1927, an experimental TV program, in which Secretary of Commerce Herbert Hoover participated, was sent over wire between New York and Washington by the Bell Telephone Laboratories. The next year Bell experimentally televised outdoor programs.

The Federal Radio Commission (predecessor of the FCC) reported that a few broadcast stations were experimenting with television in 1928. In that year WGY, Schenectady, broadcast the first television drama. Large-screen TV was demonstrated by the Radio Corporation of America (now RCA) at a New York theater in 1930. RCA tested outdoor TV pickup at Camden, N.J., in 1936.

By 1937 17 experimental television stations were operating. The first United States President seen on TV was Franklin D. Roosevelt, when he opened the New York World's Fair in 1939. That same year saw the first telecasts of a major-league baseball game, a college football game, and a professional boxing match. In 1940 the Republican and Democratic conventions were first televised. Pioneer use of coaxial cable for long-distance relay was made for the Republican convention.

The first President's message to Congress over network television was that of Harry S. Truman in 1950. The first television debate between Presidential candidates was in 1960 between John Kennedy and Richard Nixon. The first Presidential message to Congress televised in color was that of Lyndon B. Johnson in 1966.

The Journal Company of Milwaukee, now licensee of WTMJ-TV, filed the first application to broadcast television on a commercial basis. At a 1940 hearing the FCC found industry divided on technology and standards, but a committee appointed to work on the questions reached agreement on the present standards of 525 lines and 30 frames per second,* and on April 30, 1941, the Commission authorized commercial TV operations to start the following July 1, on ten commercial stations which were on the air by May 1942, six continuing during World War II.

Following the war it became evident that the available channels were too few for nationwide service. After a temporary "freeze" on the granting of new applications, the FCC first adopted the CBS method of color broadcasting. The system did not work well and was not "compatible"—it could not be seen in black-and-white on existing monochrome sets. It was replaced in short time by the RCA color system, which is the one in use today. The commission also authorized *ultra high frequency* (UHF) broadcasting, which today consists of 70 channels (14–83) along with the existing 12 *very high frequency* (VHF) channels (2 **–13).

In an apparent attempt to open up prime time (7 to 11 p.m.) to local broadcasting, the FCC imposed a prime-time-access rule during the 1971–1972 television season. Still in effect, the rule prohibits local TV stations, in the top 50 markets, from scheduling more than three hours of network programs during prime time.

How Television Works

Television broadcasting is synchronous transmission of visual and aural programs. The picture phase is accomplished by sending a rapid succession of electrical impulses which the receiver transforms into scenes and images. Here is a brief explanation of a complex process.

The scene to be televised is focused on a special tube in the television camera which has a small "screen" covered with about 367,000 microscopic

* These are technical points which will be explained in the section "How Television Works," later in this chapter.
** There is no channel 1.

dots of a special photosensitive substance. This can be likened to a tiny motion-picture screen and is called a "mosaic." The varying light from each part of the scene being televised falls upon these dots and gives them an electrical charge, the strength depending upon the amount of light falling upon the individual dots. Thus each dot becomes a tiny storage battery and the scene is formed in a pattern of electrical charges on the mosaic.

The mosaic is "scanned" by a tiny beam of electrons, no larger than the head of a pin, moving from left to right and progressing downward (just as the printed page is read by the human eye). This complete process is repeated 60 times per second, and the horizontal lines of alternate scanning are interlaced so that 30 complete pictures or "frames" composed of 525* horizontal lines are produced each second.

As the electron beam strikes each dot on the mosaic, the dot is discharged through the electron beam and the electrical impulses produced are used to modulate the signals of the television transmitter. Each time the dots are discharged by the electron beam they are recharged by the light produced by the succeeding scene as it falls upon them. The succession of individual "still" scenes creates the illusion of motion just as it does in motion pictures made on film.

The reproduction by the television receiver of the pictures transmitted is just the reverse of the transmission. The incoming succession of electrical impulses is separated from the "carrier," and after amplification is impressed on the picture-tube grid. The picture tube also has an electron "gun" which shoots out a tiny beam of electrons that moves from left to right and progresses downward on the face of the picture tube.

The face of the tube is coated with a material that fluoresces or gives off light at the point where it is struck by the electron beam. In the absence of a television signal, the whole face of the picture tube is illuminated equally by a series of closely spaced horizontal lines. When a television signal is placed on the grid of the picture tube, it controls the strength of the electron beam and hence the amount of light on the face of the tube. If the scanning of the electron beam in the picture tube is kept in perfect step with the scanning of the electron beam in the TV camera, the picture tube will reproduce the lights and shadows of the subject scene, and the succession of such scenes produces the illusion of motion.

In brief, the picture seen by the viewer is actually produced by a flickering spot of light moving rapidly across and down the face of the picture tube. The viewer sees the "whole" picture because the screen continues to glow for a tiny fraction of a second after the electron beam has passed. Coupled with the retentive ability of the eye, this continuing glow creates the illusion that the picture is there all the time. The high rate of repetition of the picture produced by the beam minimizes flicker and lends smoothness to motion.

The television transmitter is, in effect, two separate units. One sends out

---

* Television in Europe utilizes an even greater number of horizontal lines, making for a finer image on the screen.

the picture and the other the sound. Visual transmission is by amplitude modulation (AM). Sound transmission is by frequency modulation (FM).

In color television, a brightness component is transmitted in much the same manner as the black-and-white picture signal is sent. In addition, a color component is transmitted at the same time on a subcarrier frequency located between the visual and aural carrier frequencies.

Color standards are based on a simultaneous system of color transmission. Signals representing red, blue, and green are transmitted simultaneously. These are the "primary colors," and when they are combined in various amounts, they produce all of the other colors. A magnifying-glass examination of the scene on a receiver will reveal that it is made up only of red, blue, and green dots, no matter what color is being shown.* Even scenes not transmitted in color and seen as varying shades of gray to white are made up of red, blue, and green dots.

Only color receivers have the special picture tubes and the necessary circuitry to illuminate the colored dots. Under the "compatible color" system, color programs can be received in black-and-white on monochrome sets and black-and-white programs can be received as they are on color sets.

TYPES OF TELEVISION SERVICE

Television service may be expanded to new areas through use of *satellite* ** stations (regular stations largely rebroadcasting the programs of parent stations) and of *translators* (lower-power automatic installations which pick up and rebroadcast programs of parent stations on a different frequency). The FCC rules also provide that UHF stations may use *boosters* (low-power stations rebroadcasting on the same frequency) to fill in "shadow" areas. These have not proved satisfactory and none are now in operation. Rebroadcasting requires the consent of the originating stations.

Unlike AM networking over ordinary telephone wires, television networking requires special relay adjuncts. Network TV was made possible in large measure by the development of coaxial cable and microwave relay facilities. As early as 1937 motion pictures were televised and sent over the coaxial-cable link between New York and Philadelphia. Network operation was begun in 1941 by WNBT (now WNBC-TV), New York City, WRGB, Schnectady, and WPTZ (now KYW-TV), Philadelphia.

Regular coaxial-cable relay service was inaugurated between Washington and New York in 1946. The following year, microwave relay service extended as far as Boston. A midwestern relay system was opened in 1948 and was joined with the eastern system in 1949. The first link in the transcontinental relay system was opened between New York and Chicago in 1950. It reached

* This is similar to the result obtained in color print production, although in print black is added for the full-color effect.
** Not a satellite in outer space.

San Francisco the following year, and on September 4, 1951, it carried telecasts of the Japanese-peace-treaty conference.

Programs are carried between coasts now mostly by microwave, with cable used for local loops where microwave is not feasible. Although there is some private microwave television relay, most live networking is over the facilities of common carriers. American Telephone & Telegraph Company is the dominant carrier nationally.

Ultra High Frequency (UHF)

Commercial television got started in the VHF channels, with most home sets capable of receiving only VHF. Hence advertisers preferred the VHF stations and UHF had its development impeded by economic as well as technical problems. It thus remains in some degree a "special" type of TV broadcast service.

In 1956 the FCC outlined plans to promote comparable UHF and VHF television facilities as a means of extending service throughout the nation. In the years following, it considered and rejected the idea of moving all or most of TV to the UHF band. It sought the cooperation of industry to find ways to increase the range of UHF stations. It made certain areas all-UHF and took other steps to put UHF and VHF on a more competitive basis. In 1966 it revised the table of channel assignments to make additional UHF assignments.

At the FCC's request, Congress appropriated money for a test in New York City to determine the ability of UHF to provide service comparable with VHF in a locality of difficult reception because of tall buildings separated by "canyons." As a result of the tests, the Commission concluded that UHF reception, generally, was equal to that of VHF.

Also at FCC request, Congress in 1962 adopted a law permitting the Commission to require that all TV receivers be made so as to receive UHF as well as VHF channels. Industry had to convert to all-channel production by April 30, 1964. This has given substantial impetus to UHF expansion. A lingering complaint was that VHF tuning dials, which clicked into place, were earier to work than UHF, which worked like radio dials. Efforts were launched to make UHF tuning more nearly comparable with the click-action VHF tuning, and rules were adopted in 1970 to require comparability.

Community Antenna or Cable Television

Cable or community antenna television (CATV) is not a broadcast service. It augments broadcast service and it is regulated by the FCC, but CATV systems are not licensed as broadcast stations are.

CATV systems pick up the programs of broadcast stations by a central receiving antenna or by microwave radio relay. Coaxial cable, which can carry many signals, delivers them from the reception point to the homes of the subscribers.

CATV started in 1949–1950 as a means of bringing television service to communities outside the reach of broadcast signals. It spread to communities that had TV service but wanted to receive more stations. Other markets were found where there was already a choice of signals but where obstacles to over-the-air reception gave cable operators an opportunity to offer a better picture.

The FCC began to regulate CATV in April 1965 when it adopted rules for microwave-served CATV systems. It required them to carry the signals of local stations and to refrain from duplicating the programs of local commercial stations (by carrying other stations broadcasting the same programs) within 15 days of the local broadcast. In October of that year special frequencies were made available for relaying signals to CATV systems.

In 1966 the Commission required all CATV systems to carry local and nearby stations and to protect their programs from duplication, although the 15-day requirement was reduced to protecting the day of broadcast. It also set a hearing requirement on proposals to bring distant signals into communities regularly served by TV stations in the 100 largest TV markets.

The FCC proposed new CATV rules in December 1968. Adopting some of these the following October, it required systems with more than 3,500 subscribers to originate their own programming as of 1971. This was designed to bring local outlets to communities without stations. The broadcast requirements of fairness and sponsor identification were also extended to CATV.

Cable television stations carry advertising.

Educational Television

The Commission allocated television facilities for noncommercial educational use after a lengthy study in the general television proceedings. It determined that "the need for noncommercial educational stations has been amply demonstrated," that it would take longer for the educational service to be developed than for the commercial service, and that special channels should be reserved.

Broadcast Relay by Satellite *

The first live transatlantic telecast by satellite was relayed by Telstar I on July 10, 1962. More panoramic telecasts, showing life in widely distant places, were exchanged between the United States and Europe 13 days later. Telstar I and other experimental satellites were operated by the National Aeronautics and Space Administration, which continues to handle the rocket launching of privately operated communication satellites as well as some satellites in government communication and space programs.

The Communications Satellite Act of 1966 provided for the United States portion of a global system to be operated by a private corporation, the Communications Satellite Corporation, subject to Federal regulation. Comsat is owned partly by common carriers and partly by the general public. Early Bird (Intelsat I), on April 6, 1965, became the first commercial satellite to be put

---

* This refers to a satellite in outer space.

into orbit by Comsat and its foreign partners in the International Telecommunications Satellite Consortium. During the following year, some 80 hours of television were transmitted between the United States and Europe. Early Bird has since been replaced and retired.

When Intelstat II-F2 (Pacific 1) went up over the Pacific on January 11, 1967, satellite communication was established between the United States mainland and Hawaii, making live network television transmission available in the Islands for the first time. Television, however, makes up only a small part of the traffic on communications satellites around the world; telephone and teletype communications, including data transmission, dominate the loads.

Subsequent satellites of the Intelsat II and Intelsat III series increased the capability of transmitting television and commercial communication traffic across the Pacific (between the United States, the Far East, and Australia), the Atlantic (between North America, South America, Africa, and Europe), and the Indian Ocean, completing global coverage. From January 26, 1971, through August 24, 1973, the United States National Aeronautics and Space Administration successfully launched three new high-capacity communication satellites, of the Intelsat IV series, over the Atlantic, and one each over the Pacific and Indian Oceans.

TELEVISION AND ADVERTISING

Although television was developed and operated on an experimental basis for many years, it was not until 1941 that it was employed as a medium for commercial advertising. In July of that year, the Bulova Watch Company bought commercial time and started a series of announcements over WNBT, New York. It was also in July of 1941 that the Federal Trade Commission gave authorization for the commercial use of television. Therefore, it is not surprising that when the United States entered World War II, only five months later, there were an estimated 10,000 television receiving sets in the country.

Though progress in commercial television was greatly retarded by the war, experimentation and development were continued by the armed forces; by 1945 wartime improvements began to be generally available for civilian use. In that year the Federal Communications Commission allotted frequencies and thus opened up opportunities for further and more rapid development of the medium on a commercial level.

The American public was quick in its acceptance of this new form of entertainment. As has been mentioned, there were an estimated 10,000 receiving sets in the United States in 1941. By 1950, 9% of United States families owned television sets; in two years, the number had increased to 72%; and by 1975 television-set ownership stood at 97%. Advertisers were equally quick to recognize the potential of this new medium. In 1949 the expenditure for advertising on television was $57.8 million, or about 3% of total national advertising expenditures for that year. In 1974 television was receiving well over $4.8 billion—more than 18% of the total spent on advertising in the United States. In

1949 there were only 71 network advertisers and 530 spot advertisers; as early as 1955 the number of network advertisers had grown to 225 and spot advertisers had jumped to 3,355.

The rapid acceptance of television by the general public and by advertisers was reflected in the speedy growth of television broadcasting stations. In 1949 there were 48 and by 1954 there were 351 stations, 349 of which were commercial (228 VHF, 121 UHF). This figure had swelled to 697 commercial stations (513 VHF and 184 UHF) by 1974 with an additional 246 noncommercial or educational broadcasting stations. As of 1973, there were an estimated 105,100,000 television sets (black-and-white and color) in use, and the average viewing time per home per day had risen to 6 hours and 15 minutes, an increase of more than an hour since 1960.

The speed with which television facilities developed in the United States was not uniform. As a result, television-set ownership varied considerably among the different sections of the country. Ownership in the Northeast was once much greater than it was in the South; this gap narrowed tremendously, however, and in the 1970s it was no longer significant. Set saturation in the Northeast in September 1972 was 97%, while in the South it amounted to 96%.

Characteristics of the Medium

Television delivers the advertiser's sales message with the combined impact of sight, motion, and sound. With color television sets now in use in more than two-thirds of all TV homes, a fourth component has been added to this powerful selling force.

Television, probably more than any other advertising medium, delivers the advertiser's message to the family as a unit. As we have seen, it has replaced radio as a focal point in the living room, where several or all of the family often gather to view it together.

By its very nature television commands the complete attention of the viewer and often for a considerable period of time. Whereas the person listening to radio can be engaged in other pursuits and even in a different part of the house from the radio set, this is not true of television.

In television the size and type of audience are determined by the appeal of the show and by the time of day it is telecast. Competition also is a factor in determining the size of the audience that any given program will attract. In radio and television more than any other medium, the competition from other programs affects audience size. A program may inherit part of an audience from a preceding program, or benefit by acquiring additional audience from among those who tune in early for a following show. But, on the other hand, some audience of a normally popular program may be lost because another excellent program is on the air at the same time. In print media a prospect can see and read all of the advertisements that appear in any issue and read all of the magazines he chooses, but he can view only one television show at a time or listen to one radio station at a time. However, the growing use of home recording devices using audio or video cassettes allows an audience to record programs for listening or viewing at a more convenient time.

Television is a flexible medium in that its use can be expanded or contracted to match the distribution of the advertiser's product. Flexibility exists not only in terms of geographical areas covered but also in terms of time of day during which messages can be delivered. The time of the telecast may have much to do with obtaining the type of audience desired by the advertiser. However, because television, like radio, deals in units of time rather than space, availabilities are limited by the length of the broadcast day—approximately 20 hours. Therefore, advertisers are not always able to buy the time that they want.

Coverage and Circulation

In television the terms *coverage* and *circulation* are used as in radio. That is, *coverage* means the number of homes capable of being reached by a television signal, and *circulation* refers to the number of homes that actually tune in the signal.

When buying individual-market television time, the advertiser must be concerned primarily with the number of people available for his message. This is determined by: (1) the physical coverage of the station, and (2) the programming of the station. It is obvious that a home must both *be able* to tune in a station and *wish to do so* if it is to be a part of any advertiser's audience. The *ability* to tune in is a matter of physical coverage. The desire to tune in is a matter of station programming.

The *physical coverage* of a television station depends upon a number of factors. Among these are:

1. The frequency on which the station operates.
2. The amount of power employed by the station.
3. The height of the antenna at the transmitter.
4. The terrain over which it telecasts.
5. Outside interference including that caused by other stations.
6. Time period or hours when the station is on the air.

The frequency and power used by a station are important considerations to the buyer of television time because they both affect the station's coverage. In general, the lower the frequency, the better the carrying power of the station's signal. For this reason, the FCC in the 1940s set different power maximums for stations. Channels 2 through 6, operating in the lower-frequency part of the VHF band, were given a maximum of 100 kiloHertz of power, whereas channels 7 through 13, operating on the higher band of VHF, were allowed as much as 316 kiloHertz. This difference, it was believed, would equalize the coverage of the two groups of stations.

It soon became apparent that these 12 channels would not be enough to provide nation-wide competitive service in the new medium. For this reason the FCC permitted the use of ultra high frequency (UHF, channels 14 through 83). The UHF band had not previously been used commercially because of technical difficulties. However, most of the problems associated with the use of this frequency had been solved by experimentation and developmental work done during World War II, so that UHF was ready for civilian use by the time the FCC was faced with the problem of providing for the establishment of a greater number of television stations. The UHF band provided for 70 new channels, but inasmuch as ultra high frequency is higher than very high frequency its carrying power is less. The FCC hoped to compensate for this difference by permitting a maximum of 5,000 kiloHertz of power for these new stations.

Coverage of a television station, among other things, is dependent upon the height of its transmitting antenna because television waves follow what is called line-of-sight transmission; they go in a straight line from the transmitter to the receivers. Therefore, if more television receivers in an expanded or greater area are to be reached by a given station, the transmitting antenna must be higher. When only the earth's curvature blocks the line of sight, an antenna 1,000 feet high will send signals about 45 miles, a 500-foot antenna about 33 miles, and a 250-foot antenna about 25 miles. Sending over the greater distances may require more power.

There was a time when many television stations had what amounted to a monopoly of set owners in their own coverage areas. But today, few stations have such an advantage. Rather, the majority of stations share at least a part of the same coverage area with one or more other stations. In fact, it is possible, in theory, to select 60 stations for a network program that would have the same total coverage factor as another list of 90 stations. In spot television, as an advertiser adds markets to his market list, he is likely to run into an increasing amount of such *overlap* in coverage. This need not be a disadvantage. As the number of overlapping areas is increased, the advertiser's chances of obtaining TV homes that are regular viewers of at least one of the stations in any overlapped area are also increased. Also, as a result of his expanded campaign, the advertiser increases the amount of time in which his commercials are available to viewers in the overlapped areas.

Audience

The characteristics of the television audience are determined by a number of factors and would not necessarily be the same for different programs or even for the same program on different days or at different times of the year.

The characteristics of the total television audience obviously are determined by the number and kind of people who own television sets. But the audience characteristics for any particular program depend upon the time of day of the telecast, the type and quality of the program, the competing programs on other channels at the same time, the season of the year, the weather, and competing activities.

The total television audience and the population of the United States are, for most intents and purposes, one and the same. With the ownership of TV sets at 97% of United States households, according to Nielsen, "it has just about reached saturation."

The portion of the total television audience available to view a program at any particular time affects the character of the audience of individual programs.

For example, the greatest availability of people, accounting for 38% of all television viewing, is between the hours of 7:30 and 11:00 Monday through Sunday evenings. The next greatest viewing time is 4:30 to 7:30 p.m. Monday through Sunday. This period accounts for 23% of all viewing. The day part that ranks next, for 18% of viewing time, is 7:00 a.m. to 4:30 p.m. Monday through Friday.[2] Availability of men, women, and children also differs between weekdays and Saturdays and Sundays. Thus, hour of the day, day of the week, and season determine the number and type of people who watch television, and to this extent the scheduling of a program will have much to do with the characteristics of the audience it obtains. But, within the frame of available audience as set by these influences, and within the limits set by competition, an advertiser may determine his audience composition by the kind of program he elects to telecast.

So far as programs affect available audience, Nielsen reports with respect to five types offered during prime time: general drama, suspense and mystery drama, situation comedy, Western drama, and feature films. The audience composition ranged from 24.4 million to 31.9 million for the five categories, with general drama at the low extreme and situation comedy at the top. The most popular single program was "Sanford and Son," with a rating of 31.2%, a shade higher than the next two, which are "All in the Family" with 30.2% and "Chico and the Man" with 29.4%.[3]

Competition has less effect on audience characteristics than it has on audience size. That is, a program designed to appeal to children will attract children regardless of competition, but it may attract a greater or lesser number because of the quality or type of competing programs. Only 2% of all television homes in the United States today are limited in choice to 1 or 2 television stations and the average home has a choice of seven.[4] With this competitive situation, *share of audience* has become an important consideration for any television advertiser. Inasmuch as share of audience is defined as "the per cent of all homes in a program coverage area, with television sets tuned-in, that are tuned to a specific program during the average minute of its broadcast," any increase in such share of audience must come from among those people who are viewing competing programs. The only other possibility of increasing the size of the audience for any given program would be to induce people who own sets but who do not use them at the time in question to tune in to the program. This accomplishment probably would present more difficulties to the advertiser than that of obtaining an increased share of an audience that has established viewing habits at a particular time period.

Although kind and quality of program are of the greatest importance in attracting a potentially available audience, other factors also contribute to building share of audience. These are *program adjacencies, station strength,* and local promotion of the station and of the program.

Actually, an advertiser, under special circumstances does better if his program is not telecast during periods when the greatest number of sets are in use. Higher ratings are at times achieved by programs telecast when fewer sets are in use than by those telecast during peak periods of set use—even though the programs are of similar quality. These higher ratings are due to the lesser amount of competition at other than peak viewing times.

Color Television

The impact of color television can be readily seen in the figures detailing its growth. There were only 5,000 homes with TV color sets in 1955. These were a mere .01% of the 47,621,000 homes in the United States at that time. By 1975 there were 46.9 million homes capable of receiving color TV broadcasts, 68% of the more than 68,500,000 TV homes. It is interesting to note that owners of color TV sets averaged 7 hours and 5 minutes more of viewing time per week than owners of black-and-white sets only.[5]

Nielsen indicated that the ownership of color TV sets is highest in upper-income families and in larger households. As for education, ownership is highest in families where the head of the house is a high-school graduate and in those where he has one or more years of college.[6]

Rates

Rates established for individual stations almost without exception follow the number of homes each is able to deliver in the station's own area. These rates are different for day and evening and reflect the different levels of viewing during the two periods. Within the day and evening hours, rates are still further differentiated, again to reflect the available audience at different hours. For example, the most costly time in television is that between the evening hours of 7:30 and 11:00, when the greatest number of people are home and are able to view programs. This is known as *prime time*.

All television rates for time are based on a charge for one hour, and percentages are then applied to obtain rates for lesser periods of time. Half-hour rates are calculated at about 60% of the hour rates, quarter-hour rates at about 40% hourly rates.

Discounts are obtainable that reflect the number of programs an advertiser purchases within a given time period as well as the dollar-volume expenditure involved. These are termed *frequency discounts*. Contracts can be set up on a year basis, and programs run within that time can earn frequency and other discounts. Some stations insist that the programs must run without interruption throughout the year, but others will allow an alternate combination or a one-time purchase.

Special discounts may be available that do not show as such on rate cards. At times, some such notation as "special package rates upon request" will be found on a rate card. Although these special discounts usually apply to exceptionally large campaigns that go beyond the rate-card terms for frequency discounts, the advertiser would be wise to check.

Although television networks used to have a "must buy" list of stations, which was a required minimum that an advertiser had to purchase, all three major television networks have abandoned this practice. The exceptions to this are NBC-TV's "Today" program, which has available a "must buy" group and a "supplementary" group, and regional network advertisers who purchase sections of the country. Minimums required differ among the networks. Inasmuch as charges are not standard with respect to what is included in the rates quoted, it is important in each case to know exactly which charges are in the rate cards and which are not.

Spot Television

Spot television is used both by national advertisers to supplement their network shows and by advertisers with regional or local distribution for whom network television would not be practical.

A national advertiser may undertake a spot television program in any one or a combination of the following situation:

1. Where the network facility does not cover the entire market that the advertiser wishes to reach.
2. Where the network program cannot do a satisfactory job because of a special "appeal" problem or, in other words, where local program preferences are strong.
3. When network program ratings are not high enough in certain areas to carry adequate advertising weight.
4. When an advertiser decides to support his network advertising with additional advertising weight in the market to support his own market share, or to counter a competitive local campaign.

A network may have a UHF station that can't deliver all the coverage the advertiser wants. The area not covered by the UHF signal may represent a very desirable market to a particular advertiser. Under such circumstances he might elect to use a VHF station as a spot carrier to cover the desired area. It is also possible that a program is not equally popular in all places reached by a network. There may be an unusual local program in an area, which provides such strong competition that a network program can't obtain satisfactory audiences. Under such circumstances, spot programming may be desirable. It should be noted that in all of these cases the alternate TV stations could be members of the other two competing networks.

Pre-emptions

A network or station may reclaim time it has sold. Such a reclaiming of time, called a *pre-emption,* may be permanent or temporary. If permanent, the station informs an advertiser that his program (or his commercial in a preempted program) is off the air permanently; if temporary, the advertiser is put off the air for a single show or a limited time only. The one-time or temporary pre-emptions often result from special coverage of emergencies such as floods or other catastrophes where the station's facilities are used to assist in broadcasting warnings or other vital information. Pre-emptions have also taken place because of special news events such as the assasination of President Kennedy and the Apollo lunar landings. Usually, when pre-empted, advertisers get credit, an offer of an immediate makegood, or an extension of their contract. Rebates are made as an alternative to contract extensions, or upon request.

An *interruption*, as well as a pre-emption, may entitle the advertiser to a rebate. Interruptions, unlike pre-emptions, may be caused by a breakdown in the network or station facilities. Interruptions are also the result of special announcements of important news that involve less time loss than a pre-emption.

Small Advertisers

Television is a medium of national scope, of huge audiences, and of high costs. The largest advertisers of our times spend millions of dollars for TV time and millions more for TV talent. Yet television is a medium readily adaptable to the needs of the smaller advertiser. Through the use of local stations, limited markets can be reached. Through the use of spot announcements and co-sponsorship of local programs, costs can be kept within reach of modest budgets.

Results achieved through the use of television advertising by the small business are often as spectacular, relative to the situation, as those obtained by the big users of the medium. There is a sufficient weight of case histories to indicate extensive and successful use of television by a wide variety of comparatively small business enterprises.

Merchandising the Programs

In radio and television the advertiser is faced with the problem of advertising or otherwise merchandising his program. One would not expect to find an advertiser employing newspaper space to ask people to look at his magazine ad or using a car card to suggest an examination of his outdoor posters. But, any or all of these media are used from time to time to announce a radio or television program as well as to advertise the goods of the manufacturer or merchant who uses the print media and sponsors the show. Often, too, other radio and TV stations or programs are used to promote the program. In other words, radio and, perhaps today more especially, television programs are themselves a subject of advertising as well as being a medium of advertising.

The merchandising of programs is done through any or all media—newspapers, magazines, outdoor posters, car cards, point-of-purchase advertising, direct mail, radio and television commercials. In addition to the advertisements devoted entirely to the promotion of TV programs, an advertiser often gives space for this purpose in his regular product advertising. In such cases the greater portion of the advertisement is devoted to the product but mention is made of the advertiser's TV show.

Programs are also merchandised by personal appearances of the program's star or stars at conventions or other gatherings of members of the trade, dealers or consumers. At times, telegrams are sent to dealers announcing the opening of a new show. And, of course, when possible, publicity will be used to promote interest in a program.

"Speecy spicey meatballs." A scene from a classic Alka-Seltzer TV commercial produced by Doyle Dane Bernbach.

Television stations and networks also merchandise programs being broadcast over their facilities.

Commercials

In a real sense, the program of a radio or television show is comparable to the stories or editorial content of a magazine or newspaper. The commercials are comparable to the advertisements in these other media. Therefore, the advertiser must be concerned not only with the capacity of his program to attract listeners or viewers but also with the effectiveness of his commercials to sell his product. No matter how good a program may be, it will be of no value to the advertiser if his commercials are turned off or are not listened to and observed.

Commercials may be put on with live talent, or may be made on slides, video tape, or motion-picture film. If film or tape are used, as they generally are in national and regional advertising, the commercial can be aired over as many different TV stations as desired and repeated as many times as called for by contract. Film and tape also allow for special effects, such as animation. The animated cartoon has been especially popular with advertisers since the success of "Harry and Bert," The Piel's Beer commercial. "Speedy Alka Seltzer" gained a measure of popularity through the technique of animation, and more recently Levi's glamorized blue jeans in animated dazzling color and light.

CATV

Community antenna television or cable television has been growing rather steadily. The Nielsen Station Index estimates that as of Winter 1974 there were 8,619,000 households subscribing to CATV systems. This represents 13% of all TV households in the United States with the exception of Alaska.[7]

SCREEN ADVERTISING

Back in the days when villains pursued heroines through many episodes of weekly serials and the theater management asked its patrons to wait for a change of reels during the showing of a two- or three-reel feature, local merchants advertised their shops by means of slides or stills flashed on the screen. Eventually, motion pictures came to be used for advertising purposes. But in those days motion-picture projectors operated at slower speeds than they do today, and it took one minute to show 60 feet of film. Because this was the customary length of advertising films, advertising projected in motion-picture theaters became known as "minute movies." At present the same footage is projected in 40 seconds, and such names as "screen advertising," "movie advertising," and "theater advertising" are in common use. However, by whatever name it is called, advertising through the medium of motion-picture films and the motion-picture theaters is used today by local, regional, and some national advertisers. The practice is even more common in Europe, particularly in areas that have no commercial television.

While some of the types of film to be discussed here are in the realm of public relations, they are closely related to advertising and might even be considered institutional advertising. They are furnished for viewing to groups, organizations, and movie theaters, without charge. The "advertiser" or sponsor pays a distributor to circulate and place his film. Many of these films are produced solely for the purpose of showing at schools, colleges, churches and other such community groups, and at meetings. They resemble the documentaries presented in the last few years by such large national companies as Xerox, United States Steel, Alcoa, Hallmark, and others, and are known as business or sponsored films. They are distributed through such firms as Modern Talking Picture Service and Association-Sterling Films, the leaders in the field.

A survey conducted by the Society of Motion Picture and Television Engineers indicates that more than a billion dollars goes into non-theatrical and audiovisual films. "The latest available figures (for 1967) show a total of 12,750 non-theatrical films made that year—7,500 of which were produced by or for business and industrial firms. Business and industry spent $241,000,000 on films during the year with costs per film ranging from less than $10,000 to $500,000 spent on a 40-minute corporate film by a major company." [8]

More than 210 million people in school and community audiences in 22 countries (including the U.S.A.) viewed *sponsored films* during 1975, accord-ing to the 15-year-old *International Ass'n of Informational Film Distributors,* Brussels, Belgium. That's an increase of 24% above the comparable figure for 1974. The association points out that this does not include people who viewed such films in theaters and through TV (there were nearly 500,000 such show-ings in the U.S.A. and Canada alone).

The Eastman Kodak Company, which is in the business of manufacturing photographic film, produced an excellent promotional motion picture the title of which might well serve as the keynote for this section—*Movies Move People.* Examples of these business and industrial films are the several Academy Award best-short-subject winners: *Why Man Creates,* produced for Kaiser Aluminum, and Mobil Oil Corporation's *A Fable,* starring the famous French mime Marcel Marceau. Other award winners include *To Touch the Sky,* sponsored by Weyer-haeuser; St. Regis Paper's *Time to Discover;* and *Jenny Is a Good Thing,* nar-rated by Burt Lancaster for the United States government.

Screen advertising is in greater use outside the big metropolitan areas and population centers. Small-town theaters, as they did in the past, often show the advertising of local merchants (using 35mm slides or transparencies with voice over) and the more professionally prepared film of regional advertisers, in addi-tion to those distributed nationally.

A relatively new trend in screen "advertising" is the use of business or sponsored films. These are filling the gap in "short subjects," left void when Pathé, Fox Movietone, and Paramount ceased producing them. An example of a series of these new sponsored movies is a composite of segments of a number of separate industrial films edited into an overall format known as "Theater Cavalcade." It is a series distributed by Association-Sterling Films. Each runs for ten minutes and may include segments of sports, travel, fashion, science, or other subjects. A typical "Cavalcade" reel has five sponsors, each of whom has a separate two-minute story. These follow the newsreel format but are not "spot" or "hard" news stories; but rather, they are like magazine articles or newspaper feature stories that do not become dated too quickly. Promotion is extremely low-key. There is an opening or closing credit line or "logo," with discrete references in the body of the film. It is kept as unobtrusive and tasteful as possible. Association-Sterling Films estimate that over a 12-month period 1,250,000 people would see such a sponsored film in the 400 to 500 motion-picture theaters that book and play it. National advertisers who have sponsored *Cavalcade* include General Dynamics, Ford, Sears Roebuck, American Tele-phone and Telegraph Company, Clairol, Borden, Lear Jet, Noxema, and a number of others.

Since sponsored films are distributed to the theaters without charge, most are pleased to get them. According to an Association-Sterling survey of theater circuits and booking services, free sponsored short subjects are shown by al-most nine out of ten movie houses, and of these 88% would show more if they were available. They are the successors, in full color, to old black-and-white newsreels. Sponsored films answer a programming need by accompanying a single feature film and they do an excellent job in bridging the gap between two feature films. Sponsors pay approximately $10 per booking for films up to 10 minutes in length and on a graduated scale up to $20 per booking for films that run from 26 to 30 minutes. A typical booking by Modern Talking Picture Service results in 10 showings at a consequent cost of $1 per showing for the short films.

The motion-picture industry indicates that there were about 928 million paid attendances at the movies during 1972 in the United States. Moviegoers attended some 14,800 theaters, of which approximately 10,000 are the conventional or "hard top" theaters and 4,800 are drive-ins. And they spent $1,580,000 at the box office. Approximately 75% of the movie audience is 18 years of age or older. It is estimated that the seating capacity for all theaters is 8,176,000 and that they have parking facilities for close to two million cars.[9] While the overall economy suffered in the inflation-ridden recession year of 1974, movie attendance rose.

Screen advertising is produced on 35mm film, which is the size used by the vast majority of motion-picture theaters. The exceptions are the new automated minitheaters now being built in some of the large metropolitan areas and suburban shopping centers. These use 16mm projection equipment. Satisfactory enlargements or "blow ups" of 16 mm film can be made; however, far better resolution can be obtained by reducing 35mm to 16mm.

The preference for sponsored short subjects among theater owners, according to Association-Sterling, is for the one-reel short that has a running time of up to 10 minutes. Close to 74% indicated this preference, although 44.6% use two-reelers, 11 to 20 minutes in length. Featurettes, or three-reelers with a playing time of 21 to 40 minutes, were preferred by 13.8% of theater owners.[10] However, a survey conducted by Modern Talking Picture Service shows a theater preference of 58% for films of 15 minutes, 29% for 15 minutes or more, and only 13% for films under 10 minutes.[11]

Among those who booked free sponsored shorts, the greatest subject-matter preference was for travelogs. Almost 87% expressed this preference, while 84.9% opted for sports films and 45.2% for science shorts.[12] In essence the preceding findings by Association-Sterling were borne out by Modern's survey, which showed a 75% preference for travel films in theaters and 85% among theater circuits; 62% in theaters and 92% in circuits for sports, and 44% and 56% for science shorts.[13]

Sponsored short-subject films can have an additional life following their round of the motion-picture-theater circuit. Many television stations are eager to use such fare, particularly the educational TV and CATV stations. They can also be shown at airport, rail, and bus terminal waiting rooms via automated rear projection machines, and they can be shown as educational films at schools and other such organizations. For showing to all of these other audiences the film must be reduced in size to 16mm.

SUMMARY

Like radio, television is the result of the inventive genius of many men from many lands. The final product, TV as we know it today, was developed in the United States and was in limited operation by 1939. Its growth as a medium of mass communication was delayed by World War II. Following the war it grew by leaps and bounds. VHF broadcasting was joined by UHF, each of which soon gained a color capability. Both also gained a greater distance range through space satellites. In addition, CATV came on to the scene.

The first television advertising commercial appeared in July 1941 although there were fewer than 10,000 television sets in the United States at that time. By 1973 more than 96% of United States households owned TV receivers, and advertising over the medium was second in dollar volume only to newspaper advertising.

As an advertising medium, television delivers a message utilizing sight, motion, sound, and color. Close to 69% of TV homes receive broadcasts in color. Overall, television is an extremely powerful medium that delivers entertainment, news, and advertising into practically every home in the country. And 98% of the TV homes have a choice of three or more stations.

While the three major networks—CBS, NBC, and ABC—sell advertising time, national advertisers supplement their network advertising with commercials on spot television. Small advertisers and local businesses also utilize local TV stations for their advertising.

Related to television advertising is screen advertising, which is currently enjoying a revival.

QUESTIONS AND DISCUSSION SUBJECTS

1. Who was the first President of the United States to appear on television? In what year?
2. When did commercial television operations begin?
3. What are the meanings of VHF and UHF? How many channels are offered by each? What are they?
4. What was wrong with the first color television system approved by the FCC? Explain.
5. Describe how television works.
6. What is compatible color?
7. How are television programs broadcast from coast to coast?
8. What did the FCC do to boost UHF?
9. How does CATV deliver its sound and picture to the viewer?
10. What is the extent of television -set ownership in the United States?

11. Differentiate between *circulation* and *coverage*.
12. Define and explain the following in relation to television: pre-emption, rebate, frequency rate, merchandising.
13. Discuss sponsored films from the viewpoint of the audience, the theater owner, the advertiser, and the producer.

SOURCES

1. The author is grateful to the Federal Communications Commission for the use of material from the pamphlet *Broadcasting* Services, published in October 1970. This information will be found from the beginning of the chapter to the section on ''Television and Advertising.''
2. *Nielsen Television '75* (Chicago: A. C. Nielsen Co., 1975), 11.
3. *Ibid.,* 13, 18.
4. *Ibid.,* 4.
5. *Ibid.,* 5, 6.
6. *Nielson Television '71* (Chicago: A. C. Nielsen Co., 1971), 6, 7.
7. *Ayer Media Facts 1975* (New York: N. W. Ayer Co., 1975), 5.
8. Shirley D. Smith, ''PR Films—Coming or Going,'' *Business Screen* (May, 1970).
9. Motion Picture Association of America, 1973.
10. *The Use of Sponsored Short Subjects in Motion Picture Theaters—A Survey and Analysis* (New York: Association-Sterling Films).
11. *What Motion Pictures Theaters Want from Sponsored Films* (New York: Modern Talking Picture Service, 1973).
12. *The Use of Sponsored Short Subjects in Motion Picture Theaters, op. cit.*
13. *What Motion Picture Theaters Want from Sponsored Films, op. cit.*

FOR FURTHER READING

Bagdikian, B. H. *The Information Machines.* New York: Harper, 1971.
√ Chester, Edward W. *Radio, Television and American Politics.* New York: Sheed & Ward, 1969.
Klein, Walter J. *The Sponsored Film.* New York: Hastings House, Publishers, 1976.
√ Lichty, Lawrence W., and Malachi C. Topping. *American Broadcasting: A Source Book in the History of Radio and Television.* New York: Hastings House, Publishers, 1975.
Mitchell, Curtis. *Cavalcade of Broadcasting.* New York: Follett, 1970.
Quaal, Ward L., and James A. Brown. *Broadcast Management: Radio and Television.* Second Edition, revised and enlarged. New York: Hasting House, Publishers, 1976.
Stanley, Robert H., and Charles S. Steinberg. *The Media Environment: Mass Communications in American Society.* New York: Hastings House, Publishers, 1976.

Steinberg, Charles S. *The Communicative Arts.* New York: Hastings House, Publishers, 1970.

Wainwright, Charles Anthony. *Television Commercials: How to Create Successful TV Advertising.* Revised Edition. New York: Hastings House, Publishers, 1970.

★
★
★ **23**
★
★
★

Direct Mail Advertising

SOME HISTORY

The Reporter of Direct Mail Advertising stated that a "Publicity by Mail" firm, possibly the first in the world, was organized in Paris in 1864.[1] However, individual use of direct mail without the assistance of organized business firms is probably much older than this. There are three prerequisites to the use of this medium: (1) a desire to sell or exchange goods, services, or information; (2) some method of written communication; and (3) a privately or publicly operated postal system. Since all of these existed even among some ancient civilizations, it is probable that written sales messages of one kind or another were borne by courier from would-be seller to prospect in very early times.

But, if the factors necessary to the *use* of direct mail advertising were present at an early age, those necessary to its *development* as a large and important medium were much later in coming. The first known "direct mail advertising" firm came into being in the latter part of the 19th century; not until after the beginning of the present century was the medium extensively used. In fact, it even lacked a name until well into the 1900s.

In our country an official postal service predated the founding of the United States. The Continental Congress established such a service in 1775. Indeed, postal service of some sort had existed in the colonies as early as 1639. However, early American advertisers may have been somewhat discouraged by the expense associated with the use of the mails. Between 1816 and 1845 it cost 6 cents to send a letter no further than 30 miles. But, improvements in the postal service and reduction in costs of mailings came as the nation grew. By 1861 postal rates were down to 3 cents per half-ounce for prepaid mail traveling under 3,000 miles, and by 1883 postage for all first-class mail was 2 cents an ounce. In 1896 rural free delivery was started. Parcel post came in 1912; the business-reply permit was made available in 1925; and the bulk rate system for third-class mail began in 1926.

360

The means of producing direct mail was just as important to the development of the medium as was the means of sending it from seller to prospect. So fortunately, while the postal services were improving, new means of producing letters and other forms of direct mail advertising were being created. New methods of producing mailing pieces came with the invention of the typewriter in 1867 and its eventual acceptance by business, with the invention of the mimeograph in 1884 and its improvement from a flat-bed to a rotary machine in 1904, with the invention of the multigraph in 1904 and its subsequent improvement in 1906, and with the more recent application of xerography. Improvements in the graphic arts, especially in lithography and the individualizing press, also contributed appreciably to the growth of direct mail advertising, as did the later development of the computer. List building was made easier with the development of list rentals in the early 1930s; here, too, the computer has played an important part. In more recent years, much of the drudgery has been removed from direct mail handling as a result of the perfection of automatic machines.

Early Servicing Companies and Users

The Business Address Company of New York, established in 1880, is credited by Henry Hoke and R. L. Polk & Company as probably being the oldest commercial house devoted to furnishing mailing services in the United States.[2] Some 11 years later a similar company was operating in Chicago. During these years a mail-order business was organized in Bridgeport, Connecticut. The New York Life Insurance Company was using mail promotions in 1872, and the National Cash Register Company is said to have used direct mail as early as 1895. However, no sizable use of the medium was made until after the turn of the century.

Trade Journals and Organizations

The first trade publication in the direct mail field was *Postage,* which was started in 1916. About two years later a second magazine, called *The Mailbag,* came into being. In 1928 the two combined to form *Postage and The Mailbag,* which continued publication until the depression years of the 1930s. At that time it was replaced by the *Reporter of Direct Mail Advertising.* Since its founding, the *Reporter* has been the trade magazine of the field. It later expanded its name and interests to become *The Magazine of Direct Marketing.*

The Direct Mail Advertising Association was founded in 1917. In 1974 it was renamed the Direct Mail/Marketing Association. It is a nonprofit organization with a current membership of about 2,700 individuals active in direct mail and representing some 1,600 users and producers of direct mail—world-wide. Its purpose is to promote the interests of this broad membership and to help members improve effectiveness in their use of the medium. Among its services to members is a regularly published *President's Report* that gives accounts of current happenings of interest to those in the direct mail field. DM/MA, as the Association is familiarly known, also issues *The Washington Newsletter,* prepared by its Washington office and sent at regular intervals to all members in the United States. It enables them to keep abreast of legislative, postal, and government-agency matters that affect direct mail advertising. The Washington office also publishes *The State Legislative Searchlight Service,* a series of reports to help members keep abreast of the important bills affecting direct mailers in the 50 state legislatures. In addition, the Association issues to each of its members a three-inch-thick *Direct Mail Manual*—a continuing looseleaf service to which new items are added on a regular basis. A subscription to *The Magazine of Direct Marketing* is also given to each member.[3]

In 1920 the Mail Advertising Service Association International was organized to function in the interest of letter-shop operators. This association operates on behalf of the creators or producers of direct mail advertising, whereas DM/MA is more concerned with the users of the medium.

Early Practitioners

Dickie-Raymond, Inc., was founded in 1921 to provide professional counsel and service in matters pertaining to sales promotion and direct mail advertising. Because of a number of corporate changes the firm now does business as the DR Group, Inc. This company plans, writes, designs, and produces material to sell or influence selective markets. Its work covers every function of direct advertising.

R. L. Polk & Company, founded in 1870, is primarily a fact-finding organization and a publisher of city directories and direct mail advertising. Its directories cover more than 4,000 cities, towns, and communities in the United States and Canada. Polk also compiles the only national automobile and truck registration list in the United States as well as other high-quality lists. The firm pioneered the client-agency-publisher concept of selective direct mail advertising under which direct mail is planned, created, and circulated as print media are. As publishers, Polk assists clients and agencies in selecting their prospects, prepares circulation lists, publishes the advertising, and researches the results. One of the largest electronic data-processing installations in the country equips R. L. Polk & Company to imprint, address, and mail more than 3,000,000 individual advertisements a day.

DIRECT MAIL ADVERTISING TODAY

Attesting to the importance of direct mail is its third-place rank as an advertising medium—immediately behind television and well ahead of radio and magazines. During 1974 approximately $3,920,000,000 went into direct mail, accounting for close to 15% of the total dollars spent on advertising in the United States that year.

The term *direct mail advertising* is not synonymous with *mail-order advertising* or with *direct advertising.*

Mail order advertising is associated with a business in which there is no personal contact between sellers and buyers. An offer is made by the seller through any one or a combination of advertising media to send merchandise to the customer upon receipt of an order. The advertising offer may or may not be made by mail. If it is so made, then direct mail advertising becomes a medium used in the mail-order business in question. If, on the other hand, the offer is not made through the mails, direct mail advertising plays no part in this mail-order enterprise.

Direct advertising is any advertising that passes directly from advertiser to prospect without the service of commercially operated media such as newspapers, magazines, radio or television, or outdoor or transit advertising facilities. It includes advertising passed to people on the streets or as they enter retail shops, pick-ups on retail-store counters, circulars or other advertising matter delivered house-to-house by employees of the advertiser, or advertising sent through the mails—what has come to be called direct mail advertising.

Other related terms are *direct-response advertising* and the overall category, *direct marketing.*

It is apparent from the foregoing that direct mail advertising, although not synonymous with direct advertising, is a part of it—that part carried from seller to prospect by a postal service. It may take the form of letter, folders, broadsides, booklets, brochures, circulars, mailing cards, blotters, or any of several forms such as cutouts, pop-ups, or other novelties. The Direct Mail/Marketing Association has the following to say about each of these forms:

Letters are perhaps the most widely used of all direct advertising forms. Letters perform almost every function in Direct Advertising. They are actually used for more different purposes than any other direct advertising form.

. . . Letters lend the personality quotient to direct mail. They are the most adaptable, the most personal, and most flexible of all forms of Direct Advertising. For the mailer with the small list, in many cases the cost of printed matter which involves typesetting and printing-press work is prohibitive. Letters are economical in small quantities as well as in large ones. . . .

Folders are the most commonly used of all printed advertising forms, because they are comparatively inexpensive and most flexible. Size, shape, and style are unlimited. In format, folders bridge the gap between personal letters and booklets. That is the best rule to remember when considering the use of folders. Use them to precede and follow the more elaborate forms. . . . Use them for the short, direct printed message. . . . Use them for single shots or for a series. Use them when the sales message should have a compact form. . . .

Broadsides are large folders, used advantageously when the average folder is not adequate to convey the story and a booklet is not the form needed or wanted; when a smash effect is sought, particularly at the beginning of a campaign, or for a special announcement, or for special emphasis of certain appeals; when a large surface is required for pictorial and bold copy expression; when the psychology of bigness is desired.

Booklets should be used when these two other formats (folders and broadsides) are not adequate to convey the larger story, or lack sufficient prestige value or appropriateness for certain printed promotion jobs. The use of booklets is almost as great and flexible as are the functions of . . . the folder. . . . Booklets are used when the story is lengthy; when it cannot be accomplished by a folder or other lesser presentations; when dignity of approach is desired; when desired elaborateness does not reach the "brochure" classification. . . .

Brochures are the glamorous phases of Direct Advertising and should be used when an elaborate presentation of company, product, or service is called for: when there is a need or desire to go beyond the ordinary booklet and broadside format for richness, power, and impressiveness in size, illustrations, color, materials, bindings, etc.; when the presentation of a story must match the bigness of the selling job. . . .

The **circular,** or **flyer,** is the usually inexpensive form to adopt when you want to get across a strong message in a flash. Circulars are generally flat pieces up to a size that stops at the broadside category. The circular . . . can tell its story quickly, "loudly," and inexpensively.

Mailing cards [a form of Direct Advertising having great utility value]. You can logically use mailing cards when brief announcements (not confidential) are desired; when budgets do not allow for more expensive format; when a teaser idea is used to introduce a campaign; when single messages or thoughts are needed to influence prospects or obtain leads; when quick reminders are effective; when the element of time is most important; when notices, announcements, instructions, invitations, and other short direct messages lend themselves to this inexpensive, open, quick-reading format. . . .

Die cuts, pop-ups, novelties, gadgets, and **sample pieces** (the unusual forms of Direct Advertising) can be used when realism is wanted; when it is important to make a fast, single impression . . . ; when you want to show things that cannot be shown in other forms of advertising; when original, individual, and effective presentations [are desired or necessary].

Calendars are a leading form of "reminder" direct mail.[4] Together with other specialties, calendars will be considered in more detail under "Specialty Advertising" in a later chapter.

Functions

Direct mail advertising can and does do more than a direct selling job. One leading direct mail company states that there are seven distinct functions beyond that of direct selling that may be performed by the medium. These are:

1. Direct mail advertising can supplement the work of salesmen by securing leads for follow-up.
2. It can be used to pre-condition prospects in advance of a salesman's call—to make prospects more receptive and soften up sales resistance.
3. It can supply frequency of contact, at low cost, where personal contact is geographically unfeasible, or where sales potential does not warrant frequent personal calls.
4. It can be used as a medium of pure advertising to key groups of prospects—and will obtain an impressively high level of readership.
5. It can be the backbone of dealer and distributor programs.
6. It can induce people to patronize a retail store or other service conducted over-the counter.
7. It can be tremendously effective in research and market surveys—the results of which are useful in product and service development, often basic in advertising and sales planning.[5]

This handsome mailing piece promoted ad space in *Better Homes and Gardens* Garden Ideas Annual. Executed with four parallel folds to the inside, each fold opens into a new spread that functions as a design unit. *Meredith Lithography.*

Characteristics

Direct mail advertising can be the most selective and the most personal of all advertising media.

With respect to its personal character, it can range from the relatively impersonal circular addressed to ''Occupant'' or ''Box Holder'' to the highly personal letter addressing each individual by name. But in all cases it provides the

In its "Switch to the Honeywell Line" campaign, Minneapolis-Honeywell used a model train to introduce a new line of automatic controls to 115 key executives of water heater manufacturing companies. *Reporter of Direct Mail Advertising.*

advertiser with a means of presenting his sales messages directly, without any intermediary, to individual prospects.

With respect to selectivity in the audience addressed, direct mail advertising can range from no selectivity to a degree of selectivity limited only by the advertiser's ability to put together a mailing list. That is, the advertiser can use an impersonal "Occupant" or "P.O. Box" mailing and reach almost everyone in a community, or he can be more selective and send his sales messages to bald-headed men with one leg who live on the sunny side of the street, provided he can build the list to reach the last-named audience. Direct mail sent to the "Occupant" can cover as much as 93% of all United States households, according to a leading advertising agency's estimates; transients and the like make it impossible to reach all households. But if the advertiser wishes a selective audience, he can choose between men and women; he can select the income group, occupation group, or age group that promises to be the best market for his product; he can get in touch with home owners and disregard families who rent; he can send his appeals to those who have bought his product before and ignore those who have not; he can address people who have just married or those who have not yet married but plan to marry in the near future. In short, he can reach his maximum audience, without duplication and without having to reach a sizable waste circulation while doing so.

Direct mail advertising is extremely flexible with respect to (1) format, (2) geographical coverage, (3) extent of coverage, and (4) timing.

While the creative man possibly faces fewer restrictions in direct mail advertising than in any other medium, he is subject to more Federal Trade Commission control today than ever before and, like his counterpart in the other media, he gets his share of consumerists' complaints. He is also limited by the size of his budget, his own imagination, and the postal laws, which for the most part place restrictions on procedures that we hope he would not wish to employ in any event. He has control over paper stock, printing, and—within a wide range—the size of his presentation. No matter what effect he wishes to create or what problem he has to solve, direct mail offers a flexibility of format that simplifies his task. This flexibility of format is equally important to the artist and the copywriter. The mailing piece can range from a post card to a catalog; it can tell a brief sales history or a complete one backed up with ample illustrations or even swatches or other samples of the product.

In geographical coverage, direct mail advertising can be nation-wide, state-wide, or county-wide. It can be restricted to selected cities or to a particular city. It can be confined to particular neighborhoods or streets within a city. In like manner, the extent of its coverage can be great or small. A national distributor of a widely used product can send out a mailing of several million pieces; some mail order houses have sent out as many as 7,000,000 catalogs. At the other extreme, a small neighborhood store can circularize its own clientele of perhaps a few hundred people. In other words, the size of the mailing can be tailored to meet the needs of the individual advertiser. He need not buy a ready-made, fixed circulation.

Finally, direct mail advertising offers flexibility of timing. In this medium the advertiser is not bound by issue dates. He can plan and make his mailings when they are to his greatest advantage. We have already seen that the users of direct mail advertising can reach people who are about to be married. Families who are celebrating the arrival of a new baby are equally accessible. So too, the direct mail advertiser can get in touch with men who have just started a new business, people who are planning a trip to Europe, or young men and women who are about to graduate from school or college. Actually, there is very little that cannot be found out about what people are doing, and once this has been discovered they can be reached with direct mail advertising at a *time* when they are most likely to be influenced by the sales message.

It should be pointed out here that while more direct mail pieces are sent to consumers ("because there are more of 'em''), a greater number of advertisers use direct mail for industrial purposes than they do for consumer promotions and communications.

In summary, the greatest value of direct mail to the advertiser is its ability to carry the sales message of his choosing to the specific people he wishes to reach in the exact locations he wants to cover at the precise time he wishes to make the contact.

POSTAL REGULATIONS

We do not think of the *advertisements* that appear in newspapers or magazines as advertising media. The media are the newspapers and the magazines, *the vehicles that carry or present the advertisements to the market.* The same is true of radio, television, and the outdoor and transit media. The advertisements in each case may assume characteristics that are imposed by the medium employed, but the advertisements themselves are not the medium. So too, in direct mail advertising, it is the postal system that is in a sense the medium and not the letters, circulars, post cards and other mailing pieces that are used by the advertiser. These various kinds of direct mail advertising are comparable to the different kinds of magazine, newspaper, or outdoor advertising that might be used and that assume the forms they do because of the special problems and wishes of individual advertisers and because of the requirements and limitations imposed by the medium that carries them.

Therefore, to understand the potentials and the limitations of direct mail advertising, it is necessary to be familiar with the postal laws and regulations that govern it use. This constraint is basic to everything that is done in the creation and use of direct mail advertising. A summary of some of the important considerations related to these regulations will be given in this section. But for the complete and detailed information necessary to competent and safe use of the medium, the advertiser should obtain copies of the postal regulations and study them. *The Postal Manual* and *The Postal Bulletin* also furnish valuable information.

Certain things are not mailable at all; others are not mailable except under the definite, prescribed conditions of the post office. In general, dangerous or highly inflammable materials may not be sent through the mails. Indecent or obscene publications or writing or any information on how, where, or from whom they may be obtained may not be mailed. Also denied mailing privileges is any matter concerning a lottery, and, of course, no fraudulent material may be sent through the mails.

As is commonly known, mail in the United States is divided into four classes. The advertiser is concerned primarily with first-class and third-class mail, as far as his direct mail advertising is concerned.

First-class mail includes letters, postal and post cards,* airmail ** not in excess of eight ounces (whether sealed or not), matter sealed or closed against inspection, and all matter wholly or partially written, except authorized additions to second-class, third-class, and fourth-class mail.

If post cards do not conform with specifications prescribed by the post office and if they bear a message wholly or partially written or the words *Post Card* or *Private Mailing Card,* they are charged the first-class rate. However, if they are entirely in print and do not carry the words *Post Card* or *Private Mailing Card,* they are carried at third-class rates.

Second-class rates apply to the mailing of newspapers and other periodical publications and, in general, are of little concern to the users of direct mail advertising.

A large percentage of direct mail advertising is third-class. An advertiser can save money on his mailings if they qualify for third-class rates, especially if he employs the bulk-mailing privilege. Although other items may be mailed third-class, this class has its chief interest to direct mail advertisers because it includes books and catalogs of 24 or more bound pages, at least 22 of which must be printed, and circulars and other printed matter. To qualify for third-class rates, eligible mail (including printed bills or statements of account and matter prepared in facsimile of handwritten or typewritten matter by Xerox, mimeograph, hectograph, ditto, or similar reproduction processes) must be presented at the post office in 20 or more identical copies. A saving in postage is effected by using bulk mail, although bulk-mail users pay an annual fee of $30 exclusive of postage. The bulk rate applies to mailings of separately addressed, identical pieces in quantities of not less than 20 pounds or not less than 200 pieces. Postage is prepaid by the pound on the entire mailing, but it may not be less than the minimum charge per piece in any case. Unless the advertiser is a nonprofit organization, the words "Bulk Rate" or the abbreviation "Blk. Rt." must be printed either on or adjacent to the permit imprints, meter stamps, or precanceled stamps. All mail must be sorted and bundled according to ZIP codes.

Applications to mail third-class matter at special postage rates must be filed at the post office where the advertiser makes his mailings.

When the direct mail advertiser wishes replies from the recipients of his mailings, he may (1) affix a postage stamp to the return card or envelope, (2) put the burden of buying and affixing the stamp on the prospect, or (3) use a printed prepaid business-reply card or envelope. In the first case he will spend unnecessary money because he will be paying postage for material that may not be returned, usually the larger percentage of any mailing, as well as for that which is sent back to him. In the second case, it is probable that he would ma-

* Postal cards are sold by the post office and the postage stamp is imprinted on the card. Post cards are cards manufactured and sold by private companies, without an imprinted stamp.

** All domestic first-class mail travelling beyond 250 miles now goes by airmail, without additional postage.

terially reduce his returns. In the last case, no expense is placed upon the recipient of the mail, and the advertiser pays the postage for only that portion of the return-mail pieces that he actually gets back. The advertiser may obtain, without cost, a permit to use such business-reply mail, which consists of specially printed business-reply cards, envelopes, cartons, and labels. No prepayment of postage is required of the advertiser on the reply portion of the mailing, but postage is collected on each piece that is returned to him as well as on any pieces that are returned because the authorized addressee refuses them. The size and form of the reply pieces must comply with regulations prescribed by the post office.

By the use of precanceled stamps, the user of direct mail advertising may save both time and money in the handling of his mail. Furthermore, since precanceled mail is sorted and tied in packages by the sender, it requires less processing time in the post office and is dispatched more quickly. In this type of mail the postage stamps, stamped envelopes, or postal cards are canceled in advance of mailing. Precanceled stamps may not be used on boxes, cases, bags, or other containers that can be reused for mailing purposes.

Permits to use precanceled stamps must be obtained from the local post office from which the mailings will be made. Only the post office may precancel adhesive stamps, but a permit may give the advertiser the privilege of precanceling stamped envelopes or postal cards with his own cancellation mark.

Postage may be paid on any class of mail by printing meter stamps with a postage meter, which may be leased from an authorized manufacturer. These meters are made to print any or all denominations of postage and keep an automatic record of the amount of postage used. The meter must be taken to the post office to have it set for additional postage from time to time. The postage is paid at this time, usually by certified check. A license to use a meter may be obtained upon application to the post office from which the mailings will be made. There is no fee. The advertiser may use a meter stamp to prepay postage on reply mailings if the meter stamp is printed directly on the envelope or card bearing the printed address of the license holder. On printed prepaid business-reply cards or envelopes, immediately above the printed return address, the following words must be printed: "No postage stamp necessary—postage has been Prepaid by————."

The advantage to the advertiser in using meter stamps and prepaid printed indicia is that the purchase, control, and affixing of postage are made easier, and more rapid dispatching of mail by the post office is made possible.

SUCCESS IMPERATIVES

Assuming that the advertiser has a desirable product of satisfactory quality and that it is properly priced, three things are essential to the success of direct mail advertising: (1) the right mailing piece for the selling problem at hand, (2) an up-to-date list of real prospects, and (3) correct timing.

The Mailing Piece.

All advertising, regardless of the medium that carries it, must face competition. However, the kind and severity of the competition differ considerably with the medium involved. The advertisements in a magazine or a newspaper must compete for the reader's attention with other advertisements in the same publications and with the editorial content of the medium. Advertising broadcast by one station must compete both with the advertising and programs broadcast by other stations at the same time and with the other commercials on the same station. Outdoor advertising must compete with other advertising, with the scenery, and with the sundry distractions of the out-of-doors. Direct mail advertising must fight the battle of the desk top wherein it competes with orders, invoices, payments, complaints, correspondence, and other advertisements received in the same mail, with telephone calls, with personal callers, with yesterday's left-over work, and with the demanding schedule of the day at hand. If the direct mail goes to the home instead of the office, the competition is somewhat different but nonetheless real. The mailing list may be excellent, the timing perfect, but this competition still exists. Therefore, it is the job of the mailing piece to meet and overcome it.

The kind of mailing piece that will be used depends upon the product, the nature of the offer, and other factors related to the particular problems of each advertiser at any given time. There are situations that call for an elaborate brochure; others can be satisfactorily handled with a post card. In some cases the formality and dignity of a letter are necessary; on others a circular will do. Novelty mailing pieces have a wide range of use and much to be said in their favor. Many times, a novelty will catch and hold the attention of the recipient just long enough to stay his hand as it sweeps toward the waste basket and swing it in an arc that brings the mailing piece back to life and the completion of its task. Again, a novelty may strike the fancy of the recipient so that he will retain it and show it to others; thus the mailing piece does a multiple selling job. Such a piece was the die-cut figure of a trade character that held in its mouth a small, chemically treated "cigarette" that blew smoke rings when lighted. Another such piece was a pocket memorandum book with occasional line-art cartoons picturing comical situations in the trade of the men to whom it was sent. Others are die-cuts in the shape of office equipment or other figures that pop-up to three-dimensional form when the letter is opened.

That the novelty mailing piece brings results to the advertiser as well as interest or amusement to the prospect has been proven by tests. To cite but a single case, one company employing an illustrated letterhead that pictured two hands pulling on either end of a piece of cord applied a string over the picture of the cord in one-half of a mailing. The other half was sent with the picture only. Response from the letter with the string attached was 6.85%; response from the letter with the illustration alone was 3.85%.[6]

The Lists

The best of mailing pieces cannot be successful unless it is sent to people who are truly potential buyers of the product being advertised. The advertiser must, as the Direct Mail/Marketing Association says, "direct his mail to *prospects* instead of *suspects*." The list is a very vital part of any direct mail advertising program. But how does an advertiser obtain a list? How does he know that a list is a good one? If it is a good list, how may he keep it so?

Lists may be obtained in any one or a combination of three ways. First, the advertiser can build one himself, and if he is careful of his sources he should be reasonably sure of its quality. Second, he can buy one from a commercial list house. Or third, he can rent one through a mailing-list broker. Most, if not all, of the commercial suppliers of lists are thoroughly reliable so that the advertiser may be reasonably sure of the quality of the lists he purchases or rents.

If the advertiser elects to build his own list and he is a retailer, he can obtain names and addresses from his own store records—his charge accounts, deliveries, and so on. Such records provide a live and excellent list, for the names are all of people who have traded with the store before and who are most likely to do so again. Even if the advertiser is a manufacturer, company records offer a good source for a productive mailing list. People who have returned coupons from company advertisements, people who have made inquiry about the company's product or service, satisfied customers who have been induced to send in names of friends or neighbors who might be interested in what the company has to offer, people who have entered promotional contests run by the company, and purchasers who have returned warranty cards are some of the kinds of ore-bearing names that may be mined from the company's records.

Other possible sources of names and addresses for mailing lists are membership lists of clubs and associations, school and college yearbooks, city directories, trade directories, college bulletins that list staff members, telephone directories, credit-rating books, vital statistics as published in newspapers, listings of trade-show or convention participants, and automobile registrations or other county or municipal lists.

If for some reason the advertiser himself cannot build the kind of list he wants, or if he does not wish to take the time to do so, he may rent one from a commercial list house or from a list broker. Such list houses specialize in compiling lists of people engaged in specific trades or professions—people who in some way constitute a selective audience. List also may be bought or rented from the publishers of some trade and business periodicals who build them from names in areas covered by their publications and their subscribers.

When the advertiser *buys* a list it becomes his property, and he may use it as often and over as long a period of time as he pleases. But if the advertiser chooses, he may *rent* a list rather than buy one. In such a case he has only one-time use of the list. Of course, any orders or inquiries resulting from the use of a rented list supply him with names and addresses which become his property.

Rented lists may be obtained either through mailing-list brokers or from publishers of some magazines. The lists obtainable through the brokers usually are composed of names of people who have bought or made inquiry about some product and are obtained from business firms that are willing to rent them on a one-time basis. The lists rented from publishers are made up of names of present and past subscribers to their magazines and perhaps prospects and reputable people in the field known to the publisher; these people usually comprise the full market for a given product.

Possibly nothing in advertising is more perishable than a mailing list. A top-quality list completed today will start to degenerate tomorrow; indeed, the process of degeneration may have started even before the list was completed. In a year the list may have lost much of its original value; in two or three years it may be hardly worth using. The reason for this rapid obsolescence, of course, is the rapidity and all-prevailing nature of change in human society. Women marry and change their names and addresses. People are born and people die. People move, 20% of them each year—we live in a highly mobile society. People change jobs, get promoted, retire. Youngsters graduate from school. New government officials are elected. People age. Businesses are born and businesses fail. Change is constant. Therefore, a mailing list must be checked and revised or "cleaned" from time to time.

Lists may be updated and corrected in a number of different ways. The advertiser can drop names of people who have not placed an order during a specified period and add new names as orders from new customers are received. He can send a questionnaire to the names on his list asking for information on present occupations, titles, addresses, and so on. If he has a sales force he can require his salesmen to check names and addresses in their territories. Names and addresses can also be checked against new membership lists, directories, and so on, as they become available. If the advertiser is using third-class or fourth-class mail, the post office will notify him of a change of address if he prints the words "Address Correction Requested" immediately under his name and address in the upper left corner. He must pay the postage on each piece of undelivered returned mail and on each notice received from the post office.

The post office will correct, at the list owner's expense, mailing lists submitted to it. Such lists should be submitted to the post office that serves the addresses on the list. The list should be on typed or printed 3 × 5-inch cards except in the case of third- and fourth-class post offices, where lists should be on sheets. The owner of the list should identify his property by placing his name and address in the upper left corner of each card.

In servicing such a list, the post office will cross out names to which mail cannot be delivered or forwarded and will correct house, rural, or post office box numbers that are incorrect. If known, the head of the family will be indicated where two or more names appear for the same address.

Correct ZIP code numbers may be obtained by sending a mailing list to the post office serving the delivery zones represented on the list; or a copy of the

National ZIP Code Directory may be obtained from the local post office or from the United States Postal Service in Washington, D.C.

General Mailings

It may be that an advertiser is not interested in mailing to a select group but wishes to obtain wide distribution of his direct mail advertising. In such cases he will not concern himself with building a list of names but will employ a general mailing list consisting of addresses but no individual names. When using this type of mailing, the advertiser will address his mail pieces to "Postal Patron," "Occupant," "Householder," or "Resident" followed by the street and number, apartment number if one is involved, post office, zip code, and state. If the advertiser wishes general distribution of his mail pieces where there is no city or village carrier service, each piece of mail must be addressed to "Rural or Star-Route Boxholder," depending upon the type of distribution he wishes. In each case the class of boxholder addressed must be followed with the name of the post office and the state, or by the word "local."

When this type of mailing is used, one piece of each mailing must be provided for every boxholder in each class addressed. Also, all pieces of such mail for the same post office must be tied, insofar as possible, in packs of 50 with an attached slip indicating the type of distribution desired (to which type of boxholder the mail is to be sent). When packed in quantities of less than 50, the number of pieces as well as the type of distribution must be indicated. Postage must be of a kind that does not require cancellation. Occupational or other designations such as "Farmer," "Voter," and so on may not be used.

Occupant lists, like name and address lists, will be checked by the post office at the advertiser's expense. Occupant lists may be submitted to the post office either on cards or on sheets. If sheets are used, a separate one must be provided for each carrier route, and each sheet must bear the name and address of its owner. The post office will not add new ones. A code letter is used to indicate business addresses and addresses on a rural route. When an address is that of an apartment or multiple dwelling, the post office will indicate the number of families living at the address.

Timing

Just as the mailing piece and the list are important to the success of direct mail advertising, so, too, is the timing of the mailing. A mailing made too soon or too late loses much, if not all, of its effectiveness. A retailer sent out a catalog announcing gift merchandise before he had the goods in stock. Several customers attracted by the advertising came to the store only to be disappointed by its inability to serve them. However, being in a buying mood they did much of their Christmas shopping in other stores in the neighborhood that did have gift merchandise in stock. In this case a premature mailing did an excellent job of selling for the advertisers's competitors.

Obviously, a mailing that by late arrival misses the time when people make their decisions and buy will do little or no selling. A piece of direct mail selling a photographer's services may get him business from engaged couples if received before the wedding; it may do the advertiser little good if received after the ceremonies are over. Sales associated with specific events that occur at specific times can be made at those times—not too long before and rarely after. However, advertisers must keep in mind the fact that third-class mail doesn't get the same attention given priority mail such as first-class, and that they have no way of knowing when it will be delivered.

"Smart" and proper timing can add materially to the success of direct mail advertising. A neighborhood laundry had an arrangement with building superintendents to inform it when new families were moving into the area. It then timed its mailings so that the first delivery after the arrival of a new tenant brought an announcement of its services and an invitation to the newly arrived family to avail itself of them. What could be more effective than such timing? Such a family really expects no mail on the first delivery following its arrival in a new home but it does receive this letter. Obviously, the letter gets unusual attention. The name and location of the laundry are noted, and the chances are more than good that this will be the one used when the need for laundry service arises a few days or a week hence.

INDUSTRIAL ADVERTISING

Direct mail advertising lends itself equally well to the advertising of consumer and industrial goods and services. We have just seen an example of its use in a small scale, consumer-service kind of business. Let us now examine its use in a larger industrial operation.

The 3M Company, manufacturers of Scotch Brand cellophane tape, had developed a new product with a unique industrial application—a totally inert liquid called Fluorinert. It leaves no residue, doesn't harm or affect clothing or anything else with which it comes in contact, and evaporates without a trace. It is used presently as a gross leak test-bath medium for electronic components and devices such as integrated circuits. Competitive liquids, such as silicone, leave a deposit and require cleaning following the test.

In order to gain acceptance from the electronics manufacturers, 3M had to demonstrate the properties of its product. It did so by means of direct mail in a series of six mailings. The first mailing received a 10% response and by the end of the fourth the company had received 160 inquiries from less than 250 companies. (Mailings, however, had been sent to two titles in each company, for a net result of 160 out of less than 500—still an excellent response.)

Each mailing consisted of a small box containing a 3-inch-long sample bottle of Fluorinert, a small folder on which was printed a letter, and an attached self-addressed and stamped reply card. Dramatically, the first mailing asked the recipient to splash some of the sample liquid on his coat sleeve. Another asked him to dip a match in the fluid and then strike it. The 3M Company guaranteed that it would light.

Mailings were sent at two-month intervals and met the company's objective of introducing Fluorinert to prospects and placing actual samples into their hands.[7]

SUMMARY

It is conjectured that some form of direct mailing advertising, or direct advertising as it is often called, existed even in ancient times. In the United States, the official postal service was established in 1775, although some form of mail delivery was in operation as early as 1639.

As the postal service continued to expand and improve its service, the graphic arts and means of print production improved along with it.

According to the amount of money spent on it, direct mail advertising ranks in third place as an advertising medium. It is a component of direct-response advertising and direct marketing.

Direct mail advertising pieces come in a number of forms, including letters, folders, broadsides, booklets, brochures, circulars, mailing cards, and in such novelty forms as cut-outs and pop-ups.

It is a highly selective medium and extremely flexible in format, geographical coverage, extent of coverage, and timing. Advertisers who use direct mail should be familiar with the United States Postal Service regulations and rates.

Essential to the success of direct mail are the use of the right mailing piece, a current list, and proper timing.

The medium is effective in the advertising of both consumer and industrial goods.

QUESTIONS AND DISCUSSION SUBJECTS

1. In what ways do (a) direct advertising, (b) direct mail advertising, (c) mail order advertising differ?
2. Name and describe at least five uses of direct mail advertising.
3. What are the factors most important to the success of direct mail advertising?
4. Name and describe at least five different kinds of direct mail advertising.
5. How may mailing lists be obtained?
6. Lists may be corrected and updated in a number of ways. Name and describe at least four methods for accomplishing this.
7. For what reasons might an advertiser choose to make general mailings?
8. By reference to specific examples, show how timing may lead to success or to failure of a direct mail advertising venture.
9. What characteristics of direct mail make it effective in industrial advertising?

10. Give reasons for and against using third-class mail in direct mail advertising.

SOURCES

1. Henry Hoke, "The Past, the Present, the Future of Direct Mail Advertising," *The Reporter of Direct Mail Advertising,* Vol. 18, No. 5 (September 1955).
2. *Ibid.*
3. Information obtained from the Direct Mail/Marketing Association.
4. *DMAA Presents the Story of Direct Advertising* (New York: Direct Mail Advertising Association, 1956).
5. *How to Get More Money for Your Direct Mail Dollar; The Story of Dickie-Raymond* (New York: Dickie-Raymond, 1957).
6. *DMAA Presents . . . , op. cit.*
7. The Direct Mail/Marketing Association and the 3M Company.

FOR FURTHER READING

"A Consumer's Guide to Postal Services and Products." U.S. Postal Service, 1974.
"A Guide to Mail Marketing Profits." New York: Dependable Lists.
Ballinger, Raymond A. *Direct Mail Design.* New York: Reinhold, 1963.
Buckley, Earle A. *How to Increase Sales with Letters.* New York: McGraw-Hill, 1961.
Gibbs, Janet. *How Retailers Make More Money Using Direct Mail.* New York: Direct Mail Advertising Association, 1957.
"Glossary of List Terms." New York: Direct Mail/Marketing Association, 1976.
Hodgson, Richard S. *Direct Mail and Mail Order Handbook.* Chicago, Dartnell, 1974.
Mayer, Edward N., Jr. *How to Make More Money With Your Direct Mail.* Third Edition. New London, Conn.: Printer's Ink Books, 1957.
McCollum, Giles B. "The Story Behind All Those Coupons," *Reporter of Direct-Mail Advertising,* April 1964.
Psychographics . . . The Life Style of the Mail Order Buyer. New York: Dependable Lists, 1974.
Stone, Robert. *Successful Direct Mail Advertising and Selling.* Englewood Cliffs, N.J.: Prentice-Hall, 1955.
Yeck, John D., and John T. Maguire. *Planning and Creating Better Direct Mail.* New York: McGraw-Hill, 1961.

Outdoor Advertising

SOME HISTORY

Advertising first came into being out-of-doors. Long before newspapers and magazines or other media carried sales messages into the home, outdoor writings or symbolic pictures told of commercial, political, or other endeavors. Some writers date the beginnings of outdoor advertising as far back as the steles of ancient Egypt. But, since the inscriptions on these stone tablets were concerned with religious or political pronouncements rather than with commercial enterprise, perhaps they were not advertising. Nonetheless, merchants and proprietors of schools and of places of entertainment proclaimed their wares or services through outdoor advertising in Pompeii before that ancient city was buried under the ashes of Vesuvius, and outdoor advertising was known to the Rome of the Caesars.

Outdoor advertising is thus a medium of ancient standing. And it has been consistently used in good times and in bad throughout much of recorded history. In the cultural drought of the Middle Ages it took the form of symbolic picture-signs outside of taverns and other places of business. In this form it served well a society in which illiteracy ran high. Later, during the seventeenth and eighteenth centuries, it has been said that the city of London was literally darkened by swinging signs of every description.

Although outdoor advertising appeared early in colonial America, it was not until 1872 that any formal organization in the medium took place in the United States. At that time the International Bill Posters Association of North America was formed in St. Louis. Other groups followed, and in 1906 a merger was effected that created the Associated Bill Posters and Distributors of the United States and Canada. An outstanding contribution of this group was the development of the concept of measuring market coverage in terms of *showings* or of specified numbers of poster locations sold to advertisers as a package. This was significant because it could assure all advertisers of equal and fair treatment and so made the medium more attractive to national advertisers.

As time passed several industrial and sociological developments occurred that contributed to the growth of the outdoor advertising medium. The invention of the automobile and the improvement of roads, the widespread adoption of five and one-half days and later of five days as the business week, the shifting of population from urban to suburban areas, and the growth of supermarkets and suburban shopping centers—all took more people out-of-doors and kept them out-of-doors for longer periods of time. These developments, combined with the growth of population in the United States and with expanding business opportunities in general, have made outdoor advertising an increasingly important medium. The total national expenditure for outdoor advertising increased from $69 million in 1947 to more than $345 million 27 years later in 1974. A rough estimate of such expenditures at the beginning of the century places the figure at $2 million.[1]

As the outdoor advertising industry grew in size and importance a refinement in organization and operation took place. In 1925 the Outdoor Advertising Association of America, Inc. (OAAA) was formed by a merger of two existing organizations. This Association, together with the Institute of Outdoor Advertising (IOA), has done much to develop standards of practice and to standardize structures so that outdoor advertising panels have a uniform appearance across the nation.

The Traffic Audit Bureau (TAB) started operations in 1934 with the purpose of auditing and publishing certified figures on outdoor circulations, conducting special research on traffic, and furnishing data on the relative value of different outdoor locations. The TAB is covered in greater detail in Chapter 15.

OUTDOOR ADVERTISING TODAY

The individual operating unit in the outdoor advertising industry is called a *plant*. A *plant* consists of all of the facilities necessary to carry on the business of outdoor advertising on a local basis. This includes the owned or leased land or locations upon which the advertising structures are erected, the poster panels and other displays, the plant operator's shop or place of business, and the trucks and other equipment necessary for constructing outdoor displays, mounting posters, painting bulletins, and building spectaculars.

The plant operator purchases or leases locations for the erection of the displays and then subleases these locations to advertisers, together with the necessary panels or other structures. The larger poster panels, commonly called billboards by the layman, have traditionally been leased on the basis of *showings*. Although showings are currently becoming superseded by *gross rating points*, the older term remains in use and a student of advertising needs to be familiar with the concept. A *100-showing* consists of the number of poster panels regarded by the plant operator as necessary to give a daily effective

Title:	"Dog's Best Friend - Zee Napkins"
Advertiser:	Crown Zellerbach Corporation
Agency:	D'Arcy Advertising Company
Art Director:	Adrian Taylor
Copywriter:	Warren Peterson
Artist:	Gil Brunk
Poster Printer:	Stecher-Traung-Schmidt

Title:	"Great Belt"
Advertiser:	Grain Belt Breweries, Inc.
Agency:	Knox Reeves Advertising
Art Director:	Tom Donovan
Copywriter:	Ron Oakland
Photographer:	Arthur Beck
Poster Printer:	Compton & Sons

Title:	"You Should Live So Long"
Advertiser:	Volkswagen of America, Inc.
Agency:	Doyle Dane Bernbach, Inc.
Art Directors:	Bernard Rowe
Copywriters:	David Butler
Photographer:	Bernard Gardner
Poster Printer:	Diamond National Corp.

A couple of winners in the Outdoor Advertising Competition. Note the small amount or complete lack of copy.

circulation equal to the population of a given market. An advertiser has the choice of a *75-showing,* or *50-showing,* and, in some markets, a *25-showing* or less if he does not wish the complete coverage offered by the larger number of panels in the 100-showing. On the other hand, if he wishes a greater number of displays in a market he may purchase more than a 100-showing. A 200- or 300-showing would be approximately two or three times the number of panels in a 100-showing.

The numerical designations of the showings do not describe the number of panels in a showing but do indicate the relative effect. For example, the 100-showing has approximately twice as many panels as a 50-showing and four times as many as a 25-showing in any given market. Consequently, the 100-showing gives twice the market penetration and substantially greater repetition than could be obtained from a 50-showing. Outdoor markets are divided into poster zones, each having an equal portion of the main travelled thoroughfares. Generally, two panels in each poster zone are required for a 100-showing, one panel for a 50-showing.

The number of panels in a 100-showing, or any other showing of specified intensity, varies from city to city. The exact number that would constitute a specified showing in any given market is determined by the plant operator and depends upon such considerations as (1) the area to be covered, (2) the population of the market, (3) the dispersion of business, shopping, and industrial areas, and (4) the traffic flow as regulated by existing streets and boulevards.

The size of the showing bought by an advertiser depends upon the intensity of the coverage he desires. As already indicated, a 100-showing is designed to give complete and intensive coverage of a market. A 50-showing gives coverage of the same area but since it contains only half as many panels, the displays are spread out more. This results in a reduction of intensity and of repetition.

Early in 1973, OAAA began to press for the use of *gross rating points* (*GRPs*) as the primary sales unit instead of *showings.* The new system makes outdoor advertising more readily comparable between markets and with the other media. It also provides more useful data on reach and frequency and on other important marketing criteria. Essentially, GRPs "represent the number of impression-opportunities (without regard to audience duplication) expressed as a percent of the population of the market under consideration.[2] For example, a market having a population of 1,000,000 and a distribution of outdoor posters delivering 500,000 total impression-opportunities (or audited circulation) would provide 50 GRPs a day. And based on the standard outdoor 30-day contract, that distribution would deliver 1,500 gross rating points.[3] Although showings are still in use, GRPs are replacing them.*

In addition to providing the locations for outdoor advertising, the plant op-

---

* A 100 GRP Package (usually contains more panels than the 100-showing) will provide enough panels to deliver in one day a number of exposure opportunities equal to 100% of the population of the market. A 50 GRP Package will deliver daily exposure opportunities equal to half the population.

erator erects the necessary structures to carry the advertisements; he posts, paints, or otherwise places the advertisements on the structures, and maintains the advertisements for the duration of the contract period.

Values of outdoor advertising locations may change as the areas about them change. A new building may obstruct the view of a panel, or a new highway may route traffic away from a once favorable location. When such changes occur, it becomes the job of the plant operator to find new locations as good as those whose value has been reduced to destroyed.

An outdoor advertising company may consist of but a single organization serving one city, or it may be composed of several plants each serving a different market. There are some 600 or more plant operators in the United States, serving 9,000 markets. In a majority of markets there is only one outdoor advertising plant. However, there is competition in 150 markets. Local business is usually obtained through the plant's own sales force, but much of the national business is obtained through the industry's four national sales representatives.

The Outdoor Advertising Association of America, Inc., mentioned earlier, is the trade association of the standardized outdoor medium; its plant members operate more than 80% of the medium's facilities in this country.

The association advises and assists the members of the industry in matters pertaining to public, press, and governmental relations. It recommends standards for the construction, illumination, and placement of outdoor advertising panels. It established the Outdoor Advertising Foundation at the University of Notre Dame for studies on the advancement of the medium.

The Institute of Outdoor Advertising is the marketing division of the OAAA, with which it merged in 1970. Its purpose is the development of research, creative ideas, promotion, and effective uses of the outdoor medium. It is a central source of information on Outdoor, at the service of advertisers, agencies, member plants, sales organizations, and the public.

The Institute publishes the *Outdoor Buyers Guide,* issued twice a year, containing rates and panels per showing in over 9,000 markets, and the quarterly reports of outdoor advertising expenditures. It maintains liaison with agencies and advertisers on creative and research aspects of outdoor advertising.

The National Outdoor Advertising Bureau, Inc., frequently referred to as NOAB or "the Bureau," was formed in 1916. It is a cooperative organization owned and used by advertising agencies. The Bureau executes for its members all of the servicing tasks and field services that are necessary to the running of an outdoor advertising campaign, but not the creative functions. Without such assistance, each advertising agency would have to get in touch and deal separately with a large number of individual plant owners. This time-consuming and costly undertaking is eliminated by a single agency-contact with NOAB in which the organization represents the interests of its agency users among the several plant owners.

In addition to negotiating contracts and inspecting poster panels and bulletins, NOAB maintains a data-processing facility that provides agency users

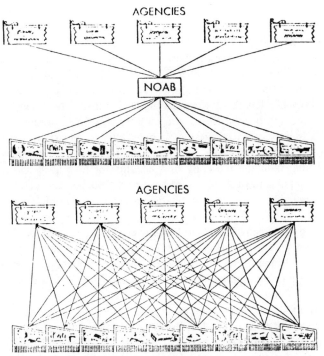

How NOAB simplifies Agency-Plant Relationships. The pattern with and without the function of NOAB. *Source:* National Outdoor Advertising Bureau.

with computerized data pertaining to the outdoor medium in every market in the United States and Canada. NOAB also publishes a complete listing of markets, allotments, and costs that contains information on every showing and every town on its record. Its Poster Contract Department, among other services, prepares poster shipping instructions and shipping labels for the lithographers and prepares and releases posting instructions to plants. Its Painted Display Contract Department, among its services, rescales or prepares from one piece of original art all mechanicals needed to fit the various sizes of painted bulletins that an advertiser may use in any given campaign.

When an outdoor advertising campaign is under way, NOAB's field representatives are available to agencies and their clients to appraise poster showings and painted displays either prior to or during the term of display. In addition, regular inspections are maintained on a continuous schedule, every major market being inspected an average of approximately three times annually. No individual agency can afford to duplicate such field operation.

NOAB services are paid for by the advertising agencies at 3⅔% from 16⅔% compensation received from plant operators (that is, the agency nets 13%). Completely confidential treatment of individual advertising agencies' figures and plans is a cornerstone of NOAB policy and practice.

CHARACTERISTICS

Outdoor advertising differs from other advertising media in that it is seen by the observer as he passes on foot, or, at greater speed, in a vehicle. Most advertising media bring the advertiser's message into the home or office, where it is seen or heard at leisure with the attention of the prospect focused upon it for an appreciable length of time. Even most transit advertising is before a seated or standing observer for several minutes at a time. Because outdoor advertising is literally seen in passing, it must tell the advertiser's story simply and quickly. This is best done by letting the picture carry the burden of the selling job and reducing the copy to a headline or to a head and subhead at most. Some of the most effective posters have had but one or two words of copy. However, the creation of an outdoor poster is not a quick and simple undertaking.

Outdoor advertising has several characteristics that offset the disadvantage of having to appeal to a market in motion. In poster advertising, the sales message is repeated many times at different locations throughout the market. Furthermore, the message remains before the public for at least a month. If a passerby misses an outdoor advertisement at one location he probably will see it at one or more of several other locations another time. If he does not see a particular advertisement today, the chances are good that he will see it tomorrow or the day after or next week.

Outdoor advertising is free to the observer (but not to the advertiser) in the sense that the observer buys nothing in order to see it. Neither need he do anything other than carry on the business of a normal day to be exposed to it. When he does see it he is likely to be at or near the market rather than seated comfortably at home with perhaps little or no thought of buying anything. To these several advantages of outdoor advertising may be added its relatively large size. The elephant, it has been said, may not be the most interesting animal in the circus parade, but it is most likely to be seen. Not only is the large size of outdoor displays an attention-getting factor, but it also gives the visualizer and layout artist the opportunity to create truly spectacular presentations.

Outdoor advertising has been subject to considerable criticism on the grounds that it spoils the beauty of the countryside and that it is a traffic hazard. Although it is true that a billboard, as someone observed, is not so "lovely as a tree," it should be recognized that a large part of this criticism springs from the unfortunate placement of advertising signs by individual businessmen and not from the placement of poster panels by the organized outdoor advertising industry. The organized industry maintains standards of uniformity of design and of exposure. It places the panels in properly zoned areas in cities, and it maintains proper setbacks on the highways where poster panels are permitted. National advertisers and outdoor advertising associations scrupulously observe federal, state, and local "highway beautification" laws.

TYPES

There are four types of outdoor advertising: (1) posters, (2) painted displays, (3) semispectaculars, and (4) electrical spectaculars. Some outdoor advertising plants handle all types; others specialize in one or two types only. About 600 plants deal in posters, about 200 in painted displays, and at least 300 in a combination of both. Most plants located in major cities handle both.

Posters

Posters are available in several sizes but the *30-sheet* is the most frequently used. The 30- and 24-sheet sizes and the bleed-size poster, which will be discussed later in this chapter, account for about two-thirds of the national sales volume of the outdoor advertising industry.

The 30-sheet poster measures 9 feet 7 inches in height and 21 feet 7 inches in length. Posters of this size get the name ''30-sheet'' from the fact that at an earlier time when printing presses were smaller than they are today, it would have taken 30 separate sheets to make up the poster. At present, usually no more than 10 to 14 larger sheets are used, but the original name still persists. Currently, there are in the United States more than 270,000 poster panels designed to accommodate this display size.

The poster design is usually lithographed on separate sheets, which are then pasted on a panel to form the desired picture and copy. The poster panels are of standard size and made of wood or of wood and metal. It is customary to place white blanking paper on the panel before the poster is pasted on. When the poster is placed in position, the blanking paper forms a mat around the advertisement that together with the frame of the panel creates an effect much like a framed picture, the over-all dimensions of which are 12 feet by 25 feet.

The advertiser buys 30-sheet poster locations in terms of showings or according to GRPs, as already explained, and must supply the plant operator with the posters. The plant operator, in turn, provides the panels erected at suitable locations, pastes up the posters, and maintains the display. The usual contract for a 30-sheet poster showing runs from three months as a minimum to one year, with any given poster remaining on the panels for one month as the standard posting period. Thus, an advertiser having a one-year contract can get 12 changes of copy during that time. Costs vary with the intensity of the showing as well as from market to market.

The plant operator so distributes his poster locations that every client buying the same intensity of showing obtains panel positions of comparable value. Some of the better locations in each showing usually are illuminated so as to provide effective night displays where after-dark traffic is heavy. The advertiser is told how many illuminated and how many unilluminated panels are in each showing.

The 30-sheet poster panel has the same outside dimensions as the bleed-size and 24-sheet panels. When the 30-sheet was first introduced a number of years ago it increased copy space over the 24-sheet poster by 25% through

All three—the 24-sheet poster (Yellow Pages), the 30-sheet poster (Coca Cola), and the bleed poster (White Horse) all fit into the same size poster panel frame. *Courtesy Institute of Outdoor Advertising.*

utilizing more of the border area. Of more recent origin is the *bleed-size poster,* which still fits the same overall panel dimensions but increases the copy space by approximately 40% over the original 24-sheet poster. The bleed-size poster uses even more of the border area and can be better compared to a bleed page in magazine advertising than the 30-sheet. Almost all plant operators now post this size on the standard poster panels at no increased space or posting cost. At present, the only additional cost is in the production of the posters.

The chief advantages of the 30-sheet poster are (1) increased legibility of about 10%, according to estimates, (2) opportunity for more dramatic copy treatment, and (3) greater readership. The bleed-size poster offers even greater advantages in these respects.

The 3-sheet poster has a printed surface of $6'10'' \times 3'5''$ and an overall dimension of $8'7'' \times 5'10''$, when mounted on the standard-size panel. These panels are usually used where space is limited and at or near retail stores, often on the outside walls of the stores themselves. Copy is held to a minimum, with the illustration dominating the display as is the case of 30-sheet posters.

Contracts for 3-sheet poster locations provide a "package deal," usually for one year. Placement is in accordance with the wishes of the individual advertiser in terms of types or kinds of locations. To a greater extent than in 30-sheet posters, the 3-sheet posters serve as a close-to-point-of-purchase reminder and are more suited to pedestrain traffic than to faster-moving motor-vehicle or rail traffic.

Posters are the least expensive form of outdoor advertising and there is no additional charge for posting color.

Painted Displays

Painted displays may take the form of painted walls or painted bulletins. Whereas posters are referred to as *"paper"* in the trade, painted displays of either type are called *"paint."* Paint is not as widely used as paper, accounting for approximately 30% of the volume of the outdoor advertising industry. There are currently about 36,000 painted displays across the nation.

Painted walls consist of advertisements painted directly on the walls of buildings. They are the cheapest form of painted display since they require no special structures. They are sold as individual units by the year. The size of the advertisement depends upon the space available and the wishes of the advertiser rather than upon any standards set by the outdoor advertising industry. This form of outdoor advertising has become less common as solid walls have been replaced by extensive areas of glass in modern urban architecture and as once-vacant properties have been built upon, concealing the formerly exposed side walls of adjacent buildings.

The painted bulletin is strictly a one-of-a-kind display. The proportions of painted bulletins are standard even though actual sizes vary. The most common size for bulletins is 14 feet by 48 feet. However, three forms in common use are: (1) the *streamliner;* (2) the *standard city* or *urban* bulletin; and (3) the *highway and railroad* bulletin.

As already indicated, painted bulletins are obtained on a unit basis rather than in terms of showings. Costs vary with locations and type of display. Contracts usually run from one to three years as a minimum and provide for one or two repaint jobs in addition to the original painting. At the time of repainting, the advertiser may change copy at no additional cost. Some bulletins have removable sheet-steel facings that can be painted in the shop of the outdoor advertising plant and then be assembled at the location of the bulletin, whereas others must be painted on location. In the latter case, the painter works from a grid of the design and with a color key. This "painter's guide" enables him to create a duplicate of the advertisement as it was conceived by the advertising agency or advertiser.

Perhaps one of the most outstanding recent developments in the painted-bulletin field has been the *embellished rotary* bulletin. These units include plastic-faced neon letters and giant cutouts which, together with the painted sections on the face of the units, are rotated or moved from one location to another every 30 days. Although not yet available everywhere, the embellished rotary is spreading and may eventually become a standard form of outdoor display.

One reason for going to the trouble of painting a bulletin rather than using a poster is that size sometimes makes the use of paper impractical. Although the use of paint makes the display less flexible than a poster and necessitates repainting when a change of copy is desired, the size of the painted bulletin is a compensating factor. Such displays, because of their large size, tend to obtain localized dominance in areas of heavy traffic where they are customarily used.

Painted bulletins generally are selected individually by an advertiser for the purpose of dominating a particular street or area. However, they may also be obtained in many large markets in a permanent rotary "package." In such cases the "package" contains enough displays to cover the most important boulevards of the city. This method of purchasing is the exceptional rather than the usual procedure, however.

Spectaculars and Semispectaculars

Electrical spectaculars are custom-built, usually one-of-a-kind displays, and are the most expensive and conspicuous form of outdoor advertising. They consist of metal frames with incandescent bulbs or neon tubing so placed as to create the illustration and copy of the advertisement. Very often the illusion of motion is achieved by the arrangement of the bulbs and by alternate lighting and darkening of segments of the design.

In addition to the initial expense, spectaculars are costly to maintain and are used, for the most part, by large advertisers. Such displays usually are located in areas where after-dark pedestrian and vehicle traffic is heavy. Therefore, rental costs for locations are high. Because of these expenses and because of the character of the circulation, convenience goods and products having a wide market are best suited to this form of outdoor display.

The larger and more elaborately constructed electrical spectaculars cost as much as $300,000 and more. They probably obtain word-of-mouth publicity in addition to the visual impact they have upon those who see them. For example, some of the spectaculars that have appeared in the vicinity of Times Square in New York City, have been topics of conversation and have obtained considerable publicity in a variety of media over areas at sufficient distance that many who have never been in New York City have heard of them or have seen photos of them.

Semispectaculars are usually painted bulletins with such additional features as threedimensional effects, reflectors, fluorescent paint, mechanical devices, or special lighting effects. They differ from the spectaculars in being equally effective for day or night display and, in general, less costly. They can be had in various sizes from 12' × 20' to 20' × 40' or even larger. They are sold on a unit basis by the year.

AUDIENCES

Outdoor advertising is unique in that its audiences come to it in the course of daily traveling about the market. This unique characteristic of the medium is inextricably linked with our mobile economy, in which 90% of our population go shopping by car. It accounts for the wide reach (number of people) and high frequency (number of exposures per person) of the medium.

Numerous surveys have shown high levels of reach and frequency for outdoor advertising. W. R. Simmons, in a study, found that a 100-showing has a reach of 89.2% and a frequency of 31 times in one month among adults.[4] Studies in San Francisco, Seattle, Los Angeles, Chicago, and New York showed consistently similar results. Outdoor advertising, it was also shown, develops its high reach rapidly, with the frequency increasing steadily throughout the month of posting. The combination of reach and frequency results in the high awareness outdoor advertising develops for the advertised messages.

While outdoor advertising reaches the entire population, it is especially likely to reach the kind of people who are the best prospects as buyers for many products and services. In the language of the trade, it delivers its highest levels of frequency of opportunity for exposure among upper socioeconomic people. People of this kind evidently can and do travel, drive cars, more than do the lower socioeconomic people.

And logic indicates that the more you drive, the greater your opportunity for exposure to outdoor advertising. The validity of this inference was demonstrated by A. C. Nielsen, in a 28-day diary study of travel patterns in Los Angeles and Orange Counties.[5] Dividing his respondents into quartiles according to the amount of annual household driving, he found that the reach among potential viewing families moved rapidly to saturation, while frequency continued to rise as mileage increased.

Following this logic, data in the W. R. Simmons & Associates studies, "Selective Markets and the Media Reaching Them," were analyzed in terms of exposure opportunity based on annual mileage. With respect to men, for example, the majority of those in the higher income and education brackets were found to be in the high-mileage driving groups, with greater opportunity for exposure to outdoor advertising. In like manner, the purchasers of many specific products or services also fell into the high-mileage driving groups. And with respect to all adults, about 46% are in the high-mileage driving category; but more than 55% of those who bought gasoline or cameras are in the high-mileage driving group. These relationships are exhibited in two accompanying tables.

MEN'S INCOME AND EDUCATION RELATED TO ANNUAL
HOUSEHOLD AUTOMOBILE DRIVING

Miles Driven during Year	All Men	Income $10,000+	College Education
10,000 miles or more	61.6%	68.4%	67.2%
Under 10,000 miles	29.4%	27.6%	27.7%
No car owned	9.0%	4.0%	5.1%

ADULTS' PURCHASES OF GASOLINE AND CAMERAS RELATED TO
ANNUAL HOUSEHOLD AUTOMOBILE DRIVING

Miles Driven during Year	All Adults	Gasoline (1)	Cameras (2)
10,000 miles or more	45.9%	55.5%	56.3%
Under 10,000 miles	38.5%	41.5%	35.2%
No car owned	15.6%	3.0%	8.5%

(1) Bought in last 3 months.   (2) Acquired in past year.

Circulation is an indication of the number of people potentially exposed to advertising. Outdoor advertising delivers the largest circulation and opportunity for exposure of any advertising medium. In addition, outdoor advertising develops high levels of readership or remembrance. This has been shown in several studies conducted by research organizations such as A. C. Nielsen, Alfred Politz, and Plan One. For example, Alfred Politz found that the average poster was remembered by 46.9% of all adults.

In other studies conducted by Nielsen and Politz using rigorous techniques, similarly high levels were found. To briefly illustrate, Politz in Los Angeles found the "Reported Recognition Average Score" for posters was

42.4%. In New York, Nielsen's "General Remembrance" average was 45% for all adults.

The averages reported in all these studies refer to total market population—not to particular segments of the population such as readers of the current issue, as is often the case in reports for other media.

COSTS AND USES OF THE MEDIUM

In terms of cost-per-thousand for daily impression opportunities, outdoor poster advertising costs average 26¢ per thousand. The average cost-per-thousand has increased over the past ten years. However, there has also been an increase in potential audience as measured by outdoor travel during the same period. Automobile registrations, gasoline consumption, and passenger automobile mileage have all increased over the same time, at least until the onset of the fuel shortage that began in late 1973; these changes indicate that on the whole an increasingly larger audience has been exposed to the outdoor advertising medium. By mid-1976, Americans were driving more than ever before.

In order to determine the best use of outdoor advertising, it is necessary first to decide upon the type best suited to the marketing strategy to be employed in any given case; that is, whether posters, painted bulletins, spectaculars, semispectaculars, or some combination or all of these types is best suited to the needs at hand.

If posters are chosen, it is then necessary to decide upon the size of the showing, the months of posting, and the markets to be covered. If painted bulletins or spectaculars are to be used, both the markets and the specific locations within markets must be selected.

The size of the poster showing to be used depends upon (1) the depth of penetration desired, (2) the importance of frequent repetition of the advertising message, (3) competitive activity in the market, and (4) the budget. The cost of a 100-showing usually runs a little less than double that of a 50-showing and includes fewer than twice as many panels. The size of the budget therefore has a very direct bearing upon the size of the showing. The level of remembrance achieved by a poster showing depends primarily upon the copy rather than upon the size of the showing. However, the amount of repetition is a result of the number of posters on display. On the basis of cost-per-thousand circulation, the 50-showing is thought by some advertisers to be a more efficient buy than the 100-showing. However, on the basis of cost-per-thousand total impression opportunities, the 100-showing is at least as efficient. Here again, it should be noted that repetition is an important consideration in outdoor advertising and should not be minimized in determining the best use of the medium. The importance of added market penetration and repetition must be weighed against the cost factor in considering the question of the size of showing to be employed.

During 1975, a 100-showing in New York City consisted of 437 panels and cost $80,507 a month. A 50-showing cost $51,795 per month for 275 panels. In Washington, D.C., 77 panels made up a 100-showing for a monthly charge of $10,849 as opposed to a 50-showing of 40 panels for $6,155.[6]

The Traffic Audit Bureau has shown that in the typical middle-sized cities of Fort Wayne, Indiana, and Cedar Rapids, Iowa, a 50-showing has nearly as great a reach as a 100-showing but that the amount of repetition is twice as great in the larger showing. However, these findings cannot necessarily be applied to larger metropolitan areas. In cities where suburban living is extensive, population and business are widely dispersed. Instead of moving from the residential section to the downtown business district regularly for daily work or shopping, people tend to move within the confines of their own area of the city. Thus, the whole population is not reachable with a minimum number of panels located on a few heavily traveled arteries; it becomes necessary to have outdoor posters located both in the area of the central city and at strategic points throughout the entire suburban area.

To achieve adequate penetration in a metropolitan market, a larger number of panels in proportion to the population is required than in many smaller cities like Cedar Rapids. It is difficult to generalize on this subject because the geographical and business characteristics of each market and the resulting traffic pattern vary considerably, as do the facilities of the individual poster plants. The number of poster showings in a market varies widely depending upon its size and importance. Small highway towns offer facilities for only a few 100-showings, whereas large metropolitan areas may offer as many as 30 to 35 places for 100-showings. Also, under some circumstances a larger showing may be more desirable in a smaller community than in a larger city. For example, in a small highway town a 100-showing may consist of a panel at each highway exit or entrance. The use of less than a 100-showing under such circumstances might well result in losing entirely that part of the outdoor audience that uses only one highway en route to market.

The question is sometimes raised concerning the comparative value of outdoor advertising in winter and summer. According to the Institute of Outdoor Advertising, with the increases in the mobility of the population and in automobile ownership, the expansion of community shopping centers, the growth in year-round play and vacation, there is very little variation in monthly traffic movements. Traffic counts continually made by the Traffic Audit Bureau further substantiate this finding.

SUMMARY

Like other advertising media, outdoor advertising originated in ancient times. Today, outdoor advertising accounts for more than $335 million of advertising revenue each year. It is represented by the Outdoor Advertising Association of America and circulations are audited by the Traffic Audit Bureau.

Plant operators erect and maintain the billboards or poster panels. Their circulation had been measured on the basis of showings. This is being replaced by a system of gross rating points.

NOAB assists its advertising agency members in all phases of outdoor advertising except the creative function.

Outdoor advertising is divided into four categories—posters, painted displays, semispectaculars, and electrical spectaculars.

Unlike most media, the outdoor advertising audience comes to it. They see it on their daily rounds, usually while in their cars.

QUESTIONS AND DISCUSSION SUBJECTS

1. What are the four major kinds of outdoor advertising, and on what basis is each obtained by the advertiser?
2. What functions are performed by an outdoor advertising plant owner?
3. What are the limitations and the advantages of outdoor advertising from the advertiser's point of view?
4. What factors are considered in evaluating an outdoor advertising location?
5. What are some of the more important factors to consider in creating an outdoor advertising poster?
6. Why would an advertiser elect to use a painted bulletin instead of a 30-sheet poster showing? In addition to a 30-sheet poster showing?
7. Is it possible to obtain any selectivity with respect to audience in outdoor advertising? How or why not?
8. How does the Traffic Audit Bureau audit and evaluate outdoor circulations and poster locations?
9. What are the functions of NOAB?
10. What are showings? What are gross rating points?

SOURCES

1. Hugh E. Agnew, *Advertising Media* (New York: D. Van Nostrand, 1932).
2. "Outdoor Reaches Consumer on Move," *Advertising Age,* November 21, 1973, 112.
3. *Outdoor Advertising and Gross Rating Points* (New York: Outdoor Advertising Association of America).
4. *She Was Crowned Miss America 1975 on a Top-Rated TV Special. But Hardly Anybody Knew Her Name* (New York: Institute of OutdoorAdvertising, 1975).
5. A diary study of travel patterns in Los Angeles and Orange Counties by A. C. Nielsen for Foster & Kleiser, a division of Metromedia.
6. *Ayer Media Facts 1975* (New York: N. W. Ayer, 1976), 20.

FOR FURTHER READING

Association of National Advertisers. *Essentials of Outdoor Advertising.* New York: Association of National Advertisers, 1968.

Barton, Roger. *The Handbook of Advertising Management.* New York: McGraw-Hill, 1970.

Grayson, Melvin J. *Billboards the Clean Medium.* New York: Outdoor Advertising Association of America, 1974.

Houck, John, ed. *Outdoor Advertising: History and Regulation.* South Bend, Ind.: University of Notre Dame Press, 1969.

This Is Outdoor Advertising. New York: Institute of Outdoor Advertising, 1972 and later editions.

$$\begin{matrix} \star \\ \star \\ \star \\ \star \\ \star \end{matrix}$$ **25**

Transit Advertising

SOME HISTORY

As early as 1850 Lord & Taylor, a department store, placed advertisements on the exterior of New York City horse-drawn streetcars. This is the earliest recorded use of transit advertising in the United States. Between 1850 and 1880, growth of this medium was slow, but with the introduction of electric-powered streetcars it became increasingly important, and by 1888 the first full-time streetcar advertising firms were in operation in Detroit and St. Louis.

Artemas Ward is credited with the first genuine use of the medium for national advertising, sometime after 1895. His dramatic promotion, primarily through car cards, of the home cleanser Sapolio to the status of a household word encouraged him to form his own company. Within four years he was able to offer transit advertising in 93 cities and 14,000 cars.

Starting in 1890, Barron G. Collier did much to organize and standardize the transit advertising business and in so doing made it increasingly attractive to national as well as to local advertisers. He even employed F. Scott Fitzgerald and Ogden Nash as copywriters. By 1917 Collier had built so strong an organization that he felt he could deny the customary 15% commission to advertising agencies without injury to himself or the transit advertising industry. Although this action is perhaps indicative of the independence that Collier had achieved for transit advertising, it no doubt retarded its development during the next 12 years, or until commissions were again granted in 1929.

After the collapse of the Collier empire and his death in 1939, some 20 Collier leases in Boston, Philadelphia, Washington, and other cities were combined to form National Transitads, Inc. This company, in addition to operating in the cities where it held leases, also served as a national selling agency representing independent operators in other cities. Shortly following the formation of National Transitads, the Loomis Advertising Company was organized and in 1949 became a part of Mutual Transportation Advertising, Inc. Of these two organizations, Mutual is the survivor under the name Mutual Transit Sales. Mutual, as did Transitads, serves as a national selling agency for the medium. The New York Subways Advertising Company, another organization formed from the Collier holdings, by 1971 was doing about 20% of the total transit advertising of the United States.

In 1942 the forerunner of today's Transit Advertising Association (TAA) was formed. At various times TAA was known as the National Association of Transportation Advertising and later as the National Association of Transit Advertising, but the original name was restored in 1961. At first based in New York City, the Association moved to Washington in 1971. Attesting to the global nature of the medium, TAA in turn is a member of the World Transad Association, based in Paris. At the time TAA was founded, some 50 companies were operating in the transit advertising field; the first job of the newly organized trade association was to bring about order and business-like procedures within the industry. A first step in this direction was the development of a standard order form by a joint committee of TAA and the American Association of Advertising Agencies. Other of TAA's activities that helped strengthen the position of the transit medium were:

1. The establishment of standards for the medium.
2. The conducting of research and the serving as a central information bureau for all transit advertising information.
3. The promotion of increased use of the medium by local, regional, and national advertisers.
4. The cooperation with other advertising associations for the improvement of advertising as a whole.

At the request of TAA, the Advertising Research Foundation in 1944 started *The Continuing Study of Transportation Advertising*. The main objectives of the study were to discover the general characteristics and riding habits of the transit advertising audience and to find out how many people aged 15 and older saw and remembered specific car cards displayed for the usual 30-day carding period in each of the markets studied. This study included 13 transit markets,* and enabled the medium to offer both quantitative and qualitative facts about its audience to actual and potential users of transit advertising space.

TRANSIT ADVERTISING TODAY

The transit advertising medium comprises three major areas of operation. They are:

* The term *market* is not synonymous with the term *city*. A market may comprise two or more neighboring cities and their adjacent suburban communities. There are approximately 380 transit markets in the United States.

1. Car cards, which are advertisements placed within subway and other rapid transit cars, streetcars, buses, and suburban railroad cars.
2. Posters, which are placed on station platforms, in stations, and in railway and airport terminals.
3. Exterior displays, which are advertisements painted or posted on the outside of streetcars and buses.

Some transit advertising companies also handle the advertising space on timetables and the various special three-dimensional and other types of platform displays and spectaculars in stations.

In the mid-1970s, new subway and rapid-transit lines provided means of transportation in a growing number of the larger urban centers in the United States. Among these are San Francisco and Washington, D.C. But buses are and have long been the chief means of intraurban public transport in the majority of communities and the chief carriers of transit advertising in most locations where the medium is available. Over 40,000 incorporated places in the United States depend entirely on buses as their means of mass public transportation. The TAA placed the number of vehicles bearing advertising, in 1972, at more than 70,000. Buses carry nearly 40 million passengers each month.

There are 380 markets available for car cards and for exterior displays. Expenditures in the medium amounted to an estimated $35,000,000 plus, in 1969. That figure doubled by the end of 1973.[1]

Organization of the Industry

The transit advertising business is conducted by independent transit advertising companies called *operators*. There are about seventy such companies in the United States. Operators and services are available for the fifty states and the District of Columbia. Each operator sells and services local accounts and in some cases regional accounts as well.

Operators bid for an exclusive lease on the transit advertising space of one or more transit companies. The operator who obtains the lease then makes this space available to local and national advertisers on a contract basis. In all but a few of the larger cities, a single operator holds the exclusive lease on all space "in, on, or about" the transportation facilities of his city. The National Outdoor Advertising Bureau, which provides such a wonderful service for outdoor advertisers, provides a similar service for national transit advertisers.

The operator places and maintains the car cards, posters, or exterior displays for the duration of the contract and provides affidavits that contract terms have been fulfilled. The advertiser must provide the cards and posters at least ten days before the desired showing date, but in most cases the operator will assist local accounts with copy, layout, and production if they desire such help. Furthermore, many operators provide merchandising services that may include getting in touch with distributors concerning the account, addressing meetings of salesmen and explaining the relation between the transit medium and their

sales efforts, aiding the advertiser's representatives with local distribution outlets and mailings of literature about the account, and telling how the advertiser
is reaching the market through his transit advertising campaign.

The operator pays the customary 15% commission to advertising agencies.
In addition, often as much as 50% to 70% of his income may go to the transit
company for the exclusive lease of the advertising space.

Car Cards

Car card space is sold on the basis of:

1. A *full run*—one card in every car in a transit system.
2. A *half run*—one card in one-half of the cars in a transit system.
3. A *quarter run*—one card in one-quarter of the cars in a transit system.
4. A *double run*—two cards in every car in a transit system.

Sometimes the term *showing* or *service* is used instead of *run*. That is, the
reference is to a *full showing* or a *full service,* or a *half showing* or a *half service,* and so on. Quarter runs and half runs are not available in all cities,
especially in the smaller communities. However, the half run, taking the
country as a whole, is the most frequently used by advertisers.

In New York City subway cars, runs double inasmuch as a full run consists of two cards in every car; thus a half run becomes two cards in one-half of
the cars, and so on. Reasons for this doubling are the length of the subway cars
and their three to six means of entrance and exit. A rider in such a car would be
less likely to be exposed to a card under the usual definition of the term *run*
than in the smaller vehicles used in many other cities. There are buses in New
York City, however, that feature only one card per vehicle.

Rates are usually based on 12 months of consecutive service with shorter
periods commanding higher rates. For example, a 6- to 11-month rate runs 5%
higher than a 12-month rate, a 3- to 5-month rate 10% higher, and a 1-month
rate 20% higher. The usual contract is for 6 months to 1 year. Space is billed
monthly, and the usual contract carries a 60-day cancellation clause.

Cards are usually changed once a month although some advertisers leave
them up longer. The placement of cards in vehicles, changing them once a
month, and normal maintenance are included in the monthly rate. However, if
cards are to be changed more frequently than once a month, a service charge is
made. Also, a monthly charge, usually about 10%, is added to the face amount
of the contract when pads, printed notices, or other detachable matter are a part
of the card. This additional charge is to cover the extra labor of replacing the
detachable elements of these so-called *take-one cards.*

It is common practice for the operator to specify an overrun (more cards
than the number needed to fill the purchased space at any given time) in order
that replacements may be made when cards become damaged or soiled, or have
been stolen. The operator informs the advertiser of the required size of the
overrun, a figure determined in terms of the length of time the cards are to be
used and the transit line on which they are to be placed.

The user of car card space may advertise several products on different cards in different vehicles or use several different pieces of copy at the same time without increasing space costs. Such practice, of course, would increase production costs of the cards. Some advertisers print on both sides of their cards so that they may be turned over in the rack on a specified date to obtain a new display. This practice affords economies in printing, shipping, and handling, but advertisers who have used it have, in many cases, found that there may be offsetting disadvantages.

The carding department of the operator keeps an exact record of each card in the vehicle it services, and the placement of cards is so arranged that each advertiser receives a well-balanced showing of cards in all side positions. Except for those, such special positions as the front and rear of vehicles, all cards are 11 inches high. The advertiser may choose among several lengths depending upon his own needs and the offerings available within specific cities. The $11'' \times 28''$, $11'' \times 42''$, and $11'' \times 56''$ cards are the sizes most commonly used. When the advertiser wishes to avail himself of unusual layouts or gain greater dominance, he may choose the giant $11'' \times 84''$ cards. Other sizes are the $22'' \times 21''$ and the $16'' \times 44''$ displays. It is apparent that an advertiser can seek media domination either by the use of the oversized giant cards or by use of multiples of the smaller cards placed at intervals around the vehicle. Such domination is more readily assured in transit advertising than in many other kinds of media because each display has a fixed maximum of advertising competition within the car or bus. That is, only a fixed amount of space is available for advertising and it cannot be expanded to meet increased demand from advertisers.

Take-one cards offer still another opportunity to the user of car card space. *Take-ones* are perforated cards attached to a pad that is affixed to either lower corner or both corners of the car card. The perforations make the individual sheets or cards easily detachable from the pad, and the viewer is invited to tear one off for closer inspection, to take home, or to mail in for the product or service.

Car cards are viewed from two possible positions—either a standing position that places them on or near the reader's eye level or a seated position that places them at an angle above eye level. Furthermore, all but a few car cards are seen by any one observer at an increasingly oblique angle as he looks toward the front or rear of the vehicle's card rack. This tends to foreshorten illustrations and condense lettering increasingly as the distance between the reader and the card is increased. For these reasons pictures should be kept simple, and copy should be set in reasonably large, medium-weight, well-spaced type.

Car cards, with the exception of the special-position cards, are uniform in size, and most of them are in color. Hence there is a degree of similarity in the unbroken line of advertisements in the side racks of vehicles. The layout artist thus has the problem of creating a card that will stand out from competition— a problem common to the creating of all forms of advertising. But its solution is made more difficult in the case of car cards because of size similarity and the

A typical subway car card (11″ x 42″). *Courtesy of the Transit Advertising Association.*

proximity of advertisement to advertisement. However, according to surveys, some advertisers have been very successful in overcoming this difficulty, achieving readership scores twice as great as competitors who used comparable space.

Important elements in the design must be kept away from the edges of the card because quarter-inch flanges on the top and bottom and a flat steel spring on each side hold the card in place in the vehicle's rack. This framing covers the edges and would obscure any illustration or printed matter that was carried to the edges of the card. A bleed effect can be obtained by carrying the background color or illustration to within an eighth of an inch of the edges of the card.

Five-ply white stock is standard for car cards, which may be varnished according to need. Full color commands no extra premium for space costs, and production costs for color in car cards are not high. Special effects are obtainable by use of fluorescent colors, foils, and three-dimensional displays in plastic or cardboard. In recent years some cities have introduced transparent backlighted units inside and outside the vehicles.

Car cards have been regarded by some advertisers and writers as "miniature billboards," and copy accordingly has been reduced to headlines and subheads. There is no objection to such copy treatment and in many cases it has proved very successful. Copy can, however, be of some length, for car cards

Never mind the "A" train.
Catch Pan Am's next 747.
To Paris.
London.
San Juan.
Honolulu.
Hong Kong.
Tokyo.
Or Frankfurt. (Soon)

Pan Am's *747*
The plane with all the room in the world.

This subway car card measures 22" x 21" and is placed at the front or rear of the car. *Courtesy of the Transit Advertising Association.*

are not seen only in passing as are billboards; they are before the reader for an extended period of time. That car cards can be treated quite differently from billboards is made apparent by the success of some of the comic-strip advertising done on car cards and of some that have been composed of copy only, carrying no illustrations.

Exterior Displays

Exterior displays, formerly called traveling displays, came into use as advertisements placed on the outside of vehicles some time after car cards had appeared on the inside. As originally conceived and used for many years, the traveling display was an advertisement placed on the front or and rear of streetcar dashboards. Because of this placement they came to be known as *dashboards* or *dashes,* and it was not until 1947 that the name *traveling display* was adopted by the trade, and later *exterior display.*

There was no uniformity in the size of the early dashes, and this tended to discourage their use by national advertisers. Because of their locations on the vehicles, the dashes were always higher than they were wide and so were displayed as vertical rectangles. It was not until buses were in common use that the traveling displays were moved to the sides of vehicles and became horizon-

A king-size poster (30″ x 144″). *Courtesy of the Transit Advertising Association.*

tal rectangular displays. In 1947 the Transit Advertising Association succeeded in standardizing the size so as to reduce production costs for advertisers and make exterior displays more attractive to national advertisers. At that time a uniform height of 21 inches and a width of 41 inches were adopted. Most markets currently offer the 21″ × 44″ display.

These displays are carried on both sides of the buses, and it is estimated that on the average they travel about 3,000 miles per month. The research committee of TAA developed a new technique for measuring potential advertising exposures of exterior displays, employing a camera capable of taking 1,600 single-frame exposures without reloading. Prior to this time, studies had been made by checkers riding bus routes and using hand meters to count the number of people who had a clear view of the exterior displays. A study conducted by the camera technique indicated a daily potential advertising exposure of 15,960 for one exterior display. This finding was based on 39 recordings taken on 10 different bus routes between 8 a.m. and 6 p.m. A study of king-size displays (see below) conducted in Philadelphia in 1959 indicated that each resident (plus the transients) was exposed at least four times to the exterior displays. This figure was substantiated by tests in Chicago in 1964 and 1965.

It is believed that best effects are obtained if such displays are produced in

Passengers as well as others along the route are exposed to this travelling display on the outside of a bus. *Courtesy of the Transit Advertising Association.*

poster style with letters not smaller than 1¾ inches in height. Bold colors are regarded as better in most cases than pastel shades.

The *traffic-ad* or *traffic spectacular* was introduced in the 1950s and has since become known as the *king-size display*. As originally developed, these spectaculars took the form of either oversized posters or painted displays on the sides of buses and streetcars. In some cases the advertisements were painted directly on the sides of the vehicles; in other cases they were painted on hardboard or were posters fixed within exterior display frames on the sides of the vehicles. At present, although the painted display is still available in a few markets, the king-size poster is in more common use. The most common available size, obtainable in most markets, is 30″ × 144″. Other exterior displays include the *queen size* (30″ × 88″) and the *taillight spectacular* (21″ × 72″). The posters obviously offer more flexibility than painted displays.

King-size bus posters are sold in showings. A *100-showing* insures the advertiser multiple coverage on every base route—both main streets and arteries—in the market. A *50-showing* gives the advertiser displays on every base route with multiple displays on important streets. Generally an advertiser can buy as many or as few positions as he needs or feels that he can afford. In most markets discounts are obtainable for 3 to 12 months of consecutive showings.

As in outdoor advertising, the cost of any specific showing varies from city to city. The justification for the differences is found in the number involved, the routes covered, and the potential audience involved.

King-size bus posters are lithographed or silk-screened on paper, mounted on Masonite panels, and inserted in frames on the sides of the vehicles. As in other forms of transit advertising, the advertiser is responsible for the art, copy, and reproduction work. The operator mounts, places, and maintains the display.

Inasmuch as traveling displays are seen on the sides of moving vehicles and sometimes at considerable distances, copy should be short, lettering large, and illustrations simple.

Recently, exterior roofline backlighted units called *busorama* were introduced. They are 22 inches high and 144 inches wide.

A new concept is *consumer bus* or *basic bus*. This consists of all of the advertising space on the inside of a given number of regularly scheduled buses. All of the advertising space on the outside of a bus is called *total bus*. And a combination of the two—all of the exterior and interior space—is *total total bus*.

Merchandising buses present an additional promotional opportunity. They are regular buses that can be chartered and turned into special mobile displays of actual products. In effect they become traveling exhibits and mobile showcases that can be driven directly to retailers and wholesalers for their exclusive viewing.

Platform Displays

Posters in standard 1-sheet, 2-sheet, 3-sheet, and 6-sheet sizes are placed on the stations of rapid-transit systems and suburban railroads.

Poster positions are sold on the basis of showings that are designated as *intensive, representative* or *minimum*. The number of posters in any one of these showings varies from city to city.

Contracts run from 1 to 12 months, but 1- and 2-month contracts do not carry rate-earning privileges. Posters may be changed monthly without additional cost to the advertiser.

Art is treated in traditional outdoor advertising poster style, and copy usually is short even though under most circumstances the reader has ample time to inspect station posters.

In recent years, *special transit displays*—subway and terminal clocks with adjacent backlighted ads—have also made their appearance.

USERS OF THE MEDIUM

Car cards and other forms of transit advertising are used by both local and national advertisers. However, local advertisers are the larger users in small markets, national advertisers in large ones. The local advertiser frequently takes advantage of the fact that he need not contract to place advertisements in an entire transit system, and uses that part of the system that serves or comes closest to serving his trading area or even the street on which his business is located.

Many national advertisers have used the medium consistently for 35 to 50 years. It has been used extensively for dealer-cooperative advertising programs. The Frigidaire Division of General Motors is credited with being the first major household-appliance manufacturer to employ the medium in this way. Both Wrigley's Chewing Gum and Campbell's Soups were long-time and very large users of transit advertising, Campbell's employing its first car cards as long ago as 1899.[2] The medium has also been used successfully by many advertisers for seasonal promotions.

Although a number of costly products like automobiles have been advertised through the transit advertising medium, for the most part it is used by advertisers who sell relatively low-priced, widely used impulse items or services.

Although the transit advertising medium can be and has been used in combination with other media to introduce new products, it probably lends itself more readily to the advertising of products that are in the competitive or retentive stages of development rather than those in an introductory stage. It is actually two media in one (exterior and interior) and is used effectively alone or as part of the media mix.

AUDIENCES

Transit advertising is an urban medium as well as a suburban one. Therefore, its audience is composed of city and suburban dwellers—a very large percentage of this group—irrespective of age, sex, or income.

The Continuing Study of Transportation Advertising, a classic historic study, shows that within the 13 markets studied an average of 80% of the total basic population were riders for at least one round trip during a 30-day showing period.

In the market areas investigated, 8 out of 10 housewives and 9 out of 10 nonhousewives used the transit systems. There was not much variation in the percentage of riders from each of the four groups studied. Young riders were somewhat more numerous than older ones according to the study, and a larger percentage of the female population than of the male rode the transit systems.

As for any advertising medium, the potential audience is perhaps of less importance to the advertiser than the actual number of people who see, read, and remember the advertising. Studies have shown that a high percentage of riders read and remember car cards to which they are exposed. Of 149 car cards tested in 13 cities, the 15 highest-scoring cards had an average audience of 42% of all riders, 43% of the women riders, and 45% of the men riders.[3]

It is also worthy of note that much of the transit advertising audience is a "constant" audience. That is, of the 8 in 10 people who ride the public transit systems, 6 make from 4 to 10 or more rides per week. It is probable that many, if not most, of these are people traveling to and from their work or shopping and so are regular or constant users of the public transportation facilities. This group provides the user of transit advertising space with a hard-core audience that is repeatedly exposed to his car cards, station posters, or exterior displays. A study conducted by the Transit Advertising Association showed that in markets of over a million population, 46% of all white-collar workers, 50% of all blue-collar men and women, 31% of all adults in households with annual incomes of $10,000 or more, and 24% of adults in households with two or more automobiles travel in public vehicles which carry advertising.[4]

CHARACTERISTICS AND ADVANTAGES OF TRANSIT ADVERTISING

Among the advantages stated for transit advertising is its relatively low per capita cost. As has already been noted, it is estimated that in the average city 8 out of 10 people aged 15 or older ride the public transit systems. The average cost per thousand (CPM) for inside space is 15¢ to 20¢ and for exterior space 7¢.

Another advantage claimed by the medium is the average length of ride and the repetition of exposure of transit advertising to riders. Studies have shown that the average ride on bus, rapid transit, and suburban lines in the United States is approximately 23 minutes, for a total, in some cases, of more than an hour per day.[5] Such rides are repeated 24 times during the course of a month.[6] For example, one study in New York City reveals that the average subway rider takes 39 rides per month.

The transit medium is a relatively flexible one that permits the advertiser to select specific cities or even specific transit lines within a given city for placement of his sales messages. Transit advertising also presents the sales messages of local advertisers within short distances of the point of purchase.

Competition from other advertisers is limited by the availability of space. More transit advertising space cannot be added to accommodate increased demands from advertisers except, perhaps, under very unusual circumstances. During a newspaper strike in New York City in the midst of the Christmas shoping season, advertisements of retail stores were pasted on some of the windows of subway cars and buses. This, however, represented a very unusual situation.

Transit advertising is available in full color with no extra space costs associated with its use. (Since the advertiser pays for the printing he will, of course, pay more for color reproduction.) Color reproduction costs are not high. Use of color, as in other media, serves as an attention-getter, aids in package identification, and presents the product in a more lifelike and attractive manner.

The crowded conditions of some city transit lines during the rush hours, periods that incidentally add appreciably to circulation counts, are somewhat short of ideal for viewing and reading a range of car cards. But despite such conditions, studies have shown a high percentage of readership for the medium as a whole.

Although it is true that an exterior display is an advertisement in motion presented to a market in motion, in the crowded streets of modern American cities bus speeds are not fast (an estimated eight to ten miles an hour) with frequent stops to take on or discharge passengers, for traffic lights, and for traffic tie-ups. Therefore, the illustration is readily visible and the copy legible to both pedestrian and motor-vehicle traffic. In addition, the sales message of the exterior display is presented near eye level and is frequently carried into sections of the city where outdoor advertising is prohibited by zoning laws or other city ordinances.

SUMMARY

The first known advertising on a public conveyance was carried by a horse-drawn New York streetcar in mid-19th century. Since that time transit advertising has become a familiar sight on metropolitan subways, buses, streetcars, and railroad cars.

Barron G. Collier, a pioneer in transit advertising, dominated the field from 1890 until his death in 1939. He was a prime mover in the standardization and organization of the industry. He even eliminated the 15% agency commission, which was finally restored in 1929. Three years after Collier's death the organization that is known today as the Transit Advertising Association was established. At that time there were about 50 transit advertising companies. Today there are some 70 companies, known as operators.

Transit advertising employs car cards posters, and exterior displays. Car cards are sold on the basis of runs. A full run means a card in every car in a particular transit system. There are also fractional and multiple runs. In some cases the terms *showing* or *service* are used instead of *run*. The most common sizes are $11'' \times 28''$, $11'' \times 42''$ and $11'' \times 65''$. New innovations include the consumer bus or basic bus, total bus, merchandising bus, and transparent or backlighted units.

Transit advertising is used by local and national advertisers. The audience is both urban and suburban. A very high percentage of that audience use the transit systems, and frequently.

A unique feature of transit advertising, like outdoor advertising, is that there is no increased space cost for full color.

QUESTIONS AND DISCUSSION SUBJECTS

1. Give examples of products and/or services that might be *better* served by transit advertising than by any other medium. Explain why.
2. What are the three major areas of operation of transit advertising?
3. Name some other areas of transit advertising operation.
4. What does an operator do?

5. Who provides the printed car cards—the operator or the advertiser?
6. Define the following, as related to transit advertising: basic bus; take-one cards; total bus; dashes; total total bus; busorama; quarter run; intensive.
7. The —— run is the most frequently used by advertisers (full, half, quarter, double).
8. How much more does the space cost in transit advertising when color is used on car cards instead of black-and-white?

SOURCES

1. "Transit Advertising Prospers," *Advertising Age,* November 1, 1973, 126.
2. *The Continuing Study of Transportation Advertising,* conducted by the Advertising Research Foundation in cooperation with the Transit Advertising Association (13-Study Summary, 1950).
3. George T. Clarke, *Transit Advertising* (New York: Transit Advertising Association, 1970), 14.
4. Sindlinger and Co., *The Transit Millions* (New York: Transit Advertising Association, 1964).
5. *Ibid.*
6. Clarke, *op. cit.,* 53.

FOR FURTHER READING

Clarke, George T. *Transit Advertising.* New York: Transit Advertising Association, 1970.
Sindlinger and Co. *The Transit Millions.* New York: Transit Advertising Association, 1964.
"Transit Advertising—Colorful History, Tremendous Future," *Bus Ride,* September–October 1972.

Point-of-Purchase Advertising

In a broad sense, point-of-purchase advertising is any advertising done at the place where the goods are sold.[1] This definition would include the use of advertising materials conceived and developed by the retailer as well as those created by or for the manufacturer. However, current usage has narrowed the concept of point-of-purchase advertising to include only those displays and advertisements or promotional pieces created by or for the manufacturer and made available through him to the retailer for use at the point where the goods are sold.

Point-of-purchase advertising differs from all other forms in that it alone delivers the advertiser's message at the location where the advertised goods or services are sold. Therefore, it serves as an attention-getter, a reminder, and an introducer of new products—and in general exerts a selling influence at a time and in a place where the prospect can act immediately upon the suggestion to buy. Furthermore, point-of-purchase advertising can draw together all the messages and art appeals used in other media and capitalize on the favorable climate created by other marketing activities.

Because the product is right at hand when a shopper sees the advertising, point-of-purchase sales messages give strong impetus to impulse buying. Point-of-purchase, conveniently known as P-O-P, is not a medium in the same sense as other media. The medium, in effect, is the retail outlet—wherever it is, whether stationary or on the move. P-O-P—the signs and displays placed in, on, at, or adjacent to the medium—might be more accurately compared to the ad that appears in the magazine (the medium), to the commercial which appears on television (the medium), or to the commercial message which may be heard on the radio. The point of purchase really is the retail outlet and P-O-P might better be called *environmental marketing,* which would include the activity of placing signs and displays at the point of purchase and in whatever way altering the environment for a particular sponsor, whether a retailer or a manufacturer of products or a purveyor of services.

P-O-P has three principal functions: to inform, to identify, and to merchandise. P-O-P is successful to the degree that it itself is not noticed but that its functions are fulfilled. Its main purpose is to perform a service for the customer by making it easier for the customer to find what is wanted and to know more about products or services, and thereby to provide a basis for buying decisions.

P-O-P as a form of marketing has its origins lost in the dim past. Signs and some forms of display were used in the early bazaars of Europe, Asia, and, North Africa. In Greek and Roman times, signs were used to designate special shops. In America, the cigar-store Indian was among the earliest of P-O-P units, designating where the products of America's first cash crop—tobacco—were sold.

By the middle of the 19th century, P-O-P began to come into its own. Calendars, clocks, posters, and racks were the most used. Today these are collectors' items—antiques—rarely seen outside museums. In the early part of the 20th century the cigarette companies were the largest users of P-O-P and thriving installation companies made money placing their printed units in the windows of drugstores, tobacco shops, and grocery stores.

POINT-OF-PURCHASE ADVERTISING INSTITUTE

Following World War I P-O-P was eclipsed by the surging forward of the print media and radio, and after World War II by television. However, P-O-P continued to grow as an industry. Because it did not have the novelty of radio and television, and had always been around, it found itself at the end of the line on promotion budgets. Between the two world wars, several attempts were made to organize the industry. But it was not until 1938, when the Point-of-Purchase Advertising Institute (or POPAI) was established, that point-of-purchase began to take its place in modern business. Today it serves such major industries as these:

Automotive supplies—passenger cars, petroleum products, trucks, tractors, trailers, etc.

Beverages—beer, liquors and wines, and soft drinks.

Foods—baked goods, candy and chewing gum, canned and processed foods, dairy and frozen foods, fresh meat, produce, and seafood.

Household goods—major appliances such as stoves, washers, refrigerators, etc.; building and garden supplies; farm supplies; hardware, paints, and floor coverings; home entertainment products; home furnishings; housewares and small appliances.

Personal accessories—jewelry and other personal items, wearing apparel, footwear.

Recreational goods—photographic equipment and supplies, records,

The OMA–Outstanding Merchandising Achievement–award is a symbol of excellence in point-of-purchase advertising. The figure is a stylized version of the cigar store Indian, one of America's earliest P-O-P advertising devices. *Courtesy of POPAI.*

record players, tape players, music and musical instruments, sporting goods, toys, books, games.

Personal products—proprietary drugs, accessories and sanitary goods, soaps, cleaners, paper goods, general toiletries, toiletries for men and women.

Miscellaneous—linens, notions, yard goods, pet supplies, personal and public services, stationery, office supplies, greeting cards, tobacco.

While these are the major product classes using P-O-P, it should be noted that almost every product made, and almost every service, can benefit from the judicious use of P-O-P at retail outlets. Among warehouse outlets also there is a growing use for P-O-P, directed to the retailer as a customer.

P-O-P VOLUME AND USE

P-O-P is today a $2-billion industry. The following figures showing annual volume indicate a trend. They are abstracted from the United States Government *Census of Manufacturers* and represent value added to shipments according to the Standard Industrial Classification:

1961	$ 722,596,000
1962	804,623,000
1963	866,249,000
1964	931,500,000
1965	1,058,333,000
1966	1,137,367,000
1967	1,225,000,000
1968	1,500,000,000
1969	1,660,000,000
1970	1,880,000,000

It must be remembered that these figures do not include any "costs of insertion" as do the comparable figures for most other forms of (media) advertising. If in some way the money spent by advertisers to place P-O-P could be calculated, the total figure would be much higher. Some advertisers use a one-to-one rule of thumb to calculate their total costs.

Perhaps a better gauge of the money spent on P-O-P would be some expenditures of individual advertisers. The top four users of point-of-purchase advertising and the annual dollar volume they spent on it in 1971 are:

General Motors Corporation	$44,000,000
Coca Cola	16,000,000
Distillers Corporation— Seagrams Ltd.	13,450,000
Procter & Gamble	9,100,000

P-O-P materials in general are divided into two categories—*promotional,* which are designed to remain in place for a few weeks or months at the most, and are usually made of corrugated board, cardboard, paper, or light plastics; *permanent,* which are designed to remain in place for six months or longer, sometimes even for years, and are usually made from wood, metal, or the more durable plastics. P-O-P dollar volume is about equally divided between these two types.

With the growth in volume and importance of P-O-P has come an increasing awareness on the part of retailers of its value to them. Large chains, with or without an emphasis on private brands, are themselves good users of P-O-P materials.

Competition among advertisers for display space in retail stores is high. This new sophistication among the retailers means that they can demand and get more and more effective P-O-P. The days of sending cheap displays together with every case of goods, whether or not the retailers wanted them, are over. The cry of "waste," often raised in the 1950s and 1960s because of such indiscriminate shipping of displays, has been stilled. For the most part, now,

P-O-P advertisers expect to "sell" their units into the stores, and ship them only on agreement.

Traffic-building "spectaculars," some costing as much as $300 per unit, are often booked in sequence in as many as 15 or 20 stores, thus assuring multiple usage of the same unit. At the lower end of the price scale may be such units as *shelf talkers* or *channel strips,* costing only pennies to produce, which may remain in place for a month or more.

It must be remembered that P-O-P does its informing, identifying, and merchandising in the store environment. It is seen only by people who are approaching a retail outlet, who are looking into the store, or who are actually in it. These people are not relaxed. They are for the most part purposeful, excited to the point where they are prepared to shop. They have money or credit cards in their pockets. They want to buy. P-O-P is designed to heighten that buying mood and to make it easy for the customer to purchase. In doing its job, it makes it easier for the retailer to "wait on" many people at once through self-guidance, self-selection, and self-service. It makes it easier for the retailer to stock more items than he could possibly handle in any other way.

Some impressive figures emerged from a 1971 study entitled *How and Why Shoppers Make Unplanned Purchases in Mass Retailing Stores.* It was based on interviews with 6,695 shoppers in six different representative sections of the country. Their responses stated why an unplanned or impulse purchase was made. Of the respondents, 73% indicated that retail-store-controlled forces were the motivators, 3% attributed the unplanned purchase to manufacturer-controlled forces, 11% named word-of-mouth motivations, and the remaining 13% gave miscellaneous reasons. Not measured, and indeed impossible to measure, were the subtle influences on those interviewed prior to their meeting with the retail-store-controlled forces—preselling and absorption of mass-media messages. Of all answers given, 50% were "Saw it displayed while shopping." Only 1% of the answers credited buying decision to the manufacturer's other advertising, although another 1% made the unplanned purchase because they liked other products of the manufacturer, and still another 1% credited the package design or label.[2]

TYPE CLASSIFICATIONS OF P-O-P

Since each P-O-P unit (which may consist of one or many pieces) is designed to do a specific job for a specific product at a specific time, or for a specific length of time, the result is an almost infinite variety of types. Beyond the general divisions into "promotional" and "permanent" that refer to its length of use, there is another general division into *indoor* and *outdoor,* referring to its place of use or location. Some of the types listed below are suitable for either indoors or outdoors, while some are not. Some of the types, shelf talkers for example, are always promotional and indoor, while others may depend upon the materials they are made of for their classification or according to time of use. The types are listed below with reference to these divisions.

Banners. Flags, pennants, and other such shapes made of cloth or plastic.

Bar and fountain units. These include any and all units designed for use on or surrounding a bar or fountain—stirrer holders, trays, bottle glorifiers, decorative backbar pieces, etc. (Tap markers, also used at bars and fountains but classified separately because they represent a highly competitive field in and of themselves.)

Cash register units. Lighted signs, clocks, wire racks are a few of the more popular forms.

Clocks. Most advertisers like to use this permanent type of P-O-P because a clock once in place, will continue to carry its message, often for years.

Counter units. Supermarkets no longer have counters, but counter units are favorites with drugstores and variety stores where floor space is at a premium and products are commonly sold over counters. Most counter units are merchandisers (they hold product), but others are samplers and testers.

Dealer loaders. These are displays that offer an advantage to the dealer over and beyond the immediate use for a particular promotion, such as a dump bin the retailer can later use for his own promotions.

Department-makers. These may be modular units which together make a total department for a single kind of merchandise, or an encompassing sign or canopy that overarches a merchandise group, or a single merchandiser that features one major item and all the necessary accessories.

Floorstands. Any display that stands on the floor, whether or not it is a merchandiser.

Floorstand (pole). Floorstands of this type may be separately classified since they are a popular group. The distinguishing feature is that a header display is supported at the top of a pole. Merchandise is stacked around the pole for easy pick-up.

On-product units. Such units are usually found accompanying large products such as appliances, or very small products which would otherwise not be noticed. There is also a kind of on-product unit which is designed to sit on a pile of products without pole support.

Overheads. These may be arches, hanging signs, mobiles, or of any type that occupies "air space."

Portable P-O-P. Units not designed for use in any particular retail location but which may be carried into the home or office. Outdoor units in this class would include trucks from which products are sold.

Premium units. Signs or displays designed to feature a premium offer.

Prepacks. These may be shelf, counter, or floor units. They hold merchandise that is packed in the display before shipping to the retail outlet. These units are always promotional, designed for throw-away once the product is sold out.

Racks. Usually, but not always, made of wire. The predominant feature is that they are tailor made in specific dimensions to hold various products

Clocks are popular P-O-P devices because of their relative permanence and continuing usefulness. This Hertz illuminated clock was a POPAI award winner. *Courtesy of POPAI.*

This floorstand display of AC auto accessories won an OMA award. *Courtesy of POPAI.*

An OMA figure was awarded to the Realemon Foods Division of Borden, Inc. for its counter or shelf display. *Courtesy of POPAI.*

415

and sizes, with a lessened emphasis for brand identification and advertising.

Shelf units. These may be shelf organizers, shelf talkers, product spotters,
etc.

Signs. There is a great range here in kind and material. They inform, identify, and advertise. They do not merchandise.

Store fixtures. The main difference between these and racks is that they are
not usually identified for a particular advertiser, although they are
frequently supplied by advertisers to retailers at cost to accommodate
particular merchandise.

Storewides. These are units consisting of numerous pieces of material,
designed to create in-store excitement for a particular event, holiday, or
season.

Tags and labels. For some types of ready-to-wear or do-it-yourself machines, these are good types of P-O-P, giving special information, identification, and advertising.

Total programs. These may consist of any of the above types along with
all the materials used to "sell" the unit into the store and to follow up
on the promotion. Sales-promotion agencies usually specialize in producing total programs. There is another type of total program, usually
distributed by franchisers, wherein the store or boutique is the central
point. A few P-O-P producer/suppliers have handled the entire gamut in
such cases, including selection of the site, preparation of legal documents, construction of the franchised unit, decoration and signing of the
interior and exterior, handling the spacing and placing of stock—with
the contracting owners taking over only on opening day.

Wall units. These can be of any size and for use indoors or out. The main
feature is that they are permanently attached to a wall.

Windows. These may vary from a single unit designed as a product glori-
fier for window use, to a complete window kit usually designed to be
flexible in size to fit the whole or part of a display window.

No list of types can be completely specific or all-inclusive. Many items
such as calendars, thermometers, table tents, and product identifiers must fall
into a miscellaneous classification. Moreover, even a general listing such as
that above must be further specified according to whether or not light and/or
motion is involved. The advertiser who wishes to promote his product at the
point of purchase can draw on a rich variety for a specific use.

DISTRIBUTION OF P-O-P

P-O-P is placed at the point of purchase in six principal ways:

1. The advertiser's salesmen "sell" the retailer on the use of the display as a
package deal at the same time they sell the product. The retailer agrees to
use the program and himself sets up the displays when the time comes

which he has scheduled for the promotion. The salesmen may return to help.

2. The advertiser's salesmen "sell" the program and the advertiser's "detail men" follow up, assembling and stocking the displays. This is most frequently done when the display is a complicated one.

3. The advertiser "sells" the displays along with his product to a warehouse-man or jobber who, in turn, "sells" to the retailer from his stock of products and displays.

4. The advertiser contracts with an installation company, which installs the signs and displays through prior arrangement with the retailer.

5. The advertiser places an ad in a trade magazine and sends out the displays to those retailers who respond.

6. When the advertiser has control of the brand, as in a franchised outlet or department, the franchise holder is expected to and usually does use the advertiser's signs and displays as a matter of policy.

The point to be noted is that in order to distribute P-O-P, a selling job is necessary. Someone somewhere must be sold on the use. This situation is entirely different from that which prevails among the mass media, where television, periodical, radio, and newspaper salesmen are continually calling upon the advertiser to persuade him to place material with them.

Most P-O-P is free to the retailer, but more expensive units usually have some arrangement for sharing the cost between the advertiser and the retailer. These arrangements would vary with the product and the type of retailing.

BUYING AND SELLING P-O-P

Less than 5% of all P-O-P sold to advertisers is handled via advertising agencies. In almost all cases the material is sold directly to the advertiser by a producer/supplier who may or may not own his own production facilities. P-O-P agencies (without production facilities) operate much in the same way as do advertising agencies. They make presentations, have a design staff, and contract for production. Producer/suppliers with production facilities seldom have the capability for all types of construction. The front office usually operates as a P-O-P agency, the factory handles that part of the production for which it is set up, and other needed services are contracted for with outside firms.

There are several reasons why advertising agencies play such a small part in the P-O-P industry. For one, their creative people are oriented toward print and broadcast media, with very little knowledge of three-dimensional construction, whereas the P-O-P man's creative people are design engineers. For another, many factors of law are involved in the design of P-O-P, concerning electrical and structural safety and protection of the public, which normally do not concern the advertising agency. Another reason is the closer relationship of the P-O-P industry to the retailing field.

The advertiser buys P-O-P most frequently through its sales-promotion manager, sometimes its merchandising manager, and in some cases through a special assistant to the marketing manager. The buyer finds it to his advantage to discuss the P-O-P program fairly early in the planning stage. If he does not have a regular supplier with whom he has found it advantageous to work on a more or less exclusive basis, he will call in two or three P-O-P men and present his marketing objectives. The P-O-P men will return with ideas and suggestions from which selection will be made.

The Point-of-Purchase Advertising Institute has worked out a code of ethics for such transactions through its Trade Practices Committee, and holds frequent seminars for purposes of updating the code and bringing it into sharper focus.

P-O-P from the Retailer's Point of View

In general the retailer will be favorable in his attitude toward P-O-P if it does most of the following things for him:

1. It spotlights an item that is normally a fast mover with a significant dollar volume.
2. It has a promotional theme that seems exciting and appealing.
3. It is of a size that is well adapted to his store, and is in keeping with store policy and decor.
4. The promotion offers a good opportunity for stimulating the sale of allied items.
5. It promotes an item that carries a substantial mark-up.
6. It fits easily into the retailer's own schedule of promotions.

Many supermarkets have been trying to make their stores look like expanded living rooms, or private clubs. Having created this rather elegant decor, they feel that special displays should be unobtrusive, match the store's wood finishes, and so on. Too wide a choice in every category of merchandise makes shopping a headache rather than a pleasure, unless there are highlights and colorful changes. The evidence for this is in the sudden resurgence of small shops and boutiques where choice is limited but exciting and the effect is cozy if bizarre.

P-O-P is a prime monotony breaker. It highlights something new or it brings attention to an old favorite. It gives a feeling of buying excitement. It serves as a reminder for messages received from mass media. It stimulates impulse purchases. It gives the customer useful information on which a buying decision can be based, and it helps to create a selling environment for the retailer.

Thus history repeats itself. Department stores went through the same syndrome. They tried to stop looking like stores and as a result, specialty shops and discount stores sprang up all around them.

The customer comes to the store for help and inspiration in reference to the goods and services he needs. He wants to be excited into making a decision. P-O-P is becoming more exciting and interesting all the time. In the future, more sophisticated use will probably answer the customer's need, even more closely.

SUMMARY

Point-of-purchase advertising, or P-O-P, comprises the displays, ads, or promotional pieces provided by the manufacturer to the retailer for use on the inside and outside of his store. It delivers the advertiser's message at the spot where his merchandise or services are sold. In addition to *inside* or *outside*, P-O-P materials are classified as *promotional* or *permanent*, depending on the length of time and use for which they were designed. Types of P-O-P include banners, bar and fountain units, tap markers, cash-register units, clocks, counter units, dealer loaders, and more.

Since there is much competition for the limited amount of space in retail stores, P-O-P materials are constantly being made better. However, they must be "sold" to the retailer by the advertiser (manufacturer).

P-O-P is a \$2-billion industry. Its trade association, the Point-of-Purchase Advertising Institute (POPAI), was established in 1938.

QUESTIONS AND DISCUSSION SUBJECTS

1. How does P-O-P differ from other forms of advertising?
2. What is the medium in P-O-P? Explain.
3. Name the three principal functions of P-O-P.
4. What major industries are served by P-O-P? What others can you think of that could use it?
5. What was a criticism of P-O-P advertising?
6. How has the industry reacted to this criticism?
7. What factors influence impulse buying?
8. Name and describe 20 of the 24 types of P-O-P advertising given in the chapter.
9. How is P-O-P distributed?
10. Why is so little P-O-P sold via advertising agencies?

SOURCES

1. All of the material in this chapter has been coordinated with the Point-of-Purchase Advertising Institute.

2. Ralph Head *et al., How and Why Shoppers Make Unplanned Purchases in Mass Retailing Stores* (New York: Ralph Head & Affiliates, 1971).

FOR FURTHER READING

Guides for Advertising Allowances and other Merchandising Payments and Services. Washington, D.C.: Federal Trade Commission, 1969.

Hayett, William. *Display & Exhibit Handbook.* New York: Reinhold, 1967.

Head, Ralph, et al. *First Time Purchase Study.* New York: Ralph Head & Affiliates, 1970.

Head, Ralph, et al. *How and Why Shoppers Make Unplanned Purchases in Mass Retailing Stores.* New York: Ralph Head & Affiliates, 1971.

Head, Ralph, et al. *How Top Supermarket Executives Consider Their Business Relations with Manufacturer-Suppliers—A Survey.* New York: Ralph Head & Affiliates, 1971.

Kress, George. *History of Point-of-Purchase Advertising.* New York: Point-of-Purchase Advertising Institute.

Offenhartz, Harvey. *Point-of-Purchase Design.* New York: Reinhold, 1968.

Point, Streater. *Shoppers' Perception of Signs and Displays—A Pilot Study.* Litton Industries, 1969.

POPAI. *Glossary of Point-of-Purchase Terms.* New York: Point-of-Purchase Advertising Institute, 1969.

POPAI. *Trade Practices and Current Procedures among Buyers and Sellers of Point-of-Purchase Advertising Materials.* New York: Point-of-Purchase Advertising Institute.

Specialty Advertising and Premiums (Sales Promotion)

SPECIALTY ADVERTISING

A leading specialty advertising salesman tells the story of making a sales call to the office of the president of a large industrial firm. The office was a spacious one, well appointed, with wall-to-wall carpeting, priceless original paintings adorning the walls, and a large picture window with a breathtaking view of the New York skyline. The specialty advertising man approached the president seated behind his massive mahogany desk. He then proceeded to ask the executive if he would mind hanging some advertising on his wall, or placing some advertising on his desk, for which the specialty advertising salesman offered him a fee.

The executive's mouth fell open as he looked at the salesman in amazement.

This never happened, of course, but in effect people do hang advertising on their walls or place it on their desks—and they don't charge a fee for it. Millions of businessmen place calendars on their walls or keep them on their desks. Most of these are specialty advertising items and they bear the advertising message or name of the advertiser. And housewives hang calendars on the walls of their kitchens, too. In fact, there are very few of us who do not have some specialty advertising items in our possession—ball-point pens or pencils with an advertiser's imprint, book covers, or a plastic wallet calendar from the local bank, to name just a few.

An insurance salesman of Auburn, New York, is credited with being the first to use an advertising specialty in the United States. In 1845, this salesman, in an attempt to obtain wider and more consistent display of his business announcements, had calendars attached to them.[1] Thus was born the idea that was to develop into a business grossing more than a billion dollars annually.[2]

The first manufacturers of advertising specialties were newspaper publishers who entered the specialty field as a side line to supplement their incomes. In 1869 George Coburn began printing advertising-carrying calendars in Hartford, Connecticut, and in 1879 another newspaper publisher in Coshocton, Ohio, produced the first advertising novelties in the form of candy boxes and school bags. In 1896 Brown & Bigelow was organized and soon became a leader in the manufacture of calendars. This firm is said to have produced the first full-color reproduction on a calendar, in 1903, and to be the originator of the "pretty girl" calendar.

Also in the year 1903 the Advertising Specialty National Association (ASNA) was formed with a membership composed in large part of calendar manufacturers.

In 1964, ASNA merged with the Advertising Specialty Guild, representing distributors, to form what is now the Specialty Advertising Association International (SAAI). The membership of SAAI consists primarily of (1) distributors, (2) suppliers (manufacturers that sell to distributors), and (3) direct selling houses—manufacturers that have their own sales forces. Suppliers make all kinds of advertising specialties, calendars, and executive or business gifts, although any one supplier may specialize in one of these three major groups.

The SAAI has produced sales training materials; it sponsors an annual Executive Development Seminar, an abbreviated college-level course held at a midwestern university; and it provides the industry with a marketplace by conducting two trade shows each year. The Association also has an ambitious public-relations program that keeps college advertising and marketing professors informed about the latest developments in specialty advertising, and a speaker's bureau that provides lecturers on the subject for college classes and for advertising, sales, and marketing organizations.

Although at one time most advertising specialties were made and distributed by the same firm, suppliers today sell through specialty advertising distributors, or "counselors" as some in the specialty medium call them. Currently, there are about 600 major suppliers of specialties, another 900 suppliers on the periphery of the industry, and approximately 3,000 distributors who together make and distribute more than 10,000 different kinds of advertising specialties.

Characteristics

The SAAI describes the medium in these words: "Take a useful article of merchandise, put an advertising or sales promotion message on it and deliver it to a customer or prospect without any strings attached and you have specialty advertising." [3] Hence, a specialty is an article that is *useful, imprinted* with the advertiser's name or message, and *given away* with no obligation to the recipient.

Although many products may be used as advertising specialties, the SAAI lists three main classifications. These are:

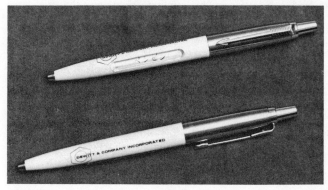

Some examples of specialty advertising award winners.

1. Imprinted advertising specialties
2. Executive gifts.
3. Calendars.

SAAI's explanation of each of these classes is as follows:

Imprinted advertising specialties. These are relatively inexpensive items produced for mass distribution. The many thousands of times in this class include ash trays, bottle openers, memo books, pencils, ball-point pens, coin purses, balloons, drink stirrers, emery boards, rulers, key tags, letter openers, watchband-calendars, litter bags, shopping bags, and the like.

Executive Gifts. These are usually the more expensive items personally and selectively given to businessmen and executives. An executive gift may be imprinted or personalized. In either case, it is a constant reminder of someone's thoughtfulness. A few of many popular executive gifts are cocktail sets, leather desk accessories, clocks, and jewelry items. A significant item in this class is the food gift—fruit cakes, steaks, cheese packages, and other delicacies. These are often packed in or with useful permanent containers, like sets of glassware or lazy susans. The intelligent advertiser selects his executive or business gifts with care, making sure that they are quality items but not so extravagant that they smack of bribery.

Calendars. Calendars represent about half the industry's business. Approximately one for each man, woman, and child in this country is produced yearly. Pretty girls, children, animals, and scenery are favorite illustrations, although some calendars have illustrations pertaining to the advertiser's products. A recent innovation is the double-duty calendar, useful also as a memo pad, cook book, child-care catalog, shopping list, or the like.

It should be noted that many advertising specialties, particularly imprinted specialties and calendars, may be combined with direct mail advertising.

At one time there was considerable seasonal fluctuation in the business as the result of increased use of advertising specialties near the Christmas holidays, but a growing recognition of their year-around use and value has tended to balance production and distribution of this medium throughout the year.

Uses of the Medium

Specialty advertising is a highly selective medium. An advertiser could choose to stand on a street corner and make his distribution only to red heads, or only to those wearing eyeglasses, for example. The medium is ideal for the manufacturer, the wholesaler, and the retailer. In addition to use as pure advertising and sales promotion, it hits the target for the politician, the trade association, the professional society; indeed, in more than a few instances it has been used successfully by churches. Specialty advertising also finds use in employee incentive programs.

One of the nation's large oil refiners and distributors of petroleum products gave advertising specialties to all of its distributors in the form of the company's trademark made up as a combination paperweight and ash tray in simulated bronze. This was done as a part of an anniversary promotion. A much smaller businessman, a beer distributor newly established in his community, helped make his business well-known through the use of wall calendars. A manufacturer of storm windows used advertising specialties as door-openers for his salesmen. A manufacturer maintained periodic contact with his distributor's salesmen by giving them loose-leaf memo books as Christmas remembrances and thereafter, at strategically spaced intervals, sending them refills for the books with accompanying letters setting forth selling points and other information that the manufacturer wished to convey. Retail stores catering to children have used advertising specialties to attract their trade. The Christmas balloon is perhaps one of the best known of this type of specialty, but by no means the only one.

These are but a few of the many uses to which this medium can be put, but they are enough to suggest the flexibility of specialty advertising with respect both to use and user.

The amount that should be spent on advertising specialties depends, as it does in other media, upon what the advertiser seeks to accomplish. If wide distribution of the specialty with the aim of building mass markets is the goal, then the less costly specialty items or calendars are probably the wisest choice. However, if the goal is the cultivation of a more limited market in the industrial field or among business executives, the executive-gift type of specialty is probably justified.

The user of advertising specialties should select items of long-lasting usefulness to recipients. The calendar is a good example of such a specialty, for if it is kept at all it will generally be retained for a year—and throughout 365 or 366 days it will be in a position to deliver its advertising message to all who see it. However, many calendars are received as each year draws to a close, and not all are kept. The advertiser who uses calendars as a specialty item should, therefore, seek to make his calendar outstanding in some aspect. In the past, the illustration was the device most commonly used in an attempt to lift a calendar above its competition. More recently, as we have seen, the dual or multipurpose calendar has come into use. Such calendars may give household hints or recipes, or may include space for shopping lists, in addition to serving as calendars. A bank located in a seaside community gives a calendar that includes the time of high and low tides with the expected rise and fall in feet for each day of the year. This calendar is so popular that residents of the community will go to considerable personal trouble to obtain one if it is not sent to them by the bank.

Other specialty items have lasting value, as well. Ash trays, rulers, letter openers, and similar items may be retained for years. Even pencils, pens, and memo pads have reasonably long life.

Successful use of specialty advertising, however, requires advance planning and programming just as does the use of other media. Specialty advertising counselors, who help develop effective programs, recommend that advertisers:

1. Define their objectives—know what the program is expected to accomplish.
2. Identify the target audience.
3. Develop a suitable distribution plan.
4. Choose an advertising theme that will reflect the product or service being offered.
5. Develop a message to support the theme.
6. Select the specialty advertising article, preferably one that bears a natural relationship to the product, service, or advertising theme.

Audiences

Because of specialty advertising's many characteristics, it is like direct mail advertising in being suitable for use by business firms, institutions, and organizations of all sizes—small, medium and large—which have the ability to separate a target audience from the mass. Since specialty advertising is a direct rather than mass medium, it enables the advertiser to reach his audience with direct control of his promotion. He picks the circulation, distribution, and cost.

PREMIUM ADVERTISING

Although the practice of giving customers free merchandise to express appreciation of patronage is one of the oldest sales-promotion tactics, the use of premiums as we know it today did not start until 1851. In that year, B. T. Babbitt offered a lithographed picture in exchange for wrappers from his soap. In this instance, the premium was employed to promote a new idea in soap manufacturing and merchandising. Laundry soap, until that time, had been cut from long bars by the shopkeeper and sold by weight. Usually, there was no identification with the manufacturer. Babbitt introduced the first soap in cake form. In addition to selling the soap in this new form, he also wished to make the buyers brand-conscious. The picture premiums that he offered were a means of accomplishing this dual purpose. Babbitt's success is measured by the fact that editions of some of the pictures he distributed as premiums ran into hundreds of thousands.

Premium offers still remain a very useful and, when correctly used, successful promotion device. The Premium Advertising Association of America (PAAA) defines a premium as usually consisting of a piece of merchandise offered in addition to, or in combination with, a manufacturer's product for the purpose of attracting new users who would not normally buy the product or who would buy it less frequently without the added inducement.

A premium differs from an advertising specialty in two important respects: (1) It usually carries no sales message, identification mark or trade name that associates it with the donor. (2) It may be obtained only on condition of fulfillment of some condition imposed by the donor.

A premium offer made in 1916 to help promote the acceptance of orange juice as a beverage. Sunkist Growers.

The value of most premiums to the consumer would be greatly reduced or entirely destroyed by a sales message or any identification imprinted upon them that readily established the fact that they were advertising or promotion devices. It is difficult to imagine a woman becoming enthusiastic over a table lamp offered as a premium with the slogan, "Eat Munchies, they're crunchy," inscribed on its base, or striving to obtain as a premium a pair of silk hose embellished with the trademark of a soap or cigarette manufacturer. On the other hand, if the premium is a package of flower seed or a garden tool, the name or trademark of the donor would detract little, if at all, from its value. But even in such cases the premium usually carries no donor-identification or sales message. Therefore, a premium is in no sense an advertising medium as is an advertising specialty. It is a sales-promotion device, which itself must be advertised if it is to accomplish its purpose.

The premium, unlike the advertising specialty, is not given away without some consideration being received by the advertiser. The recipient of a premium must purchase the advertiser's product, employ his services, attend his establishment or those of his dealers, witness a demonstration, or perform some other action of advantage to him. It is apparent from such demands placed upon the recipient that premiums may be used to introduce a new product, to win new customers for an old product, to induce customers to use more of a product, to hold customers to a particular brand over extended periods of time, or to build sales in off seasons.

Kinds of Premium Offers

There are a number of kinds of premium offers. While each is specific enough in its purposes there is some overlap. For instance, a *merchandise coupon offer* may be, at the same time, a *continuity premium* as well as a *traffic builder* and a *packaging premium*. This duplication of functions, however, does not detract from the effectiveness of premiums.

*Merchandise Coupon Offer.** Of early origin, used by the soap manufacturer B. T. Babbitt. Merchandise coupons are frequently packaged along with the product and can be accumulated and redeemed for merchandise premiums. Examples of such offers are Raleigh and other cigarette premium coupons. The coupon plan serves especially well as a device for holding customers to a particular brand. Premiums used in coupon-redemption plans range generally in value from $1 to $35, with a good share leaning toward the $2 to $6 class, but in catalog offers they go much higher. Most requests are for premium items for the home, including appliances and kitchenware. Other popular premiums are toys, cameras, sporting goods, and outdoor accessories.

Continuity Premiums. The purchaser, by continuing to buy a certain product, builds or assembles a set of premiums, such as silverware, dinnerware, or glassware. Continuity premium promotions are also very important in retail store programs. They may be given with each purchase or visit to the store, in the way steak knives were once given at Mobil ** stations, or as merchandise coupon offers. In-pack or on-pack coupons offering a discount ("cents off") on the next purchase of the product are a form of continuity premium.

Packaging Premiums. A factory-pack is a combination offer of product and premium in a unit, packed by or for the manufacturer of the product which is being promoted. Examples are: the syrup pitcher as a container for the syrup and the carafe containing coffee (container or secondary-use packs); the packages of Jell-O sold in combination with an aluminum mold and the hairbrush taped to the shampoo bottle (on-packs); the toy inside the cereal package or the Cracker Jack box and the beverage glass inside the box of detergent (in-packs). An offshoot of the combination pack is the "near-pack," such as the kites shipped along with the cereal or drink mix to be displayed with them but unat-

---

* In the main, the categories and definitions come from *PAAA Answers Questions,* published in 1970 by the Premium Advertising Association of America.

** Before the Arab oil-producing countries imposed their oil embargo during the Arab-Israeli War of 1973, with consequent shortage of oil and higher prices, oil companies in the United States frequently offered incentives to their retail customers.

Steve Allen wants YOU–
to put a little Friendship in your life.

"I just want to get this thought off my chest," says celebrity Steve Allen. "If you know what tastes good, you'll put a little Friendship on your table.

"Friendship Cottage Cheese, that is. Has a delicious taste that's very smooth. Nutritious, too—because it's made the old-fashioned way. With all natural ingredients."

ORDER A FRIENDSHIP T-SHIRT JUST LIKE STEVE ALLEN'S, ONLY $2.00. T-shirts may be 50% cotton/50% Dacron® Polyester or 100% cotton, depending upon availability from manufacturer. Colorfully printed front and back. Colorfast. Processed for minimum shrinkage. Color-contrast neck and sleeve bands. Neck band reinforced to retain shape. Youth and adult sizes. Limited quantity available. To order, send word "Friendship", cut from any Friendship Brand Food product, with $2.00 for each T-shirt. Make check or money order (do not send cash) payable to FRIENDSHIP T-SHIRT. Please allow 6 weeks for delivery.

Friendship® DAIRY PRODUCTS

TO: Friendship T-Shirt
P.O. Box 7100, Westbury, N.Y. 11592

Please send ____ Friendship T-Shirts (at $2.00 each) in sizes and quantities indicated below. Enclosed is my "Friendship" cut-out plus check or money order for $____ total.

	Small	Medium	Large	X-Large
Adult	(34-36)	(38-40)	(42-44)	(46-48)
Youth		(6-8)	(10-12)	(14-16)

Name _____

Street _____

City _____

State _____ Zip _____

The new T-shirt fad has reversed the trend of no advertising on premiums.

tached. A factory-packed premium permits fast action on high turnover products, obtains immediate sales results at point-of-purchase, permits thorough testing before complete market coverage, and allows for purchase of exact quantity of premiums needed for product run.

Self-Liquidating Premiums. promotable items of merchandise or service which "pay for themselves" entirely or in the greater part. Such premiums are usually offered for a specific proof-of-purchase, together with cash. The cash covers such costs as handling, redemption, and postage or shipping in addition to all or part of the cost of the premium. Self liquidators are also used as traffic-builders to induce visits to a retail outlet; Examples have been Texaco's * toy trucks and Goodyear's records.

Traffic-Building Premiums. Premiums are used in a variety of ways to increase consumer traffic. Examples are free premiums for visiting the store, self-liquidating premiums offered with or without required purchases, and trading-stamp plans based on purchases. Traffic-building self-liquidators range from 50¢ up for items such as mixing bowls, toys, cameras, housewares, jewelry, watches, the $1.00 Goodyear Christmas record—the choice depending on marketing factors. A lower-priced item will usually produce the best results; however, Texaco is famous for $4.95 and $5.95 self-liquidators, such as their fire truck.

Sweepstakes and Contests. A sweepstakes is a promotion by manufacturers, retailers, or others which awards prizes on the basis of chance.** Although sweepstakes are sometimes referred to as contests, the term "contest" usually involves skill. In contests, prizes are awarded not by chance but on the basis of skill or the solution of a problem according to the stated rules for the judging of entries. The contest is an excellent incentive promotion. It can stimulate consumer, sales force, and dealer interest and action to accomplish many marketing objectives. The contest can be used by the advertiser to gather ideas, methods and procedures of product use, produce re-use, and new applications for the product. Sweepstakes and contests, like premiums themselves, are often considered sales-promotional devices rather than advertising. Regardless, they do have a place in the overall marketing or advertising campaign.

Trading Stamps. Gummed stamps, given by retailers usually in the ratio of one stamp for each 10¢ of purchase, are familiar as "trading stamps." They are to be pasted in a "saver book" to accumulate up to 1,200 or 1,500, then redeemed for premiums shown in the stamp company's catalog.[4]

Dealer Premiums. Premiums given to a dealer for purchasing specified quantities of products or for coupons collected over a period of time from continued purchases. They can also be items used in dealer displays which the

---

* An inducement that became superfluous when gasoline buyers besieged service stations during and after the Arab oil embargo in 1973.

** In conducting a sweepstakes care must be taken that it is not considered a lottery, which is illegal in most states. By definition, a *prize, chance,* and *consideration* (or *purchase*) are elements of a lottery. If one of these is *not* present in an operation, it is not a lottery. Since chance and a prize are normally elements in a sweepstakes, generally purchase of the product is not required and a facsimile of the box top or label may be used in lieu of the "real thing."

dealers can keep after the displays have served their purposes. Dealer premiums can be very helpful in fulfilling many retail selling objectives: expanding distribution, stocking a line of products, and obtaining feature displays at point-of-purchase.

Sales Force Incentives. Awards to salesmen to stimulate them to extra effort to bring in additional sales or accomplish other specified objectives. Many sales objectives can be accomplished with a sales-incentive plan: exciting salesmen to increase their sales volume, adding new customers, balancing sales efforts, and inducing wholesalers' support.

Children's Premiums

Advertisers have long appreciated the importance of recognizing the distinction between buyers and users of products, and they know an appeal to the user is sometimes more effective in building sales than an appeal to the buyer. The giving of toys and other merchandise that especially appeal to children rests on the assumption that a premium of interest to the user of a product may bring better results than a premium of interest to the buyer.

Children's premiums to promote the sale of goods became increasingly popular during the years preceding 1975, when FTC regulations began to restrict them. "The Commission had proposed Guides regarding the prohibition of the advertising of premiums in advertising directed toward children . . ." [5] No doubt, television advertising with its children's programs had contributed considerably to the use of this type of premium. In such premium promotion programs, the premium offered was often a specialty item not obtainable through regular retail outlets. This is important because of a child's impatience or unwillingness to wait for a desired object.

Most children's premiums are self-liquidating. The child is asked to send from ten cents to a quarter and a specified number of box tops, wrappers, or coupons in exchange for the premium, the cash covering the manufacturer's costs associated with the offer. Package enclosures are also used in children's premium plans. In such cases, the premium is advertised as being enclosed in the package, and no additional charge is made for it.

Planning

The initial considerations in planning a premium offer include determining the specific objectives to be achieved by utilizing a premium; establishing the markets to be influenced, including the age group; selecting a premium which will appeal to the audience to be reached; planning the media program to promote the premium. [6]

Premium plans are most successful when properly combined and coordinated with all of the other promotional activities of the manufacturer. This is true of every component part of a campaign.

Premium plans are not the answer to all promotion problems. The Premium Advertising Association of America states that in general premiums are not successful in promoting proprietary items, slow-turnover merchandise, items involving pride of ownership, or gift items. But premiums can be made to succeed in the promotion of a wide range of products and services, and they deserve consideration as a part of the over-all campaign.

Selection of Premiums

A premium need not be an expensive item, but it should be something desirable to the people it is intended to influence. Furthermore, its usefulness or desirability should be readily recognized by these people; no education or advertising should be necessary to "sell" it to them. Within these limitations, a premium can be as expensive as a good leather handbag or as cheap as a plastic "secret-compartment" ring. If it is desirable to the group of people for whom it is intended, it will do its job.

Any premium should be something readily obtainable from the manufacturer in case customer demand for it exceeds original expectation and initial stocks become exhausted. If delivery of premiums cannot be made within reasonable time, refunds of money or notification of some kind as to why delivery has been delayed becomes necessary; either can be time-consuming and costly, and all precautions should be taken to make it unnecessary.

Often it is effective to offer a premium closely associated with the product it is promoting, for example, a premium toothbrush holder with the purchase of a toothbrush or tooth paste. Sometimes the premium can be associated with an idea that a company is attempting to "sell" to the public. Such was the case when the California Fruit Growers Association in 1914, started to promote the drinking of orange juice, then a new idea, and offered a juicer as a premium for orange wrappers bearing their brand and trademark. Although such association of premium and product has apparent merits, it is by no means necessary to the success of a premium plan.

Premium plans of one kind or another have been used with considerable success by both large business and small, and have accomplished all of the several goals mentioned in this chapter. However, their success depends upon correct use.

Associations

The principal associations in the premium field are the already mentioned PAAA, the National Premium Sales Executives, Inc. (NPSE—pronounced "Nipsie"), and the Trading Stamp Institute of America, Inc. (TSIA).

SUMMARY

The practice of giving useful items imprinted with the advertiser's name and/or message began in 1845. Today, specialty advertising sales exceed $1 billion annually, attesting to the fact that many people have and use these articles. Advertising specialty items are generally divided into three categories— imprinted advertising specialties, executive gifts, and calendars.

The industry has been represented by an association since 1930. The Specialty Advertising Association International (SAAI) is the current organization, a direct lineal descendent of a number of predecessor associations.

In the beginning, advertising specialties were manufactured and distributed by the same firm. Today manufacturers market their items through some 3,000 distributors.

Most advertising specialties serve as sales promotion items. Premiums, in addition to their sales promotion function, also serve as sales incentives. While no purchase is necessary to receive an advertising specialty, it is customarily required for a premium. Advertising specialties, other than executive gifts, are generally low-cost items and less expensive than premiums. Another point of difference between advertising specialties and premiums is that the latter usually carry no sales message.

Premiums or incentive awards are also given to salesmen and dealers for exceeding quotas in the sale of products or services of the manufacturers giving the awards. Other sales promotion devices are trading stamps, and sweepstakes and contests.

QUESTIONS AND DISCUSSION SUBJECTS

1. What are some of the pitfalls associated with running a contest, and how may they be avoided?
2. Discuss in as much detail as possible the factors upon which the success of a contest depends.
3. In what ways does a premium differ from an advertising specialty?
4. Name and describe three different types of premium promotions.
5. What considerations should be given the selection of a premium?
6. What are the areas of strength and weakness related to premium promotions?

SOURCES

1. Walter A. Gaw, *Specialty Advertising* (Chicago: Specialty Advertising Association International, 1972), 7, 8.
2. The Specialty Advertising Association International, Information Bureau, 1975.
3. *Ibid*.
4. *NPSE Premium Dictionary* (Union, N.J.: National Premium Sales Executives, Inc., 1974), 2.

5. "FTC Denies Petition for Ban on Food Advertising in Children's TV Programs,"
   Federal Trade Commission News Summary, April 11, 1975.
6. *PAAA Answers Questions* (New York: Premium Advertising Association of
   America, 1970), 12.

FOR FURTHER READING

"Advertising of Children's Premiums on Television." *Federal Register,* July 11, 1974,
    22505–22510.

Gaw, Walter A. *Specialty Advertising.* Chicago: Specialty Advertising Association In-
    ternational, 1972.

Herpel, George L., and Richard A. Collins. *Specialty Advertising in Marketing.* Home-
    wood, Ill.: Dow Jones-Irwin, 1972.

Luick, John F., and William L. Ziegler. *Sales Promotion and Modern Merchandising.*
    New York: McGraw-Hill, 1968.

Meredith, George. *Effective Merchandising with Premiums.* New York: McGraw-Hill,
    1962.

Nelson, Robin. "Marketing Incentives Are on the Rise Again," *Marketing/Communica-
    tions,* November 1971, 26–29.

"A Premium User's Nightmare." *Anny,* May 10, 1968.

Seipel, Carl-Magnus. "Premiums—Forgotten by Theory," *Journal of Marketing,* April
    1971, 26–34.

Special Report on Survey of Premium Usage 1974 vs. 1973. Premium Advertising Asso-
    ciation of America, February 1974.

Specialty Advertising Effectiveness Where It Counts. Specialty Advertising Information
    Bureau, October 1973.

ADVERTISING AND SOCIETY

$$\begin{array}{c} \star \\ \star\ \star \\ \star\ \star \\ \star\ \star \\ \star \end{array}\ \textbf{28}$$

The Behavioral Sciences and Advertising

Contributed by Charles Winick, Ph.D.

In most colleges, the departments that teach the sciences concerned with human behavior are usually quite separate from those departments dealing with advertising. This separation is a function of the historical development of academic disciplines, but it is unfortunate because the two areas—behavioral science and advertising—have a great deal in common.

The target of advertising is also the subject of the behavioral scientist: people functioning in a particular time and place, of one or another gender, socioeconomic status, culture, role, using certain language, responding to specific themes in the culture and to a variety of symbols. This chapter will briefly set forth some of the ways in which behavioral science can contribute to advertising.

Behavioral scientists (psychologists, sociologists, anthropologists, and economists) and advertisers are essentially concerned with the same basic subject matter: human behavior. Where they differ is in the use they plan to make of the subject matter. The behavioral scientist is interested in learning how to understand why and how people behave as they do, whereas the advertiser is concerned with attempting to influence their behavior in specific directions. Every advertiser is, whether or not he or she knows it, working in the field of behavioral science, because the goal of advertising is to communicate information and attitudes in such a way as to influence behavior.

An advertiser beginning to consider a campaign would therefore be well advised to determine whether behavioral scientists had previously considered subjects that might be relevant to the campaign. This can be clarified by looking in summary volumes, textbooks, encyclopedias, and other places where behavioral science materials are brought together.

In addition, each of the main fields in behavioral science has its own abstracting service, through which current materials appearing in scholarly journals are systematically summarized. (See "For Further Reading," at the end of this chapter.) Most moderate-sized libraries subscribe to the various abstracting series. It is possible that a researcher in one of the behavioral sciences has already studied, and published his findings in, an area that is directly relevant to some advertising problem. If so, the advertiser may be able to take advantage of the knowledge.

Subjects like the symbolism of the home, or attitudes toward shoes, or how hair styles affect the self-concept, which are of direct interest to many an advertiser of consumer products, have been explored by the various behavioral sciences for many years. Such information, although originally developed by anthropologists, sociologists, and psychologists for their own purposes, could be very helpful to an advertiser. Even one aspect of such knowledge could provide a competitive benefit to an advertiser.

Modern interest in how the behavioral sciences might contribute to advertising spurred in the 1950s, when motivation research established itself as one method for determining what consumers were "really" thinking. Proponents of this point of view, such as psychologist Ernest Dichter, argued that many motivations of consumers were complex and could only be determined by indirect methods. One of his most famous studies was conducted for Chrysler Corporation, and concluded that a man might be attracted to convertibles because they symbolized the mistress which he might fantasy about but that he would ultimately buy the sedan which represented the stability of a wife. He recommended that Chrysler put convertibles in showroom windows and stress them in advertising, because they would help attract men into the showrooms, even though they might ultimately buy a sedan.

Various procedures for tapping the unconscious and otherwise not immediately accessible motivations of advertising recipients enjoyed a tremendous acceptance by advertisers and their agencies into the early 1960s, by which time the motivational techniques became absorbed into the general body of advertising and marketing procedures.

At about the time that Dichter was helping to call attention to the role of depth psychology in advertising, sociologist Burleigh Gardner, in Chicago, was stressing that the life style of each of the several socioeconomic groups in the country was different from that of other groups. Gardner noted that the blue-collar family lived quite differently from the upper middle-class family and that the two used media differently. He stressed that what he called the Middle Majority family—middle class in terms of sociological criteria—was the major target of mass advertisers.

Dichter and Gardner were the best known proponents of the use of behavioral sciences in advertising but they were followed by many others. It may be useful to identify six typical applications:

1. Behavioral science concepts suggesting directions
2. Typologies

3. Quantification of qualitative concepts
4. Changes in professional climate
5. Improvements in the concept of the image
6. Group interviewing procedures

This list furnishes the headings of discussion hereafter.

BEHAVIORAL SCIENCE CONCEPTS SUGGESTING DIRECTIONS

One use for behavioral science concepts in advertising has been in the formulation of a problem and even in its detection. There has been a growing realization that certain broad behavioral science generalization about life in America can call attention to problems and opportunities which had previously not been perceived as such. An example of this is the concept of *megalopolis,* which has been adapted to marketing as interurbia, or the notion that the United States could be divided into some 14 major areas which were not only clear-cut geographic entities but which also were connected by road systems, public transportation, media habits, and other means, so that they constituted very distinct economic and distribution entities. This concept has led to a number of firms' examining their distribution systems and researching various alternate methods of distribution.

Another behavioral science concept that has had considerable utility in the detection and formulation of an advertising problem has been the concept of *subculture.* This has helped in developing specific questions related to the interests and needs of specific groups that constitute part of the market for a particular product. Without the clues provided by sociological and anthropological students of subcultures, advertisers would be much less sensitized to these subcultures and their importance for marketing.

Another concept that has helped launch many an advertising campaign is the notion of *perception.* The rediscovery of perception by psychologists dates from the 1950s and 1960s but the proliferation of methods for studying company and brand differences was possible only after perceptual psychology had developed its own research procedures. These procedures stress that we see and hear what is "out there" only in terms of what we bring to the perception situation.

Another area within advertising that has flourished as a result of the availability of newer procedures from the behavioral sciences is the *measurement and description of various kinds of reactions of the senses.* The establishment of much more precise vocabularies and measures for the study of the senses has led to a considerable increase in such studies. This whole area has had substantially increasing attention as a result of fairly extensive experimental work by psychologists. Not only has this experimental work developed a better vocabulary for describing these dimensions, but in addition the coincidental development of various techniques from the behavioral sciences has made it relatively easy to conduct investigations into these matters.

The discovery that changes in movement of the eye pupil occur when a person is attracted to something led, in the last several years, to a thriving use of *pupillometer studies* by advertising agencies and advertisers. The studies are employed in order to determine which headline, package, color, or shape is most provocative, persuasive, or appropriate. Because such changes in pupil activity are involuntary, they represent a valuable clue to consumer response to advertisements and products.

The behavioral science concepts of *process* and *decision theory* have also helped to call attention to the existence of a dimension of consumer behavior that could be studied systematically and objectively. The concept of process is central in behavioral science. This concept has combined with the behavioral science concept of decision theory to lead many advertisers to believe that a buying decision could be viewed as a process. This kind of study has served both to underline the complexity of many purchasing decisions and also to make knowledge of such decisions more realistic and ultimately more useful.

TYPOLOGIES

Although earlier applications of behavioral science had stressed the existence and usefulness of certain universals in human behavior, like the unconscious or the inevitable nature of repression, one major thrust of the modern advertiser is the utilization of the concept of typologies derived from or measured by the behavioral sciences. We have increasingly become aware that there is no homogeneous universe of consumers in almost any marketing research situation. Instead, we see various types of people constituting the universe of interest. It is possible to identify at least five major psychological types which have been used in advertising along with two major sociological types and two types that seem to include both psychological and sociological dimensions.

Psychological Types

Probably the most systematic attempt to use psychological typology in advertising is the administration of relatively well-established objective measures of personality to large populations of consumers on a panel. The researcher is interested in those dimensions of personality on which the various kinds of consumers appear to differ from the average, and thus in how it is possible to describe these consumers as psychological types. By a type, we mean a classification of persons who differ from the average on particular dimensions, and who can be described in terms of such dimensions.

The Edwards Personal Preference Schedule, which provides scores on each of 15 variables, is one test which has been used to establish typologies of consumers in terms of personality profiles. It increasingly has been used as a basis for classifying populations into *consumer types*. Other well known objective measures of personality that have been used in the creation of typologies are the Minnesota Multiphasic Personality Inventory and the Cattell Inventory.

A second dimension which has lent itself to psychological typology of consumers is what is perhaps the most widely used scale to evaluate personality developed since World War II: the F scale. This measure of *authoritarianism* (and its opposite) has been widely used in order to establish the extent to which particular populations might be likely to respond to specific kinds of product appeals. It has also been used to determine brand loyalty, and susceptibility to new products. Consumers' scores on the test have been shown to be highly correlated with their purchase of specific makes of automobiles and a number of other products. One serendipitous result of working with the agree-disagree scale of the F scale has been the establishment of a typology that seems to be related to some characteristics, that of *yeasayers* and *naysayers*. It has been observed, in work on the F scale, that there appeared to be some persons who consistently marked the "agree" or "disagree" side of the questions on the F scale. This has been expanded, on the basis of further research, into the finding that there are people who tend to disagree, almost regardless of the kind of question. This typology of response styles has proved to be of great utility to advertising researchers, who can take cognizance of, and measure, the bias introduced by response style.

A fourth psychological typology that has recently achieved more research use is that based on *level of aspiration*. The concept of level of aspiration, or a person's estimate of how well he is likely to do in a given task or situation, has often been used in the last few years in the construction of a typology of consumers. It has been demonstrated that a number of different kinds of purchasing behavior are correlated with high or low levels of aspiration. Advertising researchers have developed fairly effective methods, by the use of one or two key questions, for assessing a consumer's level of aspiration.

A fifth typology tapping personality dimensions that seem to be significantly related to various kinds of purchasing behavior is the psychoanalytic classification of people as *oral* or *anal types*. These two types appear to be very highly correlated with the desire to pay a higher or lower price, with preference for various colors on consumer products, with preference for various textures and shapes of packages, and with other dimensions.

These five psychological typologies represent a sampling of the many kinds of dimensions that have been found to lend themselves to typological application in advertising.

Sociological Types

Typologies have proved useful not only when they have been based on psychological dimensions but also when they have embraced sociological variables.

One of these sociological typologies is that of *vocation*. It is hardly news that a man's occupation is an important measure to know about him. Although there are some 19 realistic and effective measures of socioeconomic status, the single most effective predictor is the occupation of the head of a household. What is of interest to advertisers is that occupation probably provides better clues to a person's life style than education or even current income. As the result of the increased interest in occupation's relationship to consumer behavior, considerable advertising attention has been paid to this dimension and several typologies of occupation have been established.

Another sociological typology is that of *types of cities*. It has been obvious for many years that the life style of people who live, let us say, in San Diego, differs substantially from the life style of those in New Orleans. This has been clear enough in an anecdotal and impressionistic sense but recent work in classifying and quantifying the style of life of cities has helped to provide data toward a typology of cities. Such a typology has proved to be a major advance in the selection of cities for test purposes and in decisions involving sample selection in the nation as a whole. Being able to classify cities meaningfully provides a procedure for coping with what might otherwise be a welter of discrete and multiple classificatory variables.

Psychological-Sociological Types

A third kind of typology that has proved useful in advertising involves a combination of psychological and sociological dimensions. One such typology which draws on both psychological and sociological dimensions has been based on the concept of the various special needs, perceptions, and levels of experience that are associated with various *stages in a person's life cycle*. This concept was originally developed by Charlotte Buhler, expanding on the old German idea of *Lebenslauf,* or the kind of experience that characterizes each age group. It was first described for American audiences several decades ago but has only recently been rediscovered by social scientists and advertisers.

That there are certain broad differences between different age groups is obvious but that special levels of experience in terms of psychological needs and social behavior are appropriate for each level has only recently been empirically explored. The family life cycle as a variable has also recently been getting research attention.

Another typology that draws on both psychological and sociological concepts is the concept of the *tryer*. It has been obvious to marketers and advertisers for many years that there were some persons who tend to try new products earlier and more frequently than others. There appears to be a generalized tendency for the tryer to experiment with a variety of new products in different kinds of situations, although opinion leadership is specific rather than generalized. In view of the recent stress on opinion leadership and word-of-mouth communication, the tryer would seem to be a person whom the advertiser would wish to know a great deal about. If the tryer tries something new, he may be the kind of person who would disseminate his knowledge to his peers, as an opinion leader. Study of the tryer has moved forward on the level of both the psychological and sociological dimensions. The advertiser has increasingly tended to see the market for new products as a typology of trying and nontrying. Scales have been developed for predicting and describing the trying behavior of given groups of respondents, and thus how likely they might be to buy a new product.

QUANTIFICATION OF QUALITATIVE CONCEPTS

It is curious that the trend toward the kind of absolute represented by the polarities of a typology has flourished at just about the same time that there has been a trend toward the opposite, in the form of *scalar measurements*.

One major trend in the use of behavioral science in advertising is a tendency away from the either/or kind of measurement that characterized the earlier days of the introduction of the newer procedures. For example, the rediscovery of the unconscious led to what may have been an overenthusiastic embracing of the idea that there are certain given wellsprings of human behavior which were applicable to the United States population as a whole. A major recent stress in advertising has been the employment of several methods that permit quantification of relatively qualitative data on an index or scale.

Some techniques of this kind that have become fairly widely used are the semantic differential, the Guttman scale, and the Q sort. The *semantic differential* has attracted international attention. The procedure sets forth a number of polar dimensions which had been empirically defined, such as hot-cold. The technique offers the range of the word-association test and the precision of a statistically developed scale, each point on which was equidistant from the point on either side. This procedure helps to eliminate the ambiguity of the scales of the Thurstone or Likert type, in which there is some question about the extent to which the points on the scale were equidistant. The semantic differential also provides the opportunity of getting intensity of attitude as well as its direction. The technique is easy to administer and permits a wide variety of comparisons. It is also sensitive enough to pick up relatively slight changes over a period of time.

The Guttman scale involves a series of questions arranged in such a way that answering affirmatively to any item necessarily involves answering affirmatively to antecedent items; for example, "Are you over 5′10″? 5′9″? 5′8″?" A person who is over 5′9″ necessarily is over 5′8″ and 5′7″ as well. The Guttman scale, although developed during World War II by the Army's Information and Education Division, did not develop into a widely used research procedure until later. Although the concept of scaling and of linear attitude scales obviously has great merit in terms of economy of questioning and in terms of permitting us to rank attitudes on a continuum, it was some time before practical methods for determining the "scalability" of attitudes could be devised. They now are used quite routinely in a variety of different kinds of study. The development of scales of readiness to buy and of favorability toward television commercials stems from the adoption of the Guttman scale.

The Q sort has achieved wide adoption by advertising researchers. In the modification that has generally been the form that the test has taken, some 50 or so cards are given to the respondent, who is then asked to place them in five piles so that each pile has an equal number of cards. The cards in the pile on the right are to represent the attributes or characteristics that most accurately describe the object, product, or brand being evaluated; and the cards in the pile on the left least accurately describe the object being ranked. The piles in between represent the intermediate states of preference. This technique has the advantage of being fun for the respondent to do and of giving him the opportunity of using his hands and thus participating actively in the interview situation. It also has the advantage of being able to detect relatively subtle changes in attitude, to pick up changes over time, and to make it easy to compare attitudes found in competing companies or products.

Another technique that illustrates the same interest in quantifying qualitative material is the *picture-scale* test. This technique combines the stimulus value of a picture with the precision of a rating scale. In this technique, cartoons or drawings are presented at either end of a scale, which has no words. The illustrations, however, present what are clearly opposites, so that words are not necessary; thus, at one end of the scale, there might be a ramshackle and dilapidated house, while at the other end there might be a good-looking and well-kept modern house. There might be five or seven points on the scale that separate the two extremes. The respondent would be asked to indicate where on the scale a given kind of household product would fall. This procedure makes it possible to get quantitative data on many dimensions of products that are difficult to put into words but that nonetheless may be important. This procedure also has the merit of readily lending itself to surveys conducted by mail and thus cutting costs appreciably over what they might be in personal interviews.

CHANGES IN PROFESSIONAL CLIMATE

There are two behavioral science concepts that have not had so much of a specific effect on the conduct of advertising as their more diffuse effect on the professional climate.

One such concept is the relative agreement between proponents of objective and projective psychological tests for clinical use, which has led to a growing rapprochement between proponents of their use in marketing research. The earlier debate on these matters had conveyed the impression that the use of projective tests was an either/or matter and that the advertising researcher had to be committed either to one type of measure or to the other. The more accepting attitude toward projective tests, coupled with the publication of new data on some established objective tests, has led to a feeling that comparisons were less useful than attempts to use each kind of test as its special characteristics made most appropriate. Perhaps the most visible evidence of this new attitude is the increasing number of advertising studies which use combinations of objective and projective tests.

The other change in climate is less tangible, but certainly significant. After World War II, many students of world affairs and national events had unrealistic expectations of what behavioral science could accomplish. They assumed that there were "correct" solutions to problems of human relations that could be found by the application of behavioral science. We have developed more modest expectations about what behavioral science can accomplish, and we realize that there is as unlikely to be one "correct" solution to these problems as there is to problems of human relations, but rather that behavioral science can cast light on various possible solutions.

The same change in climate seems to be occurring in the application of behavioral science concepts to advertising. In the first flush of enthusiasm for these procedures, unrealistic expectations of their utility were widespread. We have increasingly been reminded that an advertising problem differs from one in physics or chemistry because a problem in the physical sciences is likely to have only one combination of elements or forces that can be successful. Thus, there is usually only one correct answer to such problems. The kinds of problems with which the advertiser is concerned are different in that there may be many different answers which are useful and which offer a point of purchase on some effective action. Thus, a particular problem may be able to use the concept of authoritarianism, or of *Lebenslauf,* or one of the other concepts that we have discussed. The discovery, by the advertiser, that a particular target group has specific identifiable characteristics of this type may provide clues and approaches which might not otherwise be available, although no one of these by itself might represent the "correct" solution to the particular problem.

IMPROVEMENTS IN THE CONCEPT OF THE IMAGE

The behavioral sciences have enormously enhanced our ability to identify, study, and attempt to modify brand and company images.

This is recognition of what courts recognized over a century ago when they declared the corporation to be a legal person: a company is perceived as if it were a person. It is also recognition of what accountants routinely do when they place a money value on a company's good will.

The image of a company is the end result of a person's experiences, recollections, and impressions of a company. These days, when consumer activism and corporate concern over social responsibility are so important, the concept of brand and company image has assumed new dimensions. We are interested in discovering what a company's image is because there is reason to believe that the image which people hold of a company is related to its success. This success may be in the dimension of sales, relatively favorable attitudes on the part of the public, high employee morale, good stockholder relations, and related matters.

One major direction is to determine how the image of a company or of a brand is helping or hindering sales. This is likely to be dependent on whatever qualities the company's publics associate with merit in the product or the company. An image of modernity and elegance may be just right for one company or product family whereas a "folksy" and old-fashioned image might be ideal for another. To determine the compatibility of the image of a particular company with the public's expectations of the company is one frequent goal of image research. There are well-known cases in which a brilliantly created image was inappropriate for a product or company, and had to be modified because it was actually damaging the company.

Studying the compatibility of company and image is often difficult because an image may not be simple and may have contradictory elements. How even a central image may have very contradictory elements can be seen in the methods we use to personify our own country. When the United States is presented as Uncle Sam, he is typically presented as a gnarled and emaciated old man who is usually asking the citizenry to do something unpleasant (e.g., pointing a finger and saying, "Uncle Sam wants you"). When the United States is presented as buxom Columbia, she is usually in a nourishing and comforting situation (e.g., accepting immigrants). Yet both images are immediately recognizable as representations of the United States although they are so inherently contradictory.

A company may have multiple images because it actually contains many and sometimes contradictory components which suggest different images under different circumstances. Another reason for multiple images may be that a company's different publics, because of their own roles and special interests, may be sensitized to, and thus perceive, different elements of the company. The images of the XYZ Company which are held by its neighbors, suppliers, vendors, employees, stockholders, competitors, and consumers and nonconsumers of its products are likely to be different. The relationship of the perceiver to a company, his independence of it, and how often he uses its products are relevant to the kind of image he may have of the company. A person's social and economic status, his position on a career or life cycle, and his ethnic background and personality may also be directly relevant to the image he will have of a company.

All of these dimensions are relevant to how to go about researching a company image, because the recognition of the existence of such dimensions will help to determine the kinds of questions to be put to the respondents. In the initial stages of planning such a study and pretesting its procedures, sensitization to these factors will help to suggest the kinds of respondents whose opinons, feelings, and attitudes are to be sampled. It will also suggest methods of analyzing the data in terms of respondent categories. These complexities, which are part of a thorough image study, make it practically mandatory that the researcher be able to use the full arsenal of behavioral science technique in conducting such a study.

Many social-science studies especially opinion-leader studies, have highlighted the value of the opinions of special respondent categories. Such categories may be particularly useful in image studies. Some kinds of image studies can be effectively conducted by interviewing special population groups or subsamples rather than interviewing the general population in a probability sample survey. Typical special groups might include technicians, editors of trade papers, department-store buyers, purchasing agents, security analysts, and other opinion-leader groups, or else various special occupational groups. If a probability sample study is undertaken, any special groups on which data are desired can be oversampled in order to provide adequate representation if they might not be adequately represented in the sample.

An image exists only in terms of an audience. Defining the audience defines the population whose attitudes are relevant. Thus, a central question to be answered in attempting to discover the details of a company's image is the question of who wants to know what the image is and for what purpose. The answers to these questions will be directly relevant to a number of concerns that the researcher needs to clarify before the first question can be drafted, even for a pilot study: the time and money available to do the study, the nature and extent of sampling, the kinds of questions to be asked and the method of analysis of data, whether the study will be conducted on a recurring and periodic basis, and similar concerns.

Although an attitude is usually defined as a predisposition to believe in a particular way, students of company images know that the relationship between an individual's attitude toward a company and his behavior toward it may sometimes be complex. One major reason for image research is that we assume there is a very direct relationship between expressed attitudes and behavior. We are interested in what others think of us because we expect that what they think of us determines their behavior toward us.

Just as the word for "enemy" in many primitive languages is related to the word for "stranger," so there is general agreement that a more favorable attitude is likely to be associated with more knowledge about the company. Contrariwise, a respondent usually knows less about a company which he regards less favorably. In the case of some large companies, this attitudinal dimension of the image can be studied by simply determining the two dimensions of familiarity and direction of attitude. The dimension of familiarity can usually be discovered fairly precisely.

There are a number of simple procedures for determining attitudes toward a company and the direction, intensity, and salience of those attitudes. It is important to know not only whether a respondent is favorably or unfavorably disposed toward a given company (direction), but also how strongly he holds his attitudes (intensity), and how central the particular attitude is to him (salience). Simple barometer or thermometer techniques, graduated scales, and multiple-choice questions are often employed in establishing these parameters of a respondent's attitudes toward a company. Essentially, all of the procedures used in image research can be said to be attempts to determine what the public's attitudes toward a company are.

A variety of modifications of the classical word-association technique have been made by social scientists. These modifications have generally been in the direction of making the test more objective and quantitative.

These quantitative word-association procedures may help to minimize the halo effect which is almost inevitably operative in attempts to describe a person or a company and which makes some image studies so difficult. The halo effect refers to the extent to which our central impression of a company colors our perception of all other facets of the company. It occurs because it is easier to have an oversimplified and schematic impression of a company, based on one or two salient characteristics, than to consider it in all its complexity. Presenting the respondent with a wide variety of words and phrases helps to fractionate his impressions of a company, which may be useful for purposes of image analysis. It also may suggest dimensions of the image about which he would not ordinarily have voiced an opinion, and make it easier for him to overcome his reluctance to express negative attitudes toward a company. The Semantic Differential and Q sort, discussed above, may be used.

One popular objective measure for establishing the detailed components of the respondents' attitudes toward a company is the adjective check list, which is another modification of word-association procedures. This is a procedure borrowed from personality-research methodology. It consists of a list of adjectives or phrases, usually presented alphabetically and covering a wide range of attributes of a company, its products, its personnel, and its channels of distribution. The respondent checks those adjectives which are applicable to the subject company, in his opinion. He is usually asked to repeat this procedure for the company's competitors. This procedure permits precise comparison of qualities of a company, on a quantifiable basis.

Pictorial techniques have the advantage of presenting an actual scene or illustration of some kind which is relevant to the company. They may often elicit a more detailed and penetrating kind of response from a respondent than would a verbal stimulus, because the respondent may be able to respond more freely to a picture than he would to a word or phrase.

Pictorial techniques may be relatively projective, in which case the respondent has great latitude in the nature, intensity, and length of his response. He might, for example, be given a cartoon based on a company situation, with one person in the cartoon making some remark about the company. The respondent is asked to fill in the balloon which represents the response to the remark in the cartoon. In an even more projective procedure, he might be shown a card of a thematic apperception test type in which there is an ambiguous scene involving the company, and asked to make up a story about what is happening and what will happen in the scene shown. Such a story may permit him to express relatively deep feelings about the company which he might not be able to express in any other way.

Many image studies can and do productively use a modification of the critical-incident technique to obtain useful information. This technique is a modification of a widely used personnel procedure applied to preparing job descriptions, in which employees are asked to report the critical activities in which they are engaged. The modification is based on the respondent's recalling a situation or circumstance when the company or its products may have been especially important to him in either a positive or negative way.

If the company has a symbol, seal, slogan, or colophon which it has been using for some time, an attempt should be made to elicit the extent to which it is familiar to respondents. Data on the extent to which such shorthand company symbols are known to the consumer should be obtained in any image study.

Another dimension to be considered in developing an image study is the extent to which a large corporation which has a number of subsidiary companies is or is not perceived by the public as the parent or umbrella corporation for its subsidiaries. General Motors tries more vigorously to develop a strong umbrella image than do companies like Procter & Gamble. Many a company is currently rethinking its approach to this dimension of its image, in the direction of emphasizing the parent company which had previously been de-emphasized. How aware the public is of such differences may be explored productively in an image study.

Possibly the easiest type of image study to do is that of a store, particularly a department store, because consumers are likely to have more occasion to be in contact with a store than with most other kinds of companies. For example, even though the leading New York department stores at a given price range appear to be roughly similar, their consumers hold sharply distinct images of each. These images may lend themselves to personification. Thus, we might say that Lord & Taylor could suggest a young sophisticated customer seeking high style; the store has a sense of humor about its studied feminine manner. Bergdorf Goodman can connote elegant luxury with an air of intimacy and uniqueness; unlike the other stores, it has no branches. Saks Fifth Avenue may remind the shopper of an elegant Park Avenue dining room, with an air of solidity in its many departments. Bonwit Teller may convey a feeling of conservatism and refinement.

On another level we could describe each of the stores in terms of how nice the personnel was, the store's friendliness, how much fun it was to shop, which store had the best management, which had the widest range of products, how clean and neat the store was, how convenient the store's parking and location were, the store's charge and exchange policies, specific strong and weak departments, and other specific attributes. The first or symbolic interpretation of the image of these stores would be a personified summary of those more specific qualities, but we could arrive at the former only after asking specifically about the latter. A store, like any other company, is essentially an entity which has a certain emotional tone, of which we have certain expectations, and toward which we develop certain attitudes. It is these components that constitute the image of the store or company. The task of the image researcher is to develop methods of inquiry that will permit a detailing of these characteristics.

GROUP INTERVIEWING PROCEDURES

A major application of behavioral science procedures in advertising is the use of the group interview in order to determine how consumers regard a product, product claim, television program, name, slogan, magazine, and many other items related to advertising. The group interview, in addition to discovering such material, is valuable in finding out the level of information which people have, in generating new copy ideas, and in many other purposes.

The group interview involves bringing together a sample of persons selected because they are users or nonusers or former users of a product, live in a particular area, are in a specific age or family or socioeconomic category, or for a variety of other reasons. The group format for interviewing, adopted from psychology, has a number of advantages for the advertiser.

One such advantage is the mutual facilitation that occurs as a result of hearing the views of others. Something said by A serves to trigger an idea or experience to B that B would not otherwise have recalled. Also, the group situation is nonthreatening in that it permits a person to remain silent for as long as he or she wishes, without being "on the spot" and having to talk.

Yet another advantage is that a comment or observation, which would ordinarily be held back because the person might be embarrassed in a one-to-one situation, can be made easily in a group situation.

In the course of the group interview, the group leader can get at a range of views and attitudes that would have taken much longer if the interviewing were conducted on a one-to-one basis.

Some of the most memorable advertising campaigns of recent years had their genesis in group interviews. In the hands of a capable leader, the group interview is a major tool in advertising.

OTHER BEHAVIORAL SCIENCE USES

The six areas selected for discussion are intended to be suggestive rather than all-inclusive. The behavioral sciences are so vigorously pursuing many different areas of interest that any summary of current developments is impossible, without taking more space than the entire text of this book.

Increasingly, advertisers are developing new interest in concepts, techniques, findings, and approaches from the behavioral sciences. There is every reason to believe that the yield from this exploration will continue to be fruitful.

SUMMARY

Advertising and the behavioral sciences are closely related since both are concerned with human behavior. The sciences have to do with how and why people behave as they do and advertising is interested in influencing that behavior in specific directions.

Much information has been developed by psychologists, sociologists, and anthropologists, for their own purposes, that can be of value to advertisers. This information can be found in summary volumes and in a number of abstracting series for each of the principal behavioral sciences.

One of the first behavioral scientists to relate directly to advertising was Ernest Dichter, who delved into motivation research during the 1950s. Another was sociologist Burleigh Gardner, who demonstrated that life styles differed between socioeconomic groups.

Following are six behavioral-science areas that have been applied to advertising: concepts suggesting directions, typologies, quantification of qualitative concepts, changes in professional climate, improvement in the concept of the image, and group interviewing procedures.

While the contributions of the behavioral sciences to advertising are recognized, earlier expectations of "miracle" solutions to all problems have been modified. The yield from continuing research, however, is expected to continue to be fruitful.

QUESTIONS AND DISCUSSION SUBJECTS

1. Name the behavioral sciences.
2. In what sources can an advertising copywriter possibly find behavioral science studies that might be useful to him?
3. Give an example of the result of motivation research.
4. How is the study of life styles related to advertising?
5. Identify and describe the six applications of the behavioral sciences to advertising given by Dr. Winick.
6. What is the relationship of the movement of the pupil of the eye to advertising?
7. What is meant by the term *psychological type?*
8. How does psychological type differ from the sociological type?
9. In what way does the Q sort differ from other research forms?
10. Does knowledge of a company on the part of the consumer help its image? Explain.

FOR FURTHER READING

Bonjean, Charles M., Richard J. Hill, and S. Dale McLemore. *Sociological Measurement*. San Francisco: Chandler/Intext, 1967.

Day, George S. *Buyer Attitudes and Brand Behavior*. New York: Free Press, 1970.

Dichter, Ernest. *Handbook of Consumer Motivation*. New York: McGraw-Hill, 1964.

Engel, James F., David T. Kollat, and Roger D. Blackwell. *Consumer Behavior*. Second Edition, New York: Holt, 1973.

Gardner, Burleigh B., and David G. Moore. *Human Relations in Industry: Organizational and Administrative Behavior*. Homewood, Ill.: Irwin, 1964.

Gordon, George N. *Persuasion: The Theory and Practice of Manipulative Communication*. New York: Hastings House, Publishers, 1971. (Selected chapters.)

Myers, John G. *Social Issues in Advertising*. New York: American Association of Advertising Agencies, 1971.

Pearce, Michael, Scott M. Cunningham, and Avon Miller. *Appraising the Economic and Social Effects of Advertising*. Cambridge, Mass.: Marketing Science Institute, 1971.

Psychological Abstracts. Washington, D.C.: The American Psychological Association, published monthly.

Social Sciences Citation Index. Philadelphia: Institute for Scientific Information, published annually.

Sociological Abstracts. Brooklyn, N.Y.: Sociological Abstracts, Inc., published seven times a year.

Consumerism and Criticism of Advertising

In a ruling against a Virginia law which stated that it is unprofessional for a pharmacist to advertise the price of prescription drugs, Supreme Court Justice Harry A. Blackmun, writing for the Court in May 1976 declared that advertising is necessary to the public interest:

> Advertising, however tasteless and excessive it sometimes may seem, is nonetheless dissemination of information as to who is producing and selling what product, for what reason, and at what price. So long as we preserve a predominantly free enterprise economy, the allocation of our resources in large measure will be made through numerous private economic decisions. It is a matter of public interest that those decisions, in the aggregate, be intelligent and well informed. To this end, the free flow of economic information is indispensable.

ADVERTISING AND ITS CRITICS

The primary function of advertising, as it has developed through the years and as it probably will continue to develop and be used in the future, is to facilitate the movement of goods through the channels of trade from producer to business-user or to ultimate consumer. It is in this capacity that advertising has made its greatest contributions to our society. It is around this function that most of the criticism of advertising has centered. The tool that is extensively used but not well understood will have many who question its merits. Such has been the case with advertising—the tool of marketing.

Many people do not understand the function and operation of advertising. Others, for reasons best known to themselves, are likely to misinterpret its functions and operations. Some criticize it for real or imagined faults—faults

453

inherent in a competitive economy rather than in advertising as such. Still others inaccurately imbue advertising with an aura of personification which sets it apart from those who create and employ it. So, in their eyes, we have "bad" advertising but not "bad" advertisers. Presumably, according to these critics, the men who sponsor and create this "bad" advertising would not engage in other questionable selling practices if advertising were reduced in volume or eliminated altogether.

An argument sometimes lodged against advertising is that it creates little in the way of new demand but merely effects a switching of brands. It is true that advertising results in some amount of brand switching, but this is an inherent part of any free competitive economy and would exist with or without advertising. It is a common occurrence in retail shops every day. How often do sales people suggest that a customer buy a brand other than that for which he or she entered the store?

Furthermore, to say that advertising does not build new demand but merely results in brand switching is to assume the existence of a static economy in which a more or less constant volume of goods is sold each year and where any gain made in the marketing of a particular brand must be at the expense of a corresponding loss by another brand or brands. This, as we know, has not been the case in the past, and it would be difficult to find an economist who would predict that it would be so in the foreseeable future. Our population has been and is increasing, as is demand. So, too, is the gross national product, although there was a temporary drop in 1974. Until that time, there were more people who wanted goods and more people who were able to buy larger quantities of goods than ever before. This expanding economy had given rise to increasingly great marketing opportunities. Advertising can and does do *much more* than cause people to switch brands!

Some people argue that advertising increases the prices that consumers must pay for goods. It is true that the cost of advertising, like the salesperson's salary and any other cost associated with the manufacture or marketing of products, must be a component in the price charged for the goods. But this does not mean that the price of the goods must be higher than it would be were there less advertising or none at all. If advertising builds markets more effectively and more economically than could be done by other means, then it need not make prices higher. If it builds mass markets that could not be created without it, and if these mass markets make mass production possible with lower unit cost of output, then advertising has made possible a lower price for the goods. This result occurs often. Whether or not the savings thus effected through advertising are passed on to the consumer in the form of lower prices is a decision of management, not a consequence of advertising.

When advertising is used to develop a product image that will enable a good to command a higher price in the market, this again is a decision of management. The advertising in this case *makes possible* the higher price; it does not *make it necessary*.

In sum, it can be acknowledged that advertising *makes possible* both higher and lower prices for goods, or for services. This is quite different from saying that advertising makes the prices higher, or lower.

Some critics of advertising contend that it creates desires for goods that people do not need and so results in unjustifiable purchases and economic waste. For example, a bathroom may be remodeled and modern, colored fixtures substituted for the still quite usable old-fashioned ones. The critics find it difficult to conceive of a bathtub being worn out—a new one is not *needed,* but it is desired and is purchased; a perfectly usable tub is discarded. Does economic waste result? What is meant by "needed"? Does the criticism mean that only the minimal necessities of life are needed, and nothing more? Do we really "need" anything more than a bear skin for clothing, a cave for shelter, or some roots or a loaf of bread to eat? If "need" extends to more than these, then how much more, and of what quality, and who will determine the answer? Is this criticism really a criticism of advertising, or is it a criticism of a free and democratic system of society? And is there a waste if the old bathtub is purchased by someone else who could not afford a new one, or if the metal and parts are salvaged and recycled to manufacture new products and be put to other uses?

It has been argued that advertising plays upon the emotions in an endeavor to motivate people to buy goods and services while it fails to give adequate information to enable them to buy intelligently. Much advertising does make emotional appeals. The chief function of advertising is to sell goods, services, and ideas. If an emotional appeal proves most effective in accomplishing this end, advertisers will use it. So, too, will salesmen, clergymen, lawyers, doctors, politicians, and, for that matter—even you and I in accomplishing our own purposes.

The criticism concerning lack of information is also not well-founded. Those who criticize advertising on this score seem to measure all advertising, regardless of the job it is designed to do, in terms of the mail order catalog. Much advertising is addressed to people who are *not* ready and willing to buy and who *do not* read or listen to advertising in a deliberate search for information relative to competing products. Therefore, much advertising must be designed to attract attention, stimulate interest, and excite desire. In the final analysis, the job of advertising is to set in motion human reactions that will lead to the purchase of the advertised product. This task is often most successfully accomplished by describing the product in terms of the satisfactions to be derived from its use. For this reason, advertising tends to talk in terms of sense impressions rather than measurements and qualities, and detailed information often becomes incidental in this process. Such procedure rests on sound theory, and its success is measured in the large volume of goods which advertising, through the years, helped move through the channels of trade. On the other hand, much less sound is the theory that the great majority of consumers are coldly objective, dispassionate individuals. Equally unsound is the theory that they have both the time and inclination to read or listen to a great bulk of information designed to acquaint them with all the facts that critics of advertising claim are necessary to a wise selection among the great variety of goods offered to them.

Business and advertising have always had their critics and detractors. This is not an apology or a defense for either discipline. They don't need it. Their myriad accomplishments speak for themselves.

There are dishonest and incompetent people in all professions and in all walks of life—politics, law, medicine, and even the clergy. (This does not mean, for example, that all doctors are "quacks" or that the entire medical profession engages in dishonest or illegal practices.) Business and advertising likewise have their inept and unscrupulous practitioners. Fortunately, as in the other fields of endeavor, these are in the minority. And as with the medical profession, there is nothing wrong with the system or principles of advertising. In fact, to the contrary, there is everything right with advertising. The entire apple crop should not be condemned because of a few "rotten apples."

WHY IS ADVERTISING CRITICIZED?

Why is advertising constantly "under the gun"? The answer is easy to understand: by its very nature advertising is extremely *visible*. It is constantly on display before us. No other economic activity captures our attention so much as does advertising. For the same reason, among the mass communication media it is television that bears the brunt of the attack. Radio, newspapers, and magazines escape with far less criticism.

A more deep-seated explanation for making advertising the victim is the "mirror phenomenon": Advertising is a mirror of our times and reflects what faces it. We don't like what we see and therefore attack the mirror.[1]

There is very little if anything that is created by man that is perfect; yet every system, no matter how good or positive, has its critics and detractors. To paraphrase statements made about democracy and capitalism—advertising may not be a perfect system but its the best we've been able to come up with, to date. Nothing facilitates the movement of goods through trade channels from producers to ultimate consumers as efficiently as does advertising.

THE RISE OF CONSUMERISM

At some time during the period following the Civil War, Commodore Cornelius Vanderbilt, head of the then powerful New York Central Railroad, is reported to have made the callous statement, "the public—the public be damned!" He wasn't alone. During that same period the famous showman P. T. Barnum coined the phrase, "There's a sucker born every minute." Unfortunately, this wasn't a new concept even then because, in turning back the pages of history even further we find that in ancient Rome the same negative philosophy prevailed. A common expression at the time was, *caveat emptor*—"let the buyer beware." Today, hopefully, that era is well behind us. The practice of riding rough-shod over the customer or consumer is no longer acceptable in business. In fact, the new watchword, paraphrasing the ancient Roman slogan, might well be *caveat vendor*—"let the seller beware!" Not only does government—local, state, and national—scrupulously police advertising, but consumers also make their feelings known.

For a long time marketers proclaimed that the "consumer is king," that he (or she) ruled the marketplace because of the veto power he wielded at the checkout counter. The success or failure of a product depended on the consumer's decision at the point of purchase. In reality, however, "the" consumer was only "a limited monarch" because there was no unity or organization among consumers. When Betty Furness * first went to work as President Lyndon B. Johnson's Special Assistant for Consumer Affairs, she said, "Consumers didn't even know they were having affairs. In fact, they had to be told they were consumers." [2] While this statement is a slight exaggeration—Consumers Union fought the battle from the mid-1930s—there was little leadership. Now that void has been filled. Led by government consumer affairs officials and by such independent consumer advocates as Ralph Nader, consumers have brought a great deal of pressure to bear on various manufacturers, distributors, and advertisers who have not been completely honest or fair in their dealings. And when direct appeal to the violators has not brought results, consumers have turned to such self-regulatory groups as the Better Business Bureau and the National Advertising Review Board. The latter two organizations have been most effective in obtaining compliance. And when all else has failed, violators are brought directly to the attention of the Federal Trade Commission or other appropriate governmental regulatory body.

GOVERNMENT REGULATION

Some people say that much advertising is false or misleading. Some does exist, but the amount that is of a questionable nature is relatively small. Most advertisers are basically honest; they realize that false and misleading advertising is as damaging to them as it is to the consumer. There are within the advertising business itself many codes and regulatory devices, and there are laws at every level of government—local, state, and federal—designed to keep advertising truthful and to regulate its operation in other ways.

State Control

In 1911, *Printers' Ink,* an advertising trade publication, proposed as a model for state legislation a statute designed to eliminate untrue, deceptive, and misleading advertising. It became known as the *Printers' Ink Model Statute* and today a majority of states have truth-in-advertising laws patterned after it. In part, its most recently revised edition states:

> Any person, firm, corporation or association or agent or employee thereof, who, with intent to sell, purchase or in any wise dispose of, or to contract with ref-

* Betty Furness served as Consumer Affairs adviser to the United States Government, the State of New York, and the City of New York.

erence to merchandise, real estate, service, employment, or anything offered by such person, firm, corporation or association, or agent or employee thereof, directly or indirectly, to the public for sale, purchase, distribution, or the hire of personal services, or with the intent to increase the consumption of or to contract with reference to any merchandise, real estate, securities, service, or employment, or to induce the public in any manner to enter into any obligation relating thereto, or to acquire title thereto, or an interest therein, or to make any loan, makes, publishes, disseminates, circulates, or places before the public, or causes, directly or indirectly, to be made, published, disseminated, circulated, or placed before the public, in this state, in a newspaper, magazine or other publication, or in the form of a book, notice, circular, pamphlet, letter, handbill, poster, bill, sign, placard, card, label, or over any radio or television station or other medium of wireless communication, or in any other way similar or dissimilar to the foregoing, an advertisement, announcement, or statement of any sort regarding merchandise, securities, service, employment, or anything so offered for use, purchase or sale, or the interest, terms or conditions upon which such loan will be made to the public, which advertisement contains any assertion, representation or statement of fact which is untrue, deceptive, or misleading, shall be guilty of a misdemeanor.

It is interesting to note that where states have followed the *Printers' Ink Model Statute* their truth-in-advertising laws have on the whole been more effective than those in many states where the laws were not patterned after the "model."

Possibly some of the reputation of advertising for questionable practices grew from the past when false claims were more common than they are today. But advertising was not alone in such practices. Advertising made false claims, but so too did the itinerant merchant and the shopkeeper. Honesty in the marketplace was a less common virtue than it is today. Advertising offered "sure cures" for everything from falling hair to falling arches, but the "Yankee peddler"—who seldom advertised—generated a tradition as a seller of cure-alls, wooden nutmegs, oak-leaf cigars, and horn gunflints. Thus some advertising was false, but not all, and some personal selling was false, but not all. Today, however, a survey of public opinion would probably show that not many people believe personal selling to be untruthful, perhaps because personal selling normally involves a conversation between just two individuals. Not so for advertising. What is said in advertising is public record. It is said to the masses, and it is subject to considerable repetition. As a result it makes a broader and a more lasting impression. It is a public pledge. The very things that make advertising a powerful selling tool are the things that tend to magnify its shortcomings and keep them in people's minds over longer periods of time. And it is for these reasons that it is, and must remain, honest!

False advertising was attacked by the better newspapers and magazines well before the turn of the present century and was pretty well driven from the scene during the truth-in-advertising campaigns that started about 1911. It was then that the first codes came into being and that local and national vigilance committees of the advertising clubs, forerunners of the Better Business Bureaus, were organized. However, the passing of fraudulent advertising did not remove the "trade puffery" or exaggerations prevalent in advertising copy. Much of this is within the law, and it has undoubtedly sold large volumes of goods, but it has kept the thinking portion of the general public ever aware that too much advertising deals with a "never-never land"—a fantasy environment where white teeth, fame, fortune, a wife or a husband, and a comfortable old age are to be had by the purchase of the proper brand of a variety of merchandise ranging from soap to chewing gum. It is the continuation of these practices, perhaps not by a large number of advertisers but by a relative few, that is responsible for current attitudes regarding truth or lack of truth in advertising.

The advertiser's position as to what is or is not good taste or how far "trade puffery" can go before it becomes objectionable exaggeration is complicated by the fact that not all people react in the same way to the same copy. The salesman deals with one prospect at a time and can shape his presentation to meet the situation at hand. He need never appear ridiculous to any prospect because of remarks made to another. Advertising is addressed to large numbers simultaneously. What attracts some may annoy or disgust others. Transporting readers and listeners to that "never-never land" of simple solutions to all personal problems *may* influence many to buy the advertised product, and the primary job of advertising is to sell. But, at the same time, such trips into fantasy may lead others to the opinion that most advertising is untrustworthy, and advertising cannot afford to develop poor public relations for itself. It is for these reasons that advertising as a business has developed many self-regulatory devices and has been responsible for the promotion of state legislation patterned after the *Printers' Ink Model Statute*.

Not all control is concerned with untruthfulness. All states have some laws regulating other aspects of advertising. For example, all states have laws governing the use of outdoor advertising, as does the federal government; most states have laws concerned with the advertising of particular products. In fact, so numerous are the state laws which affect advertising that *Printers' Ink* published a book in 1945 dealing only with state legislation that pertains to advertising.[3]

Federal Control

At the federal level of government the Wheeler-Lea Act, passed in 1938 and amending the Federal Trade Commission Act of 1914, is perhaps the most important control of advertising. The Commission has specific jurisdiction over the advertising of foods, drugs, cosmetics, and therapeutic or diagnostic devices. It is also responsible for the control of all "unfair competition." The Act makes illegal any untruthful or misleading statement in advertising copy. In determining whether or not an advertisement is misleading, both actual claims and any implications that might be drawn from the wording are studied by the Federal Trade Commission. If an advertisement is believed to be deceptive or misleading, the Federal Trade Commission may issue a cease-and-desist order requiring that the advertiser stop the questionable advertising within 60 days or appeal for a review of the case.

More recently, under the pressure of militant consumer groups and others, the FTC has begun to exercise even more stringent powers. The Commission streamlined its operations in 1970, substituting two bureaus—the Bureau of Competition and the Bureau of Consumer Protection—for the four that had existed before. At the same time the Commission increased the powers of its field-office lawyers to match those of the home-office staff attorneys.

In a further effort to halt false and deceptive advertising the Commission began, in 1971, to demand substantiation of advertising claims. In another more drastic move it ordered violators to use up to 25% of their advertising time and/or space for *mea culpa* purposes. That is, advertisers charged with printing or broadcasting misleading advertising are required to disclaim their previous false or misleading statements, allegations, and claims by means of "corrective advertising" and "affirmative disclosures." The first of these punitive or corrective commercials was broadcast toward the end of 1971 for Profile bread. The announcer, among other things, negated claims made on earlier broadcasts, stating clearly that Profile did not "have fewer calories than other bread" and that "eating Profile will not cause you to lose weight."

In a more recent ruling the FTC ordered that all Listerine advertising for the subsequent two years carry this statement: "Contrary to prior advertising of Listerine, Listerine will not prevent or cure colds or sore throats, and Listerine will not be beneficial in the treatment of cold symptoms or sore throats."

Other Federal agencies concerned with truth in advertising include the Securities and Exchange Commission, which has to do with the truth or falsity of advertising for stocks and bonds, and the United States Postal Service, which is concerned with fraud, lotteries, and obscenities sent through the mails. The Federal Communications Commission, through its power to grant and withold licenses, has control over radio and television stations and consequently over advertisers. Perhaps the most stringent advertising regulation put forth by the FCC was the Fairness Doctrine, which requires equal time for opposing opinions. It was applied drastically to cigarette commercials just prior to the time that the advertising of cigarettes was banned entirely from the electronic media.

To a lesser extent the Civil Aeronautics Board is concerned with airline advertising, and the Food and Drug Administration, although it is not directly involved with advertising, has a comparable interest in the labeling and sale of foods, drugs, and cosmetics. The Treasury Department, through its Bureau of Alcohol, Tobacco and Firearms, exercises strong power over the advertising of those products under its control. And the Federal Power Commission is concerned with the advertising of electric utility companies.

In May 1974 there was legislation pending in the Senate to create a superagency with power to intervene in the proceedings and actions of all other federal offices and regulatory agencies "in the interest of consumers." It had already passed the House of Representatives by a vote of 293 to 94.[4] It was shelved or killed in the Senate in September of that year.

SELF-REGULATION

Up until relatively recently and before the onset of consumerism, federal government regulations pertaining to advertising were few. Historically this "hands off" attitude stems back to the guarantee of freedom of speech and freedom of the press in the Constitution. The advertising industry itself accordingly had to maintain some measure of control and to keep its own house in order. In such a situation the self-enforcer is apt to be more conscientious in his exercise of power than outside policemen. A case in point is the ban against the advertising of distilled liquor by means of the electronic media. This is one of the self-imposed regulations contained in the *Television Code* and the *Radio Code* of the National Association of Broadcasters. Another regulation in the *Television Code* applies to "clutter" and spells out the number of "interruptions" (generally commercials) that can take place in a program. It also limits their total length of time. The Code stipulates that "the number of program interruptions shall not exceed two within any 30-minute program, or four within any 60-minute program," during prime time. At other times it allows twice the number of "interruptions." While adherence to the broadcast codes is purely voluntary, members of the NAB are expected to honor them. Observance by the industry is widespread.

Probably the most important of the self-regulatory codes, because of its general acceptance by the industry, is the *Standard of Practice* of the American Association of Advertising Agencies. An integral part of the *Standard* is the "Creative Code," which has been endorsed by leading industry organizations. These include the Advertising Federation of America, Association of National Advertisers, Association of Industrial Advertisers, National Association of Broadcasters, Magazine Publishers Association, Newspaper Advertising Executives Association, Transit Advertising Association, Associated Business Publishers, and Agricultural Publishers Association, among others.

INSERT I

The "Creative Code" reads as follows:

> We, the members of the American Association of Advertising Agencies, in addition to supporting and obeying the laws and legal regulations pertaining to advertising, undertake to extend and broaden the application of high ethical standards. Specifically, we will not knowingly produce advertising which contains:
>
> *a.* False or misleading statements or exaggerations, visual or verbal.
> *b.* Testimonials which do not reflect the real choice of a competent witness.
> *c.* Price claims which are misleading.
> *d.* Comparisons which unfairly disparage a competitive product or service.
> *e.* Claims insufficiently supported, or which distort the true meaning or practicable application of statements made by professional or scientific authority.
> *f.* Statements, suggestions, or pictures offensive to public decency.
>
> We recognize that there are areas which are subject to honestly different interpretations and judgment. Taste is subjective and may even vary from time to time as well as from individual to individual. Frequency of seeing or hearing advertising messages will necessarily vary greatly from person to person.

However, we agree not to recommend to an advertiser and to discourage the use of advertising which is in poor or questionable taste or which is deliberately irritating through content, presentation, or excessive repetition.

Clear and willful violations of this Code shall be referred to the Board of Directors of the American Association of Advertising Agencies for appropriate action, including possible annulment of membership as provided in Article IV, Section 5, of the Constitution and By-Laws.[5]

Most of the specialized associations within the advertising industry, such as those that represent the different media, also have their own specific codes and standards of practice. Some, like the Direct Mail/Marketing Association, which has its *Standard of Ethical Business Practice,* are closely attuned to consumer needs and complaints. To satisfy complainants, DMMA established a Mail Preference System. By simply requesting a form from the association or one of its member firms and returning it completed to them, a person can have his name removed entirely from all direct mail lists, or from specific types of lists according to his preference. Conversely, a consumer can also have his name added to specific lists. During the first 18 months of its existence approximately 25,000 copies of this form were returned. DMMA also has a Mail Order Action Line which assists consumers with complaints about mail order transactions. During 1973 they helped some 15,000 consumers in this regard.

As far as adjudication or regulation is concerned, the principal agency is the 60-member National Advertising Review Board, which was established in 1970.

In answer to a number of queries as to the operation of the NARB, early in 1974 the American Association of Advertising Agencies described the process of registering complaints about national advertising.

1. The complaint should be made to the National Advertising Division, c/o Council of Better Business Bureaus, 845 Third Avenue, New York 10022.
2. The complaint should detail medium, date, time (for radio or TV commercials), and a brief description of the advertisement or commercial to expedite handling. If in print, a tear sheet will be helpful.
3. Upon receipt, the complaint will be acknowledged.
4. It will then be reviewed in the National Advertising Division where most often it is negotiated successfully. If that fails, it will be sent to the National Advertising Review Board, which performs an appellate function.
5. If a complaint is not satisfactorily resolved at that level, it may be forwarded to the appropriate government agency. This has not yet proven to be necessary since most complaints have either been negotiated at the NAD level or resolved in the Review Board.[6]

CONSUMER RESEARCH

Other efforts have been made by advertisers and agencies to meet consumer demands. A research study was conducted in 1974 to update trends in public attitudes toward advertisers from a similar study conducted ten years earlier. It was designed to develop a flexible barometer for future research. Most important of all, however, its purpose was to generate information as a guide to action.[7]

The results were reassuring. They showed that "criticism of advertising is not uppermost in consumers' minds," that no drastic changes have to be made, and that since 1964 more people have come to see the need for and the importance of advertising.[8]

The paper concluded that consumers' had an overall high opinion of advertising that informed its viewers, listeners, or readers of product or service benefits. They also favored advertising that is interesting and believable.[9]

SUMMARY

The truth-in-advertising laws, both federal and state—not to mention the many controls exercised at local levels of government and by self-regulation— have done much to lessen the strength of the critics' charge of misleading advertising. Furthermore, the modern advertiser who employs the force of advertising intelligently knows that its value is not of the present only but also of the future. As advertising moves the goods of today it builds brand reputations for tomorrow and so protects long-term capital investments. Short-sighted, false, or misleading advertising cannot accomplish this.

In effect, consumerists and other activists have given advertisers a technical problem to be solved. It should not be ignored. On the contrary, consumerist cries and complaints should be heeded, and whenever they are justified there should be adjustment or compliance.

From a broader social point of view, advertising makes an important contribution to the public. The revenue derived from the sale of advertising space enables publishers to sell newspapers and magazines for far less than it would cost to publish and distribute them without advertising revenue. In like manner, the income derived from the sale of advertising time by the broadcast media makes it possible for the public to receive free radio and television broadcasts of news, educational programs, sports, and entertainment. And the industry, by means of the Advertising Council, makes a substantial contribution to public causes through many hundreds of millions of dollars' worth of free advertising each year.[10]

QUESTIONS AND DISCUSSION SUBJECTS

1. What is the primary function of advertising?
2. Discuss some of the arguments lodged against advertising. Are they justified? Explain.

3. Why is advertising so often the target of consumer and government attacks?
4. Describe the *Printers' Ink Model Statute*.
5. Which federal government agencies are concerned with the regulation of advertising? What is the extent of their power?
6. Explain the following:(a) substantiation; (b) affirmative disclosure; (c) corrective advertising.
7. Which organization bans the advertising of distilled liquor in broadcast commercials.
8. What is the gist of the "Creative Code" of the American Association of Advertising Agencies?
9. Describe the process of registering complaints against national advertising with the National Advertising Review Board.

SOURCES

1. John G. Meyers, *Social Issues in Advertising* (New York: American Association of Advertising Agencies, 1971), 41.
2. Betty Furness, "Direct Marketing Day in New York," an address given on April 12, 1973.
3. Burt W. Roper, *State Advertising Legislation* (New York: Printers' Ink Publishing Corporation, 1945).
4. "Consumer Protection Agency," *Legislative Newsletter,* Writing Instrument Manufacturers Association, Inc., May 1, 1974, 1, 2.
5. Frederic R. Gamble, *What Advertising Agencies Are—What They Do and How They Do It* (New York: American Association of Advertising Agencies, 1963), 18.
6 "Monitoring National Advertising," *4A Newsletter,* January 31, 1974, 6, 7.
7. Rena Bartos, "The Consumer View of Advertising—1974," paper presented at the Annual Meeting of the American Association of Advertising Agencies, 3.
8. *Ibid.,* i.
9. *Loc. cit.*
10. *Ad Council Report to the American People 1973–74* (New York: Advertising Council).

FOR FURTHER READING

Bauer, Raymond A., and Stephen A. Greyser. *Advertising in America: The Consumer View.* Boston: Harvard Business School, 1968.
The Challenge of Self-Regulation: Washington, D.C.: National Association of Broadcasters.
"Consumerism and the New Accountability." Papers from a panel session at the 1971 AAAA Central Region Annual Meeting. Published by the American Association of Advertising Agencies, 1972.

. Ewen, Wm. H. *The National Advertising Review Board, 1971–1975.* New York: tional Advertising Review Board, 1975.

· Howard, John A., and James Hulbert. *Advertising and the Public Interest.* Washingto D.C.: Federal Trade Commission, 1973.

' Moskin, J. Robert, ed. *The Case for Advertising.* New York: American Association of Advertising Agencies, 1973.

• Myers, John G. *Social Issues in Advertising.* New York: American Association of Advertising Agencies, 1971.

, Nicosia, Francesco M. *Advertising Management and Society: A Business Point of View.* New York, McGraw-Hill, 1974.

Powell, Lewis F., Jr. *The Powell Memorandum.* Washington, D.C.: United States Chamber of Commerce, 1971.

The Radio Code. Washington, D.C.: National Association of Broadcasters. (Editions are updated as required.)

Social Responsibilities of Business Corporations. New York: Committee for Economic Development, 1971.

• Stanley, Robert H., ed. for the International Radio and Television Society. *The Broadcast Industry: An Examination of Major Issues.* New York: Hastings House, Publishers, 1975.

. Steinberg, Charles S., ed., for the International Radio and Television Society. *Broadcasting: The Critical Challenges.* New York: Hastings House, Publishers, 1974.

` *The Television Code.* Washington, D.C.: National Association of Broadcasters. (Editions are updated as required.)

Webster, Frederick E., Jr. *Social Aspects of Marketing.*Englewood Cliffs, N.J.: Prentice-Hall, 1974.

' Wright, John S., and John E. Mertes. *Advertising's Role in Society.* St. Paul: West Publishing Co., 1974.

Advertising and the Law

Contributed by Myron D. Emery, J.D.

The advertising business, by reason of its range and variety, has a near-infinite assortment of relationships, rights, and risks that often generate need for a lawyer's viewpoint and expertise. The need may present itself more often than it does to other businesses. This chapter takes note of several aspects of the need, but obviously cannot reach all the myriad problems that might arise in the conduct of advertising and public relations. These problems grow more numerous and complex as advertisers' businesses expand and diversify, as communications resources multiply, as workers and publics organize and pursue their often conflicting viewpoints and demands.

CONTRACTS

An advertiser and an advertising agent enter into many kinds of contracts. They do business with each other according to the terms of a Letter of Appointment, a contract which states that the client and/or sponsor appoints the agency to represent it in all dealings with the media. The Letter also sets forth how the agency is to be paid by the client and by what means and methods.

The agency, in its operations, contracts with the various media in which it places advertisements. A familiar term for this contract is Insertion Order. The terms may be stipulated by the medium. The agency will, in signing this contract, state that it is agent for the client and represents him in all dealings under the contract. The contract also spells out all the various clauses that the medium requires the agency to abide by. One of the most important of these is the payment clause, wherein the agency states that it is jointly responsible with its client for the payment of any monies that become due and owing to the medium.

Account executives conduct business with an agency's clients on behalf of

the agency. An account executive performs a liaison function and has
toward both the client and the agency. He necessarily makes commitmei
the agency. His authority to make these commitments is established b
terms of a contract called an Employment Agreement. It spells out
things: How the executive is to be paid, how long he is to work, what accounts
he is to work on, and in what manner he can and cannot operate. It may include
prohibitions against working for competing agencies during and after his employment with the contracting agency. The Agreement may set forth the philosophy and policy of the agency and the expectation that the employee-executive
will conform to these. When the account executive explicitly understands all
agency policies there is less likelihood of losing a client because the executive
did not know what the policy was.

The advertising agency employs staff for business operations and creative
work and may hire talent for broadcast programs and commercials. These
employer-employee relationships involve contracts with individuals, unions,
and employment and talent agencies. Contracts also express the agency's un-
derstandings with professionals like photographers, artists, production companies, and various consultants.

Experience has often demonstrated the importance of bringing the lawyer
viewpoint into contract negotiation and decision-making. And not the viewpoint only—the lawyer is expected to contribute a special and expert familiarity
with custom, with past experience, and with law and equity as they apply to the
drafting and interpretation of contracts. Though the experienced businessman's
expertise is indispensable, so is the lawyer's.

REGULATORY COMMISSIONS AND AUTHORITIES

The advertiser and the advertising agency also seek the help of lawyers in
their relations with Federal and state administrative organizations. To name
some: the Federal Trade Commission, the Food and Drug Administration, the
Federal Communications Commission, the Consumer Protection Agency, the
Postal Service, the Interstate Commerce Commission, and the Federal Aviation
Agency. Numerous less well-known government offices also control and regulate different aspects of communication.

The Federal Trade Commission and the Food and Drug Administration
have become well-known for their policing of broadcasts against false or misleading statements that might be made in advertising. They give like attention,
less conspicuously perhaps, to advertising in the print media. The Federal
Communications Commission has comparable concerns, and it exercises the
power of licensing and licence renewal for television and radio stations. The
FCC can take false or misleading advertising into account in deciding whether
to grant renewal of a station's authorization to broadcast. The rationale for this
power is that the broadcast channels and frequencies belong to the public, that
they must not be used against the public interest, and that the FCC is the body
responsible for protecting the public and the public interest in these matters.

The Food and Drug Administration exercises authority under an even more direct protective mandate. If products in its jurisdiction are mislabeled or mis-branded, the FDA has the legal right to seize goods from the shelves, together with advertising matter describing the product, and to bring legal action pre-venting the dissemination of both the product and its advertising. Action of this kind could certainly create a great problem if the advertising agency had as-sumed or paid obligations to the media but had not yet been reimbursed by its client. The goods and advertising not having been disseminated, the client might feel that the agency had not completed its contract, might even claim that it need not pay or need not pay in full for the agency's service!

Other Federal regulatory bodies have duties and powers that bear on ad-vertising, on the work of advertising agencies, and on the uses and practices of some advertising media. Regulatory bodies of the various states, counties, and municipalities also exercise comparable functions and wield comparable author-ities in their jurisdictions.

In the presence of these strong regulatory powers and the influence that organized publics have in the commissions that exercise them, certainly adver-tisers and advertising agencies need the help of lawyers if only to keep aware of who has the powers and what the powers are. Indeed, the need goes further—lawyers maintain continuing contact with the administrative bodies in the course of representing their clients' interests; they also act for their clients in hearings and litigation both before the commissions and in the courts. And they advise and guide their clients in the effort to keep to a minimum the burden of litigation and complaint.

TRADEMARKS AND COPYRIGHTS

Advertising, by its nature as published matter, operates at all times amid trademark and copyright concerns. These concerns affect logotypes, slogans, trade and brand names, and the many rights in the ownership of creative expression—abstract, intangible, tenuous, and fragile rights that exist only through law and custom.

When a company uses a symbol like a logo to identify its products, the symbol becomes valuable and competitors may try to use it and take advantage of that value. Accordingly, laws provide that a company can protect its logo-type (and prevent anyone else from using it) by registering it as a trademark with the United States government. Applying for the registration, obtaining it, and thereafter protecting the registered item from infringement is a continuing task for the advertising lawyer.

Copyright—the right to make and distribute copies of reading matter and pictures especially—enters into advertising and mass communications in all media. Copyright registration establishes the creator's (or other owner's) prop-erty right in a created work of literature or art (and advertising is both). The ad-vertiser and the advertising agency need to protect their copyright property and—perhaps more important—to avoid trespassing on the copyright property of others. Serious financial injury and ruinous financial penalties can result from trespasses against copyright. Those exposed to these hazards need competent guidance in the law although many procedures are routine. The need for guidance is the greater because copyright property may be damaged or destroyed by carelessness or inadvertence as well as by intention or malice.

DISPARAGEMENT, DEFAMATION, PRIVACY, AND PUBLICITY

Nearly all people accept the kind of advertising that praises the production service offered. Advertising that *disparages*—that imputes fault or dissatisfaction to a competitor or a competing product or service—is regarded differently. What one may say about the competition or whether one may say anything raises both legal and moral problems for people in advertising. One cannot legally make untrue statements that discredit or disparage his competition; this offense is trade libel and the disparaged party can often recover money damages. This idea is certainly not new; as long ago as 1891 a California court made reference to business ethics and disparaging attacks upon competitors. It stated that there would be liability despite a genuine belief in the validity of the disparaging statement.

It has been generally understood that one can criticize the goods of a competitor if the statements are true and if they criticize in a way that applies merely to the personal taste or preference of the consumer. However, one must not falsely impugn the integrity of the competitor; to thrust a gray shadow over a competitor's business methods, to hold them out as questionable gives rise to many problems.

Some people hold the view that merely naming a competitor or showing his product in advertising undermines all of advertising and eventually would bring in strong intervention by the Federal government. Some have called it derogatory advertising and feel that it should not be done at all; they are, however, in the minority. Much thinking and feeling in this matter is in the area of ethics rather than that of law. The Federal Trade Commission encourages honest comparative advertising. In a recent ruling it has stated that a competitor named in an advertisement must be named in full; a competing brand cannot be called "brand X."

Statements that injure a person in his reputation may constitute *defamation—slander* if spoken, *libel* if written or published. Note that they *may* constitute defamation, for if they are true statements they may not be defamations. When such statements are in fact defamations, the injured party may recover money damages or enforce reparatory action on the defamer. Such penalties may be costly, hence advertisers and advertising people observe care not to commit defamation. Moreover, defamation can sometimes be criminal. This whole area is complex because it touches on freedoms of speech and of the press. Advertising people, therefore, may often need legal guidance.

Statements that are true and that do not constitute defamations may nevertheless create problems costly to advertisers if they invade an individual's *privacy.* An individual's right to privacy may be violated when information about his personal life is disclosed to the public without right or permission. To say of a woman that she uses a contraceptive might be an invasion of her privacy, even if in fact she uses one, unless she has given permission for the statement. To advertise that a well-known woman uses some specific contraceptive, offered for sale in the advertisement, might even more likely be an invasion of her right of *publicity.* This right is an area of privacy that is invaded when a famous person's likeness or name, or information about the party, is used in a commercial way to his or her disadvantage or without permission. Another example might be the use of a person's name or photograph in an ad or a commercial as though that person were endorsing or giving a testimonial for the advertised product. Since a famous person's rights of publicity may have great money value, violations of such rights can subject the violators to large money penalties.

Liabilities for advertising that touches the rights of privacy or publicity may be avoided by obtaining a release or waiver from the person affected. If the person is a professional model or a celebrity whose business agent arranges for testimonials and endorsements, getting the release or waiver is relatively routine, and the advertiser is protected. Getting a release from an ordinary citizen may be more difficult, as when the person is a chance participant in some event and cannot be easily found to sign a release; then, under some circumstances, the release may not be needed. But the law in this area is changing, and it differs from state to state; many details involve minute differences and distinctions. Where privacy and publicity are involved, a lawyer's guidance is emphatically needed.

REVIEW OF COPY

It is evident that an advertisement may give rise to legal problems for both the advertiser and the advertising agency. Liability can result from any type of information that an advertisement disseminates to the public. It follows that before any advertisement is published a lawyer should be asked to review, in the interest of all concerned, all copy and art. The review should deal not only with possible violation of regulations or criminal law but also and more particularly with the truth and substantiability of all statements (to avoid deception and misrepresentation) and with considerations of privacy, publicity, and copyright or trademark property. The attorney will also make sure that such words as "free," "guarantee," and "new" are used properly. Though a lawyer's review cannot eliminate all risk, the cost of such review is minuscule compared to the risk of neglecting it. The consequence is costly enough when an individual claims injury and wins damages in a legal action; when such an action presents claims for a large number of injured parties—a class action—the costs may be ruinous.

INTERNATIONAL LAW

As multinational companies become more numerous and as more products are traded across national boundaries, advertising agencies increasingly extend their operations into other countries. As they do so, they become subject to these countries' laws and need legal guidance from lawyers both in their home country and in the foreign country. Lawyers in this service need to be cognizant of the differences among national laws and systems. Risks, rights, and practices differ even among English-speaking countries. Among countries whose laws derive from other traditions and historical backgrounds, the differences are much greater.

SELF-REGULATION

It is becoming more important for advertising and public relations people to regulate themselves. Self-regulation is a purpose of the National Association of Broadcasters, through its *Radio Code* and *Television Code,* and of the National Advertising Review Board, the Better Business Bureaus, and numerous similar institutions. These can lessen the need for statutory regulation and can also deal with business matters that statutes do not touch. Even in self-regulation, however, the lawyer and the lawyer's viewpoint are needed. Self-regulatory activities must be conducted in accordance with state and Federal laws, especially with antitrust law. The drafting and interpretation of self-regulatory codes draw on the expertise and viewpoint of lawyers. Referees and arbitrators who administer these codes are often lawyers. And when the codes do not settle disputes or resolve problems, the disputes move into the courts and lawyers move with them.

SUMMARY

Like every other type of business, advertising has need of legal services. Some of these services are common to all businesses; others apply solely to advertising. Among the latter are contracts known as Letters of Appointment, Insertion Orders, and others. Attorneys also assist advertising agencies in their dealings with local, state, and Federal government regulatory organizations, bureaus, and commissions. Their opinions are also sought in matters dealing with self-regulation.

Trademarks and copyrights are other areas in which agencies require legal counsel. Such expertise is also needed when the subjects of disparagement, defamation, libel, and invasion of privacy and publicity arise. Agencies can avoid these problems by submitting their copy for legal review prior to publication.

Today, many of the large advertising agencies have branches and/or subsidiaries in other countries, making it necessary to have knowledge of the laws of each country as well as of international law.

QUESTIONS AND DISCUSSION SUBJECTS

1. List some respects in which the role of the advertising-agency lawyer is most important.
2. Describe a Letter of Appointment.
3. What is the purpose of the contract between the agency and the medium? What is it called?
4. Name some of the Federal governmental agencies that are concerned with advertising.
5. What police power has the Federal Communications Commission?
6. How do advertising agencies and their clients protect themselves against unsolicited ideas?
7. Define defamation (libel and slander)?
8. Can an advertiser name his competitor in his advertising? Can he show the competitor's product in his advertising? Discuss.
9. What is disparagement?
10. What do advertising-agency lawyers have to do with international trade?

FOR FURTHER READING

"Advertising: in the eye of the hurricane," *Sense 68, 1972.*

Annual Report of the Federal Trade Commission. Washington, D.C.: Government Printing Office, published annually.

"Consumerism and the New Accountability." Papers from the 1971 AAAA Central Region Annual Meeting. Published by the American Association of Advertising Agencies, 1972.

Federal Trade Commission, Organization, Procedures, and Rules of Practice. Washington, D.C.: Government Printing Office, 1970.

Hackett, Byron. *How to Keep Your Ads Out of Court.* New York: J. Walter Thompson Co., 1975.

Riney, Harold. *How to Write Advertising and Stay Out of Jail,* a paper presented at the 1975 Western Region Convention of the American Association of Advertising Agencies.

The Newsman's Guide to Legalese. Harrisburg, Pa.: Pennsylvania Bar Association, 1973.

The Radio Code. Washington, D.C.: National Association of Broadcasters. (Editions are updated from time to time.)

The Television Code. Washington, D.C.: National Association of Broadcasters. (Editions are updated from time to time.)

INDEX

Index

Bristol-Myers Co., 225

Broadcast media, 257, 258, 259, 322-28; advertising copy for, 119-25; and agency producer, 154-57, 161, 162; evolution of, 322-26; ratings and services for, 244-53; *see also* Radio; Television

Broadcast-media production, 154-64; and agency producer, 154-57, 161, 162; and preproduction meetings, 157; *see also* Television commercials

Broadcast Rating Council, 252

Brooker, William, 8

Brown & Bigelow, 422

Buhler, Charlotte, 442

Bulova Watch Co., 345

Bureau of Alcohol, Tobacco and Firearms, 460

Bureau of Competition, 460

Bureau of Consumer Protection, 460

Bureau of Labor Statistics, 43

Burnett, Leo, Inc., 225

Burroughs, William, 220

Bus, merchandising, in transit advertising, 404

Business Address Co., 361

Business Establishment Surveys (Hooper), 248

Business/Professional Advertising Association (B/PAA), 214

Business Publications Audit of Circulation (BPA), 237-38, 316

Business Publications Rates and Data, 311

Business Week, 314

Businesspapers, 311-18; advertising in, 312, 316-18; circulation of, 311-12, 315-16; format of, 314; industrial, 313, 314; institutional, 313, 314; merchandising, 313, 314; present-day, 311-18; professional, 313, 314; readership of, 315-16; types of, 313-14

Busorama, 404

Butler Manufacturing Co., 312

Butter, Nathaniel, 5

Byliner, 275

Cable television, 12, 54, 343-44, 354, 356

Calendars, in specialty advertising, 364, 421, 422, 424, 425

California Fruit Growers Association, 432

Campaign, advertising, *see* Advertising campaign

Campbell, John, 7, 9

Campbell's Soups, 405

Car Buyer's Guide (Ford Motor Co.), 305

Car cards, in transit advertising, 397, 398-401, 404, 405, 406

Carson, Johnny, 160

Cary, N. D., 121

Case for the Full-Service Agency, The, 192

Cassettes, 160, 346

Casting director, 156

Cattell Inventory, 440

CATV, 12, 54, 343-44, 354, 356

Caxton, William, 5

Celanese Corp., 305

Census of Manufacturers, 412

Center spread, for magazine advertisement, 304, 305

Central Registry of Magazine Subscription Solicitors, 295

Century magazine, 293

Certification marks, 68 and *n.*

Chain Store Age, 46

Chattanooga Times, 10

Chicago Business Publications Association, 312

Chicago Defender, 278

Chicago Tribune, 10, 287

"Chico and the Man" (TV program), 349

Chilton Ad-Chart Services, 55

Christian Science Monitor, 276

Chrysler Corp., 66, 305, 438

Churchill, Winston, 109

Cities, types of, 442

Cities Service Co., 66

Civil Aeronautics Board, 460

Clairol, Inc., 355

Classes, social, 44, 47

Classified advertising, 18, 283

Classified-display advertising, 18, 283

Clay, Henry, 110

CLIO awards, 164

COBOL, 221

Coburn, George, 422

Cocoa-Cola Co., 70, 71, 115, 171, 172, 175, 176, 287, 412

Cold type, 148, 149, 150